The Anzacs

GALLIPOLI TO THE WESTERN FRONT

PETER PEDERSEN

PENGUIN BOOKS

PENGUIN BOOKS

Published by the Penguin Group
Penguin Group (Australia)
250 Camberwell Road, Camberwell, Victoria 3124, Australia
(a division of Pearson Australia Group Pty Ltd)
Penguin Group (USA) Inc.
375 Hudson Street, New York, New York 10014, USA
Penguin Group (Canada)
90 Eglinton Avenue East, Suite 700, Toronto, Canada ON M4P 2Y3
(a division of Pearson Penguin Canada Inc.)
Penguin Books Ltd
80 Strand, London WC2R 0RL England
Penguin Ireland
25 St Stephen's Green, Dublin 2, Ireland
(a division of Penguin Books Ltd)
Penguin Books India Pty Ltd
11 Community Centre, Panchsheel Park, New Delhi – 110 017, India
Penguin Group (NZ)
67 Apollo Drive, Rosedale, North Shore 0632, New Zealand
(a division of Pearson New Zealand Ltd)
Penguin Books (South Africa) (Pty) Ltd
24 Sturdee Avenue, Rosebank, Johannesburg 2196, South Africa

Penguin Books Ltd, Registered Offices: 80 Strand, London WC2R 0RL, England

First published by Penguin Books Australia Ltd, 2007
This edition published by Penguin Group (Australia), 2010

1 3 5 7 9 10 8 6 4 2

Created by the Helicon Press Pty Ltd, Sydney
Cover design by Cameron Midson © Penguin Group (Australia)
Text design by Pauline Deakin and Cameron Midson © Penguin Group (Australia)
Maps by Country Cartographics
Image reproduction by Dave Deakin, Captured Concepts
Cover image E03142 from the Australian War Memorial, Canberra
Typeset in Sabon by Post Pre-press Group, Brisbane, Queensland
Printed and bound in Australia by McPherson's Printing Group, Maryborough, Victoria

National Library of Australia
Cataloguing-in-Publication data:

Pedersen, P. A. (Peter Andreas), 1952–
The Anzacs: Gallipoli to the Western Front / Peter Pedersen
9780143008460 (pbk.)
Previously published: Viking, 2007.
Includes index.
Bibliography.
Australia. Army. Australian and New Zealand Army Corps – History. World War, 1914–1918 – Australia. World War, 1914–1918 – Australia – Personal narratives. World War, 1914–1918 – Campaigns – Turkey – Gallipoli Peninsula. World War, 1914–1918 – Campaigns – Western Front.
940.44994

penguin.com.au

Contents

Maps

Ranks cited in the text are those held at the time of the action described or the command held.

Metric conversions

The following conversions should be applied to Imperial measurements cited in documents of the First World War period:

1 inch: 2.54 centimetres	1 centimetre: 0.394 inches
1 foot: 30.5 centimetres	1 metre: 3.28 feet / 1.09 yards
1 yard: 0.914 metres	1 kilometre / 1000 metres: 0.621 miles
1 mile: 1.61 kilometres	1 kilogram: 2.205 pounds
1 pound: 0.454 kilograms	1 stone: 6.35 kilograms

To my father
and in loving memory of my mother

INTRODUCTION

Dusk on 10 October 1917 found Lieutenant Paddy King and a handful of the 2/5th East Lancashires huddling in shell holes near Passchendaele, at the apex of the Ypres Salient. The 66th Division had floundered towards it through waist-deep mud but German machine-guns shattered the attack and King's party was among the few survivors. Protected by no more than a few slush-filled sandbags, under constant fire, they were exhausted, frozen and racked by cramp. Another miserable night loomed and King did not expect to see it out. Then he heard voices behind him.

King spun around. He was stunned to see three tall figures, one of them smoking. Blurting out 'who the hell are you?', King told the smoker to put out his cigarette in case a German sniper spotted the glowing end. A voice returned: 'We're the Aussies, chum, and we've come to relieve you'. The ecstatic King now realised that he knew next to nothing about the situation. 'There are no trenches to hand over, no rations, no ammunition, but I *have* got a map. Do you need any map references?' he asked. The laconic reply came: 'Never mind about that, chum. Just fuck off'. 'They didn't seem a bit bothered', King said. 'The last I saw of them they were squatting down, rifles over their shoulders, and they were smoking all three of them. Just didn't care!'[1]

The identity of these men will never be known, except that they were Anzacs. Perhaps they survived the next battle, maybe even the war. But all the Anzacs are gone now. The Australian Imperial Force (AIF) to which they belonged was the instrument of their country's first great endeavour. Their deeds and sacrifice during its course transformed Australia from a collection of disparate states into a true nation and earned it the esteem of the world. Along the way they established a tradition that gave the nation its soul. Without this inspirational force, Australia would have been a different place.

A glance at a sepia photograph or some grainy newsreel footage gives an idea of what the Anzacs were like at the time of their bequest. They recalled the war afterwards in contrasting tones, setting the warmth of comradeship and shared effort alongside the misery of privation and the shock of battle. It was the most intense period in their lives. They had escaped, temporarily at least, the humdrum existence that is the lot of all but a very few. Since their passing though, the letters, diaries and memoirs that they left have become the only means of getting to know them. Yet these writings carry an emotional risk. Browsing through the weekly letters of a soldier makes the reader part of the family to whom he addressed them. When they stop because he has been killed, the reader shares the sadness his family felt.[2]

The sorrow at such a loss can also transcend the years in other ways. Private Charles Johnston of the 56th Battalion fell at Fromelles in 1916. A highly regarded teacher, he had influenced many lives and his passing was widely felt. His parents were devastated to lose a second son, Frank, on the Somme later that year. They could not bear to tell their other children that Charles and Frank were never found. Margaret, a sister, believed that they rested in war graves in France. Curious, her son found out from the Office of Australian War Graves that Charles was commemorated on the wall of VC Corner Australian Cemetery at Fromelles, and Frank on the wall of the Australian National Memorial at Villers-Bretonneux. Her grandson subsequently visited them. Nothing was ever said to Margaret, who remained unaware of the truth to the end of her life. Far from fading with time, the deaths of her brothers had touched three generations. I am Margaret Johnston's grandson. Charles and Frank Johnston were my great-uncles.

Mention the First World War to many Australians and they immediately think of Gallipoli. The image of bronzed men storming ashore at Anzac Cove and clinging desperately to cliff-top positions is appealing, if not wholly accurate. Romance also attaches to the Light Horse, who spearheaded the advance that secured Egypt and cleared Palestine. Theirs was a war of hard riding and old-fashioned mounted charges set on a biblical stage. But there was nothing romantic about the Western Front, which summons up images of dreadful slaughter for a few acres of mud. In France and Flanders, Australia sustained more casualties than in all of the conflicts it has fought since put together. Yet the war could never have been won anywhere else and Australia made its greatest contribution to victory there. Indeed in 1918, it influenced the destiny of the world for the first time in the nation's history and arguably more than at any time since. An account of the Anzac experience must therefore focus on France and Flanders. It must also cover the New Zealanders, who have just as much claim to the title 'Anzac' as the Australians. Both called themselves 'Diggers'.

The outstanding performance of the AIF reinforced the belief, held by many Australians pre-war, that they were natural soldiers. Charles Bean, the Australian Official Correspondent and, later, Official Historian, waxed lyrically that they came from a culture that was independent, resourceful and freer from class distinction than most and hence were born with the courage, initiative and impatience essential in first-class fighting men. Another romantic notion, it fitted in well with the Anzac tradition. But it also had some substance. In his famous *Disenchantment*, British soldier–author Charles Montague remarked that Dominion troops like the Australians were 'prouder, firmer in nerve, better schooled, more boldly interested in life, quicker to take means to an end and to parry and counter any new blow' and viewed their English counterparts 'with the half-curious, half-pitying look of a higher, happier caste at a lower'. Yet the natural ability that these qualities indicated was insufficient. Gallipoli soon revealed that training was necessary as well. On the Western Front, it became even more important. Here too the Anzacs were initially caught short.[3]

Nor were the Anzac commanders and staffs any better off. The round-the-clock intensity of the fighting at Gallipoli surprised even those with previous experience of active service. Adjusting to it was a painful process, marked by all too frequent foul-ups. From mid-1916 onwards, the Anzacs were at the forefront of the attempt to breach a trench system, scientifically sited and skilfully defended, that stretched from the North Sea to the Swiss border. Both sides deployed masses of men and applied the full power of modern military technology, in the form of artillery, machine-guns, aircraft and gas, on a vast scale. New weapons such as tanks appeared. The direction of operations and the logistic support they needed became more complex than anything that had gone before.

On the battlefield the outstanding characteristic was 'the almost total lack of control once the battle started. Communications invariably broke down. Very few commanders at any level had the faintest idea about what . . . was happening on their own side, let alone "on the other side of the hill"'. Service in colonial wars was[4] of little relevance in these conditions. The generals had to start virtually from scratch. As Marshal Ferdinand Foch, the Allied Generalissimo in 1918, remarked: 'I have only one merit. I have forgotten what I taught and what I learned'. So did the Anzac commanders, who arrived on the Western Front confident that their Gallipoli experience stood them in good stead. But the ballgame was new nonetheless and they sometimes blundered badly while learning its rules. Not until the middle of 1917 did they master them to the extent of being able to capitalise on the natural ability and training of their men.

Not until 1918 did the commanders and their men become as one. Both underpinned the astonishing successes of the Australian Corps that year.[4]

Throughout the war the Anzac formations served under British higher commanders, whose Staff College at Camberley had never, even in theory, contemplated dealing with a body larger than a six-division expeditionary force. By 1917 the British Expeditionary Force (BEF) was approaching sixty divisions and each of its five armies usually contained more than six divisions. In getting used to commanding large formations, as well as gripping the tactical problems, the British generals, too, made appalling mistakes. That great Australian soldier, General Sir John Hackett, who led a parachute brigade at Arnhem and became Commander-in-Chief of the British Army of the Rhine in NATO, liked to say that the military is the only organisation that can require its members to make the supreme sacrifice. An unfortunate result is that crippling losses can result when generals have to learn as they go and when they err. The Anzacs suffered on each count at the hands of both their own generals and British ones.[5]

The following narrative dwells on the Australian soldier and his commanders in tracing the development of the AIF from its raw origins in 1914. It demystifies the lines that the generals drew on their maps and allows the soldiers to describe what advancing towards them meant on the ground. The role of Australian airmen and sailors has also been described so that Australia's military effort can be seen in its entirety. That effort has been set within the context of the British endeavour of which it formed part and against the backdrop of the wider conflict.

At the very end of his great chronicle, Charles Bean paid an immortal tribute to the AIF:

> What these men did nothing can alter now. The good and the bad, the greatness and smallness of their story will stand. Whatever of glory it

contains nothing now can lessen. It rises, as it will always rise, above the mists of ages, a monument to great-hearted men; and for their nation, a possession for ever.[6]

This book is itself a tribute to those great-hearted men and a reminder to their nation of the legacy they left it.

—ONE—

FIGHTING FOR THE EMPIRE

On 30 June 1914 Australians read that a Serbian nationalist had assassinated Archduke Franz Ferdinand, heir to the Austro-Hungarian throne, and his wife in the Bosnian capital of Sarajevo. If Russia as protector of the Slavs intervened to protect the Serbs from Austrian retaliation, the Austrians would look to Germany. Britain and France might then line up against the Germans. This bewildering array of alliance relationships had been well covered by Australian newspapers over the years. Now Australians learned that 'the peace of the world' was under threat. They were also reminded that other Balkan crises had come and gone without a major war. When the Kaiser left for his annual Norwegian cruise on 6 July, it seemed that maybe this one had fizzled out too.[1]

In any case, Australians were focussed on other issues. Frustrated by the Labor majority in the Senate, Liberal Prime Minister Joseph Cook had obtained a dissolution of both parliamentary houses at the end of June and set down a federal election for 5 September. Further afield, the tension in Ireland, where Ulster loyalists threatened civil war if London granted Irish Home Rule, grabbed attention because Australia's population of four and a half million contained a significant Irish element. Sport was also in the headlines. On 1 July Australian Norman Brookes won the Wimbledon men's singles final by beating German Otto Froitzheim in an epic five-setter.

After squaring the Rugby League test series, Australia lost the decider on 4 July 14–6 at the Sydney Cricket Ground to an English side that injuries had left three men short. The game entered legend as 'the Rorke's Drift Test'.

Australia's gaze returned to Europe when news of an Austrian ultimatum to Serbia arrived on 24 July. Emboldened by Russia, the Serbs mobilised next day, triggering a chain reaction. Austria declared war on Serbia on 28 July. The Russians mobilised on 31 July. The Germans declared war on them on 1 August and the French on the Germans a couple of days later. Germany's Schlieffen Plan, named after the former Chief of the General Staff who conceived it in 1905, aimed at smashing the French while the huge but ponderous Russian Army got into gear. It involved marching through Belgium, whose neutrality Britain had guaranteed and which it now demanded the Germans respect. Ignoring the British ultimatum, German troops entered Belgium on 4 August. Britain declared war that night. In Australia Cook told an election rally in Horsham, 'If the old country is at war, so are we', while Labor Opposition Leader Andrew Fisher famously pledged at Colac: 'Australians will stand beside the mother country to help and defend her to our last man and our last shilling'.

Australians had first gone on active service with British forces over half a century earlier in the colonial period. In 1860, during the Anglo-Maori War, the Victorian sloop HMCS *Victoria* ferried British garrison troops across the Tasman and supported operations against Maori camps. In February 1885 New South Wales sent a contingent of 770 men to help subdue dervish rebels in the Sudan. They left with great fanfare but saw no fighting, which made for an embarrassingly subdued return. Small contingents from New South Wales and Victoria also went to China when the Boxer rebellion threatened British and western interests in 1900. As they arrived after the besieged Peking legations had been relieved, another anticlimax ensued.

The first sting of action came in South Africa. When friction between Britain and the two Boer republics erupted into conflict in 1899, the Australian colonies pledged troops. Drawn mainly from their militias, the initial contingents were used as mounted infantry, ideal for the long sweeps that hunted down the Boer commandos. Wanting more of them, London encouraged the recruitment of good horsemen whether or not they had any military training. The resulting 'Bushmen' units were formed from untrained civilians in rural districts and British commanders praised their initiative, courage and hardiness. For many Australians they were proof that natural ability outweighed the value of training, the limitations of which, they thought, had been exposed by the early drubbings of British regulars. When the war ended in May 1902, 16 175 Australians had served in it, 600 of whom died.[2]

On 1 January 1901 the six colonies had federated, becoming the Commonwealth of Australia, a self-governing Dominion of the British Empire. It remained a dependency of Britain, lacking the power to declare war or make peace with another country, or to stay neutral if Britain went to war, in which case Australia could decide the extent of its involvement. The new Commonwealth inherited from the colonies military forces of 27 466 men, including 1500 regulars, and naval forces of 1659 men, of whom 239 were permanent sailors crewing 14 clapped-out ships. They were all promptly downsized. After a troubled gestation, a Defence Act was passed in October 1903. It decreed that the Australian Military Forces (AMF) would comprise volunteers who could not be compelled to serve outside Australia or its territories. Defence itself remained a backwater issue. Britain, specifically the Royal Navy, bore the primary responsibility for it – and Britannia ruled the waves. But Britannia's global position was no longer as secure as it had once been.[3]

'The weary Titan staggers under the too vast orb of its fate', Colonial Secretary Joseph Chamberlain bemoaned in 1902. Maintaining an empire on which the sun never set, Britain was in the throes of imperial overstretch. America and Germany had overtaken it industrially and along with Russia and France were challenging it militarily and imperially. The Boer War had highlighted Britain's predicament by leaving the Empire vulnerable during the three years the war lasted. It had to reshape its strategic policy to relieve the strain. 'Splendid Isolation', the avoidance of foreign entanglements, weakened as Britain concluded an entente with France in 1904 to settle colonial disputes between them. In 1907 it also reached an agreement with Russia that safeguarded India, the empire's 'jewel'. But the first step had been the Anglo-Japanese alliance of 1902, which was intended to protect British Far Eastern interests.[4]

Britain's cosying up to Japan disquieted Australians. Their fears of the Asian 'yellow peril' had just ensured that the first Commonwealth policy legislation passed was for a White Australia policy. Disquiet turned to outright concern after Japan's crushing naval victory over Russia in May 1905, which ended their war over opposing territorial claims and confirmed Japan as a great Pacific power. European developments made it unlikely that Britain could be a counterweight.

For hundreds of years Britain had fought war after war to keep one nation from dominating Europe. A European balance of power served British security interests well. But Germany had dominated Europe since trouncing France in 1870 and stripping Alsace–Lorraine from it. Under the mercurial Kaiser Wilhelm II, the Germans pursued a policy of *Weltpolitik* to achieve 'a place in the sun' commensurate with their new standing. Central to the policy was a vast naval armament programme, based on battleship construction, which butted against British naval supremacy. Though Britain responded in kind, it meant that the Royal Navy's most modern warships had to be concentrated in the North Sea at the expense of the Pacific. Moreover, the Kaiser's ham-fisted diplomacy prevented any lasting thaw in Germany's relations with the French, who were bent on recovering their lost territories. German conduct drove Britain and France closer together. They started military staff talks, which eventually examined the despatch of a British expeditionary force to France in the event of war with Germany. As the Russians already had an alliance with the French, Britain was now aligned in effect, if not technically, with the Franco-Russian camp.

With Australians perceiving a real threat to their security for the first time, the *Sydney Morning Herald* lamented the 'deplorable state' of the nation's defences. Though revolving-door governments characterised post-Federation Australia, all of them, Liberal and Labor, backed the creation of a credible navy and compulsory military service to fix the problem. As well as a response to Australia's Pacific isolation, a more self-reliant defence policy was also an expression of nascent nationalism. It did not imply any weakening of loyalty to Britain. On the contrary, Australians thought that by doing more themselves, they were strengthening imperial defence by making Britain's task easier.[5]

Hence the ships of the Royal Australian Navy (RAN), a title King George V approved in July 1911, formed a fleet unit based in Australian waters but which would 'automatically become an integral part of the Royal Navy' in wartime. When the flagship *Australia*, an 18 800-ton battle-cruiser, led the light cruisers *Sydney*, *Melbourne* and *Encounter* and the destroyers *Warrego*, *Parramatta* and *Yarra* through Sydney Heads on 4 October 1913, the hundreds of thousands of Sydneysiders gathered on the foreshores heard Prime Minister Cook say: 'May I stress for one moment the words "His Majesty's Australian Ships". The ships are none the less Australian because they are His Majesty's ships. They are none the less His Majesty's ships because they are Australian ships'. Australia was the only Dominion to acquire a navy. New Zealand funded the cost of an eponymous battle-cruiser for the Royal Navy.[6]

Compulsory military service, which included mandatory cadet training for schoolboys, was instituted in December 1909, just as Field-Marshal Lord Horatio Kitchener, Commander-in-Chief in

India and the Empire's most prestigious soldier, arrived in Australia to inspect the defences and make organisational recommendations. He called for an 80 000-strong citizen army organised into twenty-one infantry brigades, each of four battalions, as well as twenty-eight light horse regiments and fifty-six batteries of artillery. Compulsory training was blessed as the basis of the military forces, with all 18- to 25-year-old men attending short annual camps. A military college was to be set up to train the staff officers needed to run things. Kitchener also went to New Zealand, which put in place a similar scheme, albeit on a much smaller scale.

When compulsory training actually got under way in Australia in 1911, the new formations struggled to reach even a basic level of proficiency within the brief training periods laid down. Officer shortcomings were glaring and frequently commented on in the press. It also criticised commanders who planned tough and realistic exercises, such as Colonel John Monash, who was pilloried for allegedly imagining himself 'Napoleon–Wellington–Roberts all rolled into one' while directing his brigade on manoeuvres in February 1914. Checking progress at this time, the Inspector-General of British Overseas Forces, General Sir Ian Hamilton, recognised the great military potential of the men, whose 'natural soldier-like spirit, intelligence and wiry, athletic frames' were the army's best assets. He noted nonetheless that in their present state they would 'need to be in a majority of at least two to one to fight a pitched battle with picked regular troops from overseas on equal terms'.[7]

Under the Defence Act, the new army was restricted to home defence. Australia had always refrained from giving a firm commitment to furnish military forces for Britain. As its first Prime Minister, Edmund Barton, said when Chamberlain raised the question in 1902, Australia could be depended upon if the Empire was imperilled but its contribution had to stem from the spontaneous response of its people. At the Imperial Conference in May 1911, Fisher, then Prime Minister, and his Defence Minister, George Pearce, were informed that 'a European war was inevitable and that it would probably come in 1915 when the preparations that Germany was making would be complete'. Pearce did not demur when the War Office suggested that each Dominion should be given 'certain natural spheres of influence' for wartime operations. Replying that the Defence Act limited the Australian government to sending volunteers overseas if war came but that many would go, he called for the co-ordination of mobilisation schemes in case Australia and the other Dominions chose to mount an expeditionary force. The others concurred.[8]

In November 1912 the Chief of the Australian General Staff, Brigadier-General Joseph Gordon, and Major-General Alexander Godley, the British officer in charge of New Zealand's military forces, discussed joint action in the Pacific in the event of a European war. Of the adjacent German territories, they decided that Australia would seize those in the Bismarck Archipelago while New Zealand handled Samoa. If an expeditionary force were needed, each would contribute contingents, based on the number of troops it had sent to South Africa, to an 18 000-strong Australasian division, Australia therefore providing 12 000 men, or to a mounted force of four brigades, three of them Australian. In great secrecy, Major Brudenell White, Director of Operations for Australia's military forces, worked out the details of the Commonwealth's part in the scheme.[9]

On 29 July 1914 London advised that war was imminent. Exercising off the Queensland coast, the Australian naval squadron steamed to Sydney for coaling. On 2 August preliminary mobilisation, which stepped up security at vital places like seaports, was ordered. White attended a Cabinet meeting in Melbourne next day. Dusting off the plan for an Australasian expeditionary force, he stated that an all-arms volunteer force of 12 000 men could be raised and readied for sailing within six weeks. As Canada was thought – wrongly – to have offered 30 000 men, Cook thought Australia should send at least 20 000. He asked if it could be done. White concurred, adding that the six weeks' timeframe might still be possible. The offer was made. At 12.45 p.m. on 5 August, Cook announced: 'I have received the following despatch from the Imperial Government – War has broken out with Germany'. London cabled on the 6th that the British 'gratefully accepted the offer . . . and would be glad if it could be despatched as soon as possible'. Australia also put the RAN under the Admiralty's control.[10]

With few exceptions, Australians hailed the start of hostilities with heady displays of patriotism and imperial loyalty. When someone in the crowd reading the cables outside the offices of *The Age* in Melbourne began a patriotic song, the rest struck up and those with Union Jacks were lifted shoulder high. 'Rule Britannia', 'Soldiers of the King' and 'Sons of the Sea' were belted out, and 'woe betide anyone who failed to remove his hat without hesitation' during the regular renditions of the national anthem. In Sydney the Governor of New South Wales, Sir Gerald Strickland, was reminded of the revelry on the eve of Waterloo; in Adelaide the Governor of South Australia, Sir Henry Galway, urged everyone to 'keep a stiff upper lip'. The *Sydney Morning Herald* depicted Australia as embarking on a rite of passage:

> It is our baptism of fire. Australia knows something of the flames of war, but its realities have never been brought so close as they will be in the near future, and the discipline will help us to find ourselves. It will test our manhood and womanhood by an immediate local pressure, even though we may never hear a shot fired or get a glimpse of the foe.

The *Herald* reckoned the war was 'not likely to be prolonged. The pace will be too fast'. But the *Adelaide Advertiser* had no doubt that Armageddon lay ahead: 'the most frightful war of our time, a war which must surpass in horror and devastation the worst of historical wars'.[11]

Yet it began benignly for Australia, which fired probably the Empire's first shot when the German steamer *Pfalz* sailed from

Melbourne on 5 August. Reaching the Heads at Port Phillip Bay it ignored the signal to stop, whereupon the gunners at Fort Nepean lobbed a shell across its bows. Determined to proceed, the steamer's captain wrestled on the bridge with the Australian pilot, who finally convinced him to halt the vessel by saying the next shot would hit it. The day before, the Australian naval squadron under Rear-Admiral George Patey headed north in the hope of eliminating the German East Asia Cruiser Squadron, commanded by Vice-Admiral Graf Maximilian von Spee, which wireless intercepts suggested might be off German New Guinea. It was not.

On 6 August Britain asked Australia, 'as a great and urgent Imperial service', to seize the wireless stations there and in the German Pacific territories of Nauru and the Carolines, while New Zealand was called on to deal with German Samoa, essentially the division of labour Gordon and Godley had agreed upon in 1912. These stations enabled the Germans to control their warships in the Pacific and Indian Oceans and, by intercepting the chatter from allied vessels, to give them the intelligence they needed either to strike or stay out of harm's way. A 1000-strong infantry battalion, hastily enlisted in Sydney, and a 500-man landing party, recruited from ex-seamen and naval reservists, made up the bulk of the Australian Naval and Military Expeditionary Force (AN&MEF), which reached Rabaul, the colonial capital of German New Guinea, on 11 September and occupied it next day. The garrison – about sixty troops, mostly German reservists, and 240 men drawn from the native constabulary – had prepared a number of road ambushes, but the largely untrained and badly equipped Australians took to the jungle to outflank them. An Australian administration replaced the German one. The Nauru wireless station was knocked out on 9 September and the New Zealanders had occupied Samoa on 30 August. But the Japanese, who had joined the war against Germany on 23 August, took control of the Carolines, as well as the other German possessions north of the equator.[12]

The brief campaign was extremely frustrating for Patey and his squadron. He expected to continue the search for von Spee but the Admiralty decided instead that he should escort the AN&MEF and the New Zealanders. As Lieutenant William Warren, *Parramatta*'s commanding officer, lamented: 'our first and most important duty to destroy the German fleet was put subservient to the occupying of islands with troops'. The Australian submarine *AE1* also disappeared without trace off Rabaul on 20 September with the loss of all thirty-five hands. Von Spee got away. Leaving the light cruiser *Emden* to operate in the Indian Ocean, his squadron withdrew across the Pacific, as Patey had foreseen. After sinking two British cruisers off the Chilean town of Coronel on 1 November, it rounded Cape Horn and was itself destroyed off the Falkland Islands on 8 December. One Australian officer labelled its demise 'the worst piece of really good news that we have had'.[13]

It was ironic that the Australian squadron had been acquired largely on account of the perceived threat from the Japanese, who were now closer to Australia. Still, winning control of New Guinea gave Australia a buffer against Japan that would prove vital in the next war. Australia also gained a greater say in Pacific affairs. As many Australians realised, these were important strategic achievements. The AN&MEF, whose operations London praised as 'most efficiently conducted throughout', was welcomed home on a march through Sydney at the start of 1915. Having seen little combat, its moment was fleeting. The much larger expeditionary force Australia had sent abroad monopolised national attention, as it would for the next four years.[14]

—TWO—

AUSTRALIA WILL BE THERE

Offered an expeditionary force 'of any suggested composition', the War Office asked Australia on 7 August 1914 for infantry, light horse and artillery constituted as separate brigades. They could then be parcelled out among British formations, as Australian units were in the Boer War, denying the force any sense of national character. Given responsibility for raising it, the AMF's Inspector-General, William Bridges, drafted the Commonwealth's reply, which stated that it had begun organising an infantry division and a light horse brigade. A division is the smallest formation that is self-contained for fighting purposes and in the British Army of 1914, an infantry division comprised three brigades, each of four battalions, plus supporting arms and services, giving it a strength of 18 000 men. An Australian division thus organised would absorb most of the contingent being sent, while the light horse brigade, with 2000 men spread across three regiments, soaked up the rest.[1]

London agreed. The Australian government appointed Bridges overall commander and promoted him to major-general. He made White his chief of staff. Anticipating that the force was likely to be the first instalment of a wider Australian contribution, Bridges named its component formations the 1st Division and the 1st Light Horse (LH) Brigade. He needed a title to distinguish it from the AN&MEF. 'I want a name that will sound well when they call us by our initials. That's how they'll speak of us. We don't want to be called the B.L.U.F', he remarked, before hitting on Australian Imperial Force.[2]

The basis of the AIF was territorial. New South Wales supplied the 1st Brigade (1st–4th Battalions) and Victoria the 2nd (5th–8th Battalions), while the four less populous states fielded the 3rd Brigade (9th–12th Battalions). The 1st LH Brigade comprised a regiment each from New South Wales and Queensland and a composite regiment from South Australia and Tasmania. Guaranteeing that all Australia was represented, this approach also encouraged patriotism by fostering local pride in the unit provided. Retained until the Armistice, it was also the strongest factor making for *esprit de corps* in the AIF. In order to slash the time needed to equip and train, White originally hoped to fill the ranks with AMF volunteers. The New Zealanders used such a method, which directly linked the overseas force units to their home army counterparts. But at this stage of compulsory training, the AMF consisted almost entirely of 19- to 21-year-old youths.

Aware that Australia could not send away an army of boys, and wanting men who had done some military training, Bridges and White decided that at least half the force would be made up of volunteers aged twenty years or over from the citizen forces. The rest were to come from men who had served in the old militia or in South Africa or other conflicts. Enlistees could be no older than thirty-eight and had to be at least 5 foot 5 inches tall with a minimum chest measurement of 34 inches. Privates would receive 6 shillings per day, the average worker's wage after rations and quarters were taken into account. The Australian was thus the war's best-paid soldier. As well as its own personnel policies, the AIF had its own administrative structure, all of which made it a parallel army to the AMF.

The response when recruiting began on 11 August was massive. Initially the only recruiting centres were in the capital cities. In Sydney, 3600 men had been selected at the end of the first day they were open and over 10 000 had applied by 20 August. In Brisbane, 1400 applied on the first day and almost 4500 in Perth after two days. Knocked back four times in Melbourne, where 7000 volunteered in the first fortnight, one man came to Sydney and was accepted. Another joined in Sydney after riding 460 miles through Central Australia to catch the train to Adelaide, finding no vacancies there, and sailing to Tasmania where the ranks were again full. A Queensland drover walked 350 miles to Brisbane when his horse gave out.[3]

All too often, the quest ended in disappointment for the huge influx allowed absurdly demanding medical and dental standards to be set without prejudicing the recruitment targets. Men were rejected for having filled teeth let alone false ones, varicose veins, corns, and toes that were not level (which led some to have the offending digit amputated before trying again). One unfortunate with flat feet was disqualified even though he had walked the 500 miles from Bourke to Sydney. Public complaints about the injustice of inducing men to leave their jobs and families, and perhaps travel long distances only to be let down, led to the establishment of rural recruiting depots. On 3 September the Cook government advised the War Office that it could send a fourth infantry brigade and a second brigade of light horse. It was Cook's swansong for Labor under Fisher scored a landslide election win two days later. As almost 30 000 men had enlisted by the end of September, the new government offered a third light horse brigade. It, too, was promptly accepted.[4]

By the end of 1914, 52 561 men had joined. Various motives impelled them. Charles Forster wanted to uphold the traditions of the British race, while Jack Tarrant remembered that 'it was loyalty too. Everyone was King and Queen'. Others felt a moral obligation, saying that remaining behind would make it impossible to look the world in the eye again. 'You had to go', recalled Tom Usher. For Frank Parker, it was adventure. 'Forget King and Country! Who was the King? What was his name?' Those like Parker saw a means of swapping a humdrum existence for a chance to see the world. Tired of stoking on a coastal steamer, Englishman John Simpson Kirkpatrick grasped the chance to go home. As the 1914 drought had created widespread unemployment, economic reasons drove many. According to Kalgoorlie accountant Murray Aitken, the AIF was 'a real God send' that resulted in 'men who've never been better dressed nor earned so much money before in their life'. The *Sydney Morning Herald* estimated that half of Sydney's 5500 unemployed signed on.[5]

As only a fifth of the enlistees were under twenty-one, the boy army had been avoided. But the experience level was short of what Bridges and White sought. Three-quarters of the light horse had some formal military training but over 40 per cent of the 1st Division's infantry, 6098 men out of 14 693, did not. In the hope of attracting more South African veterans, the age limit was subsequently raised to forty-five. Australian discipline – or lack of it – had been frequently remarked upon in South Africa and the issue arose again. Aitken observed of the typical recruit:

> Discipline irks him, he is not used to it, & it's a thing he can never be made to thoroughly understand; every man . . . considers himself the equal of every other man, it's not in his programme to take peremptory orders but he looks upon a request almost as a command.

Harnessing the spirit of such men required officers who could perform both as leaders and commanders but, as Major-General J. F. C. Fuller has pointed out, wartime requirements sit uncomfortably with peacetime conditions. Finding officers who fitted the bill was therefore a hit and miss process.[6]

Though in overall charge of the force, Bridges, fifty-three, personally commanded the 1st Division. Australia's first chief of the general staff and the Duntroon Military College's founding commandant, he had spent his career in staff and instructional appointments. Even his five-month Boer War stint had passed on attachment to British units for instructional purposes. This background equipped Bridges to organise the AIF but it did not include regimental soldiering. Hence he had little understanding of the free-willed volunteers he led. Dour, brusque to the extent that a grunt was his conversational trademark, he was 'ruthless as to the feelings of others; he seemed to make no concessions to humanity', wrote Bean, who saw much of Bridges. Colonel Talbot Hobbs, the 1st Division's chief gunner, called him 'an uncouth, ignorant boor'. His manner discouraged initiative or frank advice, vastly increasing his decision-making load and so wasting the talent at his disposal, for Bridges had 'picked the eyes' of the AMF to get an outstanding divisional staff. White had served in an Australian mounted unit during the Boer War, attended the Camberley Staff College afterwards and so impressed its staff that, on graduating, he was loaned to the British Army for three years. His astuteness, integrity and selflessness were matched by personal charm. Eleven members of the divisional staff were generals by the war's end.[7]

Owing to the part-time basis of the pre-war army, few officers had handled 'even a brigade for more than a day or two at annual camps'. Bridges was not among them. Nor were the men he picked for the brigade commands. Colonel Henry MacLaurin, a 35-year-old Sydney barrister, was given the 1st Brigade. He had only taken over a battalion a year earlier. The 2nd Brigade went to Colonel James McCay, 49, a volatile Castlemaine lawyer who had been Defence Minister in 1904–05 and head of the Australian Intelligence Corps from 1907 to 1913. Unlike his old schoolmate Monash, who could make imbeciles feel like intellectuals, McCay did not tolerate fools gladly and made them feel like imbeciles. He freely dispensed advice to his superiors. Bridges's right-hand man at Duntroon, Colonel Ewen Sinclair-MacLagan, 46, got the 3rd Brigade. A British officer decorated in South Africa, he was capable but tended towards pessimism, as did Colonel Harry Chauvel, the 49-year-old Queensland Boer War mounted veteran chosen for the 1st LH Brigade. The brigadiers selected their battalion commanders and they, in turn, their regimental officers. Most of the 631 officers picked for the 1st Division held commissions already. Two-thirds started out in the old militia, fifty-eight were young officers under the compulsory service scheme and twenty-three came from the first class at Duntroon, which had been graduated early. The rest were largely Australian and British regulars, active and retired. One hundred and four officers had seen action; only twenty-four were new to the army.[8]

Disparate gaggles of civilians and part-time soldiers began the transformation into fighting units in mid-August. At 9 a.m. on 17 August, the 3rd Battalion, 300 strong, gathered at Sydney's Victoria Barracks. 'Crowds of men in mufti jostled each other, talking and laughing excitedly', wrote Bean's brother John, the unit's doctor. He saw the old soldiers stand quietly but take the lead when the officers told the men off into companies for the march to their new home, Randwick Racecourse, and their first army meal:

> 'The battalion will move to the right in fours. A Company, shun. Form fours, right! By the left, quick march!' snaps out the company commander, leading. The others in turn take up the cry, and the 3rd Battalion of Infantry, no longer a name, but a living entity, moves off in column of fours – a long sinuous serpent, to lunch and glory.

Uniforms were issued on 20 August, rifles six days later. A cadre group did a brief musketry course to teach the others how to use them. Recruiting in country centres started on 29 August. On 3 September the battalion was at full strength with thirty-two officers and 991 men. On 4 September its two machine-guns arrived. The band held its first practice on 16 September and the Governor-General, Sir Ronald Munro-Ferguson, inspected the battalion on 19 September. Across Australia, units took shape in more or less the same way at Broadmeadows near Melbourne, Blackboy Hill close to Perth, Enoggera outside Brisbane, Morphettville in Adelaide and Pontville north of Hobart, as well as at Randwick, Kensington and Liverpool in Sydney. Canteens selling pies, fruit, milk and chocolate quickly sprang up on the outskirts of each camp and did a brisk trade.[9]

The day began in all units with reveille at 6 a.m. followed by at least an hour of physical exercise before breakfast, after which training continued until 4.30 p.m., with an hour off for lunch. A light supper was eaten at 5 p.m. and lights went out between 9 and 10 p.m. Musketry and bayonet fighting were popular. Men also looked forward to field training, in which platoons and companies 'fought' each other, because it was competitive and hinted at the real thing. Route-marches with combat loads were grudgingly accepted as necessary to become fit. Drill, which aimed to inculcate the habit of unquestioning obedience, was regarded with amused tolerance. 'When the instructor said left turn', wrote Private George Feist of the 12th Battalion, 'one would turn right as sure as eggs, then he would condescend to tell you all about your relations etc'.[10]

Little time was spent on spit and polish. Designed for the battlefield rather than the parade-ground, the Australian uniform did not encourage it. The pure wool, pea-soup coloured outfit, with its four loose-cut roomy pockets and brass buttons oxidised black so as not to reflect the sun, was the most practical clobber of the war and its distinctive upper-sleeve colour patches, which identified a man's unit, evoked deep attachment. A hungover morning roll-call after the 11th Battalion's evening poker school demonstrated how military ritual was lampooned. Instead of responding with his regimental number when fellow cardsharp Sergeant George Mason called out his name, Private Bill Henson yelled 'Two nines and a bullet'. The parade collapsed in fits of laughter and Henson was severely reprimanded.[11]

By 21 September, six weeks after enlistment began, the first contingent was ready to sail, as Bridges and White had promised. The achievement it represented was astonishing by any standard. Almost 8000 horses as well as guns, wagons and transport had been assembled and all the men clothed and equipped. The parades in the capital cities before departure showed the public what had been accomplished. When the 2nd Brigade marched through Melbourne on 25 September, the 'swaying mile of khaki-clad figures, all with bayonets fixed', took forty minutes to pass a given point. As they swung by Parliament House, where Munro-Ferguson took the salute, 'every, arm, every boot, every head appeared to move . . . as if it was controlled by some precise mechanism', the *Argus* reported, while 'the self-control was remarkable' throughout for even cries from friends and relatives were ignored. The 1st Brigade's march through Sydney was equally impressive, and the Governor of Western Australia, Major-General Sir Harry Barron, said that the 11th Battalion in Perth looked like 'a regiment any man would be proud to command'.[12]

After embarking units from the capital city ports, the troopships were to concentrate off Albany by 3 October. When those bringing the infantry brigade and mounted rifle brigade of the New Zealand Expeditionary Force (NZEF) arrived, *Sydney*, *Melbourne*, the British cruiser *Minotaur* and the *Ibuki*, a cruiser loaned by the Japanese, would escort the combined convoy across the Indian Ocean to Aden. But von Spee's appearance off Samoa on 14 September raised fears that he might next head into the Tasman and fall on the unescorted transports creeping around the coastline to Albany. They were ordered into port. On 30 September news came that the German squadron had raided Papeete, one thousand miles beyond Samoa. Only then did the concentration resume.

The delay was a severe let-down for the men had said their goodbyes and were eager to start the 'Great Adventure', as the newspapers called it. Rumours were rife. Those that spread from idle chatter around the water carts at Broadmeadows made the name of their manufacturer, the Furphy foundry at Shepparton, a synonym for rumour thereafter. Troops regularly broke camp. The sight of them loafing about in Melbourne and Sydney led many who had been favourably struck by the farewell marches to change their minds. 'They'll never make soldiers of that lot', they said. 'The light horse may be all right, but they've got the ragtag and bobtail of Australia in this infantry.' 'Going to the front!', a Sydney newspaper manager joked, 'They'll keep the trained British regular army for the front; the nearest these'll get to it will be the line of communications!' The 'six-bob-a-day tourist' tag sprang up. But the interlude had an upside. Visiting the 2nd LH Regiment from Queensland, which had been offloaded in Melbourne, Fisher allowed them to tuck emu plumes into their slouch hats in keeping with the tradition of Queensland mounted troops. Within a year, all the light horse regiments had done the same.[13]

Thousands turned out when the day of departure finally arrived. Girls joined the ranks of the 2nd Battalion, which practically had to force its way through the crowds while marching down Bourke Street to Woolloomooloo wharf in Sydney on 18 October. In Melbourne a vast crowd swamped the guard barring access to the pier and many more gathered on adjacent Port Melbourne beach. They sang 'Auld Lang Syne' and patriotic songs like the newly written 'Australia Will Be There' long after the transports had sailed. Behind the cheeriness lurked fears unspoken but not always hidden. Soldiers gripped gifts given as a reminder of home: a watch, a pipe, a fountain pen. Signaller Bob Kenny never forgot 'the tear-dimmed eyes of the women and girls' he saw on leaving Sydney. At 6.45 a.m. on 1 November, the greatest convoy to leave Australia entered the open sea, its thirty-six ships three abreast and covering an area two miles wide and over seven long. Many of those cramming the decks threw last messages over the side in bottles that implored the finders to pass them on to their loved ones.[14]

Already the uncertainties of the Great Adventure were apparent. Germany had gained a new ally in the Turkish Ottoman Empire. Wanting to extend their influence eastward, the Germans had long courted the Turks. War Minister Enver Pasha and other principals of the Young Turks, the cabal of military officers who overthrew the Sultan in 1908, were pro-German and a German Military Mission under General Otto Liman von Sanders was modernising their ramshackle army. Enver had recently concluded a secret treaty with Germany that was directed against the Russians, who coveted Constantinople. But many Turk leaders favoured neutrality as war loomed. The outcry over Britain's clumsy seizure on 3 August, for its own fleet, of two battleships recently built in British yards for the Ottoman Navy and paid for by popular subscription ended their chances. It coincided with the arrival at the Dardanelles Straits of the German cruisers *Goeben* and *Breslau*. Letting them enter, the Turks closed the Straits on 27 September. Britain imposed a blockade on 2 October, by which time *Goeben* and *Breslau* were part of the Ottoman fleet. Departing Albany, Australians and New Zealanders knew that the two cruisers had led a bombardment of Russian Black Sea ports on 29 October. Speculation started on the likelihood of war between Britain and Turkey and disembarking in Egypt instead of England as a result.

Once the novelty of being aboard ship waned, time passed slowly. The men were put through physical exercises, musketry and theoretical work in map-reading, signalling, message-writing and tactics. Officers and NCOs attended evening lectures, sometimes learning about the subject they would teach next day. The gunners brought their guns out on deck and drilled one day a week. Spending practically all their time looking after their mounts, the busiest units were the light horse. Half the troopers fed and watered the horses, cleaned their stables and walked them around the decks during the day, and the other half attended them during the night. Only 3 per cent of the 7843 horses were lost, a sixth of what had been anticipated. A patch of squally weather two days out caused the only widespread seasickness, which the men called 'singing practice', but pneumonia was rife in some transports and accounted for most of the eleven sea burials during the six-week voyage.[15]

On 9 November the convoy neared the Cocos Islands, to the north of which *Emden* had carved out one of naval history's most spectacular commerce-raiding careers. Under its daring skipper, Captain Karl von Müller, the 3600-ton cruiser had accounted for twenty-one vessels totalling 100 000 tons, set the oil tanks at Madras on fire and sunk a Russian cruiser and a French destroyer in a Nelsonian foray into Penang Harbour. Von Müller next decided to destroy the Cocos cable and wireless station in order to disrupt Anglo-Australian communications but was unaware of the convoy's approach. At 6.30 a.m. its wireless operators picked up a message from Cocos: 'SOS. Strange warship approaching'. *Sydney* hared off westwards. Then came the muffled thuds of distant gunfire.

Sydney was twelve miles off Cocos when its lookouts sighted *Emden* at 9.15 a.m. As his eight 6-inch guns outreached von Müller's ten 4.1-inchers, Captain John Glossop planned to engage when five miles distant, supposedly outside *Emden*'s range. But at six miles there came the 'Wheeeo-Wheeeo-Wheooo' and 'But-But-But' of a salvo passing overhead and striking the water two hundred yards away. The Admiralty had not realised that German guns could shoot further by firing at an elevation of 30 degrees, whereas British guns were limited to 18 degrees. *Emden*'s shooting was excellent, fifteen of its shells striking *Sydney* in the opening minutes. Ten were duds and the shell weight was only 38 pounds, which limited the damage caused by the five that went off. Once *Sydney* found the range, its 100-pound shells were devastating. Many found their target. By 11 a.m. *Emden* was ablaze with only one gun still firing. Von Müller drove his ship onto the reef off North Keeling Island. One of the few one-on-one naval encounters of the war ended at 11.10 a.m. with *Sydney*'s famous message, '*Emden* beached and done for'. On seeing the cruiser close up, Glossop wrote:

> My God, what a sight! . . . everybody on board was demented – that's all you could call it, just fairly demented – by shock, and fumes, and the roar

of shells bursting among them. She was a shambles. Blood, guts, flesh, and uniforms were all scattered about. One of our shells had landed behind a gun shield, and had blown the whole gun crew into one pulp. You couldn't even tell how many men there had been.

Of *Emden*'s 316-man complement, 134 were dead. The rest went aboard *Sydney*, which headed for Colombo with sixteen casualties of its own.[16]

The news of *Sydney*'s triumph spread like wildfire through the convoy. Bridges declared a half-holiday and celebrations began. Lieutenant-Colonel Lyon Johnston amnestied the 11th Battalion men who were in the brig and drank champagne toasts to *Sydney*, Glossop and the dead with the officers. They shouted beer for all 2000 aboard. The 2nd Battalion was delighted when Lieutenant-Colonel George Braund, state member for Armidale in New South Wales and confirmed wowser, announced that he would stand a drink for all ranks. It turned out to be an extra issue of limejuice.[17]

In Britain *Emden*'s demise was widely publicised to counteract the shock of Coronel. Imperial poet Henry Newbolt, whose 'Vitai Lampada' urged the need to 'Play up! Play up! And play the game!' in war as much as in school sports, took lyrical licence to new heights in eulogising *Sydney*'s gunners: 'Their hearts were hot, And as they shot, They sang like kangaroos'. Australia was also jubilant, although the most common remark in Sydney was 'I'm glad it wasn't the *Melbourne*'. *Sydney*'s triumph mitigated the depressing reality that the war was not going the way Australians hoped. The Germans had towelled the Russians at Tannenberg and the Masurian Lakes, although the drubbing the Russians gave the Austrians at Lemberg partly offset their victory. Now Turkey was formally in the war on Germany's side. On the Western Front, the headlong French rush at the German frontier was slaughtered and the Schlieffen Plan wheel got to within twenty miles of Paris before stalling on the Marne. Then each side tried to outflank the other in the 'race to the sea'. Each was unsuccessful. Trenches began snaking from the Channel to the Swiss border. Instead of swift victory, deadlock.[18]

After Colombo the convoy stopped briefly in Aden. When it left on 26 November, thoughts of being sent to Egypt to fight the Turks faded for the Salisbury Plain training area in Britain was set as the final destination. But as the transports cruised up the Red Sea on the following evening, a signal arrived from Sir George Reid, the Australian High Commissioner in Britain: 'Unforeseen circumstances decide that the force shall train in Egypt and go to the front from there. The Australians and New Zealanders are to form a corps under General Birdwood. The locality of the camp is near Cairo'.

Stretched by its own massive expansion, the British Army had yet to erect hutted accommodation on Salisbury Plain, and the onset of winter weather turned the camps on the bleak expanse 'into archipelagoes of tents in a knee-deep sea of mud'. The Canadian Expeditionary Force, which was already there, suffered appallingly. Aware that the Australasians faced a worse plight because they would be going under canvas in mid-winter after a long voyage through the tropics, Colonel Chauvel, who was finishing up in London as the Australian representative on the Imperial General Staff, alerted Reid. He got Kitchener to make the change. It ensured that the Australians and New Zealanders could train in a milder winter climate before proceeding to the Western Front.[19]

The switch also suited Britain, which feared that Turkey's entry into the war might foment a revolt led by Egyptian nationalists and the seventy thousand Turkish nationals in Egypt. With Turkey now an enemy, Britain planned to terminate nominal Turkish suzerainty over Egypt and formalise its own position as the effective ruling power by proclaiming a protectorate. The appearance of the Australasians would help deter any consequent unrest. They could also be used to counter an invasion from Ottoman Syria, where a Turkish buildup was under way. Following a passage of the Suez Canal made memorable by the enthusiastic exchange of greetings with the

British territorial and Indian troops defending it, disembarkation began in Alexandria on 3 December. After a five-hour rail journey to Cairo, the new arrivals marched to camps from which they could respond promptly to any disturbances. The New Zealanders went to Zeitoun on the city's northern edge; the Light Horse to Maadi, on the Nile four miles south of Cairo; and the 1st Division to Mena, in the shadow of the Pyramids and Sphinx ten miles west of it. On 20 December they lined the streets for the proclamation of the Protectorate, which passed quietly. Their magnificent physique, 'the like of which had never been seen', was commented upon.[20]

On 21 December Lieutenant-General Sir William Birdwood arrived. A 49-year-old Indian Army cavalry officer, he had an imperial pedigree that matched his mandatory imperial moustache. The grandson of a general and the son of the under-secretary to the government of Bombay, Birdwood was born in India, educated in England and had served abroad since 1885, mainly in Indian frontier campaigns until going to South Africa as Kitchener's military secretary. A teetotaller with an occasional stammer, he had the ambitious man's flair for self-promotion. But Birdwood also took men for what they were rather than what their appearance suggested. He had commanded a brigade though not a division, and was secretary to the Army Department, Government of India, and on the Viceroy's Legislative Council before going to Egypt.[21]

The name suggested for Birdwood's new command, the Australasian Army Corps, was disliked by the national commanders, particularly the New Zealanders, and changed to Australian and New Zealand Army Corps. This was too unwieldy for telegraphic purposes. Early in 1915 Birdwood approved the acronym ANZAC, which had been derived from A.&N.Z.A.C., the initials on the stamp cut by the clerks to register correspondence at his headquarters. It came to denote the men as well. Birdwood had also proposed to Kitchener a corps of three divisions that would incorporate the fourth infantry brigade and two extra light horse brigades coming from Australia. He envisaged a mounted division and two infantry divisions, the 1st Australian Division and the '2nd' or New Zealand Division, which would be made up of the New Zealand and 4th Australian Infantry Brigades and a further brigade if one became available. As this was by no means assured, the 1st Australian LH Brigade and New Zealand Mounted Rifles Brigade (NZMR), both intended for the mounted division, temporarily took the place of the third infantry brigade in the newly named New Zealand and Australian (NZ and A) Division that Godley commanded.

Training began within a week of arrival. In the 1st Division, Bridges wanted to progress from company to brigade level exercises within two months. Divisional manoeuvres would start only if it had not left Egypt at that stage, indicating that he was prepared to go into action still without any experience of field command and with his staff unpractised in formation operations. But he set a demanding routine that was implemented six days per week. After half an hour's drill came the march through several miles of soft sand to Tiger's Tooth, Hangman's Rock, Murdering Gully, Aeroplane Waddy, and other landmarks whose nicknames denoted the unit training areas. In order to regain fitness after the voyage, men carried 70-pound packs and when they took them off, their backs, drenched with sweat, were exposed to the desert wind. A number of deaths from pneumonia resulted. Ingesting the dust thrown up by the columns made throat complaints endemic. If a sandstorm arose, conditions were intolerable.

Once in the training area, units dug simple defences and spent hours attacking them. The same exercises were done twice weekly at night, Lieutenant Hector Haslam remarking of one of the 11th Battalion's night assaults on Tiger's Tooth that they were just making sure it had not escaped after being captured in the afternoon attack. Egyptian hawkers followed the marching columns with 'oringus, leomonaht and eggs-a-cook'. Only the soldiers were visible, the 5th Battalion's historian wrote, 'until the signal was given for a smoke-o . . . when Gyppos would spring up as if by magic from the sand'. Leave was granted between 4 p.m. and the 10 p.m. Cairo curfew time for a third of the officers and a fifth of the rank and file.[22]

Egypt's ancient past was fascinating for men from a young country who belonged to a generation with a biblical grounding. 'It is a miracle how they were built', Lieutenant Ivor Margetts of the 12th Battalion said of the Pyramids. 'Solid slabs that it is impossible to place in position even nowadays.' Artillery officer Lieutenant Henry Coe had a unique insight on the mummies in the Cairo Museum: 'You can see they are awfully hungry as their tummies are all stuck to their backbones'. A guide pointed out to Private Cecil McAnulty of the 3rd Battalion the 'identical spot' on the Nile where Moses was found in the bulrushes. When asked 'which were the particular bulrushes the basket nestled against, he apparently did not hear us'. The zoo, the Citadel, pitted by Napoleon's cannonballs, and the Citadel's mosque, covered in alabaster from the Great Pyramid, were all mandatory stops on the itinerary.

Seeing the sights took a few days, after which nothing else about Egypt impressed. It was their first taste of a foreign land for most Australians and its culture was alien to theirs. Machine-gun officer Lieutenant John Campbell insisted that 'the lowest lanes in Carlton are clean and the houses palaces compared to the places in Cairo'. The Egyptians themselves were regarded according to the contemporary Australian attitude towards non-white races. 'When I am drinking tea and there is a nigger within smelling distance (15 yards), I watch my tea closely to see that he does not steal the sugar out of it', Lieutenant Coe said. Lance-Corporal George Mitchell of the 10th Battalion railed against the hawkers, 'who are low enough to take a blind man down for his socks' and 'a worse nuisance than Australian flies'. The native quarter and its 'Wozzer' (Haret el Wasser) red-light district 'surprised, nauseated and disgusted' Lieutenant-Colonel Harold 'Pompey' Elliott of the 7th Battalion. But because the more salubrious parts of the city were unofficially the preserve of the officers, the men gravitated to this area. After a long voyage, they wanted to let off steam and they had several weeks' backpay with which to do it.[23]

The upshot was that AIF's discipline hung in the balance at the end of 1914. Some of the lapses were farcical. When a captain accompanying Colonel MacLaurin berated a sentry for eating a pie and ordered him to present arms, the sentry asked MacLaurin to hold his pie while he did so. But serious misconduct was also rife. Drunkenness, venereal disease and absence without leave all soared. British military police were routinely bashed, Egyptians assaulted and robbed. Cairo residents began asking when the Australians were going to be 'tied up'. The Commander-in-Chief Egypt, Lieutenant-General Sir John Maxwell, complained to Birdwood, who asked Bridges to appeal to the national pride of all. Humiliated by the rebuke and more so when three hundred men from the 1st Division went absent in the New Year, Bridges decreed that hardcore troublemakers would be returned home. On 3 February 1915, 131 recidivists and 24 venereal cases left for dishonourable discharge in Australia.

Yet Bridges was partly to blame for the problems. 'The Sphinx has met with its human prototype', one officer said of him. Indifferent to sports, he did not bother about recreational outlets for the youthful exuberance of his command. The 11th Battalion's history commented on the 'utter lack of any systematised camp amusements for the men, such as are usually associated with any large military camp'. As Mena boasted nothing more than a YMCA tent, they took off for Cairo at every opportunity. Steps were gradually taken to discourage them. As January 1915 passed, wet canteens, kitchens and mess huts were set up. Outside the camp a shanty shopping mall developed, with 'fruitshops, bookshops, bootshops, haberdasheries, watchmakers, tailorshops, barbershops, canteens etc in all directions, and four big picture shows'. Antique dealers peddled 'priceless' artefacts straight out of packing cases marked 'Made in Birmingham', tearooms offered 'Australian Systems Afternoon Tea', and eggs-a-cook were available from the Fair Dinkum Restaurant. By February Cairo was mostly quiet. Many men saw little need to visit it.[24]

Comprising the 4th Brigade under Colonel Monash and the 2nd Light Horse Brigade under pastoralist and federal member for North Sydney, Colonel Granville Ryrie, the second Australian contingent arrived at this time. Joining the NZ and A Division, Monash's men found their quarters at Aerodrome Camp already prepared by the New Zealanders, one of the steps taken by Godley to ensure that they began well. Having the practical experience of soldiering that Bridges lacked, he provided recreational outlets for his men from the outset and had started sending New Zealand troublemakers home in mid-December 1914. An ambitious but impecunious mounted infantry officer who preferred the Boer War to Staff College, the 6 foot 6 inch Godley was nonetheless unpopular owing to his short temper, sharp tongue and forceful wife. 'Make 'em run, Alex', which she was alleged to have said while Godley reviewed some New Zealanders on parade, became his nickname, and she was later supposed to have complained because bedridden wounded did not lie to attention during her hospital visits.[25]

The latest Australians had barely settled in when the Turks attacked the Suez Canal. Three columns entered Egypt, two of them crossing the Sinai with guns and pontoons, a magnificent feat that their opponents ignored. When the columns were discovered approaching the canal towards the end of January, the New Zealand Infantry Brigade strengthened it. Some of the New Zealanders met the main assault, which the central column launched early on 3 February near Serapeum. Together with Indian troops, they riddled the Ottomans as they tried to cross. 'The slaughter was terrible', wrote Private Cecil Malthus. 'The dead were left lying, though they got most of their wounded away. The ground was strewn with all sorts of equipment. Many had even shed their boots to make a quicker getaway.' The other columns fared no better. Ordered to the Canal late on 2 February, the 2nd Australian Brigade arrived after the fighting was over.[26]

Meanwhile, training continued. In terms of hardening the men, encouraging a sense of unit identity in them and getting them used to how an army functioned, Bean was right to describe it as 'one of the finest achievements of the AIF'. In other respects, the training in Egypt was deficient. By mid-February, brigade manoeuvres were being conducted in both divisions and Godley was even starting divisional ones. Yet they differed little from the manoeuvres on pre-war camps in Australia, which followed British doctrine that had missed the main tactical lesson of the Boer War: 'the smokeless, long range, high velocity, small bore magazine bullet from rifle or machine-gun – plus the trench – had decisively tilted the balance against the attack and in favour of the defence'. The BEF was learning it the hard way on the Western Front but the information coming from there was barely reflected in the ANZAC's preparations. Lieutenant Richard Casey, Bridges's aide-de-camp and a future Australian governor-general, said after a 1st Brigade exercise: 'The disregard of cover and the advancing in face of a strong fire in the open will have to be remedied – or our troops will very soon be wiped out'.[27]

By the end of 1914, the stalemate on the Western Front weighed heavily on the War Council, the British Cabinet's military subcommittee headed by Prime Minister Herbert Asquith. First Lord of the Admiralty Winston Churchill sought alternatives to sending the new armies Britain was raising 'to chew barbed wire in Flanders', while Chancellor of the Exchequer Lloyd George urged 'bringing Germany down by knocking the props from under her'. Their deliberations coincided with more trouble on the Eastern Front, where the Germans had driven the Russians back towards Warsaw. Russia lost over a million men and had barely a week's supply of shells left when the Turks chimed in with an invasion of the Caucasus. On

2 January 1915 the Russians appealed to Britain for a demonstration to relieve the Turkish pressure. Kitchener informed Churchill: 'The only place a demonstration might have some effect would be the Dardanelles'. Dividing Europe from Asia, the Dardanelles Straits wound forty-one miles from the toe of the Gallipoli Peninsula at Cape Helles to the town of Gallipoli on the Sea of Marmara, at the far end of which was Constantinople. The defences included a minefield and forts in the initial thirteen-mile stretch to the Narrows, where less than a mile separated Chanak on the Asian shore from Kilid Bahr at the foot of the plateau straddling the Peninsula. Once the three-mile long Narrows and its minefield had been cleared and the forts beyond it reduced, the Sea of Marmara lay open.

At Churchill's behest, the Eastern Mediterranean Squadron under Vice-Admiral Sackville Carden had bombarded the forts guarding the entrance to the Straits on 3 November in response to Turkey's declaration of war. The Russian plea prompted Churchill to ask Carden on 5 January whether ships could force the Straits. He said it might be done by 'extended operations with a large number'. Churchill told the War Council on 13 January that he envisioned the fleet proceeding to Constantinople. It gave the green light even though the need to help the Russians had faded after they thrashed the Ottoman Caucasus Army at Sarikamish. The glittering strategic prizes still on offer justified going ahead. Reeling after Sarikamish, the Turks were thought likely to surrender if the fleet reached Constantinople, thereby opening the Mediterranean route to Russia and allowing munitions access. Italy, Greece (Turkey's traditional foe), and perhaps Romania and Bulgaria might be sufficiently encouraged to enter the war on the Allied side and march on Austria. All of this amounted to knocking Germany's props away. Shoring them up would force the Germans to divert resources from the Western Front, weakening them there.[28]

Comprised mostly of outdated battleships, the fleet assembled off the Greek island of Lemnos, sixty miles west of the Dardanelles, and began the attack on 19 February. But the Ottomans had sown more mines and installed mobile howitzers since the bombardment the previous November. The howitzers were hard to detect and prevented the minesweepers clearing the minefields. By 11 March the attack had stalled. Carden collapsed under the strain. His deputy, Vice-Admiral John de Robeck, renewed the attack on 18 March. The Turks had laid a new minefield near the Narrows. Four battleships struck it. Three sank. So did the naval attempt to force the Straits.

Though Kitchener had originally insisted that no troops could be spared for the Dardanelles, it was realised that they would be needed to occupy the Peninsula in the wake of the fleet and to police Constantinople after its fall. Major-General Aylmer Hunter-Weston's 29th Division, the only uncommitted British regular division, and the ANZAC were earmarked. Churchill threw in the Royal Naval Division (RND), made up of surplus marine and naval reservists, and the French contributed a division (later a corps). On 20 February, Kitchener warned Maxwell that the ANZAC should be ready to depart Egypt from 9 March but a brigade was to go to Lemnos immediately in case the fleet broke through. 'Very, very much envied', the 3rd Brigade left Mena on 28 February. On 10 March Kitchener appointed General Hamilton, who had visited Australia barely a year earlier, to command the 75 000 strong Mediterranean Expeditionary Force (MEF). Sixty-two years old and nearing retirement, Hamilton was urbane, tall, beanpole-thin and a published poet and author. He had also seen more action than any other senior serving British officer, which left him with a shattered left forearm and one leg shorter than the other. Armed with a 1912 handbook on the Turkish army and two small tourist guides on western Turkey that Kitchener had given him, Hamilton left England on 13 March. With the fleet's failure, his task was transformed. Far from merely occupying the Peninsula, the MEF would have to seize it so that the fleet could get through.

By the Turks' own reckoning, the Straits would have fallen easily had a landing been made around the time the naval bombardment opened on 19 February. Within a week, they had reinforced the two divisions they had there with two more and then a third subsequently. They thought landings would quickly follow the failure of the Narrows attack on 18 March, after which Liman von Sanders took command of the newly formed Fifth Army defending the Dardanelles. Another division arrived, giving it six altogether with 80 000 men. Believing that British naval strength would make landings difficult to stop, Liman concentrated them inland so that they could counterattack in strength once Hamilton had shown his hand to the light forces left on the coast.[29]

With no hope of strategic surprise, Hamilton sought to fool Liman as to where the main blow would fall. Next, as many men as possible had to be ashore by the time Liman worked out his intentions and began counterattacking. As that meant several landings, the 29th Division was to go in on five small beaches at Cape Helles, where the fleet could support it from the rear and both flanks. At V Beach below Sedd-el-Bahr Fort, *River Clyde*, a ten-year-old collier, would run aground and disgorge two thousand men through sally ports, doubling the strength at Helles in the first few minutes. A five-mile advance inland would then seize the Achi Baba Ridge by nightfall, gaining a springboard for an attack on the Kilid Bahr plateau. Birdwood's corps would secure the high backbone of the Peninsula, opposite the Narrows, to cut the Turks' lines of communication to Helles. The RND and French would mount feints and then go to Helles. Hamilton thought that Liman would dare not concentrate for the first forty-eight hours.[30]

On 1 April Bridges was informed that the 1st Division would embark three days hence. 'All leave stopped!' ran the order. Wanting to settle accounts with those who had 'gypped' them or infected them or both, some men launched a last foray into the Wozzer. They were ransacking a brothel when word spread that a Maori soldier had been knifed in it. Owners, bouncers and prostitutes alike were immediately turfed into the street and the furniture piled up outside and set alight. British military police beat a hasty retreat on being hit by a fusillade of bottles and rocks. When a battalion of Lancashire Territorials appeared with bayonets fixed, the crowd finally dispersed. Many Australians deplored the incident but just as many agreed with Sergeant Les de Vine of the 4th Battalion, who said that the Wozzer was merely 'cleaned up by the boys, the district being a menace to public health etc for many years'. On 3 April bonfires dotted Mena as the battalions burnt their rubbish and struck their tents. Then the NZ and A Division upped stakes. Egypt had become 'the land of sun, shit and syphillis' and the men were glad to be leaving. To their chagrin, the light horse units remained behind. Hamilton and Birdwood believed that the Gallipoli landscape precluded any role for mounted troops, at least initially.[31]

From 4 April, units entrained for Alexandria, whence they sailed for Lemnos, 625 miles across the Mediterranean. 'Dotted all over . . . are quaint old houses and windmills, grazing sheep, cattle and ponies and luxuriant crops which all suggest a scene that might be expected in France or Holland', wrote Corporal Arthur Smith, a gunner, after entering Mudros harbour. Two hundred ships, ranging from the world's most powerful battleship, HMS *Queen Elizabeth*, to *River Clyde* and grubby Thames tugs soon crowded it. On 12 April, Birdwood and Bridges were told that the ANZAC was to land on the Gallipoli Peninsula between the Gaba Tepe promontory and Fisherman's Hut three miles to its north.[32]

Behind Gaba Tepe a flat saddle, the Maidos Plain, reached to the Narrows four miles east. It was bounded to the south and north respectively by the Kilid Bahr Plateau and the Sari Bair Range, whose three summits, Koja Chemen Tepe (called Hill 971 after its height) and the slightly lower Hill Q and Chunuk Bair, offered good views of the Narrows. Birdwood was instructed to seize the inland spur of Hill 971, especially Mal Tepe, the cone-shaped feature at its

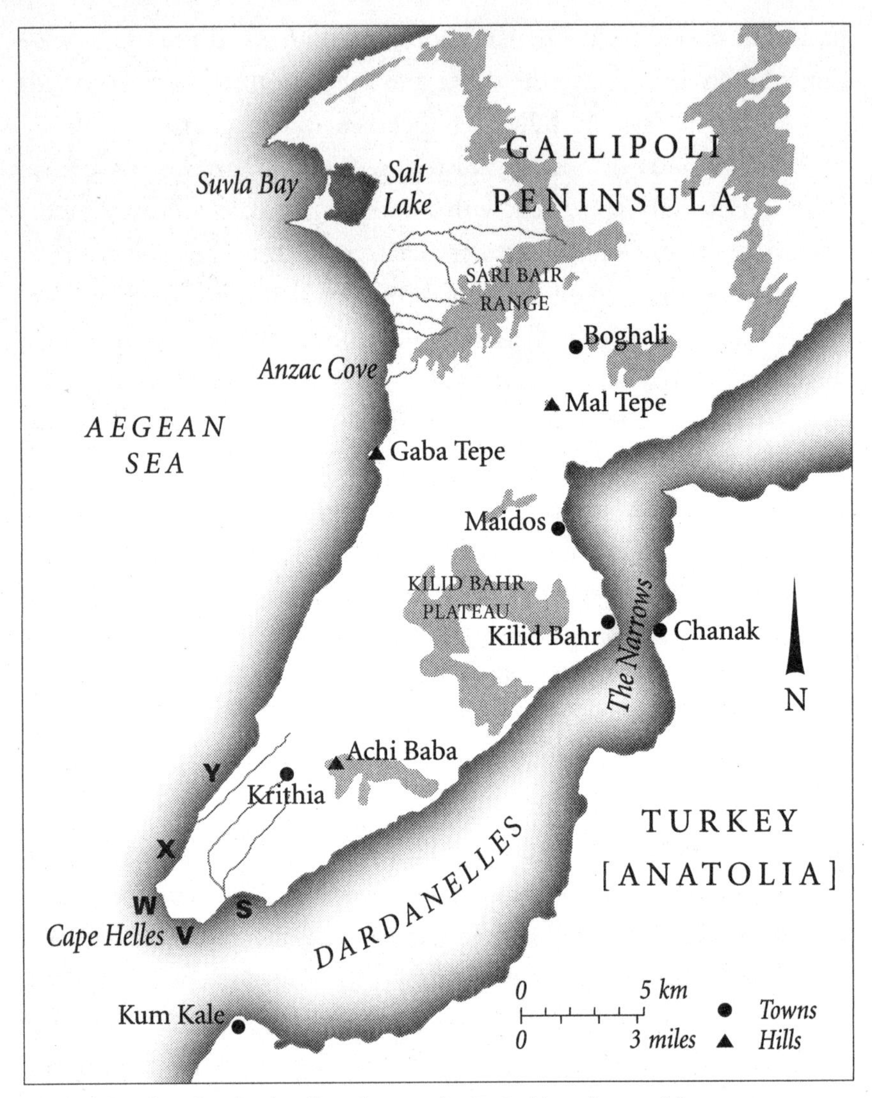

The Dardanelles, showing landing places and principal locations and features

end. The Maidos–Gallipoli Road, running over the foot of Mal Tepe and vital to the Turks holding Helles and Kilid Bahr, would thus be severed. He left Mudros on 13 April with Bridges and the brigade and battalion commanders on the battleship *Queen*, the flagship of Rear-Admiral Cecil Thursby, whose squadron would support the ANZAC. Clad in naval garb to avoid being recognised as soldiers, they peered at the coastline of the Peninsula as *Queen* slowly steamed south a mile and a half off it early next morning.

Suvla Bay hove into view, with its mile-square salt lake beyond, and then the Suvla Plain. All eyes settled on Sari Bair, which rose from the southern side of the plain, and whose three summits were each less than half a mile apart. The map also showed two eminences lying within the 700-foot contour three-quarters of a mile southwest of Chunuk Bair. One, Baby 700, was the southern shoulder of the other, Big 700, soon be known as Battleship Hill. All of these heights crowned the worst terrain on the Peninsula. Steep spurs, dissected by a maze of re-entrants, extended from the peaks almost to the beach south of Fisherman's Hut. At Battleship Hill the range divided into three ridges that headed southwest and were riven in turn by a jumble of gullies opening onto the sea. Dense low scrub cloaked peaks, ridges and re-entrants alike, except where the slopes were too precipitous for all but a few tufts to grow.

The First Ridge was the shortest. It ran from Baby 700 across a narrow saddle-back dubbed the Nek and on to a slender plateau, Russell's Top, whose seaward side was a sheer 400-foot drop. Beyond Russell's a triangular plateau, Plugge's, fell steeply to Ari Burnu, a 200-foot high knoll that formed the northern end of a sheltered beach 800 yards long, which was about to be immortalised as Anzac Cove. Hell Spit, the smaller knoll at the other end, marked the ridge's southern extremity. The Second Ridge emerged into view beyond it at a heart-shaped upland a mile and a half from Baby 700. Enclosed by the 400-foot contour and 600 yards across, the upland was christened the 400 Plateau. The northern lobe would be called Johnston's Jolly; the southern one took its name from the stunted lone pine that stood on it. Bolton's Ridge, the first of the five spurs sprouting from the plateau, hid the others and petered out 1500 yards north of Gaba Tepe, which was really the lower end of the Third Ridge. Stretching for over three miles, this ridge was the longest, and as it descended, the top of Mal Tepe behind it broke the skyline. Trenches could be seen on the Kilid Bahr Plateau and the quarter-mile long Gaba Tepe promontory, below which barbed wire glistened. Apart from scattered trenches between there and Hell Spit, the seven miles of beach to Suvla looked clear. But the hinterland of Fisherman's Hut halfway along was too precipitous for the all-important rapid advance. The landing had to be towards Gaba Tepe.

Bridges had already decided that the 3rd Brigade would be the covering force and first ashore, largely because of his faith in MacLagan, who was a trusted friend as well as the most experienced of the senior officers. MacLagan had seen the coastline from *Queen Elizabeth* two days earlier and his gaze was now fixed on Gaba Tepe. 'If that place is strongly held, it will be almost impregnable for my fellows', he remarked. Aerial reconnaissance had picked up seven gun emplacements on the promontory. Behind it were said to be another four plus an actual battery. On the available intelligence, the landing might be shelled on the way in and then taken in enfilade on the beach. Seeking maximum surprise to counter this threat, Birdwood opted to go in silently just before daylight to conceal the 3rd Brigade's approach. With luck it might be on the guns before the Turks had time to act. From the scattered trenches, Birdwood knew that there were only isolated posts on the shore north of Gaba Tepe. Landing as much of the 3rd Brigade as possible simultaneously on a wide front and quickly reinforcing it would allow the attack to penetrate, even if one or more of these isolated posts managed to pin down parts of the line. It would also reduce the effects of any shelling.[33]

Consequently, the 3rd Brigade was to go ashore in two waves on the 1600-yard frontage between Hell Spit and a point one mile north of Gaba Tepe. When *Queen* and two other battleships, *London* and *Prince of Wales*, were five miles off the coast, the 1500 men of the first wave aboard would disembark into twelve 'tows', each consisting of three lifeboats towed by a small steamboat. Off the island of Imbros, fifteen miles from Gaba Tepe, the second wave of 2500 men would transfer from their transports to seven destroyers towing more lifeboats. Getting into the lifeboats 100 yards from the beach, they were to land straight after the first wave. Part of the 9th Battalion on the right would knock out the Gaba Tepe guns, while the rest seized Anderson Knoll on the Third Ridge a mile from the beach. Scrubby Knoll, on the ridge 2000 yards north of Anderson Knoll, and Big 700 were to be taken by the 11th Battalion, and the 10th in the centre would disable the guns thought to be on the 400 Plateau before slotting in between the 9th and the 11th. The 12th Battalion was to stay in reserve. Picked up from its transports by the returning destroyers and tows, the 2nd Brigade would come in on the heels of the 3rd and extend the left flank over Chunuk Bair, hills Q and 971 and down towards Fisherman's Hut. The 1st Brigade was to remain near the beach as Bridges's reserve. Landing last, the NZ and A Division would swing through the 1st Division on the heights and advance southeast to Mal Tepe.[34]

The plan itself was nothing if not bold, with surprise, speed and the expectation of weak Turkish resistance its outstanding features. Given the terrain and the distances from the beach, the objectives were very ambitious – overly so, White told Bean postwar, but the senior commanders did not know better at the time. If the 29th Division's advance from Helles were held up, retaining them would entail prolonged defensive operations. However, the intricate terrain made a defensive battle in the area more complex than on the Western Front, and the ANZAC was inadequately trained for operations there. Like the rest of the MEF, it was not trained at all in amphibious warfare. As the last British amphibious operations, at Constantinople in 1807 and Walcheren in 1809, dated from the age of sail and were fiascos, no practical examples existed to guide it.[35]

Though the 3rd Brigade arrived on Lemnos in early March, bad weather often interfered with its practice landings. Descending the rope ladders with full equipment was no easy matter even in good conditions and the boat handling was ordinary. These things improved but direction keeping in the few night rehearsals carried out remained hit and miss. Starting its training on 14 April, by which time Mudros harbour looked like the scene of a giant regatta, the 1st Brigade had similar problems. Monash noted after a muddled landing by the 4th Brigade that the advance could be followed by the quantity of ammunition the soldiers had dropped; unless checked, 'result disastrous'. On 19 April the practices ceased. Slouch hats were withdrawn and flat-topped, peaked British field-service caps issued in an attempt to confuse the Turks over whether the Australians and New Zealanders formed part of Hamilton's order of battle. The real landing had been fixed for 23 April, and the first departures from Mudros two days earlier. A gale forced two postponements and the preliminary moves did not begin until 23 April, pushing the landings back to 25 April. Hamilton had left London forty-three days before; the planning and preparations for the Normandy invasion took over a year.[36]

In the interests of security, the men were briefed either just before leaving Lemnos or shortly after. MacLagan's special order reiterated the need to conserve ammunition 'as if it were a ten pound note', and warned against the Turkish artillery: 'We must expect to be shelled . . . but remember that is part of this game of war, and we must "stick it", no matter what the fire'. The dangers ahead were bluntly acknowledged. 'Boys', said Lieutenant-Colonel Johnston to the 11th Battalion, 'the General informs me that it will take several battleships and destroyers to carry our brigade to Gallipoli; a barge will be sufficient to take us home again!' But relief that the waiting was over, combined with a keenly felt sense of anticipation, kept morale sky high. The 11th Battalion greeted Johnston's grim words with resounding cheers. 'Joy reigns', said Lance-Corporal Mitchell. 'We are delighted beyond words at the prospect of such a chance of proving our mettle.' 'Every man was busting to get a go at the Turks', wrote Private Arthur McGuirk of the 3rd Battalion.[37]

The ANZAC left Mudros on 24 April. By early afternoon, the transports bearing the 1st and 2nd Brigades were gone and the first wave of the 3rd had transferred to *Queen*, *London* and *Prince of Wales*, aboard which was Bridges. Before leaving on the destroyer *Colne*, MacLagan called to say to goodbye. 'Well, you haven't thanked me yet', Bridges chided. Typically lugubrious, MacLagan assured him that he was grateful for the honour of landing first but added: 'if we find the Turks holding these ridges in any strength, I honestly don't think you'll ever see the 3rd Brigade again'. Bridges laughed: 'Oh, go along with you'. Shortly after 2 p.m., the battleships led the four transports carrying the rest of the 3rd Brigade out of the harbour. Cheering erupted from the French vessels and the Australians answered by trying to whistle the 'Marseillaise'.[38]

Unusually enthusiastic hymn singing marked the church services held during the afternoon. Then a hot meal was served; roast beef and Yorkshire pudding on the warships, bully and eggs on the transports. Not knowing when they would get decent food again, many tucked in but many were also too keyed up to eat. The mood was boisterous, Sergeant de Vine commenting that they were 'especially excited during teatime and sang all the time, kicking up a terrible noise'. Ammunition was distributed next, two hundred rounds per man. It was 'an unforgettable experience and produced a profound change in the behaviour of the men', wrote Private Bob Grant of the 1st Battalion. 'Whatever their preconceived ideas were of war, they were crystallising into reality now.' At dusk the covering force passed the transports carrying the main body.[39]

Around 6 p.m. companies assembled for inspection at the numbers painted on the ships' decks from which they would disembark into the tows next morning. As well as his rifle and ammunition, each man carried an entrenching tool with two empty sandbags wrapped around the handle and two or three waterbottles, whose contents had to last three days. Bully and biscuits for the same period, greatcoat, towel, a change of underclothing and socks, and personal gear were stuffed into packs looped for quick release in case a boat sank. A bundle of firewood was tied to the top. The load came to almost ninety pounds, 'enough to make a camel jib', complained Corporal David Muir of the 8th Battalion. Once inspected, the men were told to rest. Those on the battleships were the most comfortable because the crews had given them their sleeping quarters as well as cigarettes and tobacco from the ships' canteens. Those on the transports dossed down on the decks, huddling together for warmth in the chilly night. Endless cleaning of rifles and checking of gear betrayed the nervous excitement that made sleep impossible. Major Gordon Bennett did the rounds of the 6th Battalion:

Moving among them, one could see a look of determination in every man's face. They were very silent. Many were the prayers offered that night. All were anxious as to how they would behave on the morrow . . . They knew the reputation of Australia was in their hands . . . It was a solemn voyage.[40]

Conflicting thoughts gripped each man. On the one hand, Staff-Sergeant Laseron of the 13th Battalion observed, 'It is always the other fellow that is going to get shot. The fact that a bullet might get oneself . . . is somehow, inconceivable'. On the other, the possibility had to be accepted, so many dashed off a letter to their loved ones 'just in case'. Lieutenant Coe honoured his parents:

Dad, dear, I wish I could tell you all that is in my heart but words on paper seem so inadequate . . . I think the words I most appreciated from you were, 'Come back to us, Micky, as good a man as you go away.' Dad so far I have done nothing since leaving home which you and Mother would not approve of . . . For this, Dad, no credit is mine. My home training is responsible, and I thank our Father in heaven for such parents as mine. I could not wish for better.

Monash regarded the prospect of death with equanimity for he had lived a 'full and active life'. His one regret if he were killed, he confided to his wife and daughter, was the grief it would cause them. Bennett's friend, Major John Hamilton of the 6th Battalion, apologised to his wife: 'I have your testament in my hand and as I gaze at our little daughter Boyne, holding the candle and looking at me with her darling little face, I think that I have been a brute to leave you all for this life with all its danger'. Hamilton would die next day. Private David Mills of the 8th Battalion wrote similarly: 'I have kissed dear little Nan's photo goodbye. May God have mercy on my soul and care for them I have left behind. XXXXXXXXX'. He would die in three days. Lance-Corporal Mitchell looked forward rather than back: 'Here goes for death or glory. So Long All'.[41]

At 11 p.m. the covering force was off Imbros. A glorious moon shone and the sea, greeny-black in its light, was dead calm. Slinking up to the four transports, the seven destroyers took their lifeboats in tow and embarked the men. The still water allowed the use of the ships' gangways instead of rope ladders, halving the time taken in the rehearsals. 'You fellows can smoke and talk quietly', Lieutenant-Commander Wilkinson, *Ribble*'s captain, told the company of the 12th Battalion aboard. 'But I expect all lights to be put out and absolute silence to be kept when I give the order.' Sailors dispensed hot cocoa and tots of rum, so much so that the 9th Battalion company on *Beagle* was 'ready to fight the whole Turkish Army'. The refreshment locker in *Foxhound*'s wardroom was thrown open to the officers of the 10th. 'From sundry expressions dropped by several of the Naval Officers', recalled Major Miles Beevor, 'I gathered that they did not expect any of us whatever to survive the morrow'. The transhipment complete, the destroyers crawled eastwards for three miles and stopped. Not far in front but unseen were the battleships.[42]

Guided by the masked stern light of *Triumph*, Thursby's squadron had crept noiselessly into its stations five miles off Gaba Tepe.

The first wave had been roused at midnight and given a hot breakfast and a tot of rum while the boats were lowered. At 1.30 a.m., with the tows formed, the men scrambled down the rope ladders, sleeves rolled up to distinguish them from the Turks. Figures silhouetted in the moonlight one minute and lost against the water the next, the menacing outline of the shore, whispered orders, the occasional clang of a rifle butt, shuffling boots, and mumbled curses as fingers were trampled or footing lost, all coalesced into a tremendously eerie scene. The Australians may have terrorised Cairo but the naval officers marvelled at how silent and orderly they were now that discipline was essential. So quiet was the embarkation that Thursby was surprised when told at 2.35 a.m. that it had been completed. 'Cast off and drift astern', came the command and the two tows on either side of each battleship dropped back behind it.[43]

At 2.53 a.m. the battleships started pulling the tows slowly towards land, the destroyers behind them. Seven minutes later, the moon disappeared. The darkness was engulfing. At 3.30 a.m., when the battleships were supposed to be two miles off shore, they stopped. Thursby ordered 'Land armed parties'. The sailors lining the decks waved their caps in the Navy's 'silent cheer'. The painters on the twelve tows leapt as the steamboats cast off.

—THREE—

THE LANDING

As the battleships disappeared in the inky void, the tows tried to form up 150 yards apart and in line abreast. Lieutenant John Waterlow, who was to shepherd them to the beach, rode in the southernmost tow and the flotilla leader, Commander Charles Dix, in the northernmost one. Keeping station was also difficult and the line concertinaed until the tows closed to within fifty yards of one another, halving the mile-wide landing frontage. According to Bean, Waterlow steered straight ahead but the others swung away from him. According to the British Official Historian, Waterlow shoved the other tows over, crowding Dix, who did not have time to hustle them back on course. Either way, they were not heading for the landing beach but diagonally across the face of it.[1]

To Private Henry Cheney of the 10th Battalion, the hour-long run in lasted 'days'; for Lieutenant Aubrey Darnell, also of the 10th, it 'seemed to go on forever'. Hearts leapt into mouths when a pencil of light from a Turkish searchlight in the Narrows arced upward. A second beam joined it and then both abruptly vanished. At 4 a.m. the first streaks of dawn broke above the coastline. Would the Turks be surprised or were they alert and waiting, men asked themselves over and over.[2]

The Turks had known what was afoot for some hours. At 2 a.m. patrols reported to Captain Faik, commanding No. 4 Company of the

2nd Battalion, 27th Regiment (2/27th) atop Ari Burnu, that they had sighted many ships. Looking seaward through his binoculars, Faik also saw them. He told his men to stand-to. Corporal Adil Shahin was asleep on Hell Spit when the sentry started shouting, '"There's something unusual. Get up!" Then the company commander ordered us all to move up into the trenches'. No. 4 Company's 200 men were all that opposed the Australians in the first instance. They were under strict orders not to fire until the boats grounded.[3]

At 4.25 a.m., muffled oars dug into the water as the thirty-six lifeboats cast off 100 yards out. Apart from a bird chirruping, the shore was quiet, which made the next few minutes seem all the more chaotic. A plume of sparks and flame spewed from the funnel of a steamboat. Simultaneously, Dix screamed, 'Tell the colonel the damn fools have taken us a mile too far north'. A dazzling yellow light glowed for half a minute from Hell Spit. 'Seen!' someone hissed. Still the shore was silent. 'Look at that!' cried Captain Ray Leane. A man was silhouetted against the skyline. A shout in Turkish, then a rifle cracking from the top of Ari Burnu. Lance-Corporal Mitchell saw the flash: 'Klock-klock. Tension snapped. Good! The ——s will give us a go after all'.

Private Frank Loud's boat had already shoaled when the first shot rang out. It thudded into the thwarts by his ankle. 'We waited for no more but made for the sides. I went to jump but tripped & hit the briney head first'. The crisp smack of bullets striking flesh began to be heard, followed by a moan as the casualty slid to the bottom of the boat. 'Some men crouched', wrote Mitchell, 'some sat up nonchalantly, some laughed and joked, while others cursed in ferocious delight'. The machine-guns in the bows of the steamboats clattered away, covering the dash to the beach, which Cheney described as 'truly a baptism of fire and water':

I scrambled ashore as best I could, holding my rifle well above my head, but it is not a sandy bottom on that beach, it is all cobble stones and so made our progress very slow. The first act ashore was to fix my bayonet, second to divest myself of my pack. Everything was disorder now, excitement running very high.

Bullets sent sparks flying from the shingle as the first wave hurtled across a beach half a cricket pitch wide. The 9th and 10th Battalions had landed in a cluster around Ari Burnu but the seaward face of the knoll defiladed them from the Turks on top. Grounding 300 yards north of it, the 11th was tormented by a machine-gun near Fisherman's Hut further north. Instead of the anticipated strip of level ground leading to the gentle spur that tailed off the Second Ridge, a precipitous slope rose directly ahead. Dix was right. They had landed in the wrong place.[4]

The error was attributed to an unexpectedly strong current but Midshipman Eric Bush, who commanded one of the tows, averred that the current was negligible. In 1994 historian Denis Winter concluded that the first wave came ashore exactly where Birdwood wanted. Winter alleged that Birdwood secretly decided on Anzac Cove with Thursby's connivance on 23 April because it was screened from the Gaba Tepe guns. Only a very select few, says Winter, were aware of the change – MacLagan and Waterlow but not Bridges or Dix, which would have been amazing from a military standpoint. All kept an oath of silence to the grave.

Regardless of what Birdwood intended, naval limitations made arriving at the right place a flukey proposition. *Triumph*, the marker ship, had to steer from Imbros at a set speed for a set time, guided only by a magnetic compass. The resulting margin of error would have put it anywhere between Gaba Tepe and Fisherman's Hut. When the circumstances were replicated off Anzac Cove on 25 April 1990, the principal features of the coastline were too indistinct for an accurate fix to be taken. Even if this were possible in 1915, the charts available put Gaba Tepe 460 yards north of its actual location. Waterlow had to assume that the battleships were correctly positioned but the steamboat compasses, on which his and all the other tows had to rely, were 'notoriously unreliable', said Bush. So the likelihood of a glitch in the last stage was high. One occurred.

At 3.45 a.m. the shore was occasionally discernible and Midshipman Savill Metcalf, who had often seen Gaba Tepe from his action station in the foretop of *Triumph*, thought the tows were heading straight for it. Having lost sight of Waterlow next to him, he swung his tow to port away from the fortified promontory and made a second port correction fifteen minutes later when they still appeared to be going too close. The tows to Metcalf's left conformed and the line crabbed northeastwards. Waterlow failed to prevent the movement and joined it, unsure of his own location. Anzac Cove was the terminus. To put all this into perspective, the Americans, after months of preparation and with better navigational aids, still managed to miss Utah Beach by 2000 yards at Normandy in 1944.[5]

Despite their bewilderment, the men knew they had to get on as quickly as possible. Swarming up Ari Burnu in uniforms heavy with water, they pushed through waist-high scrub whose inch-long thorns shredded clothing and skin. Cheney scarcely noticed:

> We were at fever point and just made as much noise as [we] possibly could . . . I was lost in the wild mob, in the wildest of charges that I think was ever made. Everybody had taken leave of their senses and was certainly not accountable for their actions. Although I know well enough what fear is, it left me completely in that charge. Straight up that rugged, rocky precipice we went.

The first troops from the 9th and 10th Battalions soon reached the top to find that most of the Turkish platoon there had withdrawn to Plugge's Plateau. They went straight after it, scaling slopes so steep that they resorted to digging in their bayonets to haul themselves up. After twenty minutes, they clambered over the lip of Plugge's to see soldiers from the 11th Battalion appear at its northern edge. Ignoring the fire from the machine-gun near Fisherman's Hut, the 11th's two companies had rushed Ari Burnu when they saw the others climbing it. The first prisoner was taken, bringing a chorus of 'Shoot the bastard!' The Australians detested the Turks, whom they believed committed atrocities against their captives. Words spoke louder than actions and the prisoner was taken down the hill. As more Australians arrived, the Turks, including Corporal Adil and Captain Faik, withdrew across a deep gorse-covered valley towards the Second Ridge 500 yards away. In the growing light the Australians laughingly blazed away at them and at others scarpering over MacLagan's Ridge, which linked Plugge's to Hell Spit. It was not yet 5 a.m. and the battle seemed over.[6]

During the next half hour, the men on the plateau were sorted into battalion groups corresponding to the formation that the advance was supposed to be in. Those from the 10th Battalion formed up in the centre and headed towards Johnston's Jolly, now clearly visible 1000 yards to the south, from where they would go on to the Third Ridge. Those from the 9th Battalion on the right pursued the Turks towards Lone Pine, which the 9th had to cross in order to secure the right flank on the Third Ridge. Intending to strike out for Baby 700, the men from the 11th Battalion re-formed on the left of Plugge's. As the reorganisation proceeded, a new phenomenon startled Mitchell:

> There was a weird shrieking note somewhere in the air, which increased in volume every fraction of a second. It culminated in a deafening report and a cloud of smoke some thirty feet high. Simultaneously there was the swishing sound as the bullets beat down bushes and swept the earth and a devilish scream. The scream was caused by large pieces of the case as they spun through the air.

It was shrapnel from Gaba Tepe, which became particularly heavy over the deep valley crossed by the escaping Turks. Skirting MacLagan's Ridge before opening onto the sea next to Hell Spit, it was nicknamed Shrapnel Valley but its claustrophobic first half-mile, squeezed between Russell's Top and the Second Ridge, would be called Monash Valley.

The landing of the second wave was now under way. Slowing to a halt 200 yards off, the destroyers pulled their tows alongside and began disembarkations at 4.40 a.m. As heavy fire still came from the slopes either side of Ari Burnu, many of the boats were engaged all the way in. Shrapnel also spattered them. All the rowers in some boats were hit. They had to be pushed overboard so that others could take over. *Triumph* and *Bacchante* fired broadsides at Gaba Tepe but its guns, sheltered in a quarry, could not be silenced.

At 4.50 a.m. the rest of the 9th Battalion landed between Hell Spit and McCay's Hill, which ran from the southern side of Shrapnel Valley to the 400 Plateau. Brushing past a machine-gun firing from near Gaba Tepe and cleaning up the Turks on the beach, they fanned out over Lone Pine and captured three field guns. So swift was their advance that they reached the plateau before the first wave, as did the rest of the 10th Battalion, which landed halfway along Anzac Cove. Led by Lieutenant Noel Loutit, the vanguard of the 10th chased some Turks into Shrapnel Valley, where they tried to surrender. As there were too many to escort back to the beach, the Turks were shot. Loutit's party rushed on towards the Third Ridge.[7]

Distributed across all seven destroyers, the 12th Battalion was to assemble at the foot of the 400 Plateau as the 3rd Brigade's reserve. Half of it got ashore with the 9th and 10th Battalions but the other half landed under Lieutenant-Colonel Lancelot Clarke with the 11th Battalion on the northern flank. Coming in closer to the machine-gun near Fisherman's Hut, they were also engaged by Turks on Russell's Top, the ridge leading to Plugge's. Losses were heavy. Clarke told a platoon to silence the gun and ordered an advance to the crest of the Top. Captain Eric Tulloch led sixty men up Walker's Ridge, the northernmost of the two spurs that jutted seawards from it. When Tulloch got to the top, he saw Clarke lying dead.

Along with fifty men under Lieutenant Margetts, the 57-year-old Clarke had achieved an unbelievable feat. Facing the unclimbable second spur, called the Sphinx because its 300-foot vertical gravel sides and peculiarly eroded tip brought the Egyptian icon to mind, they crawled on hands and knees up the marginally less sheer cliff alongside and surprised thirty Turks. The Australians charged pell-mell. 'Steady, you fellows! Get into some sort of formation and clear the bush as you go', Clarke shouted. Pausing at the Nek, over which the Turks had fled, he was shot through the heart. As the fire died down, Tulloch's and Margetts's groups linked up and were met by some 12th Battalion men under Captain Joseph Lalor, who had waded ashore carrying a family sword. Called 'Puss-in-Boots' because he was short and liked to wear riding boots, Lalor was the grandson of Peter Lalor, leader of the 1854 goldminers' revolt at the Eureka Stockade. He had deserted from the Royal Navy as a boy, done a stint in the French Foreign Legion and helped out in a South American revolution before joining the AMF. Knowing that the 12th Battalion was in reserve, Lalor resisted his natural instinct to press on. His men dug in just short of the Nek. Those from the 11th with Tulloch, about a company, set off for Battleship Hill.[8]

MacLagan had landed at 5 a.m. and was lucky to get off the beach. Thinking some shadowy figures coming towards him were Turkish infiltrators, Major Beevor drew his revolver and waited until he could not miss before challenging them. 'Brigadier, 3rd Brigade, and Staff', came the reply. 'Beevor, we've landed in the wrong place!' MacLagan stammered, grabbing his arm and sounding very disturbed. From Plugge's at 5.30 a.m., he could see the parties from the 9th and 10th Battalions that had recently left heading for the 400 Plateau and their second wave already on it. As Brigadier Chris Roberts has written, his brigade was still in reasonable shape to reach its objectives. With the assault on Gaba Tepe no longer feasible, the 9th Battalion had at least three companies within striking distance of Anderson Knoll instead of the two originally allotted.

Most of the 10th was as close to the Third Ridge from the 400 Plateau as it would have been from the original landing site. Most of the 11th was on or around Plugge's, 800 yards nearer to Scrubby Knoll and Battleship Hill than anticipated. MacLagan had only the company of the 12th on Plugge's with him as his reserve, which was a worry. On the other hand, the 2nd Brigade was landing.[9]

Off Anzac Cove aboard *Queen Elizabeth*, Hamilton felt 'hopeful confidence in the success of this portion of his plan' and left for Helles, where a slaughter was under way. At V Beach, 'an amphitheatre designed by nature and arranged by the Turks for a butchery', sixty-four Ottomans withstood the naval bombardment and flayed the boats with fire before switching to the men crowding the gangways and sally-ports of *River Clyde*, a target 'not unlike the line of moving objects one sees sometimes in a shooting gallery at a village fair'. The sea was red for half a mile offshore. It also turned red off W Beach, 800 yards west, where another Turkish company inflicted grievous losses. The landings elsewhere went like clockwork and could have taken the Turks at V and W in rear but for General Hunter-Weston's orders to await the advance from them. Heeding the doctrine that the higher command should not meddle with the executive commander of a battle, Hamilton did not intervene.[10]

Back at Anzac the 2nd Brigade's landing began disastrously. When its transports steamed up, many of the tows that were to put it ashore had not yet returned from taking in the 3rd. Proceeding regardless, *Galeka* anchored 600 yards from Ari Burnu at 4.45 a.m. With the shrapnel making it impossible to lay in so close for long, the captain ordered a landing from the ship's boats, six of which started embarking the 7th Battalion. As the 2nd Brigade was supposed to be on the left of the 3rd, they were rowed towards the left of the rifle flashes and unknowingly headed straight for Fisherman's Hut, whose machine-gun the platoon sent by Clarke had not yet reached. It opened up when the boats were 200 yards offshore. Private Bert Heighway smelled the burning paint as bullets riddled his boat.

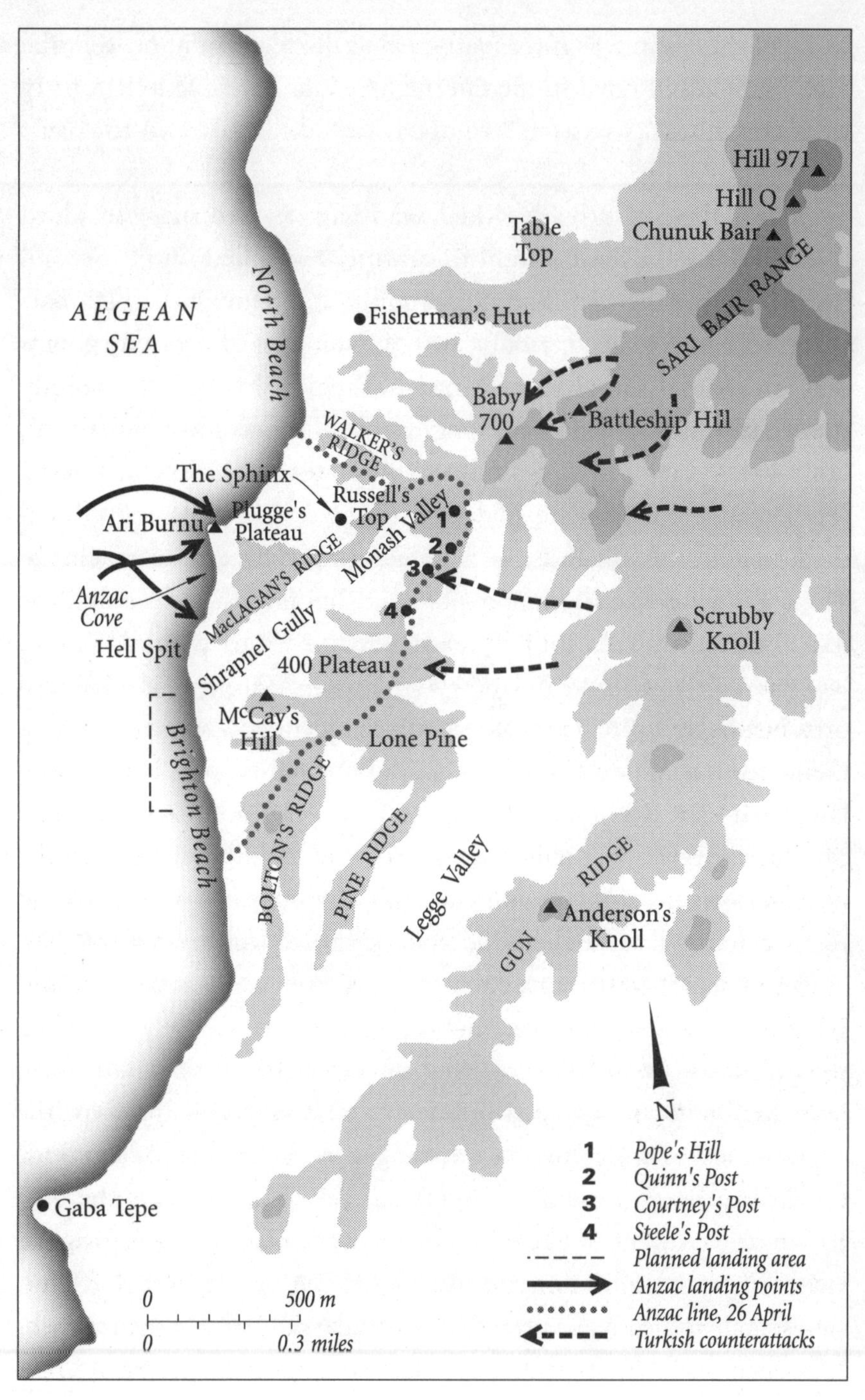

The Anzac sector

Nearly every man was hit. Finally seeing the platoon approach, the Turks bolted. Of the 140 men in the first four boats, less than forty were unscathed. A passing steamboat towed the last two to Anzac Cove.[11]

As for the 3rd Brigade, MacLagan had decided that the Third Ridge was too big and distant to capture. He halted on the Second Ridge, sending the 11th Battalion and the company of the 12th Battalion with him to occupy Baby 700, the summits of the four runnels that corrugated the head of Monash Valley below it – the Bloody Angle and Quinn's, Courtney's and Steele's Posts – and MacLaurin's Hill, which stretched towards the 400 Plateau. If, as Bean asserts, MacLagan wanted to consolidate until the 2nd Brigade arrived and then resume the advance, he was ignoring the need to reach the Third Ridge as quickly as possible and the fact that little fighting had occurred thus far. In no great strength to start with, the Turks had been driven back and the way ahead lay open. MacLagan's own justification, that cohesion had been lost because many men in their enthusiasm penetrated too far, did not stand up. When McCay landed shortly after 6 a.m., MacLagan dropped a bombshell: 'Well McCay, the position is this. I've gone to the left following the enemy instead of to the right. If you can change your plans and go to the right then it will settle the difficulty and things will be all right'.

MacLagan had feared a counterattack from Gaba Tepe all along. But the landing error shifted his right flank further away from the threat, and he was still as strong on the right as he would have been had it not occurred. Moreover, the missions of the two brigades – the 3rd to deploy as a covering screen across the beachhead, the 2nd to pass through the northern end of it to secure the Sari Bair heights – were not readily interchangeable. If the 2nd Brigade switched to the southern end, how were the heights, the 1st Division's main objective, to be taken? Understandably taken aback, McCay replied, 'It is a bit stiff to disobey orders first thing'. He wanted to assess things for himself. 'There isn't time. I assure you my right will be turned if you do not do this', MacLagan pleaded. McCay grudgingly acquiesced and set up his headquarters on the hill that was to bear his name.[12]

Landing with White at 7.20 a.m., Bridges went to McCay's Hill on learning of the 2nd Brigade's diversion and noticed men on the 400 Plateau stationary and undisturbed by firing. Neither he nor White could see anything to prevent the advance to the Third Ridge and White felt that the precious hour in which it might still be made was being lost. But Bridges suspected, from shots coming from Baby 700, that the Turks were behind his left and ordered the line to hold fast until he clarified matters on that flank. As a lengthy reconnaissance was out of the question, he merely satisfied himself from Ari Burnu that it was not threatened. He did nothing to address the problems caused by MacLagan's change of plan. The 3rd Brigade had now held the Second Ridge for almost two hours. The 1st had started landing, though behind time on account of the delays that beset the 2nd Brigade. Well over 8000 Australians were ashore with fewer than 500 Turks directly facing them. Only the men under Tulloch and Loutit, and a handful of others out in front, were seriously engaged.

On the Turkish side, the two companies from the 2/27th Battalion that faced the landing had denuded their fringe outposts to try to contain it. This greatly helped the company north of Ari Burnu because a few men could easily hold the narrow frontage leading to Battleship Hill while others came up. The Turks who had withdrawn from Russell's Top were thus reinforced when Tulloch's company bumped them short of Battleship Hill. Catching the full weight of the landing, the southern company under Captain Faik disintegrated before help arrived. Loutit's party pursued the remnants across what would become Legge Valley to the Third Ridge. 'We had trouble keeping up', Loutit later said. On his right, Lieutenant Eric Plant and a few men from the 9th Battalion probably reached the Third Ridge south of Anderson Knoll but were isolated and came back.

Two of the 10th Battalion's scouts, Private Arthur Blackburn and Lance-Corporal Phillip Robin, circled around deserted Scrubby Knoll and withdrew when Turks appeared in a valley ahead. They saw Loutit's men to the southwest.[13]

Only when Loutit halted on the Third Ridge to await promised follow-ups did the Turks he was chasing stop. At 8 a.m. he went with two men to the summit of Scrubby Knoll and saw the Narrows three and a half miles off. Rejoining the others when fired upon, Loutit noticed Australians digging in on the 400 Plateau 1200 yards rearwards. As there was no sign of reinforcements, he sent back for help. Captain John Ryder and a platoon of the 9th Battalion rushed over and lined up on Loutit's right around 9 a.m. but the Turks began pushing past them soon after. The pause had given the Turks a chance to reorganise, during which the 2/27th's 200-strong reserve company arrived from Gaba Tepe. To Loutit's annoyance, Ryder's men withdrew at 9.30 a.m., forcing his men to follow. Of the thirty-two who had started, eleven reached the Australian line with him.

With one outstanding exception, the Turks had responded cautiously to the landing. Despite Faik's sighting of the fleet around 2 a.m., no word appears to have reached the commander of the 9th Division, Colonel Khalil Sami Bey, at Maidos until 5.30 a.m. Believing that the landing was merely a feint, he ordered the 1/27th and 3/27th Battalions to wipe it out. They left at 7.30 a.m., after which Sami Bey learned that an 'enemy battalion' was headed for Hill 971. Preoccupied with the Helles landings by then, he asked Lieutenant-Colonel Mustafa Kemal, commander of the 19th Division at Boghali, to deal with it. Kemal grasped instantly that the advance towards Hill 971 was no feint but a major attack against the key ridge on the Peninsula, against which his whole division would have to be thrown, even though it was under Liman von Sanders's direct orders as the Fifth Army's general reserve. Taking matters into his own hands, he ordered the 57th Regiment, which he had intended to exercise near Hill 971 that day, to march with a mountain battery forthwith. Kemal led it himself. All was quiet when they reached Hill 971 but from Chunuk Bair Kemal saw 'a line of skirmishers' driving troops of the 2/27th Battalion towards him. The 2/27th men said they had no ammunition. He made them fix bayonets and lie down. The skirmishers took cover as well.

It was 10 a.m. Kemal sent the 1/57th Battalion down the inland side of the range towards Baby 700 and the 2/57th down the seaward side before emplacing the mountain battery on Scrubby Knoll and calling forward the 77th Regiment. His orders were unequivocal: 'I don't order you to attack, I order you to die. In the time it takes us to die, other troops and commanders can come and take our places'. Later to become Ataturk, Father of the Turkish People and founder of modern Turkey, Kemal may have been the officer Tulloch on Battleship Hill saw giving orders on Chunuk Bair. Tulloch fired at him but missed. The 2/57th Battalion drove in his left flank. He withdrew the forty men still with him towards Baby 700.[14]

As the battle seemed to have moved beyond Baby 700, a returning scout found Lalor's men at the Nek 'sitting down smoking and eating as if on a picnic'. 'Good God, sir', he said to Major Sydney Robertson, who had joined Lalor after becoming separated from the 9th Battalion, 'aren't you preparing for the counterattack?' Stunned, Robertson replied, 'I didn't dream they'd come back'. He and Margetts promptly took platoons to the far slope of Baby 700 while Lalor and the remainder stayed at the Nek. Arriving before the line was set, the 2/57th hurled Robertson's men back. Margetts's platoon pulled back to avoid being cut off. Tulloch's men reached the Nek as Kemal's mountain battery drenched the area with shrapnel.[15]

Enfilading the First and Second Ridges and Monash Valley, Baby 700 was 'the crux of Anzac', light horseman Corporal Harold Newman recalled years later. Despite his obsession with the opposite flank, MacLagan pointed to the hill from his headquarters on the Second Ridge as the Turks closed in and remarked, 'If they get that high land, we are done'. The incoming companies of the 1st Brigade that he waved towards it were being diverted onto the line above Monash Valley, which was also threatened. Exasperated, MacLagan told Bridges at 10.35 a.m. that unless his left was quickly reinforced he could not hold on. Only two companies of the 2nd Battalion were uncommitted and Bridges sent them to the Nek straightaway. Joined by the remnants of Margetts's men, they charged Baby 700 at 11 a.m. and took it. The Turks forced them back. The cycle was repeated five times during the day.

Aware that Bridges had few reserves left, Birdwood signalled at 10.45 a.m. that he was landing half of the New Zealand Infantry Brigade. They also started for Baby 700 but most ended up dispersed along the Second Ridge just as the 1st Brigade had been. The penny-packeting of its battalions there had left Colonel MacLaurin without a command. Only two companies of New Zealanders reached the Baby 700 area. Lieutenant Herbert Westmacott of the Auckland Battalion quickly found out how deadly it was:

> Cowdray was talking to me one moment, the next his blood was pouring down his face from his forehead. He gave a surprised stare, then quietly laid his head on his rifle on the ground in front of him and was dead . . . I received a blow on my right arm close to the shoulder which turned me right over . . . Reaching down I found something that seemed cold, fat and heavy at my left side on the ground. It was my own right hand. I was lying on my smashed right arm.

Meanwhile Lalor had sent the exhausted Margetts rearward and led what remained of the 12th Battalion forward from the Nek. Coming across Captain Leslie Morshead with a platoon of the 2nd, he asked them to join his men, moaning 'Oh, it's a ——', and lamenting the losses. Now swordless, Lalor was becoming unstrung. Ordering a charge, he stood, shouted 'Now then, 12th Battalion', and was sniped. On and around Baby 700 were fragments of seven battalions, worn out by the welter of disjointed advances and with no one in overall charge. Opposite them the 3/57th Battalion was deploying in the centre of the 57th Regiment, finally allowing a full regimental attack. At 4 p.m. the Turks advanced. At 4.30 p.m. the line on Baby 700 broke. Sixty men stopped the Turks at the Nek. Each one signed a message seeking reinforcements. None came. With the Turks bypassing them, they retreated along Russell's Top. The rest of the 2nd Battalion under Lieutenant-Colonel Braund held Walker's Ridge but the Top lay open. Filtering onto it, the Turks got behind the weakly held positions at the head of Monash Valley that marked the northern end of the Australian line on the Second Ridge.[16]

During the morning, the 1st and 3rd Battalions of the 27th Regiment had attacked the southern flank. The Australian 10th Battalion on the left, most of the 9th on the right and bits of the 12th intermingled were digging in across the 400 Plateau as MacLagan had ordered. With over 1000 men on a 600-yard frontage and the 7th Battalion arriving, they were in loose touch. Another 200 men were in a covering screen on the lip of Lone Pine 300 yards ahead. On the plateau when the attack started, MacLagan feared that 'if the advanced parties were thrown back, confusion would occur and they might carry the rear line back'. He sent the 9th Battalion forward to reinforce them. Parts of the 10th and 7th went too. As they started moving through the waist-high gorse, a shattering fusillade erupted. Only isolated fragments reached the screen. Hurrying back to his headquarters, MacLagan did not know that his order had left no line to speak of on the 400 Plateau except the 10th Battalion's on Johnston's Jolly. The void sucked in the 2nd Brigade like a sponge.

McCay's formation was in disarray. After its switch to the right flank, a rendezvous had been hastily set up in Shrapnel Valley but no arrangements were made to send companies on from it. They set off independently, without anyone really sure where they were supposed to go or what they were supposed to do. Confusion set in. 'We were all over the place – there was the 5th Battalion mixed up with the 6th Battalion, the 8th Battalion – all over the place', wrote Private Parker of the 5th. The line had already gone when the 5th reached the 400 Plateau and the battalion became further disorganised as it pushed on to look for it. Some men ended up on Johnston's Jolly. Others advanced over Lone Pine:

> They would reach the edge of a bit of a clearing and then a young officer would order a charge and they would push across a clear space, cheering, shot at from every angle except the rear, their bayonets flashing in the sun – and disappear in the undergrowth.

A gap opened up across the centre of the plateau as the remnants withdrew. Trying to anchor the right flank, the 8th Battalion was digging in on Bolton's Ridge to the south of it. In front of the 8th, parts of the 6th Battalion had advanced to Pine Ridge. Learning that the gap extended to Bolton's, McCay warned Bridges at 4.45 p.m. that the Turks could cut the plateau in two unless help arrived. Bridges had only the 4th Battalion available, the last from the 1st Division to land. With Baby 700 also at breaking point, he said to McCay: 'I want you to speak to me, not as subordinate to general, but as McCay to Bridges . . . Do you assure me that your need for it is absolute?' McCay did and received it. By 6 p.m. the 4th Battalion linked Bolton's to a thin line behind Lone Pine that twice-wounded Major Richard Saker, the senior surviving officer of the 5th, had cobbled together. Pine Ridge was lost. The 6th Battalion men on it fought to the end. In 1919 Bean found their skeletons in groups of three or four, the unit colour patches still discernible on the tattered uniforms.[17]

Of the 1st Division's twelve battalions, parts of ten were involved in the fight on the 400 Plateau and its surrounds. For most of the day, just the two battalions of the 27th Regiment opposed them. When their initial attacks were repulsed, the outnumbered Turks simply fired from the Third Ridge and Legge Valley at the Australians constantly moving over the plateau. Only rarely were the Turks visible. 'Their machine-guns never seemed to tire and they poured belt after belt into us', Private John Gordon of the 9th Battalion stated. 'Occasionally I would have a few shots but we had no target to shoot at, and it was bringing trouble to those near one to make too much of a show'. As standing up to dig in was fatal, Private Cheney lay on his stomach and scratched 'a molehill of earth' in front of him with his entrenching tool. So did everyone else.

Against the Turkish artillery, which more than offset the Turks' numerical disadvantage, there was no defence. By midday four batteries were in action on the Third Ridge, henceforth appropriately called Gun Ridge. Nowhere did the shrapnel fall more heavily than on the 400 Plateau. With each burst ten to fifteen feet above the ground, a hail of pellets lashed the defenceless backs of the Australians trying to avoid the torrent of rifle and machine-gun fire, which became deadlier in turn as the shrapnel shredded the vegetation and exposed them further. 'You are lucky if you stick it half an hour', wrote Private Phil Harrison. Captain Alfred Carne of the 6th Battalion never forgot 'the cries of the wounded, the cry of one for some kind hand to put an end to his misery, the ghastly look on the upturned face of the dead'. Lance-Corporal Mitchell heard and saw both. Hit in the stomach, his friend Alec Gilpin begged all day to be shot. The now familiar 'sickening thud' that signalled the man alongside him had been hit brought a ghastlier horror:

> The bullet had fearfully smashed his face and gone down his throat, rendering him dumb. But his eyes were dreadful to behold. And how he squirmed in his agony. There was nothing that I could do for him but to pray that he might die swiftly. It took him about twenty minutes to accomplish this, and by that time he had tangled his legs in mine, and stiffened. I saw the waxy colour creep over his cheek and breathed freer.

One man with half his face blown off shot himself. 'It was one long continuous cry for stretcher bearers', said Cheney. But as

Mitchell noted: 'no stretcher bearer could approach our position without being shot down'.[18]

The wounded who were evacuated faced grim prospects. Only one hospital ship, capable of handling 300 serious cases, and two transports, rudimentarily equipped for light cases, were initially available to take them. On one of these transports, *Seeangchoon*, three doctors attended 659 mostly badly wounded men, many of whom 'sat all night and well into next day with congealed blood hanging from mouths unable to speak, but with an awful appeal in their eyes imploring you to bring the doctor', wrote medic Peter Hall. Conditions on the other transports, which had to be utilised when the earmarked vessels filled, were awful. Boats and lighters went from ship to ship trying to hawk their bloodied cargoes. Midshipman Eric Longley-Cook was in charge of a lighter with a hundred serious cases:

> The hospital ship was easily marked and when I got there they just waved me away. I said: 'Well, look, I've got men dying here,' and they were screaming with pain. The hospital ship said: 'We are absolutely full up and cannot take any more wounded.' So then I went to one, two, three, four of the transports. The same story everywhere. Eventually, quite late at night . . . I went to my own ship, the *Prince of Wales*, and simply told the officer of the watch and the commander: 'I can't take them any further. These men have got to be taken aboard.' The men were hoisted up.

The extreme difficulty of disposing of the wounded afloat slashed the rate at which they could be taken off the beach. Those unable to help themselves had to lie under the scorching sun, tormented by flies and sometimes hit again by the shrapnel overhead.[19]

Wounded and unwounded alike listened for the return fire of their own guns. The 26th Indian Mountain Battery's six howitzers were landed at 10.30 a.m. and engaged Gun Ridge about midday from behind the 400 Plateau. Spirits soared but the euphoria was short-lived for the battery could be seen from Battleship Hill and almost every Ottoman gun rained shrapnel on it. Facing annihilation, it withdrew to the beach at 2.25 p.m. The 21st Indian Mountain Battery did not land until dusk and a solitary 18-pounder, from the more potent field artillery, at 5.30 p.m. Hauled up Hell Spit to the cheers even of the dying, it shut the Gaba Tepe battery down. Lieutenant-Colonel Charles Rosenthal of the 3rd Australian Artillery Brigade vehemently pressed for the landing of more field guns but Bridges probably feared losing them in a deteriorating situation. Uncertainty over friendly troop locations and problems communicating with the warships limited naval gunfire support.[20]

Being shelled by the Turks with impunity worsened the stress already felt by men who were mostly fighting in small groups, often leaderless, and unaware because of the scrub of what was happening to those six feet away. They also felt the atmosphere of outright hostility projected by the place: its baked yellow heights standing starkly against the azure sky, watching their agony with mocking indifference. Some wavering started, more so on the 400 Plateau, where the fire was heaviest, than elsewhere. Unwounded men began trickling back at 1 p.m. At 5.20 p.m. McCay reported that 'considerable numbers' were leaving.

Bean thought there may have been six hundred to a thousand stragglers on the beach by nightfall. He differentiated between them. 'The stronger sort' went back to seek instructions because they had lost their units, then promptly returned to the line. Those whose nerve had briefly failed typically helped casualties to the rear, convinced that they were 'really doing a charitable soldierly action'. They too often rejoined the fray. 'The weaker sort' skived off to safe dugouts. Captain John Gellibrand of the 1st Division's staff said afterwards that their number was negligible. Not making these distinctions at the time, commanders were alarmed at what the straggling portended. At 5.40 p.m. Bridges requested the speedy landing of the 4th Brigade, which started disembarking twenty minutes later.

Coming down to his headquarters at 7.05 p.m., MacLagan said to him: 'It's touch and go. If the Turks come on . . . on the left, I don't think anything can stop them'. McCay was similarly worried about the right. Both said that the day-long shrapnel shelling had demoralised the men.[21]

Evacuation began to be discussed. Military logic said that the Turks would bring up reinforcements and more artillery for an overwhelming dawn counter-attack. A withdrawal would avert annihilation and enable the Anzac formations to be employed at Helles. But it would hardly make for an auspicious first outing for the AIF. White recalled that Bridges 'had trouble making up his mind what to do'. Godley had no qualms and convinced him to pull out. They summoned Birdwood from *Queen* at 9.15 p.m. Landing at 10 p.m. as light rain fell, he picked his way through 'a scene of indescribable confusion' to Bridges's shelter, a niche dug into the side of a gully on the beach. Their stubbly faces pale and strained in the shadowy light, Bridges, Godley, White and Birdwood's chief of staff, the pugnacious Brigadier-General Harold Walker, were inside. According to Birdwood, Bridges and Godley demanded immediate re-embarkation. 'Walker, the little fighting cock', pooh-poohed the idea, Bean recorded, and gave Bridges a mouthful. Major Thomas Blamey of Bridges's staff reckoned that he had never been spoken to so harshly in his life. Bridges did not waver. He stressed the importance to Birdwood of prompt action. Birdwood replied that he would rather die on the spot in the morning than re-embark.

Beneath the resolute veneer, Birdwood was less certain. Briefly ashore during the afternoon, he had seen the shrapnel shelling. He reported to Hamilton at 8.45 p.m. that the position was 'not very satisfactory', the country 'very difficult', the shelling and casualties severe. Now faced with wobbling subordinates painting a worse picture, Birdwood wobbled too and dictated a note conveying their fears to Hamilton. 'If we are to re-embark', he concluded, 'it must be at once'. At 11 p.m. the note reached *Queen* for onwards transmission but because it had not been addressed in the hurry of its despatch, Thursby opened it and was flabbergasted. He headed ashore to dissuade Birdwood but also took the precaution of having the transports ready their boats to send to the beach. At that moment, *Queen Elizabeth* arrived from Helles with Hamilton aboard. Thursby crossed to it instead.

Roused from a deep sleep, Hamilton read Birdwood's message and sought Thursby's views. Thursby was dead against evacuation. Almost three days would be needed 'to get that crowd off the beach', he said. Word arrived that the Australian submarine *AE2* had penetrated the Narrows and sunk a Turkish ship. Hamilton included the news to encourage Birdwood in a reply that enjoined him to appeal to his men for a supreme effort to hold on. A famous postcript added: 'You have got through the difficult business, now you have only to dig, dig, dig, until you are safe'. Hamilton later wrote of the courage needed to face 'the various alarmist and despondent tendencies of some of my commanders, which were more frightening than the Turks'.[22]

From a much lowlier station, Lance-Corporal Hedley Howe of the 11th Battalion derided the evacuation proposal as 'sheer panic, arrived at . . . without any knowledge of the true state of affairs'. At any time before the conference with Birdwood,

> Bridges, Godley or White could have ascertained the condition of the troops by a 15-minute walk to the line at Steele's or Courtney's Posts – both pretty hot centres – where demoralisation of the troops was completely non-existent. None did so. They permitted themselves to be dominated by the fears generated during the day's tension in the relative security of headquarters by the reports of returning wounded . . . if there was any demoralisation at ANZAC that night it was in their own headquarters.[23]

In fact, the troops in the line had been digging for hours. At sunset the Turkish artillery ceased and the infantry fire became inaccurate.

Able to move about, men quickly got below ground even as the Turks continued to attack. Given away in the darkness by cries of 'Allah! Mohammed!', fierce assaults on Walker's and Bolton's Ridges were mown down. The 4th Brigade's arrival had been a great fillip. Occupying the hill, named after its commander, Lieutenant-Colonel Harold Pope, which jutted from the head of Monash Valley like a cork plugging a bottle, the 16th Battalion partly filled the dangerous gap that extended from Russell's Top. The 15th dribbled onto the Second Ridge and the 400 Plateau. By then the rest of the New Zealanders were ashore, the Otago Battalion and part of the Wellington Battalion moving into an inner defence line being dug from Plugge's to MacLagan's Ridge in order to cover the beach. The remainder of the Canterbury Battalion reinforced Braund's men on Walker's Ridge. Despite numbing fatigue, spirits had risen markedly.

Nonetheless, the initiation had been harsh. Lieutenant Casey's observation at Mena that the devastating effect of heavy fire against men in the open was insufficiently appreciated bore bitter fruit. Not enough value had been placed on machine-guns, especially on getting them forward quickly, which meant that their firepower was often sorely missed. Owing to inexperience and the shortcomings of their training, the men had to draw on their inner strength. When leaders fell or none were present, said Private Parker,

> There were quite a lot of fellows that took over – privates that probably had a little . . . Saturday afternoon experience in warfare or whatever the case may be. We eventually made a line of it, and when it came together I thought they done a mighty job to do what they did.

Casualties were well over 2000; 1800 wounded alone were embarked. The Turks had lost 2000 men, mostly from their 57th and 27th Regiments, which were now weak and exhausted.[24]

Bean rated the Landing as one of the four finest achievements of the AIF, and friend and foe alike acknowledged it as a memorable feat of arms. 'It seemed almost incredible that any troops could have done it', Captain Guy Dawnay of Hamilton's staff said. 'How they got up fully armed and equipped over the rough scrub-clad hillsides one can hardly imagine.' Another British officer described the Australian infantryman as 'The bravest thing on earth God ever made'. Hamilton felt that the Australians 'did wonders'. Calling them 'untrained (or rather irregular troops)', Godley thought that they 'landed with the most wonderful dash and carried everything before them'. 'Just absolute heroism', Sergeant Frederick Ward said, giving the New Zealanders' opinion. 'Their first effort in this difficult country was beyond all praise', remarked the Turks.[25]

The men themselves felt a collective pride in having held their own in a battle that would have tested the mettle of seasoned soldiers. They knew that 25 April would be a watershed in their country's history. Private Edward Richards of the 11th Battalion noted prophetically: 'The reckless courage and strong determination of Australia's sons will keep that Sabbath morning so clearly distinct in Australian hearts that it will appear but of yesterday'. For the first time, 'allegiance to Imperial traditions became inadequate' and being Australian was something to be treasured. Those at home felt the same way when the first detailed report, glowingly written by British War Correspondent Ellis Ashmead-Bartlett, appeared in their newspapers on 8 May. Though they were unaware that the Landing had failed, the news that the AIF had not been found wanting came as a huge relief. The 'six-bob-a-day tourist' tag lost its derisory sting.[26]

—FOUR—

STALEMATE

The anxiety in the aftermath of the Landing was greater than at any other time during the campaign. Kemal had to drive the Anzacs into the sea before they were established; the Anzacs had to establish themselves before the onslaught fell. On 26 April their task became easier. Naval gunfire knocked out some of the Turkish guns and Ottoman losses and exhaustion precluded the expected counterattack. Only 'accidental collisions or attempts by the local commander to gain some particular vantage point' took place that day. Captain Kenneth Gresson of the Canterburys saw the havoc that the navy wreaked:

The hills over which the Turks had to advance were plastered with shells by the warships . . . In the firing line the din was terrific. Behind the roar of the ships' guns – the snapping bark of the *Bacchante*'s six inch mingled with the boom of the twelve inch and the still louder and deeper boom of the *Queen Elizabeth*'s fifteen inch. In front the hills ablaze with bursting shells, dense clouds of smoke arising as pieces of hill were hurled skywards.[1]

On the 400 Plateau, the Turks profited from an Australian blunder. Visiting it shortly after midday, Bridges saw that Major Saker's position behind Lone Pine kinked back from the line on either side. He ordered it straightened, then left. Saker led the 200 men with him forward but fell in the first few yards. Only he seems to have known what the move was for. His men thought Hill 971 was the goal and kept going. Then a garbled order 'to make a general advance' reached the 4th Battalion on Bolton's, which headed northwards as well. A hail of shrapnel and machine-gun fire lashed it, killing the commanding officer, Lieutenant-Colonel Astley Onslow Thompson. A panicky retreat started. Ironically, the survivors of both assaults took up a line approximating to what Bridges wanted. Bridges was unaware that any attack had been made. Night brought some consolation when Rosenthal's field guns, finally ashore, minced Ottoman charges across Lone Pine.

Some men thought that the 4th Battalion's ill-fated advance was the spearhead of the 29th Division from Helles. Rumours of its approach swept Anzac. But the 29th, having only just secured the beaches, was too exhausted to go further. Unknown to the British, the Ottomans at Helles, badly outnumbered to start with, had been knocked about as much as those at Anzac. The remnants were entrenching before Krithia, a flyspeck of a village four miles inland at the foot of Achi Baba. With the feints that were intended to distract him from the real landings over, Liman von Sanders could concentrate against both beachheads. He sent Kemal two more regiments and some extra artillery, giving him rough parity with his opponents.

On 27 April Kemal launched an all-out attack. Dispersed by the broken terrain the fresh regiments arrived late and the Turks already in the line were tired and demoralised. The push degenerated into disjointed assaults devoid of punch. But Colonel MacLaurin and Major Francis Irvine, his brigade-major, were killed. Disdaining cover, Irvine attracted repeated pleas of 'Down Sir – you'll be sniped for certain', to which he replied, 'It's my business to be sniped at'. A sniper accommodated him. Standing in full view on the ridge that bore his name, MacLaurin was despatched ten minutes later. Monash thundered: 'such unnecessary exposure does no possible good and seriously impairs morale'.[2]

Real danger threatened only at Russell's Top. The Turks had not let up against Colonel Braund's line, which met the Top at the head of Walker's Ridge. Just after he led another bayonet charge to clear it, their attack started. Six waves of Ottomans barrelled over Battleship Hill. Shouting 'The Turks are onto us in droves', Australians and New Zealanders alike started rearwards. Braund stood in their path with revolver drawn. Salvation came from the sea. The massed formation disappeared in clouds of smoke and dust thrown up by the huge shells of the battleships, which gave the hill its name. Braund formed another line. After dark the Turks came on hourly using bombs, which were new to the Anzacs. Each time the Anzacs drove them off.

The Wellington Battalion took over on Walker's next morning. Their commander, Lieutenant-Colonel William Malone, thought the Australians 'badly handled and trained'. Braund had no plan except for 'a murderous notion that the only thing to do was to plunge troops out of the neck of the ridge into the jungle beyond'. Furious that Braund's charges had earlier cost the Wellingtons almost 200 men in their first hour in action, Malone repositioned the line where it was less exposed. But Malone was well to the rear on Walker's Ridge for most of the battle, whereas Braund had been in the thick of it. His charges secured the left flank. Malone apart, the New Zealanders praised the Australians fighting alongside them. Slightly deaf, Braund was killed a week later when he failed to answer a challenge from one of his sentries.[3]

After four days' non-stop fighting, the Anzacs were physically spent. In that time Captain Francis Moran of the 15th Battalion had 'about two decent meals' and 'what was worse, no sleep'. The earsplitting din never ceased and frayed nerves further. Distinguishing between the sounds, Captain James Durrant of the 13th Battalion left no doubt as to their effect:

The noise was terrific – bullets always make a great noise passing over a valley but we found that each shell made a roar like an express train.

> Machine-guns made it worse, and the heavy shells from the ships worse still, and the echoes from the cliffs at the back of us redoubled it, until we were nearly driven mad by the racket . . . Noise is not supposed to hurt anyone but under those conditions the strain was terrible.

It showed 'in a hundred different ways', wrote Bean. Most had 'leaden eyes'. Some 'could barely talk – almost as though they were drunk'. Others were unnaturally vivacious. Spies and snipers were seen everywhere and though men would not run from a shell, 'they would turn savagely and curse it as a dog snarls at his tormentors'. Relief was essential. On 28 April Hamilton gave Birdwood four battalions, three of them Royal Marine Light Infantry (RMLI), from the RND.[4]

The Anzacs relished the prospect of reinforcement by such a prestigious formation as the Marines. But the RMLI, like the rest of the RND, consisted mostly of raw recruits and the Anzacs' delight vanished at the sight of the newcomers labouring up MacLaurin's Hill and the 400 Plateau in a drenching thunderstorm, their pale, puny physiques crowned with silly-looking pith helmets. Lieutenant Margetts thought them 'the most amusing' soldiers he had seen. Expecting to take over a formed trench system, Private Harry Baker of the Chatham Battalion and many other Marines were nonplussed on reaching the Australian front line:

> There was what you might call a ditch about two feet deep . . . Every few yards lay a dead man. So you had to crawl over him to take up your position. There were quite a number of dead men there. You could feel them and see them – that's not a very nice experience.

One RMLI officer reportedly inquired where the officers' mess was. Calling the Marines 'children under untrained officers', Birdwood wrote that they 'are so far as I can see nearly useless . . . immature boys with no proper training'. 'The only real advantage we gained', said Lieutenant Les Bain of the 14th Battalion, 'was that they brought several machine-guns with them'. Nonetheless, their arrival allowed the done-in brigades of the 1st Division to withdraw to Shrapnel Valley to reorganise.[5]

The men stood glassy-eyed in ragged rows while the officers called the roll. 'This was the most touching sight I ever witnessed. Everybody was congratulating everybody else on their good fortune to escape injury or death', remarked Private Grant of the 1st Battalion's parade. 'We were all surprised to see each other', Margetts wrote after the 12th Battalion gathered. All too often men found that mates they hoped to see again were absent. The 1st Division had lost 4931 men, almost 500 more than the 29th Division, which amounted to a casualty rate of over one in three. 'SLAUGHTER!' exclaimed Grant. Losses notwithstanding, the respite lasted only a couple of days.[6]

Reinforced by five fresh battalions, Kemal launched a third counterattack, this time assembling in darkness to avoid giving the warships a target. The enemy had to be thrown into the sea, he told the *mehmetçiks*, the name the Turks gave to their soldiers, 'if it means the death of us all'. It almost did. At 4 a.m. on 1 May, the Marines and the 14th Battalion on Courtney's Post quickly cut down the *mehmetçiks* charging towards them. 'You couldn't see the effects, you were just firing into a kind of a big object. It didn't look like individual people', Marine machine-gunner Private Joe Clements recalled. 'It finished all of a sudden. They just turned and there wasn't anybody there anymore.' Only at Quinn's, where they threw a few bombs into the trenches, did the Turks get close to the Anzac line. Put in overall charge opposite Anzac by Liman von Sanders, Essad Pasha, a veteran general well thought of by the Germans, temporarily forbade further attacks.[7]

The line that the Anzacs held corresponded exactly with what Hamilton's chief of staff, Major-General Walter Braithwaite, reckoned was 'the irreducible minimum which must at all costs be made good'. It climbed up Bolton's Ridge in the south, crossed the 400 Plateau and ran along the Second Ridge past MacLaurin's Hill, all of which the 1st Australian Division held, to Courtney's Post where the NZ and A Division took charge. Adjacent Quinn's Post, one thousand yards from the sea, was the furthest point inland. Then came the yawning gap formed by the Bloody Angle, which was too dangerous to hold, and Dead Man's Ridge and the trench grid on the Chessboard, both occupied by the Turks. Partly filled by Pope's Hill, the gap was never completely closed. Resuming on Russell's Top below the Nek, the line headed down Walker's Ridge to isolated Numbers 1 to 3 Posts, one and a half miles along the coast from where it began. Within this perimeter lay a triangular-shaped area less than three-quarters of a mile square into which 20 000 men were crammed. The Turks beheld it as would 'a man looking down from the top of a cliff at his adversary clinging to a precarious ledge below him'.

As Monash Valley was the only avenue of communication to the beach, the future of 'the cheese-bite', as Godley called it, depended on the retention of the posts at its head – Pope's, Quinn's and Courtney's. Held by the 4th Brigade, they became the focus of the fighting for the next month. From Baby 700, the Nek, the Chessboard and Dead Man's Ridge, the Turks could fire into the back of each. The slopes behind them rose precipitously from the valley floor and could only be scaled using ropes dangled from the summit, which made resupply a Herculean task. There were also gaps between them. The forward trenches were mostly below the crests; and 'crowded like martins, in ledges and holes' on the exposed rearward slopes, were the supports. In the first three weeks, the longest period of silence was ten seconds. The stench of dead bodies was suffocating. 'You can almost fancy you are chewing it every time you breathe, it is so thick', said Lieutenant Nikolai Svensen of the 15th Battalion. Swarms of maggots crawled out of the corpses to infest the trenches, which had to be swept out regularly.[8]

Quinn's was at the apex of Anzac and its most important position. Dominated by the Turks on three sides – they were only thirty yards away in front – and with its left flank open, it could be approached only by night. The unending cacophony of exploding bombs and cracking bullets, nights spent in packed trenches staring at the crest a few yards distant, and stories of fire so intense that rifles jammed and bayonets twisted with heat as Turkish assaults were seen off, made those in Monash Valley glance up at the post 'as a man looks at a haunted house'. Hamilton said 'men live more in five minutes on that crest than they do in five years of Bendigo or Ballarat'. Major Hugh Quinn warned reinforcements: 'Don't talk too loud or they'll hear what you say. They know my name all right now and they call out "Come on, you kangaroo shooting bastards!"'[9]

Late on 30 April Birdwood ordered an offensive to improve the precarious Anzac line. Attacking northeastwards, the NZ and A Division was to seize Baby 700 at one end while the 1st Division advanced eastwards to take the entire 400 Plateau at the other. The plan was ill-conceived for the ever-expanding gap between them would have to be filled progressively as the attack developed, a feat of co-ordination virtually impossible under heavy fire. Yet it was to begin at 5 p.m. next day, allowing less than twenty-four hours for preparations. Considering the operation 'hopeless', General Walker, who had replaced MacLaurin in command of the 1st Brigade, objected forcefully to Bridges. This time Bridges listened. 'I take it on myself; the First Division will not attack', he declared. Godley was enthusiastic. The NZ and A Division would attack Baby 700 alone. But Monash felt uneasy. At his insistence, Godley sent a staff officer to see the ground on 1 May. The risks in daylight were deemed unacceptable. To reduce them, the operation was postponed to 7.15 p.m. on the following evening. After fifteen minutes' intense shelling, the 4th Brigade would assault past Quinn's to the Bloody Angle, swing north along the Chessboard towards Baby 700, and link up with the New Zealanders advancing on Baby 700 up the far side of Pope's Hill.[10]

After 'a week's irksome defensive', the prospect of finally getting stuck into the Turks sent morale soaring. The din of the bombardment raised it further. 'Come on, lads, at 'em', cried Lieutenant Cyril Geddes of the 16th Battalion, as the fire lifted. It was his last night on earth. Yelling its password, 'Yarragabbah', the 16th stormed forth, the supporting waves singing 'Australia Will Be There' and 'Tipperary'. 'Up we rushed – God it was frightful', wrote Private Ellis Silas. The preliminary bombardment had been ineffective. 'In a very few minutes the gully at the foot of the hill was filled with dead and wounded, poor lumps of clay which had once been comrades . . . all round could be seen the sparks where the bullets were striking.' The 16th Battalion only managed to get a toehold across the Bloody Angle and the 13th following took a trench below the Chessboard but could go no further. Everything now depended on the Otago Battalion reaching Baby 700 and pushing down towards them.

The Otagos had gone missing. Lieutenant-Colonel Athelston Moore had led his men from their location on Walker's Ridge to the beach, intending to turn inland at Shrapnel Valley. The longest way around, it was also the most protected. But the New Zealand Infantry Brigade's commander, Colonel Francis Johnston, and Godley failed to ensure the route was clear. The beach and Shrapnel Valley were crowded. Australian wounded thronged Monash Valley. The Otagos' attack began at 8.45 p.m., ninety minutes late, without artillery bombardment and with the Turks fully aroused. 'Line after line of our men went up', an onlooker said. 'Some lines didn't take two paces over the crest when down they went to a man and on came another line.' Two men were alongside Sergeant John Skinner:

One of them was a devout Roman Catholic and he was praying out loud to the Holy Mother Mary that he'd get hit, a blighty one so that he could get out of it, and it wasn't long before he got his wish. He and his companion were killed and I had my rifle smashed in my hand, all with the same burst of fire.

Around 11 p.m., with half his battalion casualties and the rest a shambles trying to dig in short of the Chessboard next to the Australians, Moore blundered into the Australian line, lost and 'wild with excitement'. Out of touch because the telephone lines had been cut, Godley and Johnston thought things were going well. The Canterbury Battalion was ordered to assault over the Nek and link up with the Otagos. Failure was inevitable. At 1.35 a.m. Godley gave Monash two battalions of Marines to ensure that the ground won was held. Battling the same congestion that dogged the Otagos, they reached the heights at dawn, just as a battery on Plugge's mistakenly lobbed five shells into the 16th Battalion's line. Part of it broke, carrying some Marines back with it. Others tried to slot in on Dead Man's Ridge between the Bloody Angle and the Chessboard. Marine Baker ended up alongside an Australian:

All the way to the right were men shoulder to shoulder lying on the ground. No cover at all, just lying on the very ridge. Suddenly a machine-gun cracked away at right angles to us . . . He had a good view because he was higher up and he could see exactly what he was doing. It was like mowing grass I should think for him. This machine-gun went along and killed every man . . . except the Australian and me. The Australian said: 'The bastards can't kill me. They've had lots of tries. They can't kill me'. I looked again. The machine-gun started barking again behind us . . . and covered every man again, every man. I felt the bullets thud into the Aussie and he never spoke again . . . I had a bullet through the right foot and felt as though I'd been hit by a donkey.

Giving Dead Man's its name, the corpses of the Marines lay roasting on the ridge for several days, 'like ants shrivelled by a fire' before they were kicked into Monash Valley for burial. The first attempt at a forward move had been a fiasco. Lieutenant-Colonel Joseph Beeston of the 4th Field Ambulance dealt with the bloody aftermath:

Great amount of operating, chiefly amputations, and serious abdominal cases. Some of these are very ghastly. A shell will carry the whole of the intestines away, others half of the abdomen. Nothing can be done for these unfortunate fellows but fill them up with Morphia, and await the end. The contents of the man's pockets are frequently in the abdominal cavity, sometimes clips of cartridges, and once the cap of a shell. It was a dreadful experience to see all these men, just coming into vigorous manhood, mangled and maimed with in many cases wounds that must prove fatal.

Feelings ran high. 'I did not want any more like [that]', wrote Private George McClintock of the 13th Battalion. 'It was just hell pure and simple with the gates open wide at that.' Private Henry Lewis of the Otagos called Godley 'a bloody mongrel of a general'. Shortly afterwards Bridges underscored the significance of the failure, informing Munro-Ferguson 'that we cannot get on and are really in a state of siege'. He meant that the Turks were the besiegers and the beleaguered Anzacs, with their backs to the sea, the besieged. Reinforcing the point, one hundred men of the 11th Battalion tried to raid Gaba Tepe at daybreak on 4 May. They could not get off the beach and had to be evacuated by the Navy.[11]

Hamilton now directed Birdwood to mount only minor attacks, principally to tie down Ottoman units that would otherwise be sent to Helles. Yet Helles was as stalemated as Anzac. The First Battle of Krithia on 28 April had left the attacking 29th Division 'badly bent'. Although a massive Turkish counterattack between 1 and 3 May was repulsed, the line still lay three miles short of Achi Baba and no further advance was possible without reinforcement. Kitchener had released the 42nd Division from Egypt and, on 3 May, Hamilton asked Birdwood for as many troops as he could spare from Anzac. Birdwood despatched the 2nd Australian and the New Zealand Infantry Brigades.

Landing in the shadow of *River Clyde* early on 6 May, the two brigades marched up through olive groves and flowery fields. The contrast with the wild country they had just left was striking. At 11 a.m. the 29th Division, once again, attacked with the French. 'A modern battle was taking place before our eyes, but little could be seen', Corporal Eric Moorhead of the 5th Battalion remembered. General Hunter-Weston was carrying out his specialty, the daylight frontal assault. Facing an uphill advance of over a mile across open ground, it was met instantly met by murderous fire. Though 400 yards was the maximum gain, the only change made for the following day was to start an hour earlier. An even smaller return resulted.

On 8 May Hunter-Weston had yet another go. The New Zealanders were loaned to the 29th Division for the attack, which began at 10.30 a.m. Orders were late and meagre. Lieutenant-Colonel Charles Brown gave the Canterbury Battalion the start time, smiled and said: 'I am sorry gentlemen that I cannot give you any further information'. Most of them did not get 100 yards. His uniform torn by two bullets, parched with thirst and his legs blistering in the sun, Private Frank McKenzie of the Auckland Battalion lay from 11 a.m. until nightfall saying over and over, 'Hide me Oh my Saviour hide, Till the storm of life be past'. When Hunter-Weston ordered more of the same for the afternoon, Hamilton came ashore. At 4 p.m., thinking that the whole Turkish front would collapse if only it could be pierced, he directed that 'the whole line, reinforced by the Australians, should on the stroke of 5.30 fix bayonets and storm Krithia and Achi Baba'. McCay's brigade was to head for the village on the right of the New Zealanders. He received the order at 4.55 p.m. It stated that the advance should be made with bands playing and colours flying. Neither had been brought.[12]

The 2nd Brigade was having dinner 600–900 yards behind the line when it received the word to advance immediately. Gulping down a last mouthful, the Australians hurriedly put on their gear and moved off as the bombardment, the heaviest to date, crashed down. 'It was indescribable. The noise, the dust. You just couldn't hear each other speak', wrote Private Frank Brent of the 6th Battalion. 'We thought: "Well, this is going to be a cakewalk. There's nothing to stop us."' But the ignorance of the whereabouts of the Turks made the bombardment fruitless. As soon as the Australians emerged from the olive trees onto the flat bare moorland, bullets and shrapnel lacerated them. As there had been no time for a reconnaissance, they were surprised on coming across the British front line, from where the attack proper was to start. Many thought that 'Tommies' Trench' was their objective and sought shelter in it. Accompanying the assault, Bean leapt out to rescue a wounded man. McCay turned to him and said, 'Well Bean, I suppose I will have to do the damned heroic act'. Jumping onto the parapet, he yelled: 'Now then Australians – which of you men are Australians? Come on Australians!'

When the lines went forward again, Major Bennett recalled, they were met by 'a screaming hurricane of bullets', which men crouched to avoid, 'shovels and packs held before them like shields'. A British major was overcome by what he saw:

> They were disembowelled. Their clothing caught fire, and their flesh hissed and cooked before the burning rags could be torn off or beaten out. But what of it? Why, nothing! They were as devils from a hell bigger and hotter. Nothing could stop them . . . Their pluck was titanic. They were not men but gods, demons infuriated. We saw them fall by the score. But what of that? Not for one breath did the great line waver or break. On and up it went, up and on, as steady and proud as if on parade. A seasoned staff officer watching choked with his own admiration. Our men tore off their helmets and waved them, and poured cheer after cheer after those wonderful Anzacs.

Lieutenant Bob Hooper of the 5th Battalion wrote home that the Australians, 'in truly a mark of honour', were now called 'the White Gurkhas'. They were finally stopped 500 yards from the Ottoman line, now visible for the first time since the start of the battle. The survivors entrenched frantically. In half an hour, the 2nd Brigade, already reduced at Anzac to 2900 men, lost over 1000 more. 'Have you forgotten me, Cobbers?', rang out the plaintive cries of the wounded and dying calling for stretcher-bearers. A runner answered one such call: 'You won't see them tonight, my boy – they're rarer than gold'. A wounded soldier feebly replied: 'You might let us think we will'.[13]

The 2nd Brigade's advance was the only worthwhile gain of the entire battle. Linking up with it after dark, the New Zealand Infantry Brigade had lost a further 835 men during the afternoon, reducing it to 1700. Afterwards Australians and New Zealanders alike lambasted the conduct of an offensive that had cost 6500 men, about one-third of those engaged. 'We had about as much chance of taking Achi Baba as we had of taking the Bank of England', Private Parker fumed. Colonel Malone laid the blame squarely at the feet of the British commanders, from whom, he raged, 'the New Zealand officer has absolutely nothing to learn'. A night attack was the only hope, Malone said.[14]

No sooner had the dust settled at Helles than another debacle occurred at Anzac. Alarmed by rumours of Turkish mining under Quinn's, Godley ordered an operation to ascertain the Turks' strength and dispositions opposite the post and, if possible, to take their trenches. He insisted that it proceed even after the 15th Battalion garrisoning Quinn's reported the opposing line strongly held. At 10.45 p.m. on 9 May, 100 men of the 15th charged. The Turks bolted. It seemed that the positions won could be held and three saps were dug back to the 15th Battalion's line. But the Turks counterattacked continuously from 3.30 a.m., showering bombs on the Australians who, having none, could not reply. They recaptured some of their trenches. Under blistering fire, the 16th Battalion reinforced the 15th and both tried unsuccessfully to eject them. Having lost 207 men, the Australians withdrew at 5 a.m. Godley had the temerity to remark afterwards that he 'knew all along the Turks were still present in large numbers'.[15]

With the 2nd and New Zealand Brigades absent at Helles, the mauling of the two battalions exacerbated the numerical weakness of the Anzac garrison, which now comprised just 10 000 men in the three remaining Australian brigades and the four RND battalions. The RND troops were near the end of their tether, the Marines on Quinn's once bolting when a bomb exploded nearby. Like Birdwood, Brigadier-General Charles Trotman, their commander, admitted that his men were 'quite useless'. The Australians were openly calling them 'Royal Malingerers' or, from their initials, 'Run My Lads, *Imshi*'. They left for Helles on 11 May, replaced by the 3000 men of Colonel Chauvel's 1st LH Brigade and the NZMR under Colonel Andrew Russell. The 2nd and 3rd LH Brigades arrived shortly after. At the end of April Birdwood and Bridges had called for 1000 volunteers from the Anzac mounted troops in Egypt to fight as infantry but their commanders strongly opposed the break-up of their formations to provide them. They were sent complete. Their baptism was rough. Beefing up the 4th Brigade in Monash Valley on 15 May, Chauvel's men tried to fill in the three saps linking the opposing lines on Quinn's. The attempt ended after twenty minutes with nearly fifty of the sixty involved hit.[16]

Like those who preceded them, the reinforcements were handicapped by the unsuitability of the training in Egypt for the trench warfare that had set in at Anzac. From the outset, Birdwood complained of 'reckless firing on totally inadequate objectives', which was directly attributable to the paltry training limit of seventy-five rounds per rifle. The Turks' superiority in machine-gunnery was very noticeable, Godley lamenting: 'No sooner do we capture an enemy trench than we find ourselves under the enfilade fire of one or more of their machine-guns'. Lieutenant Tom Richards, who had played rugby for both the Wallabies and the British Lions, remarked that the Turks had 'stacked themselves with them', whereas the Anzacs did not have enough. Trenches were often too deep or too shallow, lacking in loopholes and topped by parapets that were not bullet-proof. Alluding to the high toll exacted by Turkish snipers because the importance of concealment was ignored, Godley commented: 'The excellence of the enemy in this matter is a standing reproof to us'. 'Officers should carry a rifle and hide their field glasses', said Lieutenant Aubrey Liddelow of the 7th Battalion. Birdwood had his scalp grazed by a sniper's shot at Quinn's on 14 May.[17]

Wanting to give the impression that they were indifferent to Turkish fire, some officers recklessly exposed themselves to it. None did so more than Bridges, for whom the deaths of MacLaurin and Irvine were no deterrent. Yet the effect on the men was exaggerated and many ridiculed his disdain of cover during his visits because it 'drew the crabs' onto them. Ironically, Bridges seemed to be exercising a newfound caution when a sniper mortally wounded him as he dashed between a gap in the sandbag buttresses shielding the track up Monash Valley, while on his way to Chauvel's headquarters on 15 May. Remarking, 'Anyway, I have commanded an Australian division for nine months', he died at sea three days later and his body was returned to Australia for burial at Duntroon. Reflecting afterwards, Birdwood thought Bridges had doubts about his own ability to command. On the day after his death, Private John Simpson Kirkpatrick was shot through the heart while ferrying a wounded man down Monash Valley on a commandeered donkey, as he had been doing for three weeks. Whereas Bridges was soon forgotten, Simpson entered Australian folklore as the embodiment of the mateship and selflessness that Anzac came to symbolise.[18]

The edge that the Turks enjoyed in sniping and entrenching could never endanger the Anzac line. Only a massive all-out assault could do that and both Essad and Kemal still held hopes of launching one.

At Helles the lodgement was much larger than Anzac, more defensible and easier for the naval guns to support. It was also a long way from the Narrows. Conversely, Anzac directly threatened not just the Narrows but also the lines of communication to Helles. Lacking depth, it was also more vulnerable. Seeing things for himself on 10 May, Enver gave the green light for another attack at Anzac and a division was rushed down from Constantinople as the spearhead. Of the three already there, two were quite fresh. With about 42 000 men, the Turks outnumbered their opponents by over two to one, despite the return of the 2nd Brigade from Helles before the assault, which was set for 3.30 a.m. on 19 May.

On 18 May the hitherto ceaseless Turkish rifle fire waned, puzzling the Anzacs, who also wondered at the bombardment, the heaviest Turkish one yet, that began at 5 p.m. and continued until dusk. An attack seemed on the cards, especially after a British aircraft reported Ottoman formations assembling in the valleys beyond. The heaviest fusillade experienced by Australians in the war broke out from Quinn's and Baby 700 around midnight. The Anzacs were ordered to stand to at 3 a.m., half an hour earlier than usual. Shortly afterwards thousands of bayonets could be seen glinting. Then came the familiar cry of 'Allah! Allah!' set off by bugles and a band, as the Ottomans commenced human wave assaults. 'Our orders were to allow them to come quite close before opening fire', said Private Aitken. 'They were simply mowed down and yet, in spite of the terrible slaughter, they still kept coming on'. Captain Charles Duke and a corporal had 'a gorgeous time . . . For two hours we blazed away – both our rifles got too hot to hold and the bolts jammed but we got others and he got two of his chaps to load for us'. The supports begged for a place on the fire-step. Private William Tope of the 12th Battalion fought for one: 'When they had filled the trench, I found I didn't have room because there were men still filing in . . . so I pushed this chap at the end, made him make room . . . I'd felt that I'd be buried there behind if I didn't have a go'.

Taunted by shouts of 'Bucksheesh!' and 'Eggs-a-Cook!', wave after wave of Turks crumpled. Many Australians sat on the parapet to get a better shot. Subjected to five assaults, the garrison at Quinn's rose and opened fire as one man to obliterate them. As the eastern sky lightened, the Turks were silhouetted against it and made even better targets. Those skulking back to their own line were easily picked off. '*Saida*! Play you again next Saturday', yelled an Australian. Only at Courtney's Post, on which the attack fell heaviest, was the line breached and then only by nine Turks. While his mates distracted them, Private Albert Jacka of the 14th Battalion leapt into the group, shooting five and bayoneting two. The other two fled. An unlit cigarette hanging from his mouth, Jacka told his officer: 'I managed to get the beggars, Sir'. He became the war's first Australian recipient of the Victoria Cross (VC).

Each one weaker than the last, the assaults continued until late morning, when the air reeked of smoke, dust and the acrid smell of burnt cordite from the 950 000 rounds the Anzacs had blasted off. The Turks were in a state of shock, Private Memish Bayraktar of the 27th Regiment writing of 'Countless dead . . . Blood was flowing like water. At night we drank water from a creek and then in the morning realised that it was all blood'. By their own count, the Ottomans had lost over 10 000 men, of whom 3000 lay dead. The Turkish General Staff realised that Anzac could not be driven into the sea unless plenty of heavy artillery and ammunition were available. Neither was. But their own positions were also invulnerable, so the Turks reduced their garrison to two divisions and reinforced Helles. Losing 160 killed and 468 wounded, the Anzacs were unable to capitalise on their crushing victory because they had not prepared any plans for a counterattack. White always chided himself for the omission and blamed it on infant staffs that had been overburdened since the Landing. They did not, he said, 'have the experience of 1918'.[19]

The battle ended the Australians' hatred of the Turk. Before it, they showed no mercy, even firing on his burial parties. After Private

Fred Robson of the 15th Battalion captured a Turk, 'We stood him near a tree and we all had a shot at him. He tried to beg forgiveness, but we would not listen and landed about 30 bullets in him'. Lance-Corporal Harry Smith of the 3rd Battalion shared the widely held belief that the Turks used 'explosive bullets, soft nose and dum-dum and have inflicted some terrible wounds'. But as the Turks kept coming on that May morning, Lance-Corporal Mitchell marvelled at their bravery: '"Oh you poor devils", was all I could say, thinking only of the fate of the unfortunates if they got right up to us. It was a massacre'. The Australians now saw what the high velocity Spitzer-type bullet used by both sides did at close range.[20]

In view of the stink from the piles of putrefying corpses and the rapid spread of disease that they represented, both sides were anxious to bury them. Hamilton told Birdwood he could agree to a truce as long as the initiative came from the Turks. They sent an envoy under a white flag from Gaba Tepe on 21 May and a nine-hour cease fire took place three days later. Each side interred the dead in its own half of no man's land. The Australians tipped many into the communication trenches dug from Quinn's to the Turkish line in the 15th Battalion's assault on 9 May, thus filling them in. 'I don't suppose you'll find a more gruesome and sickening sight', Private Parker remarked, 'there were bloody flies and maggots and God knows what, and these fellas were swelled up like balloons'. 'Looking down I saw squelching up from the ground on either side of my boot like a rotten mango the deliquescent green and black flesh of a Turk's head', another Australian told Scottish novelist and Marine lieutenant, Compton Mackenzie. 'Nothing could cleanse the smell of death from the nostrils for a fortnight afterwards', Mackenzie wrote. Grateful for the scented antiseptic wool a Turk Red Crescent man gave him to mask it, Captain Aubrey Herbert, a Turkish-speaking British parliamentarian on Godley's staff, saw that the Turks were also appalled:

The Turkish captain with me said: 'At this spectacle even the most gentle must feel savage, and the most savage must weep' . . . I talked to the Turks, one of whom pointed to the graves. 'That's politics,' he said. Then he pointed to the dead bodies and said: 'That's diplomacy. God pity all of us poor soldiers'.

As the armistice drew to an end at 4.30 p.m., both sides exchanged souvenirs and shook hands. 'Goodbye, old chap; good luck!' the Australians called out. 'Smiling may you go and smiling come again', their opponents called back. The Turks became 'Jacko' or 'Abdul' or 'Johnnie Turk'. From then on, tins of bully beef and condensed milk were sometimes thrown into their trenches in return for boiled onions and smokes. Badges and photos were also swapped, with fire suspended to allow the retrieval of items that fell short.[21]

Even before the Ottoman attack, men had been looking seawards. The reason was the German submarine *U-21*, skippered by Lieutenant-Commander Otto Hersing, which had been spotted several times since transiting the Gibraltar Straits on 6 May. In anticipation of *U-21*'s arrival, the transports went to Lemnos and the number of battleships off the beaches was reduced. At 12.25 p.m. on 25 May, Hersing lined up *Triumph* off Anzac. In full view of both sides and with the Turks cheering wildly, his torpedo scored a direct hit. *Triumph* turned turtle and disappeared. Two days later *U-21* sank *Majestic* off Helles, again before the gaze of the two armies. All battleships and cruisers were withdrawn, emerging thereafter only when their support was actually needed. Two destroyers, one on each flank, were left to guard Anzac. Though Allied submarines also enjoyed some success, the British *E11* wreaking havoc off Constantinople, four of the six that tried to penetrate the Straits were lost, including *AE2*, whose crew became prisoners of war when it was caught by a Turkish gunboat after foundering in the Sea of Marmara.

Shortly after the sinkings, the Turks struck Quinn's. The Australians confirmed on the 9 May sortie that they were mining below it and set up listening posts. On 25 May one was fired as a camouflet to destroy the Turkish tunnel and counter-mining begun. But the Turkish picking continued. At 6 p.m. on 28 May veteran miner, Corporal Joe 'Old Ganger' Slack, warned that an explosion was imminent. At 3.20 a.m. next morning a mighty blast rocked Quinn's, blotting out the moonlight. A Turk battalion followed up. 'Grenades like showers of peas, and the noise and the flashes and confusion in the darkness, together with thick curtains of acrid smoke, made this portion of the line a terrible Hades', wrote Lieutenant Basil Fletcher of the 13th Battalion. Luckily the mine had gone off just short of the line, limiting damage, and the garrison was able to contain the Turk penetration. The task of restoring Quinn's fell to Chauvel, whom Godley had put in charge in Monash Valley, possibly because he was a regular and Monash, who was not, had objected to the Baby 700 attack on 2 May.

Going to Quinn's at 5 a.m., Chauvel ordered a charge to eject the Turks, even though it was clear that very few of them remained. Captain John Hill and others who knew the post well realised that it would be better to filter through the trenches on either side of them. The senior officers 'were not as intimately acquainted with the conditions as we were', Hill said. He urged upon Chauvel 'how disastrous a charge would be . . . and that clearing [the trenches] was only a matter of time'. The order stood. Two companies, one under Major Quinn, were told to carry it out. 'Quinn seemed very nervous about the whole business and kept asking for another minute or two'. He did not get them. Incredibly the charge resulted in few casualties because the Turks simultaneously renewed their attack and had to cease firing for fear of hitting their own men. But Quinn was killed. Nor were the Turks completely cleared. The last of them surrendered at 8 a.m. They had lost 300 men and the 4th Brigade 200. Many bearded and resembling 'dreadful scarecrows', Monash's men were immediately relieved. Bean rated their five-week defence of Monash Valley as another of the AIF's four finest wartime feats.[22]

The Turks' failure at Quinn's was another reminder that even local assaults resulted in nothing but heavy casualties. From the end of May, the Anzacs turned to improving and extending their trenches. They also gained the upper hand over the Turks. The manufacture of crude but effective bombs consisting of an empty jam tin filled with scrap metal and explosive began, enabling them to do more than just throw back the Turkish ones, which took a few seconds to explode. Production also started of a periscope invented by Lance-Corporal William Beech of the 2nd Battalion, which could be fixed to a rifle, letting the firer aim and shoot without raising his head above the parapet. It gave the garrison of Quinn's and other critical points a superiority of fire that they never lost. During June the Turkish snipers were suppressed to the extent that Monash Valley was safe in daylight. Defence stores started to arrive in quantity when the New Zealanders under Malone took over Quinn's that month. They covered the front trenches, which were also protected by bomb-catching nets, built iron-roofed terraces complete with bombproof shelters for the supports, and threw three jam-tin bombs for every bomb thrown at them. The Australians turned the tables in the underground war, exploding six mines in June alone.

Anzac now looked like a mining boom-town. Slap-up shelters perched on the hillsides and lined the gullies, all of which were scarred by streaks of orange clay excavated from the dugouts that pockmarked them. The beach, behind which the corps and divisional headquarters were wedged amongst field ambulances and logistics depots, almost disappeared under piles of stores. Brighton Beach south of Shrapnel Valley and North Beach north of Ari Burnu were pressed into service. The water teemed with men. Led by Birdwood, who would 'rather be knocked out clean than live dirty', they swam whenever the chance arose, even though Anzac Cove was frequently shelled. When the Gaba Tepe guns opened, medico

Lieutenant-Colonel John Corbin observed: 'The whole beach is quiet, not a man to be seen, no bathers, no movement . . . then quiet from the enemy and in five minutes all are back at their jobs, bathing, working, laughing as if war were a million miles away'. Sitting in his dugout, Private Richards memorably described the scene at dusk:

Straight down the ravine, and seemingly at our feet, the blue-grey water of the Mediterranean lies calm and restful. Farther away, right behind the Isle of Samothrace the sun is setting among a glorious setting of golden and crimson clouds. Slightly south the dark shape of Imbros Island looms against the horizon . . . A desultory rifle fire is the only indication that two rival armies are in the field. Around us tiny blue spirals of smoke rise clearly and slowly from the small fires, at which the soldiers are cooking their evening meal. Many of the sun and dust-stained khaki-clad warriors who have satisfied the inner man are sitting pipe in mouth discussing the events of interest . . . A convoy of mules bearing the daily rations, and a party of water carriers toil up the steep roadway which the engineers have cut into the side of the hill. Some distance away, a circle of about one hundred men are gathered about an open grave, paying their last farewells to the remains of a comrade who but yesterday was toiling amongst them. Floating down the calm still air, the clear even voice of the chaplain is distinctly heard. 'Inasmuch as it has pleased Almighty God . . .'

Hamilton found the atmosphere uplifting: 'To me this is no valley of death – it is a valley brimful of life at its highest power . . . not a murmur, not a question; only a radiant force of camaraderie in action'. [23]

—FIVE—

FROM BREAKOUT TO PULLOUT

Stalemate at Anzac, stalemate at Helles. Asked what was needed for a rapid success, Hamilton informed the War Council on 17 May that three more divisions besides the already promised 52nd (Lowland) would do. As Churchill put it, the political climate was 'sulphurous'. The iconic Admiral Lord John ('Jacky') Fisher had just resigned as First Sea Lord because he could no longer go along with the Gallipoli venture or work with Churchill. Fisher's departure fuelled the outcry over the shell shortage that had allegedly caused the BEF's latest reverse on the Western Front, at Aubers Ridge. His Liberal government tottering, Asquith formed a National Coalition with the Conservatives and Labour, as a result of which Churchill was dumped from the Admiralty. Hamilton was left in limbo.[1]

Late in May, inexpensive night advances at Helles gained almost as much ground as had been won during Second Krithia. The lines were now closer together and Hunter-Weston, promoted to lead VIII Corps, into which the British formations had been grouped, convinced Hamilton that another major attack was justified. Better prepared than its predecessors, Third Krithia on 4 June almost succeeded. But the Ottoman line held and Hamilton lost 7000 men. Had the attack been delayed for a few days, he could have used the 52nd Division, which reached Helles on 6 June, and the outcome might have been different. On 7 June Hamilton was given the three extra divisions he wanted. Coming from the New Army being raised by Kitchener, they formed IX Corps, under Lieutenant-General Sir Frederick Stopford, and were to arrive not later than the first fortnight in July. In early July two more divisions were ordered out, to arrive by mid-August. Virtually a pauper in April, Hamilton was now militarily wealthy. But so was Liman von Sanders. The three-week hiatus in London meant that the Ottomans had brought another ten divisions to the Peninsula by the time Hamilton's formations arrived.

From June onwards, Kitchener warned Hamilton to save his army for a final decisive blow. Outwardly, Hamilton concurred but he still kept hammering away at Helles after Third Krithia. Major assaults went in on 21 and 28 June and on 12 July. Though some progress was made and the massed Turkish counterattacks were mauled, these battles effectively finished off the RND and the French and ruined the 52nd Division. Hunter-Weston, who once remarked, 'Casualties? What do I care about casualties?', said that he had been glad of the chance of 'blooding the pups'. Shortly afterwards 'Hunter-Bunter' left the Peninsula with illness, having reduced the Helles army to a state of complete exhaustion.[2]

Even as the attacks went on, Hamilton had realised, like the Turks, that Anzac posed a greater threat to them than Helles ever would. He was encouraged by Birdwood, who had often heard the idea of a breakout to the north of Anzac being discussed during his visits to the line. Scouting parties sent out beyond Numbers 1 and 2 Posts by the NZMR were finding the northerly foothills and plains lightly guarded and the spurs leading up to the heights almost undefended, probably because the Turks thought their steepness made them inaccessible. Led by Boer War scouting veteran Major Percy Overton, one patrol climbed Rhododendron Ridge, which led straight to Chunuk Bair. Overton saw no Turks and only some derelict trenches on Chunuk Bair itself. Greek villagers and deserters confirmed that the Suvla Plain further north was also largely devoid of Turks.

Formally proposing the breakout to Hamilton on 30 May, Birdwood said the two Anzac divisions could do the job if reinforced by the Gurkhas of 29th Indian Brigade, who were ideal mountain troops, and another division for the subsequent advance to the Narrows. He wanted to strike early in July, when the moon had passed the full. Hamilton's enthusiasm grew with the promise of the extra divisions, though waiting for their arrival would impose a month's delay. Birdwood would get the 13th Division. As Anzac could not accommodate the rest of IX Corps, it was to go ashore at Suvla. A landing there would prevent the Turks from concentrating against Anzac. Suvla might then become a base for all the forces in the north.

Such action as there had been at Anzac in June and July was mostly to support the Helles attacks. But if the fighting hardly compared in severity, Anzac's much smaller area made the summer conditions there far worse than at Helles. It was parched brown and ankle-deep in dust with a temperature averaging eighty-four degrees Fahrenheit in the shade. Between 4 a.m. and 8 p.m. every trench and dugout became a furnace, to be shared with scorpions, centipedes and tarantulas brought out by the heat. Water was more precious than gold. 'We are only allowed one water bottle full per day for all purposes', wrote Sergeant Henry Briggs of the 3rd Battalion. 'To wash in fresh water is considered a crime, although I usually manage to get a bath, shave etc out of a small tobacco tin.' The diet was enervating. It consisted of bully beef, bacon, cheese, biscuits and apricot jam, all of which the heat rendered almost inedible. The bully could be poured like treacle from its tin onto plates too hot to touch, the jam was like syrupy juice and the biscuits were so hard that teeth frequently broke biting into them. Flies bred prolifically, prompting Colonel Beeston to remark:

We are pretty good judges of them in Australia, but Turkey has a good brand, in fact, several. There are large flies, small flies, green flies, blue flies . . . They cover everything – food is black and one has to use a wisp with the left hand while our faces are fed by the right.

A piece of muslin to cover the face while sleeping or eating was a treasured possession. The lice were ferocious and immune to lice powder. Men itched and scratched constantly. Adding to these trials were the overpowering smell – noticeable well out to sea – the unreliability of the mail and the lack of outside news. On top of everything else, labouring to prepare for the arrival of the new formations was non-stop. Water tanks had to be dragged into position and filled, ledges and shelters made for accommodation, and paths improved.[3]

The combination of depressing conditions, exhausting work, food men would rather throw away than eat and, above all, the flies, made the onset of dysentery certain. By the end of July, the month of the 'Gallipoli Trots', 80 per cent of the Anzac garrison had been afflicted and 1400 men were being evacuated weekly. 'Most of us have forgotten what solid motion means and when it happens I guess we'll think we are in the family way', Captain Gellibrand gibed. Many off-duty men slept beside the stinking latrine pits or spent the night perched on the poles over them. 'It's absolutely piteous to see great sturdy bushmen and miners almost unable to walk through sheer weakness . . . We are all the same, all suffering from sheer physical weakness', lamented engineer Sergeant Cyril Lawrence. 'The Heads', as Lawrence called them, acknowledged that the men's health was rotten but gambled that 'any change from the present conditions would be welcome, and that the stimulus of active operations would call out their reserve powers'.[4]

The ongoing arrival of reinforcements hardly alleviated matters and not just because it was greatly exceeded by the numbers of sick leaving. Training in Egypt was still below par. Many of the new men had done no fieldwork and only occasional range practices. Some of them could not load their rifles properly. Intensive efforts were made to remedy their deficiencies, even to the extent of conducting company attack exercises during the brief 'rests' some battalions had on Imbros in July. The reinforcements made their feelings known and White was haunted by the memory. He wrote long afterwards:

> No recollection is more bitter than the complaints of the men themselves that they had not had sufficient training to give them a fair chance . . . time was not available, and the need of the men was great, and ever, in consequence, rests upon our consciences a deep sense of the responsibility incurred.[5]

Widespread sickness, chronic exhaustion, inadequate training. All combined to weaken the ANZAC, which had the main role in the new offensive.

It would begin on 6 August with a feint at Helles, followed shortly after by another at Lone Pine. Godley was in charge of the breakout from Anzac that night, for which the NZ and A Division was reinforced by the 13th Division, giving him 20 000 men altogether. At 9.30 p.m. the NZMR would start seizing the Turkish posts in the northern foothills, opening the door for two assaulting columns to the main range. The right assaulting column, Colonel Johnston's New Zealand Infantry Brigade, was to swing onto Rhododendron Ridge and thence to Chunuk Bair. Commanded by Brigadier-General Vaughan Cox and consisting of his 29th Indian Brigade and the 4th Brigade, the left assaulting column was to march behind North Beach past the New Zealanders and turn inland at the Aghyl Dere, a deep, gully-ridden re-entrant. Cox's Indians would head straight upwards to Hill Q while Monash's men veered left via a long spur, Abdel Rahman Bair, to Hill 971. At dawn on 7 August part of Johnston's brigade would attack towards Battleship Hill, meeting the 3rd LH Brigade, which was to debouch over the Nek at 7.30 a.m. to seize Baby 700. Subsidiary assaults from Pope's and Quinn's by the 1st LH Brigade were to prevent any interference

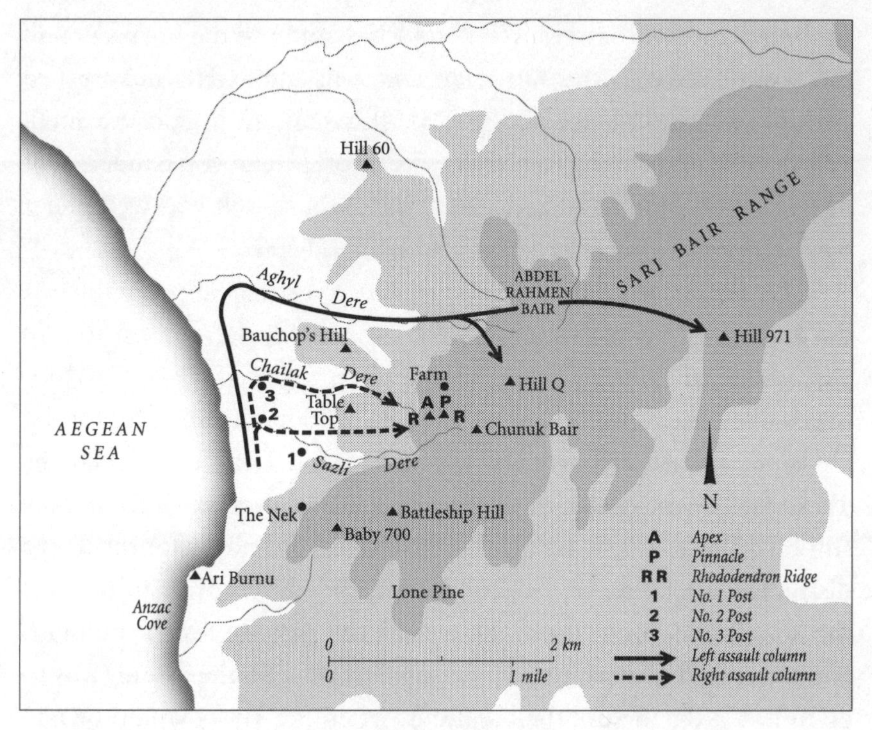

The August offensive, showing the intended routes of the assaulting columns

from the Turks at the head of Monash Valley. Starting their landing at Suvla overnight, IX Corps was to protect Birdwood's flank by taking the ring of hills a few miles inland and linking up with Anzac by evening on 7 August.

The surprise on which the whole enterprise depended was intact. Liman von Sanders had heard rumours of the offensive but did not know where it would fall. Anticipating a right hook from Anzac, coupled with a landing between it and Helles to threaten both, he moved the 9th Division, now commanded by another German, Colonel Hans Kannengiesser, south of Gaba Tepe. Kemal reckoned on a left hook from Anzac with the Sari Bair heights as the objective, just as they were on 25 April. Looking at the brutal terrain, Essad patronisingly told him it could not be done. Hence less than 3000 Turks, or 2.5 per cent of their total force in the Dardanelles, were stationed north of Battleship Hill to deal with both the breakout and the Suvla landing. Any Ottoman concerns about Helles vanished with the diversion there. Costing 3500 casualties, it gained a small vineyard. With nothing to fear on this front, Liman von Sanders sent its reserve division to Anzac, where the main assault was well under way. The Lone Pine feint got it off to a good start.[6]

The Turks considered their Lone Pine positions impregnable. At the far end of no man's land, which was bare, flat and up to 150 yards wide, they were pine-roofed and wire-girded. Baby 700 also overlooked them. Both General Walker, who had taken over the 1st Division, and White believed that assaulting Lone Pine when the Turks had nothing else to distract them, and especially while they still held Baby 700, was suicidal. Birdwood did not want the Turks distracted. As far as he was concerned, the more Ottoman reserves the attack drew onto itself, the clearer the passage for the columns making the all-important advance on Sari Bair. So the assault was to go in half a day before the breakout, when the Turks would be free to respond with everything they had. Walker and White argued with him. Birdwood finally let Walker put back the start to 5.30 p.m. so that it coincided more closely with the breakout, which would begin immediately after dark.

Tunnels were pushed out from the advanced underground firing-line that the Australians had recently finished. One tunnel that almost reached the Turkish line was to be opened as the attack went in to create an instant communications trench back to the Australian line. Pouring out of the others, the first two assault waves would only have to run forty yards to the Turkish trenches, covering the last two emerging simultaneously from the main firing-line in rear. The 2nd, 3rd and 4th Battalions from the 1st Brigade, led since Walker's elevation by another British officer, Brigadier-General Nevill Smyth VC, all contributed a company to each wave. As the assault frontage was just 220 yards, the initial blow would be heavy. With three and a half hours to go, three mines were fired in no man's land in the hope that the craters might increase the meagre cover.

Wearing white calico identification patches and fortified by rum, the 1st Brigade filed into the trenches and tunnels at 2.30 p.m. As the 3rd Brigade had starred at the Landing and the 2nd at Krithia, this was the 1st Brigade's chance and spirits were high. 'Can you find room for me beside Jim here?' implored one man. 'Him and me are mates an' we're going over together.' The desultory bombardment, which had begun two days before and destroyed much of the wire, intensified at 4.30 p.m. In the tunnels the men sweltered. 'This is hell waiting here', scribbled Private McAnulty. 'Word given to get ready to charge. Must finish, hope to get through alright.' At 5.27 p.m. the last sandbags were removed from the tunnel exits. Three minutes later the bombardment stopped. Whistles shrilled. 'Like a pack of forwards charging down a field after a football', the Australians burst into the brilliant afternoon sunlight.

Surprise was total. The attackers reached the Turkish line with few casualties but were nonplussed to find it covered by pine logs and sand. Onlookers were dismayed to see many of them start to spread out along the parapet like spectators on a sideline. The logs were too heavy to lift. Men looked instead for the entrances or for holes made by the bombardment. They jumped into them, often to be killed instantly by a waiting Turk. Bayonets were also seen flashing further back, for many other men carried on to the open communication trenches and penetrated almost to the Cup, the steep gully beyond, where the local Turkish headquarters and reserves were located.

Two Turk battalions held Lone Pine, about 1000 men in all. Of the 500 in the front trenches, half fell to the bombardment and most of the rest surrendered. But a bloody fight started against the others in the dark, fetid maze of trenches that criss-crossed the rear of the Pine like a web spun by a drunken spider. As rifles were too cumbersome for close-quarter work in the confined spaces, bombs came into their own. So did spades. Men jabbed viciously with them, decapitating heads and cleaving off faces. Knives were thrust into diaphragms. Hands and teeth became weapons. Eyeballs exploded under pressing thumbs; noses and ears were bitten or ripped off. Men strangled one another. By 6 p.m. the Australians had prevailed and were busy erecting blocks in the Turkish communication trenches.

Shortly after the feint began, Mustafa Kemal ordered the 1/57th Battalion, which had just gone into rest after forty-five days straight in the line, to Lone Pine. It had been the first unit he threw against the Landing. Entering a communication trench from the Cup, the 1/57th tried to retake the lost trenches by bombing. Six more battalions, as well as two regiments from Colonel Kannengiesser's division, were also ordered up. They passed corpses stacked like cordwood four deep on either side of the Cup. By 8.30 p.m. the 1st Battalion had reinforced the Australians, followed by the 7th and 12th Battalions as the Turkish counterattack dragged on. Others in the original Anzac front line were paying bribes and even squabbling amongst themselves to get into the action.

The bomb-fighting was the most intense the Australians ever experienced. Their jam-tin bombs were inferior and less plentiful than the German grenades the Turks had. At first the Turks used eight-second fuses, so the Australians caught and chucked their bombs back before they burst. Some went to and fro three times. When the Turks shortened the fuses, the Australians fell on the bombs with half-filled sandbags, resulting in mangled legs and genitals. Sergeant de Vine recorded a strong attack at dawn on 8 August being driven off with heavy loss, another 'very hot' bomb attack that cost the Australians dearly before it was repulsed, a third attack at 9 a.m., and then a two-hour break. Bombing as he went and cheering on those following, Captain Alfred Shout of the 1st Battalion recaptured a trench before one of his bombs exploded prematurely, smashing his hands and one side of his face and body. Still joking, he died on a hospital ship and was posthumously awarded one of the seven VCs won at Lone Pine.

Private McAnulty fell sometime between 7 and 12 August. Almost the last words in his diary were 'This is only suicide boys'. Taking a working party into an old Turkish tunnel, Sergeant Lawrence saw 'fourteen of our boys stone dead' within fifteen feet. Another dead Australian hung down through a hole in the overhead cover: 'The blood is drip, drip, drip into the trench. I sit watching it – fascinated', Lawrence confessed. Dragging out an Australian corpse from the post he was digging, Private John Bell of the 1st Battalion thought '"What a low forehead this poor fellow had." But a second glance showed me that his head was blown off by a bomb just above the eyebrows'. The only respect that could be paid to the dead was to avoid treading on their faces. Most did not even get that courtesy, as Lieutenant Margetts noted while describing a captured trench:

> [It] smelt just like a slaughter house in the cleanest parts . . . in others it is impossible to describe the smell, in other parts of the trench dead bodies were stacked in heaps in places where there was available room and in other parts where there was no room they were left in the floor of the trench and covered with a thin layer of earth and made a soft spongy floor to walk on. Of course as many as we could get rid of were thrown up to help make bullet proof parapets and barricades.

Clearing the wounded during the fight verged on the impossible. 'Their pleas for mercy were not heeded', said Private John Gammage of the 1st Battalion. 'Some poor fellows lay for 30 hours waiting for help and many died still waiting.' Lawrence came across a tunnel packed with Australian wounded, some horribly. 'One had been shot clean through the chest and his singlet and tunic are just saturated with blood, another has his nose and lip shot clean away . . . Lying beside them was a man asleep. He had been wounded somewhere in the head, and as he breathed the blood just bubbled and frothed at his nose and mouth.' They had been lying untended all night without complaint.[7]

Late on 9 August, the battle started winding down as the Turks realised they could not shift the Australians and, more importantly, that the main threat lay elsewhere. In an area smaller than a city block, the Turks lost 5000 men and the Australians over 2000 – more than 50 per cent of the 1st Brigade. Nonetheless, Lone Pine had tied up so many Ottoman formations that the northern flank remained largely undefended during the night of the breakout. For Bean, its capture was the third of the AIF's four most outstanding feats.

Three hours after the Lone Pine fighting began, the NZMR left to secure the northern foothills. Also roofed over with logs, Old No. 3 Post was the strongest of the Turk positions on them. It had been illuminated and shelled by *Colne* for the past six weeks so that the garrison would routinely take to their shelters at 9 p.m. when the destroyer's searchlight went on. Covered by its bombardment, the Auckland Mounted Rifles scaled the hill. At 9.30 p.m., when the shelling ceased and the searchlight went off, they stormed in with the bayonet, catching the Turks still in their shelters. By 10 p.m. the post belonged to the Aucklanders. Lit up by a Turkish flare as they hacked footholds into the sheer face of nearby Table Top, the Wellington Mounted Rifles stood motionless for five minutes. Remaining unseen, they took the post shortly after 11 p.m. Assaulting strongly held Bauchop's Hill and its outlier, Walden Point, at the entrance to the Aghyl Dere, the Canterbury Mounted Rifles and the Otago Mounted Rifles encountered stiffer resistance. Under strict orders to use only their bayonets, they wrestled the Turks in some cases but captured Bauchop's by 1 a.m.

Destined for Chunuk Bair, the right assaulting column, Colonel Johnston's New Zealand Infantry Brigade, was to assemble on Rhododendron Ridge after moving via the Sazli and Chailak Deres on either side of it. Turning into the Chailak Dere, the main column was held up by barbed wire and Turks missed by the NZMR, resulting in 'a concertina march – moving and stopping – moving and stopping; oh, it was deadly. Sometimes we would get long enough to sit down and sometimes we wouldn't'. The Otago Battalion at the head came across a large party of Turks near Table Top who cheerily surrendered, causing more delay. At 2.30 a.m. the column got going again. Dawn found it strung out exhausted on Rhododendron Ridge behind the Wellington Battalion. Of the Canterbury Battalion, which became hopelessly lost in the bifurcated Sazli Dere and ended up at its starting point, there was no sign. Though Birdwood had stressed that all units were to push on regardless of how other units were going, Johnston decided to wait for it.[8]

Leading the left assaulting column, the 4th Brigade had to go five miles, twice as far as the New Zealanders, and through terrain that General Cox, the column commander, described as 'mad country and very difficult'. Sergeant Albert Compton of the 13th Battalion thought beforehand that it 'would be hell all right – some of the boys are not too game – I think they are too ill to be fighting'. Before they left, men listened in silence as a bandsman from the 16th Battalion played Gounod's 'Serenade' on his cornet and they all sang the appropriately titled hymn, 'Lead Kindly Light'. 'Thoughts were for the moment swept right back to the shelter of hearts and prayers in a far off land', wrote Lieutenant Frederick Crane of the 15th Battalion. At 9.35 p.m. the 4th Brigade stepped off. It was supposed to be secure on Hill 971 six hours later.

The march quickly became a 'concertina affair' and by 11 p.m. had degenerated into 'a shuffle, slower than a funeral, with innumerable halts'. Monash went to the head of the column and found that Major Overton, who was leading it, had deferred to the local Greek guides with him and taken a shortcut into the Aghyl Dere. It was almost impassable and the 13th Battalion up front lost cohesion as it squeezed through and struck Turk snipers. Overton and the other officers were arguing over what to do. Monash rebuked them. He organised what was left of the 13th and sent it, together with the 14th Battalion, northwards to protect his flank. They should have gone another seven hundred yards along the Aghyl Dere but Overton, who would be killed later in the morning, was badly disoriented and unable to correct them.

Monash then bustled the 15th and 16th Battalions towards Abdel Rahman Bair. But the burst of physical effort necessary for the night march was giving way to sickness-induced lethargy. Men were falling asleep at every halt. Turks retreating inland from the foothills contested every yard. At 5 a.m. both battalions were totally disorganised and still a long way from Hill 971, convincing Monash that its capture was, for the moment, impossible. Around 7 a.m. Major Cecil Allanson arrived with the 6th Gurkhas, which Cox had sent forward in support. Allanson later alleged that 'Monash seemed temporarily to have lost his head, he was running about saying "I thought I could command men, I thought I could command men"'. Monash may have said as much but those with him did not corroborate the image of a man unhinged. Lance-Corporal Howe knew his staff very well and they never mentioned anything untoward. Moreover, Allanson wrote his account well after the war, a time when his good friend, the future Field-Marshal Viscount Slim, said he 'embroidered' badly.[9]

At dawn on 7 August, the 29th Indian Brigade was even further from Hill Q than the 4th Brigade was from Hill 971. Neither failure really mattered for each of the Sari Bair assaults was self-contained. The views of the Narrows from hills 971 and Q were just as good from Chunuk Bair, which also dominated the Turkish perimeter at Anzac, making it the vital ground for the whole operation. Taking Chunuk Bair would have been enough and Birdwood, though aware that Monash and Cox were held up, was far more concerned that Johnston's brigade was stuck on Rhododendron Ridge short of it. With the assault by two regiments of the 3rd Light Horse on Baby 700 also due, he faced a difficult decision.

Like the lines furrowing an old man's brow, eight successive trenches seamed Baby 700 and its approaches. The first two straddled the Nek, where no man's land's was at most sixty yards wide and enfiladed from German Officers' Trench. As Birdwood recognised from the outset that an unaided attack across the Nek would be 'almost hopeless', it was to go in with the New Zealanders' converging attack from Chunuk Bair, by which time a feint by the 6th Battalion should have silenced German Officers'. Carried out by green reinforcements, the feint was virtually wiped out. Birdwood now knew that the Nek attack would indeed be unaided but reasoned that if it went ahead, it might help Johnston's column by distracting the Turks on the northern flank of Anzac from Chunuk Bair. The risk to the Light Horse was grave but both he and Godley deemed it justified. Starting at 4 a.m., the heaviest bombardment seen at Anzac would pummel the Turkish trenches for half an hour, whereupon 600 troopers were to assault in four 150-man waves, the widest frontage that could fit on the Nek. The first two, of Victorians from the 8th LH Regiment, would take the Nek and the trenches beyond, while the West Australians of the 10th LH Regiment in the other two were to capture Baby 700.[10]

'This is what we came to do and it's better than living like rabbits all the time', one trooper said to Chaplain Ernest Merrington. The horsemen were in no doubt that they would carry the Nek and burst through into 'green and open country', wrote Bean. 'The prospect filled them with a longing akin to homesickness.' They whooped when the bombardment began and smoke and dust engulfed Baby 700. But few shells hit the foremost Turkish trenches because they were so close to the Australian line. About this time word arrived from Godley that Chunuk Bair had not fallen. Realising what was likely to happen, Lieutenant-Colonel Alex White, the 8th LH Regiment's commander, decided to lead the first wave. With a simple 'Goodbye', he left the brigade headquarters, a chain and locket with his wife and baby's photo around his neck. No explanation reached him when the shelling suddenly ceased at 4.30 a.m. with the Light Horse watches showing 4.23 a.m. Accounts differ on whether the synchronisation of watches was faulty, whether it took place at all or whether the artillery received copies of the Light Horse attack orders.

White hesitated. There might yet be a crescendo of fire. A few minutes passed. The Turks emerged from their shelters. One line sat on the parapet. Another stood behind it. They cocked their rifles and test-fired their machine-guns. 'We knew we were doomed', said Captain Leslie Hore. White yelled: 'Three minutes to go', then 'Go!' The whistles blew. The first wave clambered up the pegs and niches made in the trench wall for a quick exit. 'Come on boys, for God's sake, come on, come on!' bellowed Lieutenant Eliot Wilson. Single shots were lost in the tornado of fire and bombs that erupted. On Lone Pine, Sergeant Lawrence described the noise as a hundred times louder than thousands of policemen's rattles worked at top speed.

The first line was annihilated in thirty seconds. Observers saw it suddenly grow limp and sink to earth 'as though the men's limbs had become string'. 'Everyone fell like lumps of meat', wrote Sergeant Cliff Pinnock, who was struck by what 'felt like a million ton hammer falling on my shoulder . . . It was simply murder'. Many men were hit and flung back into the trench. Many more, including White, lay dead or dying just beyond it. Private Jack Dale survived by diving behind a fold in the ground. 'Wounded fellows were crawling past us, some with terrible wounds caused by bombs. All you could do was make way and help them past', he said. At 4.32 a.m., with Turkish bullets still slamming into the bodies and making them jerk about, the whistles sounded again. The second line rose, cheering as one and got a little farther than the first. Captain Hore saw the Turkish trenches 'aflame' as he ran, bent low towards them. Feeling a sting in his shoulder, he ducked behind a dead Turk and was shot again through the foot. Somehow he regained the Australian line.

Assaulting simultaneously from Pope's Hill, two squadrons from the 1st LH Brigade penetrated to the third line of trenches on the Chessboard. But they were isolated and under heavy fire. Major

Tom Glasgow knew no support would be forthcoming and ordered a withdrawal. Of his 200 men, 46 got back unscathed. The first wave in the adjacent assault from Quinn's was obliterated. Major George Bourne, commanding the attack, held the following waves back.

Common sense had gone missing at the Nek, where the 10th LH Regiment was clambering over the dead and wounded choking the line. Seeing the carnage, Lieutenant-Colonel Noel Brazier went to brigade headquarters at 4.40 a.m. to argue the futility of continuing. The brigade commander, Colonel Frederick Hughes, had gone to an observation post. It probably would not have mattered had he been present. A 57-year-old militia officer, Hughes had only seen action on the Victorian social circuit. Twice evacuated sick from Anzac, he was overwhelmed by command and gave his brigade-major, Lieutenant-Colonel John Antill, free rein. A regular who had served in the Boer War, Antill was eclipsed afterwards by peers such as Chauvel and White, partly on account of his bullying ways. He merited his nickname, 'Bullant'. Antill was alone at the headquarters when Brazier arrived. The two men detested each other and Antill was further incensed at Brazier for leaving the line to query orders. Antill said that an Australian marker flag had been seen on the Turkish line, suggesting that men were in it and needing support. Brazier knew that the only men in it were Turks. He told Antill that 'it was murder to push on'. Enraged, Antill shouted: 'Push on!' Brazier replied: 'Thanks, but don't forget I told you'. He returned to the line. An eerie silence, broken only by the moans of the wounded, had descended. 'I'm sorry lads', Brazier said, 'but the order is to go'.

The scenes before the second line went were replayed. Aware they had just a few moments to live, men took a last look at photos of wife or family, scribbled them a final 'I love you', removed their wedding rings and pinned them along with precious keepsakes and mementoes to the trench wall. With moist eyes, they shook hands or embraced and bid one another farewell. 'Goodbye cobber, God bless you', Trooper Harold Rush said to his mate. Faces pressed against the trench wall, they uttered a silent prayer, wondered what the impact of the oncoming Turkish bullet would feel like and steeled themselves to meet it. When the whistles blew at 4.45 a.m., there was a cheer and even laughter, recalled Trooper Alexander Borthwick, as once again the 'air became hazy with lead'. Most of the line was cut down, including Rhodes Scholar Lieutenant Alexander Turnbull and Trooper Wilfred Harper, who was 'last seen running forward like a schoolboy in a footrace'. He became the inspiration for the Archie Hamilton character in Peter Weir's film, *Gallipoli.*

Antill insisted that the fourth line must 'push on'. Brazier frantically sought out Hughes and told him that to continue 'would be nothing but bloody murder'. Hughes was thoroughly rattled. He seemed to suggest that they support a subsidiary assault from Monash Valley by a British battalion but it had already collapsed. He was still suggesting when an anguished cry went up at 5.15 a.m: 'By God, I believe the right has gone!' Apparently an officer who heard Antill's latest 'push on' had arrived on that flank and asked why it had not left. Sergeant William Sanderson noticed how the fire reduced the scrub to spikes that tore at men's puttees as they ran. 'The thing that struck a man most was if he wasn't knocked in the first three yards.' Sanderson reached the Turkish parapet. Edging back, he saw a lieutenant whose bombs had detonated, blowing his hip away. 'I can't bloody well stand it', the dying officer screamed. Sanderson and a mate tried to drag him in. The attack was abandoned. For a time, the Australian line was garrisoned only by the dead and wounded. Of the 600 who charged, 372 were casualties and 234 of them had been killed almost immediately. The Turks hardly lost a man.[11]

The Weir film implies that the horsemen were sacrificed to help the landing at Suvla, where the British were stuck on the beach and drinking tea. IX Corps's landing was indeed going pear-shaped. Though Hamilton had sought a fit and competent commander for it, General Stopford was 61, sickly and had never led in battle. But Hamilton let him water down the Suvla plan until all sense of urgency had gone. He also stood by while Stopford allowed the virtually uncontested Suvla landing, where some 20 000 men were ashore by daylight, to degenerate into chaos. Not for another thirty-six hours did Hamilton urge Stopford to get moving. Even so, Suvla was only an adjunct to the main attack and it is hard to see how it could have affected that action. Similarly, the charges at the Nek did not affect the issue at Suvla one jot. Nor were they intended to. The real reason for the sacrifice was to assist the stalled New Zealand Infantry Brigade's advance on Chunuk Bair. It came to nothing.[12]

Giving up on the missing Canterbury Battalion, Colonel Johnston resumed the advance up Rhododendron Ridge towards Chunuk Bair at 6.30 a.m. on 7 August. Kannengiesser's 9th Division was on the way as well. Originally intended for Lone Pine, it was ordered to continue northwards when Essad received the first reports of the breakout after midnight. Racing ahead of his men, Kannengiesser reached Chunuk Bair at 7 a.m. and roused the few Turks he found there. They engaged Malone's Wellingtons, who were nearing a bump called the Apex, 500 yards from the crest. Looking 'very tired', the Wellingtons went to ground.[13]

Exactly what followed in the New Zealand Infantry Brigade remains unclear. Widely held to be an alcoholic, Colonel Johnston was, according to many accounts, drunk after swigging from his rum-laced water bottle throughout the night. The brigade-major, Lieutenant-Colonel Arthur Temperley, wrote that he was 'frequently barely coherent and his judgement and mind were obviously clouded'. Temperley took the lead when the pair joined Malone at the Apex. As there was no sign of the northerly columns and a storm of fire was coming from Chunuk Bair, Malone was against going on. The others agreed. Godley was so informed. It was 8 a.m., almost three hours after the charge at the Nek, and the New Zealanders were having breakfast. Infuriated, Godley told Johnston to attack at

10.30 a.m. By then the summit was bristling with Turkish rifles for the 9th Division had arrived. The Auckland Battalion lost 300 men in clawing 200 yards to another bump called the Pinnacle. Seemingly fighting drunk, Johnston stood waving them on until his staff dragged him down. Godley agreed to delay a further attempt until 4.15 a.m. next day, 8 August. It would be part of a general assault on the Sari Bair crest line.

This time the Wellingtons found Chunuk Bair all but deserted. Apparently the bombardment beforehand had driven the Turks off. Malone's men dug in, half of them in a support line on the seaward slope. As dawn broke, the rest, occupying a Turk trench on the crest, saw the rear of the Turkish position at Anzac to the south and, ahead, the Narrows. But the light also meant that the Turks, newly arrived from Helles, on Hill Q and Battleship Hill could bring Chunuk Bair under heavy fire. The New Army battalions given to Johnston to reinforce the assault bore the brunt. Few made it to the Wellingtons. They were now alone, cut off and, with the Turks streaming back, under attack.

By 9 a.m. the line on the crest had been practically annihilated. The summit became no man's land and the Wellingtons' support line, 200 yards long and manned by their remaining two companies, the front line. They fired almost non-stop. 'The first thing we saw was heads', wrote Private Vic Nicholson. 'Then our targets got bigger as they came closer. By the time the Turks were fully in view, they were within twenty feet, bayonet range.' Malone led many bayonet charges to clear them. Nicholson also saw him constantly moving about with an encouraging word: 'It'll ease off shortly. They'll get tired of this'. By early afternoon the trench was so full of dead and wounded that the dwindling band of Wellingtons hewed out another behind it. Malone called desperately for reinforcements. Corporal Cyril Bassett won New Zealand's first VC of the war by laying and keeping open his telephone line to brigade headquarters. Around 4 p.m. 100 men from the Auckland Mounted Rifles got through.

An hour later Malone was killed by an errant naval shell. When relieved after dark, only 70 of the 760 New Zealanders who had taken Chunuk Bair were unwounded. Sleepless for forty-eight hours and without water since dawn, 'they could talk only in whispers; their eyes were sunken; their knees trembled; some broke down and cried like children'.[14]

Further north, Allanson's 6th Gurkhas almost got to the crest of Hill Q and the 4th Brigade tried again for Hill 971. Possibly too tired to command himself, Monash inexcusably put Colonel Pope in charge. The 700-yard navigational error made on 6 August was not picked up. When the Australians climbed onto what they thought was Abdel Rahman Bair for the final leg to Hill 971, they were really on the ridge before it. As they entered an oatfield, a torrent of fire erupted from the real Abdel Rahman Bair. To the 14th Battalion following, 'The 15th Battalion seemed to wilt away from in front of us and their casualties lay thickly along our line of advance'. The Turks attacked. The 15th broke. 'Everyone seemed scattered', Private Charles Smith of the 14th Battalion wrote. 'Wherever one looked, there were troops, yet no-one seemed to have any fixed objective.' The retreat was shambolic. Sergeant Tom Smith of the 14th recalled 'a mournful procession' wending its way back, 'played out, carrying and helping along the wounded, our dead left behind and in a great many cases some of the severely wounded left behind too'. It was the first time that Australians had abandoned their casualties.[15]

Godley finally set Hill 971 aside. For 9 August he ordered the attack on Hill Q renewed and a composite brigade under Brigadier-General Anthony Baldwin, made up mainly of battalions of the 13th Division, to take the crest from there to Chunuk Bair while the remnants of the New Zealanders extended to Battleship Hill. Allanson's Gurkhas took Hill Q. Six shells – most probably from Anzac, though Allanson said they were 12-inchers fired by the navy – blew them off. Johnston convinced Baldwin to reach Chunuk Bair via the Chailak and Aghyl Deres, a route that looked quicker but which was untried, instead of coming up Rhododendron Ridge behind his own brigade. Encountering congestion in the Chailak Dere, Baldwin turned his men about and plunged directly into the Aghyl Dere. The route turned out to be longer. Attacking hours late from the Farm, a ledge below Chunuk Bair, he was stopped by heavy fire. Left isolated, the Otago Battalion and the Wellington Mounted on Chunuk Bair endured a day like Malone's men the day before. When relieved that night by the 6th Loyal North Lancashires and the 5th Wiltshires, both New Zealand units had lost over half their strength.[16]

During the day, Kemal, whom Liman von Sanders had placed in command of all Ottoman forces north of Anzac, counterattacked with two fresh divisions, taking the heights inland of Suvla. Chunuk Bair was the only remaining danger point. As dawn approached on 10 August, Kemal personally led six battalions just below the Turkish side of the crest. At 4.30 a.m. he raised his whip, signalled the advance and a human wave surged down the hill crying 'Allah! Allah!' The Lancashires and Wiltshires were overwhelmed and Baldwin fell with about 1000 of his men in hand-to-hand fighting around the Farm. Chunuk Bair did not leave Turk hands again. At a cost of 12 000 men to the Anzacs, the August offensive had ended in failure.

Abysmal command lay at the heart of it. Birdwood and Godley let the hills 971 and Q battles distract them from the central purpose of getting the vital ground of Chunuk Bair. Godley admitted as much by writing that the hill could have been taken on the first night and held thereafter if the formations allotted to the other columns had been allocated to it instead. He did not attend the crucial conference that settled Baldwin's route for his attack on Chunuk Bair on 9 August. Along with Birdwood, he was still unaware that afternoon that the assault had failed and confidently told Hamilton they would have the key to the Narrows next day. Godley also took a morbid delight in watching the despatch-riders from Suvla try to reach his headquarters. Having just left the inferno on Chunuk Bair, Lieutenant-Colonel Temperley witnessed the spectacle as Godley angrily rejected his report that two-thirds of the New Zealanders had been lost:

Don't talk like a bloody fool. By God . . . I believe this fellow will get away with it after all! A man who's been in action always comes out with some cock-and-bull story about the thousands of casualties – Christ, did you see him duck that time. By God, look – look – they've got him at last, by God, they have. That was a bloody fine shot! When's the next one due to come along? And where's that fool . . . [17]

All that remained was to link the ground won to Suvla. While IX Corps advanced its right flank, the Anzacs were to take Hill 60 alongside. Flat-topped and cloaked in scrub too low to afford cover, Hill 60 is so indistinguishable from the surrounding plain that it is outlined in ink in photographs in the *Official History*. As no fresh formations remained, the remnants of the 4th Brigade, the NZMR, Cox's Indians and three New Army battalions were cobbled together for the assault on 21 August. At the last minute some of the supporting artillery was switched to support IX Corps's attack, which necessitated an abbreviated bombardment before the Anzac attack. All it did was to alert the Turks. They stood waist-high behind their parapets, shooting at the attackers still climbing over theirs. The gains were negligible, the losses crippling.

Though IX Corps failed badly, the attempt on Hill 60 continued. The 18th Battalion from the new 2nd Australian Division was thrown in on 22 August. Ordered to assault with bayonet and bomb only, Lieutenant-Colonel Alfred Chapman interjected that they had no bombs. He was told to do the best he could without them. The 18th saw the objective for the first time just before they attacked at daybreak. Until then, these green troops thought they were marching up to man the trenches. They lost over half their number. Whoever was still standing in the 4th Brigade and NZMR carried out the next attack on 27 August. Only two shells hit the trenches opposite

Monash's men and the fire against them was vicious. The 9th and 10th LH Regiments were drawn in. By the end, a false crest had been taken and the Turks kept the summit.[18]

Serious fighting at Anzac ended with the Hill 60 battles. The 54th Division, and the 2nd Australian Division, which lost the commander of the 6th Brigade, Colonel Richard Linton, when its transport, *Southland*, was torpedoed off Lemnos, took over much of the Anzac line. Captain Les Chambers of the 17th Battalion thought it 'sometimes hard to realise that you are actually at the front . . . you might as well be in George Street'. But the calm meant that the original formations could be relieved. Not only were they badly depleted – the 4th Brigade was down to 890 men – but three-quarters were judged totally unfit for active service.[19]

Battalions went for a week or more to Lemnos, where they could enjoy a decent sleep, a beer and a hot bath. There were also pleasant interludes with the nurses from the two Australian Stationary Hospitals and No. 3 Australian General Hospital on the island. 'We laughed and talked and the men flicked mosquitoes off their bare knees, forgetting the war until reminded of it by spasmodic bursts of gunfire from the peninsula', wrote Sister Nellie Pike. Virtually the only women in the theatre of operations, the nurses appreciated the break for the huge influx of casualties had stretched the hospitals to the limit. On returning to Anzac, there was great relief that the flies had gone with the onset of cooler weather. The priority was the building of shelters against the storms it brought, at this stage 'a far worse enemy than the Turks'.[20]

Storms threatened in London as well. Consternation arose when Hamilton reported that the August offensive had failed and that he needed another 95 000 men to continue operations. He was promised 25 000. Then Bulgaria threw in with Germany at the start of September, a move which the Dardanelles strategy from the outset had sought to discourage, as a prelude to a German-led attack on Serbia. Crushing the Serbs would give the Germans a direct route to Turkey, with serious consequences for Russia. Despite conflicting signals from the Greeks, who were to-ing and fro-ing over neutrality, Britain and France agreed to send 150 000 troops to the Greek port of Salonika, from where they might be able to aid the Serbs. On 25 September Kitchener told Hamilton to despatch two British divisions and a French one and suggested he should abandon Suvla. The decision was taken too late to prevent a Serb collapse.[21]

Hamilton's star was fading fast. Australian journalist Keith Murdoch was heavily involved in its demise. Briefly visiting Anzac on his way to London after the August offensive, Murdoch was shocked by the evidence of mismanagement he saw. Meeting Ashmead-Bartlett on Imbros, he agreed to take a letter from him criticising Hamilton to Asquith. Hamilton got wind of the affair and the letter was confiscated when Murdoch reached Marseilles. Once in London in late September, however, he gave his views to several politicians. A scathing excoriation of Hamilton's tactics that Murdoch had written to Australian Prime Minister Andrew Fisher was circulated as a War Cabinet paper. Hamilton was recalled on 15 October. His successor, General Sir Charles Monro, had commanded the British Third Army in France. Monro was shocked at the precariousness of the Gallipoli positions and aware that the deteriorating weather would prejudice the delivery of the stores needed for winter. Gales were already damaging the piers at Anzac. Also mindful that German heavy guns were reportedly on the way, Monro on 2 November recommended withdrawal.

Kitchener went to see for himself. Landing at Anzac on 13 November, he was greeted by the senior officers in their best uniforms and the soldiers in their usual grubby attire. 'K' thought Anzac too small to be safely held and on seeing the Turk defences at Helles and Suvla, agreed with Monro's opinion. The MEF under Monro now included the British troops at Salonika, as well as the Gallipoli command, which was renamed the Dardanelles Army and put under Birdwood. Godley succeeded Birdwood at Anzac. On 23 November the new War Committee, a small Cabinet group to whom Asquith had handed over the strategic conduct of the war, recommended withdrawal. The weather was the final arbiter. At the end of November a blizzard lashed the Peninsula, causing the evacuation of 16 000 sick, mostly from low-lying Suvla, where over 200 men drowned or froze to death. Anzac fared better but conditions were still miserable. The man sleeping in Sergeant Richard Gardiner's dugout made 'a dam of himself by keeping back a stream of water from me', while Sergeant de Vine complained that 'we have very light summer clothes, with no legs to our trousers, no singlets and shirts without sleeves'. On 7 December the evacuation of Anzac and Suvla was approved. The preliminary stage, reducing the garrisons to those needed for winter, was already under way.[22]

Responsible for the planning of the Anzac pullout, White, who had become the ANZAC's chief of staff in September, used deception brilliantly to maintain the appearance of normality while the garrison was pared down. In order to accustom the Turks to a decline in firing as troop strength fell, there was to be no shooting of any kind from 24 to 27 November and for regular periods thereafter. The Turks concluded from the 'silent stunts' that the Anzacs wanted quiet while constructing winter quarters. Given credence by the blizzard, the pretext of sending men to Imbros and Lemnos for winter continued during the intermediate stage, which was designed to reduce the garrison to the 20 000 men needed to hold Anzac for the last two nights, 18 and 19 December. Troops were ostentatiously landed in daylight to convince the Turks that Anzac was being reinforced, and taken off again with the units being withdrawn at night. The Light Horse played cricket on Shell Green. With the nightly departures and carefully guarded stores being freely distributed, rumours were rife. They were confirmed around 12 December. 'The stupendous and paralysing news' came 'like a thunderbolt from a clear blue sky', wrote Monash.

Feelings were mixed. Like Lieutenant Walter McConnan of the 8th LH Regiment, most realised that 'of course long ago we had shot our bolt'. Others felt downcast at leaving the Gallipoli undertaking unfinished. 'All that sacrifice, all that labour, all that suffering for nothing at all', Lance-Corporal Mitchell wailed. Every Anzac 'went up and down those well-known gullies moved almost to tears by the thought that . . . those narrow acres so hardly won and all those graves of our people so long defended would soon be in Turkish hands'. 'I hope *they* won't hear us marching down the deres', a soldier told Birdwood on the last day. At least 7600 Australians and 2400 New Zealanders had been killed and, respectively, 18 500 and 5000 wounded.[23]

On 19 December the front line was thinned out in three phases, the last 2800 leaving in three instalments between 1.30 a.m. and 3.15 a.m. Lance-Corporal William Scurry of the 7th Battalion invented a self-firing rifle, whose trigger was attached to a tin that overbalanced and pulled it, when filled with water dripping down from another tin. They were set to fire after the last party had gone. Of the sixteen mines held ready, none would be blown unless the Turks attacked but the two at the Nek were to be exploded at the very end to prevent them following up. Lieutenant James Connor of the 2nd Battalion, who was in one of the rearguards, marvelled at the meticulousness of the planning:

> Our feet were muffled in sandbags, equipment that might rattle was all tied together, the track was lined with flour so that you couldn't lose your way, all branch tracks were blocked up, there were different coloured lights at different places and piquets to check your party and see you knew where to go.

Lieutenant Edgar Worrall of the 24th Battalion left at 3 a.m. after firing the final shot at Lone Pine and the most trying twenty-four hours of his life. 'WOULD NOT HAVE MISSED IT FOR A

MILLION', he wrote. Half an hour later, an orange glow filled the sky as the mines on the Nek went up. The Turks began firing. There was no response. Corporal Adil's battalion sent out a scout: 'He found the trenches deserted. They'd gone!' Not a man was lost and the Suvla withdrawal went just as well. As the Turks were now expecting it, the evacuation of Helles in January was an achievement at least as great.[24]

Scarcely off Anzac, Lieutenant McConnan railed: 'The whole campaign has been a series of blunders and no doubt that fact is well known now'. Suvla, in particular, confirmed the estimate of British troops that the Australians had formed after the Marines' stint at Anzac in April. 'They can't soldier for sour apples. They have no grit, no gumption, and they muddle along', said Monash. Sergeant Lawrence echoed him: 'They won't work, they can't fight . . . helpless imbecility, sluggishness and chicken-heartedness. The British Tommy! God!!!' The New Zealanders had the same view, Lieutenant-Colonel Bill Meldrum writing of the 6th Loyal North Lancashires, who reinforced his Wellington Mounteds on Chunuk Bair: 'Only one of them fired a shot during the day – they lay in the bottom of the trench – the NZ officers kicked some of them to try to stir them up . . . the actual men were worth nothing'. Henceforth the antipodean soldiers believed that they were superior to those from Britain.[25]

From the Landing to Krithia, from Lone Pine to the Nek and Hill 60, the campaign made the notion of the Great Adventure a sick joke for the Australians. What sustained them? Bean cut to the quick after witnessing several suicidal charges. Some men took up the cry to retire. Others scoffed and demanded to know who gave the order:

> And yet strong men do that . . . they are not going to be cheated out of their job by any weak-spirited being in the force. The success of an army like ours depends on the proportion of these strong independent men there is in it. And in the Australian force the proportion is unquestionably

high – it may amount to 50 per cent or more. I have seen them going up against a rain of fire and the weaker ones retiring through them at the same time – the two streams going in opposite directions and not taking the faintest notice of one another.[26]

The spirit of the strong man was not only evident on the battlefield. It enabled men to cope with the 'mental change' brought on by the realisation that the chances of survival were grim. This awareness dawned in the May battles and was reinforced in the much more brutal August fighting. Each man quietly abandoned his dream of returning to Australia, and with no prospect of leave there, his platoon, and by extension, company and battalion, effectively became his family. The trial ahead would be even more severe.

—SIX—

THE WESTERN FRONT

The Anzacs returned to Egypt. It was tense but not because they had come back. No longer tied down on the Gallipoli Peninsula, the Turks could strike with a 250 000-strong army. Birdwood expected a powerful attack within six weeks. A more immediate crisis arose when reports on 19 January indicated that the Turks were reinforcing their 13 000 troops at Beersheba for another advance across the Sinai to the Canal. It would probably begin in a fortnight. Leaving their camps at Tel el Kebir, both Australian divisions occupied the No. 2 or Central Section of the Canal defences. It stretched thirty miles between Ferry Post in the north and Serapeum in the south, where the New Zealand Infantry Brigade had seen off the Turks a year earlier. For now, the NZ and A Division remained at Moascar, a few miles from Ferry Post. But the Turks were never seen apart from the occasional patrol. The main problem for the Australians and New Zealanders became the absorption of the 45 000 reinforcements in Egypt and the thousands more on the way.

Recruitment had soared in Australia. News of the Landing, the constant lengthy casualty lists and anger at the sinking of the British liner *Lusitania* by a German submarine in May 1915 all stimulated it. But the momentum chiefly came from the realisation that the war was not going well. Those who responded called themselves the 'Dinkums' because they were enlisting out of conviction rather than through love of adventure like the 'Tourists'. 'There are some things worth more than life,' wrote one Dinkum, Second Lieutenant John Raws, who went 'believing that the only hope for the salvation of the world is a speedy victory for the Allies'.[1]

Enlistments rose from 6250 in April to 36 575 in July, when the minimum height was dropped to 5 foot 2 inches. In New South Wales snowball recruiting began with the 'Cooee' marches, whereby a few men set out from the country to sign up in Sydney hoping that others would join them *en route*. William Morris Hughes, a leading advocate pre-war of compulsory military training, replaced Andrew Fisher as Australian Prime Minister in October. Among his first actions was a war census of eligible manpower, which showed that 215 000 fit and single men of military age were available. In November Hughes offered, over and above the monthly quota of 9500 men already being sent as reinforcements, another 50 000 men formed into nine brigades. The War Office accepted immediately.[2]

In mid-January 1916, Godley proposed forming the reinforcements into two new Australian divisions and using the 50 000 extra men for an additional division and as a reinforcement pool. The New Zealand Infantry Brigade would join a brigade constituted from reinforcements and another arriving from New Zealand in a separate New Zealand Division. All the divisions would be organised into two Anzac corps. General Sir Archibald Murray agreed. He had taken charge of the MEF when Monro returned to France to lead the First Army, and eventually succeeded General Maxwell as the commander in Egypt. Murray was appalled by what he termed 'the extreme indiscipline and inordinate vanity of the Australians', who were again thronging Cairo. As the veterans ignored what they considered petty restrictions and the new soldiers imitated them, absenteeism, brawling and mistreatment of the 'Gyppos' were again rife. Murray thought that the sooner they were all training in fighting units the better. When Birdwood reached Egypt on 19 January, after the breaking up of the Dardanelles Army, he urged the creation of an Australian and New Zealand Army because the two Anzac corps would be as strong as the original BEF. The War Office demurred but his suggestion that the additional division be formed in Australia before going overseas was adopted. It resulted in the creation of the 3rd Division. The NZMR and the Australian Light Horse Brigades would together comprise a new Anzac Mounted Division.[3]

Each of the two new Australian divisions in Egypt received a formed brigade, the 4th Brigade going to the 4th Division and the 8th Brigade, recently arrived from Australia, to the 5th. Birdwood decreed that the sixteen additional battalions needed would be created by splitting the original sixteen into two 'wings'. The first wing stayed on the Canal Line, the second went back to Tel el Kebir and the reinforcements arriving from Cairo brought the battalions in both up to full strength. Despite its Gallipoli experience, the 2nd Australian Division was left intact because it had never been properly trained.

Fearing the shock to the pride and tradition of the older units, White and many of their commanders urged the transfer of selected officers and NCOs only, as the New Zealanders were doing, but Birdwood was immoveable. His resolve 'gave a veteran character and a feeling of brotherhood to the whole force' and a common territorial identity to the sister battalions. The second wing of the 1st Brigade from New South Wales, for example, provided the nucleus of the 53rd, 54th, 55th and 56th Battalions of the 14th Brigade, the rest of which was built up of men from that state. Victorians fleshed out the 57th, 58th, 59th and 60th Battalions of the 15th Brigade, whose parent was the 2nd Brigade from Victoria.[4]

The arbitrary separation of men who had joined together and gone through Gallipoli together did create some bitterness. Even a man of Albert Jacka's standing could be the target of it. Now a company sergeant-major (CSM), he was roundly abused during a parade by a sergeant whose name he had just read out from a list of those being transferred from the 14th Battalion to the 46th Battalion:

By gum, Bert, but this is a bit of all right! No more soldiering for me! You can make out a sick report because I'm off to hospital. To think that a man has never left the battalion and been in every stunt, and now he's to be chucked out like this. Bah – I thought you were a cobber of mine!

In this, as in every other case, the bond between the old and new battalion, symbolised by the new one wearing vertically on its sleeves the same colour patches worn horizontally by its parent, quickly dissipated the resentment.[5]

The expansion created many promotional opportunities. Chauvel was given the Anzac Mounted Division. But Birdwood's attempt to appoint officers of the British and Indian armies to lead the new infantry divisions because he felt that no Australians were capable riled the Australian Government. A compromise saw Cox get the 4th Division and McCay the 5th. Major-General Gordon Legge, the architect of the pre-war compulsory training scheme, remained in command of the 2nd Division. He had led it at Anzac. The commanders of the new brigades and battalions mostly came from within the AIF. In the main, they were proven men from Anzac like Elliott and Glasgow, who went to brigades, while several former company commanders in their early twenties took charge of battalions. Veteran junior officers and NCOs were similarly promoted. Apart from the few Duntroon graduates, all officers came from the ranks and led their old comrades, a system contrary to that in the British Army. Russell, a mounted soldier, rather than Johnston, an infantryman, took command of the New Zealand Division. Along with the 1st and 2nd Australian Divisions, it formed part of I ANZAC, which was led by Birdwood with White as chief of staff. The 4th and 5th Australian Divisions made up II ANZAC under Godley. Events elsewhere had already decided their destiny.

Meeting at Chantilly at the end of 1915, the Allies, whom Italy had joined in May, formulated a strategic plan for 1916. It called for simultaneous summer offensives on the three main fronts, the Eastern, where Russia had replaced its huge losses with new conscripts, the Italian, and the Western Front, where a combined Anglo-French thrust would be launched astride the Somme River. Shortly afterwards, General Sir Douglas Haig, formerly commander of the First Army, became commander-in-chief of the BEF, and General Sir William Robertson, who had been its chief of staff, replaced Murray as chief of the Imperial General Staff in London. Their appointments brought to positions of supreme authority men who believed that the war could only be won on the Western Front and, therefore, that all British forces should be sent there except the absolute minimum required for defence elsewhere. In fulfilment of this policy, Murray intended to start transferring divisions from Egypt to France as the Turkish threat subsided with the drying up of the winter rains in March.

The third year of the war was shaped by the appreciation that Germany's military supremo, General Erich von Falkenhayn, put before the Kaiser on Christmas Day 1915. Falkenhayn contended that Russia was paralysed and France nearly exhausted. The reason the war continued, he argued, was the enormous influence that Britain still wielded over its allies. But Britain's naval supremacy and the difficulties facing a German offensive on the BEF's front in Flanders precluded a direct crippling blow against it. The only course open was to break France completely, thereby 'knocking England's best sword out of her hand'. Falkenhayn selected Verdun, a historic fortress town forming the northeastern bastion of the French front, as an objective for which France would fight to the last man and, ultimately, 'bleed to death'. After the German attack began on 21 February, Falkenhayn's prophecy seemed likely to come true.[6]

Allied plans for 1916 had to be modified. Relieving the hard-pressed French became the priority. Robertson cabled Murray at the end of February that three Australian divisions on the Western Front by April might be worth six later in the year. He told Murray: 'It will be a good thing for the Australians to get to France. It is an excellent training school and the Germans will soon put them in order'. A fortnight earlier, Murray had drafted a letter to Robertson disparaging Australian discipline and training to such an extent that White wanted the Australian Government informed so that it could decide whether troops deemed so worthless should go to France at all.[7]

Whatever his thoughts on discipline, Murray's concern over the state of training was well founded. Nearly three-quarters of the men were reinforcements. As the veterans had never led at the ranks to which they had been promoted, command experience was low. New supporting arms units that the BEF found necessary on the Western Front had to be raised. Every division now fielded a pioneer battalion for light field engineering tasks. Machine-guns were withdrawn from battalions and grouped into separate companies, one company to each brigade. Heavy, medium and light trench-mortar batteries were formed. The infantry battalions had to provide the men for these units while in the throes of their own reorganisation. The artillery's problems were worse. As each of the two Australian divisions at Anzac had nine batteries, doubling the divisions from two to four necessitated an increase from eighteen to thirty-six batteries. Murray rightly insisted that they could only go to France with the standard fifteen-battery establishment of a British division, which meant a total of sixty batteries altogether. As he had warned Birdwood on 29 February that I ANZAC would start leaving within a fortnight, the 1st and 2nd Divisions were given the partly trained batteries of the 4th and 5th. They had to re-form their artillery practically from scratch.

I ANZAC started for France on 13 March 1916. The rolling stock its embarkation move required left very little for the 4th and 5th Divisions, which were taking over the Canal Line. For the most part, they faced a three-day march across the forty miles of desert from Tel el Kebir. Even though the men were feeling the effects of recent inoculations and many had new boots, commanders decided to make the march a test and required them to carry full kit, pack and ammunition – a load of 90 pounds – in the one hundred-degree Fahrenheit heat. Major-General Cox let his brigades pack their rations and sleeping gear on the accompanying camels. Major-General McCay would not allow the 14th and 15th Brigades to do likewise.

Marching in the late afternoon cool, the 15th Brigade arrived at Ferry Post in reasonable order. The 14th preceding it in the heat of the day disintegrated. 'We were . . . foaming at the mouth like mad dogs, with tongues swollen, breath gripping our throats with agonizing pain, and legs buckling under us', Private Henry Williams remarked of the 56th Battalion. Private Johnston, also of the 56th, wrote:

> All along the route one could see the articles thrown out by the boys. Here a few cartridges, then a towel, a pair of pyjamas, trousers, oilsheet . . . some threw out a few sheets of paper to lighten the load. The boys lagged and lagged behind, hundreds needing the doctor's attention, and many fainting. Many begged and begged for water . . . I saw big Blinco the Balmain footballer drop out.

As they approached Moascar, the New Zealanders sent 'ambulances and men and water to attend to our wants', Johnston continued. 'One lot had just come in from parade, and the whole mob volunteered to march out and help our boys.' Johnston and Williams were among the thirty-eight men from the 56th Battalion who made Moascar unaided. Parched, delirious with sunstroke and occasionally naked, the 14th Brigade staggered in during the night 'like the remnant of a broken army'. On reaching the Canal Line, each battalion was paraded to hear an insulting rebuke from McCay, who said all ranks shared in the debacle and declared the 14th Brigade unfit for operations. For weeks afterwards, he made its battalions march in circles with full packs for two hours daily as punishment. McCay was loathed thereafter. The 14th's commander,

Brigadier-General Godfrey Irving, who had ridden throughout the march and been jeered subsequently during a review by the Prince of Wales, was replaced by Colonel Pope, formerly of the 16th Battalion.[8]

Both divisions held the Canal Line with little more than a battalion, which freed up the rest for training. The rebuilding of the artillery lost to I ANZAC was an enormous task. Left with less than 500 gunners, the 5th Division needed 2500 more. The newly formed infantry battalions had to give up another 100 men each and the light horse contributed most of the rest. Officers were given instruction in the mornings that they passed on in the afternoons. The few guns I ANZAC left behind were used in relays. Only elementary firing practices could be completed before the 5th Division, preceded by the 4th, left to join the other Australian divisions on the Western Front in June.

British worries about riotous behaviour when the Australians docked in Marseilles turned out to be unfounded. The local authorities remarked that I ANZAC gave them less trouble than any other troops, while the 5th Division created a record by having not a single disciplinary case when it passed through. Lieutenant Hugh Knyvett, the 15th Brigade's Intelligence Officer, was struck by the rapturous welcome:

How excited these French people were over us Australians! They pelted us with flowers and sweets, and while no one objected to the embraces of the girls, we thought it a bit too much when the men as well threw their arms around us and kissed us on both cheeks. French customs were new to us, and some of the boys thought the men were crazy.

For men fresh from the desert, the train journey to the BEF's front, 130 miles north of Paris, was a delight. 'Everywhere seemed to be running streams, avenues of trees and fields ablaze with scarlet poppies, blue cornflowers and wild marguerites', wrote Private

Williams. At each stop on the sixty-hour journey, Sergeant Harry Preston of the 9th Battalion recorded, 'we received 'coffee, vino and fruit . . . from the warm hearted French people, who made us feel that they and their beautiful country were worth fighting for'. Near Calais, 'Tommies were to be seen everywhere, and there seemed to be endless columns of motor lorries and horse transports on the roads'. The weather became bleaker as the Australians turned east for the detraining points around Hazebrouck in French Flanders. Then came the march to their billets in the local villages and farms. The absence of even middle-aged men, who were away in the French Army, made these 'sad, sad' places and the 'cheery, laughing, singing Australians' seemed a revelation. 'In some remarkable way, we seem to have awakened hope in hopeless hearts, and left happiness in cheerless homes', Captain Gordon Maxfield of the 21st Battalion felt. 'Splendid, fine physique, very hard and determined looking . . . The Australians are also mad keen to kill Germans and to start doing it at once', Haig wrote, after reviewing them at the end of March.[9]

I ANZAC began entering the line on 7 April. Six weeks later it held the right flank of General Sir Hubert Plumer's Second Army, a clear reminder that on the Western Front, where it formed a fraction of a BEF that was already fifty divisions strong, the AIF had lost the independence granted by the isolation of its enclave at Anzac. Instead of two divisions holding the line and one resting and training behind them, the normal arrangement for a corps, the 1st and 2nd Australian and the New Zealand Divisions were all needed to hold the nine miles of front that stretched from the River Lys, past Armentières, to a point opposite the Sugarloaf, a German salient. Called the Bois Grenier sector – although the Australians knew it as the Fleurbaix sector, after the half-ruined village a mile behind the line where Prime Minister Hughes reviewed the 1st Brigade in June – the area had seen no serious fighting for almost a year. Capitalising on the tranquillity, the British used it as a 'nursery' where new formations could be introduced to trench warfare.

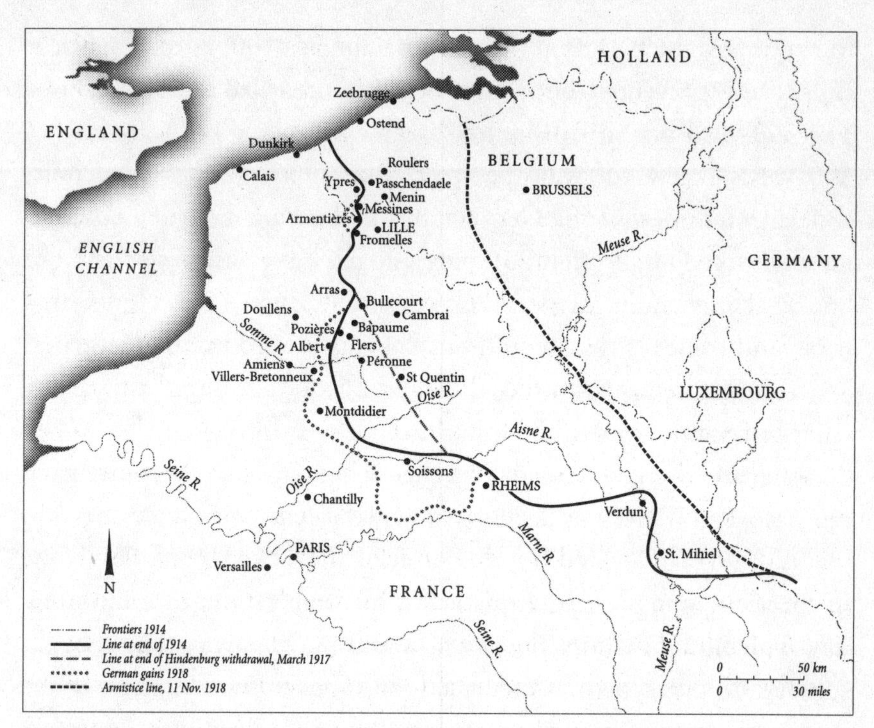

The Western Front

The opposing front lines, wrote Captain Alexander Ellis of the 31st Battalion, lay 'on one of the lowest parts of the Western Front . . . a flat, dank area about fifty feet above sea level'. Coarse, scrubby grass gradually took over as crops decayed in the abandoned fields. Beyond the German front line could be seen their second line. It ran through three villages – Aubers, Fromelles and Le Maisnil – atop a ridge that took its name from Aubers, the largest of the three. Calling it a ridge was almost a misnomer. Nowhere more than 120 feet above sea level, it was more like a flattened speed bump but still offered commanding views over Fleurbaix and other British-held villages, and the Anzac line on the plain below.[10]

As the water table was eighteen inches below the surface, diggings soon filled with slush. Both sides built upwards. Though they were referred to as trenches, the front lines were really breastworks of earth-filled sandbags. The British one ranged from nine to fourteen feet thick. A shallow support line 75–100 yards rearwards supposedly prevented both lines being bombarded simultaneously. The 300-yard line, a substantial breastwork actually located up to 500 yards rearward, was the reserve line. Counterattacking units concentrated there if the Germans broke in. Duckboarded communication trenches, spaced 250 yards apart, gave access to the front line system. A mile further back was the Second Line, comprising posts and trenches that would only be garrisoned in an emergency. More unmanned posts along the bank of the Lys, on which sat the village of Sailly, constituted the last-ditch position.

After the deep and sturdy trenches it had laboriously constructed at Anzac, I ANZAC was disillusioned by the state of these defences. In places the breastwork was not bulletproof and lacked loopholes. None of the shelters in it could withstand a hit from even a medium shell. The wire entanglements were useless and the tramway that brought supplies up overgrown. Water filled the support line and most of the communication trenches, whose shallowness sometimes left users exposed from the waist up. Refurbishment began immediately.

For the moment, the nursery lived up to its sleepy reputation. 'Oh dear! Compared to Anzac, the people here don't know what war is', wrote Monash before going to England to command the 3rd Australian Division. One soldier told Birdwood it was 'like heaven after hell', and Bean noted that 'the sound of a rifle shot rarely broke the silence'. Water was piped forward and cooked rations and fresh food were brought up from field kitchens. From the communications trenches, units walked through green fields to their billets for reasonably frequent rests and for pleasures unknown at Anzac. Field baths gave temporary relief from lice, although the rats were worse than on Gallipoli. Each village had its own *estaminet* selling wine and beer and the Australian, as the highest paid soldier in the BEF, could partake prodigiously. 'Say, pard, cut that out', he would drawl, slamming a twenty franc note onto the counter in front of his gawping British counterparts. They dreaded moving into villages the

Australians had left. Nearby Armentières meant tea-rooms, shops, canteens and YMCA recreation huts and, for those so inclined, more worldly delights.[11]

For the battalions in the line, the routine was no different to that at Anzac. Day began as it ended, with stand-to, when all men stood with rifles on the firesteps ready to repel any German attempt to take advantage of the change from night to day routine and vice versa. After an officer had checked the cleanliness of weapons, the men would be stood down, leaving one or two per platoon to keep watch on the German front line, 80–400 yards distant. Some of the remainder did fatigues, perhaps thickening the traverses that gave breastwork and trench the zigzag shape necessary both to prevent an attacker firing along them and to localise shell or bomb explosions. Others were free to rest. Every rifle was at the ready nearby and machine-guns were manned continually and trained on selected points in the line opposite or on rear areas. Night was the most active period. Patrols went out and fatigues increased to do the repair and porterage tasks that were too hazardous by day. All in all, it seemed fairly easy. 'I had the best of times in the trenches and I wish I was back again', wrote Sergeant Cec Baldwin of the 3rd Battalion in May. 'I did 3 hours work laying wire at night, and the rest of the 24 hours to myself. It suited me down to the ground.'[12]

Beginning with steel helmets to protect heads against shrapnel and splinters, equipment and weapons that would have been godsends at Anzac were issued. Each battalion received four Lewis light machine-guns, which a strong man could fire from the shoulder. In place of the crude jam-tin bomb came the Mills grenade, whose segmented ovoid body was designed to burst into numerous small fragments each capable of killing. A platoon per battalion and thirty or so men per company were specially trained to throw them. Two four-tube batteries of light Stokes mortars went to each brigade. Setting up in the support line, peripatetic mortar teams could lob twenty-two bombs per minute onto sniper or machine-gun posts pinpointed by observers in the front line. The three howitzer batteries per division could also rain their high-angle fire on the German parapet and on longer-range targets, such as communications trenches.

Yet even in the nursery, the Anzacs realised that the Western Front would be much tougher than Gallipoli and that the German, 'with his extraordinary powers of application and organisation, was an opponent infinitely more formidable' than the Turk. The omnipresence of aircraft was new and the flamethrowers that the Germans were starting to use came as a nasty surprise. Gas masks, which came in handy at Anzac to ward off the stench, had to be employed for their true purpose. The German medium trench mortar or *minenwerfer* seemed more plentiful than the Stokes and was much more destructive. Its canister-like projectile turned over and over with a 'woof, woof' sound as it arced through the air. The explosion caused a crater the size of a large room and a shock wave felt in shelters a mile away. Carried on in watery ditches and furrows, the struggle to dominate no man's land left neither side with the upper hand. German snipers were deadly and could not be suppressed. German shells fell suddenly, accurately and often on the lines and the billets. Many men were lost before the Australians realised that the cause was not spies but their own carelessness in hanging out washing in full view of the Germans or standing about in the open watching aerial dogfights.[13]

The Anzacs' first engagements were also unlike anything they had experienced at Gallipoli. On 5 May the Germans raided the 20th Battalion in the Bridoux Salient, just east of Bois Grenier, after the most concentrated bombardment the Australians had yet known. 'Some fellows' nerves gave way & they became gibbering idiots, Sergeants and all sorts, god it was little wonder . . . fighting here is simply a massacre', wrote Corporal Arthur Thomas of the 6th Battalion. For the loss of 19 men, the 62 raiders inflicted well over 100 casualties and took 10 prisoners as well as two Stokes mortars. As the latter were still secret, both Plumer and Haig were furious. The Australians were embarrassed for a long time. On 30 May the 11th Battalion at Cordonnerie Farm, three miles south of Bridoux, was struck. The German raid report stated that: 'Bodies, buried and torn in shreds, were found in great number, and also very many dead, apparently unwounded, were seen in dugouts'. Sixty yards of the front line were obliterated. The Australians lost 116 men, the Germans eight. Six of the German casualties were due to a grenade that accidentally went off after their return. General Legge admitted that the initiative lay with the enemy, who was, 'so far as he can be without actually attacking, somewhat superior in the offensive'.[14]

Launched two months after its arrival in France, I ANZAC's first offensive action was also a raid. Initiated by the Canadians in 1915, these 'minor trench operations' were originally intended to identify the Germans opposite, usually by capturing a prisoner, in the belief that a new formation signified imminent activity. Revolvers, bombs, knives and clubs were the means of mayhem. The Canadians helped prepare 66 men from the 26th and 28th Battalions assembled under Captain Maitland Foss to strike a poorly wired part of the German line near Armentières:

> The whole party was withdrawn for a fortnight to a rear area, and there went into training after the fashion of a football team before an important game. This included a sharp course of physical training, and close practice in carrying out its raid. A replica of the enemy's trench, which had been photographed from aeroplanes, was dug on the training ground and the operation was rehearsed again and again until it went almost automatically.[15]

Faces blackened and wearing unmarked British clothing to confuse the Germans, Foss's party struck on the night of 5 June as the artillery sealed off their entry point with a box barrage. The trenches were practically deserted – German policy here was to man them thinly – and only a handful of Germans were killed or taken prisoner. Caught on their return by the German artillery, the Australians lost 30 men. The raid was nonetheless considered successful. During another one on the night of 25 June, 18-year-old Private William Jackson of the 17th Battalion brought in a prisoner, carried wounded men back three times under heavy shellfire, and looked for more wounded even after a shell burst mangled his arm. He became the first Australian to win the VC on the Western Front and remains the youngest Australian to do so ever. Allied strategic needs turned these raids into the start of a whole series.

Responding to urgent French appeals to relieve the pressure at Verdun, the Russians had attacked at Lake Narocz in March but the Germans clobbered them as usual. The enthusiasm of some Russian generals for the summer offensive agreed upon at Chantilly dulled. General Alexei Brusilov, the Russian commander in the southwest, was keen. He said that his armies could take on the Austrians to divert attention from a simultaneous thrust by the northern and central armies against the Germans. The plan was approved. A plea from the Italians, who were trying to fend off an Austrian attack on the Trentino, added urgency. Launched on 5 June 1916, Brusilov's offensive caught the Austrians totally by surprise and took 400 000 prisoners and sixty miles of territory. But prolonging the offensive unnecessarily cost over a million men. The Germans halted the attack against them. Nonetheless, the Russians had done their bit. Ground down by the 'mill on the Meuse' at Verdun, the French had to skimp on theirs. By mid-June they could only spare sixteen divisions for the forthcoming Somme offensive instead of the thirty-nine originally proposed. The BEF had to assume the main role.

Giving the task to General Sir Henry Rawlinson's Fourth Army, Haig called on 28 May for as many raids as possible by his other armies in order to divert German attention from Rawlinson's preparations and wear down divisions they might use as reinforcements

▲ Private Charles Johnston. A brilliant student who became a schoolteacher, he said he saw the men who had gone to war every time he turned to his blackboard. Enlisting aged twenty-three in July 1915, Charles was dead a year later. During the Great Depression, an ex-soldier who had been in Charles' battalion called at his parents' home. He said that Charles had been wounded and was being carried back by stretcher-bearers when a German shell wiped them all out.

▲ Private Frank Johnston. Charles's elder brother, he was a clerk before joining up in December 1915, aged twenty-five. Unlike Charles, Frank was a 'larrikin'. He made corporal but was busted for going absent for two weeks to see England in June 1916. Undeterred, Frank took more time off in September. He was killed in action shortly afterwards.

◄ The AN&MEF embarks in Sydney Harbour on 18 August 1914 for German New Guinea, which was occupied after a few brief skirmishes that cost the Australians ten casualties, six of whom were killed. Having seen next to no action, many AN&MEF men joined up on returning home, to fight and die at Gallipoli and on the Western Front.

Anticipating a 'Great Adventure', a crowd of hopefuls swamps Swan Barracks, Perth, to enlist. Many have probably come from Western Australia's goldfields and other mining works, which had attracted a large number of young men and recent immigrants. Recruiting was heavily over-subscribed right across Australia.

Major-General William Bridges, commander of both the AIF and its 1st Division. Born in Scotland to a British naval officer and his Australian wife, Bridges grew up in England and Canada and came to Australia after studying at the Canadian Military College. Joining the NSW Permanent Forces in 1885 as an artillery officer, he served mainly in staff and administrative postings and had little experience of command. Though brave to a fault, his harsh manner gravely handicapped him as a leader.

▲ Recruits drilling at Blackboy Hill outside Perth sneak a look at the camera while their instructor has his back turned. Uniforms have not yet been issued. The rough and ready nature of the camp at this early stage is apparent. The camps elsewhere were no different.

▼ Crowds cheer the Wellington Battalion as it marches down Cuba Street, Wellington, to embarkation. Its commander, Lieutenant-Colonel William Malone, is the mounted officer at the centre of the photograph, while the officer leading the column may be Colonel Francis Johnston, commander of the New Zealand Infantry Brigade. Australian formations marched in similar fashion through Australian capital cities.

▲ After its battering by HMAS *Sydney*, the *Emden* was barely recognisable as a warship. Survivors cluster on the stern, below which a lifeboat from *Sydney* can be seen. The scenes aboard the hulk were ghastly.

▶ Lieutenant-General Sir William Birdwood aboard HMS *Lord Nelson*. Birdwood's indifference to danger and informal manner won him many friends amongst the Anzacs. But Birdwood was no tactician, a shortcoming that was more evident on the Western Front than at Gallipoli. After the war, he lobbied to become Governor-General of Australia but was unsuccessful.

▲ The pyramids overlook the lines of the 9th and 10th Battalions at Mena camp. Stacked rifles and gear suggest a break in training, which allows some attention to be given to the regimental mascot, a living reminder of home. The Cairo Zoological Gardens became the home of a number of mascots when their units left Egypt.

◀ Sir Alexander Godley, not quite the model of a modern major-general. Having the regimental background Bridges lacked, Godley, who also commanded the NZEF, acted pre-emptively in Egypt to prevent Indiscipline in the NZ and A Division. As a field commander he was feeble, repeatedly botching operations at Gallipoli and depending on able subordinates on the Western Front.

▲ 24 April 1915. Troops of the 10th Battalion line the deck of the battleship *Prince of Wales*, which also carried Bridges and his staff, as it leaves Mudros. After a church service, a meal and a final inspection, men wrote last letters or fiddled with their gear. With action just a few hours off, few slept.

◄ Colonel Ewen Sinclair-MacLagan. A pessimist, he thought the 'honour' of spearheading the Anzac landing, which Bridges had given to the 3rd Brigade, might result in its destruction. Sinclair-MacLagan returned to Britain in 1919 and commanded the 51st Highland Division. He died in 1948, aged almost eighty.

▲ Men of the 1st Division Signal Company going ashore at 6 a.m. By then the Turks had been cleared from the heights above the beach and the main danger to landing troops was airborne shrapnel. A soldier with a Kodak vest pocket camera (VPK) probably took this photo. There is evidence of up to a thousand private cameras at Anzac. Pictures taken with VPKs constitute about half of the 5500 photos in the Australian War Memorial's Gallipoli collection.

▼ Australians, most probably from the 1st Brigade, cross Plugge's Plateau around noon on 25 April. Stray bullets from the fighting in Shrapnel Valley are whizzing over Plugge's and the foremost men are crouching in the scrub to avoid them. This photo is one of the few of troops under fire at Anzac.

Lieutenant-Colonel Mustafa Kemal, who realised before anyone else on the Ottoman side the threat that the Anzac landing posed and hurled his division against it. Kemal would also play a pivotal role in defeating the August breakout from Anzac. His wartime exploits paved the way for a spectacular postwar career, in which he refashioned Turkey as a secular republic and led it as president from 1923 to his death in 1938.

Barges evacuating wounded from Anzac. Those able to stand or sit leave on the steam launch *Keraunos*. The number of wounded swamped both the evacuation and medical plans. By late afternoon on 25 April, casualties were being loaded on transports that had no facilities whatsoever. Many received no proper treatment until they reached Egypt or Malta.

▲ The beach towards dusk on 25 April, looking north to Ari Burnu. A wounded Australian lies in the foreground, while medics wearing Red Cross armbands tend other casualties. Stragglers, who had started back during the afternoon, are among the hundreds of other soldiers moving about.

▶ Brigadier-General Harold 'Hooky' Walker. Originally Birdwood's chief of staff, Walker's abilities and temperament were infinitely better suited to field command. He would excel as commander of the 1st Brigade and then the 1st Division. From 1924 to 1928 Walker was Commander-in-Chief, Southern Command, India. He died in 1934, aged seventy-two.

▲ Anzac Cove around midday on 25 April, showing the rugged terrain, the shelter the cove offered and the narrowness of the beach. Within a few weeks, these slopes will be denuded of vegetation and honeycombed with dugouts.

▶ Charles Wheeler's *The Charge of the 2nd Infantry Brigade at Krithia* depicts Colonel McCay standing above 'Tommies' Trench', periscope in hand, urging his men forward. The contrast between the flat, open ground at Helles and the brutal terrain at Anzac is striking.

▲ An 18-pounder from the 9th Battery in action on McCay's Hill, a seaward spur of the 400 Plateau. The Anzacs had no artillery support on 25 April but several guns landed the next day and shredded Turk assaults across the plateau that night. This photograph so impressed Lord Northcliffe, owner of *The Times*, that he scrawled 'Splendid Men' before giving it to Australian journalist Keith Murdoch.

▲ Lunch break at the 1st Australian Division's headquarters on 3 May, the day after the NZ and A Division's costly attack on Baby 700. The rear of the dugouts is cut into the hillside, offering some protection, but for the most part they are exposed to shrapnel. Major Gellibrand, centre, half-turned to camera, was once hit here. Bridges typically stands apart from the others in the dugout on the left. Major Blamey sips a brew on the right. The argument over evacuation on the night of 25 April also occurred here.

◄ Private John Simpson (Kirkpatrick), 'the Donk' (variously called 'Murphy', 'Duffy', 'Queen Elizabeth' or 'Abdul'), and a casualty they have brought down to the beach. British-born Simpson commandeered the donkey on 26 April and ferried wounded on it until he was sniped on 19 May. Aged twenty-two, Simpson became an Australian icon and remains the best-known Anzac.

Albert Jacka, possibly on Lemnos at the end of August 1915, by which time he had just been promoted corporal. Winning the first Australian VC of the war made Jacka, twenty-two, instantly famous at home and he appeared on Australian recruiting posters. He also received the £500 and gold watch that colourful Melbourne identity John Wren promised to the first VC winner.

Anzacs and Turks mingle while burying the dead during the armistice that followed the massed Ottoman attacks on 19 May. The stolid bravery of their opponents during the assault and the fraternisation of the armistice dissipated Australian loathing of the Turks. From then on they were the best of enemies.

▼ The beach in full swing, thronged with men, piled high with stores, festooned with shelters and served by piers. Watson's Pier, at the top of the photograph, was the main one. Swimmers splash about. But the instant a Turkish gun fired, not a man could be seen.

▲ Looking north from Walker's Ridge across the dreadful terrain behind North Beach that awaited the assault columns breaking out of Anzac. The high ground falls away to the Suvla Plain, on the far side of which Suvla Bay and the Salt Lake can just be seen.

▶ Australians ignore the smell and relax in a captured Turkish trench at Lone Pine on 10 August. Major David McConaghy, one of the five officers from the 3rd Battalion not killed or badly wounded in the attack, sits on the left, his hand bandaged. He would command the 54th and 55th Battalions on the Western Front before being killed near Villers-Bretonneux in April 1918.

▼ The cliff face that the Wellington Mounted Rifles scaled to seize Table Top on the night of 6 August. These troops are climbing it in daylight afterwards, which gives some idea of what the New Zealanders accomplished.

after the offensive began. The Second Army was also to prepare a separate offensive against the Messines–Wytschaete Ridge, north of Armentières. Haig envisaged shifting the main effort there if the Germans left themselves weak by using all their available reserves to check the Somme attack. I ANZAC began moving to Messines on 17 June. It also did its share in the intense raiding program Haig had ordered, launching a dozen raids from the nursery between 25 June and 2 July.

On 1 July 150 men from the 9th Battalion, under Captain Maurice Wilder-Neligan, struck east of the Sugarloaf. They lost a third of their number but inflicted seventy-nine casualties and captured a troublesome machine-gun. Shelling cost the Germans over one hundred men when the 11th Battalion raided the Tadpole strongpoint on the following night. Eighty-nine men from the 14th Battalion were raiding to the north of them at the same time. They were caught in uncut wire by shrapnel and machine-gun fire and those who got through found the line practically deserted. Almost half the raiders were lost for nothing. The hit-and-miss nature of raids was becoming evident and the Anzacs, like the rest of the BEF, came to dislike them. The few minutes they lasted were an orgy of killing, wounding and capturing. Often the killing was in cold blood, such as in 1917 when a German found tied to a post in a trench as field punishment had to be dispensed with. Getting back was always a problem because the Germans were fully alert by then. If they were ready beforehand, as was the case with the 14th Battalion, casualties were severe. '[Raids] are not worth the cost', CSM Arthur Brunton quickly concluded. 'None of the survivors want to go in any more.'[16]

At 7.30 a.m. on 1 July 1916, thirteen British divisions attacked astride the Albert–Bapaume Road over the rolling chalk uplands of the Somme on a fifteen and a half mile front. Five French divisions assaulted on a six-mile front that was mainly south of the river on their right. During the week the British bombardment lasted, the Fourth Army's 1537 guns and howitzers fired 1.5 million shells.

Owing to the long attack frontage, the fire was actually less intense than in the BEF's first offensive at Neuve Chapelle in March 1915. The Germans sheltered in dugouts up to thirty feet deep that were impervious to it. Dense wire entanglements girded their line. British shells at this stage of the war lacked a 'graze' fuse that would detonate on contact with objects as slender as a strand of barbed wire. Since they only exploded on hitting the ground, the wire belts were merely tossed about, which entangled them further. Emerging from their dugouts at the end of the bombardment, the Germans mowed down the rows of heavily-laden infantrymen plodding towards them across a no man's land that was up to 800 yards wide. When night mercifully fell, the British Army had suffered 57 470 casualties, the greatest loss in a single day in its history.[17]

Haig ordered further attacks. They resulted in more costly fighting that ended any thoughts of an offensive at Messines. On 7 July I ANZAC was ordered to the Somme. In exchange for the New Zealand Division, which joined II ANZAC in order to remain under Godley, the 4th Australian Division was to go with it after being relieved between Bois Grenier and the Sugarloaf by the newly arrived 5th Australian Division. On the same day, Godley warned II ANZAC that it was 'imperative that raids and all possible offensive should be undertaken at once' to prevent the Germans reinforcing the Somme. The 13th Jäger Battalion, which formed part of the Sugarloaf garrison, had reportedly been identified there.[18]

The 5th Division was concentrating near Hazebrouck when General McCay received Godley's order. According to Lieutenant-Colonel Walter Cass of the 54th Battalion, McCay directed him 'to do a raid tomorrow night'. Cass protested that the 54th, like the rest of the 5th Division, had yet to see the front line and had little idea of how to undertake a raid. McCay retorted that 'it had got to be done and could be done all right'. Colonel Pope, Cass's immediate superior, and Brigadier-General Edwin Tivey, the commander of the 8th Brigade, also confronted McCay. Brigadier-General Elliott of the

15th may have joined them. McCay backed down. On 10–11 July the 5th Division entered the line next to the New Zealanders. The 30th Battalion's history recorded how tense the nursery had become:

Machine-gun fire went on almost continuously . . . Shrapnel had also to be contended with, and occasionally 5.9-inch shells played havoc with our parapets . . . At night [no man's land] became a 'fairyland' by reason of the sheaves of flares which each side sent up with a view to detecting raids or the activities of patrolling parties. We were obliged to admit that the enemy fireworks were superior to our own.[19]

—SEVEN—

THE INITIATION: FROMELLES

On 13 July Haig was informed that eight German battalions had followed 13th Jäger to the Somme from the quiet northern sectors. As raiding had failed to stop them, stronger action was necessary. GHQ thought that threatening an advance on Lille, the industrial centre of Flanders and a vital rail junction for the Germans, might work. It looked again at a proposal from Lieutenant-General Sir Richard Haking for a diversion against Aubers Ridge, which blocked the western approaches to the city. Haking wanted to pinch out the Sugarloaf salient by taking 'the two main tactical localities on the ridge, the high ground around Fromelles and the village of Aubers'. The scheme involved two divisions from his formation: XI Corps, on the First Army's left flank, and the Australian division, now the 5th, on the Second Army's right.[1]

GHQ rejigged the proposal as an artillery demonstration in which the two armies would amass six divisions' worth of artillery for a three-day bombardment to make the Germans believe a new offensive was contemplated. An infantry advance would be provided for in case the opportunity for one arose. Hearing this, General Monro, the First Army's commander, decided he liked Haking's original plan better. The infantry advance ceased being an optional extra, although it was only to go as far as the German support line, 150–200 yards behind the front line breastwork and well short of

Aubers Ridge. The attack was provisionally fixed for 17 July with Haking in command.

After serving under him, Lieutenant-Colonel Philip Game, a future governor of New South Wales, called Haking 'really impossible, untruthful and a bully and not to be trusted'. He was best known for *Company Training*, published in 1913. It exalted the offensive: 'There is one rule which can never be departed from and which alone will lead to success, and that is always to push forward, always to attack', Haking wrote. An aggressive spirit would overcome firepower and unfavourable ground. As a divisional commander under Monro, he had launched repeated attacks during the First Army's disastrous assault on Aubers Ridge in May 1915. On joining Haking's shattered formation afterwards, Robert Graves wryly remarked: 'The last shows have not been suitable ones for company commanders to profit by his directions'. Haking had also recently launched an attack, similar to the one he was now proposing, against the Boar's Head Salient, a couple of miles from the Sugarloaf. It failed, with the loss of 1153 men in the two assault battalions. Haking considered their fighting value had been greatly improved.[2]

No sooner was he given the go ahead than Haking learned that instead of sending him the guns of three divisions from the Second Army, General Plumer was providing only the partly trained artilleries of the 4th and 5th Australian Divisions. The 4th Division's artillery was deemed too inexperienced to accompany it to the Somme; the 5th's was greener still. Haking scaled down the attack by employing just one division from XI Corps, the 61st (South Midland), alongside the 5th Australian Division. Commanded by Major-General Colin Mackenzie, the 61st had been starved of men, arms and equipment while languishing at the bottom of the pecking order as a second-line territorial formation in a rapidly expanding British Army. It had arrived in France barely a month before General McCay's men and been battered in the course of launching eight raids since.

At 9.45 a.m. on 14 July Haking gave McCay and Mackenzie their instructions: '[Each] Division will attack with 3 Brigades in line, each brigade with 2 assaulting battalions, and each battalion on a front of assault of about 350 yards'. Wire-cutting by the artillery would be continuous. The seven-hour bombardment before the assault was to intensify over the last three hours, during which four brief lifts were planned. In each the waiting infantry were to 'show their bayonets over the parapet; dummy heads and shoulders will be shown over the parapet, officers will whistle and shout orders'. Haking expected the sheltering Germans to man their own parapet, thinking the attack was coming. They would then be caught by the bombardment coming back onto them.[3]

The 61st Division was to take the Sugarloaf. But the position was just a stone's throw from the inter-divisional boundary. Commanders regard boundaries as unfortunate necessities because the co-ordination measures required across them can easily break down. Hence they should not be sited on or near critical locations, which the Sugarloaf certainly was. As the 'vital ground' for XI Corps, it had to be taken for Haking's attack to succeed. His setting of the boundary gravely prejudiced its chances.

At least four machine-guns had been identified in the Sugarloaf. They enfiladed both sides of the salient, where no man's land, 420 yards across, was at its widest. The ground was so flat that they were also capable of grazing fire, in which the centre of each burst does not rise above the height of a standing man, for hundreds of yards along no man's land. This combination, enfilade grazing fire with a long dangerous zone, maximises a machine-gun's lethality by enabling it to catch an assault flank on with no dead ground for cover. As the Sugarloaf could devastate both the Australian and British assaults in this way, the commanders on either side of the boundary near it had to be able to act instantly without compromising each other – not easy when they were out of touch in the heat of battle.

The 6th Bavarian Reserve Division opposite had helped smash

the 1915 attack. Their front-line breastwork, of which the Sugar-loaf formed part, was impervious to all but the heaviest shells and studded with concrete machine-gun posts. As the Anzac raiders had found, its strength allowed the Bavarians to hold it thinly. They looked to their reserve battalions to counterattack swiftly from secure locations well back. So confident were they of holding the position that the support line was abandoned. Stagnant water filled it. Moreover, the 6th Bavarian contained many men like 27-year-old Lance-Corporal Adolf Hitler, who had seen almost two years of fighting in France. Its morale was excellent.[4]

What veteran divisions under their command had been unable to do in 1915, Monro and Haking were therefore expecting two woefully inexperienced divisions to do now with next to no warning and under vastly more difficult circumstances. Of the twelve battalions in the 5th Division, six had been in the front line for two days and the other six had not seen it at all when McCay received his orders from Haking. Nevertheless, he welcomed the attack. 'The fact that his division, though the last of the AIF to arrive in France, would be the first in serious action, gave McCay much gratification', wrote Bean. He placed the 14th Brigade between the 8th Brigade on the left and the 15th on the right. The two assault battalions in each would attack in four waves. 'Clearly understand', McCay told his brigadiers, 'that each wave, so soon as it has cleared of enemy the work it gets into, goes on to the prescribed limit of attack'. This 'conveyor belt' style of moving the waves forward conformed to GHQ tactical notes. But they also warned that 'support points' must be established in rear to protect the men consolidating the new line, advice McCay neglected. The remaining battalions were to replace the assault ones in the front and 300-yard lines and also provide carrying parties.[5]

Despite their inexperience, the Australians suspected the soundness of the preparations. The artillery was not fully in position. Engineers were still working on the water-filled communication trench sustaining the 14th Brigade. The infantry had to manhandle their ammunition and stores up from the rearward dumps, an exhausting task. When the assault battalions moved forward late on 16 July, most men fell asleep on reaching the line. Only those in the first two waves had steel helmets. The rest would fight in their slouch hats.

Fate intervened to lift spirits. On 14 July Brigadier-General Elliott had shown Major Henry Howard, a liaison officer from GHQ, the Sugarloaf, 420 yards away across open ground. Elliott said that, according to GHQ's own guidelines, the 15th Brigade's attack had no hope. He asked Howard 'to tell me as man to man' what he thought. 'Much affected', Howard replied: 'Well, if you put it to me that way, I must tell you that it will be a bloody holocaust'. He promised to tell Haig what he had seen. Birdwood and White had reservations from the outset. They thought the Germans would have to be nincompoops to treat an attack by two divisions with no reserves seriously. Haig's staff was especially worried about the adequacy of the bombardment.[6]

Noting these concerns, Haig approved the attack on 15 July conditional on the artillery being sufficient. Meeting Monro and Haking next day, his Deputy Chief of Staff, Major-General Richard Butler, dropped a bombshell. The latest intelligence on the transfer of German reserves removed the urgent need for the operation. Butler asked whether it should be postponed or even cancelled. Haking resisted vigorously. He assured Butler that the artillery was adequate, warned that postponing the operation would damage morale and said he was 'very confident of success'. Haking even wanted to carry on to Aubers Ridge. Butler killed that idea.[7]

On the afternoon of 16 July, Haking ordered the start of the bombardment for 4 a.m. next morning, even though rain and mist were hampering the heavy artillery from properly acquiring its targets: strongpoints such as the Sugarloaf, and the German guns. The poor weather continued into 17 July. Haking sought a postponement.

Monro agreed. Fearing that the conditions might force further postponements, Monro also told GHQ that he wanted to cancel the attack altogether. Things had changed since Butler's visit the previous day. GHQ now thought a German counterattack on the Somme imminent, making a holding action urgent again. It replied that Haig wanted the attack carried out as soon as possible, weather permitting, so long as Monro was satisfied his resources were adequate. As he and Haking had already insisted they were, the attack was now inevitable. It would start at 6 p.m. on 19 July.

The Germans on Aubers Ridge had seen the roads behind the British line clogged with men, vehicles and horses. Villagers with whom the Australians were billeted talked openly about an operation set for 19 July. A light mist that morning heralded a perfect summer's day. Above Aubers Ridge the Australians saw a sign asking: 'Why so long, you are twenty four hours late?' The previous one had challenged them: 'ADVANCE AUSTRALIA – IF YOU CAN!' They shot it away.[8]

Gallipoli veterans and newcomers alike were awed by the bombardment. Les Martin, a machine-gun sergeant, told his brother: 'From about 11 a.m. till 6 p.m. there was not a space of a second's duration when some of our guns were not firing, the row was deafening. I put wadding in my ears while we were down in the supports waiting to go forward'. Obviously reassured, Corporal Williams relaxed with a pre-battle drink. 'We entered an estaminet, and found the place crowded to overflowing. Madame and her assistants were hard pressed to cope with the rush. The men were in the best of spirits and looked forward to the attack as if it were a football match'. When the final stage of the bombardment began at 3 p.m., the assault battalions were packed shoulder-to-shoulder in the front and 300-yard lines. The German gunners took every advantage of the overcrowding and they did not let up until after 5 p.m. Adding to the trial were the 'dropshorts' from the inexperienced Australian artillery. An engineer party was pulped and the 32nd Battalion badly hit. The casualties in the 31st Battalion forced Lieutenant-Colonel Frederick Toll, wounded himself, to combine its third and fourth waves into a single wave.[9]

As the Germans seemed to be getting a far worse battering, morale held. Sharing the danger in the front line, Elliott was sufficiently impressed to assure his men, 'Boys, you won't find a German in the trenches when you get there'. But at 5.10 p.m., too late for the artillery to respond, a message arrived warning that the wire protecting the side of the Sugarloaf facing his men was uncut. Observers noted three intact machine-gun emplacements there. The Germans were also seen to ignore the feint lifts. They realised that the blowing of whistles and waving of bayonets and dummy figures were just ruses, and of such a transparent nature, according to the 30th Battalion's history, as to cause more amusement than anxiety. One Australian wrote of those last surreal moments:

> The first thing that struck you was that shells were bursting everywhere; and you could see machine-guns knocking bits off the trees in front of the reserve line and sparking against the wire . . . When men looked over the top they saw no man's land leaping up everywhere in showers of dust and sand.[10]

The 61st Division's assault was shattered. Only on the extreme right was the Bavarian line reached. Having wiped out the 184th Brigade attacking them on the left, the Bavarians in the Sugarloaf helped Second Lieutenant Bachschneider's company deal with the neighbouring assault of Elliott's brigade. Bachschneider's men cheered as the Australians clambered over the parapet.

The first wave reached the Laies, a drainage ditch running obliquely across no man's land towards the Sugarloaf. Gravitating in that direction, the Australians were lashed by a fusillade so devastating that they thought the parapet ahead was being manned with one man per yard. 'The first wave went down like wheat before the reaper', recalled Lieutenant Knyvett. Hit as soon as it topped the parapet, the second got to the middle of no man's land. Seeing no movement ahead, the third wave pressed on towards where it imagined the first two must have been lying ready for the final rush. It was also shattered, as a machine-gun firing down the Laies turned the ditch into a deathtrap. Lieutenant Tom Kerr of the 60th Battalion saw the Bavarians leaning over their parapet, looking 'as if they were wondering what was coming next'. The fourth wave gave them their answer and they obliterated it. Private Walter Downing of the 57th Battalion saw how deadly the grazing fire from the Sugarloaf was:

> The 60th climbed on the parapet, heavily laden, dragging with them scaling ladders, light bridges, picks, shovels, and bags of bombs.
>
> Scores of stammering German machine-guns spluttered violently, drowning the noise of the cannonade. The air was thick with bullets, swishing in a flat lattice of death. There were gaps in the lines of men – wide ones, small ones. The survivors spread across the front, keeping the line straight . . . The bullets skimmed low, from knee to groin, riddling the tumbling bodies before they touched the ground. Still the line kept on.
>
> Hundreds were mown down in the flicker of an eyelid, like great rows of teeth knocked from a comb, but still the line went on, thinning and stretching. Wounded wriggled into shellholes or were hit again. Men were cut in two by streams of bullets. And still the line went on.

Wounded in the head at the start of the attack, Captain Aubrey Liddelow, now of the 59th Battalion, led a small group onto the German parapet and was hit again in the shoulder and arm. Seeing that they were alone, he withdrew them into a shell hole, where one of his men, who was also wounded, implored Liddelow to return with him for medical attention. He sent the man back but stayed himself, saying, 'I'll never walk back into safety and leave the men I have led into such grave danger – we'll wait for reinforcements'.

A German shell killed him a few minutes later. The survivors burrowed into old agricultural furrows and shell holes in no man's land. Less than half an hour had elapsed. Elliott had no idea of what had happened for another hour. He told McCay at 7.18 p.m.: 'The trenches are full of the enemy. Every man who rises is shot down'.[11]

No man's land, ahead of the 14th Brigade in the centre, was bisected by the Rue Delvas. The 53rd Battalion, on the right of the road, had to go 250 yards. Bachschneider's company, which should have been overcome by Elliott's men, enfiladed it. The first wave was held up until the second arrived. Yelling, 'Come on lads! Only another trench to take', Lieutenant-Colonel Ignatius Norris was killed on the German parapet. Twenty-one year old Duntroon graduate Captain Charles Arblaster took command. The 54th Battalion on the left of the road only had to go 100 yards and arrived at the breastwork as the Bavarians were manning it. Most of the Bavarians were killed. A few yards further on were concrete dugouts with amazing facilities. Lieutenant-Colonel Cass, the only senior officer left in the 54th, established his headquarters in one that was

> fitted with electric light, had two sleeping berths end to end giving a length in the side of about 13 or 14 feet, height about 7′6″, width 8 feet. Thickness of earth on top about 8 feet, depth (below ground level) of about 10 feet. It was reached by steps and had a passage or light to a window. It was strongly built and had an upright about 12″ x 12″ in the centre supporting a rafter of somewhat similar thickness. The ceiling appeared to be flat sheet iron papered with wallpaper. The walls were papered and even decorated with gold moulding similar to picture frame moulding. It had table, armchair, heating stove, electric bell, acetylene gas lamp similar to bicycle lamp.

Overgrown fields stretched towards Aubers Ridge. Thinking that the support line must be hidden in the grassland, the Australians struck out across it, 'like sportsmen after quail, occasionally shooting at Germans who had settled in shellholes and who now started up to run farther'.

The advance had become scattered well before the few surviving officers realised that the support line either did not exist or else was denoted by the two ditches they had crossed. Pulling the nearest men back, they set up posts along them. With German shells thickening the smoke and dust thrown up by the Australian barrage, visibility was poor. Captain Arblaster had intermittent contact across the Rue Delvas with the 54th Battalion and thought he was in touch with the 60th Battalion until bombing started on his right. It was Bachschneider's men counterattacking. Aware now that they and not the 60th Battalion were his neighbours, Arblaster left Captain John Murray in charge on the Rue Delvas while he organised the defence of the exposed flank. Unknown to Arblaster, the Bavarians were also attacking along their old front line, which was empty because McCay had directed each wave to continue on. The 53rd Battalion was in danger of being cut off. In the 54th, Cass knew only that he needed more men. At 7.36 p.m. McCay released the half of the 55th Battalion not involved in carrying duties. The imposing 6 foot 4 inch frame of Gallipoli veteran Captain Norman Gibbins led them across no man's land.[12]

Opposite the 8th Brigade, the German front line was closer than anywhere else and the Bavarians retreated hastily before the leading waves of the 31st Battalion. Colonel Toll was close behind:

> [We] swept on with the intention of capturing the second and third trenches in the first line system, but we went on and on but no trace could be found of same. It now appeared evident that the information supplied as to enemy defences and aerial photographs was incorrect and misleading. The ground was flat, covered with fairly long grass, the trenches shown on aerial photos were nothing but ditches full of water.

As they continued, Lieutenant Lawrie Trounson saved a German trapped in one from the attentions of an Australian who prodded him back under with his bayonet every time he surfaced for air. Toll's men were under heavy machine-gun fire, being shelled by the Germans and hit by Australian 'dropshorts'. They could not contact the 14th Brigade off to their right. As the only defensible position seemed to be the old German front line, Toll withdrew them to it, leaving a company under Captain Charles Mills in a ditch as a screen.

The 32nd Battalion anchored the left of the entire attack at the Kastenweg, a communication trench running past a strongpoint in the ruins of Delangré Farm. A mine had been blown in no man's land on that flank in the hope that the crater edges might shield the 32nd from the enfilading strongpoints at Mouquet Farm and the Tadpole beyond. Fire from a British brigade was also supposed to suppress them. Neither measure worked. The first wave was mauled before the Bavarians ahead of it withdrew to Delangré Farm. Unable to find the support line, Captain Arthur White, one of the few officers left, told his men to establish themselves in some ditches beside the Kastenweg. They barricaded it and eventually met the 31st Battalion's screen.[13]

At 7.30 p.m., the 8th and 14th Brigades held a disjointed line with a big gap in the centre and both flanks open. The support line they sought once ran along the muddy ditches they were occupying. While the maps showed the system as it had been, the aerial photographs taken before the battle gave a clue as to how it actually was. Haking's headquarters missed the change. The Australians lacked photographic interpreters.

Had the trenches been serviceable, the Australians could have made a new parapet facing the Bavarians simply by transferring the sandbags from the old parapet at the front to the back. Instead they stood in knee-deep water, trying to fill the few sandbags they had with soil so clayey, recalled Private Tom Donnellan of the 30th Battalion, that it 'clung to the shovel like an oyster, necessitating removal by hand, and when filled into sandbags and placed on the parapet it became slippery as an eel and could not be kept in position'. As shell-bursts choked the Laies, the water rose higher and mud scooped from the ditches had to be used. Toll called the job 'heartbreaking'. As it went on, the German artillery shelled the pocket continuously. Uncertain of the exact line occupied, the Australian gunners shelled it too.[14]

By this time the other battalions were garrisoning the Australian front and 300-yard lines. Terrible sights greeted them. Corporal Williams had come along the 14th Brigade's communication trench with the 56th Battalion. It had been pounded beyond recognition:

> The bodies of dead men lay thickly along its length. Here the [55th] Battalion moving up had suffered severely in the passage. The German shells still searched this sap and blew great craters along its length as we struggled through, trampling underfoot the dead that cluttered it. All the while we were losing men. Some of the wounded lay in pools staining the water with their blood. Dead men, broken trench-material, shattered duckboards that tripped us as we passed, the smell of the fumes of high explosives, and the unforgettable odour of death made this trench a place of horror.

Sapper Sidney Donnan and his mates decided that the Australian front line was too dangerous:

> The slaughter and confusion being worse than ever we decided to go over into the German lines and do something. Getting over the parapet we found No Man's Land a sort of hell on earth mainly through the moans of the wounded who were too numerous to get away, and the barrage was too heavy.

As ammunition, bombs, sandbags, picks and shovels were all desperately needed, the carrying parties from the 30th and 55th Battalions faced the daunting prospect of having to go back and forth between the two lines. Most did not. On reaching the old German line, they were welcomed as much as their loads. Instead of going back for another load, they were set to work digging and soon became involved in the fighting. 'The thought of being hit in the back on the return journey was too much for us, hence our inclination to remain with the fighting troops', a sergeant remarked.[15]

At this stage, Brigadier-General Charles Carter of the 184th Brigade became aware that reports of some of his men holding out in the Sugarloaf were probably baseless. He ordered another assault against it, which General Mackenzie converted into a renewal of the attack along the entire 61st Division line. As co-ordination with the Australians had to be arranged, Carter sent Mackenzie a message for Elliott at 7.52 p.m.: 'Am attacking at 9 p.m. Can your right battalion co-operate?' It reached Elliott via McCay's headquarters at 8.13 p.m. Elliott ordered half of the 58th Battalion to advance against the eastern face of the Sugarloaf. At 8.20 p.m. Haking received a firsthand report on the beating the 61st Division had taken earlier. He told Mackenzie to abort the 9 p.m. attack and try again next day. Though the cancellation was not passed on to McCay, Mackenzie informed him at 8.30 p.m.: 'Under instructions from corps commander am withdrawing from captured enemy line after dark'. Missing the importance of this message, which indicated that the assault had been called off, McCay's headquarters did not advise Elliott.[16]

Led by 21-year-old Major Arthur Hutchinson, the 58th Battalion duly attacked at 9 p.m. The Sugarloaf garrison waited until it was two-thirds of the way across no man's land before unleashing a torrent of fire that sounded like a thousand sheets of calico being rent at once. The line staggered, struggled on for a few steps and took cover in a shallow ditch. Seeking to inspire his men, Hutchinson rose and went on alone. Riddled by bullets, he died on the German wire.

Haking now learned that an aircraft patrol had seen flares in the Sugarloaf. Though the Bavarians opposing Hutchinson's attack probably fired them, he thought that some men from the 184th Brigade might still be there after all. Cancelling his cancellation order, Haking told Mackenzie at 11.10 p.m. to make 'every possible effort' to attack the Sugarloaf during the night. As the 15th Brigade would have to support it, McCay proposed throwing in Elliott's last battalion, the 57th, to assist. The likelihood of a third assault by the 15th Brigade evaporated at 12.20 a.m. on 20 July when Elliott sent McCay a message he had just received from the 58th Battalion: 'The attack of this Bde has completely failed . . . seems impossible to reorganise'. Helped by the 57th, the remnants of the other battalions crawled in. Haking again cancelled the 61st Division's attack but wanted its assault in the morning to proceed.[17]

On the other side of no man's land, the Bavarians had struck the 32nd Battalion's open left flank at dusk. The 32nd pleaded for more men. McCay released the rest of the 30th Battalion but they had already been used as carriers to replace the original carriers, who stayed on to fight, and become emmeshed in the battle too. Captain Frank Krinks and his eleven-man carrying party were drawn in when the Germans seemed about to burst out of Delangré Farm. They reinforced the barricade in the Kastenweg but were bombed into some shell holes twenty yards from it. From there they sniped at the Bavarians, who were silhouetted on the higher ground of the farm ruins when they shot at the 32nd Battalion. Another party under Lieutenant Tom Barbour encountered a legless soldier crawling back on his stumps. 'Make way please', the mortally wounded man gasped as he passed, never to be seen again. Barbour's men also stayed. Along with Krinks's XI, they beat off the counterattack.[18]

A greater danger threatened on the right flank, where Second Lieutenant Bachschneider's men were going bomb for bomb with Captain Arblaster's. After an hour, Arblaster's men ran out of bombs and withdrew. The Germans now held their old front line behind the 53rd Battalion almost to the Rue Delvas and were firing into the Australians from the rear. On the other side of the road a few yards away, Cass did not know that they were so close. But Lieutenant-Colonel David McConaghy, of the 55th Battalion, did. An original Anzac who led the 3rd Battalion through Lone Pine, McConaghy had followed Captain Gibbins's men across. He ordered blocks, covered by snipers and bombers, to be thrown up. Unable to make more headway, Bachschneider's thrust ran out of steam around 11 p.m.

After a Herculean effort, a communication trench dug from the 14th Brigade's old line reached the German front line at midnight. Gibbins started sending carrying parties back along it. Another trench inched across no man's land behind the 8th Brigade but German shelling often destroyed sections as soon as they were finished. The signallers trying to keep the telephone lines intact had a terrible time. Writing in the third person and calling himself 'Ted', 17-year-old Corporal Rowland Lording of the 30th Battalion was tracing a cable run out at 10 p.m.:

God! What sights they see out there. Huddled and stretched out bodies, khaki heaps that were once men – some of A Company digging a trench – others like themselves, making short crouching runs and flinging themselves down before anything that will afford the slightest cover.

Crump! Bang! Crash! The shells fall. Zipzipzip – zipzip! Machine-gun bullets kick up the dirt around them. A lull and they rush off again. Zipzip! Bang! Another twisted heap of khaki hits the ground.

It is Ted. He does not move. His cobbers crawl over to his side. 'Where d'you get it?' they ask him. His lips move, but they do not hear his reply. His arm is shattered and blood is gushing from his side. He cannot last much longer – they think he is going west. His eyes ask them to do something. Stan rolls him on to a groundsheet and drags him yard by yard towards the trench. Shell splinters tear through the sheet. The ground rocks from a nearby shell-burst which almost covers them with mud. Stan drags him on. Ted is in mortal fear of being hit again. At last they come to the sally-port and he is carried on a duckboard into the trench.

They give him the worst possible thing. He gulps down some rum, chokes, coughs blood, loses his breath; blood bubbles from his side, he is in the throes of death. He quietens. They give him water. If they can stop the bleeding he might survive. With a bandaged lead pencil they probe back his lung and plug the wound with a field-dressing and pieces torn from a greatcoat. They fix a tourniquet and bind his arm to a piece of duckboard. This completes their rough but honest first aid.[19]

Lording lost six ribs and his right arm and underwent many more operations before dying in a mental hospital in 1944.

By now McCay had virtually no reserves left. The Bavarians still had four battalions in reserve. Relieving Bachschneider's men just after 1 a.m., one of them attacked towards the Rue Delvas along the breastwork and ditches simultaneously. Arblaster screamed for bombs and bombers. Captain Murray further back motioned to one officer after another to head into the inferno with his men. Fewer than one in ten returned. The Bavarians' progress was inexorable. By 3 a.m. they were over the road. The 53rd Battalion was all but cut off. Arblaster knew that the only chance lay in a rearwards charge toward the breastwork. He distributed the last grenades, lined his men out and gave the signal. They crumpled in a hail of fire. Arblaster was shot through both arms and died of septicaemia in a German military hospital. The survivors crabbed back along the ditches to the Rue Delvas. Cries of 'We have been ordered to retire' and 'Our own artillery are shelling us' arose. The remnants of the 53rd broke. Sergeant Arthur Stringer rallied a dozen men and temporarily halted the Bavarians by hurling grenades from the parapet of the breastwork 'like cricketers throwing at a wicket'. Lieutenant Bill Denoon led fifty men along it. A massive bomb fight raged for the next hour, at the end of which the Australians had gained forty yards. At 4.20 a.m. Cass warned Pope: 'Position almost desperate'.[20]

Advancing through the mist at 2.30 a.m., the Bavarians swamped what remained of the 8th Brigade. A bomb shattered Captain Mills's hand and a German grabbed him, saying in English, 'Why do you not put up your hands, officer. Come with me?' Captain White ordered a charge to get back to the Australian line. He gave the signal at 3.45 a.m. Machine-guns opened up on all sides. Losses were severe and would have been worse but for the 8th Brigade's communication trench across no man's land, all but twenty yards of which had been completed. Half of Krinks's XI made it to the breastwork, where the Germans seized two of them. The others turned back and freed their mates with a flurry of punches. Krinks and three men reached friendly territory. White and many others had to claw their way back as well. Those who could not break through fought on until they were killed or captured. Lieutenant Waldo Zander of the 30th Battalion witnessed the end of a Lewis gun crew:

> After all the rest had fallen back they could still be heard firing. We could see the Bosche working in along the trench on both their flanks toward them, but they still stuck to their post and the gun kept firing. We saw some stick bombs thrown into their little stronghold – then silence!

Only Toll's men still held on but they had no bombs and their one machine-gun was smashed. They folded at 5.45 a.m. 'The retirement across no man's land resembled a shambles', wrote Toll, 'the enemy artillery and machine-guns doing deadly damage'.[21]

At 5 a.m. McCay and Mackenzie met Haking to plan the 61st Division's fresh attack. Monro was present. They had no sooner started than news arrived that the 14th Brigade's situation was critical and the 8th Brigade was back in its own line. Monro ordered a withdrawal. Thanks to another breakdown at McCay's headquarters, the order was not sent to Cass until 6.30 a.m. The Bavarians attacked again, startling Sergeant Archibald Winter of the 55th Battalion:

> God knows which way he came – we don't. He appeared to come from every direction. We were unsupported, consequently Fritz could come in on our own flanks. They had snipers everywhere and our own men were

falling fast. Then we got into close quarters with the bombs but we were only a handful and Fritz was there in his thousands.

Though wounded in the head, Captain Gibbins led several assaults to bomb them back. The withdrawal order finally reached Cass at 7.50 a.m. – eight runners were needed to get it through. He spread the word to use the 14th Brigade's communication trench across no man's land, the head of which Gibbins's party held. The inspirational Gibbins was the last to go. Finding the trench blocked with wounded near the Australian line, he climbed out and looked back at the German line. At that instant a shot to the head killed him. Corporal Williams saw those who could not reach the trench strike out across the open:

We were powerless to assist them, and had to watch them being shot down at point-blank range . . . It seemed an eternity of time until the lucky ones reached our parapets, to be pulled in by willing hands. No sooner was our field of fire clear than we blazed into the Germans who had lined their parapets to punish the retiring troops.[22]

The scene in the Australian trenches was burned into the mind of everyone who saw it. 'If you had gathered the stock of a thousand butcher-shops', Lieutenant Knyvett wrote, 'it would give you a faint conception of the shambles those trenches were'. Sergeant Martin saw 'dead bodies lying in all directions, just as they had fallen, some without heads, other bodies torn about minus arms or legs, or pieces cut clean out of them by shells'. Looking like a man 'who had just lost his wife', Brigadier-General Elliott wept openly as he shook hands with what was left of the 15th Brigade and assisted the wounded. Brigadier-General Tivey was 'quite overdone – with eyes like boiled gooseberries. The one thing he tried to assure himself of was that his brigade had done as well as those at Gallipoli'. 'They'll get used to it', McCay was overheard telling him.[23]

While the casualties in the front line could at least be tended, the plight of the wounded in no man's land was heart-rending. They 'could be seen everywhere raising their limbs in pain or turning hopelessly, hour after hour, from one side to the other'. Parched by the sun and tormented by flies and ants, they moaned for water or for an end to the agony. Unable to stand their suffering, other Australians crawled out to help. Private William Miles was looking for his officer when an English-speaking Bavarian lieutenant beckoned and told him to come back with an Australian officer to arrange a truce to collect them. Many were brought in while it was referred to McCay. Aware of GHQ's position on truces, he rejected it. Monro and Haking approved. The men took matters into their own hands, slipping out during the next several nights – 250 were found on the night of 20 July – to rescue their comrades. Sergeant Simon Fraser and his mates from the 57th Battalion had gone out to fetch a man from near the German wire when another man called out, 'Don't forget me, cobber'. He was also recovered. His cry became part of Australian folklore.[24]

Cruelty, humanity and tragedy intermingled. Preventing all attempts to save a man who had been blinded, the Bavarians let him stumble in circles near the Sugarloaf for several days before they shot him. Two Bavarians carried a wounded Australian to his own parapet, saluted and walked away. Unaware of what had happened, other Australians shot them. Captain Krinks and the three men who escaped with him went back to pick up their wounded and were returning with them when a panicky Australian sentry killed two of the rescuers with a single shot. Another Australian, hit through the arm, took food and water from the dead during the seven days it took to drag his wounded mate in.

With 5533 casualties, the 5th Australian Division was effectively destroyed as a fighting formation for several months. Considering that they had been incurred in the main over a twelve-hour period, these losses matched those in the British divisions hardest hit on the first day of the Somme. About 400 Australians were taken prisoner and the Germans paraded them through Lille to demoralise its population. The 61st Division had 1547 casualties. German losses totalled 1582, of which about 1000 were incurred against the 5th Division.[25]

Using Fromelles as an example of how not to do things, the great British military historian Sir Basil Liddell Hart decried it as 'the final link of an almost incredibly muddled chain of causation'. Chopped, changed, then stitched together at breakneck speed with more bits and pieces added, the plan was a dog's breakfast that Bean described in one of the best known passages in the Australian *Official History*:

> Suggested first by Haking as a feint attack; then by Plumer as part of a victorious advance; rejected by Monro in favour of attack elsewhere; put forward again by GHQ as a 'purely artillery' demonstration; ordered as a demonstration but with an infantry operation added, according to Haking's plan and through his emphatic advocacy; almost cancelled – through weather and the doubts of GHQ – and finally reinstated by Haig, apparently as an urgent demonstration – such were the changes of form through which the plans of this ill-fated operation had successively passed.

The British Official Historian concluded that failure was virtually inevitable:

> Even if the German defences had been completely shattered by the British bombardment, and the infantry assault had succeeded, it would probably have proved impossible to hold the objective under the concentrated fire of the enemy's artillery directed by excellent observation.[26]

The Australians, wrote Corporal Williams, felt they had been 'sacrificed on the altar of incompetence'. Elliott blamed Haking, who reprised his comment after the Boar's Head fiasco and claimed that the operation had 'done both Divisions a great deal of good'.

For most Australians, Haking was too far removed. Not so McCay. They lambasted him. His insensitive comments and rejection of the German truce offer confirmed his reputation for callousness. Though his defenders insisted that he was a victim of orders he could not realistically refuse, there is no evidence that McCay harboured any doubts about the feasibility of the attack. Indeed, he was desperately keen for his division to take part. Moreover, McCay's planning and conduct of the battle were shaky. His order to hold only the furthest line captured left the Australians without any depth and gave the Germans a free run along the breastwork behind them. The oversight that led to the 58th Battalion's suicidal charge also rested with him. McCay became the 'Butcher of Fromelles' and his headquarters staff was unwilling to work for him. As a result of soldiers' letters home, he became the villain in Australia too.

The finger-pointing was not just directed at the commanders. Contrasting the one thousand yards of German line they had taken and held for over twelve hours with the almost total failure of the 61st Division, many Australians felt badly let down. Yet again the British were not up to a tough fight. In many respects this was unfair. No man's land in front of the 61st was wider than in front of the 5th Division – on the outer flank three times as wide – and the defences facing it were just as formidable.

Describing the operation as 'some important raids', to conceal the severity of the reverse, the official communiqué also angered the Australians. Bean questioned 'the good of deliberate lying like that', because the scale of the casualties made the truth obvious. The Australian public saw through it as soon as the facts were known. From then on British official statements, which had usually been accepted at face value, were treated with scepticism.[27]

—EIGHT—

SOMME: POZIÈRES

On 10 July 1916, I ANZAC began concentrating in the Somme valley twenty-five miles west of the battlefield. Nearby Amiens, the district capital, was virtually untouched, its shops, cafés and theatres abuzz in the shadow of its imposing Gothic cathedral. Unlike the drab and crowded flats of Flanders, the countryside was undulating and uncluttered. A distant rumble and flashes on the night skyline signified the great offensive that the newcomers were keen to join.

Haig had hoped to capture most of the German second line, which ran along the Pozières Ridge, 2000–4000 yards behind the first line, on the first day. He thought that a breach might be opened through which the three cavalry divisions in Lieutenant-General Sir Hubert Gough's Reserve Army could pour to Bapaume, ten miles away. After the calamitous opening attack by General Rawlinson's Fourth Army on 1 July left the first line largely intact, the much less ambitious 'bite and hold' strategy favoured by Rawlinson was adopted. 'Bite off a piece of the enemy's line . . . and hold it against counterattack' was how he described it. Gough would tie down the Germans north of the Albert–Bapaume Road, an area dominated by the fortress of Thiepval, while Rawlinson bit and held localities south of it, the only place where the opening attack had got anywhere, in order to gain a jump-off position for an assault on the second line. These preliminary advances gained the necessary ground but were very costly. Amid concerns about the transfer of German reserves that prompted the attack at Fromelles, the assault on the second line was set for 14 July.[1]

Instead of attacking in broad daylight, as they had a fortnight earlier, the infantry would go in at dawn after the two-day bombardment ended in five minutes' 'hurricane' fire. This time Rawlinson strove for surprise. He resisted Haig's view that his formations were too inexperienced to approach at night and was vindicated when they had taken two miles of the German second line by 10 a.m. Exploitation beckoned but the cavalry was held too far back and the infantry commanders were cautious. The opportunity to capture Delville Wood and Longueval, and High Wood overlooking them, passed. Nonetheless, Haig was encouraged and ordered a third major attack. The Fourth Army was to take Longueval and the two woods and, with French support on its right, seize Ginchy and Guillemont to widen the gap just created. Stubbornly defended Pozières hemmed in the left but Haig thought that Rawlinson's advance would eventually turn it along with Thiepval. 'All that was for the present required on the left flank', Haig decreed, 'was a methodical, step-by-step advance as already ordered'. Freeing Rawlinson to concentrate on the primary attack, he made Gough responsible for it and reinforced him with the 1st Australian Division.[2]

In their training areas around Amiens, the Australians were absorbing the lessons of the recent fighting. They learned that successive objectives were now set so close that the infantry attacking one was still protected by the barrage when it lifted on to the next. GHQ tactical notes stressed that 'the assault must follow absolutely on the heels of the lift . . . This is a matter of seconds'. That meant troops creeping by night into no man's land as close to the enemy line as the bombardment allowed, so that when the fire moved on they could pounce before the Germans set up their machine-guns. Instead of every wave going to the final objective, as at Fromelles, the first wave took and consolidated the first objective, the second wave leapfrogging it to take the next objective, the third wave leapfrogging the second and so on. The newcomers also gathered that the Germans tried to isolate every assault with a massive barrage of their own, which led to prolonged artillery duels. As they practised the new methods, 'the grounding which many had previously lacked [was] to a large extent supplied'.[3]

The 1st Division started for the battlefield on 16 July, donning steel helmets as they neared Albert, the town one and a half miles behind the line that was the main base for the offensive. Its 7000 residents had mostly gone and the place was half-ruined and awash with British soldiers. Damaged by a shell, the Golden Virgin crowning Notre Dame de Brebières cathedral hung over the square like a diver about to leap. 'You could readily imagine that she had purposely leaned down over the street to bless the thousands of soldiers who pass and repass', wrote Captain Maxfield. The Australians nicknamed her Fanny after Fanny Durack, Australia's first female Olympic champion, who had won the 100 metres freestyle swimming in 1912.

After Albert came the march across the old battlefield, a riddled expanse of exposed chalk and clay that 'words cannot describe', wrote Corporal Moorhead. 'Unexploded shells, debris, equipment were everywhere among the shell craters and in the mouths of the smashed dugouts were corpses', said Private Dick Roberts of the 3rd Battalion. 'That which we took to be spongy ground that we were walking over was the bodies of dead soldiers.' Observing that many were sickened, his mate, Private 'Ned' Kelly, announced that breakfast was ready and reeled off an appropriate menu. Roberts was himself shaken when, souveniring some German dogtags, he was confronted by 'the grinning face' of their dead owner. Lance-Corporal Doug Horton of the 1st Battalion heard a British soldier call out: 'If you Anzacs can take and hold Pozières, we'll believe all we've heard about you'. Shells landing with a dull plop were dismissed as duds but men soon noticed a smell like mouldy hay.

It was their introduction to gas warfare. The Germans were using phosgene, which dissolved the membranes of the lungs.

On 20 July the 1st and 3rd Brigades took over trenches which, unlike the raised breastworks of Flanders, resembled ditches dug for drainage pipes. The shelters were holes scraped in the side just deep enough for a man to sit upright, precluding sleep. When dawn broke, Private Henry Hartnett of the 2nd Battalion looked about him:

Dead men lay thick in front of us, both British and German, mute evidence of the fierce fighting for the high ground around Pozières. In one place about a dozen British lay dead side by side in a line, a few feet apart. They had evidently been killed by the enfilade fire of a machine gun which had caught them as they advanced. It was impossible to collect their bodies for burial and they had to remain where they were until the village was captured.

Standing defiant, its hedges, orchards and ruins and the parapet of the OG Lines beyond were clearly visible.[4]

Rawlinson considered Pozières 'the key of the area'. Strung out for three-quarters of a mile along the Albert–Bapaume Road, it was an agricultural hamlet near the summit of the eponymous ridge. Gibraltar, a multi-storey concrete pillbox built into a dwelling on the road at the southwestern end, covered every major approach. At the opposite end, 'Old German' (OG) 1, the front trench of the German second line, crossed the road about a quarter of a mile past Pozières and OG2, the support line, went over 100 yards further back. The Windmill, the highest point on the ridge, rose just beyond it. Though the Germans only held the OG Lines for 500 yards east of the road following the attack on 14 July, they defied all attempts to bomb further. A switch trench called Munster Alley ran back to High Wood and the third line from their part of them. Pozières Trench, opposite it, ran forward to K Trench at the southwest corner of the hamlet. K Trench, in turn, went to the redoubt at Mouquet Farm a mile north and on to Thiepval. The surrounding fields sloped gently away, giving the German machine-gunners grazing fire in all directions. Pozières stood as a bastion. Supposed to have fallen on the opening day, the hamlet had smashed four attacks since. Its houses and the orchards behind them were in ruins, assisting the defenders even more.[5]

While stipulating a 'methodical advance', Haig's orders to Gough also directed him to capture Pozières 'with as little delay as possible'. A cavalryman like Haig, Gough had a natural impetuosity that gained him a reputation as a 'thruster'. Disinclined to act through his corps commanders, he liked to control operations directly. Seizing on Haig's instruction, Gough decided to start the assault straightaway. Summoning General Walker on 18 July, he told him: 'I want you to go into the line and attack Pozières tomorrow night'. With no time for a reconnaissance and the 1st Division not yet in the area, Walker protested vehemently and secured a 24-hour delay. Birdwood and White then weighed in and had the operation deferred another day. At this stage Haig heard about the destruction of the 5th Australian Division at Fromelles. He told Gough on 20 July 'to go into all details carefully, as 1st Australian Division has not been engaged in France before'. The attack was finally fixed for 12.30 a.m. on 23 July, when it would coincide with the Fourth Army's advance.

Walker objected just as strongly to a frontal attack from the southwest, the direction taken by previous attacks and that prescribed in Gough's 'scrappy and unsatisfactory orders'. His left flank, and the subsidiary assault of the 48th Division on some communication trenches running into K Trench beyond it, would be exposed to the Germans on the higher ground leading to Mouquet Farm and Thiepval. Walker preferred instead to attack from the southeast, where his left would be more sheltered and his right protected by III Corps's advance in Rawlinson's attack. Gough, who had not seen the ground, remained obdurate. Walker took forward Major Edward Beddington, one of Gough's staff officers and a close friend of the army commander, to explain both plans to him. They continued until Beddington asked him if it was necessary to go further. 'Not if you are convinced', Walker replied. Beddington agreed to recommend his plan. Gough came around. Walker recalled these days as 'the very worst exhibition of Army command that occurred in the whole campaign'.

Nor did matters end there. Gough envisaged the capture of Pozières over two nights, the attack on the first only gaining Pozières Trench. But a 'bite' this small would allow the Germans to reinforce the hamlet during the pause, resulting in a difficult fight through it. Birdwood and White believed that the Australians' momentum would carry them to the Albert–Bapaume Road, 500 yards past Pozières Trench, on the first night. Skirting the orchards at the edge of the village, a new trench, marked by the southern branch of the derelict light railway from Bapaume, formed a convenient intermediate objective halfway to the road. Gough again concurred. Walker devised a plan that applied the methods his men had been practising. The battalions from the 1st and 3rd Brigades in the line would attack in two waves, the first taking Pozières Trench and the second the new trench. Some of their sister battalions in rear were to go on to the road in a third wave while the rest stayed in reserve together with the 2nd Brigade.[6]

Thanks to the postponements, the preparations were thorough. Jump-off trenches were dug at night in no man's land to reduce the distance to Pozières Trench, which was up to 500 yards from the Australian line. Continuous reconnaissance resulted in so many maps that the officers 'unostentatiously' burned all but the two largest-scale sheets in order to relieve their bursting pockets, Major John Harris of the 3rd Battalion recalled. They also had intelligence on Pozières that covered every building. With 'two large, strong cellars, a dairy in the courtyard with a good vaulted cellar and a cold vaulted storeroom above that', Captain Walter Claridge of the 8th Battalion knew Monsieur Fourmier's house was 'probably the strongest in the village and likely to be turned into a fort'.[7]

The bombardment of the hamlet and its surrounds started on 19 July. Dense pink and grey smoke from the explosions shrouded Pozières, while jets of flame shot downwards from the thermite shells that were intended to set fire to anything left standing. 'The earth rocks and trembles from the sickening concussion – nothing less than the imagination of hell', wrote Corporal Thomas. Nonetheless, small parties of Germans were occasionally seen scurrying about. On 22 July, an attempt by a 100-strong party from the 9th Battalion to seize the junction of Pozières Trench and Munster Alley with the OG Lines before the main attack ended in a hail of machine-gun fire and bombs. The German artillery was not silent either, harrying the diggers of the jump-off trenches. A fresh regiment from the 117th Division held the western half of Pozières but, in the Australians' favour, a tired one from the 7th Division garrisoned the eastern half, on which their assault would fall.[8]

At dusk on 22 July the Fourth Army began the final bombardment for the main attack to the east. When the Reserve Army stepped up the shelling around Pozières at 10 p.m., the combined bombardment stood out even by Western Front standards. 'No description, however realistic, can give any idea of what it was like', wrote Private Jack Bourke of the 8th Battalion. 'The ground shook with the thunder of guns, while the whole battle line was lit up as bright as day with the thousands of rockets, flares and flashlights of every colour.' Covered by the fire, the battalions from the front line were in the jump-off trenches by midnight, sleeves rolled up and coloured tabs on their epaulettes for instant identification. Scouts stole into no man's land to lay canvas tapes 100 yards from the German line. At 12.10 a.m., the first wave edged from the jump-off trenches towards them. A few men were seen. Some machine-guns opened. Sergeant Preston was lying among the poppies:

I could see the bullets cutting their stems off right against my head . . . I lay as flat to the ground as possible, jammed the steel helmet onto my head and brought the body of my rifle across my face to stop anything that might happen to drop low . . . a man alongside of me was crying like a child and saying we will never get out of this. I kept replying yes we will!

Some Australians crept over the tapes to within thirty yards of the German line. The tension was unbearable. Those without watches constantly asked the time. Sergeant Ben Champion of the 1st Battalion could not stop urinating. At 12.28 a.m. the artillery began two minutes of hurricane fire. For the first time in their experience, the Australian gunners fired as fast as they could load. Dragged up the Albert–Bapaume Road to within 200 yards of the Germans, one Australian gun pumped 115 shells into Gibraltar. An unbroken sheet of bursting shrapnel illuminated Pozières Trench. 'The concussion made our ears ring' and it was impossible to speak to one's neighbour, wrote Champion. 'It is strange how men creep together for protection', he noted. 'Soon, instead of four paces between the men, we came down to lying alongside each other, and no motioning could make them move apart.' At 12.30 a.m. the artillery lifted to the new trench but the change was hard to see in the smoke. The three whistle blasts that sounded the attack were barely audible. Men saw their officers arise as phantom figures, took this to be the signal and 'hopped into Fritz with a yell'.

Pozières Trench fell with little resistance. Sixty Germans surrendered on seeing the rush towards them. 'All showed the strain they had been through, being shaky and rattled, and only too glad to be alive', Champion said. Too terrified to cross no man's land to the Australian line, some were shot. Private Archie Barwick's company in the 1st Battalion was still spoiling for a fight and joined the second wave as it passed through. 'On they went like a pack of hungry dogs now they had tasted blood', he wrote. Reaching the railway line, they discovered that the second objective, the 'new' trench, did not exist, except near the road. Not to be denied, the attackers pursued about thirty Germans who bolted towards the OG Lines. They killed the lot before slowing down near the Windmill, from where Sergeant Preston and two other NCOs brought them back. The chase unintentionally cleared a large swathe of Pozières for the third line, whose forward move had been disrupted by the phosgene and tear gas lacing the German retaliatory shelling of the rear area.

The only hitch was on the right flank. Advancing between the occasionally untraceable remains of OG1 and 2, the 9th Battalion took its first objective, the junction with Pozières Trench, but was pinned down by bombers using small egg-shaped grenades that could be thrown further than the Mills bomb. Private John Leak ran towards the German block, lobbed three grenades into it and jumped in when they had exploded. He was found wiping the blood off his bayonet among three dead Germans. Leak received the VC. Two machine-guns ahead prevented further progress. When the Germans counterattacked at 1.30 a.m., the Australians were driven back. The 10th Battalion stepped in but German bombers and snipers covered by the machine-gunners slowed them down. OG2 had vanished in the shelling but Lieutenant Blackburn, the man who reached Scrubby Knoll at the Anzac Landing, led seven rushes that regained 100 yards of OG1. Blackburn also won the VC. But the Australians were still 600 yards short of their goal, the Albert–Bapaume Road, and a 500-yard gap existed between them and the closest men in Pozières.[9]

By dawn, a continuous trench, four feet deep, its parapet built up with dead Germans and bristling with over twenty machine-guns, fringed the Albert–Bapaume Road through the hamlet. In the growing light, German snipers fired from the ruins. As the exhausted artillery on both sides had fallen silent, small groups of Australians moved through the hamlet throwing phosphorous bombs into the cellars and dugouts, where they thought the snipers were hiding. Forced out by the choking smoke, the Germans would be shot as they emerged, or chased and bayoneted. Having got their man, the Australians would sit down for a smoke while waiting for another German to flee. Private Roberts likened it to 'being out for a day's rabbiting'. CSM Fred Callaway of the 2nd Battalion took six prisoners, one of whom wore red crosses on each arm:

> He clung to me crying for mercy. I felt beneath his coat and got a dagger and a beautiful revolver off him. I pointed to his red cross and then to the revolver. He only cried. I lifted my revolver to shoot the swine, and he fell down and grabbed my knees, crying out for mercy. I hadn't the heart to shoot him in cold blood but he deserved it (any red cross man bearing arms is liable to be shot on sight) so I kicked him up and . . . sent them away.[9]

General Kuntze, the commander of the 117th Division, had laid down before the battle that 'not an inch of trench must be abandoned to the enemy' and every effort made, if he penetrated, 'to drive him out at once by immediate counterattack'. The first came at 5.30 a.m. as a battalion under Hauptmann (Captain) Ponsonby Lyons barrelled into the gap in the Australian line. Sergeant Preston had a grandstand view:

> The enemy came towards us like swarms of ants rushing from shell hole to shell hole . . . In our trench each man full of fight and confidence lined the parapet and emptied magazine after magazine. Men pulled one another down from the parapet to get a shot at them. The machine-guns caused great losses and artillery, which had been brought up, tore great gaps in the oncoming lines. The attack just melted away.

At 6.30 a.m. Hun hunting, souvenir hunting and digging resumed. Those who found *pickelhaube* helmets wore them; others smoked German cigars. Horton almost felt like he was on holiday: 'We lay on the parados of the trench basking in the sun. Here half a dozen would be sitting down having a meal'.[10]

The fresh 8th Battalion swept across the Albert–Bapaume Road that night. A man near Private Bourke crumpled and lay twitching on the ground. Hearing a 19-year-old soldier say 'Poor old Australia', Bourke murmured: 'A lot of meaning in that remark'. He entered an abandoned German dugout. On a nail hung a mug for 'a good boy'. Seeing cake boxes addressed in a child's handwriting and a bloody greatcoat, Bourke thought sadly of the fatherless youngster who had sent the cakes. He did not see a single German.

Patrols from the 12th Battalion further north saw a lot. Snipers had been a deadly nuisance for the 12th and Lieutenant Elmer Laing showed no mercy to those they rumbled. Seeing one of his men unearth a sniper, Laing shouted at him 'to shoot the swine or I would – so he got him'. Among the eighteen Germans from another dugout who surrendered to Captain Alan Vowles was the immaculately dressed Hauptmann Ponsonby, who introduced himself as the commandant of Pozières and explained that his grandfather was English. 'Tell him that he *was* the commandant', Vowles said to Laing, 'but that I shall be happy to relieve him!' The jocularity vanished with the distressing news that a stray shell had killed Captain Margetts.[11]

The Australians achieved the one solid success of the day. Either side of them the Fourth Army and the 48th Division made scant progress. Probably realising that the hoped for breakthrough on the Somme was unlikely, Haig turned to an attritional strategy. Local assaults were to wear down the Germans until conditions favoured a resumption of the wider offensive. On the right flank, the Fourth Army would continue grinding away at Guillemont, Delville Wood, where the South African Brigade had fought almost to the last man, and High Wood, which was proving an even tougher nut to crack. I ANZAC was to be the leading actor on the left flank. But the success at Pozières would make its role exceedingly difficult, for the hamlet's importance was such that General Fritz von Below, the commander of the German First Army, insisted that it must be regained. Fresh troops would make the attempt. The 18th Reserve Division was to be ready at 4.30 p.m. on 25 July, its path prepared by a thorough bombardment. At 7 a.m. the day before, 'Fritz commenced to return the compliment for the good times that our artillery had been giving his men for weeks past', Private Roberts wrote wryly.

For hour after hour the shelling continued. Men in the deep German dugouts were relatively safe but the majority were holding the newly made trenches. They constantly collapsed. Those left unhurt would dig frantically to extricate their mates. 'As fast as one portion was cleared, another was blown in', wrote Major Harris, whose own stretch of trench was being hit by four shells per minute. Of four men buried near Lance-Corporal Horton, one survived: his head burned, his leg broken, his arms and hands shattered. Evacuating him was impossible, so he lay in the bottom of the trench, which filled with eighteen inches of soil over the next hour. He sometimes groaned as it was removed and 'would at once turn to us and apologise for his weakness in not being able to stand the pain without a sound'. Forty-five year old Private Edward Jenkins, a renowned troublemaker in the 3rd Battalion, succoured the wounded, taking them across the open to a shelter he had built and giving them his water. A direct hit eventually blew him to smithereens. When I ANZAC finally arranged counter-battery fire at 7 p.m., the shelling eased, only to resume three hours later. By then the trench along the Albert–Bapaume Road was unrecognisable and the 1st Division was about to assault again.[12]

Gough planned to take the OG Lines astride the Albert–Bapaume Road, thereby securing the summit of the ridge north of Pozières, and then swing northwest along the crest past Mouquet Farm. He urged speedy action in the hope of cutting off Thiepval. Walker received Gough's order for the first step at 1.10 p.m. on 24 July. He was to seize a jump-off line beyond Pozières cemetery for a later attack on the OG Lines north of the road. Walker had already set down an attack on the 600-yard stretch south of it, which should have been taken at the outset, for that evening. Now having to make two attacks using the same approaches, he staggered the timings so that one would not interfere with the other. The 5th Battalion and part of the 7th would assault the OG Lines at 2 a.m. on 25 July, ninety minutes before the 8th Battalion, with the 4th bombing up K Trench towards it, headed for the jump-off position. On the flanks the British 1st and 48th Divisions would also attack.

Owing to the German shelling, few of the 5th Battalion's officers had gone forward in daylight to see the ground over which they would be assaulting. Supposed to lead the march up, the 7th ended up behind the 5th and most of it was late. The 5th arrived on time but could not find the starting tape. 'The shadow of failure already upon us, in groups, in threes, by ourselves, we crawled, none knew where as no direction had been given', Corporal Moorhead wrote. When the barrage opened at 1.58 a.m., at least the explosions indicated where the OG Lines were. 'Come on Australia, oaths and cooees and in a wild mob we tore towards [them].' The Germans had fled and the shattered lines were indistinguishable from the shell holes, from which heavy machine-gun fire came. Moorhead 'flopped in a furrow, and surrounded by the boys, realized we had taken a trench'. It was OG1. Two companies were to go on to OG2 but the confusion was so great that Captain Cyril Lillie stopped them. Another captain, 'filled to the neck with rum', roared 'Charge Australia'. Seeing some men go with him, Lillie led his forward too. German gear betrayed OG2. A German officer was brought to Lillie, crying. Lillie gave him his water bottle and said 'Have a drink'. Perking up, the German quipped, 'Thank you, Sir. Scotch I presume'. He had studied at Oxford.

The 18th Reserve Division did not take long to respond. After repulsing the British 1st Division's attack on Munster Alley, one regiment bombed towards the 5th Battalion's right. Part of another bombed down OG1 behind its left. In danger of being cut off, Lillie pulled the line back to OG1. Of the bomb fight that followed, Sir Arthur Conan Doyle later wrote:

> It was a most bloody and desperate conflict which swung and swayed down the long ditches, and sometimes over the edges of them into the bullet-swept levels between. Men threw and threw until they were so arm-weary that not another bomb could be lifted. If ever there were born natural bombers, it must surely be among the countrymen of Spofforth and Trumble and so it proved at that terrible international by Pozières village.

Stripped to the waist and covered in blood, a sergeant threw for an hour as German grenades burst all around him. One lad chased a bolting German until his throw could not miss. Covering the bombers, bursts from the Lewis gunners forced the Germans to throw from below ground level and shot off their hands when they showed above it. 'Bombs at the double – machine guns at the double – carriers at the double – more bombs at the double – strings of men going up', recalled another Australian. Part of the 7th Battalion, which had finally arrived, and the 9th and 10th were drawn in. The fight surged to and fro over forty yards of OG1 for three hours before the Germans withdrew towards the Albert–Bapaume Road. Lillie sent the officer prisoner rearwards. On leaving he 'stood to attention, clicking his heels Prussian fashion, and bowed, saying "Thank You"'. The Australians had taken only a quarter of the objective but their effort distracted the Germans from the later attack on the other side of the road.

It began badly but ended well. The divisional orders had set the operation for the following day, 26 July, and the mistake was not discovered until just before zero hour. When the assault started, the supporting barrage had already moved on. But by working closely with the Lewis gun teams, the 4th Battalion's bombers pushed 700 yards along K Trench towards Pozières cemetery, swilling German rum and coffee as they went. Nearing the cemetery, the retreating Germans were fired on by the 8th Battalion, which had advanced almost unopposed from Pozières itself. They yelled 'Mercy *Kamerad!*' but the Australians feared the presence of several hundred prisoners in their advanced position and kept on firing. Panic-stricken, the Germans took to the open and were shot down. The 4th and 8th Battalions met but the 48th Division's assault on their left failed twice and it did not link up with them until 4 a.m. on 26 July.

The 18th Reserve Division's counterattack on Pozières never got going. After parts of the division had been thrown in against the Australians early on 25 July, alarmist reports of a breakthrough led to other units from it rushing the Windmill at 8 a.m. that morning. A welter of fire met them. 'The range was about 400 and as each man appeared he got 100 bullets in him', said Corporal Moorhead. After its experience during the night, the 5th Battalion was hard-bitten:

> One unfortunate Boche having run the gauntlet of our rifle fire was getting away apparently only slightly wounded when one of our shells burst on him as though aimed, and he went up blown to pieces. Well, we cheered and laughed at the happening as though it was the funniest thing in the world.

Responsible for Pozières as commander of IX Corps, General Max von Boehn accepted that the cost of its recapture would be prohibitive. He abandoned the idea. But he continued the shelling to inflict damage and loss. The last traces of Pozières disappeared under the pounding. Only an ash heap six feet deep, pitted by shell craters lying edge to edge like the scratchings of gigantic hens, showed where it once was.[13]

'Until one has been personally subjected to such a thing, it really is impossible to conceive what it means', Birdwood said of the shelling. A French officer judged it to be as severe as the bombardments around Verdun, considered the heaviest of the war. Major Harris observed that the shells 'could clearly be seen in the last forty feet of their descent', which left no time to get out of the way. Small shells whined, large ones sounded like an oncoming locomotive and the explosions merged into a continuous ear-shattering roar. The ghastly sights as jagged chunks of flying red-hot metal effortlessly demonstrated the fragility of the human carapace also played on the nerves. Lieutenant William Joynt of the 8th Battalion was disturbed by 'the mangled remains of what had been a man – only the legs and portion of the lower part of the body remained'. Then there was the feeling of helpless vulnerability, unquestionably 'the most excruciating mental strain the war inflicted'. Bean expressed it vividly:

> Shell after shell descends with a shriek . . . each one an acute mental torture, each shrieking, tearing crash bringing a promise to each man . . . I will rend your flesh and pulp an arm and leg; fling you half a gaping, quivering man like these that you see smashed around you to lie there rotting and blackening. Ten or twenty times a minute, every man in the trench has that instant fear thrust upon his shoulders . . . and with a crash that is physical fear and pain to understand.

Eventually the strain spilled over into shell-shock, a neurosis causing psychological breakdown that was permanent in severe cases. Trying to stay alive in Pozières, Private Barwick left no doubt as to how easily it could happen:

> All day long the ground rocked & swayed backwards & forwards from the concussion . . . like a well built haystack . . . men were driven stark staring mad & more than one of them rushed out of the trench towards the Germans, any amount of them could be seen crying and sobbing like children their nerves completely gone, how on earth we stood it God alone knows, we nearly were all in a state of silliness & half dazed.

Some shot themselves. 'Expecting death every second', scribbled Sergeant Leonard Elvin of the 1st Battalion. '23 men smothered in one trench. Dead and dying everywhere. Some simply blown to pieces . . . Five left.'[14]

Strong leadership was vital. Champion saw Sergeant Rod MacGregor, a fellow NCO in the 1st Battalion, walking 'about in the open, unarmed, supervising, swearing, bullying, coaxing, whichever best served the purpose, and by his courage and contempt of shell fire, instilled into many wavering men something of his fatalism'. Major Harris marvelled at his commanding officer, 26-year-old Lieutenant-Colonel Owen Howell-Price, who was 'up and down the line all day, keeping up the men's spirits and setting them a magnificent example'. Captain Percy Binns of the 6th Battalion strode about, saying jovially: 'Buried? You're lucky you weren't hit'.[15]

On 27 July the fire increased so markedly that a German attack was feared. Lieutenant-Colonel Carl Jess of the 7th Battalion urged the artillery to pummel the OG Lines, in which the Germans might be assembling for an assault. When it did, the Germans thought they were about to be attacked and hit back with shrapnel and gas. Not until near midnight did this mighty artillery duel subside, by which time the 1st Division was past exhaustion. Its relief by the 2nd was completed during the weird calm that descended. Sergeant Edgar Rule of the 14th Battalion saw it come out:

> They looked like men who had been in hell. Almost without exception each man looked drawn and haggard, and so dazed that they appeared to be walking in a dream, and their eyes looked glassy and starey. Quite a few were silly, and these were the only noisy ones in the crowd.

The 1st Division had lost 5285 officers and men, a tally that did not include almost 400 shell-shock victims.[16]

The 2nd Division was to gain the crest of the Pozières ridge for the northward swing towards Thiepval. General Legge recalled that Gough exerted 'daily pressure' on him. Legge was conscious that his division, despite its Gallipoli service, had yet to fight a pitched battle whereas McCay's, the most junior, had already done so at Fromelles. He resembled McCay in many ways. Highly intelligent, he was prone to flights of fancy and never backward in airing his opinions. Once told that a sore throat had rendered Legge speechless, Birdwood jibed, 'I could imagine no more terrible affliction for him, and that would probably be the punishment meted out to him on the Day of Judgement'. Even though his men had only fully relieved Walker's on 27 July, Legge ordered the assault for 12.15 a.m. on 29 July. White allowed Legge's enthusiasm to allay his fear that more time was needed.[17]

Haste ruled. 'The 28th Battalion knew nothing of the position', wrote Major Arnold Brown. 'Not an officer or man had had a daylight view of the objective.' Though Legge confidently believed the artillery could destroy the wire protecting the OG Lines north of the Albert–Bapaume Road, obscuration from dust and haze hindered accurate observation by the gunners. As proper jump-off trenches could not be prepared, the northern branch of the old Bapaume railway had to suffice on that side of the road. It was 600 yards from OG1, too far to assault. Some advanced posts were dug to mark a start line halfway. It had to be reached just before 12.14 a.m., when a sixty-second hurricane bombardment was to start on OG1. In the first creeping barrage used by the AIF, the fire would then pound OG2 before advancing in three lifts to clean out the area 150 yards behind it. The Germans always lit up no man's land with flares at night. They stood every chance of detecting the move from the railway to the start line before the hurricane fire forced them into their shelters.

Aware from the digging of the advanced posts that another assault was imminent, the Germans plastered Pozières again. 'I had a terrible shaking', wrote Lance-Corporal John Cohen of the 24th Battalion. 'Two minutes before I was hit 50 [were] left out of my company 220 strong. When I was hit, 18 others were hit at the same time.' Part of the 24th in K Trench was annihilated. The 22nd Battalion also lost heavily. A fresh German regiment moved in. The units on the opposite side of the Albert–Bapaume Road also had a tough initiation. Assaulting the uncaptured stretch of the OG Lines there as soon as it entered the line late on 25 July, the 20th Battalion received a bloody nose. Next day, the 23rd Division launched the fourth British attack on Munster Alley. All the bombers of the 5th Brigade and parts of the 17th and 18th Battalions were drawn into the thirteen-hour bomb fight that followed. Throwing 15 000 bombs between them, the Australians and British gained only a few yards and at one stage the Germans penetrated the 17th Battalion's position.[18]

The Germans had the upper hand from the start in the attack on 29 July. At 11.40 p.m. their sentries saw the 5th Brigade getting into position south of the Albert–Bapaume Road. With flares turning night into day, their machine-gunners prevented it escaping the phosgene and tear gas barrage they called down. The Australians pressed themselves into no man's land until easing fire at 3 a.m. permitted a withdrawal. Across the road the 7th Brigade lined out along the railway and advanced for eight minutes towards the start line before being fired upon. They scattered across the crater field. The hurricane bombardment fell, forcing the Germans into their shelters. Staying underground only as long as the minute of shelling lasted, they emerged to rake the attack. Captain Walter Boys wrote of his company in the 25th Battalion: 'They fell around me like flies but on we went as if in a dream, while the smell of powder & din of guns, bombs etc, nearly turned my head. I reached the German barbed wire with some of my men but could not get through'.

Much of the wire was uncut. The Germans could see the Australians in the flare light frenziedly attempting to get past the entanglements, some trying to bash a path with their rifles, others using wire cutters and still others trying to wrench the stakes from the ground. They poured a hail of lead into them. The 26th Battalion was literally 'mown down', Corporal Peter Gaffney remarked. In the 28th, said Major Brown, the survivors 'ran up and down in search of an opening; others tried to climb over, but all failed'. When the last wave came up, it lay down behind the earlier ones, assuming they were lying prone waiting to assault. They were mostly dead. Eventually finding a few destroyed sections, Boys and others fought through to the OG Lines but could not hang on. Trapped in front of OG1, Boys played dead for twenty hours before crawling back 'almost off my head.'

Attacking the intersection of the Courcelette Road with the OG Lines to secure the left flank, the 23rd Battalion was untroubled by the wire. Staff-Sergeant Fred Hocking could not stop laughing at the sight of men, himself included, falling into shell holes. 'On and on we went, it seemed for miles', he wrote. The 200 men in the first wave with him had been whittled down to about forty before the first Germans were seen. The Australians were fighting mad. Hocking screamed: 'Stick the bayonet into them, take no prisoners'.

> But the Germans ran like rabbits. I saw them tearing back to their other trench. My greatest desire in life was to kill one. The dozen or so that were left set after them . . . Then biff, I was lying on the ground . . . The machine-guns having slackened a little, I looked at my leg. Little spurts of blood were coming out.

Crawling back, Hocking found the last two waves digging in on the Courcelette Road. It was so shattered by shellfire that the first two had not recognised it. Part of this new line was exposed by the 7th Brigade's withdrawal and had to be given up, leaving just a trifling gain to show for an attack which, together with the two preparatory days, cost the 2nd Division 3500 men.[19]

Haig blamed the failure on 'want of thorough preparation', which greatly annoyed him for he had warned Gough on this score. He impressed upon Gough again the need for close supervision of the Australians: 'Some of their Divisional Generals are so ignorant and (like many Colonials) so conceited, that they cannot be trusted to work out unaided the plans of attack'. As Gough was a favourite, he directed most of his anger at Birdwood and White. 'You're not fighting Bashi-Bazouks now', he snarled. Using a large wall map, Haig ran through the omissions, which he attributed to over-confidence on Legge's part. Birdwood stood like a stunned mullet but White argued back. Haig patted his shoulder and said, 'I dare say you're right, young man'. Yet Haig's ire was justified. As Bean said:

> The real cause of the defeat was that through an insufficient allowance of time for thorough preparation, the troops were forced to assemble in the open, and then, without the protection of artillery fire, to advance 400 or 500 yards against an enemy constantly expecting to be attacked.[20]

Legge wanted and was given another chance. He provisionally fixed it for 2 August. The darkness had hindered direction keeping and the identification of objectives in the first assault. Legge set the next one for 9.15 p.m., when they were still visible in the midsummer dusk. As this meant assembling in daylight, over a mile of approach and jump-off trenches would be needed to avoid detection. The artillery plan included 'demolition' bombardments interspersed with hurricane barrages to confuse the Germans as to when the real attack was coming. They replied in kind and also brought down bombardments whenever they saw the digging parties, which were mistaken for assault troops forming up. Digging thus became one of the most dreadful tasks the AIF undertook. Diggers were buried, dug out, and reburied – only to restart the work because the trenches had been obliterated. Lieutenant Alec Raws was with a 23rd Battalion digging party lost in the crater field:

> We lay down terror-stricken along a bank. The shelling was awful. I took a long drink of neat whisky and went up and down the bank trying to find a man who could tell where we were. Eventually I found one . . . so we went back and got the men. It was hard to make them move, they were so badly broken. We eventually made our way to the right spot, out in no man's

land . . . Our leader was shot before we arrived, and the strain had sent two other officers mad. I and another new officer took charge and we dug the trench. We were being shot at all the time . . . It was awful, but we had to drive the men by every possible means and dig ourselves. The wounded and killed had to be thrown on one side. I refused to let any sound man help a wounded man. The sound men had to dig.

. . . I was buried twice, and thrown down several times – buried with dead and dying. The ground was covered with bodies in all stages of decay and mutilation, and I would, after struggling free from the earth, pick up a body by me to try to lift him out with me, and find him a decayed corpse. I pulled a head off – it was covered with blood.

Legge was adamant the work must be completed. When aerial photographs showed that the 7th Brigade had made hardly any progress after two nights, he deferred the attack twenty-four hours to 3 August. White thought another day would be needed. He told Gough's staff. They fumed that Legge had said otherwise. White replied, 'Well you can order them to attack if you like', putting the responsibility squarely on Gough's shoulders. Gough approved a postponement to 4 August. At dawn next morning the Pozières crest was in Australian hands.[21]

Each using its own approach trench, the brigades assembled unseen. The first two waves continued into the jump-off trench. They crossed no man's land with plenty of cheering but little opposition as a three-minute hurricane barrage pasted OG1. Some Australians were within twenty-five yards of the fire when it lifted, catching the Germans in their dugouts or setting up machine-guns. 'The poor brutes were only too glad to surrender when they got the chance, which was not often', wrote Lieutenant Roy Phillipps of the 28th Battalion. Many in the next two waves followed the barrage lifts beyond OG2 because it was unrecognisable. Some half-buried posts of the old wire eventually revealed it, though the 27th Battalion failed to find the stretch leading to the Elbow, a kink 500 yards north of the Windmill, and returned to OG1. Twenty-one year old Lieutenant Percy Cherry of the 7th Machine-Gun Company rushed four guns into the gap that developed.

The initiative of the leaders overcame every hitch. When the opening barrage found half of the 20th Battalion still in the approach trench, the officers led it straight across the open. The retaliatory German bombardment dislocated the assembly of the 7th Brigade, causing the 26th Battalion mistakenly to enter Centre Way Trench and block the 22nd Battalion, which was leading the 6th Brigade in. Realising that the attack could hinge on whether the 22nd secured the left flank, Major Murdoch Mackay hustled it overland. Constantly losing men to the shrapnel pelting down, it reached the jump-off trench twenty-five minutes late. Barely pausing, Mackay yelled 'Come on, boys'. The Germans had time to man a machine-gun, the only one to engage any part of the attack directly. Mackay was shot through the heart but the 22nd went on to hold the left. A captured German officer remarked: 'They were in too great number to be stopped . . . fine lads'. The discovery that its jump-off trench was unfinished caused confusion in the 26th Battalion. Aware that its rear waves were still disorganised, Major Patrick Currie promptly took the leading ones on to OG2 in their place.

Such was the speed and violence of the assault that the Germans could not respond until 4 a.m. on 5 August. Cherry's machine-guns scattered a battalion of them bearing down on the Elbow in the dawn light. Urged on by an officer waving a revolver, the survivors dashed between shell holes and got close enough to bomb one of the guns before being wiped out. Cherry had traded shots with the German throughout. Their private war ended when they rose and fired simultaneously and Cherry, struck on the helmet, mortally wounded his opponent. He went over to the dying man, who took some letters from his pocket and asked him in good English to promise he would post them. Cherry agreed and the German handed the letters over, saying 'And so it ends'. Led by Captain Foss, two companies from the 28th Battalion located and occupied OG2 near the Windmill, which the 27th had missed.

All smiles now, Gough congratulated the 2nd Division for having 'inflicted a severe defeat on the enemy and secured us most valuable ground'. With the trees and rooftops of Courcelette tantalisingly close and the woods masking Bapaume in plain view further back, the Promised Land beckoned. Major Brown wondered 'why we were not sent further forward'. Private Arthur Whitear of the 24th Battalion saw German gunners get two field guns safely away. But Haig regarded the attack as just another of the attritional blows that were to continue until the next major offensive, which he envisaged starting in September. While they went on, Gough's army would play second fiddle to Rawlinson's, which had finally taken Delville Wood and Longueval. Haig also reaffirmed that Gough was not to push over the Pozières ridge but astride it towards Thiepval.[22]

Before the attack was over, Gough had typically begun pressing for renewed action. Brigadier-General Gellibrand, whose 6th Brigade held the northern flank, went forward to see whether it could immediately capture Park Lane, the next trench north. Finding that patrols had met stiff resistance, he ruled the idea out. Legge ordered him to attack that evening instead but the Germans rendered that impossible as well. If they were alarmed by the fall of Pozières, the loss of the crest had made them desperate. 'At any price [it] must be recovered', General von Below told von Boehn. He planned a more deliberate counterattack preceded by the heaviest possible bombardment. Already under fire from front and sides, the Australian salient was now deeper, enabling the German guns near Thiepval to batter it from the rear as well. Some batteries worked together, their fire crossing as it went in opposite directions and then returning to cross again. As the shells moved along, remarked a 20th Battalion soldier, 'it was like waiting your turn at the bar'. Lieutenant Raws epitomised the state of the men: 'We are lousy, stinking, ragged, unshaven, sleepless . . . I have one puttee, a dead man's helmet, another dead man's gas protector, a dead man's bayonet. My tunic is rotten with other men's blood, and partly spattered with a comrade's brains'. Raws would soon be killed by a shell. Captains Boys and Foss also died.

The 4th Division relieved the 2nd. Staggering through the bombardment, the incoming troops saw that 'scores of bodies had been partially buried in the soft earth, and bloody hands and feet protruded at frequent intervals. Boxes of ammunition and rations lay scattered about where fatigue parties had been annihilated by artillery fire'. Sergeant Rule 'came to know what that spongy feeling underfoot meant'. The shelling carved up the 48th Battalion while it searched in the dark for the 27th Battalion. But the 27th and 28th had pulled back slightly to avoid the fire, leaving the OG Lines north of the Windmill empty. Finding the Windmill also deserted, Sergeant David Twining set up a post on his own initiative to hold it. The 2nd Division's twelve-day ordeal had surpassed the 1st Division's. It lasted twice as long and cost 6846 casualties, the highest for any Australian division in a single tour.[23]

On 6 August the shelling rose to a sustained crescendo. At dawn next morning the fire lifted and three fresh German battalions started the counterattack that the bombardment presaged. They swept over lightly held OG2 and bombed several dugouts in OG1. The remnants of Lieutenant Jacka's platoon occupied one of them. His ears ringing from the explosion, Jacka darted up the stairs followed by his surviving men and shot the German sentry at the top. Seeing forty prisoners from the 48th Battalion being escorted back by a much stronger guard, he lined up the eight men nearest him, waited until the column was thirty yards away and charged. Half of the guards fled; the rest fought. Jacka recalled:

There were four Huns in a shell hole. All I could see were their heads, shoulders, and rifles. As I went towards them, they began firing point-blank at me. They hit me three times and each time the terrific impact of the bullets swung me off my feet. But each time I sprang up like a prize-fighter, and kept getting closer. When I got up to them, they flung down their rifles and put up their hands. I shot three through the head and put a bayonet through the fourth. I had to do it – they would have killed me the moment I turned my back.

The prisoners and other Australians joined in as the mêlée spread across the battlefield. Watching through his binoculars, Rule saw it develop:

I could see some of our boys standing up and firing point-blank at other men. Some figures I could see on their knees in front of others praying for their lives, and several were bayoneting Huns. It was one of the queerest sights I've ever seen – Huns and Aussies were scattered in ones and twos all along the side of the ridge. It was such a mix-up it was hard to tell who were Huns and who were Aussies. Each Aussie seemed to be having a war all on his own, and the issue was not long in doubt.

The Australians recaptured the ground they had briefly lost. So ended the German attempt to regain the Pozières crest. In the process of turning the tables, Jacka had killed at least twenty Germans and been wounded seven times, giving rise to widespread speculation that he would be awarded another VC. Soldiers looked up to him to the extent that the 14th Battalion was universally known as 'Jacka's Mob'. His superiors were less admiring for Jacka did not hesitate to upbraid them if he thought it necessary. They had the final say on gallantry awards. Jacka received the lesser Military Cross for what Bean called 'the most dramatic and effective act of individual audacity in the history of the A.I.F.'.[24]

—NINE—

SOMME: MOUQUET FARM AND BEYOND

Possession of Pozières crest enabled the northwards thrust towards Thiepval to get under way. The Australians were to advance on the intermediate objective, Mouquet Farm, with the British II Corps keeping pace on their left. Bean castigated Gough's concept as 'springing from an impossible tactical conception – that of forcing a salient gradually behind an enemy salient on a strongly fortified front . . . giving a bang with the hammer every day or two to drive the wedge in another fraction of an inch'. The width of the crest meant that the new salient would be much narrower than the one created at Pozières, restricting attacks to brigade or even battalion frontages. To avoid being skylined from Courcelette, the right flank had to keep to the lee of the crest, limiting frontages further. The German bombardments on them would therefore be even more concentrated.

Realising its importance as an outlier of Thiepval, the Germans held Mouquet Farm strongly. Two fortified communication trenches passed in front of its ruins: Park Lane and, a few hundred yards nearer the Farm, Skyline Trench. It ran past a quarry near the Pozières–Thiepval Road, which tracked up the shallow valley south of the Farm. Five hundred yards beyond Skyline Trench, the Fabeck Graben went through the Farm itself. A knuckle hid the Farm and the Fabeck until an attack was a hundred yards away.

Using this dead ground, the Germans could reinforce them unseen. They enjoyed the same advantage at High Wood, which had still not fallen. Mouquet Farm also boasted five sturdy cellars in which the garrison could shelter. Official War Office photographer Geoffrey Malins described it as 'the most wonderful defensive point that could possibly be conceived'.[1]

The 4th Brigade carried out the first attacks. At dusk on 8 August the 15th Battalion turfed parts of three German battalions out of Park Lane. But the 7th Suffolks from the 12th Division alongside were mown down. Its left flank exposed, the 15th had to withdraw. Gough extended the Australians' flank to the Pozières–Thiepval Road, giving them responsibility for the area. On the following evening the 16th Battalion took it, while the 15th reclaimed the ground it had given up. On the night of 10 August patrols from the 16th Battalion gained another hundred yards towards the quarry. Those from the 13th, which had relieved the 15th, crept along OG2 to a sunken road 400 yards east of the Farm. Counterattacks by battalions from two fresh German divisions, the 16th (Rhineland) and 24th (Saxon), on 11 August were routed, a welcome payback for the renewed agony the German shelling was inflicting on the Australians. It had been so intense that the digging of jump-off trenches for the assault planned on 12 August temporarily ceased. Badly strained, the 16th Battalion had to be replaced by the 50th, which attacked with the 7th Norfolks at 10.30 p.m. They took Skyline Trench apart from a gap at the quarry.

As the 4th Division had advanced a third of a mile in three and a half days, Gough's hopes of attacking Thiepval at the end of August were on track. The next step, the capture of the Fabeck Graben and the Farm itself on the night of 14 August, was thrown into chaos the evening before when the 48th Division, which had relieved the 12th, was ejected from Skyline Trench. Because an advance on the Farm would be enfiladed from there, Gough dropped the Farm from the plan. The 48th Division would retake Skyline Trench while the

13th Brigade, which had replaced all but the 13th Battalion from the 4th, seized the Fabeck Graben and the quarry. But the Germans had found orders in Skyline Trench for the original attack, which gave the Farm as the main objective. They interpreted any movement near it as an impending assault. On 14 August their artillery pounded the exposed Australian positions. The shelling was so brutal that shortly before the attack fell due, Lieutenant-Colonel Arthur Ross of the 51st Battalion informed Brigadier-General Glasgow: 'Both 13th CO thinks, and it is my genuine (not depressed) opinion that it would be a mistake to press the offensive further locally in this salient'.

Knowing that the 48th Division's assault would be endangered if the Australian one did not proceed, Glasgow directed it to continue. Heading off at 10.30 p.m. under a full moon, the attackers were seen by the Germans, who fired through the Australian barrage at them. The German shelling stepped up. Panicky confusion set in and both the 50th and 51st Battalions withdrew, though the 50th held on to the quarry. 'I have been to HELL and have had the luck to get back again', Captain Harry Armitage scribbled to his parents. 'I am not in a mood for writing so will stop to finish later.'

The 50th had not been able to contact the 13th Battalion, which was assaulting the Fabeck Graben on its right. Instead of falling on the Germans, the Australian barrage landed so far behind the 13th, Major Theo Wells said, that the German rifle and machine-gun fire was 'absolutely unchecked.' Captain Harry Murray led a charge through it that took 200 yards of the Fabeck. A distinguished Original Anzac, Murray had the foresight to station posts in OG1 in case he had to retreat. German counterattacks were already under way when he found out that the other battalions had failed, isolating his. Murray ordered a withdrawal. Carrying a wounded man on his back, he was the last to leave each post as his men leapfrogged through. The 48th Division took part of Skyline Trench but it was clear that Gough's advance had been checked. Having lost 4649 men, the 4th Australian Division would have to be relieved before it could continue.[2]

Over the next three weeks, the divisions of I ANZAC went in once more. With attacks launched time and again on the same narrow frontages, the advance degenerated into a repetition of the Pozières horrors on a smaller scale. 'God, it is frightful, frightful . . . Dead men everywhere', Corporal Thomas remarked. 'The stench, it gets into everything, bread, bacon, one's nostrils are full of it.' Sergeant Champion recoiled on seeing 'a row of heads and upright tips of rifles where a trench had caved in; the men had been smothered and then their heads had been cleared only to find that they were dead'. The putrid slope before Mouquet Farm became a surreal landscape of pockmarked brown that resembled 'a rough sea seen from the beach', said Captain Allan Leane of the 48th Battalion:

> Your horizon was the edges of a crater on a level with your head. When you wandered over from that shell hole into the next you came suddenly into a view of a wide stretch of country all apparently exactly the same as that through which you were plunging.[3]

Repulsing attacks was far easier than making them, as the 1st Division found, soon after it relieved the 4th. On 16 August, the Rhinelanders and Saxons charged and were shot away. Before the Australians attacked two nights later, Lieutenant-Colonel Howell-Price stood in the remains of a road cutting, the only identifiable landmark, to confirm the 3rd Battalion's position to his sceptical superiors. His message reached them too late to stop the supporting bombardment crippling its assault towards the Fabeck Graben. Last-minute changes to orders and heavy German shelling and machine-gun fire doomed a concurrent attempt by the 2nd Brigade to push beyond the Windmill. The attack was renewed twice but 'it was hotter than ever as Fritz had got his supports up', wrote Captain Percy Lay of the 8th Battalion. 'We fell back . . . as we had lost most of our officers and a terrible lot of men and we expected Fritz to attack us.' Hoping to gain surprise, the 3rd Brigade struck the Fabeck Graben in daylight on 21 August. Lieutenant-Colonel Charles Elliott risked the 12th Battalion becoming lost in an overland night march beforehand, in order 'to minimise the possibility of their being demoralised by the revolting sights they would necessarily pass in going up by the trenches'. The assault produced only another trivial gain.[4]

The 1st Division had now lost 2650 men and was relieved on 22 August by the 2nd. Carried out by the 6th Brigade, the next attack four days later concentrated against the western side of the Farm, thereby avoiding the open right flank that had dogged the assaults via the Fabeck Graben east of it. Brigadier-General Gellibrand chose to strike at dawn so that darkness covered the assembly and the advance began in light enough to see. But the German artillery hammered his men in the lead-up. One company of the 21st Battalion lost 96 men on 25 August alone. The Australians were also facing élite opponents in the 1st Guard Reserve and 4th Guard Divisions of the newly arrived Guard Reserve Corps. 'By far the finest Germans I have seen; the only troops I have ever seen taller than our own men', one Australian said. Gellibrand's attack silenced those who doubted the Farm had any underground works. The assault reached it and in some cases went further, only to be shot up from the rear by Germans emerging from concealed exits in and around the ruins. The Australians had to pull out. Lugging bombs up, Corporal Henry Taylor of the 17th Battalion was lucky to survive:

WOOF! WOOF! WOOF! went the shells, some in front, some directly behind us, while one would land directly in our path . . . a big shrapnel shell burst overhead. Peter received a pellet in the back of the neck and slumped down dead. On we went when, suddenly, a huge five-nine burst on the side of the trench; there was a scream as young Smith received a portion of the missile in the body – he died almost immediately . . . As we gazed a terrible sight met our eyes. A man was walking towards us from the direction of the front line, with the whole of the lower portion of his face shot away and all that could be seen was a big red cavity.

After losing 1268 men, the 2nd Division made way for the 4th.[5]

On 27 August bombing parties from the 4th Brigade attacked. One led by Sergeant Rule got lost *en route* to the quarry and watched from there disgusted as the supporting barrage missed its target. Rule said the job was impossible. 'It has got to go on', he was told. His men went thirty yards, found themselves nearly surrounded and withdrew. Heavy rain transformed the trenches and shell holes into a quagmire of 'sticky mud or soup'. The 13th and 16th Battalions slurped through the morass on 29 August, after being shelled by their own guns accidentally and by the German guns as usual, and took most of the Farm and the Fabeck Graben. Understrength at the outset, their rifles and Lewis guns choked with mud and bombs so slippery that the pins could not be pulled out, they were driven out by the best part of two Guards regiments using the underground workings to counterattack like ants from a disturbed nest. Captain Murray was at one stage brained by five knobkerrie-wielding Guardsmen. He shot two and the others ran.[6]

As part of an advance by Gough's army to assist an attack by the Fourth Army, the 13th Brigade tried next, at dawn on 3 September. As before, the assault initially succeeded. The 51st Battalion took the Farm but was eventually ejected in savage fighting above and below it. But the 49th Battalion held on to a chunk of the Fabeck Graben. 'This was the most fearful time of the lot', wrote Sergeant Daniel Scanlon. 'We were exposed to shell-fire of every sort, machine-guns etc.' Bombing alongside them, part of the 52nd under Lieutenant Duncan Maxwell was in dire straits until a company of kilt-wearing Scottish–Canadians arrived. The Canadian Corps had just entered the battle. Swapping stories about wheat-growing to keep from thinking about the German shells dropping around them, the Australians and Canadians fought together for the next two days. Their numbers dwindled from 350 to about 40. On 5 September, the 4th Division handed over to the Canadians and left to join the remainder of I ANZAC in the Ypres Salient, now used by both sides to rest tired divisions. The stretch of the Fabeck Graben gained was precisely that reached by Captain Murray's men three weeks earlier. The Fourth Army finally took Guillemont but failed elsewhere.[7]

'We have just come out of a place so terrible that my brain prior to this could not have conjured up anything so frightful', Captain Maxfield told his father. 'A raving lunatic could never imagine the horrors.' It made 'Hell as believed in by the ancients . . . a nice pleasant spot', said Captain Henry Davis of the 46th Battalion. In forty-five days on the Somme, the Australians had launched nineteen attacks. For most of the time they held it, the Pozières sector was the only one in which the British front forged steadily ahead. Often as not, it was the only active sector at all. The cost was 23 000 casualties. Virtually every survivor had shell-shock to some degree. For weeks afterwards, Jacka shook so badly on hearing the slightest noise that he could not sign his name for hours. Private Reg Johanesen of the 8th Battalion kept hearing the cries of the wounded for stretcher-bearers in his sleep. Their cockiness gone, the Anzac veterans admitted that they had been fighting in the minor league on the Peninsula. 'Anzac was a picnic compared to this', wrote the 4th Brigade's commander, Brigadier-General Charles Brand. If the prospects had been grim there, they were virtually non-existent now, a point eloquently made by Bean at the end of the ordeal:

> . . . there is only one way out of this war for an infantryman and that is on his back; either sick wounded or dead. There is no going back to cheering crowds – no marching through the London streets and ovations in Australian ports. They will be put at it to fight and fight and fight again – until, if not in this battle, then in the next each man gets his bullet . . . They are looking down the long straight road to the end – they can see it plain enough now, and they know that there is no turning.

The Australians had confronted the full power of modern military technology for the first time and the awareness cut deep. 'War is nothing but mechanical slaughter', trench mortarman Private Athol Dunlop reckoned. Corporal Thomas pleaded: 'For God's sake write a book on the life of an infantryman and by doing so you will quickly prevent such tragedies'.[8]

In the last letter before his death, Lieutenant Raws expressed his 'honest belief' that his brother John and many others were 'murdered . . . through the incompetence, callousness, and personal vanity of those high in authority'. His view was widely shared. Men asked whether capturing Pozières and the OG Lines were worth the cost, especially when the area beyond lay open after the attack on 4 August. Not being in a position to capitalise on the opportunity mocked the casualties. Bringing the divisions back immediately in order to batter towards Thiepval in what were nothing but secondary operations achieved nothing but further losses. Birdwood's popularity suffered as the conviction grew that he had willingly participated in a needless sacrifice. 'The soul of Anzac' temporarily became 'the arsehole of France'. 'He's a bastard of a man' was a frequently heard comment.[9]

Gough and Haig were also in the dock. Their employment of I ANZAC on the Somme evokes C. S. Forester's classic picture of the First World War generals, whom he likened to a group of savages debating how to extract a screw from a piece of wood: 'Accustomed only to nails, they had made one effort to pull out the screw by main force, and now that it had failed they were devising methods of applying more force still'. Gough was 'always for speed in trench operations, in which speed could only be of danger and of little value'. The Australians took to singing 'Take me back to Daddy Plumer's Army', a reference to the avuncular commander of the Second Army, whence they had come, whenever Gough visited them. They loathed him.[10]

Haig only enjoined caution on Gough twice, the second time after speed was seen to have contributed to the failure of Legge's first assault at Pozières. Thereafter, Haig's approach was 'hands-off'. As White remarked, 'They seem content to let each little lot plan its own attacks'. I ANZAC undoubtedly hit the Germans hard for at least six German divisions, including the two Guards formations, were relieved while it was in the line. Like body count for the Americans during the Vietnam War, GHQ treated the withdrawal rate of German divisions as a primary success indicator. But the three Australian divisions each did two stints, which meant that the Germans also saw six reliefs opposite them.[11]

I ANZAC's losses on the Somme amounted to the equivalent of twenty-three of the forty-eight Australian battalions in France. With the equivalent of another six written off at Fromelles, the need for replacements became critical and catapulted the conscription option into the spotlight in Australia. Following the manpower census, young Australian men in December 1915 were required to indicate their willingness or otherwise to enlist and if they were unwilling, to explain why. Prime Minister Hughes carried on a rousing call. The resulting surge in recruiting was brief. Enlistments dropped from 22 000 in January 1916 to 10 500 in May and an all-time low of just over 6000 in July, despite the stimulus that might have been expected from Kitchener's drowning aboard HMS *Hampshire*, which a U-boat had sunk *en route* to Russia a month before. Hughes himself was in Britain in the first half of 1916. He joined Cabinet meetings and, significantly, saw conscription adopted, which probably convinced him of the need in Australia. His return in July coincided with the first news of the losses at Fromelles and Pozières, which exceeded the available reinforcements. In August Colonel Robert Anderson, the Commandant of AIF Headquarters in London, advised that the British Army Council had decided to break up the 3rd Division, training in England under Monash, or at best borrow from it, to obtain the extra replacements needed.

Birdwood and White thought London had a hidden motive. 'The 3rd Division and apparent lack of reinforcements are being used to aid in forging conscription in Australia', White confided to Monash. In order to keep it intact, Birdwood and White wanted to bring two light horse regiments and all surplus men from Egypt as infantry reinforcements but the idea was rejected because the Australians were considered 'the keystone' of its defence. Their fallback was to seek greatly increased reinforcements from Australia. On 24 August the Army Council outlined the requirement: 16 500 instead of 11 790 reinforcements monthly for the next three months and a special draft of 20 000 to bring the divisions up to strength, including the 3rd Division, from which 2800 men were eventually taken. Birdwood and White had supplied these figures on the assumption that the casualties incurred on the Somme would be the norm. Though they proved to be much greater than the actual need, the government undertook to meet them, even though total enlistments since June only came to 16 689. Pearce told parliament that voluntarism was no longer adequate and Hughes announced the holding of a referendum on 28 October 1916 to decide if single men without dependents should be called up.

Many had already made up their minds. Those who had lost loved ones, or with loved ones fighting in France, invariably thought that allowing the unwilling to stay at home was unfair. Others could not bring themselves to send men off to be killed. Irrelevant issues also intruded. The 1916 Easter Rising in Dublin and its suppression had inflamed Irish Australia against Britain and gave a ready constituency to the Catholic Coadjutor Archbishop of Melbourne, Dr Daniel Mannix, who had 'a distrust of British motives in the war'. Accusations of disloyalty against Irish–Catholics and the animosity between Hughes and Mannix fuelled the tensions. Hughes blighted his cause by using the government's powers under the Defence Act at the start of October to call up all men between twenty-one and thiry-five for service inside Australia. It reinforced the views of those afraid of militarism, antagonised the much larger number inconvenienced by having to go into camp and raised the spectre that they would soon be in France. The referendum was defeated by 1 160 033 votes to 1 087 557, with three states also voting no. As well as dividing the nation, the issue split the governing Labor Party. It expelled Hughes, who took Pearce and twenty-four other members with him and arranged with the opposition Liberals to form a National Labor government with himself as prime minister. New Zealand had introduced conscription without any fuss in August.[12]

In the AIF the question tended to be seen more simply. After Fromelles and the Somme, many did not want to force others into the army. 'We don't want Conscriptionists here', Captain John Aram of the 57th Battalion said. That attitude angered others, like Captain Davis: 'The fools can't see that we must have them otherwise our men have died in vain'. For Sergeant Scanlon it was a military necessity: 'When we went in at Ypres 700 yards of front line trench was held by 100 men instead of about 230 men because we could not get reinforcements'. Aware of these conflicting views, Keith Murdoch in London warned Hughes before the referendum that a 'No' vote was possible. Aware that it would imperil the chance of a favourable result in Australia, Hughes asked a reluctant Birdwood to use his influence with the troops to induce them to carry the issue. Birdwood duly issued an appeal to 'The Boys' and postponed the poll for three days to allow its distribution and more campaigning, as the results in some areas where voting had already begun showed a 10 per cent majority against conscription.

The AIF result was 72 399 for and 58 894 against. According to Murdoch, the narrow 'Yes' majority stemmed from the Light Horse in Egypt, who were fighting the mounted campaign they joined up for, and the 3rd Division, which was yet to see action. He estimated that those on the Western Front voted three to one against. Where they stood naturally determined their response to the rejection of conscription at home. 'Disgraceful', raged Lieutenant Ray Evatt of the 20th Battalion, who lamented that 'the lowest class of people will nick to Australia to dodge it' in other parts of the Empire. Captain Armitage declaimed 'I am sorry to be Australian . . . and must now call myself a Britisher and be proud of that'. But Private Ernest Allan of the 49th Battalion commented that 'the boys are pleased it failed' and would have been sorry to see their mates made to join them. The defeat made the reinforcement of the divisions on the Western Front precarious for the rest of the war. For the moment Hughes suggested to the War Office that the 3rd Division remain in England to replenish the others. It disagreed: 'As already arranged the 3rd Division must proceed to France on 21 November'. The other divisions had returned to the Somme a month earlier.[13]

As Haig had thought the Germans were cracking in the lead-up to the September blow on the Somme, his concept for it amounted to 'the most grandiose vision for victory developed by any commander since Schlieffen'. If the attack, ordered for 15 September, broke through beyond Bapaume, as Haig anticipated it would, the First, Second and Third Armies were all to advance. For what would be their first big endeavour in France, the New Zealand Division had joined the Fourth Army. The New Zealanders' preparations were meticulous. Battalions 'incessantly practised the advance of assault waves . . . the avoidance of over crowding, the progress of small columns of supporting troops in rear, and the methods of communication with co-operating aeroplanes'. Tanks were used for the first time, some assembling at the Windmill. Together with the 41st Division, the New Zealanders reached Flers, a mile north of Delville Wood. 'A tank is walking up the High Street of Flers with the British Army cheering behind', the press famously reported. The Canadians seized Courcelette, the Scots Martinpuich, and High Wood also fell. Some 4500 yards of the German third line had been taken and twice as much ground gained as on 1 July for half the cost. But many of the final objectives were still over a mile further on. The unreliability of the tanks, the failure in places to use the creeping barrage lest it interfere with them, which left the infantry exposed, and the usual quick German recovery precluded any breakthrough.[14]

After the battle, Major-General Russell rued what he termed 'the waste' of the Australians and argued that they would have been better used alongside his New Zealanders and the Canadians. He was dead right. Gough no longer considered Mouquet Farm the key to capturing Thiepval. The salient I ANZAC tried to push behind it via the Farm became irrelevant for he had decided to attack Thiepval frontally. His reasons are unknown – perhaps he realised the lunacy of the original idea – but the change rendered purposeless the Australian effort and losses and justified the charge of needless sacrifice. Thiepval fell on 26 September to the 18th (Eastern) Division. In a final irony, Mouquet Farm fell shortly *after* its capture.[15]

On 25 September, the Fourth Army, with the New Zealanders again prominent, seized those parts of the German third line that it should have gained ten days earlier. His hopes of a breakthrough revived, Haig now envisioned a general advance to Cambrai. He had as much chance of reaching the moon. Cambrai was twenty miles off, five times as far as he had gone in the past three months. The advance would have to cross a valley from the high ground just taken and seize the trenches on the other side. Behind them, aerial reconnaissance had picked up Reserve (R) 1, another German defensive line 2500–3000 yards away that was anchored on Le Transloy, and R2 and R3 under construction either side of Bapaume. On 2 October the autumn rains began, turning the valley into a swamp and blinding the artillery observers. Far from being at breaking point, the Germans had brought up fresh divisions and more guns. With the odds stacked so heavily against them, assaults on 7, 12 and 18 October stalled in the valley. But Haig had no intention of stopping without anything to show, especially as the French did not halt their attacks. He justified the continuation of his own by saying their flank had to be protected and that a better winter line was needed. GHQ called on the divisions it judged most capable to launch them. The Australian divisions were on that list. But at least they would go back as part of the Fourth Army rather than the Fifth (as Gough's command was renamed).

At Ypres the Australians were absorbing replacements creamed from the training battalions in England to help replace the losses, and also raiding. They looked forward to a quiet winter. The orders for their return to the Somme arrived. Bean caught the mood: 'The men all looked very serious – sturdy and solid, but not the least buoyancy about them'. Joined this time by the 5th Division, I ANZAC began taking over the Flers–Gueudecourt area on 21 October. A fortnight earlier the New Zealand Division had left after completing twenty-three straight days in action, the longest unbroken stint by any division on the Somme, and with 7000 casualties. The Australians beheld a sea of waterlogged shell holes that started well before the old Pozières battlefield and extended beyond the front line two miles away. Marching up was a nightmare for men in sodden greatcoats that weighed forty pounds and whose soaked equipment felt 'like the load of Atlas'. Private Hartnett recalled a slog along a 200-yard stretch of communication trench:

> The mud grew worse at every step; no matter how slowly the men in front moved, those at the rear were hard pressed to keep up . . . Into this we sank, getting tangled up amongst signal wires that had fallen into the mud, going down to our thighs in many places. Perspiration poured off the struggling men trying to force their way along, step by step. The heavy breathing could be heard between their curses. Many were so exhausted that the tears ran down their cheeks and they sobbed like children . . . It took us fully an hour to struggle through that communication trench to reach the front line. The mud here was as bad. Everyone not on sentry duty was put on shovelling mud out of the trench, a hopeless task, for it ran back in at other points. Rain fell all through the long night to add to our misery. Morning showed the trench up properly. Every man was standing bogged over his knees in the mud, looking absolutely helpless. To sit down was impossible,

the banks of the trench were so wet and soft that they broke and fell in everywhere. The only thing to do was to stand up and sink down into the mud. Our feet and legs, which were clad in ordinary boots and puttees, had not been seen since they disappeared in the mud the previous night. The blood seemed to stop circulating where our legs disappeared out of sight, our feet being like blocks of ice.

The dead from the previous attacks were still in occupation. 'Hands and faces protruded from the slimy, toppling walls. Knees, shoulders and buttocks poked from the foul morass', Private Downing said. 'There was no hot food, and no prospect of it. We drank shellhole water, as it was too cold for the corpses to rot . . . We did not sleep, but waited in a torpor as the minutes crawled past.'[16]

After another attack on 23 October gained a few yards, the 5th Division was slated for the next one, scheduled for two days later but repeatedly postponed on account of the rain. Brigadier-General Elliott protested that the very idea of attacking was sheer lunacy; General McCay declared that he was not going ahead unless specifically ordered to by Birdwood. At a more senior level Lord Cavan, whose XIV Corps had been battered in the earlier assaults, told Rawlinson that he would not carry out the attack, now ordered for 5 November, until Rawlinson saw the conditions for himself. On doing so, Rawlinson agreed that the attack was impossible. Haig, who did not bother with such trifles as seeing the ground, said that it must proceed in order to help the French. With the 5th Division now relieved, the task fell to the 1st and 2nd Divisions. The 1st Battalion and bombers from the 3rd were to reduce a salient in Bayonet Trench, 500 yards north of Gueudecourt, at 12.30 a.m. In the main attack at 9.30 a.m., the 7th Brigade would strike the Maze, 2000 yards north of Flers, alongside a British brigade.

Lieutenant-Colonel Howell-Price was shot through the brain while supervising preparations for the first assault. Despite the rain, the Germans detected the attackers as they formed up in no man's land and drenched it with shrapnel, driving them back to their trench. The leading waves bridged the top with their bodies to make room for the supports crawling in underneath. When the assault started, they soon lost the barrage. Sergeant Champion watched as the Australians were convulsed by 'a hail of machine guns and bombs and we could see them moving from left to right in the very dim light, and the glare of the bursting shells, and they appeared to be trying to get through the German wire'. Badly lacerated, Private Barwick was stabbed in the leg while parrying his opponent's bayonet. 'A sharp stinging pain went through my body . . . but I kept my block and before he could draw his rifle back for another attempt I shot him dead'. Barwick was one of the few to clear the wire. Hung up in it, most men broke. Another try failed, forcing the withdrawal of the 3rd Battalion's bombers from their part of the trench. As no live Germans were to be left behind, Sergeant Arthur Matthews knew 'there would be some dirty work for somebody killing the wounded prisoners . . . and we had just got away when we heard the awful screams of the men who were being slaughtered through military necessity'.

The 7th Brigade's attack was a worse fiasco. Lieutenant-Colonel James Walker held the 25th Battalion back to wait for rations and it set off hours late when they never showed up. The guides got lost and only one company arrived in time for the assault. It joined the composite battalion that had been formed to take the place of the 25th in the meantime by robbing the other assault battalions of their reserve companies. A mix-up over timings caused the attack to start after the creeping barrage, so the 4th Guard Division, refreshed and again confronting the Australians, could fire with impunity at them. 'We couldn't hear ourselves speak for the crackle of the machine guns and the whistling of the bullets', said Private Bob Mann. Covered by enough mud 'to grow a fair patch of cabbages', Mann 'looked around to see how the rest of them were getting on. There wasn't anybody on their feet'. The British attack also failed.

On 14 November the Maze was attacked by the 5th Brigade, which had taken over from the 7th nine days before. It had been in the slough since and was in such a poor state that its commander, Brigadier-General William Holmes, had to borrow the 25th and 26th Battalions from the 7th Brigade. Barely recovered from their assault, they were now 'chopped about by our own artillery fire, which was falling fearfully short, and the Hun fairly mowed them down with m. gun fire and shells', wrote Corporal Gaffney. Observing from the flank, Captain Maxfield saw a remarkable sight as some of the Guardsmen charged the Australians:

> Curiously enough [their] efforts were quite superfluous because the attacking troops sank up to their waists in the mire and could proceed no further than the centre of no man's land. The Huns did likewise and the absurd position was created of scores of attackers and defenders bogged up to their waists in mud only a stone's throw apart.

Able to hug the barrage, the 19th Battalion and some British troops alongside took 500 yards of the Maze. Over the next two days, Holmes ordered the 25th and 26th Battalions to help by renewing their assaults but Walker and Lieutenant-Colonel George Ferguson dithered. The Germans counterattacked and regained their line. Gaffney angrily called for Walker and Ferguson to be court-martialled. Both were relieved, although, in fairness to them, Holmes's insistence on repeating assaults that had already failed without trying to ascertain why was hardly astute command.[17]

The November assaults cost the Australians another 2000 men. Though the Guards acknowledged that they attacked 'with much more dash than the average run of troops', the conditions were impossible: 'the worst ever known to the A. I. F.'. In terms of fighting efficiency, the Australians had gone backwards. Many of the replacements from England were not properly trained. In the 4th Battalion, Lieutenant-Colonel Iven Mackay would not let them enter the line until their deficiencies were rectified. The loss of so many leaders in the Pozières–Mouquet Farm attacks also told. Corporal Thomas gave as an example the lieutenants taking their platoons up to the line: 'they have no idea, they get lost and go stone mad, instead of bivouacking and then trying calmly to get their sense of direction . . . we waste time and valuable energy'. On the basis of their overall record on the Somme, though, the Australians 'were recognised as among the finest fighting machines at the disposal of the British High Command'. Major-General Launcelot Kiggell, Haig's chief of staff, included all the Australian divisions in that exclusive category of divisions 'which, if [GHQ] gave them a thing to do, would do it'.[18]

On 13 November, the Fifth Army attacked the Ancre heights and captured Beaumont Hamel and Beaucourt. They should have fallen on 1 July, 116 days earlier. As there had been little fighting in this sector since then, most of the ground, though sodden, was not so ravaged by shelling, which made for better going. Haig had the success he wanted to strengthen his hand at the Inter-Allied conference at Chantilly on 16 November that was to formulate strategy for 1917. Agreeing there to resume the Somme offensive when good weather returned in the New Year, Haig closed it down. The BEF had lost 432 000 men in advancing seven miles, or about one man per inch, over four and a half months. It inflicted 230 000 German casualties, or one German for about every two of its own. Using attritional methods at Verdun, the Germans in comparison lost 337 000 to the French 370 000. Bean commented sardonically that 'to argue Haig's method was right surely involves the complacent assumption of an extraordinarily low standard of efficiency'. The Germans might have been less able to afford the losses but Haig was wearing out his army twice as fast as theirs.[19]

The Somme's demands on the Germans forced General Falkenhayn to suspend operations at Verdun in mid-July. As one of the reasons for the Somme battle was to relieve the pressure on the

French there, that decision made its continuation into October, when there was no hope of success, unjustified. By then the French were in any case well on their way to recapturing the ground they had lost at Verdun. Dismissed for the failure of his Verdun strategy, Falkenhayn presided over the brilliant three-month campaign that all but overran Romania, which the initial success of the Brusilov offensive had encouraged to join the war on the Allied side. In Britain 1916 ended with the energetic Lloyd George replacing the lacklustre Asquith as prime minister, at the head of a new Conservative-dominated coalition. He promised a fight 'to a finish, to a knockout', but without a repetition of the Somme. For the Australians the Somme had been so dreadful that it cast a shadow over established beliefs for some. 'My God, why hast thou forsaken me?' asked medic Private Fred Brown. 'Prayer had meant for me a fruitful relationship with the unseen world of the spirit. But something had happened which made the power of that world seem pitifully weak and ineffective.'[20]

—TEN—

CHASING FRITZ

The winter of 1916 to 1917 was the severest in France for forty years. For the Australians in front of Flers and Gueudecourt, wrote Corporal Moorhead,

> Sleep was impossible. Through sheer exhaustion one dozed standing up. Owing to the muddy nature of the trench, dugouts could not be dug, tho' here and there a man was able to scratch out a ledge to sit on. With our feet and ankles in water for days at a stretch, we began to suffer. One or two became delirious, others groaned with pain, as rheumatism or cold began to take effect . . . Standing stock still to the knees in mud and water, leaning against the parapet of mud, drenched to the skin with rain, fed on cold rations, movement was practically impossible, and if one moved the mud practically held you to the spot and being very weak, every effort was a pain.

Temperatures dropped to five degrees Fahrenheit. Men warmed their hands by thrusting them into their crutches. Private Alfred Binskin of the 20th Battalion saw one man die while sitting at his post. The muddy trench walls often collapsed, engulfing the nearest occupants in slimy ooze. Lieutenant Ronald McInnis of the 53rd Battalion felt his helmet rip the skin from his forehead as it was forced downward, and his head press into his chest, around which 'it was as though an iron band were tightening, preventing any movement'. But the chief danger was trench foot, a form of frostbite in which, said Private Hartnett, 'the feet became very inflamed and painful, turning a deep red colour and swelling much above their normal size'. They then became 'burning hot' and even the slightest touch was agonising. In the worst cases, 'the flesh turned black and gradually decayed away from the bones'. Amputation became necessary as gangrene set in.

Covering the few miles to the trenches took all night, with numerous slides off the slippery tracks into the shell holes. If a man became stuck in the mud, he drowned or died of exposure unless found by rescue teams, who often had to use mules and ropes to drag him out. The struggle forward frequently defeated the ration parties, leaving those up front hungry. Several relays of stretcher-bearers, each up to eight men strong, were needed to get a wounded man to an advanced dressing station. Brigadier-General Duncan Glasfurd of the 12th Brigade died in the ten hours it took to get him back.[1]

This period represented the bottom of the morale curve for the AIF. Several men shot themselves, malingering increased and one or two deserted to the enemy. Coming from a much warmer climate, the Australians suffered from the conditions more than most but they could also have done more to alleviate them. In November the divisions were losing 200 men weekly to trench foot and the 5th Division had the highest incidence in the Fourth Army. Birdwood reprimanded McCay, telling him that Rawlinson was considering declaring it ineffective, which 'every one of us would regard as a disgrace'. He also reminded every platoon and company commander that 'his thoughts and efforts should always be to look after his men first'. Though Birdwood's appeal offended, the reluctance of many junior officers to 'mother' made it necessary. They began checking that their men regularly aired their feet and rubbed them with whale oil, that they wore dry socks, that their boots were unlaced at the top, that they discarded puttees, that they loosely wrapped sandbags around their ankles. As the supervision increased, trench foot declined.[2]

During the offensive, keeping ammunition up to the guns had been the priority for transport. Now that it was over, the priority switched to engineering materials. A great effort also went into repairing roads and laying duckboard tracks as close as possible to the line, so that timber and iron for dry standing, revetting and dugouts could be brought up more easily. Warm, waterproof clothing became available, including 65 000 sheepskin jackets sent from Australia. Battalions did only short stints in the trenches and, thanks largely to White, received hot food and canteen stores whilst there and returned to Nissen hutments and recreational facilities set up in the rear. Morale rose. When the ground froze over with the severe New Year frosts, ending the hardships caused by the mud, it improved further. The Australians still missed one thing dear to them. 'We all wish we could see the sun that we have not seen since October last', wrote Sergeant Rupert Baldwin of the 27th Battalion in February 1917.[3]

All the Australian divisions were in the line because the Fourth Army's front had been extended in preparation for the renewal of the Somme offensive in spring. On Rawlinson calling for a more aggressive policy beforehand, the 15th Battalion took Stormy Trench, a salient northeast of Gueudecourt, on 1 February but could not hold it owing to feeble artillery support and a fierce German barrage that precluded any resupply of bombs. Despite receiving only twenty-four hours' notice, the 13th Battalion left as little as possible to chance in a second attack three nights later. Every man carried six bombs, twenty carriers with 480 more trailed each company, and a reserve of 20 000 bombs was stockpiled well forward. The artillery commander worked from the battalion headquarters to ensure the close co-ordination of fire support, one of the first times this had been done in the AIF. Such was the enthusiasm that eight men deferred leave to participate. Racked with influenza, Captain Harry Murray refused to be evacuated, telling the doctor: 'I'm going to take Stormy Trench, and what's more, let me tell you, I'm going to keep it'.

Murray kept his word. The barrage was perfect and the assault threw the Germans out. But one counterattack followed another. In what he called 'the most stubborn fighting I have ever witnessed', Murray's men broke the German bombers, occasionally taking to the parapet to pelt them or running across the open to bayonet them. Despite intense German shelling, the bomb supply never faltered. In all, the 13th Battalion took 400 yards of trench but of the 140 who attacked with Murray, only 48 were left. He had led bombing parties and bayonet charges, at one stage shooting three Germans and capturing three, as well as carrying wounded, in a reprise of his performance at Mouquet Farm. Given the Distinguished Service Order then, he was awarded the VC now.[4]

As the fighting hotted up, several command changes occurred. Convinced that Australian senior officers had gained enough experience by now, the Australian government pressed Birdwood to appoint them to any vacant commands. So when General Cox left for the India Office in London, he handed over the 4th Division to Major-General Holmes, formerly the commander of the 5th Brigade and the AN&MEF before that. His standing in the 5th Division irreparably damaged by Fromelles, McCay was jettisoned at the start of January 1917. The excuse was the leg wound he sustained at Krithia. Though slight, it troubled him thereafter. Taking over the AIF training depots in England, McCay was succeeded by Major-General Hobbs, the 1st Division's chief gunner. Legge became a scapegoat for the Pozières losses. When he was evacuated to England with a timely bout of influenza in December, Major-General Smyth, VC, the British commander of the 1st Brigade, replaced him as Birdwood considered no suitable Australians were left. Legge became the chief of the general staff in Australia. The upswing in the mood of both the 2nd and the 5th Divisions was quickly noticed. So were the misgivings when the Australians returned to Gough's army in mid-February for the spring offensive. But it was no longer going to be a resumption of the Somme battle.[5]

With the cry of 'No more Sommes' reverberating across France, the French government was not going to allow a rerun. Disillusionment over the campaign's meagre results had engulfed the Commander-in-Chief, General Joseph Joffre, who was also blamed for French losses that amounted to one casualty for nearly every minute of the war thus far. General Robert Nivelle, who had commanded several successful counterattacks at Verdun, replaced him. Nivelle planned to attack the Chemin des Dames heights, above the Aisne, on 16 April on a thirty-mile front with three French armies. Other French forces and the BEF were to draw in German reserves with subsidiary attacks along the eighty-mile front running northwards to Arras. An oily English-speaking charmer, Nivelle promised to deliver within forty-eight hours the breakthrough that had eluded Joffre and Haig. This was music to the ears of Lloyd George, who considered the Somme 'a bloody and disastrous failure' and Haig 'brilliant – to the top of his army boots'. At the Calais Conference on 26 February he subordinated Haig to Nivelle.[6]

Lloyd George had other worries. It was already clear that the BEF could not be maintained at full strength even with conscription. The rules for exemption were tightened and the Women's Auxiliary Army Corps created to release fit uniformed men for front-line service. Extra troops were also sought from the Dominions. Having threatened the disbandment of the 3rd Division to sustain the other Australian formations a few months earlier, Britain now asked Australia for a sixth division. The about-turn embarrassed the Australian government, which was having enough trouble keeping up recruitment for the AIF as it stood. It agreed nonetheless. The 16th Brigade was formed in England from returning wounded as a first step. Also asked for another division, the New Zealanders raised another brigade and added it to their existing division.

On the other side of the hill, the victorious Eastern Front duo of Marshal Paul von Hindenburg and General Erich Ludendorff had replaced von Falkenhayn in August 1916. Though officially First Quartermaster-General, Ludendorff was the de facto commander-in-chief and stood for 'complete and ruthless mobilisation of all German resources in order to win a decisive victory'. It had to be achieved quickly because Germany was feeling the pinch from the British naval blockade and the Allies' greater resources. Unrestricted submarine warfare, abandoned after the outcry caused by the *Lusitania*'s sinking, seemed the best bet. Convinced by the German Admiralty that if it were resumed, Britain would starve within six months, Ludendorff urged its adoption. America was bound to declare war on Germany because its ships would be sunk but he believed that the war could be won before American strength told. Aware that this escalation precluded any hope of a negotiated peace, the moderate Chancellor, Theo von Bethmann-Hollweg, sought to capitalise on President Woodrow Wilson's isolationism and instigated a peace offer soon after the crushing of Romania. To avoid any impression of German weakness, Ludendorff insisted on the timing and that the offer must be harshly couched. It was rejected out of hand. Like other Allied troops, the Australians derided terms that would make their sacrifices futile. Mediation attempts by Wilson failed. On 1 February the U-boat campaign began. Germany's land strategy was overhauled to fit in with it.[7]

Coming from the Eastern Front, whose vast distances encouraged fluid battles, Ludendorff did not believe that ground should be held regardless of cost. At the end of September 1916, work started on the Hindenburg Line, which ran across the base of the great German salient jutting westwards between Arras and Soissons. Seventy miles long and up to thirty miles behind the front line, it would form either a backstop if the line on the Somme gave way or a new line to which the Germans could voluntarily withdraw. Though the Somme offensive had been held, Ludendorff anticipated its renewal. As his armies were badly overstretched from having to fight on practically every front, a retirement to the Hindenburg Line made good sense. The resultant thirty-mile shortening of his line on the Western Front would yield thirteen spare divisions. British and French offensive preparations for the Somme or elsewhere would be disrupted, leaving the Germans better able to absorb the blow when it came. In the meantime, the U-boats, if they had not already secured victory, would have done enough to make a decisive counterblow possible. Given the green light on 4 February, the withdrawal was to begin in mid-March when the Hindenburg Line was nearly finished.[8]

A preliminary move eliminated the awkward wedge created by the Somme offensive and left Gough's Fifth Army, which was to thrust northeastwards in order to draw the Germans away from the strike by the First and Third Armies at Arras, swinging at thin air. The Australians were preparing to attack the Maze and its offshoots, Gird and Bayonet Trenches, as part of Gough's initial advance, when the Germans withdrew towards Bapaume on 23 February. They gained a clean break, partly because of heavy fog but also because the signs went unnoticed for thirty-six hours.

Units treated the discovery that the line opposite was empty as a local matter and did not pass the information upwards. Brigadier-General Robert Smith of the 5th Brigade reckoned that the Germans were simply abandoning muddy positions. Gellibrand, temporarily commanding the 2nd Division, suspected that the quietness was due to a relief being carried out. Focussed on the small patch of mud in front of them for the past few months, commanders had lost sight of wider considerations. Australian morale skyrocketed when a prisoner captured on 24 February confirmed that the Germans were withdrawing and that a retirement all the way to the Hindenburg Line was in prospect. GHQ knew of the line but assumed until then that it was just another reserve position to which the Germans would retire if forced. Though an expeditious follow up was called for, Haig suspected that they might be luring him forward with a view to counterattacking. Not wanting to disrupt preparations for the Arras offensive either, he ordered caution.

By midday on 25 February, it was clear that the Germans had withdrawn along most of I ANZAC's line. The Maze, Gird, Bayonet and other trenches, as well as Warlencourt beyond them, were taken. Prisoners revealed that they were holding the R1 and R2 systems as their first and second lines before Bapaume. On 26 February much of the outpost line in front of R1 was captured as the Germans leapfrogged back ahead of the 3rd Brigade. But Malt Trench, on the left of the outpost line, stood firm. Believing that it was lightly garrisoned, as was the case elsewhere, and urged on by I ANZAC, Gellibrand had told the 5th and 6th Brigades to occupy it 'unless proved to be strongly held by enemy'. Both prudence and haste were implied and a shambles resulted. As it joined the Loupart Bastion, a spur shielding the Loupart Wood sector of R1 on the heights west of Bapaume, Malt Trench was indeed strongly held. Finding intact wire at the end of their half-mile advance, the Australians were repulsed. An attempt by the 5th Brigade next day and several more on 27–28 February by the 7th also failed.

Two days were allotted for the guns to cut the wire that had stopped the attacks. Few gaps had been opened when the 5th and 7th Brigades assaulted on 2 March but they sufficed for them to swarm into Malt Trench, bomb the Germans out and capture the Loupart Bastion. The Australians had now advanced up to three miles and were closed up on R1, to which the Germans had withdrawn across the whole of the Fifth Army's front. Allowing time for a thorough bombardment, Gough intended to attack it on 13 March. On the eve of the assault R1 fell quiet. The Germans had gone.

'Chasing Fritzes is the best sport I have had for some time', enthused Lance-Corporal Herbert Akhurst of the 20th Battalion. With II Corps advancing on its left, the 2nd Division occupied Grévillers village, a mile east of vacated Loupart Wood, in which orders were found suggesting that the main retirement to the Hindenburg Line had already started. Thick smoke rising from Bapaume and the villages behind it, a surge in train movements eastwards, and the commencement of withdrawals before the Fourth Army and the French all supported that conclusion. At 4 a.m. on 17 March Australian patrols found R2, which was to have been the objective of Gough's next big blow, empty. They reckoned it had been vacated thirty minutes before. Shortly afterwards the 30th Battalion was chasing the Germans though the smoking streets of Bapaume.[9]

'Fritz waits until we are ready to have a go and then clears out', wrote Captain William Braithwaite of the 22nd Battalion, acknowledging the reality of the withdrawal. 'If papers talk about our driving him back it is all rot. We are following him up.' The Germans had twice avoided Gough's blows and got away unmolested. Extensive demolitions helped them. All roads were cratered and mined, observed the 8th Battalion's chaplain, Joseph Booth. 'Any bridges have been destroyed, while the culverts have been broken up by the use of judicious bombs.' Following a scorched earth policy, the Germans had also left nothing that might be useful for their pursuers. 'All the fruit trees in the orchards are cut down close to the ground', said Lieutenant McInnis, 'houses are burnt and destroyed by mines . . . telegraph poles are cut down and the insulators smashed'. Captain Louis Roth of the 22nd Battalion saw that every well was 'either poisoned or filled with rubbish and manure'. Lethal booby traps abounded. Prized souvenirs like *pickelhaube* helmets were usually wired to an explosive. On 25 March a delayed action device obliterated Bapaume Town Hall, one of the few buildings left standing. 'Fritz is a dirty dog', remarked Braithwaite, 'the lowest of the low'.[10]

Still worried that the Germans might counterattack, Haig remained cautious. He wanted every chance of maintaining pressure on them taken but only if minimum forces could be used. Subject to these constraints, the Fifth Army was to close on the Hindenburg

Line as soon as possible in order to help the Arras offensive. Though the withdrawal had nullified the original plan of drawing the Germans away from Arras, Gough saw that by breaching the line in the Bullecourt–Quéant area eight miles distant, he could swing northward against their flank while they were fending off the main attack by General Sir Edmund Allenby's Third Army from the west. Gough told each of his forward divisions to furnish all-arms columns as advanced guards to clear the way.

Chosen because of their dynamic leadership, Gellibrand and Elliott led those from the 2nd and 5th Australian Divisions. The columns comprised their own brigades, each augmented by an artillery battery and some light horse. Dotted by the occasional wood or village, the green Bapaume plateau stretched ahead of them, blighted only by R3. Behind it, in 'outpost' villages a mile or two from the Hindenburg Line, was the German rearguard, tasked to impose as much delay as possible. Elliott had drilled his brigade in envelopment, which was tailor-made for overcoming its widely separated positions. At daybreak on 18 March the Australian columns headed out through showers and snow squalls on a five-mile front, Gellibrand's from the north of Bapaume and Elliott's from the south.

Exhilarating though it was, the open country also engendered a feeling of nakedness. Elliott's men took cover at the sound of distant firing and then gravitated towards it, abruptly changing the direction of the advance. These weaknesses marred the capture of Frémicourt, the first village they struck. But when fired on from Delsaux Farm in R3 a few hours later, they enveloped it and the defenders withdrew, leaving behind a copy of the rearguard's orders. Next day Elliott gave each of his leading companies an axis from which it was not to stray, correcting the directional problem. The Germans were manoeuvred out of Beugny, Lebucquière and Vélu and Vélu Wood. On 20 March the 59th Battalion fanned across a wide front to take Morchies and the 60th, supported by the field battery, enveloped

Beaumetz. As Elliot's column was now three miles ahead of the British on its right and facing the outpost villages of Doignies, Louverval and Hermies, General Hobbs ordered it to halt.

The breather gave the Germans a chance to retake Beaumetz. On 23 March they almost succeeded. Elliott went ballistic. Bellowing 'I'll teach the bastards to attack me', he ordered an immediate assault on Doignies and Louverval. As it would contravene Hobbs's halt order, Elliott did not want him told. Informed nonetheless, Hobbs cancelled the operation but treated the incident as a routine example of Elliott's impetuosity rather than a serious breach. Next morning the Germans tried again. Up went the cry 'They're coming, they're coming! Man your posts', recalled Sergeant Downing. 'We fired and fired until the iron-work of our rifles burnt our hands . . . At about eight the enemy retired, leaving very many dead, and all grew quiet again.' Elliott also occupied Bertincourt in the British sector because it enfiladed his flank and the British cavalry, which should have taken it, had fallen behind while trying to cross the rumpled Somme battlefield. When a cavalry patrol turned up, Elliott saw that it was too weak to hold the village and refused to leave. Birdwood reprimanded him.[11]

Gellibrand also ran foul of Birdwood. Finding R3 abandoned, his column pushed on to Vaulx-Vraucourt, where it surprised some of the garrison shaving, and finished the first day well ahead of the rest of the British front. The rusty entanglements of the Hindenburg Line could be seen three miles off. Hearing that night from Haig that the villages behind it were burning, which suggested that the Germans might be withdrawing further to dislocate the Arras offensive entirely, Gough wanted the columns quickly 'to drive in all enemy detachments'. But White, who worried that they would be heavily counterattacked if they got too far ahead to be supported, reiterated on 19 March the need to advance cautiously. Upset with the progress made that day, Gough told Birdwood at 10.35 p.m. that he hoped Noreuil and Lagnicourt, two of the outpost villages, would be occupied on 20 March. Sloppy staffwork saw this message passed on to Gellibrand virtually unchanged. Thinking that White's instructions had been superseded and temperamentally inclined, like Elliott, to harry the Germans relentlessly, he ordered at 12.50 a.m. an attack on Noreuil, a mile and a half away. Starting at 3 a.m., half of the 21st and 23rd Battalions were to steal along the spurs either side and cut the village off, whereupon the other half would assault it.

Requiring units unversed in open warfare and dead beat, after two days continuously on the move, to carry out a night attack in rotten weather over ground they had no chance to reconnoitre, the plan quickly went awry. With snow falling, some companies got lost and others, whipped by heavy fire from Noreuil, took cover behind the dung-heaps on the slope before the village. German shells fell amongst them. Gellibrand ordered a withdrawal. He estimated that 150 men with up to six machine-guns were holding Noreuil. That it was thought to be occupied only by a few snipers showed how little attention had been paid to the rearguard order captured by the 15th Brigade, which indicated likely strong resistance from the village. Hearing that 331 men had been lost in an attack they knew nothing about, Birdwood and White were shocked. 'Dear old Gelly had one of those contrary fits, which periodically affected him, and he rushed into it', said White. Birdwood harboured doubts about him thereafter.

Gough was also chastened. On 20 March he directed that the outpost villages would only be attacked when heavy guns had been brought up and after thorough preparations. Gough wanted them struck simultaneously but V Corps, which had extended southwards to relieve II Corps on the left of I ANZAC, faced more heavily wired villages and needed longer to prepare. The Australians went on alone, their own front having now expanded to eight miles. Unsuited for this second phase of the advance, the columns were dispensed with.[12]

Supported by Elliott's column in its swansong, the 7th Brigade took Lagnicourt on 26 March. While the village was being enveloped, Captain Cherry's company from the 26th Battalion assaulted through with Cherry in the van. They sent the Germans packing but within two hours the depleted line was under counter-attack. Some of the Australian posts were driven in. Corporal Edgar Morrow fired at a German machine-gun crew setting up. 'My man dropped, and "Got him", I said delightedly.' Another machine-gunner ran forward. 'He was hardly fifty yards away when I shot him in the stomach. He crumpled forward and fell on his gun. I laughed.' Then Morrow was sent flying. 'Something had hit my right shoulder like a kick from a horse, and I found my right arm useless. Blood was running down my sleeve onto my hand.' The battle was delicately poised when the Germans' morale collapsed and they began pulling back. Among the 377 Australian casualties was Cherry, who had shown such decency to the German officer he had mortally wounded at Pozières the year before. He was posthumously awarded the VC.

The 13th Brigade relieved the 7th. After a hard fight costing 600 men, the 13th wrested Noreuil from the Württembergers of the 26th Reserve Division, which much of the Australian front now faced, in a dawn envelopment on 2 April. Private Joergen Jensen won the VC for charging a German platoon that held up the advance and forcing it to surrender. Major Loutit, one of the few men who had seen the Narrows at Anzac, took over a platoon from the 50th Battalion and turned the tables on the machine-guns and bombers that had savaged the right wing of the attack and captured a number of Australians. Some 113 Germans were captured in turn. Advancing beyond Noreuil on 5 April, the 49th Battalion seized the embankment west of Bullecourt along which the Arras–Cambrai railway ran parallel to the Hindenburg Line one thousand yards away. Four miles south, the 14th Brigade took Louverval by envelopment, the 56th Battalion having thoroughly rehearsed on similar ground the previous day, and neighbouring Doignies by a flank attack. Its garrison was still eating breakfast.

On 8–9 April, the 3rd Brigade seized Boursies in a feint to cover the 1st Brigade's assault against Hermies, the strongest of the outpost villages, a mile and a half south. In freezing rain at 3.30 a.m. on 9 April, the 3rd Battalion made for the southern side of Hermies while the 2nd struck from the northwest to get behind its formidable frontal defences in the main attack. The 2nd was nearing the first German posts when 'half a dozen machine guns opened a murderous fire on us', Private Hartnett said, 'laying men low on all sides, and throwing showers of earth over those who lived through the deadly hell. Moans and groans could be heard on all sides from the wounded'. The survivors charged and the Germans fled. Trying to give away the position of Hartnett's platoon, one wounded German refused to keep quiet until CSM Frederick Payne drew his revolver. 'The effect was magical. He uttered no further complaints.' As both battalions enveloped and cleared the village, Sergeant Matthews saw a machine-gun that was holding them up dramatically knocked out:

> The lance-corporal on the left was charging a gun directly in front of him that was served and defended by eight men. From thirty yards he dropped a bomb amongst them and at twenty yards – just as his bomb burst – he was wounded in the left arm. Undaunted he continued his rush and leapt into the trench and bayoneted in quick succession the remaining three Germans. The other five had been made casualties by the bomb.

Lance-Corporal Bede Kenny received the VC for this action. As the fighting ebbed, Hartnett witnessed a German stretcher party, which had been allowed to advance unhindered because it carried a Red Cross flag, suddenly set up a machine-gun. It inflicted heavy casualties on his company. A flanking platoon knocked the gun out. Its crew got no quarter. The Australians lost 253 men but took over 200 prisoners, including four cooks captured by Matthews's party 'with sufficient, hot porridge, bacon and coffee for over two hundred men'. Adjacent Demicourt was occupied without a fight. The Hindenburg Line lay directly ahead. The brief open warfare interlude was over.[13]

As this type of warfare underpinned their pre-war military experience, the Australian commanders easily made the switch from the trenches. They handled their formations well, gaining surprise through deception and tactical manoeuvre, notably envelopment, which often resulted in complex attacks. The men had to dust off the trench cobwebs. When the advance began, good targets escaped because troops thought they were out of range or waited for orders to fire. But they adapted quickly. Elliott waxed lyrically about the 15th Brigade: 'It is lovely to see them fight . . . Their speed and dash in attack is equalled by no troops at present in the field'.[14]

—ELEVEN—

BULLECOURT: DEFEAT INTO VICTORY

Trench warfare returned with the attack on the Hindenburg Line. Seven feet deep and 150 to 200 yards apart, the front and support lines reminded the Australians of the set-up at Pozières and were dubbed OG1 and OG2. The wire was much more formidable, comprising three belts before OG1, each ten to fifteen yards wide and five yards apart and arranged in a zigzag pattern to funnel attackers into the fire of machine-guns, and a single belt before OG2. The trenches themselves followed a gentle semi-circular ridge. Skirting Bullecourt at the western end of the crest, they snaked past Riencourt, which guarded their junction with the newly dug Wotan Line. Known to the British as the Drocourt–Quéant Switch, it ran northwards behind the front system as a reserve line in case of a breakthrough at Arras. To make the junction more secure, Balcony Trench was extended from it to enclose Quéant, near the eastern end of the crest two and a half miles from Bullecourt. Quéant and Bullecourt thus stood as salients either side of a wide re-entrant. The garrison was a fresh Württemberg division, the 27th. General Otto von Moser, the sector commander, considered it among the German Army's best.

Haig wanted Gough to seize a sector of the Hindenburg Line through which the 4th Cavalry Division could pass, in order to join the three cavalry divisions that were to go through the main breach created closer to Arras by Allenby's army. Gough wanted a bigger role. As he still thought the Germans could be retiring from the Hindenburg Line on his front, great prizes seemed within easy reach. The upshot of Gough's orders on 5 April was that the 62nd Division from V Corps would attack west of Bullecourt to take Hendecourt a mile beyond it, a total advance of 4000 yards. Starting from the railway embankment reached by the 49th Battalion that day, the 4th Australian Division would go 3000 yards across the bare re-entrant east of Bullecourt to capture Riencourt, turn right and go another mile to seize the bottom end of the Drocourt–Quéant Switch. The attack was fixed for 10 April.

The 4th Division had recently completed six weeks' training at Albert and was in splendid fettle. As its task was highly ambitious, the Australian commanders were anxious. Gough deleted the switch as an objective. But crossing the re-entrant to Riencourt still necessitated a deep penetration overlooked by the Bullecourt and Quéant spurs and the assault frontage proposed, 1300 yards, was narrow. It looked like Mouquet Farm again. Staying in the lee of the Quéant spur would provide some protection on that flank but the danger from Bullecourt could only be suppressed by turning most of the artillery onto it. Already uneasy at that gamble, Birdwood and White were thoroughly alarmed by patrol reports that the guns had barely damaged the entanglements. On 8 April White said that at least another eight days' wire-cutting were necessary. Flabbergasted, Gough agreed.

On 9 April the Arras offensive opened with the most stunning blow on the Western Front to date. Emerging from laboriously dug tunnels, with its four divisions side by side, the Canadian Corps took Vimy Ridge. Third Army alongside advanced over three miles. Gough seethed because the uncut wire precluded action on his front. Clutching at straws, he seized on a scheme put up by tank officer Major William Watson. Whereas tanks had been previously penny-packeted amongst the infantry, Watson wanted his twelve machines to concentrate ahead of the infantry and crush the German entanglements, obviating any need for the artillery to do so. Gough needed no convincing. The tanks could support the Australians. He decided to attack at dawn next day, as originally scheduled.

General Holmes had twelve hours to prepare. With no time for anything else, the existing plan was simply adjusted to accommodate the tanks. At 4.30 a.m. on 10 April the 4th and 12th Brigades, each led by four tanks, were to advance either side of Central Road, which ran across the re-entrant to Riencourt. Another four tanks would move through the 400-yard gap between them, the lowest point of the re-entrant. Once through the wire, the tanks would wheel outwards and trample OG1 and 2, with the four on the left going on to Bullecourt. After the Australians had taken it, the 62nd Division was to be called forward and the tanks would lead the way to Hendecourt and Riencourt. The Australians had never worked with tanks. Though dubious, Birdwood and White were carried along by the tank officers' enthusiasm and Gough's insistence on aiding the Third Army. But the clapped out Mark II's were under-armoured training machines unable to move at walking pace. With snow falling, whether they could arrive in time from their base at Mory, six miles back, was doubtful.

The rush left soldiers bewildered. 'No details of the battle have been made known', wrote Private Wilfred Gallwey of the 47th Battalion. 'We are in complete ignorance of the part we have to take.' With just a few hours to go, disquieting reports came in from the patrols Gough had ordered out to see if the Germans were indeed retiring. They were found to be holding the Hindenburg Line in strength. The Third Army was also said to be faltering. Birdwood and White protested that the attack would be extremely hazardous, and hard to justify if the main offensive had already struck trouble. Gough's chief of staff, Major-General Neill Malcolm, replied that Haig wanted it to go ahead to help the offensive. A diminutive martinet, Malcolm intimidated waverers by giving them orders in the guise of instructions from his superiors so that they would not be questioned. Birdwood directed the attack to proceed, overruling General Holmes, who opposed it.[1]

While the argument went on, the leading units lay in the snow in a sunken road 300 yards past the railway embankment. At 1 a.m. Bullecourt was drenched in phosgene, prompting an angry German fusillade. It barely disturbed Captain Jacka, now recovered from his wounds, as he laid the jump-off tape. The sight of cane-carrying Lieutenant Reich of the Württembergers, picking up one end of the tape, did. Pistol-whipped on trying to escape, Reich complained to Jacka's superior, who replied that as Jacka had captured him, he was lucky to be alive. At 2.30 a.m. the attackers filed onto the tapes to await the tanks. Ages passed without any sign of them. At 4.15 a.m. word arrived that they had been blinded by the snow and could not make it until well after dawn. Holmes recalled his men. Amid the confusion, nobody thought to notify the 62nd Division, which had sent strong patrols towards Bullecourt in the belief the assault was still on. German machine-guns tore into them. British 'dropshorts' cleaned up the survivors. The 62nd lost 162 men.[2]

Gough rescheduled the attack for 4.30 a.m. next day. Their case strengthened by the tank fiasco, the Australian commanders again protested. Conveniently called to the telephone during the meeting, Gough returned to say that Haig regarded the attack as an urgent necessity. White later alleged that Gough concocted Haig's order and that Birdwood should have resisted more strongly. The plan was slightly altered. As the Hindenburg Line wire was now reported partly cut, the infantry would advance automatically at 4.45 a.m., fifteen minutes after the tanks started.[3]

With the decision to try again not made until the afternoon, another rush followed for units already worn out by the previous night's exertion. Lashed by the miserable weather, some had to return from quarters five miles in rear. 'I carried my rifle in my left hand, just holding it by the sling and trailing the butt through the mud', wrote Private Gallwey, about to enter his first battle. 'It was too much energy to carry it any other way.' A tot of rum failed to ward off the cold. The Australians shivered in the snow, which stretched luminously to the Hindenburg Line ahead.

At 3 a.m., when all of the tanks should have been ready, the first one arrived. Guiding it into position, Jacka ascertained that none of them could reach the wire in the fifteen minutes allowed, which meant that the infantry would get there first. It was too late to change the plan. Another tank got stuck in the sunken road. Jacka had to be restrained from shooting its crew. With the attack about to begin, only three tanks were in place in front of the 4th Brigade, none ahead of the 12th and one in the gap between them.

Bullecourt was being heavily bombarded. 'Mountains of dirt . . timber, human bodies, all were thrown up', Gallwey recalled. 'With grim and silent handshakes of farewell', the 4th Brigade rose at 4.45 a.m. The four waves stretched 'illimitably to right and left . . . a glorious sight', Sergeant William Groves of the 14th Battalion said. They soon passed the few tanks. The Hindenburg Line seemed eerily quiet until,

> With a fury of hell, the enemy machine-guns spit out incessant fire. The chaps try frantically to find a way through the frightful network of barbed wire. Here and there one of the half dozen tanks that should have . . . made passages thro' puffs foolishly and ceases to move.

Bullets glancing off the wire sparked like swarms of fireflies. Private Gallwey witnessed the fate of the many men caught in it:

> Some dropped in the middle of the wire and hung there like scarecrows wounded and helpless only to be riddled. Others got entangled and escape was out of the question. They were like birds in a snare and just had to stand there until bullets had ended their suffering.

Suddenly Major Percy Black of the 16th Battalion yelled 'Come on, boys, bugger the tanks!' Renowned in the AIF as a fighting leader, Black had been a machine-gun corporal at Anzac with his great friend Harry Murray, who thought him 'the bravest of us all'. He had told Murray before the battle: 'Well, Harry, we have been in a few stunts together, but this is my last. I'll have that Hun front line first'. Utilising damaged stretches of wire, Black got the 16th Battalion across. They captured sixty Württembergers. Going on to OG2, Black found the entanglement intact but located a gap used by their patrols. Putting the remnants of the 16th through, he was shot through the head.

'Strolling along as if death was something which only came with old age', recalled Lance-Corporal Bert Knowles of the 13th Battalion, Murray had seen Black's men mown down. 'Come on, 13th! The 16th are getting hell!' he shouted. A machine-gun fired at them even as a tank, outlined by sparks from clanging bullet strikes, crushed it. Murray's neck was grazed by a bullet as the 13th Battalion mopped up OG1 and joined in the hand-to-hand fight for OG2. The 14th and 15th Battalions had similar experiences. By 5.30 a.m., the 4th Brigade had lost over half its strength but held 850 yards of the Hindenburg Line. Efforts to reach Riencourt were shot down in the growing light and discontinued.

A blunder cost the 12th Brigade dearly. An ambiguity in its orders, which went undetected in the haste, led the 46th Battalion to assume that it was to advance fifteen minutes after its tanks, irrespective of what time they arrived, instead of at 4.45 a.m. regardless. The first tank did not appear until 4.45 a.m. Disoriented in the dark, it shot up the 46th and was then knocked out. The next came at 5 a.m. and broke down. When the assault finally began at 5.15 a.m., the shelling of Bullecourt had ceased as the attack should already have reached it. The Württembergers around the village were free to rake the open Australian flank. Pressing on, the 12th Brigade, like the 4th, found the wire untouched and awash with fire. The 48th

Battalion suffered badly in getting through. Nonetheless, by 7 a.m., the 46th and 48th occupied 500 yards of the two trenches behind it.

The gap at the Central Road separating the two brigades remained. Two companies of Württembergers held it, and the only tank to close with them was entangled in the wire. A stream of armour-piercing ammunition struck the petrol tank, which exploded, incinerating some of the crew and driving others out aflame and screaming. Another tank met a similar fate crossing Balcony Trench. Only four tanks got to the wire at all and one reached Bullecourt. With sunrise, all of them appeared to the German gunners like crawling slugs against a white background. Burning tank carcasses soon dotted it. But the 4th Division had taken most of its initial objective. Murray reported at 7.15 a.m., 'With artillery support we can keep the position until the cows come home'.

Deceived by the blanket of snow, which hid the lie of the land, the Australian artillery observers thought that Riencourt had been reached. An airman also reckoned he saw Australians near Bullecourt. Highly confident, Gough ordered the cavalry forward. It was pole-axed. Pouring out of Riencourt and Hendecourt, the Württembergers counterattacked. The Australians fired at least twenty SOS rockets to bring down a protective barrage around the Hindenburg Line. But the gunners still believed that the attack had gone well past it and continued to lay down fire well beyond Riencourt. Knowing the real situation, the infantry brigadiers braced up the artillery commander, Lieutenant-Colonel Reg Rabett. Birdwood backed Rabett. Not one Australian shell disturbed the Hindenburg Line or the villages around it.

The Württembergers struck the outer flanks of both brigades and into the gap between them. Now a corporal in the 48th Battalion, George Mitchell was on the opposite side of a traverse to a German bomber. 'Up came his head. My bullet crashed into it and his last bomb was unthrown.' Then Mitchell and a German in a pork pie cap simultaneously saw each other. 'We aimed together', wrote Mitchell.

'I fired first . . . and the German pitched back.' Another man was throwing up because the headless body of a good friend had fallen on him, bloodily 'drenching him from head to foot'. With bombs and ammunition running out, the 4th Brigade was driven inwards around 11 a.m. Pointing to the torrential fire across the re-entrant behind it, Murray yelled: 'There's only two things now – either capture, or go into that!' The chance of getting back, he said, was akin to running 'for hundreds of yards through a violent thunderstorm without being struck by any of the raindrops'. Nicked by another bullet, Murray was among the last to go.

With the 4th Brigade gone, the Württembergers bombed the 46th Battalion out of OG1, cutting off the 48th Battalion and part of the 47th in OG2. Turning the OG2 garrison about, Captain Leane led a charge that regained OG1, only for Australian shells to crash into it. Allowed to fire at last, the guns were laying down a barrage on the Hindenburg Line in the belief that it had been lost. Leane gave the word to pull out at 12.25 p.m. From the railway embankment, the Australians could be seen leaving 'with proud deliberation and studied nonchalance', helping the walking wounded, and officers bringing up the rear. Leane was not among them. Already hit, he died in a German hospital. Leane was the nephew of the 48th's commander, Lieutenant-Colonel Ray Leane, who had lost a brother Ben, the battalion's second-in-command, the day before. 'Made of all Leanes', the 48th Battalion had been known as the Joan of Arc Battalion.

During the afternoon the Württembergers shot the dying and left the wounded for the Australians to collect in an informal truce. They took 1182 prisoners, the highest number by far of Australians captured in any action during the war. Sergeant Groves was one of them. Against the Württembergers' 749 casualties, the 4th Division lost almost 3500 men, 2339 of whom were from the 4th Brigade, which had 3000 engaged. Utterly exhausted, and shattered by the death of Black, which he had refused to believe until finding his body after a desperate search, Murray could only walk a few steps at a time. Several slugs of whisky barely revived him. The 4th Brigade's senior officers 'sobbed like little schoolgirls'.[4]

Much of the Australian bitterness was directed at the tanks. 'They had been the cause of a disaster to us and they never received the least sympathy', Sergeant Rule said. To Jacka and Leane, they were 'useless and worse than useless'. Not far behind the tanks was the 62nd Division, which was traduced for sitting on its hands. But it was only to have attacked once Bullecourt had fallen. When the same reports that had misled the Australian gunners suggested that the Australian infantry was in the village, the 62nd's men on the spot knew otherwise. The 62nd stayed put. The decision was justified but the Australians regarded it as another example of the unreliability of British troops.

Australian confidence in British generalship took yet another hit. Gough himself 'broke at every stage through rules recognised by platoon commanders'. He rushed into battle using, in tanks instead of artillery, a method that was largely experimental over ground that strongly favoured the defence. Undeterred when the tanks failed once, and with their limitations impossible to remedy, he insisted on trying again immediately. Gough later admitted that the attack was launched on too narrow a front to succeed as an isolated operation. Once the Third Army's offensive stalled – and Gough knew it was in difficulty – that is exactly what the Bullecourt attack became. Afterwards, the British Army used it to illustrate how an attack should not be undertaken.

Rule listened as a teary Birdwood told the 4th Brigade that none of the Australian commanders had anything to do with the arrangements. 'It was plain to me', said Rule, 'that he shrank from being contaminated by the bloody fiasco'. The fact was that despite Gough, the tanks and the 62nd Division, the reason that the attack failed in the end lay at Australian feet. With artillery support, the Hindenburg Line could have been held. None came because Birdwood and the Australian gunners chose to ignore numerous SOS rockets from the men fighting in it. But taking the Hindenburg Line even briefly was recognised as a magnificent feat. Gough sent his congratulations. He was already gearing up for another go. Still believing that the Germans were about to withdraw, he was convinced that one more blow would succeed. The Germans got in first by putting the Australians in the unfamiliar position of themselves being heavily attacked.[5]

Heeding Haig's order to conserve forces during the advance to the Hindenburg Line, Gough had proceeded with just three divisions spread over a frontage of almost 19 000 yards. As the 4th Australian and the 62nd Divisions on reaching it were concentrated onto a 6750-yard stretch for the Bullecourt attack on his left, the 1st Australian Division had to extend across the 12 000 yards between Lagnicourt and Hermies on his right. While the 2nd Division relieved the shattered 4th on 13 April, the 1st pushed closer to the Germans to mislead them into thinking that Gough would next attack on its front rather than at Bullecourt again. This advance increased its frontage to 13 000 yards. As GHQ sought defence in depth, the 1st reached back to Bapaume in four lines. Its front line was wafer thin, comprising a string of sentry posts ahead of half-platoon piquets over 300 yards apart. These forward positions could rarely be seen by the support platoons on the grassy slopes half a mile behind. Themselves 1000 yards apart, the support platoons were invisible to each other.

General von Moser knew that this part of the Australian line was thinly held. He had also been sent a fresh division, the 3rd Guard, to bolster his own line after Bullecourt. Believing in offence as the best form of defence, von Moser proposed to attack. Keen to prevent Haig strengthening the Arras offensive, Crown Prince Rupprecht of Bavaria, commander of the German armies opposing the BEF, liked the idea so much that he also let von Moser use the two divisions adjoining his left flank, making four in all. On 15 April they were to capture or destroy as many men and guns as possible in seizing the seven villages behind the 1st Division's line, holding them for the day and withdrawing that night.

Many of the Australian posts had heard movement before the German bombardment fell at 4 a.m., signalling that an attack was imminent. When it lifted onto the villages ten minutes later, the Germans could easily be seen. The sentries withdrew to the piquets, some of which were lost. But the resistance at the piquet line allowed reinforcements to reach the supports, who then drove the Germans off. Only at the junction of the 1st and 2nd Divisions north of Lagnicourt and Noreuil, where the 12th and 17th Battalions met, did a crisis arise.

Attacking without a bombardment, the 2nd Guard Reserve Division surprised the 17th Battalion and forced its piquets and supports back. Corporal Taylor was in a group that Sergeant George Kirkpatrick gathered:

> The sergeant's first bomb made a direct hit and accounted for three Germans. The sergeant was a tall man and, as he straightened himself for another throw, an enemy officer shot him in the forehead with a revolver. Jimmy and I threw our bombs together and the resultant explosion wrote finis to that German officer and his crew. But, to our left, on top of the trench, there appeared another crowd of Germans who threw a shower of 'potato-mashers' at us. But, luckily, they landed on the parados behind us. Fortunately, more of our fellows coming up from behind us accounted for this new menace with a copious discharge of well-directed Mills bombs.

At Lagnicourt, Captain James Newland of the 12th Battalion withdrew his piquets to the southeastern corner of the village, close to where Captain Cherry had been killed three weeks earlier. Vigorously led by Newland, they closed off the exits there. Newland and Sergeant John Whittle, who silenced a machine-gun and then brought it back, received the VC.

Overrunning the rest of Lagnicourt, the Guards headed for the valley behind it, where the 2nd Australian Field Artillery Brigade was located. The 2nd could not fire for fear of hitting its own troops, some of whom started through the guns with the Germans on their heels. Taking the breech-blocks and sights, the gunners left shortly after 5 a.m., as did the 1st AFA Brigade behind them. Hastily assembled at the 12th Battalion's headquarters southwest of Lagnicourt by Lieutenant-Colonel Elliott, a mish-mash of cooks, batmen and anyone else who could fire a rifle held the attack until the 9th Battalion arrived from the rear at 6.30 a.m. By then it was daylight and the Guards had also surged across the valley to crest the rise above Noreuil, where Brigadier-General Smith had earlier called forward the 19th and 20th Battalions. The 19th Battalion arrived in time to join the 17th in stopping them 300 yards from Smith's headquarters. With the Australian guns further north pounding the area, the 20th Battalion linked with the 9th at 7.10 a.m. and cleared Lagnicourt and its valley. The 1st AFA Brigade's guns were unharmed and only five of the 2nd's twenty-one guns damaged. During the two hours they had held the guns, the Germans were more interested in looting the gunners' dugouts.

Four thousand Australians, in a little over four battalions, had held most of their line against an attack by 16 000 Germans in twenty-three battalions. The Australians had executed defence in depth to perfection. Their piquets and supports had delayed and weakened the Germans sufficiently for reserves to move up and eject them from the one objective they took. The Germans remarked on the effect of Lewis guns 'cleverly emplaced and bravely fought'. As opposed to 1010 Australian casualties, they had lost 2313. The Arras offensive was affected not a jot.[6]

General Nivelle's offensive on the Chemin des Dames, which Arras had been designed to support, began in icy rain at 6 a.m. on 16 April. As Nivelle had openly talked about it for months, the blow was broadcast like no other. Captured orders filled in any missing

▲ Officers of the 8th LH Regiment in Melbourne. Standing are Major Thomas Redford and lieutenants Edward Henty and Eliot Wilson; seated are lieutenants Keith Borthwick and Robert Baker. All except Baker fell at the Nek. He returned to Australia in 1917.

◀ The 'Bullant', Lieutenant-Colonel John Antill. De facto commander of the 3rd LH Brigade at the Nek, Antill led from the rear, demanding that the attack 'push on' even when told it was suicidal.

▼ Colonel Francis Johnston, whose New Zealand Infantry Brigade was to take Chunuk Bair. His dithering on 7 August at Rhododendron Ridge angered Godley and had disastrous consequences for the Australian Light Horse at the Nek.

▲ Wave after wave of Turks charge the Wellingtons in Ion Brown's *The Battle of Chunuk Bair, 8 August 1915*. The trench is the old Turkish one on the crest, from which the Narrows could be seen. When it was overrun, the Wellingtons carried on the fight from a support trench behind it. They were virtually wiped out and their commander Malone was killed, but they held on until relieved that night.

▼ A nursing sister and an orderly tend wounded at the 3rd Australian General Hospital on Lemnos. During the August operations, casualties inundated the hospitals and medical staff were worked off their feet. Nursing was one of the few ways Australian women could become directly involved in the war. The first draft of nurses left Australia in September 1914 and Australian nurses subsequently went wherever Australian troops fought. A number also nursed in British hospitals. In all 2139 Australian nurses served overseas and 423 in Australia.

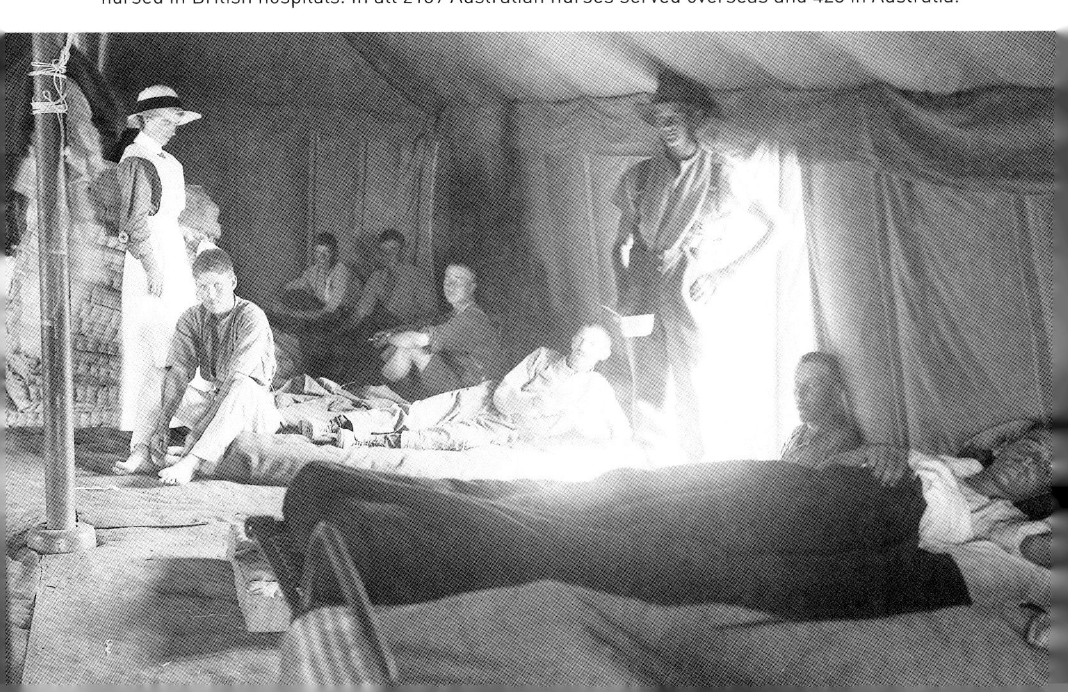

▼ Brigadier-General Brudenell White in his dugout at Anzac. Courteous, restrained, cerebral, White was the staff officer *par excellence* and his planning of the Anzac withdrawal was masterly. As Birdwood's chief of staff on the Western Front, he consistently made up for his commander's shortcomings.

◄ General (later Field-Marshal) Sir Douglas Haig, BEF Commander-in-Chief from December 1915 to war's end. Haig constantly sought to break through on the Western Front but his offensives degenerated into costly attritional slogs, as the Anzacs found in 1916 and 1917. He remains the most controversial commander in British military history.

▼ Newly issued with steel helmets, troops from the 6th Brigade show their jubilation on arrival in French Flanders. Their welcome left few Australians untouched and forged a bond that led to remarkable scenes in 1918.

▲ An aerial oblique of the Fromelles battlefield, looking southeast at the flat, bare ground over which the 5th Division attacked. Its line is the nearer. No man's land is at its widest opposite the Sugarloaf, which bulges from the German line at centre right. The Rue Delvas is the straight road that crosses the lines from the bottom of the photograph. Fromelles is near the wood at top right.

◄ Major-General James McCay. He was courageous but his harsh leadership style bred dislike and even loathing. Like the 5th Division, he had no experience of the Western Front before Fromelles. McCay commanded the AIF depots in England from mid-1917. After the war, he was appointed business adviser to the Commonwealth Government and became deputy chairman of the State Bank of Victoria. McCay died in 1930, aged sixty-six.

▲ Brigadier-General Harold Elliott. Nicknamed 'Pompey' (after Fred 'Pompey' Elliott, the captain of the Carlton Football Club), Elliott had been a Melbourne solicitor. One of the AIF's finest and most popular leaders, he foresaw the outcome when his beloved 15th Brigade attacked near the Sugarloaf.

▲ Soldiers from the 53rd Battalion enjoy a last smoke before donning their gear to 'hop the bags' at Fromelles. Of the eight men shown, five will be killed and the other three wounded.

▼ An Australian killed at Fromelles. McCay ended up throwing in almost the entire 5th Division. Only the 57th Battalion got off lightly. Had the third attack on the Sugarloaf not been called off, it too would have been decimated.

Australian prisoners from the Fromelles battle arrive at the German collecting station on 20 July. Sympathetic French civilians, who tried to give them chocolates and smokes when they were marched through Lille, received short shrift from the Germans.

The shell-damaged Golden Virgin atop the Notre Dame de Brebières cathedral in Albert was a familiar sight to every soldier of the BEF who fought on the Somme in 1916. A superstition arose that the war would end when it toppled. When the Germans took Albert in March 1918, British guns destroyed the tower to prevent them using it as an observation post. The Madonna crashed down. The war went on another eight months.

General Sir Hubert Gough. At forty-six, Gough was easily the youngest of the BEF's army commanders and a favourite of Haig. His hot temper and impulsiveness were unsuited to trench warfare and cost the Australians dearly on the Somme in 1916 and at Bullecourt in 1917. Gough was widely known as 'Goughie' but the peach-like groove in his prominent nose also earned him the nickname 'General Bumface'. The Australians called him far worse.

▲ Pozières–Mouquet Farm. The Australians called Gierich Weg, which is below Skyline Trench, Park Lane. Beyond Skyline Trench, the Fabeck Graben runs into Mouquet Farm from the right.

▲ Pre-war Pozières, looking up the main street (the Albert–Bapaume Road) towards the Windmill and Bapaume.

▼ Pozières on 28 August 1916, showing the combined effects of the British and German bombardments of the village. Centre Way communication trench crosses the main street, roughly at the point from which the previous photograph was taken.

◀ Major-General Gordon Legge. He had just taken over as Chief of the General Staff in Australia when war came. Commanding the 2nd Division at Anzac, Legge had an uneventful time. Commanding it at Pozières, he could not have had a rougher time.

▼ OG1, northwest of the Windmill in October 1916, still littered with the detritus of battle amidst shell-ravaged ground. The 2nd Division's attacks were made from left to right. After their capture, the deep dugouts, some of whose entrances are visible, were used by the Australians to shelter from the German bombardment.

▲ Brigadier-General Thomas Glasgow. Taciturn but forceful and rock-steady, Queensland pastoralist Glasgow had been a light horse commander at Anzac. He impressed sufficiently to be given an infantry command, the 13th Brigade. His – and its – finest hour would come at Second Villers-Bretonneux on 24 April 1918.

▲ Brigadier-General John Gellibrand. Tasmanian-born Gellibrand had joined the British Army, graduated top of his class from Sandhurst in 1893, served in the Boer War and attended the Camberley Staff College before returning to Australia in 1912. He was an aggressive and able commander who lived close to his men, although his eccentricities often put him offside with his superiors. The Remembrance Club he founded in Hobart in 1923 ultimately grew into the Legacy Movement.

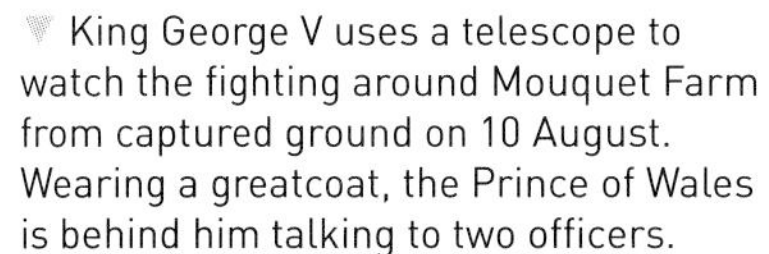

▼ King George V uses a telescope to watch the fighting around Mouquet Farm from captured ground on 10 August. Wearing a greatcoat, the Prince of Wales is behind him talking to two officers.

▲ Prime Minister William Morris Hughes raises both arms in favour of conscription in Martin Place before the 1916 referendum. As Australia was sharply divided over the issue, the campaign was bitter. When Hughes called another referendum on conscription in 1917, an even more strident campaign ensued.

▼ Major-General Sir Andrew Russell. After graduating from Sandhurst and serving briefly in the British Army, Russell returned to New Zealand in 1892 and became a pastoralist. Having excelled as commander of the NZMR at Anzac, he took charge of the newly formed New Zealand Division in 1916. He was acknowledged as one of the finest divisional commanders in the BEF. In 1940 he was made inspector-general of the forces in New Zealand. Russell died in 1960, aged ninety-two.

▼ New Zealanders after capturing and consolidating a trench at Flers. They were able to prepare thoroughly for this attack, which was launched on a wide front, unlike the narrow 'battering ram' assaults that had cost the Australians so dearly.

▲ Troops of the 1st Australian Division 'rest' in Switch Trench, part of the reserve Somme winter line, on 23 November 1916. They will spend a few days here before returning for another spell in the far ghastlier front line. During November the Australians attacked in these conditions.

▼ Privates Charles Marsh and Leo Dixon of the 30th Battalion move through the ruins of Bapaume on the morning of 17 March. The Germans devastated the area to prevent its use for billeting. Thirty Australians were killed when the town hall blew up.

▲ Major-General Talbot Hobbs. A successful Perth architect and devout Christian, Hobbs had been a gunner since joining the volunteers in 1883. He quickly won over the 5th Division after its less than happy experience under McCay. Recognising the ability of the fiery Elliott, Hobbs made allowances for him that another commander might not. He died in April 1938, aged seventy-three, *en route* to France to attend the unveiling of the Villers-Bretonneux Australian National Memorial.

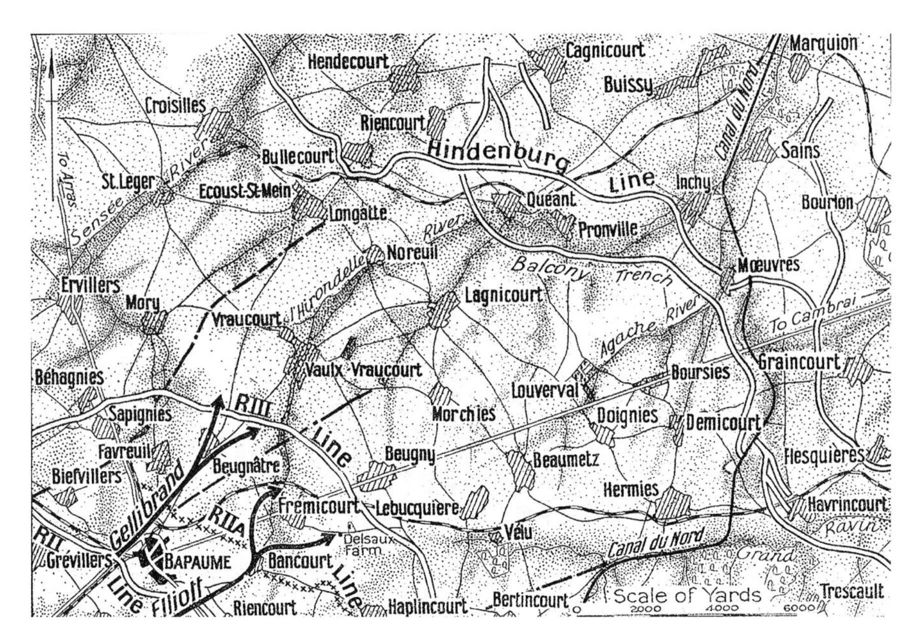

▲ The advance to the Hindenburg Line. Riencourt and Hendecourt beyond it figured in the two Bullecourt battles in April and May 1917. In the interval between them, the Germans attacked in the area of Lagnicourt and Noreuil.

▼ Men from the 2nd Division on the march, carrying typical loads for infantrymen.

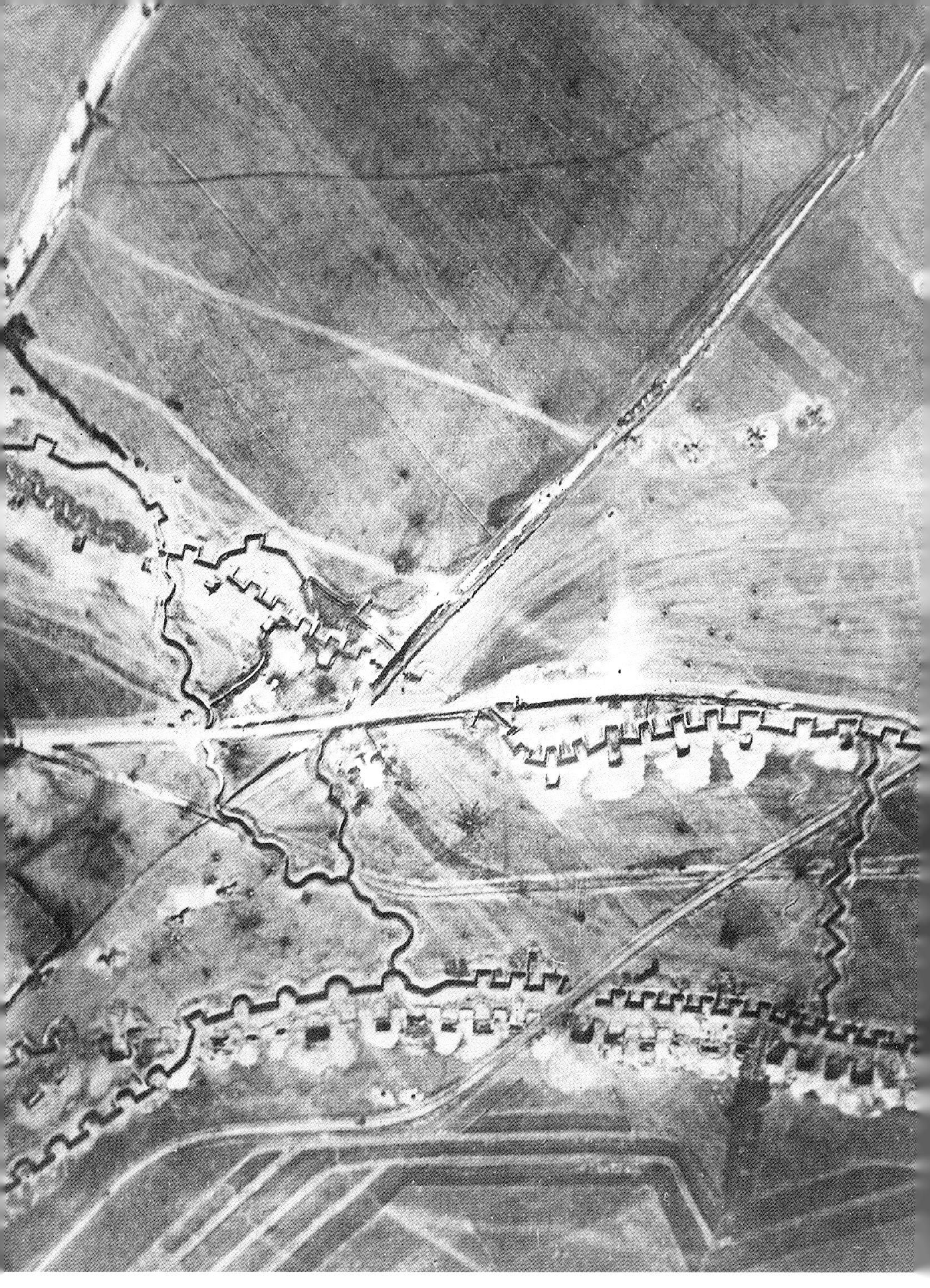

▲ The section of the Hindenburg Line assaulted by the 12th Brigade, eight days before the attack on 11 April 1917. Zig-zagging across the picture are the OG Lines, linked by cross-trenches. The bands in front of the OG Lines are wire entanglements. Another entanglement lies between them, as does the track of a trench railway. The prominent line running diagonally from the left bottom is the bed of a dismantled tramway. Bullecourt is just past the left edge of the photograph.

▲ Major-General William Holmes of the 4th Australian Division. Before the war he had been in charge of Sydney's Metropolitan Water and Sewerage Board and presided over the construction of a number of major dams. Holmes joined the New South Wales militia as a bugler in 1872, aged ten, and dropped from captain to lieutenant to serve in the South African War. He habitually reconnoitred every part of his front line but courted danger by insisting on wearing his red-banded general's cap.

▲ Major Percy Black. After years on the West Australian goldfields, Black was almost thirty-seven when he enlisted in 1914. 'I don't know anything about this soldiering game', he told an officer on joining the 16th Battalion. By the time of Bullecourt, Black held the DSO and the DCM and there was nothing about soldiering he did not know. Like Murray and Jacka, Black was a natural leader whom men followed unhesitatingly.

◀ Major-General Nevill Smyth of the 2nd Australian Division. A British regular officer, Smyth had won the VC at Khartoum in the Sudan in 1898. In 1913 he learned to fly and, as commander of the 2nd Division, occasionally flew his own aerial reconnaissances of the German line. A man of few words, Smyth was nicknamed 'the Sphinx' and often did not see eye to eye with Gellibrand. Smyth's affection for the men he had led greatly influenced his decision to emigrate to Australia in 1925.

▲ Lieutenant Walter Shelley of the 22nd Australian Machine-Gun Company looks for movement in the gaps made in the wire by the Australian artillery during the bombardment of the Hindenburg Line before Second Bullecourt. The village, which lies within the Hindenburg Line, is on the left skyline.

◀ Lieutenant Stan Dallas. Queensland-born in 1891, Dallas was an assayer and, at 6 foot 2 inches and sixteen stone, one of the biggest pilots on either side. A teetotaller, he topped the eighty-four students at the entrance exam for the RNAS in 1915. Awarded the DSO and the DSC (with bar), Dallas often used his superior flying skill to protect inexperienced pilots.

▶ Flight Sub-Lieutenant Robert Little. Rejected by the Australian Army's Flying School at Point Cook in Victoria, twenty-year-old Little went to England in 1915 and learned to fly at his own expense. A great shot, he was a superb loner in the air rather than a leader like his countryman Dallas. Little was awarded both the DSO and the DSC, with bars to each.

details for the Germans. 'The attack gained ground at most points, then slowed down, unable to follow the barrage', wrote Brigadier-General Edward Spears, head of the British Military Mission to the French. 'As soon as the infantry and the barrage became dissociated, German machine-guns . . . filled the air with a whistling sound as of scythes cutting hay'. Far from penetrating six miles as Nivelle had said it would, the advance stalled at nightfall after going 600 yards. Instead of calling it off, as he had pledged, within forty-eight hours if the offensive were unsuccessful, Nivelle prolonged it for another few days, losing over 100 000 men.[7]

On 18 April Haig heard rumours that the French wanted to sit tight and wait for the Americans. Incensed by U-boat sinkings, they had declared war on Germany on 6 April. Haig wanted to maintain the pressure. The French were facing growing disquiet over Nivelle's offensive. On 28 April General Philippe Pétain became the French chief of staff. He had stemmed the German onslaught on Verdun in 1916 but then made way for Nivelle to counterattack. Though Nivelle remained commander-in-chief, it was clear that his days were numbered. Unlike Nivelle, Pétain subscribed to 'bite and hold'. His appointment seemed further proof of waning French offensive spirit. Haig tried to prop it up by continuing at Arras. To that end, the First, Third and Fifth Armies were to assault on 3 May.[8]

The Fifth Army would carry forward the right flank using the 62nd Division and the 2nd Australian, the only one from I ANZAC still in the line following the relief of the 1st after Lagnicourt. The objectives were largely unchanged: OG1 and 2, which included Bullecourt for the 62nd, in the first phase, and the Fontaine–Quéant road, running 200–1200 yards behind OG2, in the second to gain a jump-off line for the capture of Riencourt and Hendecourt in the third, making a total advance of 3000 yards. Ten tanks were available but the Australians were only too happy to let the 62nd have them. As Gough always intended to attack again, the Hindenburg Line had been bombarded from mid-April onwards. By month's end

Bullecourt, Riencourt and Hendecourt resembled rubbish heaps and great swathes of wire had been destroyed.

In the 2nd Division, the 7th Brigade would be in reserve while the 5th and 6th Brigades assaulted respectively right and left of the Central Road, this time with no gap for the Germans to penetrate between them. With no guarantee that the 62nd Division could deal with Bullecourt, on the 6th Brigade's left flank, Brigadier-General Gellibrand planned to drench it with mortar and machine-gun fire. He was given half of the ninety-six machine-guns covering the 2nd Division's assault. Less attention was paid to the Quéant spur, where the machine-guns in Balcony Trench would be just 700 yards from the 5th Brigade's right flank. Lieutenant John Wright, the 17th Battalion's Intelligence Officer, warned that 'the field of fire was perfect, the kind of thing a machine-gunner dreams about'. Though the first attack had shown that the lee of the spur gave little protection, Wright was told 'to shut up, that artillery would keep the nest of machine-guns quiet'. Brigadier-General Smith left it at that. So did Generals Smyth, Birdwood and White. But the artillery fire-plans concentrated on the stretch of OG1 and 2 to be attacked and the three villages.

At least the preparations were thorough. Along with direction keeping in the dark, the assembly improved noticeably during rehearsals on similar terrain with mock-ups of the defences. The bayonet scabbards and entrenching tools hanging off the men's belts were tied down, after Gellibrand heard them flapping loudly against their thighs during the practices. To guard against ammunition running out, as it had in the earlier attack, four dumps were set up on the railway embankment and filled to overflowing with everything from bombs to sandbags. The infantry carried at least six bombs per man. Mats of expanding netting were issued for throwing over any wire found uncut. The Australians were confident. 'Tomorrow morning Fritz will get absolute hell pitched onto him', Captain Roth predicted.

Capturing two downed German airmen at about the same time as Captain Roth was forecasting, men from the 20th Battalion were amazed when one casually asked: 'What time is zero?' 'There's no zero! We're not thinking of attacking', Captain John McDonald shot back. 'Oh, we know you are', the German replied. 'What time do you start?' The build-up behind the British line and the increasing artillery fire had given the attack away. In anticipation, General von Moser had strengthened his line by ordering the 2nd Guard Reserve Division to take over Balcony Trench and the Quéant spur, so that the 27th Württemberg could concentrate across the attack frontage. During the bombardment they sheltered in deep dugouts in the OG Lines and in the village cellars.

In the three weeks since the first attack, spring had come and the battlefield lost its bleakness. The snow vanished, such trees as were left were blossoming, and patchy growth was sprouting in the few mildly shelled places. Like the outback's strong winds, the bombardment whipped up dense dust clouds over the German line. The haze softened the glare of the orange and green flares that the Germans fired throughout the night of 2 May. But a searchlight near Hendecourt was untroubled by shells or dust. Its beam slewed back and forth, slowing the move of the 5th and 6th Brigades onto their jump-off tapes. The Germans were also shelling no man's land heavily. 'All this time little Willie was trying to push his little tummy deeper and deeper into the earth', Captain Braithwaite said. The training paid off for the assembly was completed in good order and not detected. At 3.45 a.m the creeping barrage opened 200 yards in front. Fixing bayonets, which had been sheathed to avoid any glinting in the moonlight, both brigades headed for the Hindenburg Line.[9]

At 4.01 a.m. and again at 4.05 a.m., a pair of red flares were seen, indicating that the 5th Brigade had taken OG1 and was heading for OG2. General Smith thought his brigade was going well. It was really disintegrating. The 19th Battalion on the right had veered towards the Quéant spur, probably because its jump-off tape had been wrongly inclined. The Balcony Trench machine-guns stuttered. 'There was considerable confusion', wrote Private Ernie King of the first wave. 'I went about thirty yards and have a dim recollection of falling into a huge shell hole and was immediately wounded in the face, right arm and chest.' As the 17th Battalion alongside stayed on track, a gap yawned. The rear waves poured into it. Realising its error, the 19th changed direction leftwards. The line became densely packed, giving the flanking machine-guns an even better target. They lashed it. The German counter-barrage was also pounding the Australians. Shrapnel shells bursting at head height shredded whole groups, their flesh, blood and brains splattering those nearby.

Those who reached the wire saw the Württembergers ignoring the Australian barrage and lining the parapet to shoot. The fire became torrential. Most of the surviving Australian officers and NCOs were shot down trying to rally their men. A handful entered OG1 near Central Road – they probably fired the success flares – but were quickly cornered. Most stayed put. As dawn broke, a half-crazed officer suddenly shouted: 'Pull out – retire – get back for your lives'. The line ran back. By 4.45 a.m., 400 leaderless men were strewn along the sunken road in front of the railway embankment. Many others had gathered there. Told to investigate what went wrong, Lieutenant Wright became another victim of the danger about which he had futilely warned:

> It was daylight and I had ample opportunity to see the machine-gun barrage, which was perfect. I had to screw myself up to plunge into it and after a few steps I was hit, the bullet entering about the centre of the abdomen and passing out the left side.

A mile rearward in Noreuil, Smith could do nothing to influence the battle. Initially informed of the debacle around 4.20 a.m. and perhaps wanting more information, he did not advise Smyth, who was over two miles further back. Gellibrand had established his headquarters at the embankment. He let Smyth know precisely what had happened and pointedly suggested that Smith go up to see for himself. His own brigade had taken OG1 and 2.[10]

'Well mate, I might see you there and I might not', 17-year-old Private Robert Comb said to his mate Brown, as they set off with the 23rd Battalion. Comb never saw Brown alive again. Staying close to the shell curtain, the 23rd and the 24th ahead of it reached OG1 and 2 before the Württembergers emerged from their dugouts, and entered both trenches with little loss. Next to them on the left flank, the 22nd Battalion and the 21st following were raked from Bullecourt despite the suppressive fire Gellibrand had organised. Already in trouble, they split when the German counter-barrage struck. Heading left to avoid it, half went closer to Bullecourt. Some got to within twenty yards of OG1 before being driven back by a shower of bombs to the wire, where the others were pinned down. Veering right, the other half joined the 23rd and 24th Battalions, which had grabbed about half of the 6th Brigade's objective in the Hindenburg Line and were bombing outward to take the rest. The start of the Diagonal Road that led to Bullecourt half a mile away, and along which OG2 briefly ran, was also captured. 'Spudmaster bombs', as Braithwaite called the German 'potato-masher' stick grenades, flew thickly:

> You couldn't imagine it. One minute would be quiet, the next you would see some spudmaster bombs coming through the air and you would know you were being shown the way out. Then we would push him along with our gentle Mills which is five times the bomb than the German one and so it went on until he was gradually pushed out of our show.

Captain Maxfield led part of the 24th Battalion to the Fontaine–Quéant road. Much of the 23rd also reached it but was heavily engaged from Riencourt. The village was now clearly unattainable and at 5.47 a.m. Gellibrand ordered a protective barrage around the pocket his brigade held. It was unsupported on either flank and a wall of fire barred the way across the re-entrant in rear.

Aware that the 6th Brigade's success risked being frittered away unless its right flank was shored up, Gellibrand told one of his most trusted staff officers, Captain Walter Gilchrist, to rally the 5th's scattered troops for another try. Together with a company of the 26th Battalion sent by the 7th Brigade, he left the railway embankment with 100 men at 5.25 a.m. When the line reached the sunken road, Lieutenant-Colonel George Murphy shouted 'Come on men' to the 18th Battalion gathered there and another 200 joined it. The German machine-guns did not open until they neared the wire, where 'the stream of bullets from two guns could be seen ripping up the ground and raising two small dust clouds which gradually converged until they met'. The attack faltered. Gilchrist took charge of the handful of men who reached OG1 and began bombing eastwards. Driven back to the Central Road, he led them on again, climbing onto the parapet himself to throw. Incongruously clad in a grey cardigan, as he had discarded his jacket and helmet in the stifling heat, Gilchrist fell from sight. His bombers were driven back a second time. Once more they started forward.

On the left flank, the 62nd Division's attack had recoiled to the railway embankment. The 62nd blamed the tanks, whose form had not improved since the first attack; the tankers accused the 62nd of leaving too much to them. Gellibrand had seen the assault cut to pieces but Smyth swallowed the 62nd Division's rosy message that it was 'bombing towards the Anzacs'. He ordered the 25th Battalion to attack in support. Gellibrand protested the folly of trying to cross the fireswept open ground in daylight. Smyth overruled him. Gellibrand tested the feasibility of Smyth's order with two platoons. They were shredded. The attack lapsed.[11]

The numerous cross-trenches linking OG1 and 2 like rungs on a ladder complicated the defence of both flanks. If the Württembergers recaptured part of one line, they could zip down the nearest cross-trench and get behind the Australians in the other. The first counterattack came at 8.45 a.m. It fell heaviest on the right. Covered by Corporal Gaffney's machine-gun, the bombers threw the Württembergers back and gained 200 yards of OG1. But the line on the Fontaine–Quéant road had to be given up. Its continued viability depended on the protective barrage. The artillery had been firing for several hours at rates normally deemed unsafe and both guns and gunners were worn out. Struck by 'dropshorts' the men under Captain Maxfield and in the 23rd Battalion pulled out. Maxfield did not make it.

At the railway embankment all available men, even cooks, were called upon to resupply the pocket and help evacuate the wounded. They trundled back and forth along the partly sunken Central Road, which offered some cover. For the stretcher-bearers getting to the embankment was the easy part. From there they had to take the wounded over a mile of exposed ground to the collecting points near Noreuil. The body of a boy 'with uncovered face smiling serenely at the sky' rattled bearer Private Brown. 'If he was as happy now as he looked, how much better would it be to be with him than in this miserable mess! Did he catch that smile from Someone welcoming him Home?' Working at the advanced dressing station behind Noreuil in a tent 'awash with blood', the 2nd Division's senior chaplain, John Cue, felt deeply privileged to be among the mangled men streaming in:

I found a man . . . with his head badly knocked about, his face (what could be seen of it) covered with blood, bandaged at the advanced station; his eyes were practically covered; his jaw smashed, and so unable to speak; this battered man, unrecognisable, was vomiting blood badly at the time. I went to him to see if I could help him. He pointed to his mouth and shook his head, meaning I cannot speak, and then made signs with his hand, as if he were writing. I therefore got his paybook from his pocket and found out his next of kin and wrote it down in my book and told him what I had done. No doubt he was glad of this, but it did not satisfy him, for he still propped himself on his elbow and made the sign of writing. I concluded he wanted to write a message somehow himself, and put the pencil and book in his hand, and now I have . . . a bloodstained page with the words 'Tell him I am so sorry I was sick.' How a man, suffering as he must have been, could be so thoughtful and unable to rest until he had apologised to the wounded comrade by his side, because he had been sick on the ground between them, and had to write it because he could not speak it, is beyond my comprehension. Surely such a man is worth knowing whose action was something like our Blessed Lord's, who was so thoughtful for others, when he was dying upon the cross.

This war has broken down our shyness. One Captain put his arms around my neck and held me tightly as I whispered a prayer for him and his loved ones.[12]

At noon large numbers of Germans were observed in front of Riencourt and Quéant. Standing above the parapet to fire, the Australians forced the counterattack to ground before stopping the leopard-crawling Württembergers twelve yards out. Only on the right, where it was again strongest, did they get anywhere, reaching the Central Road. Help was to hand, for Major Brown had hustled the 28th Battalion up. The 5th Brigade remnants he passed thought they were being relieved. Before Brown could stop them, they bolted. 'I do not know whether any liquor had been issued to these men', he reported, 'but numbers of them appeared to be under the influence'. His own bombers rushed along the parapet and captured 450 yards of OG1 in the 5th Brigade's area before a shortage of bombs halted them at 4 p.m. One of the 5th's carrying parties arrived with several crates shortly after 5.30 p.m., by which time the Württembergers were back at the Central Road. Tearing the lids off, Brown's men were dismayed to find that the bombs were unprimed. The 5th Brigade let Brown down again:

> I first saw three 5th Brigade officers whom I at once asked to detail me some men for examining bombs. They replied that their men were laid out and that they would not ask them to work. I at once detailed a 5th Brigade Sergeant and 15 or 20 men who started work. Shortly after, the party had dwindled until none were left.[13]

Brown did the job with his own men. By 6 p.m. they had regained the ground lost, only to be ejected almost straightaway by a third counterattack. In a continuing cycle, the 28th Battalion pushed the Württembergers back only to withdraw itself. At nightfall, Brown received reports of men advancing behind him towards the Central Road. Word spread that the 6th Brigade was retiring. Decorated for gallantry at Pozières and Flers, Brown was hardly a panic merchant but his battalion now seemed to him to be in danger of being cut off. He ordered it to withdraw. The 28th filed down the Central Road, apart from one of its company commanders, Captain Jack Roydhouse. Formerly of the 6th Brigade's staff, he did not believe that the 6th was leaving. A quick check proved him right. Australian 'dropshorts' had briefly forced part of the 24th Battalion from its line.

For Gellibrand, the 28th Battalion's departure was 'the harshest blow that day'. Amidst reports of another German attack, he rallied its men and strung them out with his own headquarters staff along the embankment, the next line of defence if the Hindenburg Line were lost. Morale there was still sky high. Crying with rage, Roydhouse had explained what happened to Captains John Lloyd and Stan Savige, also former members of Gellibrand's staff, who were leading the 24th Battalion. They decided to hold on. Their men agreed: 'It doesn't matter at what cost, we're going to beat them', they declared. But the disruption meant that no help could be given to an attack on Bullecourt by the 7th Division, which had replaced the 62nd. It failed, as did a second.

Seeing lorries bring a fresh Württemberg regiment into Riencourt, the Australians knew the next counterattack would not be far off. The alert for it precluded rest for the few men left. None could be spared to evacuate wounded, whose growing numbers the stretcher-bearers alone could not clear. For much of the time now, the only wounded who went back were those able to do so under their own steam. The rest had to stay in the firing-line. Captain Savige recalled one whose entrails were showing through a gash in his abdomen. He lay puffing on a cigarette and when Savige said 'Stick it out lad', answered 'Don't worry about me, sir, but give the bastards hell!' Afterwards he placed a rifle between his feet and shot himself. The 1st Brigade started relieving the 6th at 1 a.m. on 4 May. Two hours later the fourth counterattack came. The 23rd Battalion, the last to leave, helped the new arrivals defeat it.[14]

Entering the battle with 2897 men, the 6th Brigade emerged a day later with 1348. Depressed by the losses, Lance-Corporal Leonard Bryant of the 2nd Field Ambulance roasted 'the Tommies on the right'. 'Bombing towards the Anzacs' instantly entered the Australian lexicon as a derisory term for British promises of help. But the 5th Brigade was also roundly criticised. Gellibrand went further, considering that the handling of the 2nd Division by its headquarters insulted his brigade's efforts. A bohemian eccentric who invariably wore a private's uniform, he broke down after Bullecourt and joined McCay's staff in England after resigning his command.[15]

'Well done, Australia!' read the note dropped by a British airman who buzzed the 6th Brigade's headquarters during the fight. Bean ranked the capture and almost single-handed defence of the Hindenburg Line as the fourth of the AIF's four greatest feats of the war. Apart from the Canadians, the 6th Brigade had achieved the only success along the entire sixteen-mile attack front. When a promised French attack on 4 May failed to materialise, Haig was all the more determined to continue British offensive action. With the First and Third Armies around Arras clearly spent, he settled on Bullecourt. Though its original aim of helping the Third Army was no longer relevant, it now stood as the exemplar of British offensive spirit.

Embarrassed at the breaking of the vaunted Hindenburg Line, the Germans were determined to restore it. The battle continued with no clearly defined purpose whatsoever.[16]

As long as the Germans held Bullecourt, the Australian pocket was endangered. Birdwood insisted on its capture. The 7th Division was to keep bashing away at the village, while the 1st Brigade extended the flanks of the pocket in order to gain the extra space needed to absorb the German counterattacks. On 4 May the 1st and 3rd Battalions bombed 200 yards closer to Bullecourt. Incensed by the Württembergers' firing on stretcher-bearers on the opposite flank, the 2nd and 4th Battalions mercilessly smashed stubborn resistance to recapture the 400-yard stretch held by the 28th Battalion the previous day. At 7 p.m. the Germans launched their fifth counterattack. Like the others, it was unsuccessful.

On 5 May the 1st Brigade moved to the left of the Central Road and the 3rd Brigade took over on the right. At 5 a.m. next morning, after a night of shelling many thought worse than at Pozières, a fiendish roar heralded a lurid orange light that banished the darkness. Storm troops were assaulting the 3rd Brigade with flamethrowers. Sergeant Pat Kinchington narrowly escaped:

> When the Germans were about forty yards away I saw a fellow shoot a jet of flame into the bank. It was the first flammenwerfer I had seen. I fired and shot the carrier through the belly; my bullet went through the flammenwerfer can, and it caught fire at the back. You could hardly see for smoke. There was a hole in the road; the man fell into it, and about a dozen men on top of him – they all appeared to catch fire.

Already shaken by the shelling, 200 men from the 11th and 12th Battalions ran back to the Central Road. Lieutenant Tom Richards with the 1st Battalion on the opposite side shouted at them. '"What will Australia think when she knows you deserted your posts and let your brother soldiers down." That shifted some back to their trench', he wrote, 'and I saw Lieut. Bruton in the end with his revolver drawn and preventing the men from going further back.' Suddenly Corporal George Howell of the 1st Battalion leapt onto the parapet of OG1 and bombed along it until wounded. Howell's action, for which he won the VC, rallied the 11th and 12th. They hurled the Germans back beyond their starting point.[17]

On 7 May, the 7th Division took the southeastern corner of Bullecourt and the fresh 9th Australian Battalion bombed down OG1 to connect. As the 1st Division, which had also borne the brunt of the Lagnicourt attack, was now used up, the 5th relieved it. When the 14th and 15th Brigades took over right and left of the Central Road on 8–9 May, Sergeant Downing felt he was entering Hades:

> We passed a Tommy lying on the ground. He was hatless. Part of his scalp was crinkled under the bloody hair, showing inches of the red skull; the fingers of one hand were smashed to pulp, the bloody puttees were twisted on his broken legs, and he was moaning, 'Keep to the left, keep to the left, they want you there, boys.' We reached the front line . . . A man with both eyeballs hanging like poached eggs on his cheeks was sitting at the bottom of the trench groaning. Someone on the parapet was babbling in delirium. A couple of slightly wounded prisoners were being led along the trench, stepping over the dead bodies, both German and Australian, that filled the bottom.[18]

In order to support the 7th Division's attempt to take the rest of Bullecourt on 12 May, the 58th Battalion had to capture the Diagonal Road stretch of OG2 and meet the British at the northeastern end of the village. Its twirling moustachioed and arts-loving commander, Lieutenant-Colonel Charles Denehy, apologetically told Lieutenant Rupert Moon, 'You've got the tough one, Mickey'. His platoon would have to knock out a concrete machine-gun post. Lieutenant Jimmy Topp announced he was turning thirty-seven on the morrow. 'A good omen', Denehy said as Topp was congratulated. German shelling savaged the 58th and the assault was held. Birthday boy Topp fell shot through the head.

Moon had been hit in the face and his men were faltering. 'Come on, boys, don't turn me down', he shouted. They knocked out the machine-gun. Hit again, Moon chased after the Germans, who took to their shelters. He sustained a third wound while shooting into the entrances to trap them inside until the bombers arrived. Within a few minutes 186 Germans surrendered. Joking 'I've got three cracks and not one of them good enough for Blighty', Moon was peering towards the next enemy position when a fourth crack broke his jaw and shattered twelve teeth. He received the VC. The 58th Battalion linked with the 7th Division after dark. On 15 May the 54th Battalion lost some ground before charging across the open to rout the Germans during their seventh counterattack.[19]

Finally deciding that the cost of trying to restore the Hindenburg Line was prohibitive, the Germans withdrew to a new position behind it. The Australian capture and defence of 'this 1000 yards of double trench line', wrote Haig, 'exposed to counter-attack after counter-attack, through two weeks of almost constant fighting, deserves to be remembered as a most gallant feat of arms'. It figured prominently in British news bulletins day after day, a French journalist remarking, 'The Australians have again captured the British communiqué'. General von Moser stated that the fighting was 'By common consent . . . much bitterer than on the Somme'.[20]

Some Australians were involved in the overhead fight, which was some of the hardest aerial combat of the war. As no Australian squadrons were in France then, they served in British ones. Perhaps the best known was Lieutenant Stan Dallas of 1 Squadron, Royal Naval Air Service (RNAS), who had six kills by September 1916. Dallas once dropped a pair of flying boots over a German airfield with a note, 'Ground Officers – for the use of', a way of saying that the German flyers had cold feet, and then shot them up when they clustered around the boots. Flight Sub-Lieutenant Robert Little had opened his account by the end of 1916 as part of the famous 'Naval Eight', 8 Squadron RNAS. Other Australians in British squadrons were Charles Kingsford-Smith, Charles Ulm, Gordon Taylor and Bert Hinkler, all of whom became renowned aviation pioneers postwar.[21]

Though these men were worlds removed from the squalor of muddy trenches, the environment in which they fought was still harsh. Pilots sat in open cockpits, close to engines that were louder than a pneumatic drill and vibrated so much their bodies shook. At the routine altitude of 10 000 feet, sub-zero temperatures, oxygen deprivation and increased blood pressure kicked in, reducing efficiency by 75 per cent. Then came the physically draining forces of violent combat manoeuvres. Lacking parachutes, pilots had no means of escaping the extreme vulnerability of their aircraft, which were flimsy, powered by unreliable engines and covered in highly inflammable doped fabric. Fire was their greatest fear. 'To watch a machine burst into flames is a ghastly sight. At first it peeps out of the tank as if almost ashamed of what it is about to do', wrote the British ace of aces, Major Mick Mannock, shortly before his death. 'Then it gets bigger as it licks its way along the length and breadth of the machine. Finally, all that can be seen is a large ball of fire enveloping in terrifying embrace.' The spectacle could be awful even when machines went straight in. Dallas watched one of his victims plummet earthwards in an inverted dive, with the dead pilot's arms hanging limp over his head. 'One can't help thinking of the chap you have shot', he wrote afterwards.[22]

The Germans formed *Jagdstaffeln* (*Jastas*) of handpicked pilots flying the latest aircraft, the best known of which was the *Jasta* led by Captain Manfred von Richthofen. Unlike the Royal Flying Corps (RFC), which always followed an offensive strategy, the Germans fought defensively. Apart from reconnaissance machines and bombers, they rarely crossed the lines. The *Jastas* simply patrolled in strength on their own side, waiting to pounce on the British machines they knew would be coming over. This combination of better aircraft flown by squadrons of the best pilots on the one hand, and the RFC's offensive policy on the other, turned the skies above the Arras offensive into a British bloodbath. During 'Bloody April', as it was called thereafter, the British lost almost half of their 360 aircraft supporting the offensive and a fifth of all aircrew. Richthofen's *Jasta* led the way, his own tally rising from thirty to fifty-two. The Australians at Bullecourt often saw the all-red Albatros scout that he flew.[23]

Among the few British aircraft that could match the Albatros was the new Sopwith Triplane, which had been test flown by Sopwith's famous Australian test pilot, Harry Hawker. One of its outstanding exponents, Dallas made April bloody for the Germans, shooting down eight. Now a flight commander with twenty kills, he would soon take over 1 Squadron. Little had also become well known after single-handedly attacking eleven Albatros, reputedly from Richthofen's *Jasta*, on 7 April and outflying them for half an hour. Crack pilot and marksman though he was, his heart-stopping landings were the stuff of legend. On 24 April he brought down a German, who glided to a perfect landing behind the British lines. Trying to land alongside, Little was stuck under the cockpit when his Triplane overturned. 'It rather looks as if I shot you down', quipped Lieutenant Neumuller, a pre-war Oxford Rhodes Scholar, as he helped Little out. By the end of May, Little also had twenty kills.[24]

On the ground, the Arras battle fizzled out on 17 May after costing the BEF almost 159 000 men. Towards the end it was a moot point whether the British, or more specifically the Australians at Bullecourt, were attacking not just to steel French offensive will but 'to prevent the Germans from finding out why so little offensiveness was apparent on the French front'. Coming on top of its earlier losses, the disappointment over the collapse of Nivelle's offensive, made all the greater because of the high hopes he had raised, was more than the French Army could stand. On 29 April a battalion refused to return to the line. A division did the same four days later.

The unrest spread like wildfire until fifty-four divisions, almost half the army, were affected. Twenty thousand men deserted. On 15 May Pétain, the one man who could restore its spirit, replaced Nivelle as commander-in-chief.

The French government was badly wrong-footed. On 4 May Prime Minister Alexandre Ribot, War Minister Paul Painlevé and their military chiefs had met Lloyd George, Haig and Robertson in Paris. The conference resolved to keep pressing the Germans, with the British delivering the next big blow in Flanders supported by the French 'with all possible energy'. The French Army's downing of tools rendered that promise hollow. 'We must wait for the Americans and the tanks' indeed became unofficial French policy, but saying as much would have terminated France's status as a major belligerent and hence its influence within Allied councils. So Pétain promised Haig the fullest co-operation while keeping the extent of his army's disarray from him. Pétain's real priority was to nurse it back to health. The main burden on the Western Front passed to the British. Indeed, they would also have to shoulder the main Allied burden in the war as a whole, for the French Army was not the only one in trouble.[25]

In the wake of the Brusilov offensive, Russia's army was tottering. It had lost 1.8 million dead and poor conditions sapped its morale. By the end of 1916 the desire for peace was overwhelming. In March 1917 strikes in St Petersburg escalated into the storming of the Winter Palace, and the Tsar abdicated. Uneasily sharing authority with the soviets or people's committees, the new Provisional Government intended to fulfil Russia's part in the joint offensive agreed upon at the end of 1916 at the Chantilly Inter-Allied conference, but the army was in no condition to do so. Elsewhere the Italians had launched the Tenth Battle of the Isonzo on 12 May but lost 157 000 men for a trivial gain. Anglo-French attacks in Salonika, a theatre that tied down half a million men, were unsuccessful.

Though their achievement at Bullecourt was one of the few bright spots on this gloomy scene, the Australians were also bruised. With the 4th Division put out of action by the first battle, the second absorbed the other three divisions of I ANZAC and cost them 7000 men. The need to replace the combined losses of 10 000 from both battles dealt a mortal blow to the 6th Division forming in England. By this time, too, I ANZAC had been continually engaged since Pozières ten months earlier, apart from its quiet interlude at Ypres. The men were tired and resentful at the lack of respite. Their mood had been apparent in the attitude of many to the election in May 1917. With support for the war effort the main issue, it resulted in a landslide for Hughes's Nationalist government. In Captain Braithwaite's company, eighty out of 200 men voted. 'They don't care who are in. Everybody is disgusted with the whole lot. They are a lot of swindlers', he wrote. 'The best thing would be to send them all over here.' Private Hartnett also acknowledged that 'few of us bothered to vote'.[26]

Before the 5th Division's stint at Bullecourt, General Hobbs warned Birdwood of complaints that British divisions were constantly being relieved. Told otherwise, Hobbs pointed out that one of the two British divisions billeted next to the 5th had been resting for three months and the other for almost two. If letters reflecting the ugly mood were published in Australia, recruiting, already poor, would fall further. Birdwood passed Hobbs's representations to Gough. Incensed that the matter had not been represented to Haig already, White stated flatly to Malcolm at the same time that he would never again agree to an Australian force serving abroad unless its commander had unfettered access to the commander-in-chief. Straightaway GHQ sent the Australian divisions to the back areas around Amiens, where I ANZAC's four-month rest was one of the longest given to any corps in the BEF.[27]

—TWELVE—

The Pillars of Fire at Messines

The 3rd Australian Division was unlike the other Australian divisions. It had gone straight from Australia to England, where companies assembled into battalions and battalions into brigades for the first time at Lark Hill on Salisbury Plain from July to August 1916. 'There is a certain air about the men', General Monash ventured soon after taking command. 'They all have a mature, independent, hard and active look, the outstanding characteristic being intelligence.' Monash thought they were superior to the originals in his old 4th Brigade. That they were virtually untrained, owing to the critical shortage of weapons and equipment in Australia, did not disturb him. Whereas much of the training given to the other divisions before they went to France was irrelevant, Monash could prepare his from the outset for the type of fighting it would shortly enter. 'There will not be a minute wasted in teaching things the men will afterwards have to unlearn', he said.

On Salisbury Plain a brigade trench system was dug 'replete in every detail with bomb stores, observers' stations, snipers' positions [and] complete wiring'. Each brigade occupied it for five days at a time to practise reliefs, patrols, raids and attacks. The climax came on 6 November when four artillery batteries, signallers, engineers and four aircraft supported an 'assault' by five battalions:

A large mine was exploded under the 'enemy' trenches, the infantry rushing the crater as the barrage formed a protective box around it. Men blocked the communication trenches as Lewis gun teams co-operated with bombers on either flank to cover the wiring parties consolidating the position.[1]

Despite losing men to replenish the other Australian divisions after their losses on the Somme, the 3rd Division arrived in France in November 1916 better fitted for the Western Front than they had been. It joined the Second Army as part of II ANZAC near the old Armentières nursery sector that Monash had left as a brigade commander.

While the other Australian divisions were briefly under General Plumer before having to endure Gough's command, the 3rd was singularly fortunate in that it remained in his army. Some say that the cartoonist Low took his inspiration for Colonel Blimp from Plumer. Appearances were deceptive. He was determined not to waste lives, which made him a disciple of 'bite and hold'. 'Trust, Training and Thoroughness' were his watchwords. Plumer's close partnership with his chief-of-staff, Major-General Charles Harington, symbolised the co-operative spirit that underpinned relations between the Second Army's staff and its men. 'They are a wonderful combination, much the most popular, as a team, of any of the Army Commanders', observed Haig's intelligence chief, Brigadier-General John Charteris. 'The troops love them.' It was a far cry from Gough, Malcolm and the Fifth Army. Plumer had also led Australians and New Zealanders during the Boer War and the mutual affection they shared then was once more evident. Like everyone else, they called him 'Daddy' or 'Old Plum'; he was delighted to be leading them again.[2]

Its sister formations thought the 3rd Division had been enjoying the good life while they were fighting hard. 'It has not declared war yet', sneered Captain Aram. Nicknames such as the Neutrals, the Lark Hill Lancers and the Eggs-a-Cook, and especially the taunts of the others that they had been 'down on the Somme', rankled Monash's men. Seeking to dispel the animosity, the 3rd began raiding and became the pre-eminent Australian division at it. Bean called its raid at Houplines on 27 February 1917 'the most important ever undertaken by Australians'. Eight hundred and twenty-four men from the 10th Brigade rehearsed for ten days on a replica of the German trenches. Monash introduced 'flavoured smoke', probably for the first time in the BEF. The preliminary bombardment included smoke and gas to inveigle the Germans into wearing their gas masks whenever they saw smoke. The final bombardment omitted the gas, enabling the raiders to attack without gas masks and catch the Germans in theirs. Reaching the third German line, the raiders occupied a half-mile stretch for thirty-five minutes, protected by a box barrage so straight, said Captain Charles Peters of the 38th Battalion, 'You could have toasted bread at it'. Monash told Birdwood:

> The whole system of enemy works was thoroughly demolished, a minimum of over 200 dead have been counted, 17 prisoners were brought back; as also a very large quantity of material, including several quite new types of Minenwerfer Fuzes, a complete portable electric searchlight plant, several medical panniers, a miscellaneous collection of rifles, helmets and equipment, and a large mass of papers, maps and documents.

In the following days the Germans struck the 3rd Division seven times but only reached its line twice. Still, Monash knew that the feeling against his formation would not entirely fade until it had been through the mill of a major battle. The opportunity came with Haig's Flanders offensive.[3]

Haig had always favoured an offensive in Flanders. Commanding I Corps during the retreat from Mons in August 1914, he had advocated moving the BEF by sea to Ostend to strike the German lines of communication. In January 1916, shortly after becoming commander-in-chief, he proposed a northeasterly drive from the

Ypres Salient to clear the Belgian coast but had to fall in with Joffre's scheme for the joint Somme offensive. He revived the project at the Chantilly conference in November. It decided to renew the Somme offensive in the spring and to carry out the Ypres operation afterwards. The ditching of the Somme offensive for Nivelle's stroke did not fundamentally affect the Ypres one, which Haig was adamant must still proceed. When Nivelle's offensive collapsed, 'there was no doubt as to where his efforts would lie'. On 7 May Haig told the army commanders that he was transferring the BEF's weight to Ypres.[4]

The BEF had twice saved the town. During First Ypres in October 1914, the original BEF was virtually destroyed while forming a salient around it. At Second Ypres in April 1915, the Germans used gas for the first time on the Western Front and pushed in the salient to within two miles of the town. They were ensconced thereafter on the high ground that overlooked both. Starting near Messines, six miles south, these heights curved northeast past Ypres through the Gheluvelt Plateau, Passchendaele and Staden, while Pilckem Ridge, an underfeature of the plateau, rose on the northern side of Ypres. Unimpressive speedbumps like Aubers Ridge above Fromelles, they gave the same commanding views. The Germans saw everything that went on in the salient below and shelled the slightest movement. Life for the British on the flats was grim and 'Wipers' etched itself into the national psyche. Shoving the Germans off the heights therefore seemed a worthwhile undertaking.[5]

The Second Army would take the first step. Unlike the other armies of the BEF, it had not participated in a major offensive. When Plumer took command during Second Ypres, he also became the custodian of the Ypres Salient. After the battle, Haig's predecessor, General Sir John French, asked him what was 'the greatest strategical and tactical objective on the Second Army Front'. Plumer pointed to the Messines–Wytschaete Ridge, 264 feet at its highest point, which commanded the communications into the salient to the north. He felt that the ridge was worth taking for its own sake and started mining operations with a view to doing so in spring 1916. By then Haig had succeeded French. Haig considered attacking the ridge if the Germans denuded it to reinforce the Somme. I ANZAC was sent to Messines for the purpose. The Somme consumed all of Haig's resources instead. But the observation the ridge gave the Germans made its capture an essential preliminary to the Ypres offensive he had in mind now. Holding it would also secure the right flank. At the meeting on 7 May, Haig asked Plumer when he could attack. 'Today, one month, sir', replied Plumer. So 7 June was the date set. 'The Second Army had its chance at last', Harington wrote.[6]

Skirting the western foot of the ridge, the ten-mile attack frontage followed a salient that bulged westwards between St Yves in the south and Mount Sorrel in the north. As well as gaining the German second line on the crest, shown on British maps as the Black Line, Plumer was to take the Oosttaverne or Green Line, a reverse slope position a mile further back, in the hope of capturing some of the German guns. That objective made IX Corps's advance in the centre much longer than those of X Corps and II ANZAC against the northern and southern shoulders of the salient respectively. Hence the Green Line was to be struck ten hours after the opening blow, which would enable IX Corps to catch up with the others for a simultaneous assault on it. As Messines was a true 'bite and hold' attack, the question of pressing on to the third or Warneton Line another mile east did not arise. The exploitation to the Green Line was 'just as far as, and no further than, the point where German numbness began to wear off'.[7]

The two years since the first hint of the attack allowed Plumer to make preparations on a scale unique in the BEF. Twenty-four mines packed with over 500 tons of ammonal ran under the German front line. In November the 1st Australian Tunnelling Company had taken over the two northernmost ones, at Hill 60 and the Caterpillar, two and a half miles from Ypres, and started digging a third mine there. Once they mastered the technique of clay-kicking, in which a digger lying on his back on an inclined plank used both feet to jab a short spade into the clay face, the Australians advanced fourteen feet daily but the attack came before their mine was completed. The work was tense in the extreme, for this squalid patch had long been the most intensively mined area of the Western Front and the Germans countermined constantly. On 24 April an Australian tunneller heard footsteps that were so loud he thought a German had broken into his tunnel. He extinguished his lamp. The sound passed six feet overhead. It came from a German gallery that had gone detected. Waiting until May 17 when the German one seemed almost finished, the Australians destroyed it by blowing up their own gallery.

As at Arras, the artillery strength needed was carefully worked out according to the amount of wire to be cut, the length of trench to be destroyed and the number of German batteries to be neutralised. The calculation came to 2226 guns, 756 of them heavy or medium, and 458 large-calibre mortars. This concentration, for which 144 000 tons of shells were dumped, represented one gun for every seven yards of front, the highest yet in the BEF. The gunners could use the new scientific techniques of flash-spotting and sound-ranging to locate the German guns. Starting on 21 May, the bombardment entered its intense phase ten days later. Augmented by the fire of 454 machine-guns, the creeping barrage would form a wall of metal 700 yards deep in order to silence machine-guns shooting at long-range through it, a favourite German tactic since the Somme. The 300 aircraft available included better machines such as the SE5 and the Bristol Fighter, which had helped the RFC recover from the mauling of Bloody April. They outnumbered the German planes two to one, enabling British aerial spotters to operate freely. Plumer also received seventy-two of the new Mark IV tanks, less vulnerable than their predecessors but just as unreliable, which he distributed among the three assaulting corps. 'No one that had not actually seen it can imagine the magnitude', 3rd Division machine-gunner Private Leslie Jungwirth said of the preparations.[8]

While the New Zealand Division, with the British 25th Division on its left, advanced in the centre of II ANZAC to capture Messines, Monash's Australians would form the right flank of the entire attack. Monash gazed at the battlefield from the observation post on Hill 63, under which the Australian tunnellers had chiselled out accommodation for two battalions. It was on the left of his division's frontage, which stretched 2000 yards eastwards to St Yves. The southern end of the Messines Ridge rose behind the Douve streamlet, its grassy slope cut by the wire and shallow trenches of the German front line. Monash, a Jew, could see the shell of Messines church on the crest. Denoting the Black Line, it had been the subject of several watercolours by Corporal Hitler, the future nemesis of his people. Harder to discern because of the sods and earth camouflaging them, concrete pillboxes dotted each line and, checkerboard-fashion, the slope between them. Though hidden, the reverse slope back to the Oosttaverne Line was held in the same way.[9]

Three things over which he had no control were clear to Monash. First, the fate of the 3rd Division's advance depended on the New Zealanders' storming of Messines because its trenches enfiladed the length of the 3rd's assault. Second, being on the flank of the salient arc meant that 'the right hand man of the 3rd . . . had to stand still while the left hand man had some three thousand yards to go', making co-ordination difficult. Last, the approach routes behind Ploegsteert Wood and Hill 63 would be heavily shelled because both were obvious locations for II ANZAC's artillery. Overall, the 3rd Division's task was 'a fairly heavy and responsible one for a staff and troops that had never before engaged in a major operation'. It became harder with the advance to the Oosttaverne Line. Whereas the 4th Australian Division, Godley's reserve in the first phase, would leapfrog the New Zealanders and the 25th Division to assault it, the 3rd was to do the job itself in its own sector. Consequently, its arrangements were meticulous even by the high standards that Plumer set.[10]

Monash told his brigadiers how they should employ even their platoons, and how many picks and shovels their battalions must carry. Visiting the Canadians to glean the lessons of Vimy Ridge, he learned that the bombardment had disturbed the ground so much that German dugouts were only visible as holes in the sides of craters. Directions on the need for careful mopping up resulted. Monash claimed that every German trench, strongpoint, farm, dugout, machine-gun, mortar, signal station, buried cable, tramway and dump identified from aerial photographs had been noted and plans made for the bombardment and capture of each one. As the 3rd Division's preliminary bombardment programme listed 446 targets, he was not kidding. Thirty-six instructions compiled into a document six inches thick covered every aspect of the attack. Monash ran through it at conferences attended by the commanders and staffs of all arms and services and, frequently, by the junior commanders. 'We are going to talk these matters out to a finish and will not separate until we have a perfect mutual understanding among all concerned', he said. On one occasion he sought the views of the engineer company commanders. 'This was a new experience for me', Major Geoffrey Drake-Brockman remarked. Many of the best British generals used the conference method but Monash was its most renowned exponent.[11]

The attack would be the first by Australian troops using the revised tactical doctrine for platoons recently issued by GHQ. Derived by the Canadians, it abandoned the notion of the platoon as just a solid line of riflemen dependent for its main firepower on attached specialists. Realising that it was the largest unit that could be directly manoeuvred under fire by one man, as well as the primary unit of attack, the Canadians included all the specialists within the platoon. It now consisted of a bombing section, a Lewis gun section and two rifle sections with a number of rifle grenadiers.

This structure made it a 'complete and independent tactical unit' that was flexible enough to meet most eventualities. The men were also cross-trained in each other's tasks, ending the guild mentality that often applied before. 'What a mistake it was not to have every man trained in bomb fighting', Private Vince Bowman of the 9th Battalion had lamented during the Pozières fighting in 1916. After watching the 3rd Division's first rehearsal for the Messines attack, Godley remarked that the application of the principles 'appears to be very good and on sound lines. The Platoon Commanders seem to have a very good grasp of what is required'.[12]

Numerous rehearsals followed on ground almost identical to that in the attack sector and against positions marked out according to the latest aerial photos of the German line. Supplementing II ANZAC's terrain model of the battlefield, the 3rd built another one for its own assault, an encircling platform giving companies in turn a bird's eye view of the divisional objectives. 'It was a splendid job showing trenches, wire, trees, trench railways . . . roads and everything of importance', recalled Captain Robert Grieve of the 37th Battalion. Monash directed his commanders to study the New Zealand Division's orders so that they understood exactly how its attack fitted in with theirs. They found that General Russell was also leaving nothing to chance. For the mopping up of the village, the New Zealanders went so far as giving each section an objective.[13]

Before the attack the 11th Brigade took over the 3rd Division's assault frontage, on which the 9th and 10th Brigades would advance. The positions below the ridge were miserable, owing to what Private Gallwey called 'bestial German practices'. He accused the Germans on the slope of arranging their latrine runoffs so that 'urine and excreta drained into the British trenches', which became especially foul after rain. But the Germans were having a far worse time. The British guns plastered them with 3.5 million shells in the eleven days before the attack, reducing Messines and Wytschaete to rubble and turning the once green ridge into a brown wasteland cloaked by a monstrous dust cloud. Stripped of their camouflage, the naked grey pillboxes stood out as perfect targets. 'All the trenches are completely smashed in', one German soldier moaned. 'No more shelter is to hand.' Ration parties could not get through and the nightly deluge of gas prevented sleep. One of the two divisions facing II ANZAC was pummelled so badly that it had to be replaced on the eve of the assault by a division previously set aside for counterattacks. The incoming division had no time to adapt to its new role. Nor was the German artillery any better off. Outnumbered at the outset with 748 guns, it had lost almost half before the battle began.[14]

At midnight on 6 June the Australian assault battalions were filing through Ploegsteert Wood. 'Pht, pht, pht' went the gas shells raining into it. The heavily laden columns had to don gas masks, 'a tremendous hardship', wrote Captain Grieve, 'because it nearly reaches a point of suffocation to be subject to continual exertion with a mask on'. High-explosive shelling added to the confusion. At 2 a.m., when their assembly should have been complete, the Australians had just cleared the wood and suffered at least 500 casualties. Thanks to their training, and Monash's decision to spread the approach over four routes to minimise congestion and delays, they still arrived in good time for the attack. Many fell asleep after gratefully drinking the water he had ordered to be stored in the jump-off trenches. Waiting to fire the Hill 60 mines, Captain Oliver Woodward, who answered the anonymous white feathers he received before enlisting by becoming the first Australian tunneller to be decorated, intently followed the second hand of his watch as it ticked around to 3.10 a.m.:

15 seconds to go, 10 seconds to go, 9, 8, 7, 6, 5, 4, 3, 2, 1 – Fire. Over went the firing switch, and with a dull roar, accompanied by a heaving of the ground, the mines exploded . . . In the determination that the firing switch would be properly closed, I grabbed the handle firmly. The switch was rather on the small side, so that when the handle was thrown over, my

hand came in contact with the terminals and I received a strong electric shock, which threw me backwards. For a fraction of a second, I could not realise what had happened but as my thoughts were collected, I perceived that all was well.

For tactical reasons, only nineteen of the twenty-four mines were set off. Londoners heard the blast and felt the 'strange early morning shock', which also shook all of southern England, wrote Voluntary Aid Detachment nurse Vera Brittain. In Lille and other nearby French towns, an earthquake was thought to have occurred. Ten thousand Germans were reckoned to have perished. Advancing immediately afterwards, future British prime minister Lieutenant Anthony Eden heard the screams of the dying above the noise of battle.

Six mines were fired on II ANZAC's front and one on either side. Captain Grieve looked in the direction of one of them:

All were on tiptoe of expectation . . . Our first warning that she was fired was by sounds like distant rumblings of thunder – then gradually getting closer – then directly to our front the earth was seen to be rising like a huge mushroom – suddenly to be flung into space with an awe-inspiring roar and the earth trembled – to us it appeared with mingled fear and relief – fear of the dread power she had stored in her bowels – relief because it had vented its fury and although she was sadly torn, its menace was gone . . . Debris of all description rained down with dull thuds for quite a time then all was over.[15]

The explosions rocked the trenches, rattling the bones of the waiting attackers. With the earth already vomiting pillars of fire, the inferno when the barrage fell was impossible to describe, Grieve recalled. 'The air screamed shells and snapped bullets and above all was the roar of the guns, the crackle of the machine guns and the hum of aeroplane propellers.' The advancing Australians were soon swallowed up in the thick cloud engulfing the ridge. Direction and order were difficult to keep and in places successive waves merged into a single line. Three smoking craters, each 200 feet across and twenty deep, broke up the 9th Brigade. Training took over again. Sorting themselves out as they went, the men headed for their designated objectives in what was the AIF 's easiest assault to date.

Cowed by the bombardment and the explosions, many Germans fled. Others quivered in their shelters or lay listlessly in the surrounding shell holes. No sooner did the Australians start bombing and bayoneting than they emerged, 'cringing like beaten animals'. 'I have never seen men so demoralised', Lieutenant William Garrard of the 40th Battalion said. It was the same for the 38th Battalion alongside. 'The enemy would not stand up to us', said Major Arthur Maudsley. 'They asked us not to kill them.' Heeding the '*Willkommen*' sign at the entrance to a shelter, Sapper Len Newton went inside. The occupants had left in a great hurry 'for not an article was missing and even such things as penknives and cigarette cases were lying about'. Newton helped himself to soda water, 'dark and heavy bread' and 'a sausage wrapped in a Frankfurt newspaper'. The only serious resistance encountered was on the right where the 33rd Battalion was machine-gunned from the area of Ultimo crater, named after the mine that caused it. Two men covered by rifle grenadiers dealt with one gun and a Stokes mortar dealt with the other. Private John Carroll won the VC for knocking out another gun and rescuing a mate seized by the Germans.

Alongside the Australians, the New Zealanders faced the steeper spine of the ridge. It was covered in huge shell holes that made for hard going in the murk. Corporal Henry Jeffery of the Rifle Brigade captured twelve prisoners after silencing a machine-gun trained on the Australians to the south. Lance-Corporal Samuel Frickleton of the 3rd Rifles received the VC for rushing and destroying two more near Messines, which was then cleared by the 2nd Canterbury and 4th Rifle Battalions. Bombing along the streets, the New Zealanders seized five machine-guns before they could come into action, rushed five from the rear and used rifle grenades to knock out two firing across the square. Private Fred White, the Canterburys' barber, took out another firing from a dressing station near the square and killed the perfidious crew. The German commander at Messines and his staff were captured.

After waiting an hour for the village to fall, the Australian support battalions leapfrogged the leading ones and resumed the advance to the Black Line. In scrappy fighting they seized three field guns and several machine-guns. By 5.15 a.m. the Black Line was being consolidated all along II ANZAC's front. Lieutenant-Colonel Morshead watched the 33rd Battalion digging in under shellfire as if it were on Salisbury Plain. The New Zealanders lost nothing in comparison, some Maori pioneers disappearing completely below ground inside an hour. Together with the 25th Division, Russell's men also pushed out 800 yards to establish posts along the Black Dotted Line, which was to protect the 37th Battalion and the 4th Division when they formed up for the afternoon attack on the Oosttaverne Line.

As the fresh units for this phase headed towards the ridge in glorious sunshine, under a sky filled with British aircraft, Private Gallwey saw the carnage that the darkness had kept hidden:

> Trenches which had reached an elaborate state of perfection were utterly destroyed. Where concrete dugouts had existed strongly reinforced with steel rails, instead of being shattered, they were completely turned upside down . . . Came upon a portion of a trench in which the sides had caved in after the explosion. Three Germans were pinned in the trench with just their heads protruding . . . Whether they were killed in the explosion or merely buried, it would be difficult to conjecture; but they were all dead men now. Machine gun fire had cut off the tops of their heads as clean as if they had been sliced with a knife. They presented ghastly sights as the blood and brains had trickled down until their faces were almost unrecognisable as human beings. I felt sick to look at such a sight.

There were so many German dead that the Australians had to pick their way through them. Nor were the casualties only German. Captain Grieve passed the remains of a 40th Battalion bridging party that had been obliterated by a shell just after throwing its bridge over the Douve, a precaution taken by Monash that ultimately proved unnecessary. 'They all lay there dead – two of them in their death struggles still retained hold of the rope carrying handles.' On reaching the ridge, the scene changed for the better. Behind was the bloody, churned up wilderness of shell holes, craters, smashed trenches and tangled wire. Ahead the Flemish lowlands, pristine green and seamed by clipped, tree-lined hedgerows, rolled away to the horizon. Closer to hand were men in shirtsleeves furiously entrenching on the Black and Black Dotted Lines in the sweltering heat. 'Yet they found time for a joke and a smoke', wrote Grieve. 'It was more like a picnic than a battle.' Along the entire front, only the 47th Division from X Corps, near Ypres, had suffered a setback.[16]

The bucolic mood abruptly vanished. Late in the morning a German aircraft penetrated the British aerial scout screen and detected the build-up on II ANZAC's end of the ridge. The surviving German guns concentrated on the area. Moving into position for the 1.10 p.m. assault on the Oosttaverne Line, the 37th Battalion and the 12th Brigade were caught in the open, the 37th losing 10 per cent of its strength. News arrived that Plumer had postponed the assault until 3.10 p.m. because the other formations and the guns were having trouble getting forward over the damaged ground. Two more hours of shelling had to be endured. At 1.30 p.m. it stepped up because the 1st Guard Reserve Division was counterattacking. The British preparatory bombardment on the Oosttaverne Line forced the Guards back to it. Also reinforced during the morning pause, the line was now held in some strength. Partly for that reason, the denuded Australians attacking it, even with tank support, had nothing like the cakewalk of their predecessors.

Pillboxes caused most of the trouble. As they were proof against a direct hit from all but the biggest shells, the garrisons could emerge unscathed, set up their machine-guns and tie down the advance. Some were loopholed, enabling the guns to fire from within. The new platoon structure lent itself to the standard drill against a pillbox, in which Lewis gunners and rifle grenadiers fired at the loopholes to cover the riflemen and bombers working around behind it. But if flanking or depth pillboxes engaged them while they did so, the drill broke down. The Australians had not encountered pillboxes on a systematic basis before and the fights around them were ferocious. Often the invariably sudden surrender of a garrison once surrounded went unrespected. Bean elaborated soberly and with great candour:

> Where such tension exists in battle, the rules of 'civilised' war are powerless. Most men are temporarily half-mad, their pulses pounding at their ears, their mouths dry. The noblest among them are straining their wills to keep cool heads and even voices; the less self-controlled are for the time being governed by reckless, primitive impulse. With death singing about their ears, they will kill until they grow tired of killing. When they have been racked with machine-gun fire, the routing out of enemy groups from behind several feet of concrete is almost inevitably the signal for a butchery at least of the first few who emerge, and sometimes even the helplessly wounded may not be spared. It is idle for the reader to cry shame upon such incidents, unless he cries out upon the whole system of war, for this frenzy is an inevitable condition in desperate fighting.

When the 47th Battalion was subduing some pillboxes in the Oosttaverne Line astride Hun's Walk (the Messines–Comines Road), Lewis gun fire at the loopholes suppressed the machine-gun inside one of them. Private Gallwey saw some riflemen creep behind the pillbox and fire through the entrance at the garrison:

> There was a noise as though pigs were being killed. They squealed and made guttural noises which gave place to groans after which all was silent. The bodies were all thrown into a heap outside the pillbox to make sure all were dead. There were five of them altogether . . . Sometimes in our hurry we leave a wounded [German] and then the duty of the mopping up party is to finish him. Their work would be light today for we are determined to kill every German we come across.

Attacking alongside the 47th, the 37th Battalion was caught by a pillbox that wiped out half of Captain Grieve's company. 'It was put out of action by the aid of Mills Grenades', his report said, 'and the company were able to get forward onto the objective'. Grieve did not mention that he was the thrower and that, covered by the dust of the explosions, he had rushed up to the loophole and rolled two bombs into it, knocking out the machine-gunners therein. So was a VC won. The Germans began bolting. Those unable to get away lay on the ground crying 'Mercy, *Kamerad!*' or embracing the knees of the Australians.

Advancing south of the Blauwepoortbeek stream next to the 47th, the 45th Battalion ran up against a large concentration of Guards, as well as pillboxes and field guns. Whipped by murderous fire, the 45th and the 49th from the 13th Brigade on the far side of the stream could get no closer than 500 yards to the Oosttaverne Line. On their left, the 52nd Battalion was on its own from the outset for the British 33rd Brigade, which should have extended the 52nd's line, did not turn up. Poor staff work sent the formation on a roundabout route over the broken ground in the heat and it was exhausted. Well-known 6 foot 5 inch Anzac and Mouquet Farm veteran Captain Arthur Maxwell led the 52nd as it rooted out eighty Germans in spreading thinly across the 33rd Brigade's objective as well as its own. When some of the 33rd eventually appeared, Maxwell moved them into position. British formations took the rest of the Oosttaverne Line. The Australians held half of it, albeit with a 1000-yard gap at the Blauwepoortbeek.

At this point the attack turned into a tragicomedy of errors. Their numbers weak – the 37th Battalion was down to 230 men – and under continuous machine-gun fire, the Australians could see a counterattack assembling. Afraid of giving away their positions, they did not fire flares to show an overflying contact aircraft where they were. At 5.30 p.m. the Germans assaulted along Hun's Walk. Blazing away from the shoulder, a Lewis gunner 'took a wide sweep of the ground in front. It requires great strength to perform such a feat', wrote Gallwey. 'I inserted clip after clip in my magazine and must have fired about thirty shots in quick succession'. The attack crumpled. 'From despair our spirits rose rapidly', Gallwey said. They fell just as rapidly for the supporting artillery, unsure of the Australians' precise location, fired a barrage that swamped them instead of the Germans. The 47th bolted for the Black Line. The New Zealanders on the ridge thought the withdrawal resulted from a counterattack that was heading for them. Believing only the Germans were ahead, they adjusted the barrage accordingly. It fell on the 37th and 45th Battalions, forcing them back too. By 9 p.m. the Oosttaverne Line between the Blauwepoortbeek and the Douve, a distance of well over a mile, lay open. A hastily organised attack by the 44th and 48th Battalions, on 8 June, regained most of the ground but pillboxes prevented the closing of the Blauwepoortbeek gap. It did not matter. On 11 June the Germans retired towards the Warneton Line.[17]

The capture of the Oosttaverne Line had been as chaotic as the seizure of the ridge was smooth. In some quarters, General Holmes's 4th Division became the scapegoat. 'Directly a portion of [it] went though us we never knew what was going on – and did not know the position in front up to the moment we came out of the line', General Russell said. But the 4th had to assault through both his division and the 25th Division, that is, along two-thirds of the corps front, and alongside the 3rd Australian. Arguably the most complex task in II ANZAC, it necessitated close liaison with all three divisions, which it was the responsibility of Godley and his staff to provide. They let Holmes down badly. Moreover, as the Black Line encompassing the ridge was the critical objective, the artillery had been organised for its defence, even though counterattacks would naturally hit the Oosttaverne Line first. The 4th Division, which mainly occupied the Oosttaverne Line, therefore depended on guns whose priority was the support of the New Zealanders and the 25th Division behind it. Haig made another apposite point to Major-General Guy Bainbridge, the 25th's commander. Bainbridge complained that 4th Division detachments 'have been wandering about in his vicinity as if they had "no leaders"'. Haig countered that the 4th 'was at Bullecourt and lost many officers'.[18]

Unexpectedly called upon so soon after that ordeal, particularly while the other Australian divisions were still resting, the mood in the 4th was grim. Morale aside, the state of the division was also questionable. Despite receiving 3600 replacements, it was still 1600 men understrength. There had barely been time to absorb the newcomers, let alone train for the attack to anything like the same extent as the rest of II ANZAC. These shortcomings placed an extra burden on the leaders, who suffered terrible casualties as a result. In the first few minutes of their assaults, the 45th Battalion lost most of its officers and the 49th every company commander killed. Prolonged shelling by their own artillery was the last straw for many leaderless men. For most of those who withdrew to avoid it, 'wandering about' in the Black Line simply meant trying to find their unit. Nor was there any reluctance to advance. Told to take a blockhouse that had already defied three attacks, Lieutenant Tom McIntyre of the 45th Battalion knew that a fourth attempt would be suicidal. He replied nonetheless: 'All right, Sir; if it is to be taken, it will be taken'. McIntyre led his men out. The German machine-guns spat. McIntyre was killed. The attack failed.[19]

The battle was gruelling for both Australian divisions. Searching for a sniper who had harassed them for several hours, soldiers from the 47th Battalion saw a branch moving above a distant shell hole. Thinking it might be the sniper, some of them wanted to fire at it but others thought they should investigate first. Two men crawled out and found a wounded Australian, whom they brought back. Private Gallwey was overcome:

The wounded man had . . . his two eyes shot away by a fragment of shell. All night he had laid in that shell hole and this morning grasped a small branch which he had used as a signal to attract attention. For a couple of hours he had been waving this about at intervals with no response. When our men got close to him, he heard their footsteps and called out. They answered him and he said 'Thank God I am in British hands'. He feared all the time he was in German lines. The poor unfortunate did not even know he was blind. Must have been unconscious for some hours and when he came to sensibility, the blood had dried and congealed with earth, forming a crust that made him believe his face was covered with mud. It was sad to hear him comment on it now, saying, 'I will be glad when I can get this mud off my face so that I can see.' No one undeceived him.

In the 3rd Division, Corporal George Carson of the 33rd Battalion wrote:

I've been knocked over by a shell covered by another and dug out, disputed the point with four Fritzies and hung onto a position for 32 hours with one man only and four dead stinking Huns. We could not get food sent up, the shelling was damnable and eventually the four Napoo Huns were so objectionable that we had to cut them up bit by bit and throw them as far away from us as possible.

From its commander down, the 3rd Division was highly praised. Of the forty-eight guns captured, the 3rd took eleven. At a cost of 4100 casualties, it had proved itself up to the standard of the others. Altogether, II ANZAC suffered almost 14 000 of the 26 000

British casualties in the battle. Godley was partly to blame. Fearing counterattacks, he overruled the protests of Russell and Monash and ordered the ridge held in strength, which exposed his corps throughout to German shelling.[20]

The stunning opening success overshadowed the later slog and evoked a joy in Britain comparable to the news of Alamein twenty-five years later. Though German losses were similar to the British, probably for the first time in a major battle, newspapers hailed 'the most sweeping and most brilliant victory won by British arms since the war began'. Some later assessments regarded it as an aberration, historian A. J. P. Taylor, for example, remarking: 'Two years of preparation and a million pounds of explosive had advanced the British front at most two miles. How long at this rate would it take to get to Berlin?' The mines for which the operation is best known, and which were its most time-consuming element, lie at the heart of this view. Yet the attack would most probably have succeeded without them, as it had at Vimy Ridge, where no mines were used. Plumer attributed the outcome principally to thorough training and rehearsal by the assault divisions and efficient counter-battery fire. Both Harington and German prisoners named the mines as only one of several factors responsible.[21]

In tactical terms, the key to the victory was the setting of limited objectives, which the infantry, moving behind the protective wall of a creeping barrage, could reach in sufficient strength to consolidate. The advance deliberately stopped well before resistance hardened, eliminating the cause of a reverse like Arras. Quick counterattacks, which the Germans were so adept at launching, invariably folded under the heavy standing barrage on the newly captured line. The tough fighting for the Oosttaverne Line did not undermine the limited approach, although it did expose two things, one peculiar to this attack, the other a general point. Going that far was Haig's idea; Plumer was never happy about it. Hence the Oosttaverne Line phase became a 'bolt-on' to the capture of the ridge. The command

and control issues, particularly in relation to the artillery, were not properly worked through. But the fumbling also showed that the army and corps staffs, used to static warfare, floundered when rapid reorganisation and redeployment were necessary. The solution was to conceive an attack in the round and prepare for it with every phase in mind from the start. What Messines had shown – and convincingly – was that so long as the objectives lay within artillery range, attacks were no longer 'foredoomed to failure and massive human loss'.[22]

For the Australians, Messines started the rebuilding of trust in British generalship. On 2 July they lost one of their own generals when a chance German salvo mortally wounded General Holmes while he was taking the New South Wales Premier, William Holman, on a normally safe route to see the battlefield. Major-General Sinclair-MacLagan, who had led the 3rd Brigade at Gallipoli and on the Somme, replaced him. The senior New Zealand officers did not get off scot-free either. Russell had two close shaves during the battle, narrowly escaping death when a shell killed Brigadier-General Charles Brown, commander of the 1st New Zealand Infantry Brigade, on 8 June, and again on the 10th when a sniper parted his hairline. Another sniper would soon kill Brigadier-General Johnston, the Rhododendron Ridge ditherer, who now led the New Zealand Rifle Brigade.

II ANZAC spent the next six weeks following up the Germans to the Warneton Line. On relieving the 25th Division, Monash's men saw that they had taken over a salient protruding towards Messines. Shelled, machine-gunned and sniped, the 11th Brigade dug a new front system across the chord during a period that became famous as the 'eighteen days'. German posts on the low Windmill Ridge blocked further progress and Monash proposed to clear them during the Second Army's feint towards Lille on 31 July, which was designed to divert attention from the offensive being launched simultaneously at Ypres. The 11th Brigade trained for three weeks for the attack, which utilised a smoke bomb developed for the Stokes mortar by Lieutenant Ambrose Varley of the 35th Battalion. Monash used it even though it had not been fully proven. The Windmill was taken, bringing the 3rd Division within 500 yards of the Warneton Line. Varley's bomb proved so successful that the BEF adopted it, Varley receiving £300 from the Inventions Board. South of the Australians, the New Zealand Division took La Basse Ville. To the north, IX and X Corps also gained useful ground. But the diversionary aspect of the operation failed because the Germans never doubted that the Ypres offensive was the main danger.

—THIRTEEN—

THEY CALLED IT PASSCHENDAELE

At meetings in London between 19 and 21 June 1917, Haig outlined his plan for the Flanders offensive to the War Policy Committee, the latest War Cabinet offshoot handling the higher direction of the war. Lloyd George's account of the presentation made Haig the possessor of history's best-known fingernail:

> He spread on a table or desk a large map and made a dramatic use of both his hands to demonstrate how he proposed to sweep up the enemy – first the right hand brushing along the surface irresistibly, and then came the left, his outer finger ultimately touching the German frontier with the nail across.

Haig's busy hands traced out the stroke he had foreshadowed to his army commanders at the start of May. After clearing both the Passchaendaele–Staden–Clercken Ridge to deny the Germans observation over the Ypres Salient, and the low ground beyond Pilckem Ridge, the advance would continue northeastwards towards Bruges. A subsidiary flanking thrust along the shore and an amphibious landing behind the German lines were to converge on it with 'the eventual object of securing the Belgian coast and connecting with the Dutch frontier'. Hemmed in by the coast and the border with neutral Holland, the Germans could not withdraw, as they had done to the Hindenburg Line. If they crumbled, Belgium would be liberated, thus achieving the immediate objective for which Britain had gone to war. Moreover, the Flanders advance would also strengthen Russian resolve and bolster the French. On 2 June the French had told Haig that their army was 'in a bad state of discipline', though without saying how bad. But they still promised six divisions, comprising their First Army, for the attack. Haig stressed he had 'no intention of entering into a tremendous offensive involving heavy losses', but to proceed 'step by step, and not to push in attacks that had not a reasonable chance of success'.[1]

Though Lloyd George had backed a loser in Nivelle and been warmer to Haig after Nivelle's failure, he was less emollient now. Clearing the Belgian coast would involve an advance of twenty-five miles, over three times as far as any advance to date. Seeing no reason to hope for anything more than a meagre initial success, he worried that Haig would resort to an attritional battle that would gravely strain British manpower. The French seemed unwilling to do more than stay on the defensive and Russia's position was 'hopeless'. Reverting to his favoured policy of 'knocking away the props', the Prime Minister wanted to beef up the Italians. Their Austrian opponents were looking shaky after the death of elderly Emperor Franz Josef in November 1916 robbed the decrepit Austro-Hungarian Empire of one of its few stabilising agents. Haig countered that the Flanders offensive was the best way of helping the Italians. Unless it went ahead, the Germans would be free to prop up the props.[2]

The offensive could not come quickly enough for the Admiralty. It had long wanted the Belgian coast cleared to eliminate any threat to the BEF's cross-Channel lines of communication. The Belgian ports were also havens for U-boats, which had sunk 373 ships, totalling 874 000 tons, in April and followed up with 285 ships, amounting to 590 000 tons, in May. Admiral Sir John Jellicoe, the First Sea Lord, reportedly told American Rear-Admiral William Sims: 'It is impossible for us to go on with the war if losses like this continue'. According to Jellicoe, a lack of shipping would prevent Britain fighting on into 1918 unless the Germans were evicted from the Belgian ports by the end of 1917. Lloyd George disbelieved him. But Jellicoe's stand put the Prime Minister in the position of having to overrule both his military and naval heads on a strategic question. He felt 'it would be too great a responsibility to take the strategy of the War out of the hands of the military'. The offensive would commence on 31 July.[3]

The Germans were far from idle while the debate went on. Using mustard gas for the first time, they launched a surprise attack on the seashore near Nieuport on 10 July and overran part of the British bridgehead across the Yser, from which the subsidiary coastal attack was to start. Most of the fifty men from the 2nd Australian Tunnelling Company, who had been mining under the German strongpoints in the sand dunes, were captured. On 12 July the Germans followed up by lobbing 50 000 mustard gas shells into the Ypres Salient. From the surrounding ridges, they had a grandstand view of the preparations for the coming offensive. General Sixt von Armin gave his chief of staff, Colonel Fritz von Lossberg, a free hand in the Fourth Army's preparations to meet it. Von Lossberg brought to a peak the elastic defence concept that the Germans had been working on since the Somme. It laid down that actions must 'not take place for or in a rigid defensive line but on a battleground of considerable depth, extending . . . far into our own position, where the enemy, at every step of his advance will be faced by more and more numerous and unexpected difficulties'. When weakened sufficiently, he could be thrown back.

Von Lossberg crammed more pillboxes into the existing lines and machine-gun posts into the intervening zones. First came the outpost zone, which was lightly held in order to minimise casualties during the bombardment and included the front line. Extending 2000 yards eastwards from it to the second (Albrecht) line, which ran along Pilckem Ridge and then the Gheluvelt Plateau, was the forward zone. It consisted of machine-guns and infantry scattered in shell holes, pillboxes and farm ruins. The battle zone was similarly organised and stretched another 2000 yards east to the third (Wilhelm) line, which crossed the Gheluvelt Plateau near Polygon Wood. Five divisions occupied these zones, each posting its three regiments side by side with each regiment posting a battalion per zone. Those in the battle zone were to carry out counter-strokes when the attacker, 'organizing the defence of a strange system of trenches', was most vulnerable. If they failed, specially trained divisions held in the rear zone, which rolled another 2000–5000 yards back to the Flandern Lines, would launch formal counterattacks. Skirting Poelcappelle, Flandern 1 passed behind Zonnebeke and Polygon Wood. Work was redoubled on Flandern 2, which branched off Flandern 1 near Passchendaele and paralleled it southwards, and Flandern 3, which tracked behind Passchendaele to Menin. Thus organised, the Germans confidently awaited the attack.[4]

Haig called on Gough and his Fifth Army to lead the offensive, a decision that Haig's admiring biographer, John Terraine, called his 'gravest and most fatal error'. Plumer was the obvious pick because he had held the Ypres Salient for two years and knew the terrain backwards. But Plumer's 'bite and hold' outlook was unsuited to Haig's purpose. Contrary to what he had said to Lloyd George, 'a limited offensive was not what Haig cherished'. According to Gough, Haig 'very definitely' viewed the battle as 'an attempt to break through', an understandable conclusion given the ambitious objectives Haig set him. He hoped to clear the Passchendaele Ridge, up to eight miles distant, by 8 August in order to catch the high tides necessary for the amphibious operation. Moreover, although recent experience argued pungently against going eight miles in eight days, Haig always emphasised the breakthrough aspect to Gough, even telling him on 28 June to try for it.[5]

Gough ordered a first day advance of 4500 yards to plant his army firmly on the ridge. Not only did this exceed the total first day advance at Messines, but Gough intended to go further if resistance was slight – so far, in fact, that he would end up beyond the range of all but his heaviest guns. Straddling the ridge on the right of the attack, the Gheluvelt Plateau, 200 feet high, was Gough's vital ground because it enfiladed the lower areas to the north. As any advance there would be limited until the plateau was secured, Haig suggested capturing it in a separate operation. Gough demurred, wanting to make the attack on the plateau 'part and parcel of the major operation, as a partial attack, even if successful, would only draw the troops employed into a very pronounced salient'. Haig relented. This was another mistake.[6]

The assault on 31 July did well on the Pilckem Ridge and poorly on the Gheluvelt Plateau. Then 'the battlefield became a bog; in every depression the flooded craters lay brim to brim like the footprints of monstrous animals in the slimy margin of some primeval waterhole'. Having amassed 3106 guns, which allowed a greater concentration per yard of front than at Messines, the artillery had fired three million shells during the eighteen-day preparatory bombardment. The intricate drainage system of dikes and culverts was destroyed and the country reverted to the vast swampland whence it had been claimed. Drenching rains flooded the ravaged terrain.[7]

Apart from the diversionary attack by II ANZAC against the Warneton Line on 31 July, no Australian infantry were involved for the first several weeks of the campaign but most of the Australian artillery took part almost from the outset. It was pounded. Though the Germans had only half as many guns as the British, they offset their numerical weakness by deploying around the rim of the salient and firing concentrically into it. With no room for alternative positions, the British guns were crowded almost wheel to wheel on the exposed Ypres flats under a storm of high explosive and mustard. The Australian artillery suffered its highest casualties of the war, losing 1375 men to the end of August, at which time the 7th Australian Field Artillery Brigade's medical officer wrote: 'All ranks are showing the effects of constant strain . . . men have been parading to me of late from debility and evident inability to stand shell-fire any longer'. Even when there was no shelling, men were incapacitated by the mustard gas, which lingered in the ground for days. Its victims were pitiful, Vera Brittain writing:

> I wish those people who talk about going on with this war whatever it costs could see the soldiers suffering from mustard gas poisoning. Great mustard-coloured blisters, blind eyes, all sticky and stuck together, always fighting for breath, with voices a mere whisper, saying that their throats are closing and they know they will choke.

The German Air Service maintained air parity over the battlefield, which gave their spotters a chance to direct the fire. Dogfights often drew in dozens of aircraft from either side. One on 26 July above Polygon Wood, whose skies served as an aerial jousting ground, involved almost a hundred. Scoring fourteen kills during the month, Captain Little brought his total to thirty-seven. Several pilots from the Australian Flying Corps (AFC) scout squadrons forming in England were attached for a few weeks' combat flying experience to British squadrons and saw their first action.[8]

On the ground, attacks on 10 and 16 August and six days of assaults on narrow frontages afterwards still left Gough barely clinging to the edge of the Gheluvelt Plateau. Shells often failed to burst in the mud and when they did go off, the explosion was barely visible. Even if the infantry could see the barrage, they soon fell behind it in the morass. Losses reached almost 70 000 by the end of August. Gough observed that 'the heart had gone out of the Fifth Army'.

On 25 August Haig transferred responsibility for the capture of the high ground to Plumer and the Second Army. Plumer demanded at least three weeks to prepare his first attack. Comprising 1295 guns firing 3.5 million shells to support an advance of 1500 yards on a central frontage of 4000 yards, the artillery concentration would be the heaviest of the war. Following the five-day bombardment, the infantry were to assault behind a Messines-style creeping barrage and dig in behind a nine-hour standing barrage. The 5th Army would keep pace on the left, making for an advance of eleven divisions on an eight-mile front. After a six-day halt to allow the artillery to be brought forward, Plumer intended to launch a second attack, similar to the first. Four such operations should take the plateau and the critical stretch of the ridge beyond. The initial spearhead would be I ANZAC.[9]

During its long rest after Bullecourt, Birdwood's corps underwent its most intense and relevant training ever. Each brigade of the 1st Division did a practice night assault on four successive objectives, leapfrogging under a creeping barrage and consolidating each objective as rapidly as possible. The 2nd Division concluded its training with an attack by the 5th and 7th Brigades, with the 6th passing through them in the final phase. Every brigade also went to a special exercise area at Lumbres to run through the latest mopping-up and pillbox fighting techniques. Recognising that the term 'Digger', by which British troops had praised the New Zealand pioneers and engineers for their entrenching exploits on the Somme, richly met their own conception of their job, the Australians now commandeered it.

The 4th Division also rejoined the other three Australian divisions in I ANZAC. Aware that the Australians wanted to fight alongside each other, Birdwood had arranged the transfer so that the divisions in his corps could always be put into battle in pairs, one pair relieving the next. The one Australian and one New Zealand division in II ANZAC would fight together but be relieved by the two British divisions that made up the rest of Godley's corps. Facing the prospect of another early return to action, after it had already been recalled from rest for Messines, the 4th Division was unimpressed with the move. 'What?' Captain Jacka shouted when Brigadier-General Brand addressed the 14th Battalion. 'Do you mean this battalion is to be flung into the line right away, in spite of all the promises made to the men?' Brand glared at him: 'Hullo Jacka – what's the trouble with you? Have you the wind up?' Jacka shot back: 'No, I'm only thinking of the men . . . I reckon it's a damned disgrace'. Brand said 'the whole bloody battalion were dopey', which prompted the 14th's officers to resign in protest. He was forced into making a humiliating public apology. But morale in the rest of I ANZAC was high. For the first time in its experience, an attack was being launched only after the most complete preparation and with maximum support.[10]

Plumer left the detailed tactical planning to the Australian commanders for I ANZAC had the main role. The rest of his army would conform to their scheme. For maximum punch, Birdwood and White shrunk the frontages for each of their two attacking divisions to 1000 yards, spread across the two forward brigades in each. They would assault in three distinct phases, each with fresh troops, and each shorter than the preceding one to allow for the progressively greater difficulties as the assault went further. One battalion per forward brigade would advance 800 yards to the first objective, called the Red Line, where a 45-minute halt allowed time for mopping up and another battalion to pass through for a 400-yard advance to the Blue Line. After a two-hour halt for more thorough consolidation, the two remaining battalions were to advance 300 yards to the Green Line. The final assault was therefore twice as strong as the initial one, though going less than half as far.

Fixed for 20 September, the attack was to cross the Menin Road, which ran southeast from Ypres through Gheluvelt, and overrun the strongpoints and woods that had defied the Fifth Army throughout August. The 1st Australian Division would clear Glencorse Wood and its outlier, Nonne Bosschen (Nun's Wood), on the plateau. Starting from Westhoek on its left, the 2nd Division was to cross the southern Hanebeek streamlet and take Anzac Spur on the far side, before joining the 1st beyond the Wilhelm Line, inside the western edge of Polygon Wood. X Corps, alongside the Australians, would capture both Inverness Copse and the Tower Hamlets pillbox complex further south. As the Australians exempted the Scots from their criticism of British troops and always got on well with them, they were delighted that the 9th (Scottish) Division would be on their left as part of the Fifth Army's assault on the northern flats.

On 16 September the Australians took over their attack front. Passing through Ypres during the night, they beheld a scene more surreal than the one remembered from the march through Albert before Pozières. A sleepy backwater with a pre-war population of 20 000, Ypres was a regional gem, whose high-gabled architecture reflected its standing as a great medieval European cloth centre. The Cloth Hall, 'a covered market in the spiky Flemish style', dated from the thirteen century and dominated the town, whose ramparts were the work of the great French military engineer, Marshal Sebastien Vauban. Now most of the population had gone, piles of rubble lined the streets, the jagged ruins of the Cloth Hall tower jutted skyward like a broken tooth, and the moat around the ramparts was a stinking swamp. Private Hartnett thought that preserving some of the ruins 'would assist the cause of peace more than the speeches of all the world's most renowned pacifists'. Dawn revealed the usual cloud of dust and smoke over the German positions, which were being bombarded without let-up. September had been as fine as August was wet and, though low-lying areas were still waterlogged, parts of the heights were so dry that shells ricocheted.[11]

The approach march began in the drizzly dusk of 19 September. By 11 p.m. rain was falling steadily, turning the ground to mud again. Gough wanted to postpone the attack. Armed with a forecast of improving weather, Plumer refused. The Australians filed into shell holes along the jump-off tapes. At 4.30 a.m. a heavy bombardment fell on the 3rd Brigade opposite Glencorse Wood, mauling the 9th and 10th Battalions. They pressed onto the foremost tapes to clear it. No one knew whether the Germans had seen the assembly. But they rumbled the 2nd Division, after capturing a lost Australian officer stupidly carrying the operation order. At 5.37 a.m. 'annihilation fire' descended, as the 2nd shivered in no man's land. Like those in the 1st, the men closed up beyond it and were ready when the creeping barrage signalled the start of the attack three minutes later. With cigarettes and pipes lit, the Diggers advanced. In the rear waves with the 7th Battalion, Lieutenant Alex Hollyhoke saw how close the leading waves were to the fire:

There was the continual swish swish of shells overhead – some high, some low – some indeed too low. With shells bursting around, many indeed were the narrow escapes. Most men were hit at times by flying pieces of high explosive or shrapnel. Unless a man was badly hit, all went eagerly on.

Bean wrote: 'The advancing barrage won the ground; the infantry merely pounced on any points at which resistance survived . . . in this battle the infantry were little more than a necessary adjunct to the artillery's effort'. But the guns were unable to subdue the German artillery. Though the 121st and the Bavarian Ersatz Divisions opposite were tired and due for relief, they had the most powerful supporting artillery on the German front. It shelled the Australians for twenty-five minutes after the advance began. Attack formations disintegrated as all the waves coalesced into one dense line ahead of the German fire. In the event, the creeping barrage saved the advance to the Red Line by forcing most of the enemy machine-gunners to stay under cover until the Australians were upon them. Many Germans were dazed and waved white handkerchiefs or bandages at the Diggers but some fought. Lance-Corporal Horace Parton of the 5th Battalion struck both types:

Fritz was only too eager to cry 'Mercy *Kamerad*' and in most cases got it. There are some who do not get mercy, they get in a blockhouse and fire on our chaps with machine-guns, but when we get up with them, they throw up their hands and ask for mercy but very rarely get it, which is quite right.

Both divisions were baptised into the pillbox fighting that the 3rd Division and the New Zealanders had got to know at Messines. When a pillbox held up the 6th Battalion in Glencorse Wood, now just a cluster of tree trunks, Second Lieutenant Frederick Birks rushed it and reached the rear entrance, whereupon the garrison surrendered. Shortly afterwards, he led his men against another strongpoint occupied by twenty-five Bavarians, of whom ten were killed and the rest captured. Falling himself next day, Birks was awarded a posthumous VC. Lieutenant Graham Leaver's platoon from the 10th Battalion got behind a pillbox that had pinned down the 11th. When Leaver was shot through the head at point blank range, his platoon 'went mad'.

> Corporal Harry Hodge rushed forward, shot the machine-gunner, and overturned the gun . . . the Germans tried to surrender, but the excited troops filled the place with bombs until, growing tired of killing, they allowed a remnant – an officer and 40 men – to go to the rear as prisoners.

Some men got bogged in the flooded Hanebeek, which had swollen to a width of 100 yards, and had to be helped out. By 6.09 a.m. the Red Line had everywhere been reached. The advance to the Blue Line, which crossed the Wilhelm Line, was even easier. Lieutenant Arthur Hull of the 18th Battalion planted the Australian flag on top of Anzac House, a big artillery observation post that lent its name to Anzac Spur. The bombardment had pounded the Wilhelm Line into oblivion. Cyril Lawrence, now an engineer lieutenant, saw a casual response when a distant machine-gun opened:

> Despite warning, our men will not keep down until there is a thud and a man standing up collapses. Stretcher-bearers quick! Too late – clean through the head . . . for a few minutes the men keep down, but they are strange fools, these Australians, and it seems part of their nature to court danger. In ten minutes they are walking about again as they would in their garden at home.

At 7.45 a.m. the Blue Line was being consolidated. During the two-hour pause there, the Diggers smoked the German cigars they had found in abundance. Those appointed as 'newspaper boys' distributed copies of the *Daily Mail* and *Daily Mirror*, which Lieutenant-Colonel Wilder-Neligan had obtained for the 10th Battalion. 'It really is rather comical to think of a whole line of men lying in shell holes, each reading his daily paper, in the middle of an attack of this description', wrote Birdwood. The relaxation was short-lived because firing from pillboxes and shell holes on the near side of the protective barrage became intolerable. They had to be taken out during the break.

Led by Captain Frederick Moore, Diggers from the 5th Battalion surrounded the blockhouse at Black Watch Corner, on the southern corner of Polygon Wood. Its garrison motioned to surrender but Moore was shot dead as he ran towards them. Only a great effort by other officers prevented his men slaughtering the Bavarians. Those in a two-storey pillbox, cleared at the same time, were less fortunate. The Australians thought the battle was over because the men on the lower level surrendered. Unaware they had done so, the men on the upper level shot one of the Australians. Incensed, the Australians bayoneted every prisoner. In no mood to spare one who pleaded for mercy, a Digger whose bayonet was not on his rifle grimly fixed it and killed him. Clearing the other pillboxes took only a few minutes but a 'dropshort' mortally wounded Major Frederick Tubb, a Lone Pine VC. By 10.30 a.m. the Australians were on the Green Line.

Owing to the standing barrage, the two German counterattack divisions could not begin deploying until 6 p.m. On seeing them the Australians called on the guns again. Replying instantly, they crumped the Germans north of Polygon Wood for forty minutes and no counterattack came. At 7 p.m. the Germans tried again in the Reutelbeek Valley to the south. The Diggers had mixed feelings when the answering barrage pulverised them for an hour. Some 'simply sat down and laughed. They knew the Germans could not get through it, yet they were praying for the Germans to get through'. The Battle of the Menin Road was over, with the 41st Division's repulse at Tower Hamlets the only setback. Costing 21 000 men, over a quarter of them Australian, the success was not cheap. German losses were similar and their morale was rattled. The Australians were elated for the plan had unfolded almost flawlessly. 'If only every attack could be carried through so cleanly', one wrote. Using the same formula, the next two attacks were.[12]

On 22 September, the 4th and 5th Divisions started relieving the 1st and 2nd for the capture of the rest of Polygon Wood and Flandern 1 beyond it. To be launched four days later, this second step would clear most of the Gheluvelt Plateau. Engineers and pioneers laboured to complete loop roads across craterfields poisoned by lingering mustard gas that would enable the artillery to move closer to the line just taken. Up ahead the 4th Division peered at a desolate moonscape broken only by half-sunken pillboxes. The 5th in Polygon Wood was at the near end of what had once been a Belgian Army training ground, complete with a rifle-range stop butte and a racecourse that had been used not just by the cavalry but by Belgium's equestrian team. Fir saplings had surrounded them but all that remained, wrote Lieutenant Sinclair Hunt of the 55th Battalion, was 'a forest of charred and splintered stumps standing about three or four feet high' amidst thick undergrowth, craters and pillboxes, with the butte at the far end giving the Germans unbroken views.

Aware that an assault on the rest of the Gheluvelt Plateau was imminent, Crown Prince Rupprecht ordered a spoiling attack in order to buy time to strengthen his counterattack forces, which had proved insufficient at Menin Road. Its objective was the Wilhelm Line south of Polygon Wood, which formed a salient owing to the German retention of Tower Hamlets. At 5.30 a.m. on 25 September, the 50th (Prussian) Reserve Division punched up the Reutelbeek in the wake of a bombardment that was reputedly the heaviest to support a single German division during the war. The British guns isolated the assault by mid-morning. But the 98th Brigade from the 33rd Division, which was next to the Australian 15th Brigade in Polygon Wood, careered back 700 yards. The 58th Battalion swung its flank around to face the Germans. Battered by the bombardment, its position was precarious. Brigadier-General Elliott sent the 60th Battalion, under Lieutenant-Colonel Norman Marshall, both to reinforce it and to support a counterattack by the 98th Brigade. Shelled on the way, the 60th lost over 100 men. The counterattack barely got started. At 7.05 p.m. Elliott ordered the 57th Battalion forward. With only the 59th Battalion left, he told Major-General Hobbs at 8 p.m. that his brigade could not attack next morning. But it was too late to give the job to the 8th Brigade, which Hobbs held in reserve. He ordered Elliott to proceed.

Originally slated for the second phase of the assault, the 59th Battalion would now take the first objective, the Red Line, along the eastern edge of Polygon Wood. 'So you know what to do?' Elliott asked Lieutenant Colonel-Charles Mason. He nodded. 'Well, then go and do it.' Elliott had no time to say more for he was organising the six-mile move up of the 29th and 31st Battalions, which the 8th Brigade was giving him for the final 400-yard advance to the Blue Line. Elliott hurriedly briefed their commanders around midnight. He was assured that the 98th Brigade would restore the right flank. But one of its two battalions got lost and the other waited for it. Elliott's men would have to look after the flank themselves.

Lieutenant Hunt was one of the Diggers waiting along the Australian line:

Half an hour to go. A fog had fallen and we could see Fritz flares only hazily through it. Ten minutes. A man rose here and there to tighten a belt or to stretch his cramped limbs. Three – the fog was more dense, and sections became very restless as they quietly fixed bayonets and prepared to advance. A gun behind boomed louder than the rest, suddenly the whole earth seemed to burst into a seething bubbling roaring centre of eruption and, as at the touch of an enchantress's wand, out of the ground sprang a mass of men in little worm-like columns – each wriggling its way forward to a sparkling shouting seething line of earth, fire and smoke in front of them.

Bean called the barrage 'the most perfect that ever protected Australian troops'. It rolled on 'like a Gippsland bushfire', throwing up a cloud so dense that compasses had to be used to keep direction. Taught to hug the fire at all costs, the 29th and 31st Battalions closed up onto the 59th in the 15th Brigade's assault on the southern half of Polygon Wood. It degenerated into a single, thick, ragged line. Around twenty machine-guns were firing through the barrage and the line rippled constantly as platoons darted back and forth to knock them out. The 5th Division's pre-battle training bore fruit:

Instantly, a couple of Lewis gunners would open on the defenders, and rifle bombers would drop their volleys of grenades all around them. Under cover of this fire a couple of parties would work round the flanks of the obstruction and in a few minutes further resistance was impossible. It would all happen so quickly that the check to the general advance was imperceptible and touch with the barrage was never lost.

By 6.45 a.m. the 15th Brigade was consolidating the Red Line.

As the 98th Brigade had still not shown up, the commanders of the 29th and 31st Battalions refused to expose the right flank further by continuing. The impasse was solved when the 59th Battalion reached the Blue Line while surrounding some pillboxes onto which the 14th Brigade alongside had driven a counterattack. Around midday the 2nd Royal Welch Fusiliers advanced on the right. They took some ground but pulled back when the Germans were seen massing across the Reutelbeek at 4 p.m. The Australians rallied many Welchmen who kept going rearwards – sometimes at pistol point. At nightfall Colonel Marshall led a raid into the 98th Brigade's area that finally secured the open flank. Elliott arrived early next morning to reorganise the new line. 'It was the only time during the whole war that I saw a brigadier with the first line of attacking troops', wrote Fusilier Frank Richards. That afternoon the Welch braved heavy fire to gain the Blue Line alongside Marshall.

The rest of the Australian attack was relatively uneventful. As the 14th Brigade cleared the northern half of Polygon Wood, whimpering boys emerged from many pillboxes holding out hands full of souvenirs. Their rifles were still racked inside, Lieutenant Hunt recalled. Brushing aside slight resistance, two platoons of the 53rd Battalion scaled the butte and bombed the dugout entrances in it. About sixty Germans, mainly medical staff, surrendered. The Blue Line also fell readily. Comprising several hundred yards of Flandern 1, it was unrecognisable apart from a few shreds of wire. The artillery and the Australian machine-guns smothered the two counterattacks the Germans tried to launch during the afternoon.

Altogether, seven divisions from the Second and Fifth Armies had attacked on a six-mile front and been successful everywhere except on the flanks. On the right the 39th Division was repulsed before Tower Hamlets and the 3rd Division from the Fifth Army, next to the Australians on the left, stalled before the Windmill Cabaret hillock north of Zonnebeke. The two Australian divisions suffered a third of the 15 000 British casualties. Plumer singled out the 15th Brigade's effort in holding the German counterstroke and then taking much of the 98th Brigade's objective. He 'went so far as to thank Elliott for saving the British army from disaster'. That Elliott had to cope with news received during the battle that his brother George, the 56th Battalion's doctor, had been killed and that he himself was facing likely financial ruin, redounded to his credit all the more.[13]

Bite and hold attacks had now foiled the German system of elastic defence in depth twice. On 30 September General von Armin ordered a partial return to the old system of holding the forward positions in strength and launching deliberate counterattacks from them. Not only would the resulting losses be no heavier 'than those incurred when lying inactive under enemy fire', but 'The enemy must hold his forward zone in great strength and thus provides a better target for our artillery'. These changes were in place to meet the third step on 4 October.[14]

From the Gheluvelt Plateau the ridgeline swung northwards through Broodseinde, whose capture would leave the Second Army facing Passchendaele. The Anzacs were again the spearhead but on a grander scale. It had been thought that I ANZAC would be too tired for another attack but the 1st and 2nd Divisions had emerged so fresh from Menin Road that they were able to join II ANZAC, as originally desired by Plumer and Harington. Sideslipping slightly northward to bring its line of advance directly onto the ridge, Birdwood's corps retained the central role. II ANZAC, which had been warned for it, instead replaced V Corps from the Fifth Army on I ANZAC's left. Both corps would cross the northerly continuation of Flandern 1 from Polygon Wood before reaching the final objective, the Blue Line. It corresponded roughly to the line held in 1914 by the 'Old Contemptibles', as the Kaiser called the BEF then. As usual, Gough's army would prolong the attack on the left, while X Corps buttressed the Australian flank on the right. In all, twelve divisions were to assault on an eight-mile front. To deceive the Germans as to the day and hour, the artillery would fire *en masse* when the creeping barrage opened at 6 a.m. The shelling beforehand was to be much more limited than in the earlier attacks.

I ANZAC's preparations were easily made, not least because its formations knew the ground. Their orders largely consisted of those for the previous steps. II ANZAC had to recast its plans at the last minute. Attacking on the northern side of the derelict Ypres–Roulers railway, the 3rd Division was to take the Windmill Cabaret before fighting through the pillboxes in the marshy valley of the northern Hanebeek to the Blue Line. It would link up there with the 2nd Division on the crest of the ridge on its right and with the New Zealand Division assaulting the Gravenstafel Spur, an offshoot of the ridge, on its left. Monash's 1900-yard assault was the longest but the only pause came on the Red Line well before halfway. He ordered an additional halt either side of it to leapfrog fresh battalions through. General Russell did the same for the New Zealanders. Spirits soared with the realisation that four Anzac divisions were attacking shoulder to shoulder. The feeling was particularly noticeable amongst Monash's men. Bean saw them on the march up: 'The 3rd beside the 2nd and 1st will make a splendid combination – all keen to win and keep their reputations and their place in the force'.

Light rain began falling during the move forward. Learning from the earlier attacks, all the assault battalions squeezed up behind the jump-off tape in order to escape the retaliatory German barrage when the attack opened. Some units were in position at 4 a.m. and had to lie in watery shell holes for two hours chilled to the bone. Newcomer Private Verdi Schwinghammer of the 42nd Battalion betrayed his rawness:

> About half past five I saw many red and green lights go up from the German positions and remarked to the corporal how pretty they looked. He said, 'Now we are for it. The Germans have taken a tumble that we are going to attack them, and now they are sending up their SOS signals to their artillery'. Almost immediately a heavy barrage descended on our positions.

Crowding forward to clear the German barrage expected at zero hour, the densely packed Australians were badly pummelled when it fell half an hour beforehand. Captain Braithwaite thought that a shell landed on every part of the lip of his shell hole. 'I was quite certain that I would not get out of it alive and so was everyone else', he said. 'I was buried twice and have never been 1/100 as frightened in my life before.' 'Five minutes seemed like an hour', Private Hartnett said. 'Being the only one with a watch in our section, I was kept busy, for every few minutes someone poked his head around the corner to ask the time.' I ANZAC, the worst hit, had lost one man in seven when his watch finally showed 6 a.m.

Behind us, as far as the eye could see, the sky suddenly became red with the flashes of guns. Our artillery had opened. Their mighty roar sounded sweeter to our ears than the finest music. Our faces fairly shone with joy at the sudden turn of events in our favour.

Almost as soon as the British barrage began and the Anzacs stepped off, the German barrage ceased. Hartnett was reassured when a giant Lewis-gun corporal got up from a shell hole. 'He took a cigarette from his pocket, lit it, picked up his gun, and strode off with a cheery "Come on boys", to his mates.' The leading waves of I ANZAC had just caught up with the barrage when they saw a line of men rise with bayonets fixed thirty yards ahead. I ANZAC and the Germans were attacking simultaneously.

The barrage that crunched the Australians had been intended to pave the way for a counterattack by the 212th Regiment to recapture some of the ground lost between Polygon Wood and Zonnebeke on 26 September, in accordance with von Armin's new policy. But the Australian barrage had caught the Germans at the moment of their assault. The Diggers ran towards them. Someone yelled, 'They're your own chaps – don't fire'. The reply was swift: 'Mind your own bloody business'. The shooting continued. 'I never had such an enjoyable time', wrote Braithwaite. 'As soon as they saw we were in force, they either up with their hands or rushed off to Berlin.' German dead, most with bayonet wounds, soon littered the area. The rain ceased.

Following the remnants of the 212th, the Australians met the 4th Guard Division, their old opponent at Mouquet Farm, which had just taken over the sector. They quickly felt the stronger forward defence that was the second result of the German tactical changes. The 1st Brigade had a difficult time outflanking the large Molenaarelsthoek pillbox complex, and the pillboxes confronting the 2nd Brigade resisted stubbornly. Nineteen-year-old Private Walter Bradby saw the occupant of one start towards him. 'I aimed point blank at his stomach and pressed the trigger. Down he went, on his right knee, and covered his face with his hands.' Bradby shot two more and was upset to find that they looked younger than himself. The Red Line was reached at 6.45 a.m. But the 2nd Brigade had to fight through the hour's pause to silence the Guardsmen defending the headquarters, observation posts and a battery crowding the ridge-top at the Crater, near Broodseinde crossroads. As well as the artillery headquarters, two battalion staffs and the guns were captured.

Attacking next to the 2nd Brigade, Lieutenant Adrian Ball and his platoon from the 24th Battalion seized another pillbox. Sending the prisoners off, Ball returned to his men, who were smoking German cigars and getting stuck into Rheinwein, a bottle apiece. Suitably primed, they sent some convivial messages to the Guards after finding two crates of carrier pigeons. Expecting updates on the battle, the Guards read instead: '*Deutschland Über Alles! Ha! Ha!*' 'Hock the Kaiser, – I don't think', and a request from Ball himself for certain information of an obscene and personal nature. The remaining pigeons were plucked and stewed.

Alongside I ANZAC, the leading battalions of the 3rd Division had tried to avoid the opening German barrage by creeping towards the line opposite. The 37th was thirty yards from the Germans on the Windmill Cabaret, upon which the northern wing of the 212th Regiment's counterattack had assembled. Together with the 43rd Battalion, it stormed the position at 6 a.m., catching the Germans totally unawares. The Australians killed over 350, mostly with the bayonet. Resistance stiffened near Flandern 1, where the barrage pulled away over the swampy ground. The Diggers were on their own but the injection of fresh battalions at the intermediate halt ensured that their momentum continued. The 11th Brigade captured a battalion headquarters. But ten machine-guns tore at the 10th, some shooting from the Gravenstafel, which the New Zealanders had not yet overcome. Sergeant Lewis McGee charged fifty yards to knock one out with his revolver. Killed afterwards, he received a posthumous VC. One by one, the others were silenced. By 9 a.m. the 3rd Division was on the Blue Line, where it quickly dug 'perhaps the most complete and accurately-sited front and support lines ever made by Australians in battle'.

Going over the flattened rubble of Broodseinde hamlet, I ANZAC reached the Blue Line about the same time. The Diggers looked southeast over the green Flemish lowlands and saw another world: copses and hedgerows swaying in the wind and cows grazing in the fields as farm carts trundled by. Even the Keiberg, the spur that descended from the ridge directly in front of them, was still covered in grass. Given the panoramic view, the German counterattacks were seen a long way out and scattered by the artillery.

The Anzacs took most of the 4600 prisoners. 'Terror was written all over their faces', said Private Hartnett. Many were wearing thick glasses, 'which drew from our lads the greeting, '"Good morning, Professor'". On the northern flank the Fifth Army took much of Poelcappelle. The rest of the Second Army on the right of the Australians advanced its line, though failing to capture the elusive Tower Hamlets. Some commanders wanted to go further and an exultant Charteris screamed at Harington: 'Now we have them, get up the Cavalry, now we have them on the run – push on, push on'. Plumer dropped the idea after Birdwood said that the artillery was too far back to give close support and casualties had been heavy. They totalled over 8000 in the four Anzac divisions.[15]

The German Official History spoke of 'The black day of October 4th', while Ludendorff said that the battle 'was extraordinarily severe, and again we only came through it with enormous losses'. On the Anzac front four German divisions had been crippled. 'The idea of holding the front line more densely', Ludendorff added, 'was not the answer'. The Germans reinstituted the lightly held outpost zone and greatly increased the depth of the zones behind it. Sensing their desperation, Monash ventured: 'Great happenings are possible in the very near future, as the enemy is terribly disorganized . . . and our next two blows will be very severe'. Set for 9 and 12 October, they were to take Passchendaele.[16]

Late on 4 October the heavy rains re-turned and the battlefield degenerated into a quagmire so deep that field guns needed timber platforms laid on a bed of fascines and road metal. They started sinking after firing a few shells even then, and soon red flags marked positions where guns had sunk altogether. 'Barrages were, in consequence, feeble and wild, no protection to the infantry after the first round.' On 7 October, Gough and Plumer jointly proposed ending the campaign. But Haig thought that the strongest defences had been reduced, while Charteris insisted that the Germans were about to fold. After Broodseinde he declared that they had no reserves within easy reach of the battlefield, reinforcing Haig's view that the next attack 'will probably give opportunities for exploitation'. Bean felt terribly anxious: 'I suspect that they are making a great bloody experiment – a huge gamble and no more than that; a deliberate attempt to see how it works'.[17]

As Passchendaele lay directly opposite II ANZAC, Godley's corps had the main role on 9 October. Its two British divisions, the 49th and 66th, had not fought at Broodseinde and would launch the attack. Only twenty-five guns, a quarter of the normal number, were able to support the 66th. The 5th and 6th Brigades from the 2nd Australian Division, which would secure II ANZAC's right flank by advancing to the Keiberg, were in a sorry state. 'We walked up to our knees in mud and have been wet through now for four days but have to do another hop over first thing in the morning', wrote Private William Vincent of the 21st Battalion. Since Broodseinde, both brigades had been helping the engineers. Worn out and lacking shelter from the dreadful weather, hundreds were evacuated with fatigue and trench feet. Many others, it was believed, 'temporarily deserted'. The average strength of the Australian assault battalions dropped to seven officers and 150 men. Opposite the two Anzac corps, three fresh German divisions entered the line on 5 October.

The battle took its name from the village of Poelcappelle because the Fifth Army and the French advanced half a mile there. X Corps also made some minor gains. But II ANZAC's attack in the centre failed. The approach marches of its divisions in a howling gale took up to twelve hours and some units were still late. Those that arrived for the 5.20 a.m. start could barely discern the weak barrage. The 49th Division hardly got past the jump-off line, leaving the left of the 66th enfiladed in the muddy Ravebeek Valley. It made little headway. With easier going on the ridgeline, the right reached Passchendaele but was also enfiladed because the neighbouring Australians had already gone back. It retired too. The lateness of parts of the 66th Division had left the 5th Brigade's flank open and it was struck from the 66th's sector as well as meeting stubborn resistance ahead. Struggling to the Keiberg, the 5th lacked the strength to hold it and withdrew. Unsubdued machine-guns checked the 6th Brigade. A raid by the 10th Battalion on Celtic Wood further south, which was intended to spread the German artillery, cost 71 of the 85 raiders and completed a disastrous day.[18]

Even Charteris now told Haig that there was no hope of success in 1917. Haig would have none of it, saying of Poelcappelle: 'It was simply the mud which defeated us . . . The men did splendidly to get through it as they did'. The attack on 12 October would go ahead. Godley, who had little idea of the situation forward, was enthusiastic. The 3rd Division and the New Zealanders would assault. On the suggestion that I ANZAC might participate, Birdwood told Plumer that the objectives were 'far beyond the capacity of my troops in their exhausted condition'. They would do no more than safeguard the right flank as before.

Little thought was given to the fact that the six-day minimum to organise such attacks in good weather had now been whittled down to three in bad. 'Things now rushed. No time to prepare, refer to orders as we go along', Monash told his brigadiers. 'Matters were very incompletely attended to . . . or had to be almost totally neglected.' To give the infantry a chance in the mud, the creeping barrage needed to be much slower and, therefore, required much more ammunition than hitherto. Even if it had been possible to get the shells forward, the bogged guns could only have fired a fraction of them. The option of getting more guns up did not exist. Guns 'stuck in the mud on moving', reported Brigadier-General William Burgess, the 4th Australian Division's chief gunner.[19]

Nonetheless, the 3rd Division was expected to advance 2500 yards to reach the final objective, the Green Line, a quarter of a mile past Passchendaele. Despite the greater difficulties, its assault would be 1000 yards longer than at Broodseinde. An alarming discovery extended it still further. The plan was based on reports that the 66th Division had not withdrawn all the way to its old front line after its assault on 9 October. After going forward late that afternoon to find a headquarters for the 9th Brigade's attack three days hence, Brigadier-General Rosenthal said that it well may have. Similarly, troops from the 10th Brigade could see no one in front of them. Events next day removed all doubt that the area ahead was empty. When Lieutenant Walde Fisher of the 42nd Battalion went up the Ravebeek valley towards the 66th,

> The slope . . . was littered with dead. I got to one pillbox to find it just a mass of dead, and so I passed on carefully to the one ahead. Here I found about fifty men alive, of the Manchesters . . . Never have I seen men so broken or demoralised. They were huddled up close behind the box in the last stages of exhaustion and fear. Fritz had been sniping them off all day, and had accounted for fifty-seven – the dead and dying lay in piles. The wounded were numerous – unattended and weak, they groaned and moaned all over the place.

No doubt about it, said Fisher, 'the line was practically the same as before the last attack', which meant that the 3rd Division would have to cover another 650 yards in the next one. Its advance would now be the longest undertaken by a division in any of the Second Army's attacks. Monash 'personally used every endeavour to gain a twenty-four postponement. The chief decided that every hour's postponement gave the enemy breathing time'. It was decided to start the 3rd Division's barrage 300 yards further back but increase its rate of advance so that it caught the general line of the barrage within 500 yards. Yet Poelcappelle had shown that the infantry struggling through the mud soon lost the barrage at the existing rate. Given the limited supply of shells, extending the barrage would also dilute its intensity. Firing from the undamaged ground beyond, the German gunners had no such problems.[20]

Hit by high explosive and gas, the approach march fumbled through the darkness and pouring rain. Each man gripped the equipment of the man in front. If he lost touch, those ahead had to go back. 'We were slipping and sliding all over the place and falling into shell holes and to make matters worse, we were losing men every few yards', wrote Private John Hardie of the 33rd Battalion. Dawn was breaking when the barrage opened at 5.25 a.m. It seemed as if a few pebbles were being tossed into the mud. The 40th Battalion 'made no attempt to conform to it', because 'there was really nothing to conform to'. Attacking the Flandern 1 pillboxes on the Bellevue–Meetcheele Spur on the left of the Australians, the New Zealanders faced disaster. Their patrols had reported the night before that the dense wire protecting Flandern 1 was intact. The feeble shelling left it unscathed and merely splashed mud on the pillboxes. Trying to get through, the New Zealanders fell in droves. Private Bill Smith saw Sergeant Jock Stewart get shot through the heart but Jock's younger brother Harold, who was nearby, did not. 'When he realised it, Smith said, 'we couldn't hold him':

He crawled back on his stomach to where Jock was lying, and got hold of his body and dragged him back to the road where we were sheltering. The machine-gun bullets were splashing up the mud all around them. Harold got right through them all. Then, just as he reached us he eased himself up slightly to pull Jock down below the road surface, and a German sniper put a rifle bullet through his throat . . . His blood gushed out all over me . . . Whatever was left of the N. Zedders was just a disorganised rabble, so much so that the Germans had become very cheeky. They weren't bothering to take cover, they had come out and were perched on top of their concrete forts picking off any fool who showed his nose.

Smith saw Maoris form relays to evacuate the wounded. 'They carried them in their arms like children.' Within a few hours, the New Zealanders had lost 3000 men. 'Things are bloody, very bloody', Lieutenant-Colonel Morshead in the 33rd Battalion next to them reported.

'After we had gone about 100 yards we were all being bogged', wrote Sergeant Thomas Dial of the 34th Battalion. The Bellevue machine-guns ripped into the 10th Brigade as it struggled along the Ravebeek through 'gluey mud, generally knee-deep, and in some places, waist deep'. Rallied by Major Lyndhurst Giblin of the 40th Battalion, the survivors reached the first objective, the Red Line, 1000 yards distant. A group of twenty Diggers crept into Passchendaele, whose red brick church rose like a beacon above the ruined village. Realising they were alone, they turned back and ran into the 9th Brigade. It, too, had got to the Red Line, largely because Captain Clarence Jeffries, also of the 34th Battalion, outflanked a pillbox that held up the advance with severe loss. Jeffries was killed while silencing another pillbox and received a posthumous VC. But its capture enabled the advance to continue to the Blue Line, 600 yards short of Passchendaele. Holding 300 yards of front, Dial and five others were among the few men left. German machine-guns and snipers were sweeping the line, and presently artillery firing over open sights began pounding it as well. With the Germans dribbling down the Bellevue–Meetcheele Spur behind them, the remnants of the 10th Brigade withdrew. Now virtually isolated, the 9th did likewise, as did the 47th and 48th Battalions from I ANZAC, which reached the Keiberg.[21]

'Our dead lay everywhere, it was the worst slaughter I have ever seen', said an Australian doctor. He sobbed at the sight of so many casualties. The Germans mercifully left the stretcher-bearers alone: 'Many pointed to where wounded were lying – Hun snipers pointed to where their victims were'. The bearers were soon exhausted: 'To carry a wounded man from the front line to the R.A.P. was a terrible undertaking. The distance to be covered was less than a thousand yards but it took six men, four, five and even six hours to do the trip'. As Lieutenant Carson wrote, the plight of numerous unwounded was also awful: 'We were bogged up to our armpits and it took anything from an hour upwards to get out. Lots were drowned in the mud and water.' They haunted Lieutenant Russell Harris:

> The feeling of frustration of having been unable at times to go to the help of men in those mudholes is still a painful memory. It was impossible to shut one's ears to their cries, and when silence came it was almost like a physical blow, engendering a feeling bordering on guilt.

The 3rd Division had lost 3000 men. Comparing the casualties to the ground gained, Messines and Broodseinde both cost the division less than one man per yard. Passchendaele cost it over thirty-five men per yard. Going up afterwards, official Australian war photographer Frank Hurley saw how the battle had affected the Australians. 'Under a questionably sheltered bank lay a group of dead men. Sitting by them in little scooped out recesses sat a few living; but so emaciated by fatigue and shell shock that it was hard to differentiate.' 'Our men are being put into the hottest fighting and are being sacrificed in hare-brained schemes like Bullecourt and

Passchendaele, and there is no one in the War Cabinet to lift a voice in protest', fumed Monash.[22]

By this stage, many of the underlying reasons for the offensive were no longer valid. One of them, the need to deprive the U-boats of the Belgian ports, should never have arisen. Less than a quarter were based there and they could easily have been shifted back to the principal bases on the German coast if the Belgian ones fell. Moreover, the U-boat threat had been contained with the replacement of independent sailing by the convoy system. Convoys were hardly more conspicuous on the ocean wastes than single ships and made far more efficient use of the available escorts. Though some of its ships patrolled off Australia, where the raider *Wolf* sank several ships with mines in 1917, as well as the East Indies, Malaya and India, the RAN was heavily involved in the anti-submarine fight. Australian vessels joined North Sea patrols, escorted Scandinavian convoys and contributed to the Otranto Barrage, an attempt to seal off the Adriatic. The work was numbingly wearisome. *Sydney* enjoyed a rare thrill when the Zeppelin L43 tried to bomb it. But *Australia* 'never saw a battle or fired a gun in action'. Her crew seethed at missing the war's biggest naval encounter, off Jutland on 31 May 1916, after a collision with the *New Zealand*, which did participate and whose captain donned Maori warrior's garb for it.[23]

On land an assault at Verdun in August and their solid performance at Ypres were clear evidence of the French recovery. As a combatant, Russia was moribund before the campaign started. Launched against the Austrians on 1 July, its own offensive began well but collapsed when resistance hardened and German reserves led a counterattack. Clearing Galicia, the Austro-German advance headed for the Russian border on the heels of a disintegrating army. Already under challenge from Lenin's Bolsheviks, the revolutionary extremists on the soviets, the authority of the Provisional Government crumbled further. Prime Minister Alexander Kerensky became preoccupied with the internal chaos and his own survival.

Switching tack, Haig now argued that every effort should be made to defeat the Germans before they could transfer troops from the Eastern Front. That became a new argument for continuing the Ypres offensive. He also wanted a winter line that was not under German observation from the Passchendaele end of the ridge. Yet the British had held two-thirds of the ridge since Broodseinde, which gave them observation over much of the German line. It did not follow that the British line was so disadvantaged that Haig necessarily had to improve it. But, as Bean saw, Passchendaele was now an obsession from which 'it would take the impact of a travelling planet' to deflect him.[24]

So the battle ground on, though Haig called off the amphibious landing. The Canadian Corps, which had been carrying out diversionary attacks at Lens, took over the advance on the ridge. Its very able commander, Lieutenant-General Sir Arthur Currie, insisted on a return to the 'bite-and-hold' policy of short assaults launched only after maximum preparation. After five attacks between 26 October and 10 November, with the Australians supporting the flanks of the earlier ones, the Canadians did what II ANZAC had been ordered to do in two attacks and finally took Passchendaele. By then Haig admitted that he had created a 'very sharp salient' against which the Germans could easily concentrate their artillery, and hence a partial evacuation could not be ruled out. To that end, the BEF had lost 275 000 men, including 70 000 dead, in conditions far worse than the Somme. The Germans also suffered severely, probably losing 200 000 men but they had a replacement army in Russia. Britain had only the one. As John Keegan says of Haig's handling of it: 'On the Somme he had sent the flower of British youth to death or mutilation; at Passchendaele he had slipped the survivors into the slough of despond'. 'I died in hell. (They called it Passchendaele)', Siegfried Sassoon wrote. The British Army was near the end of its tether. So were the Australians.[25]

—FOURTEEN—

CRIME AND PUNISHMENT

General White considered its participation in the Flanders offensive 'perhaps the best performance of the AIF up to that date'. But the effects on the Diggers were telling. 'They have not the same spirit at all as the old men we had. The difficulty once was to restrain their impatience for action', Elliott observed. 'Now we find men clearing out to avoid going into the line at all.' It was the same after any big offensive, and not just in the Australian divisions, for a rise in disciplinary problems went hand in hand with exhaustion. They had leapt in the New Zealand Division after its long stint on the Somme in 1916. But the Australians had a reputation within the BEF for indiscipline as a matter of course. It had preceded them from Egypt and, in British eyes, they had lived up to it in France. Seeing Australians for the first time, Gunner Lieutenant Patrick Campbell was unimpressed: 'They were unlike any of our divisions . . . They were noisy and swaggering, they did not march on the road, they just walked, they seemed to be without any kind of discipline'. Their unwillingness to salute or say 'sir', their slovenliness, drunken behaviour and absenteeism were legendary. They liked to encourage the legend but it did have another side.[1]

With no prospect of home leave, the Diggers were engaged half a world away in battles that left little prospect of survival. Like all red-blooded men in their situation, they were going to enjoy themselves when the chance offered. 'Eat, drink and be merry, for tomorrow we die' made sense, particularly when they were paid handsomely enough to do the first three very well. Birdwood, who understood Australians better than most British officers, linked such things as absenteeism to the national character, remarking that they 'absolutely and simply' could not realise it was an offence to head off to the nearest French town after a hard battle. Bean observed that even after four years of war, they did not have 'the habit of automatic, subconscious response to command'. Some occasionally challenged the small print of King's Regulations by stepping forward three paces on parade to fart. Decorating Lieutenant Joe Maxwell with the VC and Lieutenant Edward Mattner with the MC early in 1919, George V recalled his visit to Australia over the next few minutes. As a conversation of that length was unprecedented in Palace routine, the Lord Chamberlain led a horde of officials in asking what the King had said. 'Well', drawled Mattner, 'he said, "I'm sick of this turnout. Let's go down to the corner pub and have a couple of beers."' The Lord Chamberlain gave Mattner, a future president of the Australian Senate, a good bollocking.[2]

By the same token, discipline *within* Australian units was usually first-rate as long as they were well led. Most of the dud commanders had been weeded out by 1917. Mackay, Howell-Price, Wilder-Neligan and Morshead, to name a few, were no-nonsense disciplinarians who regarded saluting and smart turnout as indicators of their battalions' professionalism and *ésprit*. The men upheld their values because they were proven leaders who looked after them and showed flair in battle. Elliott, Glasgow, Gellibrand and other successful brigadiers also had exacting standards that they insisted must be observed. Woe betide any man who failed to salute Elliott. The point was that the men of the 15th Brigade did so willingly. Nor were the divisional commanders any different. Before taking over the 3rd Division, Monash said to a young Digger who had not saluted him: 'I am nothing but a mere brigadier-general, my boy, but one of these days some second-lieutenant is going to come along here and reprimand you severely for your lack of observation'. Once in command, he admonished Brigadier-General James Cannan because some men in the 11th Brigade were not wearing hat-badges:

I attach no particular importance 'per se' to the absence of a badge . . . but if it is evidence of laxity on the part of the platoon officer or NCO's, it assumes a totally different aspect. If a man is allowed to go about for weeks with[out] . . . a badge, one wonders whether he is also allowed to go about with a rusty rifle or without a gas mask – or some other essential deficient.

At Polygon Wood, Welch Fusilier Private Richards commented on the 'excellent spirit of comradeship' between Australian officers and men. By then most of the regimental officers were men who had shown leadership qualities whilst in action as more junior officers or as soldiers. Though still friendly with his old mates, the officer from the ranks knew that he was no longer one of them. He had learned from personal experience that discipline was not just a necessity but an advantage. 'The boozer soon goes to the pack – he is an impediment, so I make a practice of getting rid of my drunks quickly', Captain Armitage said. As long as his men fought well, Jacka forgave their misdemeanours out of the line but only up to a point, and he administered his own justice. When one came back from a village fighting drunk, Jacka said: 'Well, Nugget, you can have what you like. Either come up before me in the morning, or else take me on for a few rounds'. The crowd formed a ring. Whack, whack, whack. 'Now, Nugget, off you go and have a sleep, and don't let me catch you at this again. You'll get all the fighting you want in the near future.'

Fed up with what he considered constant ignorant harping criticism by British officers on the AIF's unruliness, Monash produced what is still the best rejoinder to it:

> Discipline does not mean lip service, nor obsequious homage to superiors, nor servile observance of forms and customs, nor a suppression of individuality . . . In the Australian Forces the soldier was taught that personal cleanliness was necessary to ensure his health and well-being, that a soldierly bearing meant a moral and physical uplift which would help him to rise superior to his squalid environment, that punctuality meant economy of effort, that unquestioning obedience was the only road to successful collective action. He acquired these military qualities because his intelligence taught him that the reasons given were the true ones . . . In short, the Australian Army is proof that individualism is the best and not the worst foundation upon which to build collective discipline.

Haig counted the Australians 'among the best disciplined troops . . . Because when they are ordered to attack, they always do so'. But on one aspect of discipline, the use of the death penalty to deter desertion, the Australian generals were at one with their British counterparts and Haig in particular.[3]

Under Section 98 of the Australian Defence Act of 1903, only mutiny, desertion to the enemy – not simple desertion – and certain forms of treachery were punishable by death. The sentence had to be confirmed by the Australian governor-general rather than a commander in the field. Unlike the Canadian, South African and New Zealand governments, which agreed to their soldiers being tried and punished under the British Army Act, the Australian government insisted on the primacy of Section 98 when its troops served under British command. With the small number of capital offences it specified effectively excluding the death penalty, return to Australia in disgrace was the severest instrument of discipline for Australian soldiers. But for men whose nerve had gone at Fromelles, Pozières and Mouquet Farm, the concept of duty as a noble and overriding ideal faded, and being shipped home in disgrace held no sway. Courts martial had convicted 288 Australians of desertion by the end of 1916. Birdwood, Rawlinson and Haig wanted Section 98 waived, thereby putting the AIF on the same footing as the rest of the British Army. Fearing the effect on recruiting, the Australian government refused.[4]

In the first six months of 1917, during which I ANZAC fought the twin battles of Bullecourt and the 4th Division was recalled from rest for Messines, Australians comprised 171 of the 677 convictions for desertion in the entire 62 divisions of the BEF. These figures represented an average of 34.2 convictions in each Australian division, as opposed to 8.87 in the rest. Holmes, Glasgow and Monash wanted Section 98 amended so that the death penalty could be applied to a few cases. They believed it would cut the desertion rate by 90 per cent. Haig took up the matter again, promising the most sparing use – in cases 'where desertion was most deliberate and an example badly needed'. Again the Australian government said no. But absences and desertion peaked during Third Ypres. The number of Australians in military prisons in July, proportionately four times that of British and other Dominion soldiers, rose by the end of the year to six times more than for all other Dominion soldiers combined and eight times the rate in the British Army. On 5 November Birdwood asked Defence Minister Pearce to approve the publication in all Australian newspapers and in AIF orders of deserters' names, towns of enlistment and sentences. With reinforcements down to a trickle and the desertions and imprisonments shrinking the AIF's ranks further, Pearce agreed. The measure came into effect in January 1918 and the first list was cabled to Australia in March.[5]

At the same time, AIF attitudes to shell shock softened. Like their British counterparts, Australian commanders throughout 1916–17 tended to believe that it was merely a convenient excuse for malingering. But as Sassoon observed, every man became 'windy . . . It was just a question of time'. Graves put the time at between a year and fifteen months, after which 'he was often useless'. By the end of the Flanders campaign, many veterans had fought in every battle since Pozières, some, like Harry Murray, since Gallipoli. He told close colleagues, 'I have to go up to the line by myself now, so that they do not see me duck at the shells'. Private Leak, a Pozières VC, deserted at Passchendaele, was caught six days later and given a suspended life sentence. In December 1917 Birdwood formally acknowledged that cases involving nervous breakdown were very different to those of deliberate desertion to avoid action. He directed that 'the medical aspect of the case should be carefully gone into before the man is charged with desertion'. From May 1918 onwards, long-service men suffering from 'nerves' were withdrawn from the line and generally sent to support units.[6]

The Diggers were not sympathetic to deserters because they increased the burden on the majority who soldiered on. Irrespective of what the commanders thought, though, condemning them to death was something else again. The reading out to Australians on parade of reports on executions 'evoked only a sullen sympathy and a fierce pride that their own people had refused this instrument to its rulers'. Together they had a resounding answer to the question asked so eloquently by Captain Alan Herbert: 'Ought anyone who *volunteers* to fight for his bloody country be shot?' In the British Army and the armies of the other Dominions that formed part of it, 3080 soldiers received the death penalty and it was carried out in 346 cases. Alone among the armies, the AIF possessed 'the privilege of facing death without a death penalty'.[7]

It was also alone in remaining a volunteer army. On entering the war in April 1917, the Americans introduced the draft for overseas service and Canada enacted conscription in August after a debate as divisive as that in Australia a year earlier. Even so, lack of men after Passchendaele necessitated the break-up of the 5th Canadian Division, which had been forming in England. The New Zealanders were also forced to disband their 4th Brigade. Having been at the forefront of four of the Ypres campaign's eleven major attacks, the Australians had suffered 38 000 casualties. But the number of monthly reinforcements needed to bring them up to strength again was less certain. Hughes put it at 7000, Pearce at 6000, while Birdwood and the British Army Council reckoned on 5500. Whichever figure was chosen, it greatly exceeded the 2500 men monthly to which enlistments had dropped at the end of 1917.

Though Hughes had pledged during the election in May that the return of his government would not mean the imposition of conscription, the collapse of recruiting led him to announce on 7 November that the question would be put to the people once more. The second conscription campaign was 'more strident, more bitter and even more uninhibited' than the first. Declaring that he would not continue to govern unless the proposal was passed, Hughes squared off again against Archbishop Mannix. In what was probably the most violent political struggle in Australian history, 'overripe eggs and unripe fruit took the place of argument at many meetings'. Hughes took to carrying a revolver and was famously hit by an egg at the Darling Downs town of Warwick on 29 November. The vote went against him, the 'No's' winning by a slightly larger margin than in 1916 and in four states outright, as opposed to three then. Despite furious Labor protests, Hughes stayed on with the assent of Munro-Ferguson, the Governor-General, after receiving a vote of confidence from his Nationalist Party colleagues.[8]

As before, the AIF voted in favour but this time the margin was even narrower, 103 789 to 93 910, or 10 000 votes. Voicing the opinions of many, Captain Braithwaite had told his parents: 'Do not vote for conscription on any account. Australia has sent enough to the war and if we did empty the remaining men out, it would only cripple her and not make the slightest difference to the result of the war'. Giving substance to Elliott's observation of the widespread tiredness and the slump in morale, Braithwaite was 'absolutely sick to death of the whole show' and 'knew of no-one who is not of the same mind'. Private Walter Bishop of the 55th Battalion heard an outburst from his mate 'Nugget':

Haig couldn't win a dogfight, let alone a war. What the hell has he ever done towards winning? He plans a stunt, sends thousands of men over the top, gets a lot of us killed, captures a few prisoners, then we dig in. Swapping valuable lives for filthy, bloody shell holes will never win the war. We really lose, because the Germans just fall back a bit onto good country and we have more of the shell-holed mud to contend with.

Some Diggers confided to Bean: 'I'm quite ready to let Fritz keep what he's got and shake hands with him'.[9]

A spell of leave in Blighty – England – the ancestral home of most Australians, was a means of escape for those lucky enough to get it. After calling in at AIF Headquarters at Horseferry Road in London to store their rifles and packs, draw pay, ration tickets, tourist 'drum' and often a new uniform, men would 'do' the capital. Private Thomas Linney and his mates visited 'the Abbey, St. Paul's, the Houses of Lords and Commons, the Zoo and other places. We had some great fun trying to find our way around . . . We thought the tube railway a wonderful burnout'. Going further afield, Lieutenant Joynt visited the village made famous by Longfellow's poem 'The Village Blacksmith', and found 'the old smithy still there and the spreading chestnut tree propped up by stout oak stays'. Those with English relatives would head off to look them up, even if that meant going as far as Scotland at one extreme or Cornwall at the other. But the theatres, music-halls and pubs also beckoned because the call of history and family co-existed with the need for entertainment, which meant life. Staying at a 'swank' West End hotel, Lieutenant Williams saw a 'stunner'. She ignored him. When he sat down at her table nonetheless, she snarled at him: 'Look here, Australia, what do you take me for?' Leaning across the table, Williams replied: 'The prettiest girl that I have seen in London'.

For an instant her face was expressionless, then she threw her head back and laughed. 'There is no doubt about you Australians; your effrontery carries you through'. She went on: 'Well as long as you do not take me for one of these women who frequent these hotels to be picked up by you Colonials, we know where we stand'.

They went out together for two days before the inevitable station farewell. 'I feel sick at heart when I think that within a few days you will be back in France again', she said, lips quivering. 'You and your pals laugh at the dinner-table at your life in the army, but I know that there is a hideousness you do not speak of, for it is in your eyes in your unguarded moments'. They kissed and never saw each other again. Years later, Williams could still recall 'the freshness of her youth with her dark head and eyes of limpid brown'.

With the great reputation they had won at Gallipoli enhanced by generous publicity, the Australians invariably received warm hospitality in England. But their high pay naturally drew the type of women condemned by Williams's acquaintance. Lieutenant Harold Westaway of the 27th Battalion thought the pretty young girls he saw in English hotel bars 'a disgrace – their behaviour awful. Worse than Egypt or France'. Nor was England in winter – cold, wet and overcast – attractive. Moreover, Blighty leave only came about once a year.[10]

Those Australians who sustained a Blighty wound remained in England until they had recovered, which could take weeks or even longer. Those sent to the Queen's Hospital at Sidcup in Kent stayed for months on end. Specialising in facial and maxillary wounds, it had an Australian 'pavilion' and, together with the Brook Street Hospital in London, did pioneering work in plastic surgery techniques. Visiting Sidcup, Australian nurse Matron Gertrude Moberly's stomach turned but the rule was '*Always* to look a man straight in the face [because] he's watching your face to see how you're going to react'. As soon as Matron Moberly left, she 'sat by the roadside and cried and cried, for my heart felt like bursting, likewise my head'. Writing from a hospital in Northampton after being wounded at

Passchendaele, Private Hardie admitted that he would never have got to England 'if it hadn't been for one of the nurses . . . who was an Australian. She used to do her best to get all the Aussies across. There seems to be a great difference between our nurses and the others'. Australian nurses staffed hospitals as far afield as India and Salonika, as well as those in Egypt and France.

Exempted from the Defence Department's policy of not employing females in any military capacity, nursing was one of the few ways Australian women could contribute tangibly to the war. Unlike in England, there was no substantial labour shortage to force them into military-related jobs. Hence 'the tag that in war women must "wait and weep" was perhaps an apt description of the role of most Australian women'. Envisaging a similar function to the Women's Auxiliary Army Corps in Britain, some formed the Australian Women's Service Corps at the end of 1916 but the government virtually ignored it. Others joined organisations such as the Red Cross and the Australian Comforts Fund, which sought to ease the lot of Australian soldiers abroad. They supplied items ranging from well over a million pairs of knitted socks – extremely useful on the Western Front – to Christmas 'billies' packed with goodies designed to raise spirits. Not surprisingly, though, the ongoing experience at the front was a much more important determinant of morale. Events there revived it. Ironically, the most important stemmed directly from the chronic manpower shortfalls that the Australian divisions faced.[11]

In June 1916 the Australian government pressed for the creation of an Australian Army but Haig rightly considered that five or even six divisions were insufficient. Lobbying intensified in 1917, particularly after disquiet was expressed about the way the Australians were employed at Bullecourt. It culminated in October with a more modest proposal to group the Australian divisions in a single corps instead of the arrangement that split them between I and II ANZAC. Haig demurred again, thinking that a corps of five divisions was too large a command for one man to handle and the system of reliefs within it would be too complex. A corps of four divisions avoided the problem because two could be in the line with the other two ready to relieve them. When the manpower crisis intervened, Birdwood and White suggested that the 4th Division, which was the most battle-worn, should temporarily become a depot division to supply reinforcements for the others. Besides averting the 4th's breakup, their proposal meant a corps of the magical four divisions. Haig agreed and the Australian Corps came into being on 1 November 1917. He allotted it as many Australian units as possible, including the two Australian siege batteries and No. 3 Squadron AFC, which flew artillery-spotting, infantry co-operation and bombing sorties in its lumbering RE8s. It had arrived in France on 9 September, the first Australian squadron to do so. With 50 000 non-Australian troops attached, mainly British heavy artillery, labour battalions and American engineers, giving it a strength of 166 000 men, the Australian Corps was the largest corps at Haig's disposal.

The creation of the Australian Corps came as a total surprise and was greeted with joy, though it meant a parting of the ways with the New Zealanders. They now belonged to XXII Corps, as II ANZAC became. Grouping the Australian divisions together in a single formation took full advantage of one of the AIF's major strengths, its homogeneity. When Australian divisions attacked alongside each other for the first time on the Menin Road, their enthusiasm was striking. One commander estimated that the effectiveness of his formation had been increased by a third. British generals, on the other hand, were slow to recognise that keeping divisions together in their own corps helped morale and hence efficiency. The British Official Historian, Brigadier-General Sir James Edmonds, believed that what British troops envied most was 'the corps formation of the [Australian and Canadian] divisions which gave them many advantages'. He maintained that Haig should have tried harder to achieve it with British divisions. The Australians applied the policy at all levels. Reinforcements joined battalions from their own state and returning wounded went back to their old units, which was often not the case in the British Army. Edmonds lamented that recovered casualties and drafts 'e.g. of Irish and cockneys, were sent to Scots units, Lancashire drafts to Yorkshire battalions etc, etc. Thus officers and men hardly knew each other and there was little to bind them together'.[12]

Four months recuperating, refitting and training at Messines during a mild winter gave morale another great boost. As casualties and sickness were minimal, the steady flow of returning wounded temporarily eased the manpower shortage. Five raids were launched across the fields and marshlands separating the opposing lines in the Lys valley, of which the 3rd Division carried out four. Monash devised new methods to ensure surprise and inflict losses, such as raiding the same position twice over seven hours, 'the time that it would probably take to restore the situation and garrison'. In another raid, twenty silhouette figures in no man's land were raised and lowered by wires from an outpost to divert attention from the real objective 400 yards away. The Germans were completely deceived and riddled the targets. But nightly patrolling was the main method by which no man's land was dominated. Australian patrols took prisoners on 14 out of 25 attempts, while the Germans took Australian prisoners on 10 out of 54 attempts but left prisoners or identifications themselves on 42. The Australians regarded the patrolling as a training activity and it did much to maintain their confidence and proficiency.[13]

Though the 1917 campaign was over for the Australian divisions, the British fought one more battle. In contrast to the tragedy in the mud before Passchendaele, the Third Army under General Sir Julian Byng won a brilliant success at Cambrai on 20 November, when an attack led by 381 tanks penetrated five miles for the loss of 4000 men. The 55th Australian Siege Battery took part as well as No. 2 Squadron AFC, which had arrived in France two months earlier. Flying the peculiar reverse-stagger DH5 scout, it carried out low-level bombing and strafing attacks. But the casualties suffered in Flanders left Haig insufficient reserves to exploit the breach and the Germans regained most of the ground lost in an equally brilliant counterstroke. The 4th Australian Division was rushed into close reserve at Péronne on 3 December in case they went further, effectively ending its brief stint as a depot division. Wanting to prevent another costly attritional offensive in 1918, Lloyd George withheld men from Haig, forcing a reduction in the number of battalions in a British division from twelve to nine. Comparing the two armies, Lieutenant-General Sir Henry de Lisle judged that the best British division was only as good as the average German one. Henceforth, the spearhead of the BEF would be its Dominion troops.[14]

Except for Palestine, the other fronts were equally depressing. In August 1917 the Italians had launched their eleventh offensive on the Isonzo. Though fizzling out after trivial gains like the rest, it brought the Austrians to crisis point. They sought German help. With the Eastern Front well in hand, Ludendorff could send seven divisions despite the ongoing demands of the Flanders arm-wrestle. They formed the core of an Austro-German Army that struck down the Isonzo at Caporetto on 24 October. When bad weather and fraying supply lines finally stopped it on the Piave ten days later, the advance had gone eighty miles, within striking distance of Venice, and had captured nearly 300 000 prisoners. Almost 400 000 Italians deserted. Surprising even themselves, the Germans had sparked one of the war's most dramatic routs. Five British divisions were sent from the Western Front under General Plumer, together with six French ones, to shore up the Italians. They arrived too late to be of use.

The debacle had one positive outcome. It made the Allies recognise that the existing system of directing the war effort through informal liaison and occasional conferences was inadequate and that a more rigorous basis for co-operation was essential. Appropriately meeting at the Italian city of Rapallo on 5 November in the midst of the crisis, the British, French and Italian prime ministers, with American agreement, established a permanent Supreme War

Council that would sit at Versailles, under the aegis of the political leaders of all four nations, to co-ordinate Allied strategy. An Inter-Allied Staff, independent of the national military chiefs, would advise them. Shortly after the conference, French Prime Minister Painlevé was rolled in the Chamber of Deputies and replaced by an irascible patriot and former doctor, the 76-year-old radical, Georges Clemenceau. As colourful as Lloyd George but blunter and less devious, he also doubled as War Minister.

More dismal news arrived on the heels of Caporetto from Russia. In October the Germans had followed up their capture of the great Baltic city of Riga by taking several Baltic islands. With Petrograd (the former St Petersburg) now threatened, the tottering Provisional Government proposed shifting the capital to Moscow. The Bolsheviks derided the idea as a counter-revolutionary move to leave the cradle of people's power to the Germans. Their call to defend Petrograd won widespread support. Troops supposedly loyal to Prime Minister Kerensky refused to enter the city and on 24–25 October the Bolsheviks seized control. Lenin announced the formation of a new government with himself as chairman. Talks begun with the Germans at Brest-Litovsk resulted in a ceasefire on the Eastern Front on 15 December. But hostilities resumed after subsequent negotiations broke down, and a treaty was not signed until 3 March. Meanwhile, the Germans were able to transfer thirty-five divisions westwards. Ludendorff planned a decisive blow before the American build-up tilted the strategic scales against them. He intended to shatter the BEF. With the northern flank of the Western Front sundered, the French would collapse in turn.

Operation *Michael* dwarfed all previous attacks. It was to be launched on 21 March on the fifty-mile front between Croisilles, near Arras, and La Fère on the Oise. Advancing on Bapaume and Péronne respectively, the Seventeenth Army on the right and the Second Army in the centre would then cross the old Somme battlefield and swing northwest, enveloping Arras and driving the BEF back towards the Channel. As well as protecting the left flank, the Eighteenth Army was to draw in French reserves that might otherwise help the British and sever the connection between the British and the French. Six thousand six hundred and eight guns and howitzers, 3534 mortars and over 700 aircraft would support the three armies. Two lesser attacks were also prepared. *Mars* would follow on the Arras flank after a few days, and *George* might be launched in April in Flanders.[15]

Though the BEF was understrength, its front was longer than ever. Lloyd George had agreed in principle to a French demand the previous September that Haig should extend his line. Both armies had roughly the same number of battalions but the French were holding 325 miles and the British 100. As the British were attacking virtually single-handed then, Haig could legitimately decline to do as much as the French wanted. But now the British were on the defensive like the French. Clemenceau revived the issue at the Supreme War Council in December and Haig had to take over another 25 miles. The area between Arras and St Quentin, behind which aerial reconnaissance from January onwards detected the most extensive preparations for the German attack, thus lay entirely opposite the British.

Haig was in a cleft stick because the need to retain the Channel Ports required him to be strongest further north. Part of the German blow would therefore strike the Third Army, whose 14 divisions held 28 miles of front about Arras. Holding a 42-mile front that included the old French line with only 15 divisions, the Fifth Army stood in the way of the main thrust. Haig was unfazed. His only fear, as he told both the War Cabinet and the King, was that 'the German would find our front so strong that he will hesitate to commit his Army to the attack with the almost certainty of losing very heavily'. Together with Pétain, he stymied the Supreme War Council's scheme for a general reserve that the Inter-Allied Staff, chaired by General Ferdinand Foch and renamed the Executive War Board because it now had a command function, could send to the point of greatest danger. Asked in February to contribute 10 of the 30 divisions sought, Haig said it was to late to comply. He was also loath to restrict his own freedom of action by surrendering divisions to an independent authority. Instead, he had agreed with Pétain, who was like-minded on the issue, that they would help each other out.[16]

Meanwhile, the BEF was not just going over to the defensive for the first time since 1914, but adopting the layered defensive tactics recently used by the Germans against it. The Australians at Messines worked feverishly on each layer, beginning with the wired redoubts in the Forward Zone. Like the German one, it was to dislocate the onslaught, which would then break itself against the Battle Zone 2000 yards rearward. The Rear Zone, essentially a second position, was at least four miles further back. Though the Australian sector did not appear to be directly threatened, increased German shelling of the rear areas on 9–10 March and night raids by giant Gotha bombers on nearby Bailleul ramped up the tension. Directed to hold an exposed post 'at all costs', Lieutenant Frank Bethune gave orders to his machine-gun section that caught the Australian mood:

1. This position will be held, and the section will remain here until relieved.
2. The enemy cannot be allowed to interfere with this programme.
3. If the section cannot remain here alive, it will remain here dead, but in any case it will remain here.
4. Should any man, through shell shock or other cause, attempt to surrender, he will remain here dead.
5. Should all guns be blown out, the section will use Mills grenades, and other novelties.
6. Finally, the position, as stated, will be held.[17]

—FIFTEEN—

LIGHT HORSE

While the Australians on the Western Front waited for the Germans to advance, the Light Horse waited in Palestine to advance again. The two theatres were vastly different. Even at its fiercest, the fighting in the Middle East never approached the intensity of the offensives in France and Flanders. Gains of tens of miles at little cost were common. As the distances made mobility essential, the horsemen were indispensable to the Egyptian Expeditionary Force (EEF), into which General Murray had grouped British forces in Egypt in March 1916.

The Light Horse were mounted infantry, whose job was to scout, probe and raid. Their sturdy Australian walers were unsurpassed for the work, sometimes going seventy hours without watering. In a fight horsemen dismounted to use rifle and bayonet, unlike cavalry, which fought on horseback with sword and lance. The four-man section was the smallest working unit. In battle, one man kept the section's horses under cover. With a quarter of its strength thus occupied, a light horse regiment dismounted for action rarely had even 350 'bayonet-carriers' available. A dismounted brigade of three regiments was not much stronger than a full-strength infantry battalion.[1]

Nearly all of the Australians who served in South Africa were mounted troops. Many joined the AIF's light horse brigades, which were therefore well versed in mounted operations before they left Australia. At Gallipoli the horsemen fought purely as infantry. Their commander, General Chauvel, learned like his troopers. Birdwood initially thought him slow and indecisive: 'He has always struck me as taking the gloomiest view . . . and he never seems to put life into things as he might'. But Chauvel improved and temporarily led the 1st Division in the last weeks at Anzac. Then Birdwood found him 'much more alert and resourceful [and] more ready to assert himself and come to a decision'. When the Anzac Mounted Division was formed in Egypt, half the men and nearly all the officers were Gallipoli men. They combined the skills acquired there with the mobile techniques recalled from South Africa and applied the whole to the desert. They knew their enemy, the Turk, thoroughly. As Australia was unable to supply guns, four batteries of British territorial horse artillery supported them.[2]

Once the threat of a Turkish invasion across the Sinai from Palestine subsided with the passing of the cool winter weather early in 1916, I and II ANZAC and most of the 300 000 troops gathered in Egypt after Gallipoli went to the Western Front. But Egypt still had to be garrisoned and lesser attacks towards the Suez Canal could not be ruled out. So Anzac Mounted remained. The 1st LH Brigade patrolled on the edge of the Nile Valley, 140 miles from Cairo, against raids by marauding Senussi Arabs. The 2nd and 3rd LH Brigades sortied into the Sinai from the Canal Line. On 11 April a composite force rode fifty-two miles to wipe out a small Turkish post at Jifjafa. Such operations practised the horsemen in procedures that became standard. Aircraft scouted ahead and dropped reports, enabling them to advance swiftly. Camels lugged water and feed for the horses and also humped the wirelesses that kept Chauvel in touch.

Convinced that a passive defence on the Canal would be 'wasteful in men and material', Murray aimed 'to push out across the Sinai towards its eastern frontiers'. On 7 April a brigade of British yeomanry (the Territorial Army's cavalry), later known as the 5th Yeomanry, occupied Romani, twenty-three miles east of the Canal, Oghratina, eleven miles further on, and posts in the Qatiya oasis area that stretched in between. Though all three were astride the coastal road, resupply from the sea was difficult. Murray planned to extend the railway from Qantara on the Canal to Qatiya, which would then become the springboard for a sixty-mile advance to El Arish. From there he could strike swiftly into Palestine.[3]

April 1916 belonged to the Ottomans. In Mesopotamia (modern Iraq), a classic example of 'mission creep' had seen the occupation of Basra by a small Anglo-Indian force at the end of November 1914, to secure Britain's oil supply, expand into a corps advance up the Tigris towards Baghdad. Major-General Charles Townsend's 6th (Poona) Division neared the city in October 1915 but stiffening resistance forced it back to Kut al Amara, seventy miles downriver. The Turks laid siege. On 29 April 1916 Townsend and his 10 000 troops surrendered. They included some men of the Australian Half-Flight, which the Australian government had despatched following a request from the Indian authorities in February 1915. Coming so soon after the withdrawal from Gallipoli, Kut was a serious blow to British prestige. By the time it was retaken at the end of the year, 200 000 Anglo-Indian troops had been sent to Mesopotamia.[4]

In the Sinai on 23 April, a strong Ottoman raiding force overwhelmed Qatiya and Oghratina and briefly reached the Canal Line at Dueidar. Chauvel's formations were the only ones in a position to intervene. Brigadier-General Ryrie hustled the 2nd LH Brigade to Qatiya, followed by the NZMR under Brigadier-General Edward Chaytor, the first New Zealander to graduate from the Camberley Staff College. The Turks were gone. They had not approached Romani. But the horsemen found there abandoned officers' messes replete with gin, whisky, champagne, cake and carpets. The effects of five English lords were recovered. 'They were not the right people to put at this sort of job', Ryrie commented sardonically. That the

Yeomanry officers had been among the severest critics of their discipline in Egypt increased the Australians' scorn.[5]

The 2nd LH Brigade set up at Romani with the NZMR behind it. The 1st LH Brigade joined them at the end of May. Now commanded by 'Bullant' Antill, despite his miserable performance at the Nek, the 3rd was still detached to the Canal Line. Chauvel received the remnants of the 5th Yeomanry in lieu. When the railway reached Romani in May, the 52nd (Lowland) Division arrived and began work on positions that ran six miles northwards to the sea from Katib Gannit. Together with Mount Meredith and Mount Royston, it was one of three dunes, each around 220 feet high, that were outliers of Wellington Ridge on the southern flank of the Romani tableland. Romani's elevation above the desert plain made it an ideal defensive location.

Over the next few months the horsemen patrolled deeper into the Sinai. 'It is awful country for horsework, the loose shifting sand making travelling painfully slow', wrote Lieutenant Maurice Pearce of the 1st Regiment. With the onset of summer, the heat was almost unendurable. Temperatures regularly rose above 120 degrees Fahrenheit in the shade. The patrols started moving by night, listening to the howls of jackals while navigating through the featureless terrain using compass and the stars, and resting where possible during the day. Thirst, flies, fleas, lice and body odour were constants. Encounters with the Turks were fleeting.[6]

At this stage General Murray had just the mounted troops and four weak territorial infantry divisions. Whereas the Ottomans could call on German pilots flying the latest aircraft, Murray relied on two squadrons flying BE2c's, underpowered two-seaters that had a well-deserved reputation as Fokker fodder. 'We depended mainly on luck', said Captain Richard Williams of the Australian No. 1 Squadron. The Germans overflew Murray's positions at will. On 1 June they bombed the 1st LH Brigade at Romani, killing eight men and thirty-six horses and stampeding 300 horses into the desert.[7]

'Enemy reported in force at Oghratina', wrote Lieutenant James Greatorex of the 1st LH Brigade machine-gun squadron on 21 July. Commanded by a German, General Friedrich Kress von Kressenstein, a strong Turkish column had marched by night from El Arish. The 1st and 2nd LH Brigades reconnoitred and harassed it. Slowed by the blistering heat, lack of water and the effort of moving guns, the column reached Qatiya on 2 August. Murray and Chauvel were cheerful. It would bump the prepared position at Romani. They thought the Turks would put in a holding assault against the main fortifications while trying to envelop the right flank, which the 1st LH Brigade defended. They planned accordingly.[8]

The 1st LH Brigade stretched three miles from the 52nd Division at Katib Gannit via Mount Meredith to Hod el Enna. Pivoting on Katib Gannit, it was to fall back slowly, drawing the Turks onto the soft sands between Wellington Ridge and Mount Royston. Chauvel forbade elaborate defences lest they swung further south to bypass them. Then Chaytor's New Zealanders, joined if possible by the 3rd LH Brigade, would strike the exposed Turkish southern flank. They were controlled by Major-General Herbert Lawrence, the commander of the northern section of the Canal Defences, whom Murray put in charge of the battle. An Anglo-Australian mobile column, under Lieutenant-Colonel Leslie Smith VC, was formed on horses and camels to help. The Turks could bring about 14 000 rifles to bear against the 10 000 at Romani. If they avoided the 52nd Division in the main position, the bulk would fall on the 800 rifles of the 1st LH Brigade.

At 10 p.m. on 3 August the 2nd LH Brigade returned to Etmaler Camp behind Wellington Ridge, the day's patrolling over. They noticed some Turks following. Apart from a few shots, all was quiet until midnight, when the 2nd Regiment reported thirty Turks approaching Hod el Enna. Five hundred were assembling behind them. The Turk advance guards had discovered that the Australians were on the intended forming-up place for the assault. They halted while plans were adjusted. At 1 a.m. 'Allah! Allah! Finish Australia!' babbled from thousands of throats. Heavy firing erupted. Little hummocks tufted with bushes gave the Turks excellent cover. At 2 a.m. they were thirty yards out. Some blundered into several 'Cossack' posts, from which a few horsemen would fire a sudden fusillade before galloping rearwards. Several Australians were bayoneted as they mounted their horses. Major Mike Shanahan of the 2nd Regiment came across four troopers who had been outflanked. Two jumped onto his horse. With each of the others clinging to a stirrup, Shanahan dashed to safety.

At 2.30 a.m. 8000 Turks charged Mount Meredith. Many had discarded their boots to run faster over the loose sand. At 3 a.m. Mount Meredith was abandoned. The fighting was so close that one big Queenslander dragged another man onto his horse and discovered he was a Turk. 'Bullets were making little spurts of flame all around us, owing to the phosphorous in the sand', Lieutenant-Colonel Bourne recalled. Troop covering troop, the 1st LH Brigade withdrew to Wellington Ridge. But the resistance had also led the Turks to feel for the Australian flank. Pouring past Hod el Enna, masses of them headed for Mount Royston beyond it. Chauvel directed the 2nd LH Brigade to extend the 1st's flank there. A battalion from the 52nd Division took over the left of the line, releasing more men for the threatened right. A squadron of Gloucesters from the Yeomanry bolstered it as well. But the Turks, with their superior strength, made steady progress. The horsemen fell back.

Taking Wellington Ridge at 7 a.m., the Turks were 700 yards from Etmaler Camp. Detached from the NZMR to the 2nd LH Brigade, the Wellingtons blocked them. 'If they get through my line here', Lieutenant-Colonel Meldrum told Brigadier-General John Royston, 'they can have the damned camps'. A 56-year-old South African, Royston led the 2nd in the absence of Ryrie on leave. 'Galloping Jack' went through fourteen horses as he rode amongst the troopers, a bloody bandage from a leg wound trailing behind him.

'Stick to it. We are winning now', he shouted. 'They are retreating in hundreds.' Worn out by their long advance through the soft sand, their thirst increasing with the rising sun, the Turks were faltering. When they tried to advance from Wellington Ridge at 8 a.m., the territorial batteries crunched them. Stalled and with their left flank exposed, they were ripe for the planned counterstroke. But the plan was fraying.

Murray had wanted General Lawrence to move his headquarters close to Romani for rapid decision-making. Lawrence was worried that the Turks might skirt Romani and make for the Canal. He stayed at Qantara. The direct telephone line to Romani was cut early in the battle. Chauvel could not get through to Lawrence until 7.25 a.m. He ordered Chaytor to Mount Royston, together with the Yeomanry. Holding off 2000 Turks at Mount Royston, the horsemen saw Chaytor's column appear at midday. Attacking at 2 p.m., the New Zealanders and the Yeomanry struck stubborn opposition but were close enough for a bayonet charge four hours later. Five hundred Turks surrendered. Chauvel had arranged for the 156th Brigade from the 52nd Division to assault Wellington Ridge at the same time and for the 1st and 2nd LH Brigades to advance as well. The 156th started late, met heavy fire and halted. Unwilling to risk his tired and weak brigades continuing alone, Chauvel stopped them. The 126th Brigade from the 42nd Division, which Lawrence ordered forward from the Canal, arrived too late to take part. So did the 3rd LH Brigade. Colonel Smith's column missed out too.

At 4 a.m. on 5 August, Chauvel's brigades attacked with a brigade from the 42nd and 52nd either side. Gaunt, red-eyed and grimy, the horsemen advanced with bayonets fixed. The Turks were in worse shape. Only on Wellington Ridge did they put up a fight. The line did not waver. The Turks broke. By 5 a.m. 1500 prisoners had been taken. The rest of the Turks scuttled towards Qatiya. At 6.30 a.m. Lawrence gave Chauvel command of all mounted troops to pursue them. The 3rd LH Brigade was to make for Hamisah, a few miles south of Qatiya, to outflank the Turks. The other brigades would head for Qatiya itself.[9]

By 4 p.m. the 3rd LH Brigade had taken 425 prisoners at Hamisah. The regiments were keen to push on but came under desultory shelling. Antill decided to withdraw, removing from the battlefield a brigade, which, as regards strength and freshness, was equal to any two of those going to Qatiya. Royston later replaced Antill. Lacking swords, the 1st and 2nd LH Brigades and the NZMR at Qatiya drew bayonets and tried a massed cavalry charge. The 5th Regiment went for a palm hod half a mile off. Trooper Ion Idriess heard that some guns had been spotted there:

We rode knee to knee; to right and left were excited faces and flashing steel; and our bodies felt the massed heat of the horses that tugged and strained as the squadrons broke into a swift canter. Then a horse reared high as it screamed and we went into a mad gallop, the horses' mouths open and their great eyes staring as the squadrons thundered on.

The hod was empty. On seeing the horsemen, the Turks had moved the guns. They waited until the squadrons started to reassemble under the palms before ripping into them. Dates rained down. The Turks had lain masses of fronds between the palm trunks for extra concealment. All three Anzac brigades were clawing dismounted towards them:

You were all concentrated just in your section and often for mad, hysterical moments, just in yourself. You saw a Turk's head in a bush, you saw his moustache, you saw his eye glaring along his rifle sights. You fired too, with breath in your belly, then rushed screaming to bayonet him, to club him, to fall on him and tear his throat out and he met you a replica of the berserk frightened demon that was in yourself.

The last drops of water boiled in water-bottles. Reaching a pond, the leading Anzacs gulped eagerly from it. 'The Turks saw the target. A bullet smashed a man's temple and his blood sprayed the clear water surface. We pulled him out and thrust down our bottles again.' The attack had stalled. Chauvel called a halt. Lieutenant Stewart Macfarlane of the 1st Light Horse was relieved:

This was the worst experience I have ever had. We only had 1 bottle of water for 35 hours, and we all had an awful time from thirst. The horses were 56 hours without water and for 44 hours in the saddle.

The Turks retired on their own terms. At Bir el Abd, they had 6000 men in strong fortifications. Chauvel's 3000 horsemen attacked them on 9 August and pushed in some posts. The Turks counter-attacked. The outnumbered horsemen had to pull out. A flurry of shells struck the 8th Regiment's horses, 'draping the desert bushes with legs and entrails of horse-meat. Horses scream frightfully when in agony', Idriess wrote. 'No matter what hail of death is around a man he sort of forgets his own peril, but an unexplainable fear shivers through him when horses scream like that'.[10]

Anzac Mounted sustained over 900 of the 1130 casualties that the five days of fighting cost. The Turks lost more than 9000 men, including 4000 prisoners. Though not a big engagement, certainly by Western Front standards, Romani was one of the war's decisive battles. Ending the threat to the Canal, it also wrested the initiative from the Turks. The credit lay with the Light Horse. On the first day Chauvel had controlled the withdrawal of the flank and prevented its envelopment. He praised his horsemen. Worn out after harassing the Turks for a fortnight beforehand, 'their pluck, dash and endurance [were] beyond all description'. The way troops and squadrons covered each other as they pulled back spoke volumes for their training. That the Turks were not completely destroyed was due to Lawrence. Well to the rear, he was out of touch and had placed the exploiting formations too far back. In December 1917 Lawrence became Haig's chief of staff.[11]

The pursuit showed the strengths and limitations of the Light Horse. Their mobility meant that only they could follow up the Turks. Once in contact, they transitioned seamlessly from fast-moving horsemen to small groups of riflemen advancing by rushes under the covering fire of their machine-guns. Once again, training as much as dash underpinned the speed with which the attacks were mounted. It kept the Turks off balance. But at Qatiya and Bir el Abd, the Turks held the initial assault. Lacking the strength and firepower to continue against their well-fortified positions, Chauvel had to break off both actions.

Two raids on Mazar and Maghara, garrisons on the way to El Arish, were the only actions carried out between August and December, enabling the horsemen to snatch a rest. That usually meant camping in the palm hods or a spell in tented areas further back that offered decent chow, beer and sports. There were no village billets and *estaminets*, as on the Western Front, and leave to Cairo was rare, which made for frequent monotony. In another difference to the Western Front, the desert war was often more principled. Just before Romani a German pilot dropped a note asking the Australians to mark their ambulances better in order to prevent them being bombed. The friendly respect for the Turks that emerged at Anzac continued. Idriess admired the way they hauled their guns to Romani by endlessly laying planks before the gun-wheels. On 19 August the 5th LH Regiment stumbled on sixty-eight Turks crazy with thirst. The Australians helped the Turks into their saddles and led the horses for five miles until transport was met.[12]

During the interlude General Murray restructured his command. As GHQ in Cairo was 140 miles from Romani, Lieutenant-General Charles Dobell took charge of the forces on the Canal and in Sinai, collectively known as Eastern Force. He had cleared the Cameroons in a well-run minor campaign but lacked wider experience.

Conversely, Lieutenant-General Sir Philip Chetwode, a cavalry leader, arrived from the Western Front to command the advanced troops in Sinai, now called the Desert Column. The eighteen camel companies, twelve of them Anzac, were grouped into the Imperial Camel Corps under Brigadier-General Smith and added to Chauvel's command. It was twice as strong as a light horse brigade and more heavily armed. Anzac Mounted, as it stood, was established as the backbone of the forces in Egypt. Murray protested vigorously when Birdwood proposed denuding the Light Horse to reinforce the understrength Australian infantry divisions after the Somme.

Murray now planned to advance to El Arish, as the precursor to the conquest of Palestine. Since its 1600-man garrison was strongly entrenched, the 42nd and 52nd Divisions would attack the town while the horsemen isolated it. The railway and the water pipeline that the infantry needed to advance were still thirty miles from El Arish when the Turks were reported to be retiring. On 20 December Chetwode ordered Chauvel to envelop it by next morning. During the 23-mile night march to cordon off the town, the horsemen left the waterless Sinai for the solid ground on the fringe of the Palestine plains. 'The hard going for the horses seemed almost miraculous after the months of sand', wrote Brigadier-General Frederick Cox of the 1st LH Brigade. 'As the shoes of the horses struck fire on the stones of the bed of the wady, the men laughed with delight.' Dawn revealed the squalid mud houses of El Arish. Amidst a noisy welcome, the chief sheik surrendered it.[13]

Wanting to block the two easterly routes from El Arish, the Turkish rearguard had divided to occupy Rafa, just inside Palestine on the coastal road to Gaza, and Magdhaba to the southeast, which straddled the track to the El Auja railhead. They were twenty-five miles off and thirty apart. Chetwode directed Chauvel to ride against both forthwith. Word arrived from No. 1 Squadron, which had plastered Magdhaba, that the village was well defended. Chetwode decided to concentrate wholly against it.

At 4 a.m. on 23 December, the horsemen saw the campfires of the Magdhaba garrison four miles away. The nearest water was back at El Arish. Chauvel had a few hours at most to take Magdhaba. At 9 a.m. the Camel Corps assaulted directly while the NZMR and the 3rd LH Brigade swung northeast to cut off the Turks. A few were seen leaving. Brigadier-General Royston went with the 10th Regiment on a wide sweep behind them. At 10 a.m. a pilot reported signs of a general withdrawal. Chauvel ordered his reserve, the 1st LH Brigade, to go in on the right of the cameliers. The pilot was mistaken. The Turks laid down torrential fire. Progress was snail-like. The water situation was critical. At 1 p.m. Chauvel ordered a withdrawal. But the battle had moved ahead of him.

Receiving Chauvel's order, Brigadier-General Cox applied the Nelsonian blind eye. 'Take that damned thing away and let me see it for the first time in half an hour', he told the runner. Having dismounted 1000 yards from the central Turkish redoubt, Cox's men were working by rushes towards it, with the cameliers alongside. By 2 p.m. they were 100 yards away. They charged. The Turks capitulated. Machine-guns were hurried up to the redoubt. They helped the other assaults. The 8th Regiment and the New Zealanders were on the left. 'Fixing bayonets we had a lovely charge that swept all before it', said Captain Albert Wearne. The 10th Regiment galloped over a redoubt and attacked it from the other side. Confronted by five Turks, Royston brandished his cane and yelled at them in Zulu. They gave up. At 4.30 p.m. it was all over. The Turks sustained nearly 400 casualties. Almost 1300 were captured, as against mounted losses of 146. Dazed after three nights with little sleep, the horsemen had hallucinations of well-lit streets and houses and weird animals on the ride back to El Arish.[14]

After a rain and gale lashed Christmas, Anzac Mounted, the 5th Yeomanry and the cameliers rode for Rafa on 8 January 1917. Close to the Palestine boundary, Lieutenant-Colonel Charles Mackesy of the Aucklanders galloped ahead, removed his hat and thanked God for allowing him at last to enter the Holy Land. Lieutenant Macfarlane saw 'thousands of acres of barley'. Starved of pasture for months, the walers had to be restrained from grazing. Rafa was encircled by dawn. 'Hard position to take with mounted men', thought Sergeant Ronald Ross of the 3rd Regiment. 'Flat, grass sown and fenceless country sloping down for over a mile before four Redoubts.'

The horse artillery started a short bombardment. For the first time on this front, air observers using wireless corrected the fire. Among them in No. 1 Squadron was Lieutenant Ross Smith. With his brother Keith, he would make the first England–Australia flight in 1919. At 10 a.m the NZMR assaulted from the north, the cameliers from the south and the 1st LH Brigade from the east. They dismounted up to 2000 yards out. The line was thin once the horse-holders dropped back. By 11 a.m. the 3rd Brigade and the 5th Yeomanry had been thrown in. The Turks had excellent fields of fire and seemingly limitless ammunition. They stood on their parapets to shoot. Water was a problem. Aircraft reported 2500 Turk reinforcements approaching. Chetwode and Chauvel conferred. At 4.25 p.m. Chetwode gave the word to withdraw. The 5th Yeomanry started back. The other brigades ignored the order.

Pouring as much fire as they could into the key redoubt, the New Zealanders bayonet charged it. The Turks shot waywardly. Chetwode was watching. The New Zealanders 'took the bit in their teeth and stormed over the hill yelling like fiends and sent the Turks flying', he wrote. 'It was a most inspiring and gallant sight.' The cameliers launched another tempestuous charge. Captain George Smith led one of the Australian companies. He had been feuding with Captain 'Mac' McCallum, who led a New Zealand one. Reason prevailed. 'Tomorrow we leave for the front; some of us may not come back; let us shake', Smith said. They did. Smith was now killed at the head of his company, while McCallum was already dead. The Turks fixed bayonets. The cameliers yelled louder. The Turks surrendered. 'It

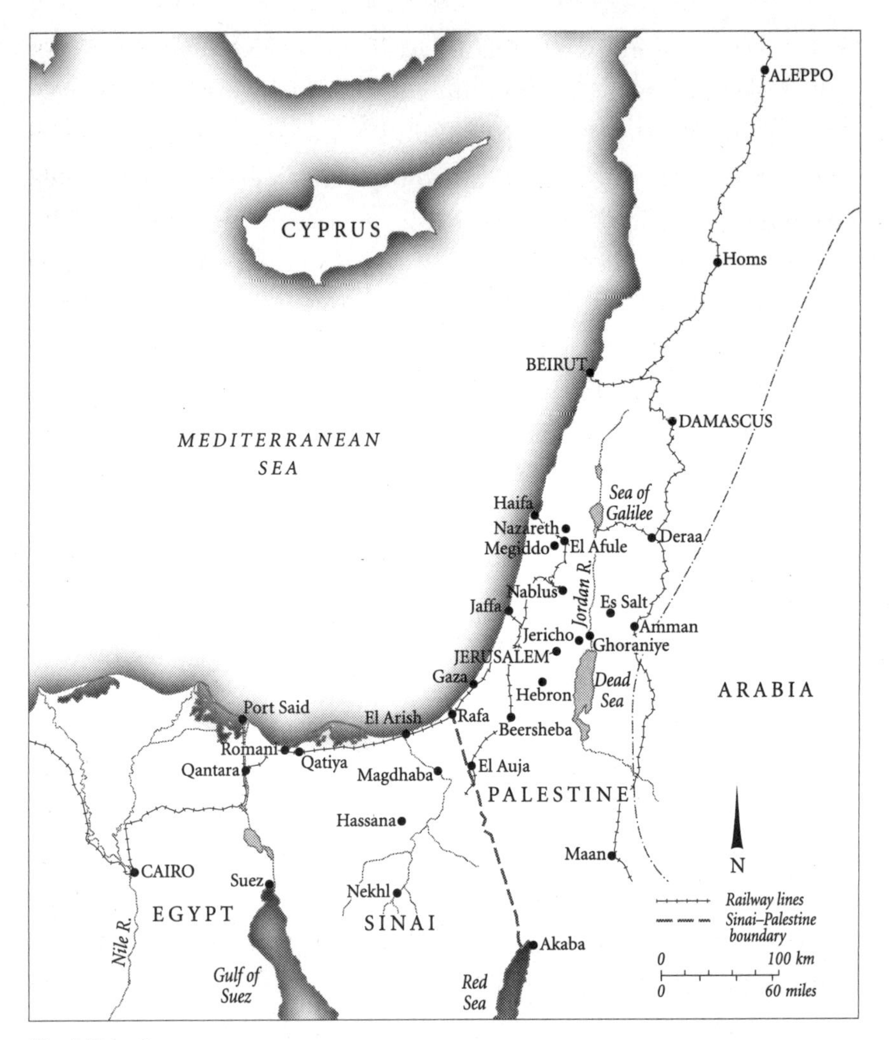

Sinai–Palestine

was all over (including the shouting) in 15 minutes', said Lieutenant Greatorex. The 5th Yeomanry joined the last stages of the battle. Mounted losses came to 476 men. The Turks lost almost 2000, including 1434 taken prisoner. Their reinforcing column was beaten off. With the elimination a month later of the posts at Nekhl and Hassana in the south, the Sinai was cleared of Turks. The mounted troops, four-fifths of them Anzacs, had done the job practically on their own.[15]

So valuable had the mounted arm proved that Murray expanded it in February. The 4th LH Brigade, which had been disbanded to feed the others on Gallipoli, was reconstituted under Brigadier-General John Meredith. The 22nd Yeomanry Brigade joined the 1st and 2nd LH Brigades and the NZMR in Anzac Mounted under Chauvel, while the 3rd and 4th LH Brigades, together with the 5th and 6th Yeomanry, formed the new Imperial Mounted Division. As they comprised half of it, many Australians were miffed by the title. The appointment of a British officer, Major-General Sir Henry Hodgson, to command Imperial Mounted rankled too. General Ryrie wanted all the Australian brigades together in a single division. Chauvel realised that Murray's arrangement was the best way of utilising the less experienced yeomanry. Stronger in mounted troops, Murray was now weaker in infantry. With the departure of the 42nd Division for France, he had only the 53rd Division from western Egypt, which replaced it in Eastern Force, and the 52nd and 54th left. A new infantry division, the 74th, was forming from dismounted yeomanry.[16]

At the start of March the Turks withdrew from their last outposts before Gaza. Twenty miles from Rafa and two miles from the sea, Gaza stood amongst cactus hedges at the southern end of the lush Philistia Plain. It had been captured by conquerors from the Pharaohs through to Napoleon, with Alexander and Ptolemy between. Murray thought that the Turks had 4000 men there, 2000 in Beersheba, twenty-eight miles to the southeast, and perhaps 9000 in posts and redoubts linking the two. Taking Gaza would turn this line and open the way to Palestine. The railway and the water pipeline had advanced sufficiently to sustain Eastern Force in the Gaza area for twenty-four hours. It had to fall in that time. Then the navy could resupply over the beach.

Chetwode's Desert Column had the task. He planned a *coup de main*, a surprise strike like Rafa or Magdhaba but on a larger scale. Attacking frontally, the 53rd Division was to take Ali Muntar knoll, 300 feet high, and then Gaza, a mile beyond it. Skirting

Sire Ridge on the town's eastern side, Anzac Mounted would reach the coast northeast of Gaza to prevent the garrison escaping. Facing eastwards, the Imperial Mounted Division and the Camel Corps were to protect Chauvel's flank. All the mounted units and the 54th Division were to help the 53rd Division if it got into trouble.

No. 1 Squadron bombed the railway north of Gaza. Shot down on 20 March, Captain Douglas Rutherford pranged near some Turks. Though badly wounded in the leg, Captain Frank McNamara landed alongside Rutherford and picked him up. Owing to his injured leg, McNamara lost control on take-off and crashed himself. Setting fire to his plane, he and Rutherford started for Rutherford's, which they reached just ahead of the Turks, McNamara's wound notwithstanding. They got it going and McNamara flew the seventy miles to El Arish. He became the war's only Australian air VC.

Anzac Mounted set out at 2.30 a.m. on 26 March. As it crossed the rugged Wadi Ghuzze, five miles in front of Gaza, dense fog reduced visibility to twenty yards. Gallopers went up and down keeping units in touch. At 6 a.m. the fog lifted. The 7th LH Regiment in the lead charged a Turk patrol. German airmen ran towards two nearby aircraft. Getting airborne just in time, they strafed the Australians. The Gaza–Beersheba Road was crossed. Many small parties of Turks woke to find the horsemen upon them. Six miles east of Gaza, the column turned for the sea. 'Two funny little coaches that might have come out of Queen Anne's reign' were intercepted on the coastal road. They carried the commander of the Turkish 53rd Division and his escorts. The dishevelled Australians troopers guffawed at the immaculate Turkish general. He nervously offered them smokes from a gold cigarette case. A trooper fished a butt from his own pocket and offered it to him. By 10 a.m. all the mounted formations were in position.

The 53rd Division, which should have been centre stage, had been held up at the Wadi Ghuzze by the fog. Major-General Alister Dallas waited for it to lift. He lost two hours. Chetwode tried to contact Dallas to tell him to get a move on. Dallas was away from his headquarters on a reconnaissance. Neither Chetwode nor Dobell went forward to take control. They fumed instead. Not until midday, when all surprise had been lost, did the 53rd assault. The Australians saw the long, straight lines start for Ali Muntar. They had 4000 yards of open ground to cover. 'Every yard must have seemed death to them', wrote Idriess. 'We could see in between the smoke-wreaths that when each line jumped up, it left big gaps.' The 54th Division was committed. Ali Muntar was not captured until late afternoon. The Turks still held Gaza.

Giving up on Dallas, Chetwode had ordered Chauvel at 1 p.m. to take the town. Chauvel redeployed his brigades. At 4 p.m. the 2nd LH Brigade galloped down from the north and the NZMR from El Sire with the 22nd Yeomanry alongside. Ahead were the cactus hedges, ten feet high. The horsemen reached them. General Ryrie saw 'our men and Turks firing at each other through the cactus, not more than six feet apart. Some of our fellows were shooting off their horses . . . they could see them better from up there'. Others were hacking through the cactus with their bayonets. 'It was just berserk slaughter', Idriess wrote:

> A man sprang at the closest Turk and thrust and sprang aside and thrust again and again – some men howled as they rushed, others cursed to the shivery feeling of steel on steel – the grunting breaths, the gritting teeth and the staring eyes of the lunging Turk, the sobbing scream as the bayonet ripped home. The Turkish battalion simply melted away: it was all over in minutes. Men lay horribly bloody and dead; others writhed on the stained grass, while all through the cactus lanes our men were chasing demented Turks.

By dusk all three brigades were in the town. Out to the east, the Imperial Mounted Division was holding off Turk relieving columns. 'Retire, retire, retire!' The message reverberated around the streets. 'But we have taken Gaza', Chauvel wailed. Chaytor wanted the order in writing. Ryrie felt a huge blunder had been made. The horsemen cursed the 'unbelievable folly of the Higher Command', which had robbed them of victory. The British infantry were even more bitter. They had sustained nearly all of the 3500 casualties.

Dobell and Chetwode thought time had run out. Gaza was unsubdued, one of the Turk relieving columns was reportedly 3000 strong, the horses had not been watered since the day before. Neither general knew that Ali Muntar had fallen, that the mounted brigades had watered their horses at pools they found, that the fight in Gaza was virtually won, and that the Turk columns showed no sign of continuing against Imperial Mounted in the darkness. Murray and Dobell glossed over the failure. Estimating Turkish losses at 7000 – they were actually 2500 – Murray told the War Office that 'it was a most successful operation' and that 'it had filled our troops with enthusiasm'. 'How can we believe the news of our victories in France, when we read such lies as this!' asked Trooper Idriess. General Dallas was sacked.[17]

Neither Murray nor Dobell thought twice about another attack. Murray's glowing reports persuaded the War Cabinet. Delighted by the recent fall of Baghdad, which erased the embarrassment of Kut, it sought in Palestine a repeat of the progress being made in Mesopotamia. All three infantry divisions would attack Gaza frontally. The Imperial Mounted Division and the cameliers were to assault dismounted on their right to drive the Turk flank towards Beersheba, with Anzac Mounted to the southeast holding the Turk reserves. Augmented by warships and beginning two days before, the preliminary bombardment would be the heaviest in Palestine to date. Six tanks and 2000 gas shells were available. Neither had been used against the Turks previously. Murray was confident, Dobell even more so. With precious mounted troops about to be used as straight infantry, Chetwode and Chauvel were not. Expecting another attack, the Turks had brought down men and guns from as far north as Damascus and transformed the defences. A series of well-wired redoubts dotted their line.

At 7.15 a.m. on 19 April the attack began. The gas was ineffectual. Penny-packeted along the line, the tanks made easy targets. Despite its promise, the bombardment hardly troubled the Turks. They mowed down attack after attack. Some infantry joined two companies of Australian cameliers under Captain Archibald Campbell, who were following the tank 'Nutty' in an assault on Tank Redoubt. Of the 200 cameliers who started with 'Nutty', 100 were left when it was knocked out. They charged over the 350 yards to the redoubt. Thirty were left. Together with twenty infantrymen, they hoed into the 600-strong garrison, which panicked and broke. A German officer stood before Campbell, revolver drawn. A shell landed between them, blowing the German to pieces. Campbell stayed in one piece. When the Turks counterattacked, he sent six runners back to ask for support but none made it. Campbell told the survivors to withdraw. He was one of five unscathed men in his 102-strong company.

The Atawineh Redoubt defied the Imperial Mounted Division. Screaming 'O Jerusalem', Captain Wearne felt as though he had been whacked in the head by a pick-handle and pitched forward, blood pouring down his face. 'The bullet struck the side of my head and, turning upwards, ploughed its way along the skull over the top of the head and out the other side', he wrote later. Repelling two weak thrusts on the right flank, Anzac Mounted got off lightly. At 3 p.m. a wireless intercept stated that the Turks had the situation well in hand. Dobell called time. He had lost 6000 men, 547 of whom – the equivalent of one and a half regiments – came from Imperial Mounted, and 345 from the cameliers. The Turks were elated. If they had been fortunate to avoid defeat in the first battle, they had decisively won the second.[18]

On 21 April Chetwode replaced Dobell as commander of Eastern Force. Chauvel became the first Australian and the first officer of a Dominion army to lead a corps when he took over the Desert Column. In May Murray reorganised it. With the return of two yeomanry brigades from Salonika, he formed a complete Yeomanry Division under Major-General Sir George Barrow. Anzac Mounted, now led by Chaytor, transferred the 22nd Yeomanry to it. Imperial Mounted lost the 6th Yeomanry and was renamed the Australian Mounted Division, much to the joy of the Australians. General Allenby, who had commanded the Third Army in the Arras offensive on the Western Front, replaced Murray in June. Arras had ended badly for Allenby, with three of his divisional commanders formally protesting his piecemeal attacks on narrow fronts. Haig seized the chance to offload a rival. As a cavalryman, Allenby now had opportunities denied him by the more formidable conditions of the Western Front.

Bulk, voice, temper, presence: everything about Allenby was massive. 'The Bull' quickly impressed his personality on the EEF. 'At last we had a commander who would live amongst us and lead us', said Corporal Roy Dunk of the 10th LH Regiment. Allenby shifted GHQ out of Cairo and set up near Rafa. Abolishing Eastern Force command, he reorganised the EEF in August into three corps directly under his own command. Chauvel led the Desert Mounted Corps, which comprised the three mounted divisions and the cameliers. He became the first Australian lieutenant-general. Formations from Salonika increased the infantry divisions to seven. They were grouped in XX Corps under Chetwode and XXI Corps under Major-General Edward Bulfin. More guns arrived and the superb Bristol Fighter began replacing the obsolete aircraft used hitherto. Disillusioned by the prospects in France after the Somme and the Nivelle fiasco, and anxious to boost morale at home, Lloyd George had told Allenby, 'Jerusalem by Christmas'. Allenby adopted a plan devised by Chetwode to get under way.[19]

As the toughest defences were at the Gaza end of the line, Chetwode proposed to feint against Gaza and seize Beersheba at the other end. It was less strongly held because the Turks thought the lack of nearby water limited operations there. For that reason Beersheba and its wells would have to be taken in a day. Then the whole position could be enveloped. Allenby ordered XX Corps to strike Beersheba from the southwest while Desert Mounted pounced from the east. Once Beersheba had fallen XXI Corps would attack between Gaza and the coast, with Desert Mounted riding across the Turks' line of retreat. Elaborate deception measures, which included an officer on patrol dropping fake orders, convinced the Turks that the main blow would hit Gaza. Sent to organise the recapture of Baghdad, General von Falkenhayn realised that if Allenby broke through, his advance could ultimately cut off the Turks in Mesopotamia. He sent the Seventh Army, waiting to move on Baghdad, to help the Eighth under Kress von Kressenstein in southern Palestine. Only two divisions had arrived when Allenby attacked on 31 October. He had twice the infantry and eight times the mounted troops of the Turks. At Beersheba 40 000 men confronted 5000.

Since Second Gaza, Chauvel's divisions had each spent a month in the line on the Beersheba flank, followed by a month's training and a month's rest. Operations did not stop entirely. Reconnaissances accustomed the Turks in Beersheba to seeing mounted troops come and go. Nearby Asluj and Khalasa were known to have been the sites of ancient cities. Their wells and cisterns were located and restored, providing enough water for Desert Mounted to concentrate in the area before the attack.

With the Yeomanry forming Allenby's reserve, Chauvel was left with the two Anzac divisions. They set off at 6 p.m. on 30 October. 'A full moon shone silver-white on a white metalled road', Trooper Idriess wrote. 'We knew it led to Beersheba.' It was twenty-five miles off in a shallow depression. The redoubt on Tel el Saba hill defended the eastern side of the town. Anzac Mounted attacked it at 10 a.m. Meeting heavy fire, the horsemen dismounted a mile out. Not until

3 p.m. did they get close enough to rush the redoubt. XX Corps had taken the western defences two hours before. It would be dark in another two hours. Chauvel was running out of time.

Australian Mounted was in reserve, with the 4th LH Brigade its nearest formation. Brigadier-General William Grant led the 4th, as Meredith had been invalided home. 'Put Grant at it', Chauvel ordered. Grant's regiments were dispersed to avoid bombing. By the time he assembled them four miles southeast of Beersheba, it was 4.30 p.m. Every man knew that unless the town was captured by nightfall, they would have to retire to water the horses. If that happened, said Sergeant Pat Hamilton, 'the Gaza–Beersheba front would not be outflanked, the whole attack would have failed, and we would be back where we were'. Starting at a slow trot and holding their bayonets, the horsemen shook out to five yards interval over the first half-mile and then galloped headlong.

'All I could do was ride my horse, wave my bayonet round my head and yell', one trooper said. The Turkish artillery opened but the horsemen were fleeting targets. They passed quickly through the shelling. Turkish machine-guns started up and were silenced by the horse artillery. Turkish riflemen began firing and many in the leading wave went down. The rest galloped harder. 'We came in so fast that the Turks lost their range and fired over our heads', said a trooper. Captain Charles Abbott's troop pulled out in front because his horse 'insisted on following a small track, which must have been used by the Turkish patrols going out and returning'. For Idriess the last half-mile was 'a heart-throbbing sight':

> My glasses showed me the Turkish bayonets thrusting up for the bellies of the horses – one regiment flung themselves from the saddle – we heard the mad shouts as the men jumped down into the trenches, a following regiment thundered over another redoubt, and to a triumphant roar of voices and hooves was galloping . . . right into the town.

Parties of forty or more Turks surrendered to lone Australians. Trooper Tom O'Leary had a gun crew wheel their gun into a side street to prevent another regiment claiming it as a trophy. 'We did not believe that the charge would be pushed home. That seemed an impossible intention', a captured German officer said. 'I have heard a great deal of the fighting quality of Australian soldiers. They are not soldiers at all, they are madmen.' Losing sixty-three men, Grant's brigade took over 1000 prisoners. Attacking along the coast on 2 November, XXI Corps outflanked Gaza. Allenby wanted Kress von Kressenstein to keep his forces there, while XX Corps seized the Tel esh Sheria and Hareira strongholds behind the Gaza–Beersheba Line. Desert Mounted was to arc further around through the Judaean hills to the coast. But the Turks were strengthening the inland flank.[20]

Before the Beersheba attack, the 2nd LH Brigade blocked the Hebron Road five miles north. Further north were a few hundred Arabs under Lieutenant-Colonel Stewart Newcombe. He was a colleague of Lieutenant-Colonel Thomas (T. E.) Lawrence, the best-known of the British military advisers sent to help Sherif Hussein after he raised the standard of revolt against the Turks in the Hejaz in June 1916. Getting on well with Feisal, the ablest of the Sherif's sons, Lawrence guided the Arabs in attacks on the Hejaz railway and isolated Ottoman posts. In July 1917 they seized Akaba, at the head of the Red Sea, which put them 130 miles from the EEF. Feisal's Arab Northern Army became part of Allenby's strategy. In return for arms, ammunition and a monthly gold subsidy, it was to harry the Turks beyond his right flank. Newcombe's party had come much closer.

The Turks thought that these moves on the Hebron Road presaged an advance astride it to Jerusalem, thirty-five miles distant. Overrunning Newcombe's Arabs, their reserves blocked Desert Mounted's attempt to reach Tel el Khulweilfe in the Judaean Hills, where there was good water. On 7 November Chetwode took Sheria and Hareira, creating a gap through which the mounted troops could pass. The 1st LH Brigade captured the ammunition dumps at Ameidat station but neither it nor the 2nd LH Brigade could go further. The 4th LH Brigade also met stiff opposition. But the horsemen had pushed far enough to see long columns of Turks withdrawing along the coast from Gaza. They captured many stragglers but the rearguards, bolstered by German machine-gunners and Austrian artillery, kept the main body out of harm's way. The chance to destroy the Eighth Army had gone.

Allenby switched the main drive to the coastal flank. Australian Mounted stayed in the Judaean Hills to secure the inland flank, while the rest of Desert Mounted kept touch with the Turks ahead of XXI Corps on the coast road. The advance was exhilarating. From the Jewish villages of Deiran, Wadi Henein and Richon le Zion came fruit, wine, bread and solid friendships. At Jaffa oranges were plentiful. At Ludd, Lieutenant William James and forty men from the 1st LH Regiment caught a Turk column and took 300 prisoners. The two Turkish armies diverged, the Seventh retiring northeast to cover Jerusalem and the Eighth heading north to hold the line of the Nahr Auja stream, a few miles past Jaffa. Horsemen and cameliers established posts on the far side but were driven back across. That suited Allenby, who sought to convince the Turks that he was continuing the coastal drive while really concentrating against Jerusalem. The slog towards it was primarily an infantry affair, conducted in miserable weather brought on by the winter rains. On 8 December, the 10th LH Regiment linked the 53rd and 60th Divisions in the final assault. After a day of bitter fighting on the western approaches, the Turks withdrew. On 11 December Allenby walked through the Jaffa Gate into the city, a deliberate contrast to the Kaiser's triumphal entry on horseback in 1898. The British people had their Christmas present.

Nothing more could be done until the ground dried out. The mounted divisions rested on the Mediterranean near Gaza. Many visited the Holy Places. 'We were taken on a tour of the Via Doloroso and the place where Jesus was crucified – also the Garden of Gethsemane', wrote Corporal Charles Livingston of the 6th LH Regiment. 'We were told that the olive trees were the same trees growing during the time of Jesus'. For Staff-Sergeant Harry Langtip of the 4th LH Regiment, the Holy City was a big disappointment. 'The place is really dirty, in fact it is just a big native village.' After long months in the saddle, rowdiness was inevitable. Though not matching the indiscipline that had occurred in Cairo, it was sufficiently troublesome for Chauvel himself to speak to some leave parties 'like a father' before they left for Jerusalem.[21]

Apart from Palestine, the Allies had nothing to crow about at the end of 1917. On the Western Front, Third Ypres had fizzled out in the mud and the initially promising attack at Cambrai ended up just another failure. The Italians were thumped at Caporetto. The Russians were out of the war. The Americans were still barely in it. Amidst this gloomy scene, Jerusalem's fall shone like a beacon. For Lloyd George, it vindicated the idea of knocking away Germany's props. He urged a major offensive to eliminate Turkey from the war by seizing Aleppo in Syria. The Supreme War Council conditionally approved it on 30 January 1918. Going to Aleppo would require double Allenby's present strength but also permit an easing of the Mesopotamian campaign. The extra troops could come from there.

In the meantime, Allenby struck out for the Jordan. On 19 February the 60th Division advanced astride the Jericho Road through a tangle of steep, rocky hills with Anzac Mounted on its right. The Turks withdrew on being outflanked by the horsemen, who descended into the Jordan Valley and entered Jericho on 21 February. On the far side rose the forbidding hills that shielded the lands of Moab and Gilead in the Trans-Jordan. Striking into Moab, Allenby intended to take Es Salt, ten miles east of the river, and destroy the Hejaz railway at Amman, another ten miles east on the fringe of the Arabian Desert. It was the lifeline for the 20 000 Ottomans south of the town, whom Feisal's Arabs were raiding. Anzac Mounted, the cameliers and the 60th Division set out in a downpour on 22 March.

As the Jordan rose in flood, the crossing had been delayed for three days, precluding surprise. When the 60th Division was unable to bridge the river at Ghoraniye, opposite Jericho, sappers from an improvised Anzac bridging train swam across a few miles downstream and dragged pontoons into position. The infantry took the Es Salt Road into the hills but the tracks used by the mounted troops were impassable. Both the NZMR and the 2nd LH Brigade often had to lead their horses single file in the freezing rain. General Smith remarked that 'The camels were carried up by the men'. On 25 March the 1st LH Brigade took Es Salt without a fight and the 60th Division occupied it to provide a secure base for the raid on Amman. Given plenty of warning and tipped off by friendly Arabs, the Turks had garrisoned Amman with 4000 troops and fifteen guns. They outnumbered and outgunned the attackers.

General Chaytor's men dismounted a mile and a half from the town on 27 March. They were halfway to it when the Turks unleashed hell. The attack failed, although sections of the railway were destroyed that night. Reinforced with two battalions from the 60th Division, Chaytor tried again the following afternoon. The outcome was the same. Chaytor decided on a night assault. Early on 30 March, the New Zealanders took Hill 3039, directly below which lay Amman, but were held up from the old Roman citadel. Anzac Mounted withdrew. Es Salt was evacuated on 1 April. Fearing Turkish retribution, its Christian inhabitants fled. The horsemen and cameliers lifted women onto their saddles or rode with sleeping children in their arms through the icy rain. Several hundred Turks had been captured at a cost of 1200 men, over half of them Anzacs. The effect cut deep. In the 6th LH Regiment, which suffered almost 100 casualties, 'horseholders, sole survivors in many sections, leading the saddled horses of their missing mates, silently echoed the "empty saddle" appeal of Sydney recruiting picnics'. The railway was quickly repaired.[22]

The Turks were always going to react strongly to Trans-Jordan operations. From Amman, Allenby could threaten Deraa, forty miles north, where the Hejaz railway bifurcated. One track went to Damascus; the other ran to Haifa on the coastal plain of Sharon. Taking Deraa would thus cut the main Turk supply line west of the Jordan, paving the way for an advance on that side to Damascus itself. Seeking to make the Jordan more secure, the Turks attacked on 11 April but were unsuccessful. They also made Es Salt the headquarters of their Fourth Army, which now comprised all forces beyond the river, and moved 5000 troops to Shunet Nimrin in the foothills astride the Es Salt road.

These developments served as a red rag to the Bull. On 20 April Chauvel took over the Jordan flank from Chetwode, with orders to seize both Shunet Nimrin and Es Salt as a preliminary to another advance on Amman and thence to Deraa. The operation would deny the Moab wheat crop to the Turks and help Feisal's Arabs. Allenby fixed it for 30 April to suit the local Beni Sakr Arabs, who promised full co-operation. While the rest of Australian Mounted dashed for Es Salt, the 4th LH Brigade was to seize the Jisr ed Damieh bridge, over which the Es Salt Road ran, to prevent the Turks reinforcing from the west bank. It was fifteen miles north of Ghoraniye. Turkish preparations for another crossing at Mafid Jozele, five miles south of the bridge, were missed. The build-up for an attack that the Turks were themselves planning on 4 May also went unnoticed. Moreover, Chetwode had feinted strongly against Shunet Nimrin on 18 April. Perhaps Allenby ordered this operation before deciding on Chauvel's sortie. But the Turks had been on alert since.

Leaving Ghoraniye before dawn on 30 April, the 4th LH Brigade heard the din off to the right as the 60th Division assaulted Shunet Nimrin. Not expecting the northwards gallop to Jisr ed Damieh, the posts on the valley floor were brushed aside. But rapidly increasing resistance meant that the Damieh crossing could only be engaged by the horse artillery. Visiting General Grant that afternoon, Chauvel was concerned to see his 800 men strung out across an eight-mile front. He sent the 4th back to more secure positions astride the Es Salt Road. The Turks promptly expanded the Damieh bridgehead. Grant was concerned that only one squadron occupied Red Hill, which dominated the surrounding plain. He wanted Chauvel to put a regiment there. Chauvel was in a quandary, made worse by the news that the Turks had completed a pontoon bridge at Mafid Jozele. On the one hand, success depended on holding the river line. On the other, he was reluctant to commit his slender reserves so early in the battle. Chauvel turned Grant down.

Brigadier-General Lachlan Wilson had commanded the 3rd LH Brigade since Royston's return to South Africa the previous October. It reached Es Salt at 4.30 p.m. The 9th and 10th LH Regiments dismounted, charged and overwhelmed the outlying redoubts, whereupon Wilson hurled the 8th LH Regiment at the town. It galloped through. The commander and staff of the Fourth Army narrowly escaped. This achievement, 'one of the cleanest and most decisive pieces of light horse work in the campaign', blocked the main route from Shunet Nimrin. The Beni Sakr were to have cut the lesser route at Ain es Sir. But they waited to see which way the wind blew. When the Turks held Shunet Nimrin they decided the battle was lost and skulked off. The Turks could now either leave or reinforce Shunet Nimrin. Chauvel found out next morning. He ordered the 2nd LH Brigade from Es Salt to join the 5th Yeomanry and strike it from the rear in conjunction with another assault by the 60th Division. The Turks repelled all attacks.

Disaster befell the 4th LH Brigade. During the night over 5000 Turks crossed the Damieh bridge. More still waited to cross at Mafid Jozele. Shortly after 7 a.m. on 1 May the Turks struck. 'They looked like ants crawling along the white banks of the Jordan', said Trooper Bill Smyth. By 10 a.m. the 4th had been driven off the Es Salt Road. Red Hill was lost. So were nine guns when Grant ordered a withdrawal. 'Every man for himself', Smyth was told. The horsemen finally stopped the Turks on a line covering the Umm es Shert track, the one remaining exit route for the brigades in the hills.

No. 1 Squadron also reported the Turks massing around Es Salt, where Wilson's men were using captured German bombs and living off the land. At 4 p.m. on 3 May Chauvel told them to pull out. Next morning Major Arthur Olden of the 10th LH Regiment saw the Turks attack in great style 'with a triumphant cry, which, however faded away as they made the startling discovery that their expected and long-denied quarry wasn't there!' Over the next two days, the Australian airmen bombed and machine-gunned the Turks to help the men on the ground break clear. The horsemen sustained 397 of the 1649 casualties the operation cost. Apart from those left on Gallipoli, the nine guns captured by the Turks were the only ones permanently lost by the Australians in the war. The 4th, the men of Beersheba, 'absolutely showed the white feather', said Trooper Gorden Birkbeck of the 1st Machine-gun Squadron.[23]

The failure of the two Trans-Jordan thrusts were not the only crosses Allenby had to bear. Ludendorff's concurrent attacks on the Western Front had created an insatiable demand for men. Between March and May, Allenby sent the 52nd and 74th Divisions plus another ten battalions to France. Re-formed as machine-gun companies, most of the yeomanry also went. Indian formations, some coming from Mesopotamia, replaced the 60 000 troops Allenby provided. Indian cavalry regiments fleshed out the old Yeomanry Division, which became the 4th Cavalry Division, and permitted the formation of the 5th Cavalry Division. Less suited to the Jordan hills than the desert, the Camel Corps was disbanded and its Anzacs incorporated into the new 5th LH Brigade. The 5th took the place of the yeomanry in the Australian Mounted Division, which also adopted the sword. Desert Mounted now comprised four divisions. But it was in the same position as the rest of Allenby's army. As most of the incoming formations were raw, the EEF had gone backwards in terms of effectiveness.

Though Allenby temporarily shelved thoughts of taking the offensive, he had already decided to break through on the coastal plain. To that end, he appreciated that the Amman and Es Salt actions kept the Turks riveted on the Jordan. As they would expect Allenby to strike wherever Desert Mounted was located, it remained in the valley. 'The prospect of spending mid-summer in that delightful spot, 1200 feet below sea level, and where the thermometer reached 128 degrees, was not a very pleasant one', Colonel Bourne laconically wrote. Besides the furnace-heat, the atmosphere was oppressive and dust, snakes, mosquitoes and flies were ever present. Sickness rose alarmingly. One Australian trooper remarked: 'Well, I reckon God made the Jordan Valley, and when He seen what He'd done, He threw stones at it!'[24]

The Jordan period was the horsemen's harshest experience of the war. But it ensured, as Allenby hoped, that the Turks watched the area closely. On 14 July 1000 Germans from the 'German Asiatic Column', ostentatiously sent to support them in 1917, attacked the Abu Tellul Ridge. Its fall would render the Ghoraniye bridgehead untenable. The 1st LH Brigade shot down repeated assaults. One post was eventually overrun. 'Get to them, Granny', General Wilson said to Lieutenant-Colonel Cecil Granville of the 1st LH Regiment, which was in reserve. The horsemen galloped to the crest, dismounted, fixed bayonets and charged. Though the Germans outnumbered them, the shock was terrific. The Germans broke. Over 100 were killed and 358 captured. Liman von Sanders, who had replaced von Falkenhayn, was angry. The Turks should have attacked too. Poorly fed and lacking basic necessities, they were in a wretched state. Many of their draught animals were too weak to haul guns. Allenby had twice the numerical strength of Army Group F's three armies. As regards morale, supply and, now, training, his three corps were far superior. His railway had reached Jerusalem. Allenby was ideally placed to attack. To avoid the winter rains, he had to do so in September.[25]

Allenby aimed to destroy Army Group F. XXI Corps was to smash a path through the Eighth Army on the Plain of Sharon for the 4th and 5th Cavalry Divisions and Australian Mounted. Swinging over the Carmel Range west of Samaria, they would descend on the Esdraelon Plain near Megiddo. After cutting the railway to the coast at El Afule and Beisan, forty miles from their current position, and capturing Nazareth, von Sanders's headquarters, the horsemen were to take the Jordan crossings below the Sea of Galilee. The Seventh and Eighth Armies would be trapped, as XX Corps was to advance through the Judaean Hills towards Nablus and also seize the Damieh crossing. Feisal's Arabs were to destroy the railway at Deraa beforehand, disrupting the Fourth Army's retreat. When it started to pull out, Anzac Mounted on the Jordan would strike. Breathtaking in its boldness, Allenby's scheme was helped by Liman von Sanders. Whereas von Falkenhayn sought defence in depth, Liman put everything in the shop window, although his long line left him little option. The advance would be hard to stop if the line were broken. As Allenby had concentrated 35 000 infantry against the 8000 Turks on the coastal plain, it probably would be. The battle was named after Megiddo, the ancient Armageddon. It was exactly that for the Turks.

To conceal the move of the horsemen to the coast, dummy camps were set up in the Jordan Valley. Mules dragging sleighs maintained the dust clouds the troops routinely raised. Anzac Mounted made 15 000 dummy horses to replace the real ones that had left. Chauvel's headquarters remained standing and lit. Buying up barley around Amman, Lawrence's agents hinted to the Beni Sakr that it was needed for a large British cavalry force. Prying German aircraft were driven off. No. 1 Squadron accounted for all fifteen downed in the lead-up to the battle. Major-General William Salmond, the theatre air commander, rated No. 1 among the finest squadrons in the air force. It received the only Handley-Page heavy bomber sent to the Middle East.[26]

Flying this machine early on 19 September, Captain Smith bombed the central telephone exchange at El Afule. Other aircraft struck the Seventh and Eighth Army headquarters at Nablus and Tul Keram respectively, as well as Nazareth. For several vital hours, the Turks were rendered deaf and dumb. At 4.30 a.m. the 300 guns on Sharon erupted. XXI Corps burst forth. At 7 a.m. Desert Mounted started over the battlefield where Richard the Lionheart had beaten Saladin on another September day in 1191. 'The great column streamed northward without even its vanguard being checked', wrote the British Official Historian. 'It seemed that the clock had been put back and warfare had recovered . . . the pageantry whereof long-range weapons had robbed it'. Getting amongst the Turks fleeing Tul Keram, the 5th LH Brigade captured 2000. The two Indian cavalry divisions crossed the Carmel Range. Taking El Afule, the 4th Cavalry Division entered Beisan at 4.35 p.m. on 20 September. Liman von Sanders fled with a few clerks when the 5th Cavalry Division arrived at Nazareth.

The remnants of the Eighth Army headed for Jenin, at the southern end of the Esdraelon Plain. Australian Mounted intercepted them. With swords drawn, the 1st LH Brigade fell on Jenin from the rear. Lieutenant Peter Doig's troop in the lead charged an outlying camp and took 1800 prisoners. The 10th LH Regiment pushed down the road whence the Turks had come. Lieutenant Reginald Patterson's troop of twenty-three men encountered a strong column in the dark. They opened fire. Saying a large force was behind him, Patterson called on the Turks to surrender. In the morning, General Wilson found he had 8000 prisoners, five guns and two aeroplanes. The 5th Cavalry Division captured Haifa on the coast.

The collapse of the Eighth Army unhinged the Seventh, now led by Mustafa Kemal, which had doggedly resisted XX Corps in the hills before Nablus. By evening on 21 September, it was retreating towards the Jordan. Next morning Anzac Mounted took the Damieh crossing but the twenty-five miles north to Beisan remained open. As the 4th Cavalry Division moved to close it, No. 1 Squadron drenched the Turks with bomb and bullet. Almost 1000 vehicles and eighty-seven guns were abandoned in the panic-stricken chaos. What followed, when the gap was closed on 23 September, 'was but a rounding up of cattle by the cavalry'. The Seventh Army, too, had been destroyed. Only the German Asia Brigade escaped.[27]

East of the Jordan, patrols from Anzac Mounted listened for signs of the Fourth Army's withdrawal. 'Finally on the night of 21/22 September we heard the rattle of transport wheels and the chase was on', said Lieutenant Ronald Hopkins of the 6th LH Regiment. The Turks made for the railhead at Amman, for which the Maan garrison 120 miles south was also heading. Following up, Chaytor's men easily took Es Salt on 23 September. Amman fell two days later but the rearguard had given the main body the chance to get clear. On 28 September the Maan garrison, 6000 strong, reached Ziza, seventeen miles away. A warning to surrender went unheeded. Ali Bey Wahabay would not capitulate to a force too weak to protect his men from the 10 000 Beni Sakr who had been circling them for days. He wanted to wipe out the Arabs and then surrender. General Ryrie and the 2nd LH Brigade broke the stand-off. Taking two sheikhs hostage to make sure the Arabs stayed their hand, they joined the Turks for the night. 'Go on Jacko, give the bastards hell!' the Australians yelled when the Turks fired at their tormentors. Next morning the Turks formally surrendered. Losing 139 men, Chaytor's force had taken 10 300 prisoners in nine days.[28]

'What about Damascus?' Allenby had asked Chauvel on 22 September. 'Rather!' Chauvel replied. When the formal order arrived three days later, Australian Mounted was advancing on Semakh, at the southern end of the Sea of Galilee, and Tiberias, halfway up the western side. With the Turks in disarray, German machine-gunners were at the core of the resistance from now on. Liman von Sanders told those at Semakh to defend it to the last man. 'Form line and charge', Major John Parsons shouted when they opened up on the

11th LH Regiment. The horsemen galloped at the 'tiny pinpoints of light dancing along the muzzles of the guns like flickers of lightning'. There was no artillery support. Almost half the 200 horses were hit. The horsemen dismounted. General Grant sent some machine-gunners to the left of the village. They raked it. The horsemen forced their way in. A close-quarter fight raged for the next hour. Semakh fell. Losing seventy-eight men, the Australians killed 100 Germans and took 365 prisoners. By contrast, the 3rd LH Brigade easily captured Tiberias and camped on the shores of Galilee afterwards. Arab boatmen charged extortionate prices to cross. 'No wonder that other bloke walked', the horsemen gasped.[29]

At nearby El Mejdel, other Arabs sniped at the Australians. They caught and shot six, solving the problem. The Anzacs considered the Arabs treacherous and cruel. Idriess called them 'the ghouls of the battlefields'. Seeking loot, they snared weak patrols, killed stragglers, stripped wounded and dug up dead. El Mejdel was only one example of the Anzacs' anger boiling over. During the retreat from Amman in April, Arabs in the village of Ain es Sir fired on the Wellingtons. They dragged the firers out and killed them. At the end of 1918 an Arab murdered a New Zealander. He was tracked to the village of Surafend. When the British authorities did nothing, the Australians and New Zealanders surrounded it. Removing the women and children, they killed or wounded over thirty of the men and torched the village. Publicly rounding on Anzac Mounted, Allenby withheld decorations and awards. The Anzac horsemen could never understand why Arab outrages seemed to be tolerated while their retaliation was not.[30]

From El Mejdel and Tiberias, Australian Mounted was to cross the Jordan at Jisr Benat Yakub, fourteen miles north of Galilee, and continue over the Golan Heights to Damascus, seventy miles distant, followed by the 5th Cavalry Division. The 4th Cavalry Division would head east of Galilee to Deraa, try to destroy the Fourth Army, and then ride for the city. If the Turks escaped, it was to drive them north towards the other two divisions. Feisal's Arabs would operate with the 4th. Frequently attacked by German aircraft from Deraa, they were crumbling. On 22 September Lawrence sought help. Next day Captain Smith and two other Australian pilots downed four German planes and bombed the Deraa strip, eliminating the menace.

The advance began on 26 September. Though harried by the Arabs and under relentless Australian air attack, the Fourth Army left Deraa before the 4th Cavalry Division arrived. The Arabs were already there, ransacking and killing the Turkish wounded. General Barrow stopped them. Sick, hungry, even lacking boots, the promise of refuge in Damascus was all that kept the Turks going. German machine-gunners prevented the cavalry finishing them off. But the 4th's artillery crumped the columns. The 5th Cavalry Division also joined the 4th in raiding them.

Clearing the western side of Galilee, Australian Mounted reached the Benat Yakub bridge. It had been destroyed, and the German rearguard forced the horsemen to use distant fords. An envelopment by the 3rd LH Brigade on 29 September dislodged 1500 Turks and Germans at Sasa. From dust clouds off to the east came the sounds of the guns battering the withdrawing Fourth Army. Damascus was twenty miles away. The Official Historian of the Light Horse, Henry Gullett, wrote of the next day's advance:

> The men, unshaven, dusty, their eyes bloodshot from lack of sleep, rode with the bursting excitement of a throng of schoolboys . . . With swords flashing in the early sunrise, little parties of three and four men raced shouting on bodies of Turks ten and twenty times their number.

When a Turkish column hurriedly made a stand on the ridge either side of Kaukab, the 5th LH Brigade outflanked it while the 4th charged. For the first time the German machine-gunners ran. The 5th LH Brigade reached the Barada Gorge on the western side of Damascus, along which the road and railway to Beirut ran. On its way to cut the Homs Road, north of the city, the 3rd LH Brigade moved west of the 5th during the afternoon but the terrain was impossible. Brigadier-General Wilson decided to ride through Damascus next morning. Meanwhile a large Turkish column was trying to escape up the gorge. 'They were simply mown down', said Trooper Stanley Billing of the 8th LH Regiment. 'The road was blocked with dead and wounded men, dead horses, mules and donkeys, and a flock of about thirty sheep and goats which had got into the line of fire.'

Led by the 10th LH Regiment, the 3rd LH Brigade started for Damascus at 5 a.m. on 1 October. A flurry of shots rang out as they entered, most of them fired in greeting by the Arabs. The Turkish authorities had fled and the 20 000 Turkish troops in the city were too exhausted to do anything. Revolver drawn, Major Olden strode into the Town Hall. 'In the name of the City of Damascus, I welcome the first of the British Army', declared the Emir, Said Abd el Kader, the leader of the notables who had raised the Hejaz flag above the building. They were controlling Damascus until the arrival of Feisal's Arabs. Getting his written assurance that they would encounter no resistance, Olden led the horsemen northwards. Freed from Turkish rule, the Damascenes joyously 'clung to the horses' necks, they kissed our men's stirrups, they showered confetti and rosewater over them'. Clear of the city by 7 a.m., the 3rd LH Brigade harried what remained of the Fourth Army, which was labouring on to Homs and Aleppo. On 2 October the 9th LH Regiment charged a column near Khan Ayash, fifteen miles from Damascus. The 100 Australians captured 1500 men as well as the only standard taken by the AIF in the war. It was the Australian horsemen's last fight, though Chauvel directed the 5th Cavalry Division's subsequent advance to Aleppo. It arrived on 26 October.[31]

In the two-and-a-half years since leaving the Canal, the Anzac horsemen had advanced 500 miles and captured 50 000 Turks. Their own losses, less than 2000 dead from all causes and 6000 wounded, paled alongside the horrific toll in the Anzac Divisions fighting the Germans. Such was the nature of the war in Sinai and Palestine, 'a giant picnic' compared to 'the hell of France', said Frank Hurley. It was easier on trooper and general alike. A relative failure on the Western Front, Allenby emerged from the Palestine campaign with claims to greatness. Chauvel, too, handled his formations with aplomb but was never confronted with the tactical problems faced by the Anzac generals in France.

Australian and New Zealander worked more closely together in Sinai and Palestine than on the Western Front. Australian regiments were detached to New Zealand brigades and New Zealand regiments to Australian brigades. Moreover the low casualties allowed exceptionally close associations to develop amongst all ranks, which further increased effectiveness. Tactical skill was just as important, since the horsemen lacked numbers and artillery. The result was total dominance of the Turks. Murray said that the horsemen were his most valuable troops. Allenby attributed the completeness of the Megiddo victory to the action of Desert Mounted. But the fight against Turkey was always a sideshow, Lloyd George's views notwithstanding. It contributed little to the defeat of Germany and the winning of the war. That could only be achieved on the Western Front. The Anzacs there were to contribute mightily to the campaign that brought the end about.[32]

—SIXTEEN—

STEMMING THE TIDE

To Australians at the start of 1918, Villers-Bretonneux was just a name on area maps of the Somme. It stood on the edge of the Santerre, a great agricultural plateau on the southern side of the river. The crop-covered fields around the town and the mills within it ensured reasonable prosperity for its 5200 residents. Two miles to the northeast, the village of Hamel nestled at the foot of a bald hill, 260 feet high, that the Germans called the Wolfsberg. Hill 104, on the northern side of Villers-Bretonneux, was the highest point of the Santerre. 'Altogether it was a delightful setting for anything but grim war', wrote Australian gunner Ralph Keegan. But Villers-Bretonneux was also important strategically because it barred the way to Amiens, whose urban sprawl and cathedral could be seen ten miles westwards. An important railway centre, Amiens was vital to the BEF's logistics chain. The ruler-straight Roman Road and a trunk railway from the east both ran through the town to the city.

Until the Fifth Army arrived, upon the extension of the British front southwards in January 1918, Villers-Bretonneux had been in the French sector. The defences ahead of it were wretched, not least because the French, following a live and let live policy with the Germans and knowing that they would be leaving anyway, had neglected them. Nevertheless, the town was twenty miles behind the front line. Only a breakthrough could threaten it and that was an unlikely prospect if past experience was any guide. British and French offensives had gained about a mile a month and never looked like breaking through. The local farmers were so relaxed that General Gough had to stop them filling in a nearby trench system. Known as the Amiens Defence Line, it had been built by the French in 1915 to protect the city. Starting at Ribemont on the Ancre, its inner line crossed the Somme at Sailly-le-Sec and straddled the Wolfsberg before going over the Roman Road three miles east of Villers-Bretonneux.[1]

At 4.40 a.m. on 21 March, the most spectacular offensive of the war opened. It 'seemed as though the bowels of the earth had erupted', said a British machine-gunner on the receiving end of the bombardment. Stormtroops advanced like a tide surging over a rocky shore, penetrating at weak points, ignoring their flanks and bypassing strongpoints, which the following waves took out. The right of the Third Army was pushed back but the Fifth Army crumbled. By 23 March the Germans had opened a breach forty miles wide. The French took over Gough's right flank. His left passed to the Third Army after Haig made the Somme the boundary between it and the Fifth Army. Gough was left only with XIX Corps. Some of its divisions were down to brigade strength.[2]

Contrasting the dramatic advance in the south with the slower progress in the north, Ludendorff shifted the weight of the attack leftwards. The Second Army was to advance astride the Somme towards Amiens. But when it reached the shattered ground of the 1916 Somme battlefield, on 25 March, the artillery and logistics could not keep up. Ordering the drive on Amiens to continue, Ludendorff strengthened the right wing of the Eighteenth Army, which was still advancing rapidly alongside the Second against the French. On March 28 the Seventeenth Army would launch Operation *Mars* to 'shake and smash' the British around Arras, with Operation *Georgette* (a lesser *George*) to follow on the Lys.

Australian airmen were helping to slow the offensive. No. 2 Squadron, which had switched to the outstanding SE5a at the end of 1917, and No. 4 Squadron, which arrived in France with its Sopwith Camels at the same time, bombed and strafed the Germans from dawn to dusk. Captain Arthur Cobby flew with No. 4:

> The job consisted of getting to the line . . . as fast and often as one could, and letting the enemy on the ground have it as hot and heavy as possible . . . The air was full of aircraft, and continuously while shooting up the troops on the ground we would be attacked by enemy scouts . . . The smoke of the battle mixed with the clouds and mist above rendered flying particularly dangerous.

For their part, the Diggers could see that the outcome of the war was being decided. They itched to enter the fight. 'Our physical fitness was something to marvel at and morale, too, never have I seen it better', wrote Captain Peters.[3]

On 25 March the 3rd and 4th Australian Divisions began moving south. Next day the 4th Brigade relieved the exhausted 19th Division from IV Corps at Hébuterne, where a gap had opened in the Third Army's line. Defending the village had reduced the 19th to 2000 men. Some of them wept on seeing the Diggers. On 27 March, the Australians beheld wave after wave of Germans advancing with wagons and guns strung out behind them. Together with the artillery, they held the tide. Further German attempts to get through were repulsed. The 4th Brigade stayed at Hébuterne for another month. Lieutenant-General Sir George Harper, IV Corps's commander, would not entrust it to anyone else. Rushed into southern part of the gap, the New Zealand Division gave the Germans a bloody nose too. They spent the rest of the war in IV Corps.

The 3rd Division concentrated on 26 March near Doullens, ten miles west of Hébuterne. Monash guessed that there had been 'a great conference between the British and French High Command, for the square was packed full of motor cars and brilliantly uniformed French soldiers'. One of the most momentous meetings of the war, it had stemmed from a crisis in the allied high command. Under the arrangement between them, Haig was relying on Pétain to help his right while the Third Army held onto Arras. With the Fifth Army stuck in reverse gear, Pétain argued that helping it was like throwing good money after bad. If the German drive on Amiens continued, he would have to fall back to cover Paris instead. Haig was thunderstruck because the Germans would then achieve their aim of splitting the British and French. He instigated the Doullens proceedings. Joining him were Lord Milner from the War Cabinet, and General Sir Henry Wilson, now the Chief of the Imperial General Staff, Robertson having resigned in February to protest the creation of a general reserve outside national command. President Raymond Poincaré, Clemenceau and Foch sat with Pétain. Foch was adamant: 'We must fight in front of Amiens, we must fight where we are now'. At Haig's urging, he was made Generalissimo, giving the Allies something like a supreme commander. Foch immediately directed that both armies must stay in touch to cover Amiens.[4]

Almost while the conference had been in session, VII Corps, which held the line north of the Somme, had swung behind the Ancre, leaving the ten-mile front across the triangle of ground between it and the Somme virtually undefended. Lieutenant-General Sir Walter Congreve VC had misinterpreted an earlier order to retire only if 'the tactical situation imperatively demands it' as a direction to fall back regardless. Nothing but a small scratch force in the old Amiens Defence Line, screened by the 2nd Cavalry Brigade, held the triangle. Gough's flank on the Somme was six miles eastwards. Should the Germans jump the Somme in this gap, they could outflank the Fifth Army and then continue on the southern side of the river before recrossing to turn the right flank of the Third Army. They would then have a clear run to Amiens.

The calamity brought the Australians to the Somme. 'You're going the wrong way, Digger. Jerry'll souvenir you and your —— band too', retreating British troops shouted. Hordes of French refugees shuffled westwards with whatever belongings they could carry. 'One old lady I saw was being wheeled along in a wheelbarrow', wrote Private Arthur Sindrey. 'One old couple passed me arm in arm, all they had was a shawl and a loaf of bread.' '*English soldat no bon!*', these people said. Shouting '*Vive l'Australie!*', they embraced '*Nos Australiens*!' Hearing the Diggers say '*Fini retreat – beaucoup Australiens ici*', which quickly became one of Australia's great national statements, many returned to their villages.[5]

'Thank heavens – the Australians at last', gasped General Congreve when Monash reached his headquarters at 1 a.m. on 27 March. He directed the 3rd Division to occupy the triangle. Its battalions began arriving at 8 a.m. and deployed without interference. Meeting Congreve just after Monash, General Sinclair-MacLagan was ordered to secure the high ground on the Ancre. Force-marching through the night, the 12th and 13th Brigades passed through the villages they had known as rest areas in 1916. The 12th Brigade went on to relieve the 9th (Scottish) Division, which was strung out in foxholes along the embankment of the Albert–Buire railway. It had been fighting continuously since 21 March. 'Thank God', the exhausted Scots said as they left in the moonlight. 'You'll hold him.'[6]

Advancing in the triangle on 27 March, the Germans tried to cross to the southern bank of the Somme between Sailly-le-Sec and Sailly-Laurette, a mile further east. Delighting in the pristine countryside with its 'green fields, wheat crops [and] sheep and cattle browsing unconcernedly', Monash's Australians in the Amiens Defence Line watched the cavalry in the screen ahead holding them off. Blocked up front, the Germans switched their effort to Cérisy, a mile short of Sailly-Laurette and four and a half miles behind the left of the Fifth Army on the river. They were over by 2 p.m. Gough had received the 1st Cavalry Division from the Third Army and used it to reinforce the Amiens Inner Line from the Somme to the Roman Road. In order to protect the Third Army's right flank if the Germans still punched through, Monash's reserve, the 9th Brigade, guarded the river crossings. Fortunately, the French were also releasing Fifth Army formations that had fought under them. The 61st Division, the first to arrive, was to counterattack early next morning.[7]

In the midst of these developments, Gough learned that he was to be relieved by General Rawlinson, then British Military Representative on the Allied Executive War Board. With the Fifth Army badly mauled, he became the scapegoat that the British retirement demanded. Yet the bits of his army that Gough still led were on the line that Foch at Doullens had expected him to hold. That meant at least 2000 Germans were now behind the remnants of XIX Corps. With no time to brood, Gough obtained Foch's consent at 3 a.m. on 28 March for its withdrawal. The 61st Division counterattacked in the meantime. By 1918, the 61st, which had been carved up with the 5th Australian Division at Fromelles, 'reckoned it had been unlucky at everything it had attempted and called itself the Sixty-worst'. But it got to within 200 yards of the Germans, after charging them over 2500 yards of bare ground. The Germans reached the Wolfsberg, where they were belted in turn by the 1st Cavalry Brigade and some scratch forces.[8]

The Australians had mixed success. At noon on 28 March, Congreve told Monash that Foch wanted more ground gained in the triangle as soon as possible to pave the way for an offensive that he and General Byng had in mind for the Third Army. Gough had also urged the capture of Sailly-Laurette to secure the Fifth Army's left flank. Monash ordered an afternoon attack towards Morlancourt. He left the details to the two brigade commanders. Their plans did not mesh. He failed to co-ordinate them. Brigadier-General Walter McNicoll of the 10th laid on a formal assault on the left. At 5.13 p.m. the 40th Battalion advanced. Brigadier-General Cannan on the right instructed the 42nd and 43rd Battalions to snaffle the ground ahead

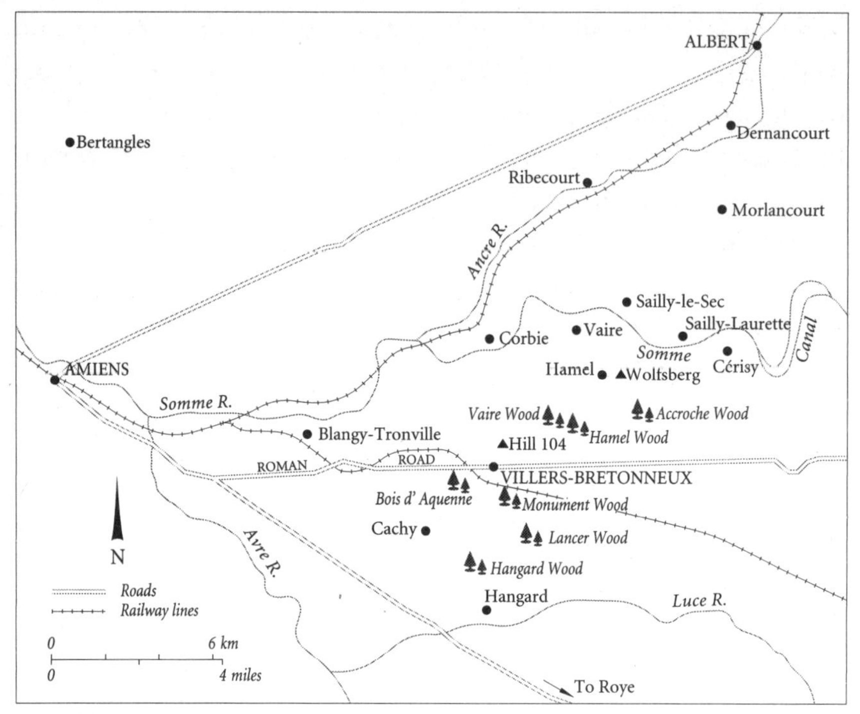

Villers-Bretonneux and Hamel

with patrols. They started late, leaving the 40th unsupported. With little artillery yet in range, it bumped two oncoming German regiments. The 40th gained about 500 yards. At dusk, the 39th came up. In drizzling rain, both battalions clawed out another 500 yards. Cannan directed the 44th Battalion to take Sailly-Laurette. Slithering down the steep slopes above the village, it was ambushed 300 yards short. The 3rd Division lost 300 men.

On the Ancre the story was different. Guarding the level-crossing on the railway north of Dernancourt, Sergeant Stanley McDougall of the 47th Battalion heard troops marching in the dawn mist. Running along the embankment to warn his platoon, he saw the Germans of the 50th (Prussian) Reserve Division, which had opposed Elliott's men at Polygon Wood, emerge from the murk. They bombed a Lewis gun. McDougall picked it up and shot them down. He continued along the embankment, hosing the Germans.

When some broke through at the crossing behind him, McDougall, who won the VC for this action, took them on as well. Defying heavy German shelling, the 48th Battalion stood waist high above the embankment to fire into the masses in front it. Lieutenant Mitchell charged one group:

> I reached the nearest, an officer. His hands were at his waist, unbuckling his equipment. 'Up! Up! Up! Damn you!' I said, thrusting the long barrel of my Smith and Wesson in his face. He apologised in broken English, French and German. By this time a host of our men had gathered around. He explained that there was beer in his bottle and socks in his pack.

It was all bluff because the Australians were hopelessly outnumbered. When the 47th Battalion ran out of bombs, they threw stones. The artillery pounded the Germans as well. Nine attacks were seen off. Dazed after seventy-two hours without rest, the Diggers were greatly cheered by the news that Operation *Mars*, which was supposed to prise open the Third Army's line at Arras, 'turned out to be just another classic Western Front offensive . . . By the end of the day the Germans had failed to gain a single lodgement in the British battle zone'.[9]

When Rawlinson formally succeeded Gough at 4.30 p.m. on 28 March, the Anglo-French front was solid everywhere except at its junction, where the Fifth Army and the French First Army met on the River Avre. On 29 March the Fifth Army's line held but the French left buckled. Worried about Rawlinson's flank, Haig sent the 9th Australian Brigade to Cachy, a hamlet a mile and a half southwest of Villers-Bretonneux, for use in counterattacks. Elliott's brigade replaced it on the Somme crossings.

Realising that Operation *Michael* was all but dead, Ludendorff ordered the Sixth Army to mount *Georgette* within ten days. But he was too close to Amiens to resist trying to grab it. Eight divisions attacked on 30 March. The Fifth Army's right fell back towards the

Bois de Morgemont, immediately behind which was Hangard Wood, a mile south of Villers-Bretonneux, and, in the valley of the Luce below the wood, Hangard village. A German drive up the Luce to outflank Villers-Bretonneux threatened. At 12.30 p.m. Lieutenant-General Sir Herbert Watts, the commander of XIX Corps, ordered the 9th Brigade to deal with it. Brigadier-General Rosenthal gave the job to the 33rd Battalion under Lieutenant-Colonel Morshead. A curt exchange followed:

When are we to do it? Now.
Any artillery? No.
Do you know where the British line is? No.

Supported by the 12th Lancers and the 34th Battalion, the 33rd struck out at 3.10 p.m. For Private Hardie, 'It was a lovely sight. Our great long columns of Infantry in battle order and the Lancers riding alongside in their squares with gleaming lances and swords. It was just like some of the scenes I have read about of troops going into battle'. About 4.35 p.m the 33rd reached the Bois de Morgemont, which the 12th Lancers had already cleared. On Morshead's recommendation, it was called Lancer Wood thereafter. The Australians admired the cavalry. They were 'the true British soldiers', said Morshead.

Advancing in drizzling rain at 5 p.m., the Australians were 200 yards past the wood when they came into view of the Germans on the higher ground. 'The boys started to drop all around, slowly at first but quicker as we got closer', Hardie recalled. 'I kept watching the little puffs of steam the red hot bullets made in the sodden fields'. The Australians charged. Some reached the German line. 'The enemy screamed and howled for mercy but all he got was the bayonet . . . Our lads didn't fire a shot but used the bayonet something awful', Hardie wrote. 'They passed over our wounded and dying coming up and it roused their blood.' Too weak to regain the old British front line, the two battalions dug in along the edge of the wood. They saw the Germans massing on the skyline for a counterattack at 11 p.m. 'We opened up and in less than no time there wasn't a Hun showing', said Hardie. Of the 200 Australian casualties, the 33rd Battalion suffered 168.[10]

North of the Roman Road, the cavalry ejected the Germans from Hamel. Across the Somme, the 18th Division tried a long daylight advance with little artillery support against Monash's men, just as the latter had done against the Germans two days before. Avenging that setback, the Diggers disdained cover in their excitement to shoot at a target they had only ever dreamed of. Three times the Germans came on; three times, wrote Monash, the 11th Brigade 'swept their lines, wiping them out one after the other . . . The ground in front of us was literally covered with enemy dead'. The Australians lost 150 men, the 18th 2000 in what it called 'a miscarriage such as the division had never before suffered'. Still Ludendorff could not let go of Amiens. After a pause to give his tired divisions a rest, and enable the roads to be repaired so that enough ammunition could be brought up for an annihilating bombardment, the next attack was set for 4 April.[11]

During the break, the 35th Battalion replaced worn out British units in front of Villers-Bretonneux. Covering the 2800 yards between the Roman Road and the railway, the 35th held the longest and most exposed part of the Fifth Army's line. The hastily dug section posts spread along the frontage were unprotected by wire and cut off by day. As there was nothing between them and the town, two and a half miles back, Lieutenant-Colonel Henry Goddard, the 35th's commander, ordered his reserve company to dig a support line a mile ahead of the town. With the work pushing Goddard's men to the brink, Rosenthal moved the 33rd Battalion to the town to help. It would man the support line when finished.

Still largely intact, Villers-Bretonneux was now virtually in the front line. Its inhabitants, apart from a few old people and a mother and her children, had gone. An Australian who had seen the woman stacking some belongings onto a cart, told her: 'You needn't go, Ma. The Aussies are here. Best stay where you are', and helped her carry them back into her house. Though there had been looting during the retreat, much remained – '*beaucoup vin* and champagne, poultry, tinned food and vegetables', Private Walter Smyth said. Rather than let it go to waste, the Australians helped themselves. Shivering in the sodden fields, the 35th Battalion greatly appreciated the supplementary delicacies that came up with the hot meal each night.[12]

When III Corps began returning from the French sector, Rawlinson relieved XIX Corps. In terms of their fitness for action, the 18th (Eastern), 14th (Light) and 58th Divisions were hardly a great advance over the outgoing divisions. All three had been in the front line when the Germans attacked; and in the week that followed the 18th Division lost 2445 men, the 14th 3197 and the 58th 832. They were worn out. The 18th was only a shadow of the division that had captured Thiepval during the 1916 Somme offensive. Led by Major-General Richard Lee, it took over from the Luce to the Roman Road on 31 March, which put the 35th Battalion under Lee's command. Tensions soon arose. 'I hate the Aussies, as does all British Tommies', said Private Robert Cude of the 7th Buffs, who were alongside them.

Aware of their reputation for indiscipline, Lee feared widespread drunkenness among the Australians. Encountering some carrying sacks and guessing what they contained, he struck the sacks with 'a thick oak stick, and caused cascades of red and white wines to flow freely down the Australians' backs'. Lee would have been beaten up but for the timely arrival of some Australian officers. Yet his men were doing the same. 'We have our choice of wines of all qualities and age, but our attention is drawn to the champagne that is present in large quantities', wrote Cude. Among the Australians, Elliott did his bit for poor relations. To curb the looting of liquor by British stragglers in the riverbank town of Corbie, he directed that 'the next officer caught looting would be summarily hanged in the Corbie market square, and his body would be left swinging there as a deterrent'. The looting stopped immediately. 'None seemed willing to make themselves a test case', Elliott observed.[13]

On 2 April, the Fifth Army was renumbered the Fourth, reviving the title of the army Rawlinson had led on the Somme in 1916. Next day German aircraft buzzed the front line and the artillery started shelling it. Night brought torrential rain, during which the 6th and 7th Londons, the first units of the 58th Division, arrived in Villers-Bretonneux. They were to relieve the 35th Battalion on the following night. At 3.45 a.m. on 4 April, the 7th Buffs captured a prisoner who said the Germans would attack at dawn. From 5.15 a.m. Villers-Bretonneux, surrounding villages and the front line were smothered with high explosive and gas. From 6.15 a.m., the shelling concentrated on the forward area. At 6.30 a.m., the wet and cold infantry of XIV Corps north of the Roman Road and XI Corps south of it started out towards the equally miserable defenders.

The 14th (Light) Division was the most miserable of the lot. Having moved into the Amiens Inner Line across the Wolfsberg during the night, it had not seen in daylight the ground it was supposed to defend. It had been on the move for the two previous nights. It had fought poorly during the retreat. On 21 March 'its forward positions fell quickly; many men surrendered, and some hasty flights to the rear were observed'. Struck now by the 4th Guard Division, it lost Hamel and backpedalled to Hill 104. Many also headed for Vaire on the Somme, where Captain Harold Ferres and his company from the 58th Battalion were protecting the crossing. Ferres made 'strenuous efforts' to rally them but 'the officers leading the retirement, when remonstrated with, protested that their orders were to fall back'. A furious Elliott in Corbie directed Ferres 'to compel them to fight'. Ferres collected about 500 stragglers and they dug a line of posts to Hill 104. Thanks to the artillery, which fired over open sights, the line stood. Late in the afternoon the 15th Brigade crossed the Somme to occupy Hill 104 with the cavalry.

In the 35th Battalion's line south of the Roman Road, Captain Gilbert Coghill was finishing a chicken and champagne breakfast at 6.30 a.m. when the light of a burning house showed the 9th Bavarian Reserve Division preparing to attack. Passing the order to open up only on his signal, he leapt onto the railway embankment where every post could see him. When the leading waves were forty yards away, Coghill raised his arm. He was instantly shot through it. The fire going the other way obliterated them. Another attack came at 7 a.m. The Australians minced it. But the 7th Buffs next to the railway broke. Coghill floundered 500 yards through the mud to find their commander. He assured Coghill, 'We'll stand by you, Anzacs'. His men reoccupied the line, thought better of it and left again. The 14th Division had already scarpered. Outflanked on right and left, the 35th Battalion fought its way back and took up a new position behind the empty support line. With the help of the 33rd Battalion and cavalry reserves, the attack was halted there. Rosenthal was directed to move the 34th and 36th Battalions either side of Villers-Bretonneux to block another breakthrough. They were in position by 1 p.m. Not so heavily hit, the line to the south held.[14]

Major-General Graf Bernhard Finck von Finckenstein, of the 4th Guard Division, wanted to renew the attack north of the Roman Road, where the greatest gain had been made and the new line was very fragile. He was overruled. The only formation that could have undertaken the assault had to be retained as a reserve and Monash's artillery across the Somme enfiladed XIV Corps. So XI Corps struck south of the Roman Road at 4 p.m. It sliced through the 18th Division, which careered back up to 3000 yards, losing Lancer Wood, the eastern half of Hangard Wood, and Monument Wood and Farm on the southern edge of Villers-Bretonneux. The 7th Queen's burst onto the 36th Battalion, which had assembled in a hollow behind the Farm. The 7th Buffs hurtled back to the town. Left hanging by the Buffs again, the right of the 35th Battalion bent rearwards to form a defensive flank. Thinking a withdrawal was under way, the rest of the 35th pulled out. Only part of the 33rd Battalion remained on the Roman Road. Villers-Bretonneux lay open.

At 4.45 p.m. Major Henry Carr of the 35th Battalion dashed into Goddard's headquarters in the town yelling that 'the whole line had retired'. The headquarters was now the most advanced position. Lieutenant-Colonel John Milne of the 36th Battalion was there. Goddard turned to him. 'Colonel, you must counter-attack at once.' Milne raced back to the hollow. 'Company commanders to assemble at the double', he shouted. Milne told them: 'The enemy has broken through on our immediate front and we must counterattack at once'. 'How far shall we go?' asked Captain John Bushelle. 'Go till you're stopped and hold on at all costs'. Milne had also seen a 'stoutly built figure, with overcoat and walking stick', whom he thought was the 'CO of the Queen's'. It turned out to be Brigadier-General Edward Wood, who commanded the 55th Brigade, to which the Buffs and Queen's belonged. He was re-forming the Queen's behind the Farm when Milne's adjutant turned up with 'a cordial invitation' to co-operate on the right flank. Wood said he would personally lead this part of the attack. The Australians shook out. Milne walked along them, turned and said: 'Good-bye, boys. It's neck or nothing'.

At 5.15 p.m., the line went forward at a brisk jog. It crested the lip of the hollow just as waves of Bavarians emerged from Monument Farm. They recoiled but recovered swiftly. A crunching fusillade broke from the hedges and buildings. The assault diverged. Captain Bushelle led the northern half along the railway for 1500 yards to outflank the Bavarians. They started to withdraw. The southern half was closer to the fire. It lost badly. Second Lieutenant Albert Amess, who had been blown up and sniped, was the only officer left. He urged on the Queen's, who were stalled. Three runners died and Amess was sniped again before his message got through. The advance restarted. Amess was hit a fourth time before the southern half linked up with Bushelle's men. Monument Farm and Wood had been regained. But the new line was almost a mile long, and the gaps in it were huge because the 36th Battalion had lost 150 men, a quarter of its strength. With night falling, Milne used the 6th Londons to fill them. His after-action report stated: 'Owing to the rapidity of our counter attack and the intensity of enemy fire, it was impossible to bother about prisoners, only three being sent back'. Arch-Australophobe Cude thought the 36th Battalion's effort 'simply wonderful'.

North of the railway, Captain Raleigh Sayers reorganised the 35th Battalion for a charge. The Germans broke before it. Sayers tackled three in a shell hole. Unarmed because he had left his revolver at Goddard's headquarters, he brained one with the man's steel helmet and strangled the second; the third bolted. On the Roman Road the 33rd Battalion was withdrawing to avoid being cut off. The 17th Lancers appeared. They were thrilled by the 33rd's response: 'The whole line appeared to halt, as if with surprise at what they saw, then mechanically turn about and advance. It was a wonderful moment'. Dismounting, the cavalry opened up with their Hotchkiss guns, the Australians joined in, and three armoured cars sent by Rawlinson barrelled up the road with Vickers guns blazing to lend a hand. The Germans wilted and the 33rd and the Lancers extended southwards to link up with the 35th and 36th Battalions. Reinforced by the 34th Battalion, they advanced to their old support line early next morning.[15]

Though Villers-Bretonneux was saved, the Germans came within a whisker of taking it. They had also advanced two miles against the French First Army. The Somme front was the only one that still seemed to offer them some hope of success. Ludendorff was determined to keep pressing there. Even if Amiens were not reached, the Allies might be deterred from sending troops to Flanders to counter *Georgette*. On 5 April the Germans tried three times to reach Hill 104. Each one was shredded. They had no success across the Somme either.

Since the assault on 28 March, the 4th Division had beaten off sporadic probes around Dernancourt. Australian pioneers dug a reserve line on the heights a mile behind it. But the long, bare slopes precluded reinforcement of the front line along the railway embankment during daylight. To prevent the Germans capturing the embankment and possibly breaking through on the Ancre to Amiens, General Sinclair-MacLagan on 4 April ordered it held as the divisional 'main line of resistance'. Prisoners captured that day revealed that the Germans would attack next morning. Pre-dawn patrols reported them massing northeast of Dernancourt. Mist had reduced visibility to 150 yards when XXIII Reserve Corps assaulted at 9.30 a.m. The attack fell mainly on the 12th Brigade holding the embankment between Dernancourt and Albert.

Dernancourt was 'a mass of roaring, shouting Germans', wrote pioneer Private Fred Klingner. 'Their losses there must have been frightful.' One Stokes mortar battery lobbed 370 bombs into them, its entire supply. But the Australians were unsupported by artillery because the mist hid their signalling rockets. Sheer weight of numbers eventually told. After three attempts, the Germans overran the right of the 47th Battalion at 10 a.m. Soon they were pouring through, even dragging a field gun along. The 52nd Battalion and the rest of the 47th were unaware until they were fired on and shelled from the rear. Together with the 48th, which held on under Captain Frederick Anderson until almost cut off, they fought their way to the support line halfway up the slope. Part of it was lost too. The Diggers withdrew to the reserve line. At 5.15 p.m. the 45th and 49th Battalions counterattacked from it. Coming under 'a devilish fire, a tremendous tattoo of machine-guns', said Lieutenant-Colonel Alexander Imlay, watching with the 47th, they drove the Germans part way down the slope.

In the heaviest attack made against them during the war, the Australians lost 1100 men, including some captured. The Germans lost 1600, many from the 50th (Prussian) Reserve Division that spearheaded the assault. Perhaps remembering the knock they had received at Dernancourt a week before, not to mention at Polygon

Wood, some Prussians acted brutally towards the Australian prisoners. They asked one group who they were. A man answered 'Australians'. He was shot. Another prisoner, wounded in both arms, was punched in the mouth on identifying himself as Australian. Still another was horsewhipped. Yet after the war the Prussians were found to have erected on a 48th Battalion post that had fought to the end two wooden crosses. The inscription read: 'Here lies a brave English warrior'.[16]

Georgette began on 9 April, a date chosen partly because Ludendorff wanted to attack before British troops relieved the poorly trained 2nd Portuguese Division around Neuve Chapelle. Struck in heavy mist by the German Sixth Army, it collapsed spectacularly. The British First Army, to which the Portuguese were attached, consisted of divisions cut to pieces during *Michael*. Some resisted stubbornly but the 40th Division gave way, letting the Germans through. Armentières was abandoned. The German Fourth Army advanced north of the city, overrunning the winter line the Anzacs had built at Messines and taking Fleurbaix. Several Australian artillery units and some tunnellers narrowly escaped capture. The Germans were now within striking distance of Hazebrouck, a railway junction essential for the resupply of the BEF in Flanders. Keen to build up forces for a counter-offensive against the salient that *Michael* had extended towards Amiens, Foch would not help Haig directly, although he moved the two French reserve armies to the Doullens–Amiens area to release some British reserves. On 11 April Haig issued an order that became famous:

> There is no other course open to us but to fight it out! Every position must be held to the last man: there must be no retirement. With our back to the wall, and believing in the justice of our cause, each one of us might fight on to the end. The safety of our homes and the freedom of mankind alike depend upon the conduct of each of us at this critical moment.

Haig's words had a special ring for the 1st Australian Division. The last of the Australian divisions to arrive on the Somme, it was marching up to relieve the 3rd Division in the triangle on 10 April. Flinging Lieutenant Joynt a map of the Hazebrouck area, the 8th Battalion's commander, Lieutenant-Colonel John Mitchell, remarked, 'There is your new map, Joynt. The Huns have broken through up north and they are sending us back again . . . when we reach our destination be prepared to get out of the train and go straight into the fight'. The shelling of Amiens station by long-range guns east of Villers-Bretonneux disrupted the 1st Division's departure on 11 April. General Harington was waiting on the platform when the first men arrived at Hazebrouck next day. 'The 1st Australian Division is the only formed body of troops now between here and the Channel Ports', he told them. The leading units set off to occupy an 'army line' five miles distant that arced across the front of Nieppe Forest, blocking the main approach. British troops were drifting back. 'Mind you don't get drowned in the Channel', the Australians shouted at them. On 13 April four battalions from the 1st and 2nd Brigades were strung out along the six-mile front. Two divisions would normally have held it.

Inspecting his posts, Lieutenant Joynt saw some of his men clad in frock coats, top hats, long dresses and Parisian gowns, found in the wardrobes of an abandoned farm. They were dancing to a quadrille playing on a gramophone. He rocked with laughter. Soon the 29th Division started streaming through Vieux Berquin, a village just ahead. 'Boy, is this your post?' a colonel asked Lieutenant Leslie McGinn. 'Yes, Sir.' 'You are going to make a fight of it?' 'Yes, Sir.' 'Well, give me a rifle, I am one of your men'. Joining McGinn, the colonel said he was disgusted with his own men. For the first time in the regiment's history, they had abandoned a position they were ordered to hold. Suddenly telling McGinn, 'My boy, you can report that the 1st Lancashire Fusiliers held the village to the last man', the colonel strode back to Vieux Berquin. He settled in with some stragglers he had rounded up. The Australians heard firing in the village throughout the night as the colonel kept his word. They also witnessed the 4th Guards Brigade fighting until only handful remained. Some of the survivors insisted on joining the Australians in what was now the front line.

Parts of four German divisions attacked early on 14 April. Corporal Percy Turvey of the 3rd Battalion remarked that it was 'like firing into a haystack – one could not miss'. Running into a wall of machine-gun fire and artillery, the Germans went to ground. Lieutenant Fred Jarvis played *Die Wacht am Rhein* on a tin whistle in the hope of provoking them to continue attacking. They blasted two of Joynt's advanced posts out with field guns. Joynt called for a runner to tell the neighbouring posts to cover the gap. Private William Parfrey volunteered. Under torrential fire, he delivered the message. The gap was filled. As Parfrey came back, he signalled Joynt:

> I made towards him, he stopped running and opened his mouth to speak and then suddenly collapsed with the words on his lips unspoken. I dropped alongside him to find the blood gushing from a bullet hole in his neck. I tried to stop the flow but found the bullet had made a hole the size of an apple in his throat and that it was hopeless trying to block the flow without choking him, the gash was too big.

When reinforcements arrived, as a result of an alarmist message given to Lieutenant-Colonel Mitchell by a bolting Tommy, Joynt had the situation in hand and was hard put to find a use for them. The Germans did not reach the Australian line anywhere else. Crown Prince Rupprecht postponed the next assault until 17 April to allow time for a thorough bombardment. By now Foch had finally made some French formations available. The French 133rd Division moved in before Meteren, north of the 1st Division. When the blow came, the fire from the Australians and the supporting artillery was so devastating that many Germans stayed under cover. The French shattered the attack on the Meteren flank. Ludendorff abandoned the attempt to reach Hazebrouck. He swung north, taking the painfully earned gains of the 1917 Ypres campaign and Mount Kemmel, one of the few dominating heights in Flanders. But the Germans were unable to exploit the success. *Georgette* was over.[17]

On the Somme the Australians had been briefly brought back to earth. On 6 April the 5th Brigade, the first of the 2nd Division's formations to arrive, took over the Fourth Army's right flank between the Roman Road and the French at Hangard. Wanting to drive the Germans farther away from Amiens, Foch ordered an Anglo-French offensive south of Villers-Bretonneux. The eastern half of Hangard Wood, lost on 4 April, was to be recaptured by the 5th Brigade as an urgent preliminary. Brigadier-General Smith looked at the map rather than the ground. He did not seem to realise that his advance would finish up below the muzzles of the Germans near Lancer Wood. As Smith needed all four of his battalions to hold a line 6000 yards long, the assault force had to be light. Early on 7 April, two companies from each of the 19th and 20th Battalions spread across the 2500-yard attack frontage. Aerial reconnaissance reported Hangard Wood weakly held. In fact, two battalions from the 24th (Saxon) Reserve Division occupied it.

Unseen machine-guns cut up the 19th Battalion. Eleven survivors under Lieutenant Percy Storkey burst through the thick undergrowth onto the north–south ride. Two Saxon companies twenty yards behind them were flaying those still in the open. The closest Saxons heard the Australians and turned around. Storkey shouted charge 'as if the whole battalion were following'. He had to shock the Germans into surrendering because there would be no second chance. Pausing to reload was out of the question. The Australians used rifle butts and bayonets. Several Saxons were found later with their skulls smashed in. The furthest away were reluctant to surrender. Storkey shot three and his men grenaded others. The rest put their hands up. Fifty-three were captured. Storkey received the VC.

But when his men reached the edge of the wood, they immediately came under brutal fire from the Saxons on the higher ground about Lancer Wood and had to withdraw. The 20th Battalion alongside staved off three counterattacks before having to pull out as well. Considering the small numbers involved, the loss of 151 men was excessive. Bean called the attack 'a particularly interesting example of the way in which an operation, readily sketched in with a sweep of the pencil by higher authority, and formulated in a fluent order', ended up with a harassed company commander trying to achieve the impossible.

The Franco-British offensive was cancelled with the opening of *Georgette* on 9 April. Three days later a local German attack took Hangard in the morning and a heavy shell slammed into Lieutenant-Colonel Milne's headquarters in the afternoon. He died instantly. Lieutenant-Colonel McConaghy, original Anzac, Lone Pine veteran and inspirational figure at Fromelles, also died when the 54th Battalion's headquarters on Hill 104 was pulped. Though the French recaptured Hangard, the cemetery and copse adjacent to it remained in German hands. Smith agreed to an attack on the copse by the 18th Battalion, in conjunction with a French assault on the cemetery. The 18th's commander, Lieutenant-Colonel George Murphy, was reluctant. He knew the copse was strongly held and the approaches were exposed. But orders were orders. Attacking on 15 April, one company routed the Germans north of the copse but was forced back by a strong counterattack. Another company took the copse but was cut off and overrun. Half of the 180 men involved were casualties. Contact with the French, who took the cemetery, was never possible. The 5th Brigade had lost heavily in poorly planned actions directed at objectives of questionable value. Its morale, sky-high a week or so earlier, sagged. Absence without leave skyrocketed.[18]

By this stage, Villers-Bretonneux was 'a most horrible ruin, a revolting sight of torn and gutted houses and littered streets, littered too with dead here and there among the splintered glass, smouldering beams and heaps of bricks', wrote Australian war correspondent Frank Cutlack. But it was still the '*vin blanc*' sector to the Australians, many of whom now wore women's underwear they had purloined instead of their usual lice-infested garments. The presence of von Richthofen's Circus, so called because its machines were brightly painted, and the low cloud ceiling, which kept combats close to the ground, made the air fighting interesting. Von Richthofen himself scored four kills around the town, bringing his total to eighty. On 21 April Sergeant Cedric Popkin of the 4th Australian Machine-gun Battalion accounted for the most famous fighter pilot of all time as he tried to clear the Morlancourt Ridge. For years the credit went to Canadian pilot Captain Roy Brown but modern research puts Popkin's claim beyond doubt.[19]

Four days earlier a three-hour bombardment had drenched Villers-Bretonneux with gas. Forgetting that the environs were dripping with toxic chemicals, troops removed their respirators when the shelling ceased. Colonel Morshead was among the 271 casualties in the 33rd Battalion. The gas attack interrupted a reorganisation begun on 13 April. Until then, the Somme had been the boundary between the Australian Corps and III Corps, respectively north and south of the river. But the emergencies on the southern side had necessitated the cross-grouping of Australian brigades in British divisions and the 5th Australian Division replacing the 14th (Light) Division in III Corps altogether. On the northern side, the 8th Division, a British formation, had replaced the 1st Division in the Australian Corps on its departure for Flanders. Haig wanted the Australians made solely responsible for the Somme. Rejoining its parent formation, the 5th Division slipped northwards astride the river. The 15th Brigade went into reserve at Blangy-Tronville, four miles west of Villers-Bretonneux, and the 14th Brigade held the northern shoulder of Hill 104. III Corps, with the 8th Division transferred to it, stretched from there to Hangard.

Holding the town and its surrounds, the 8th Division was regarded highly enough to be one of the first three British divisions that, along with all of the Dominion ones, received additional Lewis guns when the allocation was doubled at the start of 1918. But it had lost almost 5000 men in the March retreat. Their replacements were the boy-recruits that Lloyd George was now pouring across the Channel, after previously withholding them from Haig's clutches. They were barely trained and their physique was 'much below average'. The Australians pitied the youngsters but were more concerned about them losing Villers-Bretonneux, in which case the Australian flank on Hill 104 would be turned. None worried more than Brigadier-General Elliott. He put the 59th and 60th Battalions at Blangy-Tronville on stand-by. They were to send patrols into Villers-Bretonneux at the first sign of an attack in order to keep him informed. Prisoners taken on 23 April revealed that it would come next morning. Ludendorff was seeking to divert attention from the attack on Mount Kemmel.[20]

Following a gas-laced hurricane bombardment, the Germans assaulted in dense fog at 6 a.m. on 24 April. They were using tanks, thirty-ton A7Vs, whose slab armour hung over the tracks like a crinoline skirt to shield their eighteen-man crews. Three led the 228th Division north of the railway directly against Villers-Bretonneux and six more supported the 4th Guard south of it, while the remaining four moved with the 77th Reserve Division against Cachy. Horrified to see them lumbering out of the gloom, the young British soldiers broke. British gunners stopped one tank as it crawled along the railway west of the town and three British tanks fought the first tank-versus-tank duel against three German ones in the fields south of it. The German tanks withdrew after knocking out two of their opponents, whereupon a company of British Whippet light tanks ran amok against the 77th Division, stopping it short of Cachy. But by mid-morning the Germans held Villers-Bretonneux and a pocket four miles wide and one deep around it that included the southern end of Hill 104, Monument Farm and the rest of Hangard Wood.

◀ Major-General John Monash. He kept abreast of tactical developments on the Western Front and his training of the 3rd Division reflected what it would face there. Monash's skills and those of his New Zealand counterpart, Major-General Russell, contributed greatly to the effectiveness of II ANZAC.

▼ Though the photograph shows German shells pummelling Messines Ridge on 8 June, the view is as it would have been when the ridge was under British bombardment. The 3rd Division crossed the Douve, which runs through the middle of the picture, in this vicinity. Trees lining Hun's Walk are on the skyline to the right.

▲ The New Zealand Division trains on ground similar to that across which it will advance to capture Messines. The men move in artillery formation, which aims to spread companies out in order to minimise the effect of German shelling. A line of widely-spaced skirmishers would have preceded the unit shown here.

▼ Rear view of a pillbox at Messines. Near ground level at either end are the entrances, with receptacles above them for ammunition and bomb storage. The netting on the roof held camouflage to conceal the pillbox from aerial observation.

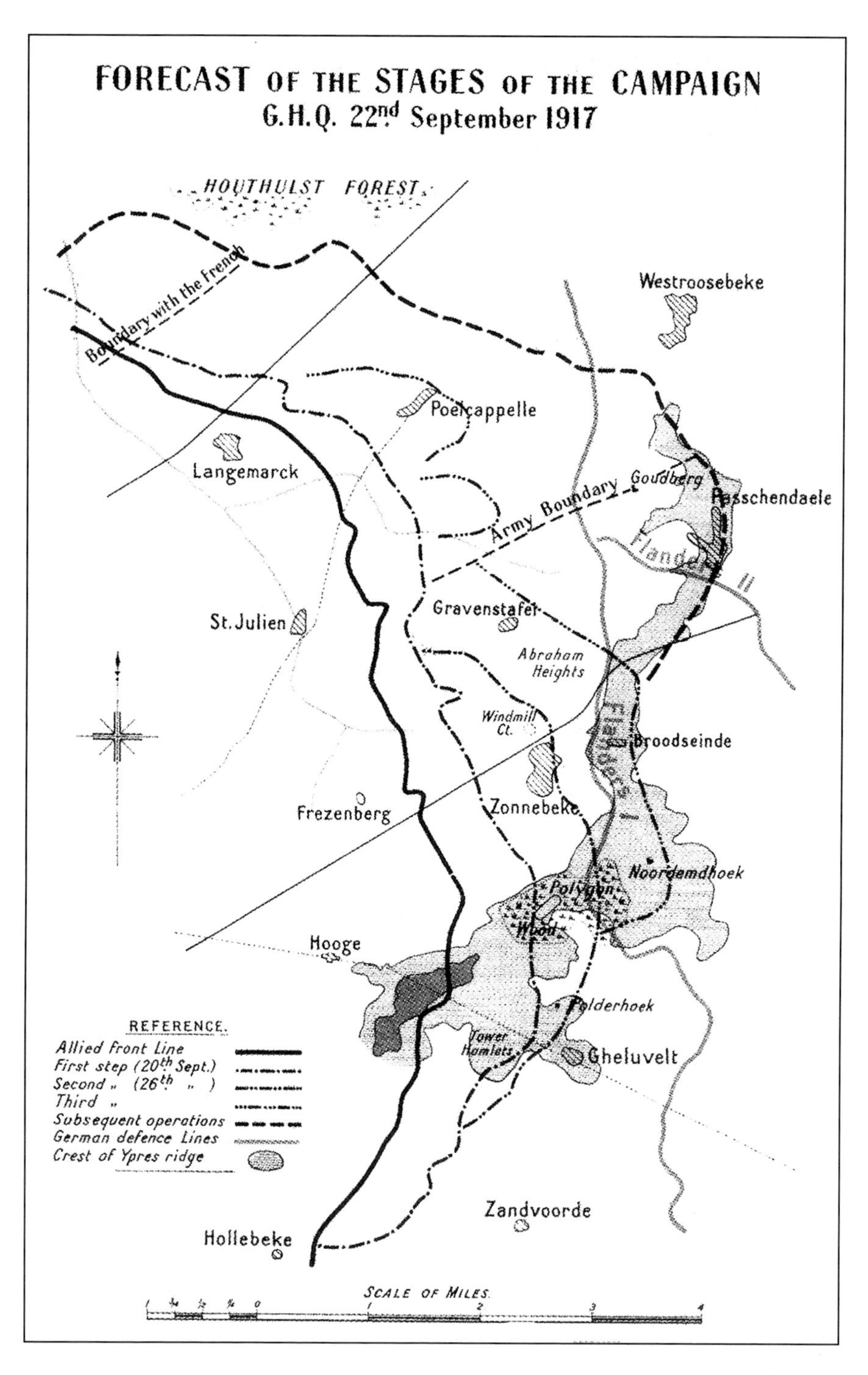

A British official map showing the Ypres attacks. The 'first', 'second' and 'third' steps respectively correspond to the Menin Road, Polygon Wood and Broodseinde battles. 'Subsequent operations' encompasses the Passcehendaele assaults.

▲ An Australian column passes the ruined Cloth Hall, while marching through Ypres on its way to the front line in the salient. These ruins were as symbolic of Ypres as the precariously leaning Golden Virgin was of Albert. This photograph was taken by Frank Hurley, who had earlier established his reputation as the photographer/cinematographer on the Antarctic expeditions of Sir Douglas Mawson and Sir Ernest Shackleton.

▼ Australian infantry purportedly 'going over the top' to resist a German counterattack at Zonnebeke. Taken by Frank Hurley, it is in fact a composite based on other photographs he took at the same time. Hurley added low-flying aircraft in a later version. He justified 're-touching' on the ground that he had witnessed such scenes but was unable to capture them owing to the technical limitations of his camera.

▲ Stretcher-bearers struggle through glutinous mud. The conditions on 9 and 12 October made their work, and the plight of the wounded they carried, agonising.

▼ Dead and wounded Australians and Germans in the Ypres–Roulers railway cutting east of Broodseinde after the attack on 12 October. Facing the camera on the far right is Private Austin Henderson of the 38th Battalion. Though this well-known photograph is usually credited to Frank Hurley, Hubert Wilkins, another Australian official photographer, was also in the cutting at the time.

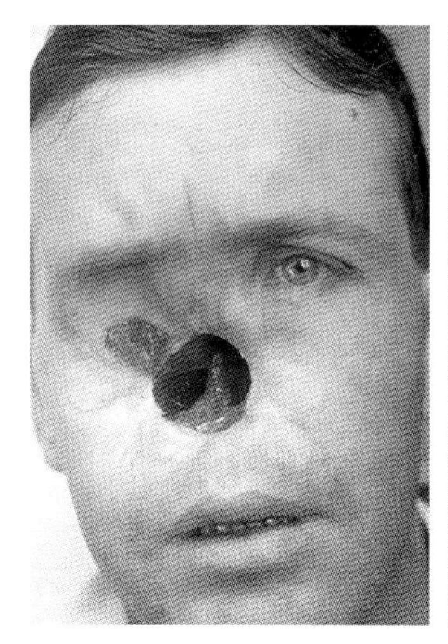
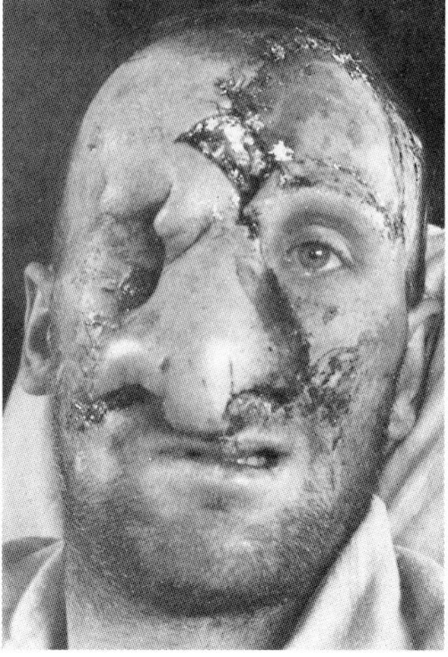

Those Anzacs who sustained disfiguring wounds usually spent long periods at the Queen's Hospital at Sidcup, as numerous operations were needed to give them something resembling a face. The soldier above is Private S, twenty-one, of the 33rd batallion, shown on 4 August 1918 after surgical procedures following his wounding (left) and on 25 March 1919, shortly before his return to Australia (right). For men in their twenties like this, to carry on their lives required great mental strength on their part and the understanding of those around them.

Though this picture was taken before the first contingent sailed in 1914, it shows typically equipped light horsemen. The slung rifles reinforce the point that they are not cavalry but mounted infantry, though the difference in 1918 was miniscule. Trooper Williams Woods (right) was one of the first light horsemen to die at Gallipoli.

◀ General Sir Harry Chauvel. Commissioned into the Queensland Permanent Forces in 1896, Chauvel gained experience of leading a mounted unit in action during the South African War. Diplomatic but shy, he was a man of great integrity. He became Chief of the General Staff in 1923 and was promoted general shortly before his retirement in 1930. Chauvel was recalled to duty in 1940 as Inspector-General of the Volunteer Defence Corps, Australia's Home Guard equivalent, a post he held until his death, aged almost eighty, in March 1945.

◀ Brigadier-General Edward Chaytor. Severely wounded in South Africa, Chaytor had a key role in raising the NZEF and was twice wounded at Gallipoli while on the staff of the NZ and A Division. He took over the NZMR at the end of the campaign. As his wounds attest, Chaytor was invariably close to the action. He got on well with Chauvel. After his retirement in 1924, Chaytor lived in England, where he died in 1939, aged seventy-one.

▼ Australian cameliers of the Imperial Camel Corps. The first companies were raised in January 1916 to operate against the Senussi Arabs in Egypt's Western Desert and manned by rejects from the Australian infantry battalions. Though camels could carry heavier loads, they lacked the speed of horses and were much less suited to the more fertile country of Palestine, into which the mounted formations eventually advanced.

◀ Australian Light Horse on the Bethlehem–Jerusalem road pass the walls of Jerusalem. The Tower of David rises in the centre. Between it and the church on the left is the Jaffa Gate clock-tower, through which Allenby entered Jerusalem after its capture.

▲ The 4th LH Brigade has just struck the Turkish trenches in George Lambert's *The Charge of the Australian Light Horse at Beersheba*. Leaving the tangled mass of wounded and dying soldiers and horses in the foreground, the rest of the line gallops towards the town, which can be seen on the left skyline.

◀ Led by Chauvel, units of the Desert Mounted Corps ride through Damascus. Law and order had broken down after Allenby, on instructions from London, directed that control of the city be handed over to Feisal's Arabs. Chauvel's show of force on 2 October restored calm.

▲ The 28th Battalion practises bayonet fighting. Rifles would be given a half-twist at the end of the thrust, which made the blade easier to extricate from skin and muscle. Their willingness to close with the bayonet and their proficiency with it helped the Australians establish a psychological ascendancy over German and Turk.

▼ Gassed Australians outside a dressing station near Villers-Bretonneux. The eye bandages indicate probable exposure to mustard gas, a blistering agent also called 'yellow cross'. Though this well-known photograph was taken in May 1918, the scenes after the Villers-Bretonneux gas attack of 17 April would have been similar. By the end of the war, one in four shells fired on the Western Front was a gas shell.

▲ 'Mephistopheles', one of the German tanks used in the attack that took Villers-Bretonneux on 24 April, after its capture in July by the 26th Battalion in Monument Wood. A British artist painted the scene on the side, probably in retaliation for the German one on the front showing 'Mephisto' clobbering a British tank. A radiator and a fuel tank lie on the ground. Today 'Mephisto' is on display at the Queensland Museum in Brisbane.

▼ A German machine-gun post overrun by the 15th Brigade during its charge at Villers-Bretonneux. The 15th had developed its own bayonet technique, which proved extremely effective. This crew were probably victims of it.

▲ Australians in a support trench after the battle of Villers-Bretonneux. Behind them, smoke rises from the village, which the Germans are shelling. One shell has landed near the trench, wounding the Digger who is making his way back. Putting an umbrella salvaged from the town to good use, another Digger has resumed his siesta on the parapet. Still another keeps off the sun with a sombrero. The wire entanglements are newly erected.

▼ Australians on the outskirts of Hamel with a Mark V tank that had been disabled in the attack on 4 July 1918. A tricolour flies from the ruined house beyond. Captain John Moran hoisted himself onto the roof to raise it when the assault reached the village.

Sergeant Richard Travis VC. A horsebreaker and farmhand, Travis was born in 1884. His reputation as a scout emerged towards the end of the Gallipoli campaign and burgeoned on the Western Front, where he led a scouting section called 'Travis's Gang' and carried out lone nocturnal patrols. Travis also held the DCM and MM. He was blasé about rank and dress but meticulous in his military work.

The attack on 8 August would feature the all-arms co-operation practised so successfully by the Australians at Hamel. In fact, it was developed further, because this time artillery would advance with the infantry. Taken during the actual attack, this photograph shows troops of the 5th Australian Division, with artillery and a Mark V Star tank, waiting for the second phase of the advance to start.

Australians surround an 11-inch railway gun, soon to be known as the Amiens gun, on 8 August after its capture by the 31st Battalion earlier in the day. The words 'captured' and 'Australia' (partly obscured) have already been painted on the carriage.

▲ A company from the 21st Battalion leaves Elsa Trench at 1.30 p.m. on 1 September, as the 6th Brigade renews its assault on Mont St Quentin. That night the hill was theirs.

▼ Private James O'Hehir (right) and other Diggers from the 45th Battalion snipe at Germans scampering up the far slope in the attack on 18 September. The weight of the bayonet makes aiming more difficult, reducing the chances of a hit. By this stage of the assault, the old British front and outpost lines have fallen and the 45th has captured a German howitzer battery.

▲ *Breaking the Hindenburg Line*, by Will Longstaff, shows tanks and infantry in action in the battle. The wire has been breached. In many respects, Longstaff emphasised drama at the expense of reality. With fighting going on a few yards away, for example, German prisoners would not have been left to their own devices around a machine-gun.

▼ Monash, Birdwood and Harry Murray after their arrival in Australia at the end of 1919. Enlisting as a private, Murray ended the war as a lieutenant-colonel commanding the 4th Machine-Gun Battalion. Having won the DCM, the DSO (and bar) as well as the VC, and been made a CMG, Murray remains the most decorated of all Australian servicemen, and is usually considered the most highly decorated infantryman of the British and Empire armies in the First World War.

▲ Bullecourt Digger Robert Comb casts soil from Pozières onto the coffin of an Unknown Australian Soldier in the Australian War Memorial's Hall of Memory on 11 November 1993. Standing opposite, Governor-General Bill Hayden has already cast a sprig of wattle. Prime Minister Paul Keating is on the right. The ceremony touched the nation's heart, the Governor-General remarking that it brought out 'a degree of reverence, a display of sentiment . . . rather uncharacteristic of us Australians'.

◄ The Bullecourt Digger, a memorial to great-hearted men, whose spirit and achievements transcend the years.

Thanks to his patrols, Elliott knew what had happened before anyone else. The 59th and 60th Battalions set off at 9.45 a.m. Angered by reports of unnecessary British withdrawals, he directed: 'All British troops to be rallied and reformed as our troops march through them . . . and on any hesitation to be shot'. General Hobbs countermanded this instruction, as well as the move of Elliott's battalions. The Australians had not reckoned with the commanders of III Corps, Lieutenant-General Butler, and of the 8th Division, Major-General William Heneker. Butler had recently been deputy chief of staff at GHQ, in which capacity he was involved in the on-the-run decision-making before Fromelles. His bullying manner made him many enemies. Heneker was an unimaginative martinet whose 'eagle eye could detect an unshaven chin, the need for a haircut, a grease stain, or an unpolished button, at a considerable distance'. Possibly because they felt that accepting help would be a humiliation, Butler and Heneker insisted that the 8th Division could handle things. In reality, it was no longer a cohesive formation and its attempts to eject the Germans came down to a failed counterattack by the 1st Sherwood Foresters around midday.

Lacking the confidence of Butler and Heneker, Rawlinson had ordered the Australian 13th Brigade, in reserve north of the Somme, southwards at 9.30 a.m. III Corps appeared to him to be doing nothing. Exasperated by the inactivity, Rawlinson told Butler at 11.30 a.m to have Heneker contact Hobbs with a view to counter-attacking during the afternoon. Warned by his brigadiers that a daylight assault would be massacred, a fact amply demonstrated by the Foresters, Heneker recommended a night operation to Butler. Still waiting for Butler's answer, Heneker was not very forthcoming when he called Hobbs. Not until 3.30 p.m did Hobbs find out that the 15th Brigade would be attacking north of the town to meet the 13th attacking south of it in the old British front line. Elliott issued his orders at 4.15 p.m.

Brigadier-General Glasgow had met Heneker a few hours earlier. Heneker outlined the plan. Glasgow had not seen the ground and insisted on reconnoitring. Rejoining Heneker at 2.30 p.m., Glasgow said he would attack eastwards from a line north of Cachy. Heneker objected: 'But you can't do that. The corps commander says the attack is to be made from Cachy'. This meant a northeasterly assault that would put the 13th Brigade much closer to the 77th Division. Glasgow refused. 'Tell us what you want us to do, Sir, but you must let us do it our own way.' Heneker relented. Seeking surprise, Glasgow did not want the barrage to precede the attack. Heneker agreed. Glasgow foreshadowed an assault at 10.30 p.m. Heneker ordered him to start at 8 p.m. Glasgow refused. Heneker replied that Butler wanted to attack then. Glasgow snapped. 'If it was God Almighty who gave the order, we couldn't do it in daylight.' They finally settled on 10 p.m. Heneker did not summon Elliott to this conference. The decisions reached required new orders from Elliott at 5.15 p.m. that extended the 57th Battalion well south of Villers-Bretonneux to meet Glasgow's left flank. On joining Elliott at 8 p.m., Glasgow worried that the 57th might get entangled in his own advance. Elliott switched it back to the northern side of the town.

'Went to bed thoroughly depressed', wrote Bean, 'feeling certain that this hurried attack would fail hopelessly'. Sergeant Downing thought there was not 'the remotest chance of success'. Facing an assault of 4000 yards, both brigades were tired: the 13th because it had forced marched all day, and the 15th because it had been subjected to heavy gas shelling in the early morning and waited in suspenseful anticipation since. The lateness of the orders meant rushed preparations. The Germans had been given a long time to get ready. But whatever happened, the morrow would be Anzac Day. Every Digger drew strength from the thought.[21]

Captain Hubert Essame of the 2nd Northants, who were to mop up behind the 13th Brigade, was much impressed by the calmness of the Australian battalion commanders giving their orders in the twilight. The company commanders had ten minutes to brief the platoon commanders. The men got their orders on the run. With the 50th Battalion following, the 51st and 52nd would advance on Monument Wood. Captain Billy Harburn of the 51st was emphatic: 'The Monument is your goal and nothing is to stop your getting there. Kill every bloody German you see, we don't want any prisoners, and God bless you'.

No sooner had the advance begun than flares shot up like Roman candles from the Bois d'Aquenne, the wood on the left of the 13th Brigade. Enfilade machine-gun fire ripped into Captain Harburn's men. Lieutenant Clifford Sadlier commanded the flank platoon:

> We wondered what had struck us. Before we had gone 50 yards, 39 out of the 42 in my platoon were in the mud either dead or wounded. I hit the deck and saw that Charlie Stokes from another platoon was still alive and 2 bombers . . . had also escaped the fire. I knew that if we did not clean out the edge of that wood, the 51st Battalion would be sitting ducks.

Sadlier told Stokes, sergeant of the adjacent platoon, to collect his bombers. Stokes found six. That made ten men in all. They charged. A German shouting '*Kamerad!*' shot Sadlier point blank in the thigh. Sadlier killed him and knocked out two machine-guns. Hobbling at a third with his revolver, he killed its crew too. Another wound paralysed his arm. With only two men left, Stokes took over. He destroyed another three machine-guns, using captured German bombs when his own ran out. Sadlier received the VC. Stokes was also recommended. Higher authority decided that only one should be given for the action. Stokes got the Distinguished Conduct Medal instead.

As the rest of the line advanced, a flurry of shots rang out in front. 'Bomb the bastards', someone yelled. Grenades were thrown. The subsequent rush found remnants of the 8th Division in a forward trench. Unaware of the counterattack, they had thought the Germans were behind them. As the line approached the wire protecting the trench, the fire became intense. Several machine-guns were on the far side but the deadliest fired along the wire from the corner of the Bois d'Aquenne. Sergeant Stokes silenced it. Australian dead hung off the wire next day. Calling it English, Guards Company Sergeant-Major Elfeldt saw the 52nd Battalion attack:

> The leading men fall but others charge on. These too are mown down, but new waves always come on cheering in their place and rush forward into our machine-gun fire . . . As the line gives way, the English machine-gun fire strikes it from front and flank. The English follow hard on our heels. With great uproar they sweep through the dark night. Where at some points an attempt is made to put them on their defence, their machine-gun fire soon breaks down the resistance, and mows down many of our troops.

The 51st Battalion routed a Guards counterattack in a wild mêlée. Other Germans surrendered. 'No prisoners', went the cry. In the middle of an attack the Australians did not know what to do with them. The Germans fled towards Villers-Bretonneux. Few made it. Lance-Corporal Cec Burt and Privates Reg Helyar and Bertie Denman blundered into a strongpoint manned by forty men. Helyar grenaded it and Burt threatened the Germans with his damaged Lewis gun, which could only fire single shots. They surrendered nonetheless. The 18-year-old Denman shouted, 'What shall we do with them? Shoot them? Stick them?' Helyar was brusque: 'For God's sake shut up. Cec's gun is useless and my bombs are napoo. This crowd could eat us if they liked'. This time the Germans were led rearwards. As the advance closed on Monument Farm, its garrison saw 'a dense crowd of khaki uniforms and plate helmets' and let fly a devastating fusillade. The assault was stopped just short of its objective. The British 54th Brigade gained some ground alongside the Australians.[22]

By excluding the 5th Division from the planning until late afternoon on 24 April, Butler and Heneker ensured that the 15th Brigade, which had been ready to counterattack since early morning, ended up doing so almost two hours late. Rushing from Blangy-Tronville, the 59th and 60th Battalions, with the 57th behind them, formed up west of Hill 104. The 228th Division's line was out of sight on the far side of the summit. Starting up the slope, the Australians crabbed towards Villers-Bretonneux. It was burning. The flames were behind the Germans. They could see nothing. The Australians advanced a mile unopposed. At 12.40 a.m., two flares went up. A machine-gun opened. They had been detected.

Charging like a horde of Viking berserkers, the Australians unleashed a banshee yell that the 13th Brigade heard while fighting over a mile away. 'For the time being', wrote Bean, 'the men had thrown off the restraints of civilised intercourse and were what the bayonet instructors of all armies aimed at producing – primitive, savage men'. The 15th Brigade had perfected what Elliott called 'the throat jab', a thrust 'under the chin and upwards into the spinal chord' that was 'most difficult to parry . . . Struck thus a man dies easily, quickly and painlessly, often without a cry or a movement'. In a mêlée, he said, it made the 15th invincible. The 5th Division's history records:

A storm of enemy machine-gun and rifle fire was poured into the oncoming ranks but checked them not at all. A hundred enemy flares lit the terrible scene in vivid light, in which the Germans read too well their fate. Shriek following shriek marked the toll of the deadly bayonets and good round Australian oaths were ripped out in quick succession as the panting men plunged forward to the next victims. The German defences were arranged in a series of strong posts distributed in depth . . . if for a moment the slaughter slackened, it was only because new victims were wanted and, in the dark, they were not easy to see. But soon the enemy flares would shoot up again from strong points not yet reached. Those flares were the death warrant of many a German that night, for, guided by them, the assailants knew exactly where their enemies lay.

At 6 a.m., the 57th Battalion and the 2nd Royal Berkshires started through Villers-Bretonneux itself. Lewis gunners sprayed the front of any building from which fire came while bombers grenaded the back. The 2nd Northants charged the southern side and the town was largely cleared by nightfall. At 1 a.m. on 26 April, the 13th and 15th Brigades linked up on the eastern side. A few hours later, they watched the French Moroccan Division attack towards Hangard Wood with 'great panache, the sounding of trumpets and beating of drums, terrible losses and hardly any territorial gain'.[23]

Though the old British front line was nowhere reached and Monument Farm remained in German hands, Villers-Bretonneux had been saved a second time. Amiens was no longer threatened. The achievement was almost entirely due to the Australian counterattack, which cost the 15th Brigade 455 men and the 13th 1009. III Corps lost 9500 men, including 2400 taken prisoner. German losses were about 7500. Lieutenant Mitchell saw what these figures meant when the 12th Brigade took over the line south of the Roman Road:

A Digger came to me with a sandbag, half-filled. 'I found this by a dead bloke. Have a look over it' . . . Very few things contained so much concentrated tragedy as the contents of that sandbag. They were all letters, unsealed and uncensored. Some of the letters were pierced through and crimson-stained . . . I could see everything clearly. These were the letters written by our 13th and 15th Brigade men before they were rushed into the attack. Without a chance to post them, they had carried them on to battle. And they had died. The unknown gatherer had been struck down during his kindly task.

Now the sacred duty had fallen to me, from the hand of death, to deal rightly by them. Long I pondered the problem. It would not be fair to just frank and send them on. False hopes might be raised that the sender still lived . . . That afternoon I spent writing a short explanatory note on each letter. I strove for words to ease the blow, yet did not attempt to raise vain hopes.[24]

The counterattack raised the Australians' fighting reputation even higher. Foch spoke afterwards of their 'altogether astonishing valiance'. On the British side, Brigadier-General George Grogan of the 8th Division, who fought alongside them, called it 'perhaps the greatest individual feat of the war'. Another British officer, Major Neville Lytton, said much the same:

> The Australians made . . . one of the most astounding manoeuvres of the war . . . the battlefield discipline of the Australians must be absolutely perfect, no matter what their billet discipline might be . . . Even if the Australians achieved nothing else in this war, they would have won the right to be considered among the greatest fighting races of the world.

The training of the Australians, as much as their soldierly qualities, underlay such assessments. Their superior bayonet fighting and small unit tactical skills carried the battle. A German machine-gun officer was full of admiration:

> The line dropped, but, as soon as the guns were turned elsewhere, it rose and advanced again. He swung his guns around to meet it, and again it dropped. This happened three or four times, and then he found an Australian machine-gun firing from behind his flank. Thus, he said, the attack was on his troops and round them and past them before they realised that they were confronted by a critical situation.

Butler graciously acknowledged the Australian effort but from Heneker not a word of appreciation was forthcoming.[25]

As the Australians made no allowance for the poor state of the British divisions, their derisive estimate of them hardened. Captain Braithwaite thought that many were 'as good fighters as the Chinese Labour Corps'. 'Some of these Tommy Divisions are the absolute limit, and not worth the money it costs to put them into uniform', Monash complained. Himself British-born and, unlike Monash, involved at first hand, Hobbs remarked: 'The conduct of some of the [British] troops through the ignorance, neglect, or I am almost tempted to say – but I won't, I'll say nervousness – of their officers has had a very depressing effect on me and disgusted many of my officers and men'. Birdwood felt impelled to urge senior Australian commanders to put a stop to 'disparaging comparisons' between Dominion and British troops: 'We are of the same blood, and the creation of friction by criticism is only playing the German's game'. The Germans had already drawn the distinction, saying after Dernancourt: 'The Australians and the Canadians are much the best troops that the English have'. On this they were at one with the French, who proclaimed: 'The English are useless. It's the Scots, the Australians and the Canadians who do all the work'. The New Zealanders might well have been added. Haig entrusted the Dominion troops with the defence of strategically important locations. He kept the Canadian Corps around Arras. When Hazebrouck was threatened, he recalled the 1st Australian Division to buttress it. The Australian Corps safeguarded Amiens. To that end, he ordered it to swap places with III Corps, which shifted north of the Ancre. The Australians now held the BEF's right flank. But the defensive battles had cost them 15 000 men. The 9th, 12th and 13th Brigades, which had borne the brunt, disbanded the 36th, 47th and 52nd Battalions respectively to maintain their other battalions, thereby becoming three-battalion formations like British brigades.[26]

At the end of May, the final 'Australianisation' of the corps occurred. In October 1917 Birdwood had been promoted to general, making inevitable his eventual appointment to army command. When Haig reconstituted the Fifth Army, he offered it to him. Birdwood was reluctant to leave the corps, until Haig pointed out that he would be denying an Australian the chance to command it by staying. As his successor, Birdwood selected Monash, who had proven himself as a divisional general and was senior to the only other real contender, White. He took White with him to the Fifth Army as its chief of staff. Glasgow and Rosenthal replaced the last senior British commanders in the AIF, Walker and Smyth, in charge of the 1st and 2nd Divisions. Gellibrand, who had returned from England in November 1917 to command the 12th Brigade, succeeded Monash in the 3rd Division. Sinclair-MacLagan and Hobbs continued to lead the 4th and 5th Divisions. All were Australian or had lived in Australia for many years, except for Sinclair-MacLagan. Having instructed at Duntroon before the war, he was regarded as an honorary Australian.

—SEVENTEEN—

MONASH AND THE ORCHESTRATED BATTLE

Born in Melbourne on 27 June 1865 to Jewish parents from Prussian Poland, John Monash spoke fluent German, graduated in engineering, arts and law from Melbourne University and became a pioneer of reinforced concrete construction in Australia. Major engineering works gave him experience of large-scale enterprises. Like the great Western Front offensives, they required the organisation, direction and support of labour and the assembly and maintenance of resources. The principles guiding Monash in these projects were equally applicable to high command: foresight, flexibility, co-operation, economy, delegation of authority and an awareness of time. After the war he reflected that a background such as his was 'far more useful for general applications to new problems than the comparatively narrow training of the professional soldier'. By 1914 Monash was a wealthy man but his success did not come easily. He had often worked for expenses only, hoping to win lucrative contracts later on, battling to support his wife and daughter. This adversity was akin to what Clausewitz called 'the frictions' experienced at every level of wartime command. Overcoming them developed 'robustness' in Monash, 'the ability to withstand the shocks of war', which the great soldier–scholar Field-Marshal Lord Wavell put at the top of his list of qualities a successful general must have.[1]

Monash's thirty years of militia service was more serene. Much of it was in a technical arm, the Garrison Artillery. The relationship between technology, the development of modern weapons and the changes they wrought on warfare fascinated him. 'Fighting machinery', he concluded, had replaced physical force and brute courage. In March 1908 he took command of the Victorian section of the fledgling Australian Intelligence Corps. It prepared mobilisation and interstate troop movement plans, which Monash regarded primarily as logistics problems. He thought of logistics as an operation of war in an age when that term applied exclusively to combat: 'I believe that the task of bringing the force to the fighting point, properly equipped and well-formed in all that it needs is at least as important as the capable leading of the force in the fight itself'.

As each plan took shape, Monash's ability to conceive it unfolding was often evident. He could also visualise the shape of terrain from a map. This power of creative imagination was a priceless asset given the scale of operations on the Western Front. Monash's last pre-war appointment was as commander of the 13th Brigade. A trinity that he constantly espoused underpinned its training: unity of thought, policy and tactical method. Monash made the same appeal in every formation he led subsequently.[2]

At Anzac Monash experienced the soldiers' war firsthand because the cramped conditions meant that headquarters were virtually in the front line. As his exhausted and dysentery-ravaged 4th Brigade responded to call after call during the breakout in August 1915, he saw the limits to which men could be pushed. In the attack on Hill 60, a last-minute change of plan resulted in heavy casualties. From then on Monash adopted Napoleon's aphorism, 'Order, Counterorder, Disorder'. Once issued, he insisted, orders should not be modified unless absolutely necessary for the success of the operation.

As commander of the 3rd Division, Monash set a benchmark for meticulous planning and preparation. Messines confirmed his belief in limited objectives that the assaulting infantry could reach in sufficient strength to defeat counterattacks. 'So long as we hold and retain the initiative, we can in this way inflict the maximum of losses when and where we like', Monash maintained. 'It restores to the offensive the advantages which are natural to the defensive in an unlimited objective.' Told to plug urgently the gap between the Somme and the Ancre in his final battle as a divisional commander, Monash relied on his ability to visualise ground and a plan unfolding, as he dictated his orders by candlelight from the instructions he had scribbled on three scraps of paper. The episode demonstrated Monash's 'great powers of grasp and lucid expression at their best – the officers to whom they were read . . . recognized, with a flash of pride, "the old man's" masterly touch', wrote Bean. 'The situation that called for each phase of action was clearly explained, and the action then crisply ordered.'[3]

Haig favoured Monash's promotion to corps command. They first met when Haig reviewed the 3rd Division in December 1916 after its arrival in France. 'On parting he put his arm around my shoulder', Monash wrote, 'and with much feeling and warmth, he said – "You have a very fine division. I wish you all sorts of luck old man".' It was an uncharacteristically emotional display by Haig, a man whom Birdwood described as lacking 'any great human sympathies, and . . . inclined to regard men more as part of a machine than human beings'. Haig considered Monash 'a clear-headed, determined commander', and in his diary gave him perhaps the greatest volume of unmitigated approval of any one man. For his part, Monash's respect for the Commander-in-Chief was based on the way he bore his weighty responsibilities rather than his military acumen, which Monash did not rate highly.

The Western Front confirmed what Monash realised before the war: that morale, discipline and an offensive spirit alone could not defeat sophisticated military technology. It had to be countered by technology as well. The infantry would benefit most:

> [Its] true role was not to expend itself upon heroic physical effort . . . but to advance under the maximum possible protection of the maximum possible array of mechanical resources . . . guns, machine guns, tanks, mortars and aeroplanes . . . to be relieved as far as possible of the obligation to fight [its] way forward.

The emphasis on the physical was not at the expense of the moral. 'Personally I have always found it to pay well closely to consider the psychology not only of the enemy, but also of my own troops', Monash said in April 1918. Hence his insistence on looking to the Diggers' welfare in order in order to keep them in fighting trim. Erecting optimism into a creed and 'feeding the troops on victory' were other means of creating and maintaining *ésprit*.[4]

The differences with Birdwood were obvious. Birdwood relied heavily on White because his own vision was so narrow. Inspecting Anzac in its last days, the one thing Birdwood noticed was the signal wire, which he wanted reeled up. White was flabbergasted: 'Heavens! What does he think we are doing here – why I would gladly have left all the guns behind if we could only get the men off safely'. Looking back on leaving the Australian Corps, White could not recall Birdwood ever having drafted a plan, and as for his much vaunted visits to the trenches, 'he never brought back with him a reliable memory of what he had seen . . . He would say that so and so had a couple of companies overlooking such and such a post . . . I would find out later that this was completely wrong'. Like Haig, Birdwood was 'not a master of the weapons and tactics of his day', whereas Monash 'understood the ingredients of battle right down to the part played by the individual infantry soldier'. Monash's opinion on his predecessor was the same as White's: 'Birdwood was always "buzzing about", looking people up, perambulating all over the place, barely ever at Headquarters and not really exercising any command at all'. Monash spent as much time as he could at his headquarters, planning, organising and directing. By remaining there:

> Everybody knows where to get me, at a moment's notice, for immediate discussion or reference, and rapid decision; I can have before me all the time, a complete and not a partial picture of what is going on, and . . . I can at all times reach every possible subordinate with the minimum of delay. I take leave to describe my method as scientific and efficient, and the other method . . . as dilettante and futile.

From Monash's standpoint, his creative imagination or 'seeing through other men's eyes', as one of his staff put it, made it unnecessary to go forward. 'He could tell you which duckboard needed repairing but never in his life went near a front line trench', recalled General Harington. Though his method worked most of the time, the dreadful conditions before the attack on Passchendaele was an exception that really needed him to see things for himself. It proved that Monash was fallible.[5]

Not all agreed with Monash's appointment. Bean and Keith Murdoch were among those who felt that the corps command should have gone to White. Whereas they considered Monash an intriguer – Bean writing of 'the ability, natural and inborn in Jews, to push themselves' – White was thought to be morally upright and Monash's equal militarily. Claiming that their views were widely held, Murdoch approached Prime Minister Hughes, then *en route* to England. Monash's biographer called this conspiracy 'perhaps the outstanding case of sheer irresponsibility by pressmen in Australian history'. White had no part in it and his relationship with Monash remained impeccable. Within the AIF, there was minimal objection to Monash's preferment. But his robustness was tested over the next two months by having to command in the knowledge that outside forces were trying to replace him.[6]

Rawlinson, his army commander, disliked Monash on religious grounds, likening him after the war to the Secretary of State for India, Sir Edwin Montague, whom Rawlinson called 'a clever, slippery, creepy crawley jew who will always back you if he thinks you are winning and have no scruples about sticking you in the back if he thinks you look like a loser'. But there was no animosity in their professional relationship. The pair worked well together. In any case, at this stage of the war, the army commanders and even Haig himself were becoming less relevant to the day-to-day conduct of operations. The increasing complexity and expertise of the forces they commanded made detailed intervention inappropriate. II ANZAC, whose reputation rested on the skill of Monash and Russell and owed little to Godley, was an early example of this trend. Like the Canadians under Currie, the Australian Corps under Monash knew its business and Rawlinson applied only the lightest touch.[7]

Monash knew that he was fortunate to have taken over such a wonderful fighting machine. The corps was its peak, its prestige and morale were soaring and, with a higher proportion of veterans than the rest of the BEF, it had gained an ascendancy over the Germans it was never to lose. Exemplifying the superiority achieved, patrols used stealth to ambush, cut off posts and take prisoners. The Diggers dubbed these tactics 'peaceful penetration', the term applied by the British press to the spread of pre-war German trade through the Empire. Capitalising on the fluid conditions, it was designed to create more room for defence by advancing the line locally and became a competitive private war that gave free rein to individual initiative, patience and bushcraft.

A typical instance occurred on a hot May morning near Morlancourt. Lieutenant Alex Irvine of the 18th Battalion guessed from the stillness in a troublesome machine-gun post opposite that the Germans were asleep. Organising a raid in ten minutes, he jogged across no man's land with eighteen men and returned in another ten minutes with twenty-two prisoners and the machine-gun. The Australians did not fire a shot and suffered no casualties. The Germans were unaware until that evening that their post had gone. Haig said of the 3rd Division on 9 May:

> During the last three days [they] advanced their front about a mile . . . The ground gained was twice as much as they had taken at Messines last June, and they had done it with very small losses; some 15 killed and 80 wounded; and they had taken nearly 300 prisoners.

At Hazebrouck, wrote Lieutenant Hubert Chedgey of the 1st Battalion, 'We fight in open fields, among hedges and farm houses'. The cover enabled German posts to be snaffled at will. Arriving opposite the Australians in mid-June, the 4th Bavarian Division had lost so many by the end of the month that its commander, Prince Franz, Crown Prince Rupprecht's brother, said that the situation was a disgrace to the division. Its relief, the 13th Reserve Division, fared no better. On 11 July, men from the 1st and 4th Battalions cut out over 1000 yards of its front line, taking 120 prisoners and eleven machine-guns without the knowledge of the higher authorities on either side. Sergeant Richard Travis and his six-man 'gang' from the 2nd Otagos were at the forefront of the New Zealanders' peaceful penetration activities at Hébuterne. Travis's aggression and skilful use of ground were legendary and earned him the sobriquets 'King of no man's land' and 'Prince of Scouts'. 'We get no sleep at nights', said a German captured by the New Zealanders. 'You have to look out like a watch-dog here. Otherwise Tommy comes over and snatches you out of your trench.' The Germans came to dread the Anzac sectors, more than one regiment expressing relief when its 'bloody tour' opposite them ended.[8]

Minor attacks increased the pressure. During May, sharp advances by the 3rd and then the 2nd Division captured Ville-sur-Ancre. Thinly spread across a mile-long frontage in the 2nd Division's attack on 19 May, the 22nd Battalion was held up soon after the start. Sergeant William Ruthven charged a machine-gun, forced the occupants of one dugout to surrender and rushed another, taking thirty-two prisoners. He received the VC. The 2nd Division reached the edge of Morlancourt in June, the Germans lamenting that in a few minutes 'a complete battalion had been wiped out as with a sponge'. In Flanders, the 10th Battalion surrounded and took Merris with the loss of thirty-five men as against the 300 casualties it inflicted. During the British capture of Meteren, the 9th Battalion seized a mile of the line south of it. The New Zealanders advanced up to a mile in their sector, gaining Rossignol Wood. A revolver in each hand like a Western gunfighter, Sergeant Travis charged two machine-guns and knocked them out before shooting four Germans who charged him. Killed a few days later, Travis was awarded a posthumous VC.

Perhaps the most notable Australian casualties were in the air. On 27 May Captain Little, with forty-seven kills to his credit, was blinded by searchlights while attacking a Gotha bomber and fatally wounded. Flying alone four days later, Major Dallas was bounced by three Fokker Triplanes and killed. His official score stood at thirty-two. His unofficial tally was closer to fifty.[9]

On the wider stage, Ludendorff sought to mount *Hagen*, a final crushing blow against the British in Flanders. First he had to make sure that the French would be unable to help them. His eyes settled on the Chemin des Dames, Nivelle's old battleground, from where he could threaten Paris. Pétain had expected him to strike there in March and fortified it accordingly. When nothing happened, the defences were run down. Foch was so confident that the area would stay a backwater that he arranged with Haig for five crippled British divisions to recuperate there in return for three French divisions sent to Amiens. But General Denis Duchêne of the Sixth Army ignored previous experience and packed the forward positions. The bombardment opening Operation *Blücher* on 27 May shattered them.

By nightfall the German First and Seventh Armies had gone thirteen miles and were over the Aisne and Vesle, the longest advance in one day since the Western Front took shape. By 30 May they had captured Soissons and were on the Marne, where the German tide ebbed in 1914, less than fifty miles from Paris. One million people fled the capital, which was being shelled by 'Big Bertha'. Ludendorff had planned to stop on passing over the Chemin des Dames, in order to launch the more important finale against the British. He fed *Blücher* with fresh troops instead. Stiffening resistance and overstretched lines of communication forced a halt on 3 June, after it had punched a salient forty miles deep. Ludendorff thrust again from Noyon on 9 June. Lacking surprise, this attack was foiled.

Blücher rocked the French. Their criticism of the British Army diminished, especially since the tired British divisions on the Chemin des Dames fought better than the French formations. Pétain was stunned at the ease with which his troops had given way – the Germans took 65 000 French prisoners. Clemenceau called it a 'lamentable rout'. Both castigated Foch for being 'hypnotised by the north'. They thought that the Germans were making an all-out effort against the French. Foch did not believe it for the Germans had not reduced their reserves opposite the British in Flanders. Nor would he denude the British front of its reserves to reinforce Pétain. Some help came from the American Expeditionary Force. Its commander, General John Pershing, allowed his 2nd and 3rd Divisions to fight in the battle, even though he wanted the Americans to have their own front instead of being parcelled out amongst the French and British. They were pouring into France, 800 000 arriving in May and June alone. Ludendorff's offensives had now cost over half a million irreplaceable men without causing an Anglo-French collapse. Allied spirits rose.[10]

When *Blücher* began, Foch asked Haig to tie down German reserves by launching local attacks. Monash thought that the most useful operation that the Australians could carry out was the recapture of Hamel. As commander of the 3rd Division, he had urged an attack there because German guns at nearby Accroche Wood troubled his right flank on the northern bank of the Somme. The 2nd Division was now so far ahead on the northern bank after its advance on Morlancourt that these guns were firing into its rear.

Taking Hamel would also gain more room for the defence of Villers-Bretonneux. It would also require a full division. Fearing heavy casualties at a time when the Australian Corps could ill-afford them, White strongly objected when Rawlinson proposed the attack as a feint in support of the Anglo-French offensive south of Villers-Bretonneux that Foch had mooted in April. 'If we have to carry out a perfectly valueless attack at the cost of a division which it is earnestly desirable not to waste – there seems to me something very much wrong in our scheme of arrangements', White said. The Australian manpower position had deteriorated since then.[11]

Now the tactical situation was different and Australian intelligence did not think much of the Germans opposite. The 43rd Reserve Division astride the Somme and in Hamel was rated 'average'. Holding the line from the village to the Roman Road, the 13th Division had been mauled during the attack on Dernancourt, after which it needed a month's break. The 108th Division south of the Roman Road was classed as a 'trench' formation: 'as a fighting division it is not of the best as it has spent most of its time on the RUSSIAN front'. On 22 June the Australians put total German strength in the sector at 2790 backed up by a reserve of 2860. With undermanned companies averaging around fifty rifles, the Germans were, in fact, considerably weaker. But their defences were naturally strong.

Except on the Somme flats, the German front line was nowhere more than 400 yards from the 4th Australian Division's line on the main spur of Hill 104 and followed a sunken road below it to Vaire Wood. Hidden by the brow of the spur, Pear Trench redoubt enfiladed attacks towards the Somme or, in the other direction, past Kidney Trench redoubt. In common with the German policy of turning woods into death traps, Vaire Wood and Hamel Wood, which formed its eastern end, were fortified. German artillery observers on the Wolfsberg behind Hamel had magnificent views over the 2700 yards separating them from the Australians. The old Amiens Defence Line crossing the hill 'has been cleared out in places and wired', Australian intelligence said. Though the line between Vaire Wood and the Roman Road consisted mainly of rifle pits, the area was devoid of cover and ironing-board flat. Australian and French attempts to take Monument and Hangard Woods, on similar ground south of it, had been roughly handled. Like White, Monash concluded that the cost of attacking Hamel outweighed the gains.[12]

Meanwhile, Brigadier-General Anthony Courage's 5th Tank Brigade, which supported the Fourth Army, had re-equipped with the new Mark V tank. At 4.6 m.p.h., it was almost 1 m.p.h. faster than the earlier Mark IV, had more armour protection and greater endurance. It was also mechanically reliable. Monash was among the senior commanders to whom the Mark V was demonstrated. Major-General Hugh Elles, the Tank Corps's commander, predicted that it 'would so increase the capacity of infantry and artillery that decisive defeat might be inflicted on the Germans before winter'. Impressed, Monash 'resolved to propose an operation for the recapture of Hamel, conditional upon my being supplied with the assistance of tanks, a small increase of my artillery and an addition to my air resources'. Rawlinson maintained that he put the concept to Monash. Who convinced whom that an attack on Hamel was possible immediately if tanks were employed will probably never be known. Bean suggested that both Monash and Rawlinson conceived the idea simultaneously.[13]

Hard, crop-covered and largely free of shell holes, the terrain was good tank country. Running down to the Somme, the Hill 104 spur would protect the approach of both tanks and infantry before they advanced to the Blue Line. It ran from the river across the Wolfsberg to the Roman Road. But the tanks would be vulnerable in Hamel village and Hamel and Vaire Woods. Then as now, tanks do not like built-up or wooded areas because they constrain the mobility and manoeuvre on which their effectiveness and security depend. Partly for that reason, Monash dismissed Accroche Wood as an objective even though it shielded the troublesome German guns. Its capture necessitated going another 1000 yards. The extra casualties incurred would make a counterattack harder to hold off. Monash was adamant: 'This is a limited objective we are going for, and no consideration is going to prompt me to allow exploitation beyond the line chosen. On no account will an attempt be made to go chasing after those guns'. Besides, the Wolfsberg, which would be captured, lay between the Somme and Accroche Wood. It offered good views of the wood and blocked much of the view from the wood over the river.[14]

Monash briefed Courage on 19 June. Courage sent him his plan next day. Four tank companies, forty-eight tanks in all, would attack in three waves. By crushing the German wire, the fifteen in the leading wave took the place of a preliminary bombardment. They were then to move as quickly as possible towards the Blue Line to demoralise the Germans, cut off their retreat and block reinforcements. The twenty-one tanks in the next wave would lead the infantry forward and the nine tanks in the last one were to subdue remaining opposition. Three tanks would be left as a reserve. Heavily influenced by the Cambrai attack, Courage's scheme embodied the doctrine of Lieutenant-Colonel J. F. C. Fuller, later to become the most famous of Tank Corps officers. It sacrificed some of the tactical requirements of other arms to ensure that the tanks had unimpeded mobility. The creeping barrage was dispensed with because its linear shape and slow pace restricted tank movement. The infantry would have to stick close to the tanks, 'so that they may at once make good any opportunity the Tanks create and free the Tanks to continue their advance and so keep the battle moving forward'.

Using the tanks in this way, Monash calculated that he could cover the four-mile attack frontage with ten battalions, of which two formed the reserve. As the Australian battalions averaged around 550 rifles, the density would be less than one man per yard of front for an advance of a mile and a half. Even allowing for the greater strength of positions attacked in earlier campaigns, it was, by their standards, a tiny infantry commitment. At Broodseinde the 3rd Australian Division employed eight battalions to penetrate 1900 yards on a frontage of 1000 yards. Ludendorff allotted to one division on 21 March 1918 the frontage Monash was giving to each of his battalions now. Monash also opted for a composite infantry force, to be commanded by General Sinclair-MacLagan, so that the losses did not fall entirely on the 4th Division, in whose sector most of the Blue Line lay. Its 4th Brigade would attack in the centre, with the 11th Brigade from the 3rd Division assaulting across the Somme flats on the left and the 6th Brigade from the 2nd Division between Vaire Wood and the Roman Road on the right. Haig approved the plan on 25 June. For good measure, Monash obtained another two tank companies to augment the 8th Tank Battalion, which had been allotted to him. He had sixty tanks in all.

The plan was not well received. Monash had not reckoned on the legacy of the 4th Division's disastrous experience at Bullecourt. It had attacked there without a creeping barrage on account of the tanks, just like Monash was proposing now, and been hung out to dry when they failed miserably. Sinclair-MacLagan and the brigadiers all urged the retention of the creeping barrage with the infantry advancing close behind it. That meant combining the first two tank waves and no lightning capture of the Blue Line. It was a dramatic revision of the concept, which 'ceases to be primarily a tank operation', wrote Monash. 'It becomes an infantry operation in which the slight infantry power receives a considerable accretion by the addition of a large body of tanks.' He had strong arguments in favour of his own scheme. The Mark V tank was much more capable than its predecessors and would be advancing over ground that was no obstacle. But Monash deferred to the doubters. Had he overruled them, Sinclair-MacLagan and his commanders would have attacked half-expecting a repetition of Bullecourt, an attitude inconsistent with Monash's emphasis on confidence and optimism. It was not the only example of his use of psychology before the battle.[15]

Monash subordinated the tank commanders to their infantry counterparts. Each battalion worked with the tanks alongside which it would attack. The tanks demonstrated that they could manoeuvre in any direction, were as fast as running infantry and impervious to the armour-piercing ammunition their crews invited the Australians to fire at them. To talk to the tank commander, the Diggers were told: 'Just ring the back-door bell' by tugging on the rope at the back of the tank. Their greatest worry, a tank accidentally running over a wounded man in the crops, was addressed by having a soldier guide each fighting tank and three accompanying every reserve tank. Keeping 'open house', the tank crews took the Diggers for joyrides and allowed them to drive. After 1 July the tank officers moved into the battalion bivouacs. The result went a long way towards exorcising the Bullecourt demons:

> The fame of the Tanks, and all the wonderful things they could do, spread rapidly throughout the Corps. The 'digger' took the Tank to his heart, and ever after, each tank was given a pet name by the Company of Infantry which it served in battle, a name which was kept chalked on its iron sides, together with a panegyric commentary upon its prowess.[16]

The artillery had to be greatly reinforced for its expanded role. Monash obtained eleven extra brigades of field artillery which, when added to the eighteen Australian ones, yielded 326 guns or howitzers. Four heavy artillery brigades joined the nine already in the corps, making 313 heavy guns available. Over 200 of them were to engage the German guns. Starting 200 yards ahead of the tanks and infantry, three belts of fire 600 yards deep made up the creeping barrage. It was to lift 100 yards every three minutes. One-tenth of the ammunition was smoke shell. Doubting that the 6th Brigade on the exposed Santerre could dig itself in by daylight, Monash arranged for a heavy battery to fire desultorily on the area beforehand. The shell holes were mapped so that the Diggers knew where the cover was. Rawlinson asked Haig for a squadron of heavy bombers to strike villages and woods where German reserves might be quartered.

Employing the technique used by the Germans in *Georgette* and *Blücher*, aircraft were to parachute ammunition to the infantry. Captain Laurence Wackett of No. 3 Squadron, who would become a postwar pioneer of aviation in Australia, designed the release mechanism. Barrages and diversionary operations on the flanks would confuse the Germans as to the sector under attack. Harassing missions with flavoured smoke were fired daily from 26 June, so that they would not regard the smoke as unusual at zero hour. Guns, ammunition and stores were moved forward at night and camouflaged by dawn, when No. 3 Squadron flew 'police patrols' to report on anything that German pilots might see. From 27 June other aircraft flew 'noise patrols' over the German line from dusk to dawn to drown the noise of the tanks' assembly. Conferences assumed a new importance because as little as possible was committed to paper. The final one on 30 June lasted four and a half hours, as Monash worked through an agenda listing 133 separate items. Subsequently, 'no fiddling with the plan was permitted'.[17]

Diggers also met Yanks. Just before Monash started the planning, five American divisions began training in the BEF's rear. With the ongoing worry of another German offensive against the British, Pershing agreed to move two of them, the 27th and 33rd, close to emergency defensive positions behind the Third and Fourth Armies respectively. Rawlinson hit on the idea of using troops from the 33rd Division, an Illinois National Guard outfit, to swell the Australian battalions in the Hamel attack under the pretext of giving them a chance to get some experience. Monash asked him for 2000 men and confirmed 4 July, American Independence Day, as the date of the attack to make the proposal more attractive. Haig approved. The 33rd's commander, Major-General George Bell, and his superior, Major-General George Read of II Corps, were enthusiastic. On

29 June an American company joined each of the ten Australian battalions.

The Americans were big men who reminded the Diggers wistfully of themselves at the start of the war. 'We felt today as though we had been walking among ghosts', Bean wrote on encountering them. 'Wherever one goes one is struck more and more by their likeness to the men of the old 1st Divn at Mena Camp and behind the lines in Gallipoli.' When an Australian sarcastically asked an American, 'Are you going to win the war for us?', he replied, 'Well, we hope we'll fight like you'. Lieutenant-Colonel Joseph Sanborn, commander of the 131st Regiment from which some of the Americans came, gave their perspective on the Australians: 'from the first when our soldiers came in contact with them they mixed well and took kindly to each other'. The warmth was reciprocated. Private Harold Shapcott of the 42nd Battalion found the Americans to be 'very fine chaps, ready and eager to learn and not above taking advice'. Lieutenant Rule was glad to have them on board:

> These Yanks view things just the same as we do, and their general trend of ideas was very sensible indeed. They were all men in the prime of life; and such a mixture – one could see among them all the nations under the sun . . . When their names were called, I could hardly keep from laughing, and I felt very grateful to my boys that they had not inflicted such names on my roll book. I heard our C.O. say to one of their sergeants: 'I wish we had some of those Austrians in front of us,' and we got the shock of our lives when he quite calmly replied: 'You know, I was born in Austria, and my father was a Pole'.[18]

Prime Minister Hughes and his deputy, Sir Joseph Cook, called on the Australians on 2 July, while on their way to a meeting of the Supreme War Council in Paris. When Monash told them that the men they were seeing would shortly be going into action, the firebrand Prime Minister was uncharacteristically humbled:

Hughes, as often as not, lay at full length on the ground, looking into the faces of the soldiers and chewing a stalk of grass. He seemed wrapped up in the men, and was gazing into their faces all the time. I suppose that he was thinking to himself: 'Within thirty-six hours these men will be out there advancing under the bursting shells, going straight into the thresh of the machine-guns . . . and here they are laughing at Joe's old jokes, wrapped up in his speech as if they were at a picnic'.[19]

Pershing had just visited II Corps. He was unaware that the Americans were about to attack with the Australians. He exploded on finding out. The use of his partly trained troops contravened the agreement with Haig, whereby they could only be committed to action in an emergency. Hamel was not an emergency. Pershing told Read that they must not participate. Rawlinson informed Haig, who ordered them withdrawn. The Americans had arrived in two contingents, an initial group of four companies and a second of six. Both Read and Rawlinson thought the direction applied only to the six. At 4 p.m. on 3 July, Monash learned that the original four companies also had to come out. He told Rawlinson that it was too late to comply and that if the Americans did not participate, he would call the attack off. In that case, no Australian would fight beside an American again. Unless Monash had a decision by 7 p.m., the latest by which cancellation orders could be issued if they were to reach the assault battalions in time, the attack would proceed. Rawlinson wailed that he might be sent home if it did not. Monash replied that keeping the confidence of the Americans and the Australians in each other was more important than preserving an army commander. Rawlinson went to Haig. While he waited, Monash gave a briefing that betrayed not the slightest hint of tension. Bean listened:

There is no question that the old man gave us, as always, a very able discourse indeed. Very few men could have done it. He stood up at his desk there so as to get at the map, and gave it to us without a note – names of battalions and everything . . . The thing has been planned with a thoroughness like that which went before Messines – every particle of the plan, down to the action of companies, being known to the corps commander.

Haig's response arrived with a few minutes to spare. The improvement of the position before Amiens was so important that the attack must go ahead, even if the American companies could not be withdrawn before zero hour.[20]

The tanks left their leaguers at 10.30 p.m. German searchlights and anti-aircraft fire probed for the aircraft blotting out their noise. At midnight the infantry ate a second hot meal, after which they began filing onto the jump-off tapes. Each man received a tot of rum. Lieutenant Rule asked himself the familiar questions: 'What luck this time? Who would get it in the neck? Did the Hun know we were going to attack? Did he know the time? Was he waiting? What sort of barrage would he put down? Could we get beyond it before it fell?'

At 3.10 a.m. on 4 July a gigantic sheet of lightning ripped from the gun lines. Tracers from 111 Vickers guns drew spider web patterns in the sky. The ground in front of the Australians was quaking and aflame. At his headquarters at Bertangles, five miles north of Amiens, Monash kept his nerves steady by sketching the head of the French *poilu* who had chauffeured Hughes two days before. Lieutenant Rule rose from the damp grass:

Not a bit of use to try and get the men to double, for in the roar of the guns and of the shells bursting ahead it was impossible to hear your own shouts. All we could do was to keep going steadily forward, and hope to God that the Hun would be slow in answering his SOS signal, otherwise the chances were we would be cut to ribbons. Just as his SOS – two red lights – went up, two heavy shells fell, one just in front of my platoon, and the other on the right of the company. When we were twenty yards further on, down they came again . . . a piece from one which burst closest to me hit me in the seat of the pants with an awful wallop . . . For the next hundred yards I held onto it until I managed to push it into a fold of my trousers where it no longer burnt my flesh.

As most of the guns had not been ranged by registration but fired from map-based calculations, 'dropshorts' were inevitable. They cost the 15th Battalion fifty men. The smoke screens and the fountains of dust thrown up thickened the dense fog. Shell bursts appeared as dull glows and then disappeared altogether. The Australians gauged the barrage line from the flashes of air-bursting shrapnel. Until they took their lead from them, the keen but inexperienced Americans blundered into the barrage one minute and lost it the next. The gloom affected the tanks even more. In the rehearsals, they had caught up with the infantry by four minutes after zero, when the barrage made its first lift, but at 3.14 a.m. most were nowhere to be seen. Trying to find the battalions to which they were attached and avoid running over dead and wounded, they were still groping forward, guided by officers with compasses.[21]

Attacking Pear Trench, the 15th Battalion had gone barely 200 yards when machine-guns opened up and bombers hurling grenades rose from the crops ahead. Charging them, the Australians stumbled into intact wire, behind which the redoubt was untouched. Owing to the lack of observation over it, the barrage had fallen either side. The Diggers should have lain down and awaited the tanks as instructed. But the three allotted to Pear Trench had lost their way in the murk. Uncertain whether they would arrive at all, the 15th assaulted using fire and movement. The Lewis gunners stood and sprayed over the crops. Clearing the wire, the riflemen rushed the two machine-guns holding up the advance. A third gun began firing. Private Henry Dalziel leapt into the gun pit and killed two of the gunners. He spared the third because 'the youngster fought so well'. Dalziel became the one thousandth recipient of the VC. Around the sunken road at the rear of the redoubt, the Germans threw grenades even as those in front surrendered. Infuriated by what they considered to be 'white flag treachery', the Australians moved along the road killing any Germans they found. Forty dead ones were subsequently counted in 'a very small sector'. The 15th Battalion's run of bad luck was over. It reached the eastern tip of Hamel Wood uneventfully. Its tanks turned up there.

Attacking alongside the 15th Battalion, the 16th faltered before uncut wire at Kidney Trench. Its tanks had not yet caught up either. Seeing a gap in the wire, Lance-Corporal Thomas Axford tore through, hurling grenades that stunned the machine-gunners. He bayoneted ten Germans and captured several others. Axford received the VC for this action, which broke the back of the resistance. Entering Vaire Wood, the Australians stretched out in extended line behind the barrage and advanced firing from the hip like a bunch of gunfighters. They drove the Germans into the fire and cleared the wood by 3.50 a.m. Hamel Wood fell next. Amongst the 16th Battalion's prisoners,

> One party of about a dozen . . . was led by a German who laughed when one of the diggers said to him, 'Finis le Guerre.' 'Yes, he replied, my —— oath.' He said he learned the English language on the Boulder mine in Western Australia, and had been called back to the Fatherland early in 1914.

Machine-guns in a concealed trench pinned down the 13th Battalion on the other side of Vaire Wood. The Australians pointed out the danger to a tank. When they saw it pirouetting on top of one of the guns, the rest of the Germans in the trench put their hands up. Advancing between the 13th Battalion and the Roman Road, the 6th Brigade came closest to Monash's ideal of mechanical resources helping the infantry forward. The barrage was 'perfect'. Private Isaac Betteridge said that the 23rd Battalion's leading wave was punchy from hugging it so closely:

> Our own front had a lot of smoke shell that burst in great sheets of fire 30 feet across and looked like golden rain. The old fashioned hell couldn't be as bad and the line of men dropping and lying still, staggering back wounded or lurching drunkenly forward into shell holes, falling over the wire, buffeted by explosions till they looked like devils in their proper environment. Suddenly the enemy trench stood out in front. A line of white cut into the green of the wheat-field. The crowd were firing for moral effect. Some were swearing in a sort of strangled undertone. The reason was to open one's mouth was to get it full of the acrid fumes of the explosions. He had not many machine guns. We had the shelter of his trench before he got them going. Into the trench, had to walk over two dead Huns. In a dugout was a poor scared creature that whined and cried like a kiddie that is afraid of the dark. Our officer called on him to come out. The whining continued, to be cut short by a shot. Hope his conscience don't worry him later. The trench we were in was a regular shambles. The sides spattered with blood. Dead men lying everywhere.

Shielded by the flank smokescreen, the tanks 'had severe fighting and did great execution, their action being of the greatest service'. All in all, the attack progressed with 'the ease of a field day'.

The 11th Brigade on the Somme flats was given almost half the tanks because it faced no man's land at its widest, 800 yards, and its objectives included Hamel and the Wolfsberg. On the outskirts of the village, which the shelling had turned into an inferno, the 43rd Battalion met men from the 43rd Reserve Division. Leading an American platoon, Lieutenant Ivor Symonds outflanked a post hidden by a beet pile, killing fifteen Germans and capturing forty. Dense smoke disoriented the Australians at Notamel Wood on the northern side of Hamel. Picking out the treetops against the shell bursts, 44-year-old Captain John Moran yelled parade-ground orders to get his company back on course but a machine-gun near the village halted the leading platoon. Crawling to a tank, the platoon sergeant rang its bell and when the door opened, pointed out the gun to the tank commander. The Germans just managed to flee before their position was flattened. Private Shapcott was fascinated:

It was a weird sight to see these ungainly objects waddling up at the toot, in response to signals from the infantry and approach a machine gun possie with blazing guns. If they did not manage to put the machine gun out of action with their fire they continued straight on and went right over the gun and crew and emplacement and flattened the whole lot out!

As the 43rd Battalion prepared to attack Hamel, Lance-Corporal Francis Shaw spotted a machine-gun two hundred yards away. Charging it, he killed a German officer who rushed at him firing a revolver. When Shaw reached the post, eight Germans lay dead around the gun. A ninth attacked him. Drawing his own revolver while they grappled, Shaw smashed the German's skull and shot him. Three more machine-guns opened up. Shaw led an assault on one that yielded seventeen prisoners and a tank flattened the other two. Corporal Thomas Pope, an American, charged yet another machine-gun and bayoneted its crew, winning the US Army's first Medal of Honor in France. Specially designated sections cleared the cellars and dugouts in the village, capturing 300 prisoners. Conditioned by the flavoured smoke to spend the nights sheltering there, some had their gas masks on and did not realise they were being attacked until the Australians arrived. 'Everywhere the enemy was unprepared for the assaulting troops', the 43rd Battalion's War Diary said. Having noted on air photographs the faint signs of a buried cable, Lance-Corporal Boyce Schulz traced it to a deep dugout, where he took the surrender of a battalion commander and his staff. Accepting a bet, Captain Moran ignored lurking snipers by climbing onto the rafters of a ruined house and raising a French tricolour.

Dawn had broken when the 44th Battalion started up the Wolfsberg for the Blue Line. Capitalising on the excellent fields of fire from the old Amiens Defence Line, the 43rd Reserve Division's machine-guns were in action well before the Diggers got close. As the barrage was mainly shrapnel now, the tanks could move underneath it without risk, allowing the infantry to hang back. The tanks trampled the German posts or fired point-blank into them with grapeshot. With the way ahead clear, the 44th Battalion rushed the crest, capturing dugouts crowded with men – fifty in one, forty in another and a battalion headquarters in a third. To Bean, on the northern heights of the Somme, the Wolfsberg seemed

> like the skyline, so full was the valley of smoke from our smoke shell. Almost immediately after we saw the first tank – and then three or four on either side of it on the skyline behind Hamel and crawling up the hill. Then we could make out a thick line of infantry between the various tanks – at first I thought they were stationary, but they must have been going on to their last objective.

By 4.43 a.m., ninety-three minutes after the attack started, the Blue Line had been reached along its length. Six hours later it was everywhere wired in and the support trenches in rear were down. Four carrier tanks had delivered the ammunition and defence stores normally carried by 1250 men. The artillery dispersed Germans gathering for counterattacks during the day but at 10 p.m. the 43rd Reserve Division's reserve battalion burst forth to recapture a small part of the Wolfsberg. One-half of the Australian pincer attack to pinch the Germans out was held up. The other half hurtled on, thanks largely to Private James Lynch, a giant who had been an axeman before the war. Throwing grenades and wielding a club, he drove the Germans before him but was shot through the head as they broke.[22]

The battle cost the Australians 1200 casualties and the Americans 176. German losses amounted to over 2000 men, 177 machine-guns, two field guns, thirty-two trench mortars and three anti-tank rifles. Over 1600 prisoners were taken. It was the BEF's first major offensive success since the opening day at Cambrai eight months earlier. No battle within his previous experience, wrote Monash, 'not even Messines, passed off so smoothly, so exactly to time-table, or was so free from any kind of hitch'. The closeness between conception and execution led him to coin the famous analogy: 'A perfected modern battle plan is like nothing so much as a score for an orchestral composition, where the various arms and units are the instruments, and the tasks they perform are their respective musical phrases'. Monash was the conductor.[23]

At the Supreme War Council, Lloyd George and the Prime Ministers of Canada, New Zealand and Newfoundland asked Hughes to cable their congratulations to Monash. Clemenceau decided to visit the Australians instead of making his weekly call on a French division. Wheezing, through emotion and asthma, he enthralled the Hamel veterans gathered around him on 7 July with an address in English that entered Australian folklore:

> When the Australians came to France, the French people expected a great deal from you because they had heard what you have accomplished in the development of your own country. We knew that you would fight a real fight, but we did not know that from the very beginning you would astonish the whole continent. I shall go back tomorrow and say to my countrymen; 'I have seen the Australians. I have looked in their faces. I know that these men will fight alongside of us again until the cause for which we are all fighting is safe for us and for our children'.

Sinclair-MacLagan led three cheers for France and Clemenceau remarked '*De jolis enfants*', as he left. Haig was delighted with this 'nice success'. Monash's position as corps commander was secure and a steady stream of commanders from other corps and armies in the BEF arrived at Bertangles to study his methods. GHQ included his orders in two instructional pamphlets it published on the battle. They attributed the success to 'the care and skill as regards every detail with which the plan was drawn up', not least the maintenance of secrecy that ensured surprise, and the excellent co-ordination and co-operation of infantry, tanks, artillery and aircraft that made Hamel an all-arms battle.[24]

From Monash down, the Australians recognised that the tanks had given them the real edge. After the battle, twenty-six machine-guns were dug out of a trench crushed by a single tank. They had survived the creeping barrage and could have inflicted crippling losses, as the bloody attack on Pear Trench showed. It caused most of the 15th Battalion's 240 casualties, easily the heaviest of any of the assaulting battalions. Elsewhere the mere approach of a tank often induced surrender. Tanks returning with cheering wounded and 'Dinkum Chum', 'Humdinger' and other nicknames chalked on their sides testified to the revolution in the Diggers' opinion of them. Lieutenant-Colonel Fuller thought that the reputation of the Tank Corps owed more to Hamel than Cambrai. Of the sixty tanks used, only three broke down and the Germans knocked out just one of the five that were disabled. No Australian or American wounded were run over.[25]

The tankers were unstinting in their admiration of the Australians, who 'never considered that the presence of the Tanks exonerated them from fighting, and took instant advantage of any opportunity created by the Tanks'. Before the tanks caught up or whenever a tank was not to hand, the GHQ reports noted, the Australians fought their way forward making full use of their own weapons, especially the bayonet and bomb. The standard of infantry platoon leading was especially praised. Bean was adamant that the battle would have ended differently without top-shelf infantry.[26]

As for the Americans, Monash said they 'acquitted themselves most gallantly'. The Diggers praised them as well, though observing that they had the fault of all first-class fighting men who lack experience – excessive keenness. They invariably looked to the Australians, and in practically every way, as the 13th Battalion found:

'I guess we're shark troops now,' one of a party of Yanks visiting us after Hamel remarked. Thinking he was referring to collecting souvenirs from Fritzs, and not being willing to take second or even equal place with anyone at that, our 'Souvenir King' took out a heap of German watches, marks, photos, soldbuchs, feldpostbriefs, revolvers and daggers, and proudly retorted, 'You'll have to be Some Shark Troops to beat that little heap, I guess, Guy.' 'I wasn't referring to souvenirs, Aussie. I said I guess after that battle we'll be regarded as shark troops like you Australians. Shark Troops – SHARK Troops like you. S-H-O-C-K – shark troops.' The Digger's perplexed look vanished.[27]

Hamel did not make Monash the first exponent of blitzkrieg as some of his admirers have claimed. For a start, the objective was limited. As the operation was effectively an experiment, Monash wanted to maximise the chances of success and opted for what seemed possible, rather than being seduced by what seemed desirable. Nothing like the German armoured thrusts across France and Russia in 1940–41 was intended. The Mark V's were incapable of carrying them out anyway, although in this respect one tank historian wrote: 'In relation to the machines at his disposal, Monash's tank-infantry tactics have rarely been equalled, and probably never surpassed'. His own claims about the battle were also exaggerated. Far from originating in a desire to allay the 'anxiety and nervousness of the public' or to get commanders to 'think offensively', Hamel was launched for local tactical reasons. As for an 'electric effect' that 'stimulated many men to the realisation that the enemy was not invulnerable', General Charles Mangin had probably never heard of Monash when the French Tenth Army attacked on the Matz River with 144 tanks in mid-June and advanced two miles to break the German thrust from Noyon; or on 28 June when two of his divisions took 1200 prisoners; or on 3 July, when another 1000 prisoners were captured.[28]

On 15 July, Ludendorff launched *Friedensturm*, a last attempt to draw Allied reserves away from Flanders to clear the way for

Hagen. He renewed the attack on the French from the *Blücher* salient to envelop Rheims and again threaten Paris. Forewarned by the build-up, Pétain insisted on a system of defence-in-depth. The blow east of Rheims was smashed but the westerly one penetrated beyond the Marne before the French, with five of the enormous 28 000-strong American divisions on their order of battle, halted it. Instigated by Foch, Mangin's Tenth Army, with the Sixth Army alongside, unleashed a counterstroke on 18 July with twenty-three divisions, four of them American, backed by 2000 guns and 350 tanks. Advancing six miles, it captured 25 000 prisoners and 400 guns. His army racked by the first outbreaks in Europe of a worldwide influenza epidemic, Ludendorff was in a high state of nervous excitement, irritable and unable to eat. He called off *Hagen*. The Germans realised that Foch's regaining of the initiative signified *der Wendepunkt der Kriegslage*, 'the turning point of the war situation'. It also influenced Allied thinking in the manner Monash attributed to Hamel. But Hamel was the model for the more important British offensives that followed. It was 'a textbook victory, a little masterpiece casting a long shadow before it'.[29]

—EIGHTEEN—

ADVANCING TO VICTORY

On 6 July 1918 Sergeant Walter Brown of the 20th Battalion was chatting to a sergeant from the 21st, which the 20th was relieving. The sergeant pointed to where a German sniper might be. Half an hour went by without a shot being fired. Brown set off towards the suspected sniper's nest. A shot rang out. It missed. Brown charged, chucking a bomb as he ran. He hit the ground when it fell short. Silence. After several minutes, Brown resumed his solo attack. He arrived at an empty trench. A machine-gun was perched above a dugout at the far end. Brown reached the dugout at the same time as a German emerged. The German yelled '*Kamerad!*'. Brown clocked him. The German went down. More Germans came from another dugout. Holding his remaining bomb menacingly, Brown motioned towards the Australian line. They headed off with him following. Handing the thirteen prisoners over, Brown thought nothing of the incident. But the news of his foray, which gained him the VC, spread like wildfire throughout the Australian Corps.

General Monash was highly impressed. 'It was difficult to imagine men exhibiting greater dejection and poorer morale', he said of Brown's prisoners. Peaceful penetration was to proceed apace. The 2nd Division took Monument Farm by this means and by 14 July had secured Monument Wood. Monash had originally proposed taking it in a sequel to Hamel. The German commanders admitted that the Australians enjoyed complete ascendancy. Regarding the constant loss of ground to them, General Georg von der Marwitz, the commander of the Second Army, declared: 'Troops must fight. They must not give way at every opportunity and seek to avoid fighting; otherwise they will get the feeling that the enemy is superior to them'. Monash was determined to capitalise. But he always remained uncertain of his role in inspiring the great offensive that followed on 8 August.[1]

Meeting Rawlinson and his chief of staff, Major-General Archibald Montgomery, almost daily between 4 and 20 July, Monash impressed upon them that the Australian Corps could undertake an offensive on a decisive scale if its front were reduced, the 1st Australian Division returned to it and the Canadian Corps advanced on its right. On 15 July they told Monash that the Canadians would be available and asked him what he needed in tanks and guns. Monash claimed that this conversation was 'really the genesis of the whole plan'. On 21 July Rawlinson, Monash, Currie and Butler met to 'elaborate the outlines'. So went Monash's account. He described himself as 'the prime mover' but undeserving of 'the whole credit'. Many of the AIF's senior officers believed that Monash was at the heart of it, particularly his own chief of staff, Brigadier-General Thomas Blamey. He staked Monash's claim very strongly afterwards. Patriotic journalism promoted the view, sometimes with the added claim that the AIF thus 'won the war.' The reality was different.

From the time he became Generalissimo in March, Foch wanted to attack on the Somme to safeguard Amiens. *Georgette* stymied the Anglo-French offensive he proposed in April. He revived it with Haig in May. The British role would comprise a surprise assault by the Fourth Army to gain the Morcourt–Harbonnières ravine, five miles distant. Haig intimated to Rawlinson that he would receive the Canadian Corps for it. Rawlinson described the plan to Birdwood and White. They started work on the Australian role. *Blücher* caused

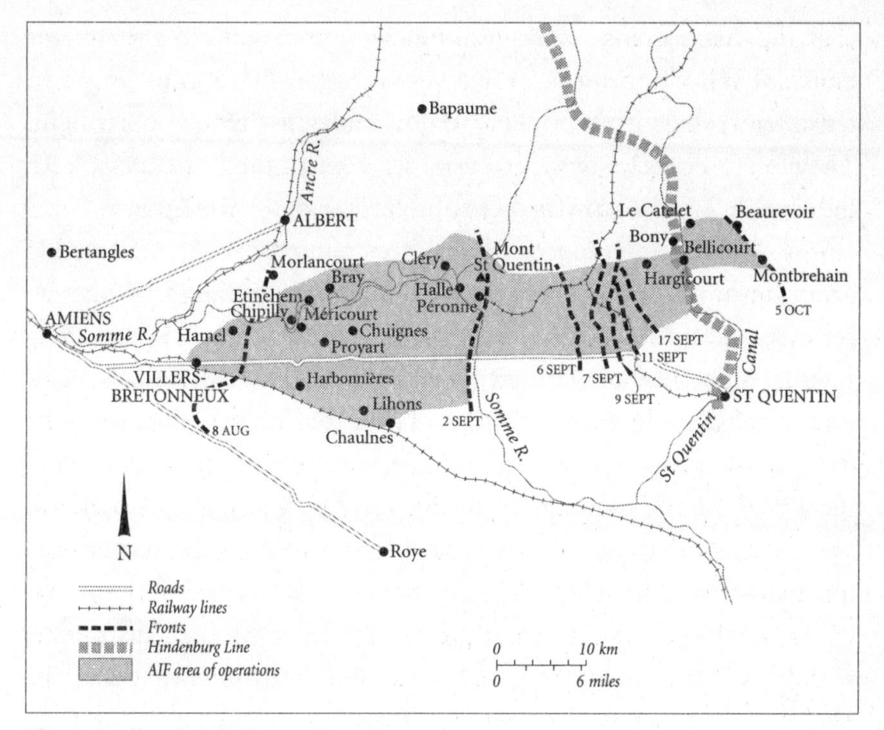

The Australian Corps advance in 1918

another postponement. Birdwood and White headed off to the Fifth Army. Seeing the Australians' ascendancy over the Germans, and also because the Santerre plain was ideal for tanks, Rawlinson resurrected the scheme. He sent Haig detailed proposals on 17 July. Haig approved them two days later.

By then the French counterstroke on the Marne had ended German offensive aspirations. Foch could unleash the Allied counteroffensive. On 24 July he outlined a series of blows to Haig and Pershing. The French would again strike on the Marne, the Americans, now with their own sector in Lorraine, were to pinch out the St Mihiel salient southeast of Verdun, and the British would have the leading role in the Anglo-French advance before Amiens. Rawlinson would assault on 8 August on an eleven-mile front between Morlancourt and Démuin with the Australians and Canadians, respectively left and right of the railway, south of the Somme and III Corps north of it. Advancing in three stages, they were to reach the old Amiens Outer Defence Line seven miles away. Some 2000 guns and 552 tanks, as well as armoured cars and cavalry, would support them. The French First Army was to advance next to the Canadians, with the French Third Army further south attacking on 10 August.

As a corps commander, Monash was removed from the strategic direction of the war. He may have thought along the same lines as Foch, Haig and Rawlinson but never knew that they had been considering an offensive on the front held by the Australians since April. Rawlinson also encouraged him to think that he was the instigator to dissuade Prime Minister Hughes from imposing restrictions on the use of the AIF. Bean's conclusion was appropriate: 'Monash did not devise the August offensive, though of course he was responsible for many of the details of the plan for his own Corps'.[2]

Spread between the Somme and the railway, the Australians were to advance over five miles. Monash complained that the first objective or Green Line, 2000 yards distant, fell short of the German gun line. Rawlinson shifted it 1500 yards eastwards to prevent the Germans withdrawing their artillery during the 100-minute pause before the start of the 5000-yard advance to the Red Line. Its capture would put Amiens outside the range of all but the heaviest German guns. The finger-shaped Chipilly Spur, around which the Somme curved sharply opposite Morcourt, also concerned Monash. Its guns enfiladed the left of his advance. But Chipilly was in Butler's sector. Having little confidence in III Corps, Monash wanted Rawlinson to extend the Australian line over the river so that it fell in his sector. Rawlinson compromised by adjusting Butler's objectives to enable III Corps to concentrate more on taking Chipilly. The last part of the Australian attack was the 1500-yard advance past Harbonnières to the Blue Line. Arriving from Flanders just before the battle, the 1st Division would be in reserve.

The five-mile frontage of the assault necessitated two divisions attacking side by side. Its depth necessitated leapfrogs, which favoured the divisions attacking first because they could assemble as close as possible to their objectives. Those destined for the later phases had to leapfrog them after marching from concentration areas well to the rear and through positions already captured. In the deep penetration now proposed, they would have to march a long way. By placing those divisions, the 4th and 5th, closest to the start line, Monash shortened the distance by almost three miles. The 2nd and 3rd Divisions would leapfrog them to attack the Green Line and be leapfrogged in turn for the advance to the Red Line by the 4th and 5th, whose reserve battalions were to carry out a third leapfrog to the Blue Line. Leapfrogging within divisions had become commonplace but it was rarely practised between divisions. Monash was now ordering two leapfrogs by two divisions next to each other. He acknowledged the complexity but trusted 'the intelligence of the troops and the sympathetic, loyal and efficient co-operation' of commanders and staffs. Calling the plan 'John Monash's masterpiece', Bean wrote that 'the elaborate placing of the brigades and the timing of their starts so that each punctually took up its post in the intricate task, affords what will probably be the classical example for the launching of such operations'.[3]

At least twenty-four tanks supported each division. Moving up during the pause on the Green Line, a field artillery brigade, as well as an engineer and a machine-gun company, would support the advance of each infantry brigade to the Red Line. Thirty-six Mark V Star tanks, stretched Mark V's that could carry up to three infantry machine-gun teams, were laid on for the attack on the Blue Line and armoured cars tasked to cause havoc beyond. The extra punch and flexibility given by these groupings meant that the creeping barrage could be dispensed with for the later phases, which would take on the character of open warfare. Conversely, said Monash, the attack on the Green Line in the set-piece first phase reproduced 'the conditions of Hamel on a much larger scale'. The methods employed to preserve surprise at Hamel were again applied.

As the Canadians could not take over their assault frontage, then held by the French, without giving the game away, the 4th Division occupied it instead. Seeing the Australians extend their line, the Germans would hardly expect an attack. The 4th was told that the outgoing French divisions were needed on the Marne. It had just held an uproarious race meeting at Allonville, for which the two Australian fighter squadrons had flown in. Some of the pilots got nicely 'shickered', wrote Lieutenant Rule. One shed his plane's wings trying to fly through a hangar. The Canadians started assembling behind the Australians. Those who saw them were stunned. 'Canadians?' said Sergeant Downing. 'We thought they were at Arras.'[4]

Noting the change in the Australian line, the Germans raided on 4 August, taking five prisoners. They knew nothing of the coming attack. But the incident that most threatened security occurred across the Somme, where the 5th Division took two trenches and 128 prisoners near Morlancourt on 29 July. The Germans waited until they had brought up the 27th (Württemberg) Division, the Australians' foes at Bullecourt, before hitting back. III Corps relieved the 5th Division in the interim. Striking on 6 August, the Württembergers regained the ground lost and captured 282 men from the 18th and 58th Divisions. Some were in the know but the Germans learned nothing. Worried about his flank, Monash made 'such an outcry' that Rawlinson told Butler the offensive had already begun for III Corps. It was to regain immediately the ground lost.[5]

While III Corps's counterattacks on 7 August made little headway, the Diggers listened to an appeal from Monash for every one of them to carry on to 'the utmost of his power, for the sake of AUSTRALIA, the Empire and our cause' in the battle next day, 'which will live for ever in the history of our homeland'. On hearing this message, 'all were thrilled, morale was never so high', wrote Lieutenant Joynt. Hearts went into mouths at sunset when a flukey German shell lobbed amongst sixteen carrier tanks at Villers-Bretonneux. All but three were soon ablaze. Again the Germans suspected nothing. Fog rolling in lent a ghostly touch to the assembly. Lance-Corporal David Wilson of the 24th Battalion, part of the garrison holding the right of the Australian line, countered with an earthy touch. Overindulging on the rum ration he was doling out, Wilson spewed lustily just before the 24th made way for the assault brigades of the 2nd Division and went into reserve. The sights he saw going back impressed him despite his spinning head:

Guns were moving from all directions. Tanks were crawling about and one had to be careful he wasn't run down as it was terribly dark. Planes were flying low overhead to drown the noise of the tanks and the gun limbers moving about. There was men everywhere and one had to keep close to his next man in case he lost his company. I shall never forget it. The organization was wonderful.[6]

3.30 a.m. The fog was so dense that visibility had dropped to about twenty yards. Out of the blue a bombardment thumped the Australians and Canadians either side of the railway. It was covering a raid that hit a trench just vacated by the last of the advanced Australians screening the assembly. 4.15 a.m. All quiet again. 4.20 a.m. Fourth Army's 2000 guns spoke.

Downing thought the dawn had been flung skyward:

There was a titanic pandemonium . . . The lighter, more metallic notes of thousands of field guns were blended in one long-drawn chord. The hoarse and frantic rumble of the sixty-pounders, the long naval guns, the great howitzers, was like the rapid burring of a thousand drums. The light pieces were like trombones, for there were no individual sounds except the bark, bark, bark of an eighteen-pounder battery close behind us. And always, thrutter, thrutter, thrutter went the heavies.

White smoke curled over us and hid the flaming skies. There was a thrumming as of gigantic bumble-bees, and a low chug-chug-chug, as the ugly noses of the tanks poked through the fog above us. We hastily scattered from the path of one, and found ourselves almost beneath others. They went forward in a line, scarcely thirty yards between them. They were in scores, and their vibrations sounded through the fog from every side, like another layer of sound on the bellow of the guns. Then a rattling of machine-guns told us that the lads in front were at grips with the enemy.

The fog rather than the totally surprised Germans broke up the advance. At least one platoon held hands to stay together.[7]

Attacking next to the Canadians, the 7th Brigade struck the only intact wire met that day. As the tanks had not caught up, Second Lieutenant Alfred Gaby of the 28th Battalion found a gap, reached the strongpoint holding up the assault and walked along the parapet firing his revolver. Fifty Germans surrendered. Gaby was killed three days later, unaware that he had won the VC. With the arrival of the tanks, the Australians pulled ahead of the Canadians and bombed a post pinning them down. The 5th Brigade alongside moved as a gaggle of intermixed units. Lieutenant John Lane of the 18th Battalion described the tactics as 'someone telling anyone he met that there were some Germans down in some corner he had passed or where he had seen them; collecting a few men and going round and grabbing the Germans'. Further north, the 9th Brigade rooted them out of Accroche Wood. On the Somme flats outstretched hands could not be seen in the fog. The Germans could only fire blindly. Homing in on their shots, the Australians silenced them.[8]

The German guns were reached as the fog began to lift. No fewer than 504 of the 530 arrayed against the Fourth Army were identified before the attack. Four hundred and fifty heavy guns lavishly supplied with ammunition took them on. The German gunners were for the most part killed or driven off. Their guns were easily captured. 'This stunt is remarkable . . . for the lack of enemy shell fire', observed Gunner Charles Rea. By 7 a.m., the 2nd and 3rd Divisions were on the Green Line and digging in. Moving up for the next phase, the 4th and 5th Divisions passed columns of prisoners going back. Lieutenant John Barton of the 54th Battalion laughed when his platoon sergeant yelled 'Good day, Fritz', to an old German who was carrying one of his boots as he limped along. Without batting an eyelid, Fritz 'replied in perfect English, "I am going to England", and he seemed quite pleased about it'. Lance-Corporal Wilson thought that the only Germans unhappy at being captured were the officers.[9]

At 8 a.m. the sun broke through, revealing a scene that remained indelibly printed on the minds of the 50 000 Australians who beheld it. 'Everything was on the move forward, guns, tanks, ambulances and everything that was used in an offensive', wrote Wilson. 'No man's land of yesterday was a spot now that one could rest in peace and quiet'. Captain Daniel Aarons of the 16th Battalion saw 'our artillery galloping into action, unhitching the guns and the drivers galloping the horses away again . . . and almost within a few seconds the guns were in action'. From the heights behind the British line, Charles Montague looked across the Somme almost in disbelief at the tearing apart of the German line: 'The marvel seemed real, the road lay open and dry across the Red Sea . . . the object of all dream and desire seemed to have come'.[10]

At 8.20 a.m. the advance to the Red Line began, the tanks taking the place of the creeping barrage. No longer blinded by the fog, the German gunners further back started firing over open sights. Covered by an extemporised barrage from the accompanying artillery, the Diggers and the tanks headed towards them, the tanks forcing the gunners into cover while the infantry attacked. But the gunners fought well, crippling most of the forty tanks lost out of the 142 that started with the Australians.

Munching breakfast, the 15th Brigade pinched out Bayonvillers on the 5th Division's front. The 8th Brigade skirted around the north of the village, where two batteries blasted several tanks before they were captured. By 11 a.m. the Red Line had been reached. Both the 8th and 15th Brigades took off for the Blue Line without waiting for the tanks assigned to help. At 1.15 p.m., Monash signalled Rawlinson: 'Australian flag hoisted over Harbonnières at midday'.

On the 4th Division's front on the Somme flank, the 15th Battalion was stalled in Cérisy until the rest of the 4th Brigade crossed the lower Morcourt Valley behind the village and outflanked it. In the valley the Australians found stores, hutted officers' messes and canteens replete with cigars and liqueurs, sixty horses and hundreds of unresisting troops. The 12th Brigade had captured 500 Germans in the upper part of the valley. As it was too steep for the 12th's tanks to negotiate, they remained at the edge covering the infantry, which crossed in short rushes. The 45th Battalion had seized twenty-nine guns beforehand, each appropriately marked by a Digger following with a tin of white paint and a brush. Over the Somme, III Corps had failed to take the Chipilly Spur, as Monash expected. Its guns became 'the chief instrument of the enemy's resistance on the Australian front'. The German gunners complained that they had too many targets. They laid into the 4th Brigade as it re-formed on the Red Line. Sixty men were soon hit. Some of the batteries attached to the 4th caught up. Ferocious short-range artillery duels followed but the German guns could not be suppressed.

Abandoning the Mark V Star tanks that were supposed to take them, on account of the unbearable conditions inside, the 16th and 48th Battalions pressed on to the Blue Line. The few Mark Vs were disabled, leaving the Diggers to advance against heavy machine-gun fire. A bullet ripped the eyelet holes from one of Captain Aarons's leggings. 'I must say that the boys exercised considerable craft and commonsense in their movement', he said of his company's short rushes. Seeing Germans pouring out of Méricourt, the next village east, and into the old Amiens trenches, Aarons's men fired at them but also yelled '*Kamerad!*'. Over fifty surrendered. Though the 4th Division was now beyond the Chipilly Spur, its flank remained exposed to the feature. At Monash's direction, Sinclair-MacLagan deployed the 1st Brigade along the Somme facing it.[11]

Meanwhile the cavalry had passed through. Monash had been given the 1st Cavalry Brigade and a company of Whippets. They were to operate beyond the Blue Line. Crossing it north of Harbonnières, one cavalry column was fired on from three trains on the nearby railway. Two steamed off and smoke belched several times from a hump on the third. Just as this train started up, the cavalry engaged it and a British aeroplane bombed the loco. The 'hump' turned out to be an 11-inch railway gun used to shell Amiens. Arriving soon afterwards, the 31st Battalion captured it. German machine-guns eventually forced the cavalry's retirement. Its combination with the Whippets was a failure. Left behind in the early stages, the Whippets forged ahead whenever resistance was met, 'a continuous shuttle movement' ensuing. But the sixteen armoured cars with the Australians wreaked havoc, ranging over two miles out to shoot up headquarters, transport columns and billets in Vauvillers, Proyart, Framerville and Chuignolles. British aircraft did likewise. 'Aeroplanes were in the sky in hundreds', wrote Aarons, who counted over seventy at one point. They dropped ammunition and bombed and strafed whenever the opportunity arose.[12]

Except for the extreme flanks, the Australian Corps was on the Blue Line by 1.15 p.m. For the loss of 2000 men, it had taken 7295 prisoners, 173 guns and enough engineering material to last it for the rest of the war. Major George Cook, Sir Joseph's son, told his father: 'Monash seems to be making good. I have seen nothing to equal it. It puts fresh heart into one to see evidence of the master hand'. Calling the flawless execution of the double leapfrogs a remarkable demonstration of the 'discipline and high organization of the Australian Corps', Rawlinson waxed lyrical: 'The Canadians have done splendidly and the Aussies even better'. The Canadians took 6000 prisoners and about the same number of guns as the Australians. Montague heard the Aussies say that night: 'The Canadians were all right, of course, but the Tommies! Well, we might have known!' It was an obvious dig at III Corps. The French were also successful, taking 3500 prisoners.[13]

For fifteen miles south of the Somme, the German line had been ripped open. 'August 8th was the black day of the German Army', wrote Ludendorff. '[It] put the decline of its fighting power beyond all doubt'. But the German reaction was swift. By early afternoon six divisions had been ordered to the area instead of the five GHQ expected. Next day Crown Prince Rupprecht believed he was well placed to halt the advance. His confidence was justified. If the attack had been a model of co-ordination and organisation, the follow-up was anything but.[14]

On 26 July Foch and Haig had agreed that the advance should go five miles after the first day to a line drawn between Chaulnes and Roye, through both of which ran a railway supplying the Germans facing the French. During the following week, the Germans withdrew on the Marne. Foch thought they were crumbling. He urged a deeper penetration. Haig told Rawlinson to advance another fifteen miles to Ham. Extending the penetration from seven to twenty-seven miles, his decision transformed the attack into an unlimited offensive. Rawlinson always favoured limited offensives. Reviewing Rawlinson's orders, Haig felt that the impetus would cease at the old Amiens Outer Line. Haig impressed the more distant objectives on him on 5 August. Next day Rawlinson informed General Currie that the exploitation would be made on his front. Most of the cavalry was deployed there for the purpose. The line south of Chaulnes lay ahead of Currie's men, whose divisions fielded at least 12 000 bayonets each, as opposed to 7000 in each Australian formation. They had also seen much less recent fighting. The Australians would advance their right flank in conformity.

The 1st Australian Division was to drive for Lihons, four miles distant, with the 5th initially, and then the 2nd, on its left. 'In order to minimise casualties', Rawlinson decreed that 'considerable artillery' and 'a strong body of tanks' would support the Australian advance. But most of the artillery was still moving forward and only 145 tanks were fit for action in the Fourth Army. The 1st Division received fourteen, the 2nd and 5th seventeen between them. Rawlinson left the start time to Currie, even though the responsibility was his, as formations other than the Canadians were involved. Montgomery said that everyone at Fourth Army Headquarters was 'so busy congratulating everyone else' that things slipped. He blundered too, countermanding the relief of a Canadian division even though it was under way. The Canadians had to draft fresh orders. They were not completed until 1 a.m. Monash could only tell his division commanders to confer with Currie's to save time. Orders were still being disseminated in the 1st Division two hours before the attack was due to begin at 10 a.m. It had no chance of being ready.[15]

The 15th Brigade held the line next to the Canadians. They asked Brigadier-General Elliott for help. With Hobbs's approval, he agreed. The 58th and 60th Battalions were simply told to advance until the 1st Division showed up. Attacking without a barrage but with a single tank lent by the Canadians, both battalions were pinned down by withering fire just beyond Harbonnières. Helped by the tank, part of the 60th and some Canadians outflanked the southern end of the strongpoint. The 58th worked around the northern end. When the Germans began to break, the Australians charged. They captured 300 men and twenty-one machine guns. The Canadians acknowledged their 'very great debt' to Elliott's men. Up with the action, Elliott had been giving directions to the tank commander when a bullet grazed his backside. He continued to supervise proceedings with his trousers around his ankles while medics attended to him. It was one of the sights of the war, said Lieutenant-Colonel John Scanlan of the 59th Battalion. Attacking Vauvillers next to the 15th Brigade, the 8th Brigade lost four of its tanks to a single anti-tank gun before surrounding the village and taking 150 prisoners.

At 1.45 p.m., when the 1st Division finally caught up, the first stage of its advance had already been made by the 15th Brigade. Lihons lay two miles ahead in the lee of a bare, gentle hill that gave its defenders terrific fields of fire. German field batteries quickly disabled most of the tanks, leaving the 2nd Brigade with an assault reminiscent of its attack at Krithia in May 1915. Attacking in extended line then, it did so in short rushes now. On the way the 8th Battalion seized the massive timber and railway supply dumps near Rosières. Reaching the foot of Lihons hill, the 7th Battalion charged the Germans blocking its path. Grinding towards the crest, the Australians captured three field guns. The 7th's flank had been open for the entire attack.

The 2nd Division should have been alongside. Monash had directed it to attack 'in conjunction with the 1st'. Rosenthal and Glasgow were to co-ordinate the details between them. Monash should have done it. Wires got crossed. The 2nd Division's planning conferences did not conclude until 1.30 p.m. Its advance did not begin until three hours later. Most of its tanks were knocked out in taking Framerville, a few miles north of Lihons. Another ill-coordinated advance left the Canadians and the cavalry well short of Roye. More seat-of-the-pants planning characterised the operations on 10 and 11 August, which resulted in the capture of Lihons and nearby Rainecourt. By then the Fourth Army had only thirty-eight tanks left. Rawlinson primarily, but also Currie, Monash and their divisional generals, had mishandled the transition from a limited-objective attack to open warfare with an unlimited advance. They underestimated the time needed to disseminate orders and the communication difficulties caused by the absence of the elaborate telephone networks to which they had become used in static warfare. The three days after 8 August furnished 'a classic example of how not to follow up a great attack'. They cost the 1st Australian Division over 1500 men. Among the dead was Lieutenant Murray Aitken, the original Anzac who had commented on discipline in 1914.[16]

On the Somme flank satisfaction replaced frustration. Fed up with the harassment from the Chipilly Spur, Monash finally persuaded Rawlinson on 9 August to give him responsibility for the northern bank of the river. A six-man patrol under Quartermaster-Sergeant Jack Hayes of the 1st Battalion crossed and met a company of the 2/10th Londons from the 58th Division. Stalled half a mile from Chipilly, the Londons advised Hayes not to go on. The Australians rushed the village. It was deserted. Working up the reverse side of the spur, Hayes's men took several German posts in rear, capturing seventy Württembergers. They handed them over to the Londons following. The German artillery had already withdrawn. Early on 10 August, the 13th Brigade crossed the Somme and the 3rd Division relieved the rest of the 4th on the southern bank. Suffering from strain and insomnia, Butler was temporarily replaced by Godley as commander of III Corps.

Seeing that the Somme now followed a series of U-shaped bends, of which the Chipilly Spur was the first, Monash decided to take the next two that night by 'a species of investment'. At 9.30 p.m. the 13th Brigade was to advance along the Bray–Corbie Road north of the river and punch through the German line to seal off the Etinehem Spur. At the same time, the 10th Brigade would swing through Proyart from the Roman Road to cordon off the Méricourt Spur south of the river. A few tanks were to accompany each column, mainly in the hope of panicking the Germans, who would hear but not see them. Monash instructed the two brigadiers directly, to avoid misunderstandings. 'The German is in a condition of great confusion', he said. 'We only have to hit him without warning and roll him up.' Bean called the plan 'ingenious'. It was certainly bold.

The 13th Brigade's advance sent the Germans packing to Bray at the far end of the Etinehem Spur. The 10th Brigade was sent packing by the Germans. As soon as the column started, a German aircraft skimmed along it dropping bombs. The Germans on the ground let fly a tempest of machine-gun and armour-piercing fire.

High-explosive and gas shells rained down. Private Sindrey looked to his maker:

As we lay there trying to find cover when there was none, the bullets were knocking sparks out of the road beside our heads, whistling between us and missing us by inches . . . It seemed impossible that any of us could live through it, and I am convinced that it was God Himself that saved me. We struggled on for some distance along the road, but it was impossible to go on. The tanks were the first to turn it up, and when they started to come back we left the road and dug ourselves in.

Progress was out of the question. The 37th Battalion in the lead lost its commander, Lieutenant-Colonel Ernest Knox-Knight, and over 100 others were killed. Outflanked by the 13th Brigade's advance north of the Somme, and by the capture of Lihons in the south, the Germans evacuated Proyart on 11 August.[17]

The knock confirmed that opposition on the main front south of the Somme was increasing. Moreover, the advance was at the edge of the French sector of the 1916 battlefield, a wilderness of old trenches and entanglements that would slow it down, just as it had the Germans in March. Currie impressed the point on Haig on 10 August. So did Monash when Haig visited him next day. Haig wanted to shift the offensive north. Foch agreed. The Third Army would advance on Bapaume, with the Fourth Army staying put until it could mount another set-piece attack. Haig outlined the plan to General Byng, who joined him at Bertangles. When Rawlinson heard that Haig was accompanying Monash to a conference with his divisional generals at Villers-Bretonneux, he arranged a meeting there with Currie and the other corps commanders. Haig thanked the Australian generals, saying 'You do not know what the Australians and Canadians have done for the British Empire in these days'. Tears rolled down his cheeks. Sir Henry Wilson, Foch and Clemenceau turned up. It was decided that the Fourth Army, with the Canadians leading, would make 'a cut and dried attack' on the Chaulnes–Roye line with the French on 14 or 15 August. The King knighted Monash on the steps of Bertangles on 12 August.[18]

'Currie not anxious to attack', Rawlinson noted on 13 August. The Canadians faced difficult terrain. Aerial photographs showed that they were up against heavy wire entanglements too. Currie recommended the return of the Canadian Corps to its familiar stamping ground at Arras. As the shrewd commander of a highly distinguished Dominion force, Currie, like Monash, could not be ignored. Uncomfortable with the continuation of the battle himself, Rawlinson urged Haig next day to postpone the renewal of the Fourth Army's attack. Haig agreed. Elated by the French progress alongside it, Foch was livid. He told Haig to stick to the original plan. Haig told Foch that he was responsible for the safety of the British Army. Foch backed down. Byng's offensive would start on 21 August. III Corps and the 3rd Australian Division north of the Somme were to carry forward its right flank by advancing on the line Albert–Bray next day. The rest of the Australian Corps would attack on 23 August. On leaving for Arras, Currie told Monash: 'there are no troops who have given us as loyal and effective support as the Australians, and I am sure I speak for all Canadians when I say that we would like to finish the war fighting alongside you'.[19]

The lull permitted a much-needed rest. Monash complained about the impossibility of relief while the Corps had to hold a line nine miles long. Rawlinson temporarily reinforced him with the British 17th and then the 32nd Divisions. Every Australian division got a brief respite between 12 and 23 August. Those in the line carried on peaceful penetration. North of the Somme, the American 131st Regiment, whose use Pershing had permitted in the emergency on Chipilly Spur on 8 August, joined the 13th Brigade in a Liaison Force that gave Monash another division in all but name. It was disbanded when the 3rd Division took over its line on 20 August. Two days later the 1st and 4th Canadian Divisions came under

Monash's command before going back to Arras, briefly expanding the Corps to eight divisions. Monash constantly controlled more troops and far more important operations than Birdwood did as an army commander.[20]

Though the RE8s of No. 3 Squadron worked continuously with the Corps, the two Australian scout squadrons were above them at this juncture as well. No. 2 Squadron had earlier been one of the first selected for 'circus' work, in which crack squadrons were grouped together for offensive flying operations. No. 4 became one of the highest-scoring Sopwith Camel squadrons. For a time it specialised in balloon-busting, in which Captain Cobby led the way. In June 1918 both squadrons joined the 80th Wing of the Royal Air Force, into which the Royal Flying Corps and the Royal Naval Air Service were combined at the start of April. They often flew together as a circus. After supporting the Fourth Army, the two squadrons returned to their base at Reclinghem in Flanders. They were at the heart of attacks on the German airfields at Haubordin and Lomme on 16 and 17 August, which involved over sixty aircraft from the 80th Wing and reportedly destroyed fifty-four German machines.[21]

Crossing the northern edge of the old Somme battlefield, Byng's offensive started well, taking 2000 prisoners. On 22 August, III Corps regained Albert and the 3rd Australian Division seized Happy Valley above Bray. The heavily defended village could now be captured through envelopment. But a German counterattack drove the 47th Division next to the Australians back almost to its start line, leaving their flank exposed. Gellibrand's men held on but the attack on Bray had to be postponed. Next day the 1st Australian Division advanced almost two miles to secure the Chuignes Valley, south of the river.

The 1st Brigade swept through patchy resistance on the Somme flank to Chuignolles. Astride the Roman Road, the 2nd Brigade had a harder time. Heard as they moved up, half its tanks were lost to a counter-barrage. The remainder greatly helped the Diggers.

One silenced twenty machine-guns along the rim of strongly held St Martin's Wood, which the Diggers then had to clear, as the tanks could not keep up in it. A Digger started playing a piano he found in an abandoned hut. He was still tickling the ivories when terrific fire from Plateau Wood 500 yards further on halted the 6th Battalion. Following with the 8th Battalion, Lieutenant Joynt took two platoons to outflank the wood. He led four Diggers along a communication trench towards it. No sooner had they bombed a dugout than twenty Germans appeared behind them. The leader dropped his rifle when Joynt threatened him with a revolver. The rest did likewise. Then the survivors from the dugout emerged with their hands raised. One seemed about to cry. Lieutenant Les McGinn 'took three or four very slow menacing strides towards the cringing Hun, and bringing his face close to him, said "BOO!" The Hun collapsed on his knees'. The men offered Joynt a choice of ratted watches. He selected one. The situation was 'perfectly absurd', Joynt wrote.

> Twenty or more Huns all standing with their hands held high, with our Diggers 'ratting' them and McGinn and myself looking on with one Hun still on his knees. The reaction was so great that I started to laugh – one minute or second ago all was lost, at best we were prisoners or more likely dead men, and now our lives were safe and we were triumphant. I couldn't stop laughing, then McGinn joined in and we just couldn't stop. I suppose it was a sort of hysteria after the strain we had been through. We leaned against the wall of the trench and laughed and laughed – it was some time before we could stop.

Two Diggers took the prisoners back. The men Joynt had left came up the trench for the attack. The Germans in the wood broke. The Australians captured 100 without loss. Joynt received the VC.

Lieutenant Lawrence McCarthy of the 16th Battalion won another. The 16th protected the right flank of the 32nd Division, which advanced alongside the 1st Division to take Herleville. When the 32nd's right was held up, the 16th bombed towards it. Bombs ran out at a trench block. Followed by Sergeant Fred Robbins, McCarthy leapt the block, shot a sentry and silenced a machine-gun blazing away at the main attack. Using German bombs, he killed an officer trying to rally his men and, with Robbins, bombed the trench sap into which they fled. Forty Germans surrendered just as two British soldiers arrived. Fifteen Germans were dead. McCarthy had captured 700 yards of trench. 'I have never heard of anything so remarkable', wrote Captain Aarons, whose company was fighting with his. Bean called it perhaps the most effective individual action in the AIF next to Jacka's counterattack at Pozières.

The day belonged to the Australians. At a cost of 1000 casualties, the 1st Division took one-quarter of the 8000 prisoners captured by the Third and Fourth Armies. Though disabled by the Germans, a 14-inch naval gun, the largest that fired on Amiens, also fell into its hands. At 1 a.m. on 24 August, the 10th Brigade took Bray. Advances either side distracted the garrison from the main assault, which entered the village at three points and quickly cleared it. The Third Army was within two miles of Bapaume, which the New Zealanders had a tough time trying to envelop.[22]

Reviewing the effect on the Germans of the recent operations, Haig declared that 'Risks which a month ago would have been criminal to incur ought now to be incurred as a matter of duty'. The Third Army continued the main thrust, with the First Army joining it on 26 August to extend the attack northwards over the Scarpe River past Arras. Advancing astride the Somme, the Fourth Army was to guard the right of the Third. Rawlinson told Monash on 24 August to 'keep touch' with the enemy: 'no opportunity will be missed of making ground towards Péronne'. But Haig denied Rawlinson reinforcements because his was the subsidiary offensive. On 25 August Rawlinson announced that the Fourth Army would 'mark time and await events elsewhere'.[23]

Monash disagreed. Prisoners confirmed numerous indications that the Germans were withdrawing to the main Somme bend. Some said they were retiring to the Hindenburg Line ten miles east of it. The Australian line was about to be shortened with the French extending north to Lihons, allowing the 4th Division to be rested. Believing that the Australian 'reserve of striking power' was being underestimated at a time when the Germans were on the run, Monash embarked on a private war. He circumvented Rawlinson by falling back on his earlier directive to 'keep touch'. Through aggressive patrolling, Monash instructed on 26 August, 'advantage will be taken of any opportunity to seize the enemy's positions and to advance our line'. By 28 August, the 3rd Division had reached Cléry after capturing Suzanne, Vaux and Curlu. On the southern bank, the 2nd, 5th and 32nd British Divisions were nearing the Somme bend.[24]

At Cléry, the Somme abruptly abandons its northerly direction to follow a westerly course after making a left-angled turn past Péronne. This section of the river was canalised but unfordable marshes extended 1000 yards from the canal. Overlooking the river and the main bridge into the town was Mont St Quentin, 300 feet high. A good division, the 2nd Guard, defended it. The hill also dominated Cléry, lying at the foot of the Bouchavesnes Spur and connected by a footbridge to Omniécourt on the opposite bank. Vauban's ramparts rose sixty feet to enclose Péronne. From the line reached on 28 August, Monash knew that the Germans would have to withdraw over the Somme next day. That afternoon he ordered a frontal assault on the river line, hoping to catch them before their retirement was complete. The 2nd Division was to secure the bridge, the 5th and the 32nd were to seize crossings further south. But every crossing was under torrential fire. Monash decided to turn the line of the Somme from the north. At 5 p.m. on 29 August, he ordered the divisions on the southern bank to sidestep left, which brought the 2nd Division to Omniécourt. Crossing there once the 3rd Division had taken Cléry and Bouchavesnes, it was to pass behind the 3rd and attack Mont St Quentin at 5 a.m. next morning. The 5th Division following would go through to capture Péronne.

After marching all night, the 5th Brigade reached Omniécourt at 4 a.m. on 30 August. The crossing was unapproachable because the 3rd Division had not yet reached Cléry. It was full of Germans. The 5th made for another crossing at Feuillères, two miles west. Hopes of launching the attack at 5 a.m. had gone. Monash postponed it twenty-four hours, giving the 9th and 10th Brigades more time to secure Cléry and Bouchavesnes. They were exhausted. Closing up on Cléry, the 38th Battalion was dazed after almost ninety hours of continuous action. Fighting through the village, a company from the 40th Battalion took fifty-nine prisoners, more than its own strength. Finally completing its circuitous crossing, the 5th Brigade reached Cléry during the afternoon, whereupon the 20th Battalion cleared the knoll above it from which the attack on the Mont was to begin next morning. 'So you think you're going to take Mont St Quentin with three battalions! What presumption! However, I don't think I ought to stop you! So, go ahead and try – and I wish you good luck!', a disbelieving Rawlinson told Monash.

Five field and four heavy artillery brigades supported the attack, a powerful concentration. As there was no time to arrange a creeping barrage, they engaged selected localities well ahead of the infantry. The 5th Brigade was down to 1340 all ranks, an average of 330 per battalion. Assaulting at 5 a.m. on 31 August, the 17th and 20th Battalions yelled their heads off to convince the Guards they were much stronger. The Germans were dumbfounded as the Australians, finding gaps in the wire, tore through. Seven hundred were captured when the 20th Battalion on the left cleared Feuillaucourt and the 17th on the right moved through Halle halfway to Péronne. 'It all happened like lightning, and before we had fired a shot we were taken unaware', the Guards said. The skilful co-operation of rifle grenadiers and Lewis gunners was particularly noticeable. Now able to use the Omniécourt bridge, the 19th Battalion arrived in support. The Guards reserve counterattacked. Lieutenant William Guard of the 20th Battalion shot two who got close. Shrapnel was bursting ten feet over his men:

> A man on my right, firing from a kneeling position, fell forward with a shell splinter piercing his steel helmet. Enfilading and rear fire from our left were playing havoc and I ordered the men about me to retire to a line of trenches some 200 yards to the rear.

Clinging to a line just below the crest, the 5th Brigade repulsed five counter-attacks during the day. Monash ordered the 3rd Division to take the rest of the Bouchavesnes Spur in order to secure the left flank on the Mont. 'Casualties no longer matter', he told General Gellibrand.

The 6th Brigade, 1334 strong, attacked the summit of the Mont at 6 a.m. on 1 September. Lance-Corporal Wilson saw the Guards standing to shoot at the Australians: 'I lay the gun on one whom I thought was an officer and gave him a burst and he burst into flames and fell back. I must have hit bombs he was carrying or his ammunition'. This time the Guards fought to the end and the Australians needed two attempts to gain the summit. The aid post of Major Donald Coutts resembled a charnel-house. 'We were kept going continuously all night. About 10.30 p.m. two men were brought in and I had to amputate one man's arm at the shoulder, and the other man's leg through the right thigh – I had to use a razor for this.'

Attacking Péronne, in and around which were parts of three German divisions, the 14th Brigade also had great difficulty crossing the Somme. Taking ten hours to complete an approach that should have taken three, it finally assembled near Cléry at 8 p.m. on 31 August. Advancing below the 6th Brigade next morning, it met ferocious fire from trenches protected by barbed wire. Lewis gunners stood to shoot over men ripping up the pickets. The Germans fled. On the left, the 53rd Battalion turned an abandoned field gun onto them before it was stopped at Anvil Wood by a fusillade from the town. The 54th, alongside it, enjoyed more success, reaching the moat on the river side of the town. Ignoring his mates' yell, 'Mack, you are a dead man', Lieutenant Don McArthur scouted a trench near a footbridge. Mortally hit, he gasped: 'I am happy to die, the war is now won and I have lived to see it and like Nelson I can say thank God I have done my duty'. Further west, Corporal Arthur Hall noticed that the ramparts seemed empty. Much of the 54th entered Péronne there. Taking five men, Hall pressed beyond the town centre, capturing Germans as he went. From the last house on the far side, he saw twenty lining the ramparts. 'After stationing a man at each door or window that afforded a good view', he said, 'I went to the corner of the building and gave the order to fire. The Germans immediately surrendered'. Machine-gun fire forced Hall back and the Germans retained this part of the town. In all, his tiny band had taken seventy prisoners. He won the VC.

Hustling his brigade over the Somme to attack Flamicourt, across the moat to the south of Péronne, Elliott tumbled into the river. 'Pompey's fallen in the Somme', clogged the 5th Division's telephone lines. Elliott commanded trouserless while his pants dried out. Despite the inspiring sight, his men could make no progress. Monash ordered a renewed assault for the next day. General Hobbs protested that the 5th Division was exhausted. Monash 'was compelled to harden my heart and to insist that it was imperative to recognise a great opportunity and to seize it unflinchingly'. The 15th Brigade cleared the rest of Péronne. With the 7th advancing well beyond the Mont, nothing more could be done until III Corps caught up. At a cost of 3000 casualties, the Australians had hammered five divisions and taken 2600 prisoners in evicting the Germans from one of their key bastions in France.[25]

'Within Australian experience of the Western Front', wrote Bean of the battle, 'it was the only important fight in which quick, free manoeuvre played a decisive part. It furnishes a complete answer to the comment that Monash was merely a composer of set-pieces'. The tactics were left 'largely to divisional, brigade, battalion and even platoon commanders; they were sometimes brilliant and sometimes faulty'. But Monash himself admitted that the outcome was due 'first and chiefly to the wonderful gallantry' of tired soldiers in understrength units who repeatedly attacked strong positions without tanks and, sometimes, without the usual artillery support. Rawlinson was astounded, reportedly telling Monash that it was 'the finest single feat of the war'. Haig, too, was amazed. Some contend that the effort was wasted because Ludendorff intended to withdraw anyway to the Hindenburg Line. But he also wanted to winter in an intermediate line to the west, while its defences were thoroughly prepared. On 2 September the Canadian Corps broke through the Drocourt–Quéant Switch Line near Bullecourt. With the Somme line lost to the Australians the same day, he had no choice but to retire to the Hindenburg Line forthwith. It faced the entire length of the Fourth Army's front.[26]

On 5 September the pursuit began, with each brigade screened by a squadron of light horse as it advanced. The old British reserve line, overrun during the March offensive, was taken by peaceful penetration on 11 September but Monash foreshadowed that the front and outpost lines would have to be taken by a set-piece attack. Rawlinson concurred. The Hindenburg Outpost Line was included in the objectives. It gave excellent observation over the Hindenburg Line and the Reserve or Le Catelet Line a mile beyond. Rawlinson and Byng advocated striking them before German morale recovered sufficiently to make the cost prohibitive. The War Cabinet was already worried about the cost. Attacking the Outpost Line would test the feasibility of assaulting the main system. Haig told Rawlinson to do it as soon as possible. It was fixed for 18 September.

With IX Corps replacing the 32nd Division in the southern part of the line held by the Australians, Monash's corps now comprised only the five Australian divisions. The 4th Division on the right would strike towards Le Vergieur next to IX Corps, while the 1st Division on the left advanced towards Hargicourt alongside III Corps. By this time, said Monash, 'the methods of the Corps were becoming stereotyped . . . we all began to understand each other so well that what I had to say could be taken for granted'. As only eight tanks were available, he ordered the building of dummy tanks, which would be placed where the Germans could see them. The attack began in dense mist but the Australians were now used to keeping direction in such conditions. By 10.30 a.m., the 1st Division had taken Hargicourt and was on the Hindenburg Outpost Line.

The 4th Division took Le Vergieur but was stopped 500 yards short of the Outpost Line. General Sinclair-MacLagan ordered artillery brought up to lay down a creeping barrage for another attack at 11 p.m. Lieutenant Rule thought the fire 'very tame'. In pelting rain, the 14th Battalion went around to the trenches captured by the 1st Division and bombed southwards to meet the 46th Battalion. Tracers flicked around their heads. 'Now's your time, rush them', yelled the Lewis gunners. Screaming like lunatics, Rule's men did. The Germans fled and the two battalions met. On either side the British had been unable to reach the Outpost Line, though the flanking division in IX Corps said that it had. Joining a small patrol that proved otherwise, Private James Woods of the 48th Battalion rushed a post that held six machine-guns and fought off a counterattack. 'You will I suppose be pleased to hear that I might get some decoration out of it', Woods wrote to his sister. He got the VC. For the loss of 1360 men, the two Australian divisions took 4300 prisoners and seventy-six guns, well over a third of all the captures by the Third and Fourth Armies that day. German officer captives said their men would not now face the Australians.[27]

Butler was back in command of III Corps. After it had spent two days trying to reach the Outpost Line, he asked Monash to assist by taking over the southern 500 yards of III Corps's line. Monash agreed. Knowing the ground, the 1st Brigade got the job. It was just being relieved. On receiving the order, 119 men from the 1st Battalion went rearwards in protest at being called upon to make good British failures as well as having to fight on their own front. All but one were convicted of desertion, given up to ten years' imprisonment on Dartmoor and pardoned after the Armistice. The incident reflected the fatigue of the men. It had been evident before the Outpost Line attack, which was the last action fought by the 1st and 4th Divisions in the war. 'We were thoroughly worn out and discontented all round', wrote Lance-Corporal Eric Russell of the 58th Battalion, then down to 170 men. Private John Nixon-Smith in the 31st thought it was 'time they gave us a *rest*'.

Monash himself was tired. Blamey observed that he had become very thin and the skin hung loosely on his face. He rode in his car for long periods in silence. But his attitude was moulded by the obvious decline of the British Army, which, he pointed out on visits to the brigades, was no less overworked than the Australians, and by the obvious demoralisation of the Germans, whom he wanted to hit as hard and as often as he could. Yet only the Australians and Canadians were able to win constantly, so it was inevitable that 'they should be called upon to yield up the last particle of effort of which they were capable'. Notwithstanding their longing for a rest, many Diggers agreed. As Corporal Robert Campbell of the 55th Battalion maintained:

> All this hard fighting is necessary. There is only one way of finishing this war and that is by force of arms. If they make peace by negotiations . . . the Hun will make war again in a few years' time . . . To prevent anything like that ever happening, we *must* win *this* war . . . and the only way to win is on the battlefield.

Monash rotated the divisions frequently. Mechanical resources permitted attacks with inferior numbers: 'I welcome any pretext to take the fewest possible . . . into action', he said. 'So long as [battalions] have thirty Lewis guns it doesn't very much matter what else they have'. When attacking, they now headed directly for points of resistance, ignoring the interval between them. But Prime Minister Hughes feared that if the Australian Corps declined, Australia's voice at any peace conference would decline too. In London before the 8 August battle he had sought the power of veto over its future use. He was ignored. With the Australians playing such a prominent part in that success, Hughes stayed his hand until mid-September. He allegedly told Monash then that his job depended on the Corps being rested by mid-October.[28]

More troubling for Monash was Hughes's announcement on 12 September that 800 original Anzacs were to be sent to Australia immediately for two months' furlough. Together with the losses in the fight for the Outpost Line, it was the final factor necessitating the disbandment of more battalions. The War Office had been concerned about the numerical weakness of the Australian battalions in June, when only eleven of the fifty-seven were at the establishment strength of 900. As numbers dwindled further, it insisted in late August on the reduction of the Australian brigades from four battalions to three, as in the British Army. Three had already been reduced. Although the four original brigades were exempted, a battalion in each of the other eight was ordered to disband on 23 September. Elliott's influence persuaded the 60th to break up but the other battalions refused, though their officers heeded the decision. Taking their lead from the 37th, they 'went on strike', electing their own leaders and asking to go into the next battle in their old units. Monash deferred action for another fortnight, when the battle would be over. Starved of reinforcements, they would have to disband voluntarily.

Reassured by the relatively easy Australian success against the Outpost Line, Haig directed the Fourth Army to attack the main Hindenburg Line. Planned for 29 September, the operation would be the principal British stroke in the series of hammer blows by which Foch planned to conquer territory held by the Germans since the beginning of the war, as distinct from ground they had captured in their offensives between March and July. Three offensives were to precede it. Having eliminated the St Mihiel salient in mid-September, the American First Army would join the French Fourth Army to thrust between Rheims and the Meuse, 100 miles south of the Australians, on 26 September. Next day, the British First and Third Armies, followed by the French First Army, were to strike at Cambrai, with the British, French and Belgians in Flanders attacking towards Ghent, seventy miles north of the Australians, on 28 September. The salients created would be so acute that the Germans would have to retire between them and thus along the front as a whole.

The Australian Corps would have the main role in the Hindenburg Line assault. On its front, the St Quentin Canal, on which the defence rested, ran through a tunnel that began at Bellicourt and emerged 6000 yards north near Gouy. The Germans could counter-attack from it through concealed passages and airshafts. Above them, up to six belts of wire girded several lines of trenches and pillboxes that protruded 1200 yards westwards to enclose the village of Bony. Gillemont and Quennemont Farms were strongpoints in the Hindenburg Outpost Line 1500 yards further west that should have been captured by III Corps. As the 1st and 4th Divisions were now resting, Monash had only three divisions to tackle these formidable positions, which were held by five German ones. Rawlinson offered him the 27th and 30th Divisions from the American II Corps, which was in GHQ reserve and now available for any task. He readily agreed. Each was fresh, three times stronger than an Australian division and, though inexperienced, dead keen, as those who fought at Hamel had shown. Attacking across the tunnel, they were to capture the Hindenburg and Le Catelet Lines. The Australian divisions following would assault the third and last part of the Hindenburg system, the Beaurevoir Line, two and a half miles beyond. Tanks would support each division and the four-day bombardment would include the first British use of mustard gas.

Monash knew he was asking a lot of the Americans. He figured that the Germans opposing them, badly shaken from recent battles, would be further jolted by the bombardment. Moreover, the American part was still simpler than the long open-warfare advance without a creeping barrage to the Beaurevoir Line that fell to the Australians. In IV Corps too, the experienced New Zealanders were invariably used for exploitation rather than the set-piece phases. To help the Americans, a specially formed Australian Mission advised them down to battalion level. But Monash soon had cause for worry. Despite repeated assaults, III Corps was still 1000 yards from the Outpost Line. Monash had made it the start line for the attack on the Hindenburg Line. He now wanted to pull the start line back. Rawlinson insisted on the 27th Division taking the ground on 27 September. The 106th Regiment tried. Lieutenant Rule explained what happened:

> All our officers told the same story about how the Americans attacked. If a machine-gun was hundreds of yards away, they'd go straight at it, and in nine cases out of ten get wiped out. You don't catch our lads doing this now, though they used to do it on the Peninsula.

Some Americans made the Outpost Line but many others were scattered in front of it, which precluded the option of starting the creeping barrage for the coming attack from the 27th's present position. On 28 September Monash told Haig he was in 'a state of despair'.[29]

Both American divisions went over at 5.55 a.m. next day. Thinking an attack imminent, the Germans had moved their artillery during the night. It escaped the British counter-battery fire and thumped them. On the left, many of the tanks with the 27th Division ran into a forgotten British minefield or were knocked out by anti-tank guns. Unprotected by a creeping barrage, the assault broke down before the Outpost Line, as it had two days earlier. The result for the Australians, said Lieutenant Arthur Fullard, was 'Fritz firing wildly through smoke with [artillery] and machine-guns in all directions . . . why we were not all wiped out, goodness knows'.

The Australians had moved up in great spirits but found themselves being whipped from Gillemont and Quennemont Farms, which the Americans should have taken. Though under strict orders not to become enmeshed with the Americans, the situation seemed so dangerous that the 10th and 11th Brigades began launching local assaults without artillery or tank support to gain breathing space. 'The Yanks were heartily cursed', said Private Shapcott. 'The advance was very slow and difficult – progress was made by yards, and hand-to-hand fighting was encountered.' 'Americans are still wandering about everywhere', said Lieutenant McInnis a day later. 'No-one can direct them to their HQ!' Lieutenant Barton encountered several parties all asking the same things: '"Have you got any water" and "Have you seen our Lieutenant?"'

Aerial reports received at Australian Corps headquarters suggested that the 27th Division was doing well. Prisoners claimed that the Hindenburg Line had been reached. Disturbed by the lack of reliable information, General Gellibrand went forward at 9.50 a.m. and saw the Americans pinned down, with the 3rd Division held up behind them. Monash maintained that the Americans had reached their objective. 'We have had the report absolutely confirmed from a number of places', Blamey insisted. Only a few German pockets must be holding up Gellibrand's men. He was ordered to attack at 3 p.m., without artillery support on account of the Americans ahead. Advancing a few hundred yards, the 10th and 11th Brigades took Gillemont Farm but against such heavy fire that nothing more could be attempted in daylight. Private Shapcott gazed at the Hindenburg Line wire: 'There were rows and rows of it, as thick as it could possibly be. It had not been broken to any great extent by either the barrage or the Yanks'. But the door to the Hindenburg Line had already been opened.

Able to attack from the Outpost Line with a creeping barrage, the 30th Division did not have the problems of the 27th, though its left was halted by enfilade fire from Quennemont Farm until the 3rd Division took it. With the tanks crushing the wire, the rest got to the tunnel, took the entrance at Bellicourt and reached Nauroy in the Le Catelet Line. Their advance was helped by the 46th Division from IX Corps alongside, which crossed the canal 'on rafts, life-jackets from Channel packets and anything else that would float' and captured intact the Riqueval bridge in a great feat of arms. Moving behind the 30th, the 5th Australian Division struck posts that the Americans had missed in the fog. Lieutenant-Colonel Scanlan personally directed a tank in crushing one that held up the 59th Battalion. He was leading his men through the first belt of wire when his adjutant screamed at him. Scanlan's dive into the barbs saved his life:

> 30 yards from us was a Fritz strong post. A Fritz had stood upon his parapet and taken aim but I fell before he pressed the trigger. There I was acting as a scout for my Battalion. I left a Lewis Gun team to clean up those Huns and directed the companies still on [and] came upon a sight which, in spite of the seriousness of the situation, made me laugh. A big Digger wearing an American raincoat was holding up a dozen prisoners at bayonet point, and making the unhappy devils dance about . . . I have never seen men so cowed and frightened as these Huns; they were crying for pardon, and dancing Highland flings all about this grinning Digger.

The 5th Division linked up with the Americans in Nauroy and the 46th Division next to it.

For much of the day, Gellibrand expected his reserve to be swung northwards through this penetration. But the order was not given until after Monash had conferred with Rawlinson late in the afternoon. Next morning, the reserve brigades of the 3rd and 5th Divisions were to attack along the Hindenburg Line and Le Catelet Line respectively, securing the tunnel as far as its northern entrance and taking Bony. The rest of the 5th Division was to strike eastwards towards the Beaurevoir Line. 'Slow and methodical hand to hand fighting, in a perfect tangle of trenches', wrote Monash, raged on 30 September. 'Machine-gun bullets were thick enough to nearly jam in the air', said Lieutenant Barton, and the German shelling was intense. When the flank thrust stalled, Monash ordered Gellibrand to mount a set-piece frontal assault at dawn. Gellibrand wanted to stick with the flank attack. The pair argued. Monash relented. His exhaustion was showing.

1 October went well. Realising they were outflanked, the Germans abandoned Bony and withdrew to the Beaurevoir Line, up to which the Australians closed. 'Damn it! If you can do it, do it now!' Elliott demanded, on hearing that the 57th Battalion could go further. But the Germans were firmly ensconced. 'All done up', the 3rd and 5th were relieved by the 2nd Division. Private Schwinghammer grabbed the chance to satisfy himself that the tunnel did not contain a 'corpse factory' where the Germans boiled down their dead for fat, as many Australians believed. It was chock-a-block with casualties.[30]

After weathering a severe gas bombardment during the night, the 5th and 7th Brigades successfully attacked the Beaurevoir Line with just 2500 men on a 6000-yard frontage on 3 October. So widely spread were they that few platoons knew what the others were doing. 'You Australians are all bluff', a captured German officer blustered. 'You attack with practically no men and are on top of us before we know where we are.' As the 6th Brigade was still reasonably fresh, it struck Montbrehain, two miles southeast, two days later. Tough resistance from fresh troops and a heavy counterattack had to be overcome before the village fell with the loss of 450 men. It could have been easily captured with far fewer casualties as part of a larger operation. But Haig was anxious for the attack because possession of Montbrehain removed the final obstacle to a deep cavalry exploitation of the breaching of the Hindenburg Line. Perhaps for this reason, Monash, Rosenthal and Blamey thought it worthwhile. Captain Braithwaite was among the Australian dead. With the withdrawal of the 2nd Division, the Australian Corps had left the line. It did not return.[31]

The end was near. Driven back by an Allied offensive from Salonika on 15 September, the Bulgarians sought an armistice that was signed at the end of the month. The collapse of their last offensive on the Piave in June shattered the Austrians, and the Italians trounced them at Vittorio Venetto on 23 October. The Austrians threw in the towel. Turkey did likewise on 1 November. Though the Germans were being driven back remorselessly, they always managed to patch up their line. But the constant bad news and the capitulation of allies, plus the starvation caused by the British naval blockade, caused widespread unrest at home. On 1 October a moderate government headed by Prince Max of Baden assumed office. Like von Hindenburg, Ludendorff realised that an armistice was essential. He resigned on 26 October. The German High Seas Fleet mutinied at the end of October and the Kaiser abdicated on 9 November. At 11 a.m. on 11 November the armistice came into effect.

On the Sambre River a few days earlier, the New Zealanders had participated in some of the last fighting. The Australian flying squadrons also remained in action, Captain Cobby amassing twenty-nine kills to become the AFC's top-scorer. At a cost of 21 243 casualties, just over a quarter of whom died, the Australian Corps had taken 29 144 prisoners, 338 guns and countless machine-guns and trench mortars, as well as liberating 116 towns and villages in 344 square miles of territory. These figures represented about 22 per cent of the captures of the entire British Army, of which it comprised just over 8 per cent, in the last phase of the war on the Western Front.[32]

—NINETEEN—

REFLECTIONS

'It became obvious, early in October, that the war was nearing its end', wrote Lieutenant Rule. 'There was no cheering, no undue excitement. I think we all grinned', Corporal Edgar Morrow of the 28th Battalion recalled of the announcement of the armistice. 'But the event was too big to be appreciated all at once, and by the time we had appreciated it, the novelty of there being no war had worn off.' 'The War has become such a habit that it has become impossible to realise what peace would really mean', said Captain Graeme Stobie of the 6th Battalion. 'I hardly know what to write about Mum', Gunner Rea ventured. 'We seem lost without the war. When it was on we always had something to occupy our minds, but now it is different.' Too many men had been killed for any sense of rejoicing. 'One sits and ponders sadly of those many pals who are "gone to that home from which no wanderer returns"', 2nd Battalion stretcher-bearer Corporal Roger Morgan remarked. Some were still fighting in Russia. Several Australians had gone there mid-year, as part of a 560-strong British military mission, to advise anti-Bolshevik forces with a view to reopening the Eastern Front. About 120 were in the two-brigade relief force that safeguarded the mission's evacuation in late 1919, during which two Australians, Corporal Arthur Sullivan and Sergeant Samuel Pearse (posthumously), won the only VCs of the campaign. Another fifty Australians had earlier formed part of a composite brigade, led by Major-General Lionel Dunsterville, that sought to counter the Ottomans and Germans, and secure the oil, in the Trans-Caucasus and Persia (modern Iran).[1]

The 7th LH Regiment, together with the Canterbury Mounted Rifles, spent six weeks at the end of 1918 on the Gallipoli Peninsula as part of the Allied occupation force. All of the light horse regiments had vied for the honour. Apart from No. 3 Squadron AFC and No. 3 Australian Casualty Clearing Station, the AIF in France did not form part of the army of occupation that entered Germany in December, though the Canadians and New Zealanders were included. Not that the Diggers minded. As Captain Norman Nicolson of the 14th Field Artillery Brigade wrote, the question for them was 'How soon can we get home to be civvies again?' Appointed Director-General of Repatriation and Demobilisation to plan and oversee the massive task of returning the AIF to Australia, Monash began the work in London on 21 November. He persuaded Prime Minister Hughes that the men must not go back by regiments, which the government favoured, but according to a priority determined by their length of service, a principle to which the Diggers themselves clung. Some 180 000 had to be kept intelligently occupied until ships became available. Monash urged their leaders to imbue them with a 'reconstruction morale', which would create 'a vision of the needs of Australia in the future days of peace, so that each one would be keen to reinstall himself as a useful member of his nation'. Bishop George Long's Education Scheme gave substance to the vision, allowing every man awaiting repatriation to study at government expense any subject he believed might be of value to him in civil life.[2]

Anxious though the Diggers were to go home, the departure of the first drafts early in 1919 occasioned deep melancholy. By making a man's mates his chief reason for being, the war had drawn men closer than brothers. Now that it was all over, they were going their own ways and the units that had been their home were breaking up. 'The battalion, our father and mother of unforgettable years, was drifting to pieces', wrote Lieutenant Mitchell. 'The links that connected us with the unforgotten dead seemed to be snapping one by one. As each draft left, mateships were sundered'. 'The AIF was slowly dissolving and becoming a mere memory', said Lieutenant Rule. 'For all the dreadful implications of war, which the soldier barely realises when he is in the thick of it, it *is* something to have known men as they truly are'. When the first men of the 40th (Tasmanian) Battalion left, the scene was truly poignant:

For quite two days before . . . there was a feeling of irresponsibility about all of us. We drank in fellowship together, pledged ourselves to meet again in Tasmania . . . and for once felt sorry that the war was over. Those of us who remained stood in the rain and watched the draft move off. Farewells were shouted, mostly facetious farewells, with reference to future meetings in favourite Tasmanian hostelries. But as the column moved beyond us we stood watching them in silence as they plodded away from us through the mud and rain, till they passed out of sight.

The men of the light horse had the additional sorrow of having to leave their faithful walers behind in Egypt and Palestine. Some shot their mounts rather than see them sold off to the Arabs. The horsemen's embarkation was interrupted when most of them were called upon to restore order after an anti-British uprising erupted in Egypt early in 1919. But all had left for Australia by September. Only 10 000 Australian troops remained in England at the end of that month. On 1 April 1921 the AIF officially ceased to exist.[3]

The Diggers ended the war with the same qualities as they began it: initiative, resilience, a rough humour concealing an inner nobility, disrespect of authority in its outward forms and, above all, loyalty to a mate. If there is such a thing as an Australian tradition of warfare, then the image of the Australian soldier as a man who embodies those qualities forms an important part of it. But any similarity between the Diggers of 1914 and 1918 ends there. On this point, British Official Historian Edmonds advised Bean in 1927: 'Anything tending to demonstrate that war can be entered on without preparation or training . . . by a number of individuals simply because they are brave, have natural fighting instincts and are fine specimens of manhood is to be deprecated'. He was right. Inadequately trained, the Gallipoli men were essentially enthusiastic amateurs. The then-Private Aitken observed in 1915 that the Australian was 'a fighter', in the sense that he had 'separate individuality and priceless initiative', as distinct from a soldier who had been 'drilled and trained' to form 'a component part of a huge machine'.[4]

Those who fought at Gallipoli believed that anything thereafter would be child's play. In the case of the Light Horse campaigns, they were more or less right. They were dead wrong as regards the Western Front. The brutal reality of the 'industrial warfare' struck there came as a great shock and, much more so than Gallipoli, showed that the attributes of the soldier were also necessary. Rawlinson remarked of the Australians' early days in France that they were fine fighters but not soldiers. Fromelles and Pozières made the point, though Rawlinson probably overstated his case at least with regard to Pozières. The successful attacks on the village and the ground gained towards Mouquet Farm reflected training the Australian divisions had done beforehand that incorporated the lessons learned thus far on the Somme. At the same time, the exploits of Jacka, Murray and others in these battles and at Bullecourt proved that initiative and resourcefulness were priceless even in 'industrial warfare'. Those qualities were also evident in the Australian follow-up of the German retirement early in 1917 and in peaceful penetration in 1918.

From Messines onward, thorough training combined with experience and natural ability to make the Australian soldier a master of his trade. Lavish artillery support made his task easier but its essential nature remained. Despite the shattering bombardments at Third

Ypres, clever minor tactics, frequently rehearsed, and spontaneity were often required to reduce the German pillboxes. The outcome at Villers-Bretonneux owed little to the artillery but everything to the skill and dash of the Australian assault. Training also paid off in the co-operation between infantry and tanks at Hamel and in the teamwork of the infantry sections on Mont St Quentin.[5]

The Americans illustrated how the Australians had benefited from training and experience. If their physique reminded the Diggers of themselves in 1914, their tactical naïvety did as well. The American commanders admitted lack of proficiency throughout their formations and recognised that they would have to learn, as their Australian colleagues had, in order to remedy it. As General John O'Ryan, commander of the American 27th Division, said: 'The rough and ready fighting spirit of the Australians had become refined by an experienced battle technique supported by staff work of the highest order'. The Doughboys were fighters. Though they had lost none of the qualities that made them fighters, the Diggers were also soldiers. Judgements on how good they had become are perhaps best left to the soldiers who fought with and against them, rather than to historians almost a century afterwards.[6]

Captain Essame, who had fought on the Somme in 1916, been wounded alongside the Australians at Villers-Bretonneux and who rose to become a general in the British Army, thought the Australian soldier in 1918 'the best infantryman of the war and perhaps of all time'. Some had reached that conclusion months beforehand. After Polygon Wood a British general told the 5th Division: 'You men have done very well here'. 'Only as well as ability and opportunity allow', a Digger shot back. 'Very well put young man, very well put indeed', the General retorted, 'but you have undoubtedly the best troops in the world'. British gunner Lieutenant Campbell, who formed a poor impression of the Australians on encountering them during the March retreat, soon changed his mind and remarked that 'they were magnificent soldiers'. He wished his battery was behind an Australian division. Rawlinson was overjoyed when the Australians came south to the Fourth Army at this time. He now considered the Diggers to be crack troops. Edmonds thought the Australians in 1918 'the finest'. In 1919 Marshal Foch declared the Australian 'the greatest individual fighter in the war'. As for the Germans, a sergeant-major from the Guards maintained that the Germans 'considered that the Australian troops were about the finest in the world, and the Germans were loth to attack them'. Generally, however, they thought the Australians and Canadians about equal. The New Zealanders were no less highly regarded but the fact that they comprised just a single division meant that they tended to be lumped in with the Australians.[7]

Just as it did the Diggers they led, the war moulded the Australian commanders. They were unprepared for Gallipoli and, generally speaking, bumbled through the campaign. Bridges's replacement by Walker was as timely as it was providential. Starting with the debacle on 2 May and ending with the shambles at Hill 60 after the bungled advance on Sari Bair, Birdwood and Godley floundered from one battle to the next. Facing tougher conditions on the Western Front, the Australian generals performed unevenly. McCay was out of his depth at Fromelles, while Walker displayed sound generalship at Pozières but Legge, at least initially, did not. Second Bullecourt reflected little credit on the senior command but the improvement thereafter was noticeable. II ANZAC benefited from having two outstanding divisional commanders, Monash and Russell, who carried their mediocre superior, Godley. By mid-1918 the divisions of the Australian Corps were led by men who had been fighting – and learning – for over three years. They thoroughly grasped the principles that underpinned success. Apart from Sinclair-MacLagan, all were citizen soldiers yet they were indistinguishable from professionals like him. The regimental officers had also become outstanding leaders and tacticians. Able generals, dynamic officers, superb soldiers. Edmonds summed it up: 'Nothing too good can be said of the Australian divisions of 1918'.[8]

All these things testified to the good fortune that Monash enjoyed in taking over the Australian Corps when he did. It was also at its zenith when the Germans were in decline. But Monash also made his own luck. The open mind, robustness, intellect and creative imagination evident in his pre-war civil and military careers were sharpened by his experience at Gallipoli and on the Western Front before he became corps commander. By then Monash's ideas on fighting were highly developed and fully proven. They gave the infantry every conceivable assistance and did not commit the Diggers to assaults on distant objectives that they would reach too weak to hold. Monash's technical mastery of all arms and tactics, particularly surprise and deception, was unsurpassed among his contemporaries, and he attached equal weight to logistics. His practical philosophy of 'unity of thought and policy and a unity of tactical methods throughout the corps', enabled the tremendous potential inherent in the grouping of the Australian divisions together to be fully realised. Monash's strengths far outweighed the flaws in his command style or the few mistakes he made.

The Australian Corps could not have won its successes without Monash's skill as its commander. It is hard to conceive Glasgow, Rosenthal, Gellibrand, Sinclair-MacLagan, Hobbs and even White, good as they were, rivalling his achievements. They were 'simply not comparable in intellect, articulateness or personal magnetism'. Outstanding as a light horse general in the desert, Chauvel would have been an unlikely corps commander on the Western Front. The New Zealander Russell perhaps might have been. He so impressed Haig as a divisional commander that Haig offered him command of a British corps in June 1918. Staying with his division, Russell was never tested in the higher role. Of the Anzac generals, Monash stands supreme. Under him, the Diggers 'went into action feeling, usually with justification, that, whatever might lie ahead, at least everything was right behind them'. There can be no higher praise.[9]

Over the four years of war, Australia enlisted a total of 416 809 men, a mind-boggling effort for a country of about four million people. Over half the eligible white male population joined up, of which 80 per cent, or 331 781, took the field, mostly on the Western Front. In all, 59 342, almost 20 per cent, were killed – over 46 000 on the Western Front – and 152 171, nearly 45 per cent, wounded. The overall casualty figure amounted to 215 585. Hence only one out of every three Australians who went overseas got through unscathed, at least physically. The concentration of men in arms that were exposed at the 'sharp end', over 210 000 in the infantry and more than 30 000 in the light horse, explained this grim statistic. Putting it into a wider perspective, the Australian casualty rate proportionate to forces fielded was the highest in the British Empire. Proportionate to population, it was second only to New Zealand, which suffered 58 526 casualties out of a population of 1.3 million. Some 2700 Australians belonged to the aerial component of the AIF, the Australian Flying Corps, and about 200 served as aircrew with British squadrons. Australia was the only Dominion to contribute a significant naval force.[10]

The war efforts of the Dominions won the right for their governments to be represented at the peace conference that opened in Versailles in January 1919. But they exercised no votes additional to those of Britain, which, with America, France and Italy, formed the Council of Four that steered matters. Nonetheless, Prime Minister Hughes, who led the Australian delegation, clashed heatedly with President Wilson. Germany had been stripped of its overseas territories and Hughes sought Australian control of the German Pacific colonies that Australia seized in 1914. His demand represented the security concerns that informed Australian pre-war foreign policy. He stood firm against the Council's insistence that they should be administered as trust territories according to a mandate laid down by the projected League of Nations. That arrangement might see them fall under hostile foreign sway. Wilson reminded Hughes that he spoke only for a few million people. Hughes countered: 'I speak for 60 000 dead. For how many do you speak?'

A compromise allowed the mandatory nation to apply its own laws in the relevant territory. On this basis Papua–New Guinea and associated islands south of the equator were entrusted to Australia and Samoa to New Zealand. They formed a buffer against Japan, which had advanced closer on being entrusted with the former German islands north of the equator. Hughes also resisted the Japanese call for a national equality clause in the League covenant. It would result in unrestricted immigration, threatening the White Australia policy. Unwilling to give him a platform on such an inflammatory issue, Wilson called for a unanimous vote, which he knew would not be carried.

On the matter of reparations, of which he was a leading advocate, Hughes lost. The Fourteen Points, which Wilson had enunciated in January 1918 as the basis for a peace honourable to all combatants, limited Germany's liability for war costs to the damage done to civilians and their property. Facing stronger domestic clamour on this issue than any other, Lloyd George and Clemenceau sought much greater restitution. A compromise that included the capitalised amount of war pensions in damage to civilian property failed to produce an agreement and the decision on a final sum was postponed. Australia would clearly not get the £364 million that the government estimated it had outlaid on the war. Its claim was eventually fixed at about £80 million, of which it received £5.6 million. Hughes and Sir Joseph Cook signed the Versailles Treaty for Australia in the great ceremony in the Hall of Mirrors on 28 June 1919, five years to the day since the assassination of Franz Ferdinand.[11]

By giving Australia a recognised place among the nations, the AIF's successes endowed Australians with a new confidence in themselves. The process started with the news of the landing at Anzac, which erased the doubts expressed when the 'six-bob-a-day tourists' left about their capacity to make good. It was completed by the Australian contribution to the final campaign in 1918, with the Australian Corps confirmed as an élite of the British Army, its victories lauded and its leaders acknowledged by friend and foe alike. Thereafter, the country that in many respects still consisted of six colonies in 1914 was a nation tried and true and considered itself such. 'We lost our reverence for England. We no longer gloried in the Empire and the army that Kipling wrote about before [1914]', said Brian Lewis, who was a boy in Melbourne during the war. 'In 1914 the most important political news published in our papers came from London; after the war it was news of the Commonwealth government that had first place.' But the imperial attachment remained firm despite the upsurge in nationalism – if for no other reason than the continuing rise of Japan made Australians look to the Empire and the Royal Navy as essential to their security. The Japanese shattered this belief by capturing Singapore, the British naval base that was supposed to protect Australia, in 1942. That is another story.[12]

The AIF's other great achievement was the prominent role it played in the defeat of Germany. Its significance has been eroded over the years by the view that Imperial Britain manipulated Australia into expending its manhood in a European quarrel in which it had no interest. Were that quarrel lost, though, Australia would have been different. The penalties imposed on Germany – reparations, part-occupation, loss of empire and some of its European territory, which were also applied in varying degrees to its allies – give some idea of the harsh measures that might have been imposed on Britain and its empire if Germany had won. With the Royal Navy gone and the German Navy all-powerful, Australia could have done little to resist. It could not have looked across the Pacific, as America had retreated into isolationism. Together with the other Dominions, it had to join Britain to see off the threat. Australian and Imperial interests were at one. Germany's defeat was vital for Australia's future. The men of the AIF were fully aware of that. 'They knew they were fighting an important struggle that had to be won to avoid disastrous consequences.'[13]

Peace brought mixed fortunes. Accepting the chairmanship of the infant State Electricity Commission of Victoria in August 1920, Monash planned and supervised the development of the state's power scheme, his greatest engineering project. Aged 66, he died on 8 October 1931. His military and civil achievements, centred on the numerous lives his generalship saved, entitle him to be called the greatest Australian. White retired from the army as Chief of the General Staff in 1923, was recalled to that position in March 1940 and died in a plane crash near Canberra airport five months later. Gellibrand, Glasgow and Elliott all went into federal politics, the last two as senators. Glasgow became the first Australian High Commissioner to Canada. Increasingly bitter as the years passed at having been denied the divisional command he expected to receive in May 1918, Elliott committed suicide in March 1931.

Albert Jacka, too, met a sad end. He went into business and became mayor of St Kilda. When the business fell victim to the Depression, he took on a job as a travelling salesman but his health deteriorated. Jacka died on 17 January 1932. His body lay in state, eight VC winners carried his coffin and General Brand gave a magnificent eulogy at his funeral. Returning to Australia with Monash and Birdwood, Harry Murray drew adoring crowds wherever he went. He settled on the land, served in the Second World War and died aged 85 after a car crash in 1966. George Mitchell also served in the next war and died in 1961. William Joynt, Wilfred Gallwey, Les de Vine, Peter Gaffney, Henry Taylor, Henry Hartnett and Ion Idriess all came home.

There were also shades of the 'generation of men who, even though they may have escaped its shells, were destroyed by the war', whose story Erich Maria Remarque told so poignantly in *All Quiet on the Western Front*. Many found the adjustment to peace difficult. 'One has settled so much down to this life that one will feel more or less like a duck out of water', wrote Captain Duke. A third of those who took advantage of the soldier-settler schemes, whereby they were helped to take up farming, failed – although in numerous cases the land allotted was unsuitable. The disabled or disfigured had to learn to cope. Others had to overcome the demons of the mind. Tedium, pettiness and a sense of futility beset all but a few. Today legions of counsellors would besiege the returnees; in those days there were none. Then came the Depression with its degrading effects. All the while, there was an unbridgeable gulf between those who went and the rest. Australians who had not experienced it directly wanted only to put the war, with its endless casualty lists and its shortages and disruptions, behind them. They did not want to hear about the fighting. The Diggers did not want to talk about it to them. They felt that only those who had shared in their experience could understand and empathise.[14]

In peace, therefore, the AIF veterans became an exclusive brotherhood. Lieutenant Rule dedicated his *Jacka's Mob* 'To that grand companionship of great-hearted men, which, for most of us, is the one splendid memory of the war'. Their leader, Monash, was 'deeply moved by the fellowship of the AIF in which he was humbly proud to participate'. At the other end of the scale, Gunner Francis Anderson said how hard it was 'to break away from the boys and each time I went into the City we met and still talked shop'. When the Australian government sponsored the return of forty-seven Gallipoli veterans to the Peninsula for the seventy-fifth anniversary of the campaign, many of them engaged in silent conversation at the grave of a comrade at Lone Pine while touching his headstone. Others ran their fingers across a familiar name on the Memorial Wall. And on 11 November 1993, when the coffin of an Unknown Australian Soldier from the Western Front was interred in the Hall of Memory at the Australian War Memorial in Canberra, Private Robert Comb, the Bullecourt veteran, acknowledged the brotherhood's bonds as he cast a handful of soil from Pozières on it. 'You're home, mate', 'Combsy' told him.[15]

Despite their passing, there are reminders of these men and their deeds everywhere in Australia. Even the smallest town has a monument bearing the names of the locals who went, with a cross alongside denoting those who did not return. Gallipoli, Lone Pine, Pozières, Bullecourt, Hamel, Beersheba, Jacka, Monash and a host of names like them are listed in the street directories of most cities, often several times over. Monash's name also graces a Canberra suburb and a Melbourne university. His face is on the nation's largest denomination dollar note. The Australian War Memorial abounds with relics, from a boat used by the 13th Battalion at the Anzac Landing and logs from the overhead cover at Lone Pine, to the barrel of the Amiens gun. While these naturally draw plenty of attention, the exhibit that brings the Digger alive perhaps more than any other often attracts just a cursory glance. It is the uniform worn by Private George Giles of the 29th Battalion and the rifle, equipment and personal gear he carried during the fighting above Morlancourt on 29 July 1918. Somme mud cakes them. At the Queensland Museum in Brisbane can be found 'Mephisto', the last surviving A7V tank, which the Germans used in the attack on Villers-Bretonneux.

The spirit of the Great War Diggers is rekindled on Anzac Day. It permeates the dawn services and the marches. More Australians visit Anzac itself than any other Australian battlefield. It has almost become a rite of passage for young Australians and thousands of them, as well as older ones, congregate on the beach every 25 April. But the beach represents the easy part of the campaign. The real epic occurred on the ridges inland and to the north. Going there when the crowds have gone is the only way of encountering the ghosts of the men who held them. The stillness is uncanny. Walking up Monash Valley towards Pope's, Quinn's and Courtney's Posts by day, you feel distinctly uneasy. Do so at night, stumbling repeatedly as you blunder through the clinging undergrowth, and unease turns to outright anxiety. The ghosts abound. You see the vague shapes of Diggers against the black sky and hear their muffled voices as they pass, helping a wounded comrade or coming from the beach with ammunition and water, ignoring the shrapnel bursting overhead.

On the Western Front the ghosts emerge at night as well. At Fromelles arcing flares and the flashes of exploding grenades, whose dull crumps often drown out the harsh cacophony of machine-gun and rifle, light up the area. Mud-covered figures splash along the ditches, in response to the unceasing call for more grenades and men to throw them. Awful moans come from the wounded sheltering in the German breastwork, which rises like a dam wall. Standing on a farm track that crossed the OG Lines in the fields northwest of Pozières, you are surrounded by Jacka and his men as they tear into the field-grey hordes. Their wild eyes fail to see you, just as you fail to see the twinkling lights in the village or hear the occasional juggernaut pounding along the Albert–Bapaume Road. Lying out on the jump-off tape at Hamel you feel clammy in the damp mist. You are thankful that the racket from the aircraft overhead is drowning out the noise of the tanks moving up. When the barrage starts, the sky in rear disappears in a continuous white flash and a few seconds later the ground in front erupts in sea of red flame. The concussion rattles every bone in your body and clods of earth rain down like giant hailstones. Your ears ache from the din and you barely hear the whistle that tells you to head off. But you know it's time to go anyway. You hug the barrage, pray that no rounds drop short and hope that the tanks are coming.

Crowning the Wolfsberg above Hamel is the Australian Corps Memorial. Set amongst the trenches of the old Amiens Defence Line, its curved black granite walls bear the Australian rising sun badge and scenes from the battle. From it can be seen the tower of the Australian National Memorial on Hill 104 at Villers-Bretonneux, whose screen walls enshrine the names of 10 892 Australians killed in France who have no known grave. The 1298 missing from Fromelles are etched on the wall at VC Corner Australian Cemetery on that battlefield. In the nearby Australian Memorial Park on the German front line, the bronze statue *Cobbers* depicts Sergeant Fraser carrying a wounded comrade back to the Australian line. Between the OG

Lines at Bullecourt is another bronze, this time of a Digger in full marching order. It is a tribute to 'hope, pride and optimism' which, together with determination, resilience and mischievous humour, are all apparent in the unforgettable expression on the Digger's face. His mates rest beneath the headstones in the cemeteries that dot the landscape from Ypres to the Somme, Australians whose hair never got the chance to turn grey.

They were tough men and they came from a strong people. Today they are all together again, marching on as an immortal army. At the going down of the sun, and in the morning, we will remember them.

ABBREVIATIONS

AFA	Australian Field Artillery
AFC	Australian Flying Corps
AIF	Australian Imperial Force
AMF	Australian Military Forces
AN&MEF	Australian Naval and Military Expeditionary Force
ANZAC	Australian and New Zealand Corps
AV	*Australian Victories in France*
AWM	Australian War Memorial
Bde	Brigade
BEF	British Expeditionary Force
Bn	Battalion
C-in-C	Commander-in-Chief
CMG	Companion of the Order of St Michael and St George
Comd	Commander
CSM	Company Sergeant Major
D	Diary
DCM	Distinguished Conduct Medal
DFC	Distinguished Flying Cross
Div	Division
DSC	Distinguished Service Cross
DSO	Distinguished Service Order
EEF	Egyptian Expeditionary Force
F-M	Field Marshal
GHQ	General Headquarters
HQ	Headquarters
IWM	Imperial War Museum, London
JAWM	*Journal of the Australian War Memorial*
JM	John Monash
JRAHS	*Journal of the Royal Australian Historical Society*
KC	Liddell Hart Centre for Military Archives, King's College, London
L	Letter
LH	Light Horse
MC	Military Cross
MC	Monash Collection, AWM
mg(s)	machine-gun(s)
MEF	Mediterranean Expeditionary Force
ML	Mitchell Library, State Library of New South Wales
MM	Military Medal
MP	Monash Papers, NLA
NAM	National Army Museum, London
NLA	National Library of Australia
NZEF	New Zealand Expeditionary Force
NZMR	New Zealand Mounted Rifles (Brigade)
Opord	Operation Order
OH	*Official History of Australia in theWar of 1914–18* (volume number follows)
RAN	Royal Australian Navy
Regt	Regiment
RFC	Royal Flying Corps
Sqn	Squadron
TNA (PRO)	The National Archives, (Public Records Office), London
VC	Victoria Cross
WD	War Diary

NOTES

Full details of letters and diary entries can be found under 'Manuscripts' in the Bibliography. Where multiple references are made to the same primary document, only the first reference is given. Book titles have been abbreviated.

INTRODUCTION

1 Macdonald, *Passchendaele*, p. 201.
2 Keegan and Holmes, *Soldiers*, p. 259.
3 *OH I*, p. 47; Montague, *Disenchantment*, pp. 158–9.
4 Carver, *War Lords*, p. xi; Hackett, *Profession*, p. 148.
5 Sheffield, *Forgotten Victory*, p. 131; Hackett, *Profession*, p. 148.
6 *OH VI*, p. 1096.

1 FIGHTING FOR THE EMPIRE

1 *Sydney Morning Herald*, 30 Jun. 1914.
2 Belfield, *Boer War*, p. 115; Grey, *Military History of Australia*. p. 56.
3 C. D. Coulthard-Clark, 'Formation of the Australian Armed Services, 1901–14', in McKernan and Browne, *Australia. Two Centuries*, p. 123; *Oxford Companion to Australian Military History*, p. 203.
4 Andrews, *Anzac Illusion*, p. 18; Strachan, *First World War. I. To Arms*, p. 13.
5 *Sydney Morning Herald*, 9 Aug. 1905; Grey, *Military History of Australia*, p. 85.
6 Souter, *Lion and Kangaroo*, p. 147.
7 Kitchener, *Memorandum*; *Leeton Call*, 28 Feb. 1914; Hamilton, *Report on Inspection*.
8 Pearce, *Carpenter to Cabinet*, pp. 81–2; Grey, *Australian Army*, pp. 33–4; Mordike, *Army for a Nation*, p. 240.
9 Pugsley, *Anzac Experience*, p. 61; *OH I*, pp. 27–8; Bean, *Two Men*, p. 90.
10 *OH I*, pp. 16–17, 28-9; Souter, *Lion and Kangaroo*, p. 211.
11 *Age*, 4 Aug. 1914; *Adelaide Advertiser*, 4, 5 Aug. 1914; Souter, *Lion and Kangaroo*, p. 212; *Sydney Morning Herald*, 6 Aug. 1914.
12 *OH IX*, pp. 44; *Robertson, Anzac and Empire*, p. 19; *OH X*, pp. 23–5, ch. 5.
13 Warren, L, undated; *OH IX*, p. 126.
14 Robertson, *Anzac and Empire*, pp. 20-1.

2 AUSTRALIA WILL BE THERE

1 Bean, *Two Men*, p. 21.
2 *OH I*, p. 36.
3 Gammage, *Broken Years*, pp. 6–7; *OH I*, p. 44; Souter, *Lion and Kangaroo*, p. 215.
4 Welborn, *Lords of Death*, pp. 44-5; Robson, *First AIF*, p. 29.
5 White, 'Motives for Joining Up', *JAWM*, Oct. 1986, p. 10; *Gallipoli: The Fatal Shore*, ABC TV Doco, 1988; Aitken, L, 27 Jan. 1915: Andrews, *Anzac Illusion*, pp. 44–5.
6 *OH I*, p. 60; Aitken, L, 29 Aug. 1915; Fuller, *Generalship*, pp. 27, 88.
7 *OH I*, pp. 64, 66; Coulthard-Clark, 'Bridges' in Horner (ed.), *The Commanders*, pp. 15–16; Howe to Bazley, 24 Nov. 1963, Bazley Papers, AWM.
8 Hill, Chauvel, p. 54; *OH I*, p. 54.
9 Wren, *Randwick to Hargicourt*, pp. 9–10; *OH I*, p. 85.
10 Feist, L, undated.
11 Belford, *Legs-Eleven*, p. 9.
12 *Argus*, 29 Sept. 1914; Belford, *Legs-Eleven*, p. 18.
13 Bean, *Anzac to Amiens*, p. 46.
14 Adam-Smith, *Anzacs*, pp. 30-1.
15 Godlee, D, 1 Nov. 1914; *OH I*, p. 99.
16 *Sydney–Emden* fight: *OH IX*, p. 565; Stevens, *Royal Australian Navy*, p. 40.
17 Belford, *Legs-Eleven*, p. 26; Taylor and Cusack, *Nulli Secundus*, p. 45.
18 Robertson, *Anzac and Empire*, p. 30; Adam-Smith, *Anzacs*, p. 44.
19 *OH I*, pp. 110–11.

20 Brugger, *Australians and Egypt*, p. 22.
21 Rhodes James, *Gallipoli*, p. 60.
22 Training in Egypt: Belford, *Legs-Eleven*, p. 46; Harvey, *From Anzac to the Hindenburg Line*, p. 19.
23 Attitudes to Egypt: Margetts, L, 9 Jan. 1915; Coe, L, 17 Jan., 28 Mar. 1915; McAnulty, D, 21 Apr. 1915; Campbell, L, 27 Feb. 1915; Mitchell, D, 10 Dec. 1914, 2 Jan. 1915; Elliott, L, 22 Feb. 1915.
24 Indiscipline: Gammage, *Broken Years*, p. 39; Coulthard- Clark, *Heritage*, p. 140; H. J. Smith, L, 31 Jan. 1915.
25 Carlyon, *Gallipoli*, p. 127; Glen, *Bowler at Gallipoli*, pp. 20–1.
26 Malthus, *Anzac*, p. 33.
27 *OH I*, p. 125; Pakenham, *Boer War*, p. 574; Casey, D, 17 Mar. 1915.
28 Origins of Gallipoli campaign: Gilbert, *First World War*, p. 121; Churchill, *World Crisis*, I, p. 529, 533, 543.
29 Turkish General Staff, *Short History of Turkish Operations*, pp, 10, 14; Liman von Sanders, *Five Years in Turkey*, p. 61.
30 Hamilton, *Gallipoli Diary*, I, p. 98.
31 *OH I*, p. 213; de Vine, D, 2 Apr. 1915.
32 A. Smith, L, undated.
33 *OH I*, p. 222; Winter, 25 April, p. 133.
34 ANZAC Opord 1, 17 April 1915, Item 367/156; 3 Bde Opord 1, 21 April 1915, Item 367/175, both AWM25; 1 Div Opord 1, 18 April 1915, Item 4, 3DRL/8042, AWM38.
35 White, 'Notes on the Gallipoli Expedition', undated, Item 36, 3DRL/8042, AWM38.
36 Monash to COs, 20 Apr. 1915, MC.
37 Belford, *Legs-Eleven*, pp. 59–60; Mitchell, D, 23 Apr. 1915. McGuirk, L, 30 Jul. 1915.
38 Bean, *Two Men*, p. 53.
39 de Vine, D, 24 Apr. 1915; Grant, 'World War One Memoirs', PR 89/90, AWM.
40 Austin, *Cobbers in Khaki*, p. 80; Bennett in *Sydney Morning Herald*, 25 April 1939.
41 Laseron, ML; Coe, L, 21, 23 Apr. 1915; Monash to wife, 24 Apr. 1915, NLA; Adam-Smith, *Anzacs*, p. 61; Winter, *25 April*, p. 85; Mitchell, D, 24 Apr. 1915.
42 *OH I*, p. 247; M.F. Beevor, 'My Landing on Gallipoli', MSS0761, AWM, p. 3.
43 Thursby, 'Power of the Navy', *Reveille*, Mar. 1932, p. 53.

3 The Landing

1 *OH I*, p. 250; Aspinall, *Gallipoli*, I, p. 174.
2 Cheney, 'Outline of Experiences', undated; Darnell, L, 27 May 1915.
3 Broadbent, *Gallipoli*, pp. 54-5.
4 Landing: *OH I*, p. 252; Mitchell, D, 25 Apr. 1915; Loud, D, 13 May 1915.
5 Landing error: Bush, *Gallipoli*, pp. 98, 111; Winter, *25 April 1915*, ch. 11, and 'The Anzac Landing – the Great Gamble?', *JAWM*, Apr. 1984, p. 19; Frame, *Shores of Gallipoli*, pp. 199–209.
6 *OH I*, pp. 258–9.
7 *OH I*, p. 338.
8 *OH I*, p. 273; Belford, *Legs-Eleven*, p. 77.
9 Beevor, 'My Landing on Gallipoli', pp. 11–12; Roberts, 'The Landing at Anzac: a Reassessment', *JAWM*, Apr. 1993, pp. 28–9.
10 Helles landings: Aspinall, *Gallipoli*, I, p. 180; Liddell Hart, *First World War*, p. 233; A. Moorehead, *Gallipoli*, p. 99; Liddle, *Men of Gallipoli*, p. 126.
11 McMullin, *Elliott*, p. 127.
12 Bean, *Anzac to Amiens*, p. 91; Winter, *25 April*, p. 189; W. E. Cass, 'Early Events of the 2nd Infantry Brigade at Anzac 25.4.15', 3DRL/8042, AWM 38.
13 Roberts in *JAWM*, p. 31; 'The Military Adventures of John Rutherford Gordon', PR89/085, AWM, p. 10.
14 M. Kemal (Ataturk), 'Memoir of the Anafartalar Battles', Box 76/75/1, IWM, pp. 5-9.
15 *OH I*, p. 293.
16 Baby 700: Newman's interview with author, 14 Jun. 1980; *OH I*, pp. 309, 430–1; Pugsley, *Gallipoli*, pp. 126–7.
17 400 Plateau: Winter, *25 April*, pp. 163, 201; Broadbent, *Boys Who Came Home*, p. 50; *OH I*, p. 401; Bean, *Gallipoli Mission*, p. 190.

18 Gordon, 'Military Adventures', pp. 13–14; Harrison, 'Account of Landing', undated, PR91/005, AWM; Carne, 'Essay', undated, 2DRL/0013, AWM; Mitchell, D, 25 April 1915.
19 Hall, L, 2 May 1915; Steel and Hart, *Defeat at Gallipoli*, p. 75.
20 Rosenthal, D, 25 Apr. 1915; Travers, *Gallipoli*, p.76.
21 Bean, D5; Gellibrand to Bean, 27 Jun. 1927, Item 27, 3DRL/7953, AWM38; *OH I*, p. 454.
22 Evacuation proposal: 'Notes on the Gallipoli Expedi-tion'; Ashmead-Bartlett, *Uncensored Dardanelles*, p. 48; Birdwood to Bean, 14 August 1922, Item 36, 3DRL/8042, AWM38; Coulthard-Clark, *Heritage*, p. 160; Bush, *Gallipoli*, p. 108; Hamilton to Lady H, 29 April 1915, File 7/1/4, Hamilton Papers, KC.
23 Howe to Bazley, 24 Nov. 1963, Bazley Papers, AWM.
24 Broadbent, *Boys Who Came Home*, p. 56; *OH I*, pp. xxiii, 566; Aspinall, *Gallipoli*, I, p. 199.
25 *OH IV*, p. 488; Dawnay to wife, 29 Apr. 1915, File 69/21/1, IWM; Robertson, *Anzac and Empire*, p. 76; Pugsley, *Gallipoli*, p. 115; Bean, *Gallipoli Mission*, pp. 351–2.
26 Richards, L, 15 May 1915; Gammage, *Broken Years*, p. 85; *Age*, 8 May 1915.

4 STALEMATE

1 Hart and Steel, *Defeat at Gallipoli*, p. 131.
2 Bean, D6, 27 Apr. 1915, Monash to wife, 18 Jul. 1915, MP.
3 Pugsley, *Gallipoli*, p. 168, Travers, *Gallipoli*, pp. 84–5.
4 Moran, L, 6 May 1915, 1DRL/508, AWM; Durrant, '13 Bn AIF', MSS143, AWM224; *OH I*, p. 531.
5 Margetts, L, 23 May 1915; Steel and Hart, *Defeat at Gallipoli*, p. 136; Birdwood, D, 28 Apr. 1915, Birdwood Papers, AWM; Bain to Wanliss, 17 Nov. 1921, '14 Bn History', MSS143/22, AWM.
6 Grant, 'World War One Memoirs'; Carlyon, *Gallipoli*, p. 231.
7 Kemal, 'Memoir', p. 13; Hart and Steel, *Defeat at Gallipoli*, p. 139.
8 Anzac: Bush, *Gallipoli*, p. 106; F. S. Rosenskjar, 'With the Australians on Gallipoli', 2DRL/0432, AWM, p. 28; Robertson, *Anzac and Empire*, p. 80; *OH I*, p. 527; Cutlack, *War Letters*, p. 36; Svensen to Bean, 24 Jul. 1922, Item 18, 3DRL/8042, AWM.
9 Quinn's: Hamilton, *Gallipoli Diary*, I, p. 258; Little to Bean, 8 Feb. 1924, Item 18, 3DRL/8042, AWM.
10 *OH I*, p. 583, Schuler, *Australia in Arms*, p. 138.
11 Baby 700 attack: Longmore, *Old Sixteenth*, p. 46; Silas, D, 2–3 May 1915; Pugsley, *Gallipoli*, pp. 176–7, 182; Durrant's account, Item 11, 3DRL/8042, AWM; Hart and Steel, *Defeat at Gallipoli*, p. 143; *OH I*, p. 597; Beeston, D, 3 May 1915; McLintock, D, 23 Sept. 1915; Shadbolt, *Voices of Gallipoli*, p. 24.
12 Helles: Moorehead, 'Reminiscences', 3DRL/7253, AWM, p. 4; Pugsley, *Gallipoli*, p. 194; Hamilton, *Gallipoli Diary*, I, p. 211.
13 Krithia attack: Hart and Steel, *Defeat at Gallipoli*, p. 163; Wray, *McCay*, p. 134; Bennett, 'The Battle of Krithia', *Smith's Weekly*, 20 Sept. 1930; Rhodes James, *Gallipoli*, p. 154; Austin, *White Gurkhas*, pp. 120, 129; Fewster, *Gallipoli Correspondent*, pp. 96-7.
14 Pugsley, *Gallipoli*, pp. 197-9.
15 Pedersen, *Monash*, pp. 78–9; Chataway, *15th Battalion*, p. 35; Monash, D, 10 May 1915, MP.
16 W. A. Forsythe, D, 4 May 1915, '13 Bn AIF', MSS143, AWM224; Monash, D, 8 May 1915, MP.
17 NZ & A Div to Bdes, 26 Apr. 1915 and Godley's comments on Force Order 8, 17 May 1915, both MC; Richards, D, 11 Jun. 1915; NZ & A Div Special Order, 5 May 1915, MC; Liddelow, D, 2 May 1915.
18 *OH II*, p. 130; Coulthard-Clark in *Commanders*, p. 17.

19 Turkish attack of 19 May: Aitken, L, 19 May 1915; Duke, L, 29 May 1915; Broadbent, *Boys Who Came Home*, p. 73; *OH II*, pp. 143, 150; White to Bean, 2 Feb. 1924, Item 13, 3DRL/8042, AWM.
20 Robson, D, 27 Apr. 1915; H. Smith, D, 8 May 1915; Mitchell, D, 19 May 1915.
21 Armistice: Broadbent, Gallipoli, p. 164; Mackenzie, *Gallipoli Memories*, p. 83; Herbert, *Mons, Anzac and Kut*, pp. 138–42.
22 Quinn's 29 May: Fletcher, D, 30 May 1915, and Hill, Pope and Durrant to Bean, 18, 22 and 23 September 1922, all in Item 17, 3DRL/8042, AWM; '13 Bn AIF', MSS143, AWM224; *OH IV*, p. 488.
23 Description of Anzac: Birdwood, *Khaki and Gown*, p. 262; Corbin, D, 12 Jul. 1915; E. Richards, L, Jun. 1915; Hamilton, *Gallipoli Diary*, I, p. 258.

5 FROM BREAKOUT TO PULLOUT

1 Aspinall, Gallipoli, I, p. 349; *Churchill, World* Crisis, II, p. 784.
2 Rhodes James, *Gallipoli*, pp. 210, 231.
3 Conditions at Anzac: Pedersen, *Images of Gallipoli*, Melbourne, 1988, p.16; Briggs, L, 19 Jul. 1915; Beeston, D, 24, 29 Jun. 1915.
4 Men's health: Gellibrand to brother, 4 November 1915, Gellibrand Papers, AWM; Rhodes James, *Gallipoli*, p. 222; *OH II*, p. 373; East, *Gallipoli Diary of Sergeant Lawrence*, p. 46; Butler, *Medical Services*, I, pp. 248, 252–3.
5 White, 'Some Recollections on the Great War', 1 Apr. 1921, White Papers, AWM.
6 Kemal, 'Memoir', p. 28.
7 Lone Pine attack: Bean, *Anzac to Amiens*, p. 145; McAnulty, D, 6–8 August 1915; de Vine, D, 6, 8 August 1915; Lawrence, *Gallipoli Diary*, p. 69; Bell, L, 21 Oct. 1915; *OH II*, pp. 532, 566; Margetts, L, 20 Aug. 1915; Gammage, D, 8–9 Aug. 1915.
8 Pugsley, *Gallipoli*, p. 279.
9 4 Bde night march: Cox in *Final Report of the Dardanelles Royal Commission*, p. 33; Compton, D, 6 Aug. 1915; Crane, 'Concert in Reserve Gully', *Reveille*, Aug. 1938, p. 33; *OH II*, p. 585; Rhodes James, *Gallipoli*, p. 272; Pedersen, *Monash*, pp. 105-6; Rhodes James to North, 28 Feb. 1964, Item I/3/402, North Papers, KC.
10 Birdwood to Hamilton, 'Proposals for Using Reinforcements', 1 Jul. 1915, Item 23, 3DRL/8042, AWM; Hamilton, *Goodbye Cobber*, pp. 269, 277, 287.
11 Nek action: Brazier to Bean, 19 Mar., 13 Apr. 1931, Item 27, 3DRL/7953, AWM; Burness, *The Nek*, pp. 24, 101, 105, 117; Lawrence, *Gallipoli Diary*, p. 64; Pinnock, L, 15 Aug. 1915; Borthwick, L, 22 Aug. 1915, PR01729, AWM; *OH II*, pp. 619-20.
12 Lee, *Soldier's Life*, p. 205; Prior, 'The Suvla Bay Tea Party: a Reassessment', *JAWM*, Oct. 1985, p. 31.
13 Kannengiesser, *Campaign in Gallipoli*, p. 206.
14 Wellingtons on Chunuk Bair: Pugsley, *Gallipoli*, pp. 282–8, and *Anzac Experience*, p. 104; Shadbolt, *Voices of Gallipoli*, p. 93; Waite, *New Zealanders at Gallipoli*, pp. 220–3; *OH II*, p. 679.
15 4 Bde on 8 August: Dare to Bean, 3 Mar. 1931, undated accounts from both Smiths, all in Item 23, 3DRL/8042, AWM.
16 Davies, *Allanson of the Sixth*, p. 51; Pugsley, *Anzac Experience*, p. 111.
17 Assessment of commanders: North to Bean, Items I/3/77, North Papers; North, *Gallipoli*, pp. 238–31; Hickey, *Gallipoli*, p. 286.
18 Hill 60: Pedersen, *Monash*, pp. 116–19; *OH II*, p. 740.
19 Chambers, L, 26 Oct. 1915.
20 Laffin, *Damn the Dardanelles!*, p. 170; Monash to Steward, 12 Nov. 1915, MC.
21 Aspinall, *Gallipoli*, II, p. 365; *OH II*, p. 767.
22 Gardiner, D, 26 Nov. 1915; de Vine D, 12 Nov. 1915.

23 News of evacuation: Cutlack, *War Letters*, p. 92; McConnan, L, 21 Dec. 1915; Mitchell, D, 21 Dec. 1915; Masefield, *Gallipoli*, p. 176; *OH II*, pp. 882, 909.
24 Connor, L, 24 Dec. 1915; Worrall, D, 19 Dec. 1915; Broadbent, *Boys Who Came Home*, p. 127.
25 Monash, *War Letters*, (typescript), MC, p. 108; Lawrence, *Gallipoli Diary*, pp. 58–9; Pugsley, *The Anzac Experience*, p.111.
26 Bean, D6, 29 Apr. 1915, *D17*, 26 Sept. 1915; *OH II*, pp. 426–9.

6 THE WESTERN FRONT

1 *OH III*, pp. 419–20; Raws, L, 12 Jul.1915.
2 *OH XI*, p. 871; Grey, *Military History of Australia*, p. 101.
3 *OH III*, p. 57
4 Bean, *Anzac to Amiens*, p. 189.
5 Rule, *Jacka's Mob*, p. 35.
6 Horne, *Price of Glory*, London, p. 44
7 Robertson to Murray, 1 Mar. 1916, Item 8/1/20, Robertson Papers, KC; *OH III*, p. 57.
8 Desert march: Williams, *Gallant Company*, p. 25; Johnston, L, 31 Mar. 1916, Author's Papers; *OH III*, p. 291.
9 Knyvett, *Over There*, p. 140; Williams *Gallant Company*, p. 42; Preston, 'Notebook', 2DRL/0811, AWM; Maxfield, L, 9 Jun. 1916; Haig, D, 27 March 1916.
10 Nursery sector: Ellis, *Fifth Australian Division*, p. 88.
11 Monash, *War Letters* (typescript), MC, p. 195; Birdwood to Munro-Ferguson, 3 May 1916, Birdwood Papers; *OH III*, p. 119; Winter, *Death's Men*, p. 47; Dunn, *War The Infantry Knew*, p. 288.
12 Baldwin, L, 21 May 1916.
13 *OH III*, p. 118.
14 Thomas, L, 9 May 1916; *OH III*, p. 216; 2 Bde to bns, 17 May 1916, Item 213/1(2), AWM 25.
15 Ellis, *Eye-deep in Hell*, p. 79; *OH III*, pp. 244–5.
16 Brunton in Gammage, *Broken Years*, p. 153.
17 Farndale, *Artillery*, p. 144; Prior and Wilson, *Command on the Western Front*, p. 169; Keegan, *First World War*, p. 314; Middlebrook, *First Day on the Somme*, p. 96.
18 *OH III*, p. 328; 'Historical Note. Fromelles', undated, Item 243b, 3DRL/606, AWM.
19 Sloan, *Purple and Gold*, pp. 63-4.

7 THE INITIATION: FROMELLES

1 Haking to First Army, 9 Jul. 1916, XI Corps WD, Jul. 1916, Item 1/22, Roll 774, AWM 4.
2 Haking, *Company Training*, p. 103; Travers, *Killing Ground*, p. 48; McMullin, *Elliott*, pp. 205-6; Graves, *Goodbye*, p. 95.
3 XI Corps Order 57, 15 July 1916, XI Corps WD.
4 Sugarloaf and 6th Bavarian Division: Pedersen: *From-elles*, pp. 27-8, 40–1;
5 *OH III*, p. 335; 'Instructions for Brigadiers', 15 Jul. 1916 and Order 31, 16 Jul. 1916, 5 Aust Div WD, July 1916, Item 1/50, Roll 836, AWM 4; GHQ SS.109, 'Training of Divisions for Offensive Action', 8 May 1916, MC.
6 Elliott, 'Private Memoranda on Supercession', 25 May 1918, Elliott Papers, AWM.
7 *OH III*, pp. 347-8.
8 Macdonald, *Somme*, p. 170.
9 Martin, L, 31 Jul. 1916; Williams, *Gallant Company*, p. 55.
10 *OH III*, pp. 358, 362; Sloan, *Purple and Gold*, p. 72.
11 15th Bde's attack: Knyvett, *Over There*, pp. 153-4; *OH III*, pp. 365-6; Downing, *Last Ridge*, p. 8; *OH III*, pp. 364–6.
12 14 Bde's attack: Corfield, *Don't Forget Me, Cobber*, p. 147.; 'Report on Condition of German Trenches', 22 Jul. 1916, 14 Bde WD, Item 23/14, Roll 26, AWM 4; Bean, *Anzac to Amiens*, p. 229.
13 8 Bde's attack: After Action Reports, 21 Jul. 1916, 31 Bn WD, Item 23/48, Roll 66, AWM 4; 'Report on

Operations 19/20 July 1916', 32 Bn WD, Item 23/49, Roll 67, AWM 4.
14 Sloan, *Purple and Gold*, p. 76.
15 Williams, *Gallant Company*, p. 57; Donnan, L, 3 Feb. 1934; Sloan, *Purple and Gold*, p. 80.
16 *OH III*, pp. 392–4; Messages, 19 Jul. 1916, 5 Aust Div WD.
17 Messages 19 Jul. 1916, 15 Bde WD, Item 23/15, Roll 28, AWM4.
18 Corfield, *Don't Forget Me, Cobber*, pp. 229.
19 Lording, *There and Back*, pp. 171–3.
20 *OH III*, p. 419.
21 8 Bde withdrawal: Ellis, *Fifth Australian Division*, p. 104; Zander, 'Narrative of Experiences', 2DRL/0171, AWM; 31 Bn Report.
22 14 Bde withdrawal: Winter D, 19–20 Jul. 1916; Williams, *Gallant Company*, p. 62.
23 Knyvett, *Over There*, p. 155; Bean, D52, 20 Jul. 1916; Corfield, *Don't Forget Me, Cobber*, p. 83.
24 *OH III*, pp, 437, 441.
25 *OH III*, p. 442.
26 Liddell Hart, *First World War*, p. 325; *OH III*, p. 350: Miles, *France and Belgium, 1916*, II, p. 134.
27 Australian reactions: Williams, *Gallant Company*, p. 68; XI Corps Report, 24 Jul. 1916, XI Corps, WD; Wray, *McCay*, p. 204; Bean, D52, 20 Jul. 1916.

8 SOMME: POZIÈRES

1 F. Maurice, *Rawlinson*, London, 1928, p. 130.
2 *OH III*, p. 465.
3 'Miscellaneous notes from divisions which have taken part in recent operations', 17 Aug. 1916, White Papers; *OH III*, p. 471.
4 Move to Pozières: Maxfield, L, 13 Oct. 1916; Charlton, *Pozières*, p. 127; Moorehead, 'Reminiscences', p. 28; Roberts, 'Memoirs', PR00395, AWM, p. 39; Horton, 'With the 1st Battalion at Pozières', 1DRL/0359, AWM, p. 7; Hartnett, 'The 2nd Battalion', 2DRL/0840, AWM, p. 63.
5 *OH III*, p. 455.
6 Background to Pozières attack: *OH III*, p. 468; Farrar-Hockley, *Goughie*, p. 188; Walker to Bean, 13 Aug. 1928, Item 34, 3DRL/7593, AWM; Haig, D, 20, 22 Jul. 1916; 1 Div Order 31, 21 Jul. 1916, 1 Div WD, Roll 809, AWM 4.
7 Harris, 'General Account' undated, 1DRL/0338, AWM, p. 7; Claridge, L, 10Aug. 1916.
8 Thomas, L, 1 Aug. 1916.
9 Pozières attack 14 July: Bourke, L, Aug. 1916; Champion, D, 19–26 Jul. 1916; Preston, 'Notebook'; Barwick, D, 23 Jul. 1916; Callaway, L, 10 Aug. 1916.
10 *OH III*, p. 546; Horton, '1st Battalion', p. 18.
11 Laing, L, 30 Jul. 1916; *OH III*, p. 542.
12 Roberts, 'Memoirs', PR00395, AWM, p. 41; Harris, 'General Account', p. 22; Horton, '1st Battalion', p. 21.
13 25 Jul. attack: 'Report on Operations', 3 Aug. 1916, 1 Div WD; Moorehead, 'Reminiscences', pp. 28, 30; Lillie, 'Reminiscences', PR85/010, AWM; Conan Doyle, *British Campaign in France and Flanders*, pp. 192-3; *OH III*, pp. 565, 573.
14 Shelling: Birdwood to Allen, 12 Aug., to Pearce, 1 Aug. 1916, Birdwood Papers; Winter, *Death's Men*, pp. 117–18; Joynt, D, 26 Jul. 1916; Ferguson, *Pity of War*, p. 341: Bean, D58, 4 Aug. 1916; Barwick, D, 24 Jul. 1916; Elvin, D, 25 Jul. 1916.
15 Champion, D, 26 Jul. 1916; Howell-Price, L, 1 Aug. 1916; *OH III*, p. 580.
16 Rule, *Jacka's Mob*, p. 61; *OH III*, p. 593.
17 Legge to Bean, 25 May 1934, Item 4, 3DRL/7953, AWM; Birdwood to Munro-Ferguson, 31 Dec. 1916, Birdwood Papers.
18 Preparations for 29 Jul. attack: Brown, 'The Old Windmill', *Reveille*, Oct. 1932, p. 3; Cohen, L, 29 Jul. 1916.
19 29 July attack: 'Report on Operations', 29 Jul. 1916, 2 Div WD, Roll 820, AWM4; Boys, L, 2 Aug. 1916; Gaffney, 'Experiences 1915–18', PR91/084,

AWM, p. 30; Hocking, L, 16 Aug. 1916; *OH III*, p. 642.
20 Haig, D, 29 Jul. 1916; Bean, *Two Men*, pp. 136–7; *OH III*, p. 643.
21 Preparations for 4 Aug. attack: 2 Div Order 37, 3 Aug. 1916, 2 Div WD; Bean, *Letters from France*, p. 129, *Two Men*, pp. 138–9; Raws, L, 8 Aug. 1916; Haig, D, 4 August 1916.
22 4 Aug. attack: Welborn, *Lords of Death*, p. 115; *OH III*, pp. 685, 694; Whitear, 'Narrative', 2DRL/0439, AWM, p. 9.
23 Aftermath: *OH III*, pp. 699, 702, 724; Raws, L, 4 Aug. 1916; Wanliss, *History of the 14th Battalion,* p. 135; Rule, *Jacka's Mob*, pp. 63–4.
24 Rule, *Jacka's Mob*, pp. 70–3: *OH III*, p. 720.

9 SOMME: MOUQUET FARM AND BEYOND

1 Mouquet Farm: Bean to Gellibrand, 14 Sept. 1944, Gellibrand Papers; Gliddon, *When the Barrage Lifts*, p. 336.
2 4th Division attacks: *OH III*, pp. 763, 770, Armitage, L, 17 Aug. 1916; Wells, 'First Stunt: Vivid Impressions', *Reveille*, Aug. 1932, p. 34; Murray, 'His Hardest Battle', *Reveille*, Dec.1935, p. 33.
3 Thomas, D, 16–17 Aug. 1916; Champion, D, 9–17 Aug. 1916; Leane, L, 9 Aug. 1916.
4 Austin, *Cobbers in Khaki*, p. 130; Newton, *Story of the Twelfth*, Hobart, 1927, p. 230.
5 *OH III*, pp. 802, 822; Taylor, 'The Mob that Shot the Camel', MSS0863, AWM, pp. 83–4.
6 Rule, *Jacka's Mob*, p. 99; White, *Fighting Thirteenth*, p. 72.
7 Scanlon, L, 21 Dec. 1916.
8 Maxfield, L, 15 Aug. 1916; Davis, D, 10 Aug. 1916; A. Ekins, 'A Private War', *Age*, 14 Nov. 1998; Austin, *Cobbers in Khaki*, p. 122; Brand, 3 Sept. 1916 to Monash, MP; Bean, D60, 3 Oct. 1916; Dunlop, D, 28 July 1916; Thomas, L, 9 Jun and D, 25 Jul. 1916.
9 Raws, L, 19 Aug. 1916; Bean, D60, 3 Oct. 1916.
10 Forester, *The General*, p. 173; Edmonds to Bean, 16 Nov. 1927, 3 Jul. 1928 and Bean to Edmonds, 28 Apr. 1928, Item 34, 3DRL/7953, AWM38; Farrar-Hockley, *Somme*, p. 221.
11 *OH III*, p. 871.
12 Conscription referendum: Robson, *First AIF*, pp. 85–90; White to Monash, 26 Aug. 1916, MP; Grey, *Military History of Australia*, p. 115; *OH III*, pp. 866–8.
13 Conscription referendum in AIF: Aram, L, 3 Dec. 1916; Davis, L, 17 Oct. 1916; Fitzhardinge, *Little Digger*, p. 209; Evatt, L, 3 Jan. 1917; Armitage, L, 5 Nov. 1916; Allan, L, 8 Mar. 1917; *OH III*, p. 893.
14 Prior and Wilson, *Somme*, p. 222; Sheffield, *Somme*, p. 124; Stewart, *New Zealand Division*, p. 64; Pigeon, *Tanks at Flers*, p.168.
15 *OH III*, p. 876; Prior and Wilson, *Somme*, p. 184.
16 *OH III*, p. 890; Hartnett, '2nd Battalion', pp. 118–20; Downing, *Last Ridge*, pp. 17–18.
17 Flers/Gueudecourt attacks: Champion, D, 1 Nov. 1916; Barwick, D, 5 Nov. 1916; Matthews, 'Diary of Experiences', 2DRL/0219, AWM, p. 7; Doneley, *Black over Blue*, pp. 68–9; Gaffney, 'Experiences', pp. 50, 57; Maxfield, L, 1 Dec. 1916.
18 Bean, *Anzac to Amiens*, p. 267; *OH III*, pp. 889, 929, 958; Chapman, *Mackay*, pp. 79-82; Thomas, L, 6 Nov. 1916.
19 Prior and Wilson, *Somme*, pp. 300–1; Brown, *Verdun*, p. 159; *OH III*, p. 946.
20 Wilson, *Myriad Faces*, p. 406; Brown, 'Autobiography', MSS1360, AWM, p.11.

10 CHASING FRITZ

1 Moorhead, 'Reminiscences', p. 35; Binskin, D, 16 Nov 1916; McInnis, D, Nov. 1916, PR00917; Hartnett, '2nd Battalion', pp.122-3.

2 Gammage, *Broken Years*, p. 179; Birdwood to officers, 11 Nov 1916, to McCay, 1 Dec 1916, Gellibrand Papers.
3 Baldwin, D, 9 Feb, 1917.
4 Stormy Trench: Hatwell, *No Ordinary Determination*, p. 141; Winn, 'Stormy Trench', *Reveille*, Feb. 1938, p. 7; Murray, 'Capture of Stormy Trench', *Reveille*, Dec. 1937, p. 10.
5 Coulthard-Clark, *No Australian Need Apply*, p. 152; Birdwood to Pearce, 24 Jan. 1917, Birdwood Papers.
6 Horne, *Price of Glory*, p. 312; Holmes, *Western Front*, p. 142.
7 Barnett, *Sword-Bearers*, p. 274.
8 Asprey, *German High Command*, p. 303.
9 Advance to Bapaume: *OH IV*, p. 66; 10 Sadler, *Paladin*, p. 110: Akhurst, L, 23 Mar. 1917.
10 Braithwaite, L, 26 Mar. 1917; Booth, L, Feb. 1917; Willey, 'My Experiences during the War', MSS1471, AWM, p. 9; McInnis, D, 27 Mar. 1917; Roth, L, 30 Mar. 1917.
11 Elliott's advance: McMullin, *Elliott*, pp. 267–76; Downing, *Last Ridge*, p. 53.
12 Gellibrand's advance: *OH IV*, p. 179; White to Bean, 15 Jan. 1930, Item 258, 3DRL/6673, AWM.
13 Capture of outpost villages: Morrow, *Iron in the Fire*, pp. 45–6; Hartnett, '2nd Battalion', pp. 174-80; Matthews, 'Experiences', pp. 31–2.
14 McMullin, *Elliott*, p. 281.

11 BULLECOURT: DEFEAT INTO VICTORY

1 Genesis of Bullecourt attack: *OH IV*, p. 267; Watson, *Company of Tanks*, pp. 44–6; Gallwey, 'Siver King', MS1355, AWM, p. 1690; Farrar-Hockley, *Goughie*, pp. 227–8.
2 Rule, *Jacka's Mob*, p. 169.
3 Bean, D113, 30 May 1918; *Two Men*, p. 154.
4 Bullecourt attack: Gallwey, 'Silver King', pp. 1726, 1733; Murray, 'Bravest Man in the AIF', *Reveille*, Dec. 1929, p. 8, and 'Memories of First Bullecourt', Dec 1936, p. 59; Groves, 'Experiences', 2DRL/0268, AWM, pp. 5, 11; Willey, 'Experiences', pp. 10–11; Hatwell, *No Ordinary Determination*, pp. 170, 288; B. Knowles, 'Bullecourt Tragedy', *Reveille*, Apr. 1931, p. 15; *OH IV*, pp. 340, 317; Mitchell, D, 11 Apr. 17; Rule, *Jacka's Mob*, p. 184.
5 Aftermath: White to Bean, 15 May 31, Edmonds to Bean, 25 Jun. 30, and Gough to Edmonds, 31 Aug. 30, all in Item 30, 3DRL/7593, AWM; *OH IV*, p. 351; Walker, *Blood Tub*, p. 104; Rule, *Jacka's Mob*, p. 185.
6 Lagnicourt: *OH IV*, pp. 393, 399, 401; Taylor, 'Mob that Shot the Camel', p. 117; Downing, *Last Ridge*, p. 56; Matthews, 'Narrative', p. 36; Walker, *Blood Tub*, p. 117; Bean, *Anzac to Amiens*, p. 336.
7 Spears, *Prelude to Victory*, p. 492; Keegan, *First World War*, p. 355.
8 A. Horne, 'Pétain' in *The Swordbearers*, pp. 61–2.
9 Lead-up to 2nd Bullecourt: Andrews and Jordan, 'Second Bullecourt Revisited', *JAWM*, Oct. 1989, pp. 36–40; Roth, L, 2 May 1917; Braithwaite, L, 11 May 1917.
10 5th Bde attack: *OH IV*, pp. 433, 435; King, D, 3 May 1917, PR83/018, AWM; Sadler, *Paladin*, p. 131.
11 6th Bde attack: Walker, *Blood Tub*, pp. 4, 137; *OH IV*, p. 448; Sadler, *Paladin*, p. 132.
12 Wounded: Butler, *Medical Services*, II, pp. 144–9; Brown, 'Autobiography', p. 19; Cue, 'With a Chaplain During a Battle', 1DRL/0625, AWM.
13 Walker, *Blood Tub*, p. 146.
14 Walker, *Blood Tub*, pp. 148–9; *OH IV*, p. 484.
15 Bryant, D, 3 May 1917; Sadler, *Paladin*, pp. 137–40.
16 *OH IV*, p. 488.
17 *OH IV*, p. 493; T. Richards, D, 7 May 1917.
18 Downing, *Last Ridge*, pp. 65–7.
19 58 Bn attack: McMullin, *Elliott*, pp. 286–9; *OH IV*, p. 530.

20 Terraine (ed.), *Haig's Despatches*, p. 102; Bean, *Anzac to Amiens*, p. 344; *OH IV*, p. 541.
21 Jones, *King of Air Fighters*, p. 68.
22 Winter, *First of the Few*, pp. 147–50, 163; Dallas, L, 29 Aug. 1916.
23 Simkins, *Air Fighting* p. 44; Winter, *First of the Few*, p. 156.
24 Dallas, L, 15 May 1917; Little, www.diggerhistory.info, Oct. 2005.
25 French military unrest: Wilson, *Myriad Faces*, p. 456; *OH IV*, p. 550.
26 Braithwaite, L, 24, 29 Apr. 1917; Hartnett, '2nd Battalion', p. 198.
27 Walker, *Blood Tub*, p. 170; *OH IV*, p. 684.

12 The Pillars of Fire at Messines

1 3 Div training: Monash, *War Letters* (typescript), MC, p. 207; Monash to Locke, 28 Aug, to Durrant, 2 Oct. 1916, MP; Pedersen, *Monash*, p. 147.
2 Harington, *Plumer*, p. 79; Charteris, *At GHQ*, p. 226; Powell, *Plumer*, p. 151.
3 Aram, L, 13 Nov. 1916; *OH IV*, p. 567; Peters, 'The Raiding Days', MSS1887, ML; Monash to White, 27 Feb. 1917, MP.
4 Liddell Hart, 'Genesis of Passchendaele', c.1934, Item II/1934/61, Liddell Hart Papers, KC; Sixsmith, *Haig*, p. 132.
5 Wilson, *Myriad Faces*, pp. 458–9.
6 *OH IV*, p. 555; Harington, *Plumer*, p. 84.
7 Liddell Hart, *First World War*, p. 393.
8 Messines preparations: Edmonds, *France and Belgium, 1917*, II, pp. 41–2; Terraine, *Western Front*, p. 230; Jungwirth, 'Experiences', PR89/063, AWM, p. 9.
9 Coombs, *Endeavours*, p. 57.
10 Jackson to Liddell Hart, 4 Oct. 1935, Item 1/516/14, Liddell Hart Papers, KC; *OH IV*, p. 576.
11 Pedersen, *Monash*, pp. 165–6; Monash to Grimwade, 9 Dec. 1916, MP; Drake-Brockman, *Turning Wheel*, p. 117.
12 Griffith, *Battle Tactics*, pp. 77–8; Bowman, D, 24 Jul. 1916; Notes by Murray, 8 Apr. 1917, MC.
13 Grieve, 'Experiences', 2DRL/0260, AWM, p. 4; Stewart, *New Zealand Division*, p. 183.
14 Gallwey, 'Silver King', p. 2127; Farndale, *Artillery*, p. 188; Holmes, *Western Front*, p. 159.
15 Mine explosions: Woodward, 'Hill 60 Mines', MSS0717, AWM, p. 24; Barrie, *War Underground*, p. 214; Brittain, *Testament*, p. 356; Gilbert, *First World War*, pp. 336–7.
16 Messines Ridge attack: *OH IV*, p. 595; Maudlsey, L, 17 Jun. 1917; Newton, L, 16 Jun. 1917; Stewart, *New Zealand Division*, pp. 187–95; Morshead, L, 7 Jun. 1916; Gallwey, 'Silver King', pp. 2134, 2136.
17 Oosttaverne Line: *OH IV*, pp. 624, 627; Gallwey, 'Silver King', pp. 2167–8, 2205.
18 Pugsley, *Anzac Experience*, p. 226; Haig, D, 9 Jun. 1917.
19 *OH IV*, pp. 631–2, 673, 734.
20 Gallwey, 'Silver King', p. 2257, Carson, L, 16 Jun. 1916; *OH IV*, pp. 681–2.
21 Powell, *Plumer*, p. 193; Taylor, *First World War*, p. 190; Haig, D, 'Proceedings of Army Commanders' Conference', 14 Jun. 1917; Harington, *Plumer* pp. 94–5; '2 Army Intelligence Summary', 1–11 Jun. 1917, MC.
22 Pedersen, *Monash*, pp. 175–6; Prior and Wilson, *Passchendaele*, p. 65.

13 They Called it Passchendaele

1 Lloyd George, *Memoirs*, II, p. 1277; Haig, D, 2 Jun. 1917; GHQ OAD 434, 7 May 1917, Haig D; Edmonds, *France and Belgium, 1917*, II, p. 102.
2 Lloyd George, *Memoirs*, pp. 1299–1300; Terraine, *Road to Passchendaele*, p. 156.
3 Gilbert, *First World War*, p. 328; Simms, *Victory at Sea*, pp. 6–7; Lloyd George, *Memoirs*, p. 1298.
4 German defences: 'Experience of the German 1st Army in the Somme Battle', 3 May 1917, and 'Principles of

Command in the Defensive Battle in Position Warfare', 21 Sept. 1918, White Papers; Holmes, *Western Front*, pp. 154–5.
5 Terraine, *Haig*, p. 337; Fuller, *Conduct of War 1789–1961*, p. 171; Edmonds, *France and Belgium, 1917*, II, p. 127.
6 Gough, *Fifth Army*, p. 195; Sheffield, *Forgotten Victory*, p. 204.
7 *OH IV*, p. 721; Farndale, *Artillery*, p. 195.
8 A. Ekins, 'The Australians at Passchendaele' in Liddle (ed.), *Passchendaele*, p. 232; Brittain, *Testament*, p. 395.
9 Macdonald, *Passchendaele*, p. 160; Edmonds, *France and Belgium, 1917*, II, pp. 238–9.
10 *OH IV*, pp. 732–3; Rule, *Jacka's Mob*, p. 250; Grant, *Jacka*, p. 134.
11 Menin Road preparations: 3 Div to II ANZAC, 8 Aug, 1917, MC; Holmes, *Fatal Avenue*, p. 102; Hartnett, '2nd Battalion AIF', p. 283.
12 Menin Road attack: Hollyhoke, 'Journal', 3DRL/1465, AWM; *OH IV*, pp. 761, 764, 786 790; Parton, L, 26 Sept. 1917; Yule, *Sergeant Lawrence Goes to France*, p. 131; Birdwood to Pearce, 16 Oct. 1917, Birdwood Papers.
13 Polygon Wood attack: Hunt, 'Narrative', 2DRL/0277, AWM, pp. 5–6; Farndale, *Artillery*, p. 208, McMullin, *Elliott*, pp. 310, 331; *OH IV*, pp. 813, 825; Ellis, *Fifth Division*, p. 246; Richards, *Old Soldiers*, p. 251.
14 German Records Relative to Australian Operations, Class. 111.05, AWM25.
15 Broodseinde attack: Bean, D65, 28 Sept. 1917; Schwing- hammer, 'Narrative', 2DRL/0234, AWM, pp. 16–17; Braithwaite, L, 14 Oct. 1917; Hartnett, '2nd Battalion AIF', pp. 266–9; *OH IV*, pp. 845, 866; Bradby, Polygon Wood and Broodseinde', *Stand-To*, Sep-Oct. 1963, pp. 21–2; Macdonald, *Passchendaele*, pp. 192-3; Harington to Edmonds, 15 Dec. 1932, 3DRL/7953, AWM.
16 *OH IV*, p. 876; Ludendorff, *War Memories*, p. 490; Cutlack, *War Letters*, p. 198.
17 Terraine, *Haig*, p. 369; Haig, D, 28 Sept., 5 Oct. Bean, D90, undated.
18 9 Oct. attack: Prior and Wilson, *Passchendaele*, p. 161; Vincent, D, 8 Oct. 1917; Ekins in Liddle, *Passchendaele*, pp. 239–40.
19 Charteris, *At GHQ*, p. 259; Haig, D, 8–10 Oct. 1917; Birdwood, *Khaki and Gown*, pp. 316–17; Monash, 'Notes for Conference', 7 Oct. 1917, MC; Horner, *Gunners*, p. 160.
20 Rosenthal, D, 9–10 Oct. 1917; *OH IV*, pp. 906–7; Cutlack, *War Letters*, pp. 199–200.
21 Passchendaele attack: Hardie, 'Narrative', PR00519, AWM, p. 4; *OH IV*, p. 912; Stewart, *The New Zealand Division*, p. 282; Macdonald, *Passchendaele*, pp. 206–9; Morshead to 9 Bde, 12 Oct. 1917; Dial, 'Passchendaele', 2DRL/1195, AWM.
22 Aftermath: Birnie, L, 26 Oct. 1917; Fairey, *38th Battalion*, p. 28; Carson, L, 25 Oct. 1917; 'The 27th in the Menin Road Battle', *Stand-To*, Jan–Mar, 1966, p. 4; Pedersen, *Monash*, p. 203; O'Keefe, *Hurley*, p. 64; Cutlack, *War Letters*, p. 202.
23 *OH IX*, p. 262.
24 Bean, D90, 10 Oct. 1917.
25 Wilson, *Myriad Faces*, p. 482; Keegan, *First World War*, p. 395.

14 CRIME AND PUNISHMENT

1 White to Bean, 17 Jun. 1932, White Papers; Elliott, L, 31 Dec. 1917; Campbell, *Ebb and Flow*, p. 51.
2 Birdwood to Munro-Ferguson, 4 Apr. 1917, Birdwood Papers; Bean, 'Sidelights of the War on the Australian Character' in *JRAHS*, No. 4, 1927, p. 211; Gammage, *Broken Years*, p. 230.
3 Sydney *Sun*, 1 Apr. 1918; Monash to Cannan, 2 May 1916, MP; Armitage, L, 5 Nov. 1916; Rule, *Jacka's Mob*, p. 199; *AV*, pp. 292–3; Birdwood to Pearce, 12 Nov. 1916, Birdwood Papers.

4 Wahlert, *Other Enemy*, pp. 58–9.
5 J. Peaty, 'Haig and Military Discipline' in Bond and Cave, *Haig*, p. 210; Pedersen, 'Thou Shallt Not Kill', Ypres Conference paper, 2000.
6 Babington, *Shell-Shock*, pp. 96, 104–5; Sassoon, *Memoirs*, p. 32; Graves, *Goodbye*, p. 143; Bean, D84, 25 Aug. 1917; Ekins, 'A Private War', *Age*, 14 Nov. 1998; Birdwood to Div. Comds, 11 Dec. 1917, MP.
7 Herbert, *Secret Battle*, p. 125, Babington, *Example*, p. 245; *OH V*, p. 32.
8 Conscription referendum: Robson, *First AIF*, pp. 141, 171–2, 181; Fitzhardinge, *Little Digger*, pp. 286–9.
9 Braithwaite, L, 7 Aug. 1917; Bishop, *Hell, Humour and Heartbreak*, pp. 134–5; Bean, D95, 30 Dec. 1917.
10 Linney, D, 18 May 1917; Joynt, D, 19 Dec. 1916; Williams, *Gallant Company*, pp. 135–7; Westaway, D, 4 May 1917.
11 Macdonald, *Roses*, pp. 149, 228–9; Adam-Smith, *Anzacs*, p. 294; Hardie, L, 30 Oct. 1917; McKernan, *Australian People*, pp. 65–80.
12 Formation of Australian Corps: Bean, D165, 28 Sep. 1917; Edmonds to Bean, 27 Jun. 1928, 26 Jun. 1929, 2 Sep. 1932, Item 34, 3DRL/7953, AWM38.
13 Monash to Aust. Corps, MC, to White, MP, both 1 Dec. 1917; *OH V*, pp. 41–4.
14 Winter, *Death's Men*, p. 212.
15 German offensive: Edmonds, *France and Belgium, 1918*, I, p. 149; Holmes, *Western Front*, p. 192.
16 Haig, D, 2 Mar. 1918; Wilson, D, 30 Jan, 18 Mar. 1918, Wilson Papers, IWM.
17 *OH V*, p. 110.

15 LIGHT HORSE

1 Hill, *Chauvel*, pp. 48–9.
2 Birdwood to Hamilton, 5 Jun. 1915, File 5/10, Hamilton Papers, KC; Birdwood to Pearce, 8 Nov. 1915, Birdwood Papers, AWM.
3 *OH VII*, pp. 48, 50-3.
4 Keegan, *First World War*, p. 323.
5 Gammage, *The Broken Years*, p. 127; *OH VII*, p. 92.
6 Pearce, L, 23 Aug. 1916.
7 *OH VIII*, p. 33.
8 Greatorex, D, 21 Jul. 1916.
9 Romani: Mitchell, *Light Horse*, p. 45; Bourne, *2nd Light Horse*, p. 40; *OH VII*, pp. 151, 157, 159;
10 Pursuit: Idriess, *Desert Column*, pp. 135, 138–40, 175; Macfarlane, D, 5 Aug. 1916.
11 Bean, *Anzac to Amiens*, p. 282; Hill, 'General Sir Harry Chauvel' in Horner (ed.), *The Commanders*, p. 71 and *Chauvel*, p. 81.
12 Idriess, *Desert Column*, p. 156; Wetherell, L, 20 Aug. 1916; *OH VII*, p. 162.
13 *OH VII*, p. 209.
14 Magdhaba: *OH VII*, p. 221; Wearne, L, undated.
15 Rafa: Powles, *New Zealanders in Sinai*, p. 69; Macfarlane, D, 9 Jan.1917; Ross, D, 9 Jan. 1917; Pugsley, *Anzac Experience*, p. 136; Adam-Smith, *Anzacs*, p. 241; Greatorex, D, 9 Jan. 1917.
16 Hill, *Chauvel*, pp. 96–7.
17 First Gaza: Idriess, *Desert Column*, pp. 246, 252, 263; Mitchell, *Light Horse*, p. 61; *OH VII*, pp. 282, 294, 296.
18 Second Gaza: *OH VII*, pp. 312–5, 334; Wearne, L, 26 Apr. 1917.
19 P. Simkins, 'Haig and the Army Commanders' in Bond and Cave, *Haig*, pp. 84; *OH VII*, p. 357; Dunk, 'Battle of Beersheba', PR00469, AWM; Gilbert, *First World War*, p. 325.
20 Beerhseba (3rd Gaza): Wilson, *Myriad Faces*, p. 500; Idriess, *Desert Column*, pp. 318, 325; Hamilton, 'The Stretcher-Bearers at Beersheba', 3DRL/3826, AWM, p. 4; E. Ritchie, *Crusaders of the Southern Cross*, Sydney, 1998, p. 221; Abbott, L, 8 Oct. 1973; *OH VII*, p. 404.
21 Livingston, 'Some Memories of an Anzac', PR88/30, AWM, p. 13; Langtip, D, 23 Apr. 1918; Hill, *Chauvel*, p. 140.

22 Amman: *OH VII*, pp. 561, 584; Berrie, *Furred Hats*, p. 128.
23 Es Salt: *OH VII*, pp. 610, 634; Smyth, D, May 1918; Birkbeck, D, 1 May 1918; Olden, *Westralian Cavalry*, p. 240.
24 Jordan interlude: Bourne, *2nd Light Horse*, p. 71; Preston, *Desert Mounted*, p. 189;
25 *OH VII*, p. 667.
26 *OH VIII*, p. 146.
27 Megiddo: *OH VIII*, p. 146; Falls, *Egypt and Palestine*, II, p. 514; Liddell Hart, *First World War*, p. 560.
28 Mitchell, *Light Horse*, pp, 95, 97; *OH VII*, p. 727.
29 *OH VII*, pp. 728, 732; Mitchell, *Light Horse*, p. 99; Gammage, *Broken Years*, p. 140.
30 Gammage, *Broken Years*, p. 145; Idriess, *Desert Column*, p. 181.
31 Damascus: *OH VII*, p. 747; Billing, L, 16 Nov. 1918; Olden, *Westralian Cavalry*, p. 283.
32 *OH VII*, p. 533; O'Keefe, *Hurley*, p. 97; Pugsley, *Anzac Experience*, p. 33; *Chauvel*, p. 173.

16 STEMMING THE TIDE

1 Keegan, 'An Even Break', MSS1333, AWM; Gough, *Fifth Army*, p. 225.
2 Holmes, *Western Front*, p. 197.
3 Cobby, *High Adventure*, p. 50; Peters, L, 15 Apr. 1918.
4 Cutlack, *War Letters*, p. 224; Pitt, *1918*, p. 95; Barnett, *Swordbearers*, p. 326.
5 *OH V*, pp. 271, 174–7; Sindrey, L, 26 Sep. 1918.
6 *AV*, p. 26; Mitchell, D, 27 Mar. 1917.
7 Brahms, *The Spirit of the Forty-Second*, p. 65.
8 Middlebrook, *Kaiser's Battle*, p. 92.
9 Mitchell, D, 28 Mar. 1918; C. Barnett, 'Offensive 1918' in Frankland and Dowling, *Decisive Battles*, pp. 78–9.
10 *OH V*, p. 302; Hardie, L, 24 Apr. 1918; Reports, 31 Mar., 6 Apr. 1918, 33 Bn WD, Item 23/50, Roll 69, AWM4.
11 Monash to Birdwood, 30 Mar. 1918, MC; *OH V*, p. 235.
12 Macdonald, *Last Man*, p. 344; Smyth, D, c.5 Apr. 1918.
13 Australians and British: Pedersen, *Villers-Bretonneux*, p. 37; Nichols, *Eighteenth Division*, p. 306; Cude, D, 26, 31 Mar. 1918; McMullin, *Elliott*, p. 374.
14 German attack 4 Apr: Middlebrook, *Kaiser's Battle*, p. 327; 58 Bn WD, 4 Apr. 1918, Item 23/75, Roll 96, AWM4: *OH V*, pp. 319–20.
15 Aust counterattack: Goddard, 'Villers-Bretonneux Mar. 30 – Apr. 6 1918', 3DRL 2379, AWM; *OH V*, pp. 339–40, 346–7; Cude, D, 5 Apr. 1918.
16 Dernancourt: Klingner, D, undated, PR91/099, AWM; *OH V*, pp. 364, 397, 404, 412, 418.
17 Lys offensive: Joynt, *Channel Ports*, pp. 65, 75–9, 87; *OH V*, p. 467.
18 Hangard: Reports, 7 April, 20 Bn WD, Item 23/37, Roll 53 and 5 Bde WD, Item 23/5, Roll 11, both AWM 4; *OH V*, pp. 503, 507.
19 Cutlack, *Final Campaign*, p. 122; Taylor, 'Mob That Shot the Camel', p. 141; N. Franks and A. Bennett, *Red Baron's Last Flight*, London, 1997, p. 114.
20 Boraston and Bax, *Eighth Division*, p. 199: 22 Durham Light Inf WD, 4 Apr. 1918, WO95/1702, TNA.
21 German attack on Villers-Bret: *OH V*, pp. 549, 574–5; Essame, *Battle for Europe*, p. 109; Bean, D112, 24 Apr. 1918; Downing, *Last Ridge*, p. 125.
22 13 Bde attack: *OH V*, pp. 579–80, 590–1, 595; Browning, *Fix Bayonets*, pp. 159, 164.
23 15 Bde attack: 15 Bde WD, 25 Apr. 1918; McMullin, *Elliott*, p. 409; Ellis, *Fifth Division*, p. 298; Blaxland, *Amiens*, p. 130.
24 *OH V*, p. 637; Mitchell, *Backs to the Wall*, pp. 210–11.
25 *OH V*, pp. 638, 641–2; Lytton, *Press and General Staff*, pp. 163–4; McMullin, *Elliott*, pp. 409–10.
26 Criticism of British troops: Braithwaite, L, 7 Apr. 1918; Monash to wife 4 Apr. 1918, MC: Hobbs, D, 27 Apr. 1918;

Simkins, 'Absolute Limit', p. 2; *OH V*, p. 417; Holmes, *Western Front*, p. 202.

17 MONASH AND THE ORCHESTRATED BATTLE

1 Wavell, *Generals*, p. 15; Monash, 'Leadership in War', 30 Mar. 1926, MP. For Monash's development as a general, see Pedersen, *Monash as Military Commander*, Melbourne, 1985.
2 Monash, 'Staff Duties in Operations' (USI lecture notes), 18 Jun. 1911, MP.
3 Monash to Rosenhain, 14 Jun. 1917, MP; *OH V*, p. 177.
4 Cutlack, *War Letters*, p. 151; Terraine, *Haig*, p. 215; Monash, 'Leadership in War' and *AV*, p. 96; Monash to Meyer, 1 Apr. 1918, MP.
5 Bean, D113, 30 May 1918; White to Gellibrand, 8 Jun. 1917; Sixsmith, *Haig*, p. 164, and *British Generalship*, p. 140; Monash to Swinburne, 20 Jul. 1925, MP; Jackson to Liddell Hart, 4 Oct. 1935, Liddell Hart Papers; Harington to Edmonds, 27 Jan. 1932, 3DRL/7953, AWM38.
6 Bean, D91, 18 Oct. 1917; Serle, *Monash*, p. 328.
7 Rawlinson to Montgomery, 8 May, 9 Sept. 1920, Montgomery-Massingberd Papers, KC; Prior and Wilson, *Command*, p. 305; *OH VI*, p. 42.
8 Peaceful Penetration: Haig, D, 9 May 1918; Chedgey, L, 23 Apr. 1918; *OH VI*, p. 408; Pugsley, p. 286; Bean *Anzac to Amiens*, p. 456;
9 *OH VI*, p. 240.
10 *Blücher*: Holmes, *The Western Front*, p. 202; Cruttwell, *Great War*, p. 526; *OH VI*, pp. 163, 169; D. Trask, 'Entry of the USA' in Strachan (ed.), *Oxford History of the First World War*, p. 247.
11 Bean, D95, 30 Dec. 1917; *AV*, pp. 43–4.
12 Hamel defences: Fourth Army Intsum 189, 25 Jun. 1918, Item 350/6, AWM26; 'Notes on Enemy Opposite', c. 4 Jul. 1918, Item 243/14, AWM25; Aust. Corps, 'Forecast of Available Enemy Infantry', 22 Jun. 1918, Item 361/2, AWM26.
13 Elles, 'Defensive and Offensive Use of Tanks', 3 Jan. 1918, Item 481/8, AWM26; *AV*, p. 44; Maurice, *Rawlinson*, p. 221; Bean, *Anzac to Amiens*, pp. 459–60.
14 Bean, D116, 3 July 1918.
15 Plans: Courage to Monash, 20 Jun. 1918, MC: Pedersen, *Hamel*, p. 47; Monash, S4671/1 to Fourth Army, 26 Jun. 1918, Item 361/2, AWM26.
16 *AV*, pp. 49–50; Laffin, *Hamel*, pp. 61–2.
17 Monash to Rawlinson, 5 Jul. 1918.
18 Americans: *OH VI*, pp. 259–60, 262; Shapcott, 'War Babies', MSS 1369, AWM, p. 186; Rule, *Jacka's Mob*, pp. 298–9.
19 Bean, D116, 2 Jul. 1918.
20 *AV*, pp. 53–4; Bean, D116, 3 Jul. 1918.
21 Rule, *Jacka's Mob*, pp. 301–3: Cutlack, *War Letters*, pp. 249–50.
22 Hamel attack: *OH VI*, pp. 290, 297; Longmore, *Old Sixteenth*, p. 183; Betteridge in Austin, *Forward Undeterred*, pp. 168–9; 5 Tank Bde Report, 13 Jul. 1918, Item 358/17, AWM4; Shapcott, 'War Babies', p. 194; 43 Bn WD, 4 Jul. 1918, Item 23/60, Roll 79, AWM4; Bean, D116, 4 Jul. 1918.
23 *AV*, p. 56
24 Pedersen, *Hamel*, p. 111; 'GHQ Notes on Recent Fighting No. 19', 5 Aug. 1918; SS218, 'Notes by Fourth Army on the Operations of the Australian Corps Against Hamel', both MC.
25 Tank Corps WD, 6 Jul. 1918, Item 358/17, AWM26; Blaxland, *Amiens*, p. 149; Fuller, *Memoirs*, p. 287.
26 *OH VI*, p. 329.
27 *AV*, p. 59; White, *Fighting Thirteenth*, pp. 146–7.
28 Orgill, *The Tank*, p. 64; *AV*, pp. 44, 64.
29 *OH VI*, p. 455; Terraine, *To Win a War*, p. 85.

18 ADVANCING TO VICTORY

1 Peaceful penetration and effects: *OH VI*, pp. 345, 380.
2 Origins of Amiens offensive: Monash

to Bruche, 10 Oct. 1919, MP; Serle, *Monash*, pp. 37–40; Bean to White, 30 Jun. and White to Bean, 27 Jun. 1935, White Papers.

3 Monash, 'Allotment of Infantry to Objectives', c. 23 Aug. 1918, MC and *AV*, p. 95; Bean, 'Monash the Soldier', *Reveille*, 31 Oct. 1931, p. 2.

4 Rule, *Jacka's Mob*, pp. 311–12; Downing, *Last Ridge*, p. 135.

5 Bean, D116, 7 Aug. 1918.

6 Joynt, *Channel Ports*, p. 128, and D, 7 Aug. 1918; Wilson, D, 8 Aug 1918.

7 Start of attack: Downing, *Last Ridge*, pp. 138–9.

8 *OH VI*, pp. 534, 544.

9 Prior and Wilson, *Command*, pp. 314–15; Rea, D, 8 Aug. 1918; Barton, D, 8–9 Aug. 1918.

10 Aarons, L, 17 Aug. 1918; Coutts, D, 8 Aug. 1918, PR83/155, AWM; Montague, *Disenchantment*, p. 127.

11 Advance to Red and Blue Lines: Monash to Fourth Army, 1.15 p.m., 8 Aug. 1918, MC; *OH VI*, p. 571.

12 Fuller, *Decisive Battles*, p. 290.

13 *OH VI*, p. 600; Cook, L, 2 Sep. 1918, MC; Rawlinson to Allenby et al., 28 Aug. 1918, Rawlinson Papers, NAM; Montague, *Disenchantment*, p. 128.

14 Ludendorff, *War Memories*, II, pp. 679, 684; GHQ, 'Reinforcement of Somme Front', 6 Aug. 1918, MC; Herbertson, 'German Records', p. 206.

15 Exploitation: Sheffield, *Forgotten Victory*, p. 241; Montgomery, '8 August 1918', *Royal Artillery Journal*, LVI, 1929, p. 7; Nicolson, *Canadian Expeditionary Force*, p. 410.

16 Lihons: McMullin, *Elliott*, pp. 468–9; Pedersen, *Monash*, pp. 251–2; *OH VI*, p. 684.

17 Etinehem–Proyart: *AV*, p. 138; Bean, D116, 10 August 1918; Sindrey, L, 26 Sept. 1918.

18 Monash to wife, 11 Aug. 1918, MC; Hetherington, *Blamey*, p. 47.

19 Rawlinson, D, 13 Aug. 1918; Prior and Wilson, *Command*, pp. 335–6; Serle, *Monash*, p. 351.

20 *OH VI*, p. 733.

21 *OH VIII*, pp. 348-9.

22 Chuignes: Joynt, *Channel Ports*, pp. 152–4; Aarons, L, 24 Aug. 1918; *OH VI*, pp. 743–60.

23 GHQ OAD 911, 22 Aug. 1918, File I/2/2, Dill Papers; 4th Army to Corps, 24 Aug. 1918, Montgomery-Massingberd Papers.

24 *AV*, pp. 166–7; Aust. Corps Battle Instruction 10, 26 Aug. 1918, MC.

25 Mt St Quentin/Péronne: Guard, 'Account', undated, 2DRL/0879, AWM; *AV*, pp. 181, 194; Wilson, D, 31 Aug – 2 Sep. 1918; *OH VI*, pp. 822, 874; Coutts, D, 31 Aug – 1 Sept. 1918; Barton, D, 22 Sep. 1918; Hall, 'Recollections', PR87/085, AWM; McMullin, *Elliott*, pp. 476–7.

26 *OH VI*, p. 873, *AV*, p. 177; Pitt, *1918*, p. 217; Holmes, *Western Front*, p. 209.

27 H. Outpost Line: *AV*, p. 222; Rule, *Jacka's Mob*, pp. 326–7; Woods, L, 22 Oct. 1918; *OH VI*, pp. 931–2.

28 Tiredness: Russell, L, 6 Sept. 1918; Smith, L, 23 Sep. 1918; Blamey, 'Disliked Show', *Reveille*, 31 Oct. 1931, p. 10; *AV*, p. 202; Campbell, L, 2 Oct. 1918; Bean, D116, 8 Sep. 1918;

29 Americans: Rule, *Jacka's Mob*, p. 335; O'Ryan, *27th Division*, p. 300; Haig, D, 28 Sept. 1918.

30 H. Line: Fullard, D, 29 Sept. 1918; Shapcott, 'War Babies', p. 257–8; McInnis, D, 30 Sept. 1918; Barton, D, 29 Sep, 1 Oct. 1918; Blamey to Gellibrand, 1.10 p.m., 29 Sep. 1918, Item 489/1, AWM26; Smithers, *Monash*, p. 268, Scanlan, 'Account', and Baker, 'Narrative', both PR00983, AWM; Sadler, *Paladin*, pp. 179–80; Britton, D, 1 Oct. 1918; Schwinghammer, 'Narrative', p. 45.

31 *OH VI*, p. 1021.

32 Pedersen, *Monash*, p. 292.

19 REFLECTIONS

1 Rule, *Jacka's Mob*, p. 337; Morrow, *Iron in the Fire*, p. 266; Stobie, D, 11 Nov. 1918; Rea, L, 2 Dec. 1918; Morgan, D, 11 Nov. 1918.

2 *OH VI*, p. 1057.

3 Mitchell, *Backs to the Wall*, p. 281; Rule, p. 340; Green, *The Fortieth*, pp. 202–3.
4 Edmonds to Bean 19 Sep. 1927, Item 7, 3DRL/7953, AWM38; Aitken, L, 29 Aug. 1915.
5 Rawlinson in Andrews and Jordan, 'Second Bullecourt Revisited', p. 43.
6 O'Ryan in Bean, 'Relations of the AIF with the Americans', Series 10, Class. No. 354.151, AWM38.
7 Essame, *The Battle for Europe*, p. 3; Gammage, *Broken Years*, p. 226; Campbell, *Ebb and Flow*, pp. 60, 82; Edmonds to Bean, 27 Jun. 1928, Item 7, 3DRL/7953, AWM38; Foch in H. S. Gullett, 'Our Splendid Dead', Melbourne *Herald*, 25 Apr. 1925; *OH V*, pp. 417, 676.
8 Pedersen in *Australia. Two Centuries*, p. 186; Ed-monds to Bean, 14 May 1936, Item 34, 3DRL/7953, AWM38.
9 Monash: Monash, 'The History and Constitution of the Australian Army Corps', 3 Oct. 1918, MC; Serle, *Monash*, p. 375; Pugsley, *Anzac Experience*, p. 243; *OH VI*, p. 1092.
10 *OH XI*, p. 874; Grey, *Military History of Australia*, pp. 119–20.
11 Versailles: Fitzhardinge, *Little Digger*, p. 396; Bean, *Anzac to Amiens*, p. 527.
12 B. Lewis, *Our War*, Melbourne, 1980, pp. 2, 361.
13 Robertson, *Anzac and Empire*, pp. 264–7; See also Moses, *Australia and the Kaiser's War.*
14 Duke, L, 14 Nov. 1918; Serle, *Monash*, p. 396; Gammage, *Broken Years*, p. 268.
15 Coverage of the interment ceremony in *JAWM*, No. 24, Apr. 1994, p. 10.

BIBLIOGRAPHY

OFFICIAL SOURCES

Australian War Memorial, Canberra

AWM4. AIF formation and unit war diaries, 1914–18.
AWM25. Written Records, 1914–18.
AWM26. Operations Files, 1914–18.
AWM38. C. E. W. Bean Papers.
War diaries and notebooks. 3DRL/606.
Miscellaneous papers. 3DRL/6673.
Official History Correspondence. 3DRL/7953.
Records used in writing the Official History. 3DRL/8042.
AWM224. Unit Manuscript Histories.
Kitchener, Lord. *Memorandum on the Defence of Australia*. Melbourne, 12 February 1910.
Hamilton, Gen. Sir I. *Report on an Inspection of the Military Forces of the Commonwealth of Australia*. Melbourne, 24 April 1914.
Final Report of the Dardanelles Royal Commission. London, 1917.
Turkish General Staff, *A Short History of Turkish Operations in the Great War. I. The Dardanelles Campaign*. Constantinople, 1922.

The National Archives, London

WO95. War diaries of British formations and units pertinent to AIF actions.

OFFICIAL HISTORIES

Australia

Bean, C. E. W. *Official History of Australia in the War of 1914–18*. Sydney, 1921–42.
——. I. *The Story of Anzac*. 1921.
——. II. *The Story of Anzac*. 1924.
——. III. *The AIF in France, 1916*. 1929.
——. IV. *The AIF in France, 1917*. 1933.
——. V. *The AIF in France During the Main German Offensive, 1918*. 1941.
——. VI. *The AIF in France During the Allied Offensive, 1918*. 1942.
Gullett, H. S. VII. *The AIF in Sinai and Palestine*. Sydney, 1923.
Cutlack, F. VIII. *The Australian Flying Corps*. Sydney, 1923.
Jose, A. W. IX. *The Royal Australian Navy*. Sydney, 1943.
Mackenzie, S. S. X. *The Australians at Rabaul*. Sydney, 1942.
Scott, E. XI. *Australia During the War*. Sydney, 1936.
Butler, A. G. *Official History of the Australian Army Medical Services in the War of 1914–18*. Melbourne, 1930–33.
I. *Gallipoli, Palestine and New Guinea*. 1930.
II. *The Western Front*. 1940.

Canada

Nicolson, G. W. L. *Canadian Expeditionary Force 1914–19*. Ottawa, 1962.

New Zealand

Official History of New Zealand's Effort in the Great War.
Waite, F. *The New Zealanders at Gallipoli*. Auckland, 1921.
Stewart, H. *The New Zealand Division*. Auckland, 1921.
Powles, C. G. *The New Zealanders in Sinai And Palestine*. Auckland, 1922.

United Kingdom

Aspinall-Oglander, C. F. *Gallipoli*. 2 vols, London, 1929, 1932.
Falls, C. *Egypt and Palestine from June 1917 to the End of the War, II*. London, 1930.
——. *France and Belgium, 1917. I. The German Retreat to the Hindenburg Line and the Battle of Arras*. London, 1940.
Edmonds, J. E. *France and Belgium, 1917. II. Messines and Third Ypres*. London, 1948.

——. *France and Belgium, 1918. I. The German March Offensive*. London, 1935.
——. *France and Belgium, 1918. II. March–April: Continuation of the German Offensives*. London, 1937.
——. *France and Belgium, 1918. III. May–July: The German Diversion Offensive and the First Allied Counter-Offensive*. London, 1939.
——. *France and Belgium, 1918. IV. 8th August – 26th September: The Franco-British Offensive*. London, 1947.
——. *France and Belgium, 1918. V. 26th September – 11th November: The Advance to Victory*. London, 1947.
Miles, W. *France and Belgium, 1916. II. 2nd July 1916 to the End of the Battles of the Somme*. London, 1938.

OTHER SOURCES

Manuscript

AUSTRALIAN WAR MEMORIAL

Aarons, Capt. D. S. 2DRL/0166; Abbott. Capt. C. L. PR86/300; Aitken, Lt J. M. 1DRL/0013; Akhurst, L/Cpl H. G. 1DRL/0015; Allan, Pte E. 1DRL/0027; Aram, Capt. J. T. PR84/087; Armitage, Capt. H. E. 1DRL/0053; Baker, Lt E. A. PR00983; Baldwin, Sgt C. C. 2DRL/0324; Baldwin, Sgt R. T. J. PR00557; Barton, Lt J. H. PR00261; Bazley, A. W. 3DRL/3520; Bell, Pte J. B. 2DRL/0189; Beeston, Col. J. L.2DRL/206; Beevor, Lt-Col. M. F. MSS0761; Billing, Tpr S. PR83/053; Binskin, Pte A. W. PR83/047; Birnie, Pte A. PR 84/068; Birdwood, Field-Marshal Lord. 3DRL/3376; Booth, Chap. J. J. PR84/336; Borthwick, Tpr A. H. PR01729; Bourke, Lt J. 1DRL/0139; Bowman, Pte V. A. 1DLR/0141; Boys, Capt. W. G. 1DRL/0142; Braithwaite, Capt. W. M. PR00349; Briggs, Lt H. F. 1DRL/0152; Browne, Pte F. E. MSS1360; Bryant, L/Cpl L. C. PR00142; Callaway, 2Lt F. W. PR87/237; Campbell, Lt J. D. 2DRL/0034; Campbell, Cpl R. J. 3DRL/5087(B); Carne, Capt. A. G. 2DRL/0013; Carson, Lt G. 2DRL/0185; Chambers, Capt. L. K. 2DRL/0049; Champion, Lt B. W. 2DRL/0512; Chedgey, Lt H. V. 2DRL/0178; Cheney, Sgt H. A. 1DRL/0199; Claridge, Capt. W. G. 2DRL/0240; Coe, Maj. H. J. 2DRL/0491; Cohen, L/Cpl J. 1DRL/0204; Connor, Lt J. M. PR90/110; Corbin, Lt-Col.. J. PR00176; Cue, Chap. J. A. 1DRL/0625; Dallas, Maj. R. S. 2DRL/890; Darnell, Maj. A. H. 1DRL/0233; Davis, Capt. H. S. 2DRL/0547; de Vine, Sgt A. L. 1DRL/0240; Dial, Sgt T. W. 2DRL/1195; Donnan, Spr S.K. 2DRL/0712; Duke, Capt. C.R. 2DRL/0562; Dunk, Cpl R. J. PR00469; Dunlop, Pte A.C. PR006786; Elliott, Brig-Gen. H.E. 2DRL/0513; Elvin, Sgt L.R. 2DRL/0209; Evatt, Lt R. S. 2DRL/0160; Feist, CSM G. S. 1DRL/0280; Fullard, Lt A. F. PR01029; Gaffney, Cpl P. PR91/084; Gallwey, Cpl W. D. MSS1355; Gammage, Pte J.K. PR82/003; Gardiner, Sgt R. J. 1DRL/0305; Gellibrand, Maj-Gen. J. G. 3DRL/6541; Goddard, Brig-Gen. H. A. 3DRL/2379; Godlee, Sgt F. L. PR01507; Gordon, WGCDR J. R. PR89/085; Grant, Pte R. A. PR89/180; Greatorex, Lt J. J. 3DRL/6776; Grieve, Capt.. R. C. 2DRL/0260; Groves, Sgt W. C. 2DRL/0268; Guard, Lt W. 2DRL/0879; Hall, Lt A. C. PR87/085; Hamilton, L/Sgt. P. M. 3DRL/3826; Hardie, Pte J. PR00519; Harris, Maj. J. R. 1DRL/0338; Harrison, Pte P. H. PR91/005; Hartnett, Pte H.G. 2DRL/0840; Hobbs, Lt-Gen. J. J. T. PR82/153; Hocking, S/Sgt F. R. PR88/161; Hollyhoke, Lt A.H. 3DRL/1465; Horton, L/Cpl D. 1DRL/0359; Howell-Price, Maj. P. L. 1DRL/0363; Hunt, Lt S. E. 2DRL/0277; Joynt, Capt. W. D. 2DRL/0765; Jungwirth, Pte L. A. PR89/063; Keegan, Gnr R. M. MSS1333; King, Pte E. G. PR83/018; Klingner, Pte F.W. PR91/099; Langtip, S/Sgt H. PR00053; Laing, Lt. E. W. 1DRL/0404; Leane, Capt. A. E. 1DRL/0411; Liddelow, Lt A. 1DRL/0417; Lillie, Capt. C. M.

PR85/010; Linney, Pte T. E. PR00436; Little, Capt. R. A. 3DRL/6858; Livingstone, Cpl C. H. PR88/030; Loud, L/Cpl. F. PR89/132; McAnulty, Pte C. A. 1DRL/0422; McConnan, Lt. W. A. PR01577; Macfarlane, Lt S. 2DRL/0211; McGuirk, Pte A. O. PR89/156; McInnis, Lt R. A. PR00917; Margetts, Capt. I. S. 1DRL/0478; Martin, Lt L. J. 1DRL/0483; Matthews, Sgt A. E. 2DRL/0219; Maudsley, Maj. A. J. 1DRL/0487; Maxfield, Capt. G. L. 2DRL/0489; Mitchell, Capt. G. D. 2DRL/0928; Monash, Gen. Sir J. 3DRL/2316; Moorhead, Cpl E.W. 3DRL/7253 (PR85/010); Moran, Capt. F. 1DRL/0508; Morgan, L/Cpl R. 2DRL/0218; Morshead, Lt-Gen. Sir L. J. 3DRL/2632; Nixon-Smith, Pte J. S. 2DRL/0271; Parton, Cpl H. A. PR00259; Pearce, Lt. M. E. PR89/125; Pinnock, Sgt. C. C. 1DRL/0547; Preston, Sgt H. 2DRL/0811; Raws, Lt J. A. 2DRL/0481; Rea, Gnr C. PR00184; Richards, Lt E. J. 2DRL/0301; Richards, Lt T. J. 2DRL/0786; Roberts, Pte R. PR00395; Robson, Pte F. PR84/172; Rosenskjar, F. S. 2DRL/0432; Ross, Sgt R. C. PR01032; Roth, Capt. L. C. 1DRL/0554; Russell, L/Cpl E. PR87/096; Scanlon, Sgt D. J. PR90/105; Schwinghammer, Pte V. G. 2DRL/0234; Shapcott, Pte H. S. MSS1369; Silas, Pte E. 1DRL/566; Sindrey, Pte A. G. 3DRL/7514(A); Smith, Cpl A. H. PR84/365; Smith, L/Cpl H. J. 2DRL/0318; Smyth, Pte W. PR00927; Smyth, Tpr W.E. PR00633; Stobie, Capt. G. 2DRL/0196; Taylor, Cpl H. G. MSS0863; Thomas, Cpl A. G. 3DRL/2206; Vincent, Pte W. P. PR84/261; Warren, Lt W. 1DRL/0597; Wearne, Maj. A. E. PR01739; Westaway, Lt H. W. PR00268; Wetherell, Capt. H. 2DRL/0747; White, Gen. Sir C. B. B. 3DRL/6549; Whitear, Lt. A. E. 2DRL/0439; Wilson, L/Cpl D. T. PR86/341; Winter, Sgt A. T. PR89/163; Woods, Pte J. P. PR00325; Woodward, Capt. O. H. MSS0717; Worrall, Lt E. S. 1DRL/0607; Zander, Capt.. W. H. 2DRL/0171.

IMPERIAL WAR MUSEUM

Ataturk Papers (Mustafa Kemal, Memoir of the Anafartalar Battles).
Cude, Pte R. Diary.
Dawnay, Maj-Gen. G. P. Papers.
Wilson, Field-Marshal Sir H. Papers, 1917–18.

LIDDELL HART CENTRE FOR MILITARY ARCHIVES, KING'S COLLEGE, UNIVERSITY OF LONDON

Dill, Field-Marshal Sir J. G. Papers, 1917–18.
Hamilton, Gen. Sir I. Diaries and Papers, 1914–18.
Liddell Hart, Capt. Sir B. H. Papers.
Montgomery-Massingberd, Field-Marshal Sir A. A. Papers, 1918.
North, J. Papers re Gallipoli.
Robertson, Field-Marshal Sir W. Papers, 1916–18.

MITCHELL LIBRARY, STATE LIBRARY OF NEW SOUTH WALES, SYDNEY

Barwick, Sgt A. A. ML MSS1493/1; Britton, Sig. C. J. ML MSS1396; Compton, Sgt A. R. ML MSS1243; Hall, Pte P. ML MSS 2768; Laseron, Sgt C. ML MSS1133; McClintock, Pte G. T. MSS2783; Peters, Capt. C. H. MSS1887; Rosenthal, Maj-Gen. Sir C. MSS2739.

NATIONAL ARMY MUSEUM, LONDON

Rawlinson, Field-Marshal Lord. Papers, 1914–18 and Diary, 1918.

NATIONAL LIBRARY OF AUSTRALIA, CANBERRA

Casey, Maj. R. G. MS 6150; Monash, Gen. Sir J. MS1884.

NATIONAL LIBRARY OF SCOTLAND, EDINBURGH

Haig, Field-Marshal Earl. Papers and diary, 1916–18.

Books and articles

Adam Smith, P. *The Anzacs*. Melbourne, 1978.

Andrews, E. *The Anzac Illusion.* Cambridge, 1993.
Andrews, E., and Jordan, B. G. 'Second Bullecourt Revisited', *JAWM*, No. 15, Oct. 1989.
Ashmead-Bartlett, E. *The Uncensored Dardanelles*, London, 1928.
Asprey, R. A. *The German High Command at War.* NY, 1991.
Austin, R. J. *Cobbers in Khaki: The History of the 8th Battalion, 1914–19.* McCrae, 1997.
——. *Forward Undeterred: The History of the 23rd Battalion.* Rosebud, 1998.
——. *White Gurkhas.* McCrae, 1976.
Babington, A. *For the Sake of Example.* London, 1985.
——. *Shell-Shock.* London, 1997.
Barnett, C. *The Sword-Bearers.* London, 1986.
Barrie, A. *War Underground.* London, 1990.
Bean, C. E. W. *Anzac to Amiens.* Canberra, 1968.
——. *Gallipoli Mission*, Sydney, 1990.
——. *Letters from France*, Melbourne, 1917.
——. 'Monash the Soldier'. *Reveille*, Vol. 5, No. 2, 31 Oct. 1931.
——. 'Sidelights of the War on the Australian Character', *JRAHS*, Vol. 13, No. 4, 1927.
——. *Two Men I Knew.* Sydney, 1957.
Belfield, E. *The Boer War.* London, 1993.
Belford, W. C. *Legs-Eleven. The Story of the 11th Battalion in the Great War.* Perth, 1940.
Berrie, G. L. *Under Furred Hats.* Sydney, 1919.
Birdwood, W. R. *Khaki and Gown.* London, 1941.
Bishop, B. *The Hell, the Humour and the Heartbreak: A Private's View of World War 1.* Kenthurst, 1991.
Blaxland, G. *Amiens: 1918.* London, 1981.
Bond, B., and Cave, N. (eds). *Haig: A Reappraisal Seventy Years on.* Barnsley, 1999.
Boraston, J. H., and Bax, C. E. O. *The Eighth Division 1914–1918.* London, 1926.
Bourne, G. H. *History of the 2nd Light Horse Regiment.* Swanbourne, 1994.
Bradby, W. J. 'Polygon Wood and Broodseinde'. *Stand-To*, Vol. 8, No. 5, Sep–Oct. 1963.
Brahms, V. *The Spirit of the Forty-Second.* Brisbane, 1938.
Brittain, V. *Testament of Youth.* London, 1978.
Broadbent, H. *Gallipoli: The Fatal Shore.* Melbourne, 2005.
——. *The Boys Who Came Home.* Sydney, 1990.
Brown, A. 'The Old Windmill'. *Reveille*, Vol. 6, No. 2, Oct. 1932.
Brown, M. *Verdun 1916.* Stroud, 1999.
Browning, N. *Fix Bayonets: The History of the 51st Battalion AIF.* Bayswater, 2000.
Brugger, S. *Australians and Egypt.* Melbourne, 1980.
Burness, P. *The Nek.* Sydney, 1996.
Bush, E. W. *Gallipoli.* London, 1975.
Campbell, P. J. *The Ebb and Flow of Battle.* London, 1977.
Carlyon, L. *Gallipoli.* Sydney, 2001.
Carver, M. (ed.). *The War Lords.* London, 1976.
Chapman, I. *Iven G. Mackay. Citizen and Soldier.* Sydney, 1975.
Charlton, P. *Pozières.* Sydney, 1986.
Charteris, J. *At GHQ.* London, 1931.
Chataway, T. P. *History of the 15th Battalion.* Brisbane, 1948.
Churchill, W. S. *The World Crisis 1911–1918.* 2 vols. NY, 1993.
Cobby, A. H. *High Adventure.* Melbourne, 1981.
Coombs, R. *Before Endeavours Fade.* London, 1976.
Conan Doyle, A. *The British Campaign in France and Flanders 1916.* London, 1918.
Corfield, R. S. *Don't Forget Me, Cobber.* Melbourne, Rosanna, 2000.
Coulthard-Clark, C. D. *A Heritage of Spirit.* Melbourne, 1979.
——. *No Australian Need Apply: The Troubled Career of Lt-Gen. Gordon Legge*, Sydney, 1987.
Crane, F. W. 'The Concert in Reserve Gully'. *Reveille*, Vol. 11, No. 11, Aug. 1938.

Cruttwell, C. R. M. *A History of the Great War 1914–1918*. London, 1982.
Cutlack, F. M. *The Australians: Their Final Campaign, 1918*. London, 1919.
—— (ed.). *War Letters of General Monash*. Sydney, 1935.
Davies, H. *Allanson of the Sixth*. London, 1991.
Dennis, P. et al. *The Oxford Companion to Australian Military History*. Melbourne, 1995.
Doneley, R. J. *Black over Blue: The 25th Battalion at War*. Toowoomba, 1997.
Downing, W. H. *To The Last Ridge*. Sydney, 1998.
Drake-Brockman, G. *The Turning Wheel*. Perth, 1960.
Dunn, J. C. *The War The Infantry Knew*. London, 1987.
East, R. (ed.). *The Gallipoli Diary of Sergeant Lawrence*. Melbourne, 1981.
Ellis, A. D. *The Story of the Fifth Australian Division*. London, 1920.
Ellis, J. *Eye-deep in Hell*. London, 1977.
Essame, H. *The Battle for Europe 1918*. London, 1972.
Fairey, E. *The 38th Battalion AIF*. Bendigo, 1920.
Farndale, M. *A History of the Royal Artillery: The Western Front, 1914–18*. London, 1986.
Farrar-Hockley, A. *Goughie: The Life of Sir Hubert Gough*. London, 1975.
——. *The Somme*. London, 1964.
Ferguson, N. *The Pity of War*. London, 1998.
Fewster, K. (ed.). *Gallipoli Correspondent*. Sydney, 1983.
Fitzhardinge, L. F. *The Little Digger*. Sydney, 1979.
Forester, C. S. *The General*. London, 1979.
Frame, T. *The Shores of Gallipoli*, Sydney, 2000.
Frankland, N., and Dowling, C. (eds), *Decisive Battles of the Twentieth Century*. London, 1976.
Franks, N., and Bennett, A. *The Red Baron's Last Flight*. London, 1997.
Fuller, J. F. C. *The Decisive Battles of the Western World*. 3 vols. London, 1963.
——. *Generalship: Its Diseases and Their Cure*. London, 1933.
——. *Memoirs of an Unconventional Soldier*. London, 1936.
——. *The Conduct of War 1789–1961*. London, 1977.
Gammage, W. *The Broken Years*. London, 1975.
Gilbert, M. *The First World War*. London, 1994.
Glen, F. *Bowler at Gallipoli*. Loftus, 2004.
Gliddon, G. *When the Barrage Lifts*. London, 1987.
Gough, H. *The Fifth Army*. London, 1931.
Grant, I. *Jacka VC*. Melbourne, 1989.
Graves, R. *Goodbye to All That*. London, 1976.
Green, F. C. *The Fortieth: record of the 40th Battalion, AIF*. Hobart, 1922.
Grey, J. *A Military History of Australia*. Cambridge, 1990.
——. *The Australian Army*. Melbourne, 2001.
Griffith, P. *Battle Tactics of the Western Front*. London, 1994.
Hackett, J. *The Profession of Arms*. London, 1983.
Haking, R. C. B. *Company Training*. London, 1913.
Hamilton, I. *Gallipoli Diary*. 2 vols. London, 1930
Hamilton, J. *Goodbye Cobber, God Bless You*. Sydney, 2004.
Harington, C. *Plumer of Messines*. London, 1935.
Harris, R. H. 'The 27th in the Menin Road Battle'. *Stand-To*, Vol. 10, No. 3, Jan-Mar, 1966.
Harvey, N. *From Anzac to the Hindenburg Line. The History of the 9th Battalion AIF*. Brisbane, 1941.
Hatwell, J. *No Ordinary Determination*. Fremantle, 2005.
Herbert, A. *Mons, Anzac and Kut*. London, 1919.
Herbert, A. P. *The Secret Battle*, Oxford, 1982.
Hetherington, J. *Blamey. Controversial Soldier*. Canberra, 1973.
Hickey, M. *Gallipoli*. London, 1995.
Hill, A. J. *Chauvel of the Light Horse*, Melbourne, 1978.
Holmes, R. *Fatal Avenue*. London, 1992.
——. *The Western Front*. London, 1999.

Horne, A. *The Price of Glory: Verdun 1916*. London, 1962.
Horner, D. M. (ed.). *The Commanders*. Sydney, 1984.
——. *The Gunners: a history of Australian artillery*. Sydney, 1995.
Idriess, I. *The Desert Column*. Sydney, 1938.
Jones, I. *King of Air Fighters*. London, 1986.
Joynt, W. D. *Saving the Channel Ports*. Melbourne, 1975.
Kannengiesser, H. *The Campaign in Gallipoli*. London, 1927.
Keegan, J., and Holmes, R. *Soldiers. A History of Men in Battle*. London, 1985.
Keegan, J. *The First World War*. London, 1998.
Knowles, B. 'Bullecourt Tragedy'. *Reveille*, Vol. 4, No. 8, 30 Apr. 1931.
Knyvett, H. R. *'Over There' with the Australians*. London 1918.
Laffin, J. *Damn the Dardanelles!* Melbourne, 1985.
——. *The Battle of Hamel*. Sydney, 1999.
Lee, J. *A Soldier's Life. General Sir Ian Hamilton 1853–1947*. London, 2000.
Liddell Hart, B. H. *History of the First World War*, London, 1970.
Liddle, P. H. *Men of Gallipoli*. London, 1976.
—— (ed.). *Passchendaele in Perspective*. London, 1997.
Longmore, C. *The Old Sixteenth*. Perth, 1929.
Lording (a.k.a. 'A. Tiveychoc'), R. E. *There and Back*. Sydney, 1935.
Lloyd George, D. *War Memoirs of David Lloyd George*. 2 vols. London, 1938.
Ludendorff, E. *My War Memories 1914–18*. 2 vols. London, 1919.
Lytton, N. *The Press and the General Staff*. London, 1920.
Macdonald, L. *Somme*. London, 1983.
——. *The Roses of No Man's Land*. London. 1980.
——. *They Called It Passchendaele*. London, 1978.
——. *To the Last Man. Spring 1918*. London, 1998.
Mackenzie, C. *Gallipoli Memories*. London, 1929.
McKernan, M. *The Australian People and the Great War*. Sydney, 1984.
McKernan, M., and Browne, M. *Australia. Two Centuries of War and Peace*. Canberra, 1988.
McMullin, R. *Pompey Elliott*. Melbourne, 2002.
Malthus, C. *Anzac:A Retrospect*. Auckland, 2002.
Masefield, J. *Gallipoli*.
Maurice, F. B. *The Life of General Lord Rawlinson of Trent*. London, 1928.
Middlebrook, M. *The First Day on the Somme*. London, 1975.
——. *The Kaiser's Battle*, London, 1978.
Mitchell, E. *The Light Horse*, Sydney, 1978.
Mitchell, G. D. *Backs to the Wall*. Sydney, 1937.
Monash, J. *The Australian Victories in France in 1918*. London, 1920.
Montague, C. E. *Disenchantment*. London, 1922.
Montgomery, A. A. '8 August 1918'. *Royal Artillery Journal*, LVI, 1929.
Moorehead, A. *Gallipoli*, South Melbourne, 1975.
Mordike, J. *An Army for a Nation*. Sydney, 1992.
Morrow, E. *Iron in the Fire*. Sydney, 1943.
Moses, J. A. *Australia and the Kaiser's War*. Brisbane, 1993.
Murray, H. W. 'Bravest Man in the AIF'. *Reveille*, Vol. 3, No. 4, 31 Dec. 1929.
——. 'Capture of Stormy Trench'. *Reveille*, Vol. 11, No. 4, 1 Dec. 1937.
——. 'His Hardest Battle'. *Reveille*, Vol. 9, No. 4, Dec. 1935.
——. 'Memories of First Bullecourt'. *Reveille*, Vol. 10, No. 4, 1 Dec. 1936.
Newton, L. M. *The Story of the Twelfth*. Hobart, 1927.
Nichols, G. H. *The Eighteenth Division in the Great War*. Oxford, 1922.
North, J. *Gallipoli: The Fading Vision*. London, 1936.
O'Keefe, D. *Hurley at War*. Sydney, 1986.
Olden, A. C. *Westralian Cavalry in the War*. Melbourne, 1921.
Orgill, D, *The Tank: Studies in the Development and Use of a Weapon*. London, 1970.

O'Ryan, J. F. *The Story of the 27th Division*. NY, 1921.
Pakenham, T. *The Boer War*. London, 1979.
Pearce, G. F. *Carpenter to Cabinet*. London, 1951.
Pedersen, P. A. *Fromelles*, Barnsley, 2004.
——. *Hamel*. Barnsley, 2003.
——. *Images of Gallipoli*. Melbourne, 1988.
——. *Monash as Military Commander*. Melbourne, 1985.
——. *Villers-Bretonneux*. Barnsley, 2004.
Pigeon, T. *The Tanks at Flers*. Cobham, 1995.
Pitt, B. *1918. The Last Act*. London, 1984.
Preston, R. M. *The Desert Mounted Corps*. London, 1921.
Prior, R. 'The Suvla Bay Tea Party: a Reassessment'. *JAWM*, No. 7, Oct. 1985.
Prior, R., and Wilson, T. *Command on the Western Front*. Oxford, 1992.
——. *Passchendaele. The Untold Story*. Carlton, 2003.
——. *The Somme*. Sydney, 2005.
Powell, G. *Plumer*. London, 1990.
Pugsley, C. *The Anzac Experience*. Auckland, 2004.
——. *Gallipoli. The New Zealand Story*. Auckland, 1984.
Rhodes James, R. *Gallipoli*. London, 1984.
Richards, F. *Old Soldiers Never Die*. London, 1933.
Roberts, C. 'The Landing at Anzac: A Reassessment'. *JAWM*, No. 22, Apr. 1993.
Robertson, J. *Anzac and Empire*. Melbourne, 1990.
Robson, L. L. *The First A.I.F.* Melbourne, 1982.
Rule, E. *Jacka's Mob*. Sydney, 1933.
Sadler, P. S. *The Paladin: A Life of Maj-Gen Sir John Gellibrand*. Melbourne, 2000.
Sanders, O. Liman von. *Five Years in Turkey*. Maryland, 1927.
Sassoon, S. *Memoirs of an Infantry Officer*. London, 1978.
Schuler, P. F. E. *Australia in Arms*. London, 1916.
Serle, G. *John Monash: A Biography*. Melbourne, 1982.
Shadbolt, M. *Voices of Gallipoli*. Auckland, 1988.
Sheffield, G. *Forgotten Victory*. London, 2002.
——. *The Somme*. London, 2003.
Simkins, P. *Air Fighting 1914–18*. London, 1978.
Simms, W. S. *The Victory at Sea*. NY, 1927.
Sixsmith, E. K. G. *British Generalship in the Twentieth Century*. London, 1970.
——. *Douglas Haig*. London, 1976.
Sloan, H. *The Purple and Gold. A History of the 30th*
Battalion. Sydney, 1938.
Smithers, A. J. *Sir John Monash*. London, 1973.
Souter, G. *Lion and Kangaroo*. Sydney, 1992.
Spears, E. H. *Prelude to Victory*. London, 1939.
Steel, N., and Hart, P. *Defeat at Gallipoli*. London, 1994.
Stevens, D. *The Royal Australian Navy*. Melbourne, 2001.
Strachan, H. *The First World War. I. To Arms*. Oxford, 2001.
—— (ed.), *The Oxford Illustrated History of the First World War*. London, 1998.
Taylor, A. J. P. *The First World War*. Ringwood, 1972.
Taylor, F. W., and Cusack, T. A. *Nulli Secundus: A History of the 2nd Battalion*. Sydney, 1942.
Terraine, J. *Douglas Haig, The Educated Soldier*. London, 1963.
—— (ed.). *Sir Douglas Haig's Despatches*. London, 1979.
——. *The Road to Passchendaele*. London, 1977.
——. *The Western Front*. London, 1970.
——. *To Win a War*. London, 1978.
Thursby, C. F. 'Power of the Navy: Made Landing Possible'. *Reveille*, Vol. 5, No. 7, 31 Mar. 1932.
Travers, T. *Gallipoli 1915*. Stroud, 2002.
——. *The Killing Ground*, London, 1987.
Wahlert, G. *The Other Enemy? A History of the Australian Military Police*. Melbourne, 1999.

Walker, J. *The Blood Tub*. Staplehurst, 2000.

Wanliss, N. *A History of the 14th Battalion*. Melbourne, 1929.

Watson, W. H. *A Company of Tanks*. Edinburgh, 1920.

Wavell, A. P. *Generals and Generalship*. London, 1941.

Welborn, S. *Lords of Death*. Fremantle, 1982.

Wells, T. 'First Stunt: Vivid Impressions'. *Reveille*, Vol. 5, No. 11, Aug. 1932.

White, R. 'Motives for Joining Up'. *JAWM*, No. 9, Oct. 1986.

White, T. A. *The Fighting Thirteenth*. Sydney, 1924.

Williams, H. R. *In Gallant Company*. Sydney, 1933.

Wilson, T. *The Myriad Faces of War*. Cambridge, 1986.

Winn, R. C. 'Stormy Trench'. *Reveille*, Vol. 11, No. 6, 1 Feb. 1938.

Winter, D. *Death's Men*. London, 1978

——. *First of the Few*. London, 1982.

——. 'The Anzac Landing: The Great Gamble?' *JAWM*, No. 4, April 1984.

——. *25 April 1915*. St Lucia, 1994.

Wray, C. *Sir James Whiteside McCay*. Melbourne, 2002.

Wren, E. *Randwick to Hargicourt: History of the 3rd Battalion AIF*. Sydney, 1935.

Yule P. (ed.). *Sergeant Lawrence Goes to France*. Melbourne, 1987.

Newspapers

Adelaide Advertiser, Age, Argus, Sydney Morning Herald, Smith's Weekly and some local papers, e.g., *Leeton Call*.

Miscellaneous

Author's interviews with AIF veterans, 1979–83.

Johnston, Pte C. W. Letters held by author.

Little, Capt. R. A. Information on www.diggerhistory.info. Accessed Oct 2005.

Newton, Sapper L. L. 16 Jun. 1917: www.abc.net.au/australians online. Accessed Oct 2005.

Pedersen, P. A. 'Thou Shalt Not Kill'. Paper given at 'Unquiet Graves' Conference, In Flanders Fields Museum, Ypres, Apr. 2000.

Simkins, P. 'The Absolute Limit: British Divisions at Villers-Bretonneux'. Unpublished paper.

Gallipoli. Feature film directed by Peter Weir, screenplay by David Williamson. Associated R & R Films, 1981.

Gallipoli: The Fatal Shore. Australian Broadcasting Commission 'Four Corners' Television Documentary, repor-ted by Chris Masters and produced by Harvey Broadbent, 1988.

ACKNOWLEDGEMENTS

This book could not have been attempted without the unstinting support of two people. My father's encouragement and practical help were ceaseless. Dad, I owe you more than I can say. The same goes for my partner, Patricia Simpson, who went out of her way to make sure that I had nothing on which to concentrate but my writing. Month after month she accepted uncomplainingly that my mind was off with the ghosts of the AIF. Darl, you are a princess!

Special thanks, too, to Valerie Haye of The Helicon Press, whose idea this book was. Her faith in my ability to undertake it, and patient understanding during the course of the project, were always sources of strength. I thoroughly appreciated her editorial prowess. Pauline Deakin, the book's designer, went to great lengths to ensure that the illustrations resonated elegantly with the text. Her expertise was indispensible. Robert Sessions, Publishing Director at Penguin, offered every assistance throughout.

The hospitality extended by Brigadier Chris Roberts and his wife Judy during my many stays in Canberra to research at the Australian War Memorial touched me deeply. Chris was also a font of wisdom on the Gallipoli campaign and read parts of the manuscript. In addition, I benefited from many discussions on Gallipoli with Colonel Michael Hickey and Harvey Broadbent. Major-General Steve Gower, Director of the Australian War Memorial, Professor Frank Clark of Macquarie University, and Dr John Besemeres and Kyle Wilson of the Australian Office of National Assessments gave generously of their time in offering valuable insights on various aspects of the narrative. I alone am responsible for any errors that remain.

Diane Melloy Follet helped enthusiastically with the research in Australia. Jeffrey Russell, Librarian at the Queen Elizabeth II Army Museum, Waiouru, tirelessly answered my many queries on the New Zealand side of the story. My good friend and colleague, Jon Cooksey, chased up details in Britain. I have valued his perspectives on the Western Front and the discussions we had while walking the battlefields together. Nicolas Goret assisted with matters French. To other colleagues, too numerous to name, who have helped in one form or another over the years, thanks.

No request was too difficult for Ian Smith, Senior Curator of Official and Private Records, Ian Affleck, Senior Curator of Photographs, and Andrew Jack, Assistant Curator, Photographs, at the Australian War Memorial. They readily answered questions and tracked down documents and photographs, invariably at short notice. Their dedication is inspiring. The late Ursula Davidson and John Renfrew of the Royal United Service Institution of New South Wales gave me the run of its wonderful library. I would also like to express my gratitude to the reading room staff at the National Library, Canberra; the Mitchell Library, State Library of New South Wales, Sydney; and the Imperial War Museum and the National Archives in London. Thanks for their help in years past to the staff at the Liddell Hart Centre for Military Archives, King's College, University of London; the National Army Museum, London; and National Library of Scotland, Edinburgh.

Lilian Coulton of the National Archives of Australia provided service records as soon as I needed them. Dr Bruce Taylor of the Australian Society of Plastic Surgeons, Lisa Poulier of the Royal Australasian College of Surgeons, and Dr Frank Chen all helped with the medical aspects. The computer expertise of Tom Cohen made the normally laborious task of compiling the index so much easier. Pat Morrissey made sure I saw everything at Leuralla, the Evatt family home.

The Downing family kindly allowed me to use excerpts from Walter Downing's memorable *To the Last Ridge*. The excerpts from Edgar Rule's *Jacka's Mob* and Ion Idriess's *Desert Column* appear courtesy of Harper Collins Australia. For permission to quote from personal papers and diaries, and to reproduce photographs and artworks, I thank all those institutions and individuals listed in the Bibliography and Sources of Illustrations. If I have inadvertently infringed copyright held by another person, I offer my sincerest apologies. Omissions drawn to my attention will be rectified in any future edition of this work.

SOURCES OF ILLUSTRATIONS

ALEXANDER TURNBULL LIBRARY, WELLINGTON

Crowds cheer the Wellington Battalion (G-17072-1/4), Sir Alexander Godley (G-1336-1/1), barges evacuating wounded from Anzac (F-8784-1/4), Anzac Cove on 25 April (F-65278-1/2), cliff face scaled by Wellington Mounted Rifles (F-58065-1/4), the New Zealand division training (G-012753-1/2), Brigadier-General Edward Chaytor (F-013282-1/1), Sergeant Richard Travis VC (F-103803-1/2)

AUSTRALIAN WAR MEMORIAL, CANBERRA

AN&MEF embarks in Sydney Harbour (A03272), recruits drilling at Blackboy Hill (A03404), the *Emden* (EN0235), Lieutenant-General Sir William Birdwood (H10400), Colonel Ewan Sinclair-MacLagan (E00062), men of the 1st Division Signal Company (A02781), Australians cross Plugge's Plateau (G00907), beach towards dusk on 25 April (PS1659), Brigadier-General Harold 'Hooky' Walker (ART03349), 18-pounder from the 9th Battery (A00879), lunch break at the 1st Australian Division's headquarters (G00033), Charles Wheeler's *The Charge of the 2nd Infantry Brigade at Krithia* (ART09558), Private John Simpson (J06392), Albert Jacka (P02141.003), Anzacs and Turks burying the dead (H03954), the beach in full swing (H03500), looking north from Walker's Ridge (G00410), Australians in a captured Turkish trench (G01126), Officers of the 8th LH Regiment (P00265.001), Lieutenant-Colonel John Antill (G01330), Colonel Francis Johnston (G01325), tending wounded at the 3rd Australian General Hospital (J01386), Brigadier-General Brudenell White (C01815), troops from the 6th Brigade (EZ0003), aerial oblique from the Fromelles battlefield (E05990), a dead Australian soldier (A01566), Australian prisoners (A01552), the Golden Virgin (H08482), Pozières on 28 August 1916 (EZ0095), Major-General Gordon Legge (A03754), OG1 (E00007), King George V (H15924), troops of the 1st Australian Division (E00575), Major-General Talbot Hobbs (E00179), Private Charles Marsh (E00374), men from 2nd Division (EZ0120), Major-General William Holmes (13340), the Hindenburg Line (A01121), Lieutenant Walter Shelley (E00603), Major-General Nevill Smyth (P05148.001), pillbox near Messines (E00552), Australian column passes Cloth Hall (E04612), Ypres–Roulers railway cutting (E03864), Australian cameliers (B01627), George Lambert's *The Charge of the Australian Light Horse at Beersheba* (ART02811), Australian Light Horse on the Bethlehem–Jerusalem Road (B01609), Desert Mounted Corps (H10659), 28th Battalion (E00684), gassed Australians (E04851), Amiens gun (A00006), company from the 21st Battalion (E03139), Will Longstaff's *Breaking the Hindenburg Line* (ART03023), Bullecourt Digger Robert Comb (PAIU1993/198.28)

BATTYE LIBRARY, STATE LIBRARY OF WESTERN AUSTRALIA

Swan Barracks, Perth (009559D)

NATIONAL LIBRARY OF AUSTRALIA, CANBERRA

Australian infantry resisting German counterattack (23478258)

PARLIAMENT COLLECTION, WELLINGTON

Ion Brown's *The Battle of Chunuk Bair, 8 August 1915*

ROYAL AUSTRALASIAN COLLEGE OF SURGEONS, MELBOURNE

Private S, of the 33rd Battalion, after surgery and before returning to Australia

MAPS

Pozières-Mouquet Farm, advance to the Hindenburg Line (Australian Official History), the Ypres attacks (British Official History)

PRESS SOURCES

Major-General William Bridges, 9th and 10th Battalions at Mena Camp, troops of the 10th Batallion on the Prince of Wales, Prime Minister William Morris Hughes (*Sydney Mail*); General Sir Douglas Haig, Private James O'Hehir and other Diggers (*The Times History of the War*)

PRIVATE COLLECTIONS

Private Charles Johnston, Private Frank Johnston (Peter Pedersen)

INDEX

ALSO FROM PENGUIN

Gallipoli: The Fatal Shore

HARVEY BROADBENT

It was an adventure to die for. A daring attempt to force the Dardanelles and capture the Turkish capital Constantinople. For the Allies it was the Trojan War and crusade combined. Once again Europe would prevail over an ancient enemy.

History records otherwise. The Gallipoli Campaign was to become one of the most savagely contested for the First World War and end in defeat and controversy. Over 400 000 Allied troops were killed and wounded as the Peninsula became a killing ground as deadly as any on the Western Front. The raging battles of the landing, the defeats at Krithia and on the Suvla plain, the desperate Australian assaults on Lone Pine and the Nek, the heroism of the Gurkhas at Sari Bair, and of the New Zealanders at Chunuk Bair resonate down the years in many nations.

Written by Harvey Broadbent, a leading authority, *Gallipoli: The Fatal Shore* situates this remarkable story within its multinational context. Illustrated with photographs and artworks form collections in Australia, Britain, New Zealand and Turkey, this is a fascinating insight into the campaign in which national identity was forged.

Sea of Dangers

GEOFFREY BLAINEY

Two ships set out in seach of a missing continent: the *St Jean-Baptiste*, a French merchant ship commanded by Jean de Surville, and the Endeavour, a small British naval vessel captained by James Cook. In *Sea of Dangers*, distinguished historian Geoffrey Blainey tells the story of these rival ships and the men who sailed in them. Just before Christmas 1769, the two captains were almost close enough to see one another – and yet they did not know of each other's existence.

Both crews battled extreme hardships including scurvy, storms and loneliness; but they also experienced the euphoria of 'discovering' new lands, and the fascination of meeting peoples so different they may as well have come from separate worlds.

This is the most revealing narrative so far written of Cook's astonishing voyage along the east coast of Australia. It also casts new light on the little-known voyage by Jean de Surville; Blainey argues that the Frenchman was in the vicinity of Sydney Harbour months before Cook arrived. Eventually Cook set out to explore the hazardous Barrier Reef and find a way through Torres Strait, while the Frenchman searched for a mysterious Jewish colony in the South Pacific.

In *Sea of Dangers* Blainey once again takes us on a vivid journey through history, challenging accepted views.

Tobruk 1941

CHESTER WILMOT

The gripping first-hand account of the battle that made the Rats of Tobruk an Australian legend.

March 1941. The Allied forces have suffered one brutal defeat after another. Hitler's forces have already brought the swastika from Poland to the Pyrenees, from Norway to North Africa – the conquest of Egypt, and the rich oil fields of the Middle East, lie next on the horizon. All that stands in their way are a few Australian brigades defending a town called Tobruk.

For eight months the Australian Imperial Forces were the frontline defenders of the North African coastal fortress, battling almost unbeatable odds in the dust and the heat of the Libyan desert. Under the command of General Morshead, the Australian troops used unorthodox methods and sheer grit to withstand the superior might of General Rommel's elite 'Afrika Korps'.